www.wadsworth.com

www..wadsworth.com is the World Wide Web site for Thomson Wadsworth and is your direct source to dozens of online resources.

At *www.wadsworth.com* you can find out about supplements, demonstration software, and student resources. You can also send e-mail to many of our authors and preview new publications and exciting new technologies.

www.wadsworth.com
Changing the way the world learns®

6th Edition

Wrightsman's Psychology and the Legal System

EDIE GREENE
University of Colorado at Colorado Springs

KIRK HEILBRUN
Drexel University

WILLIAM H. FORTUNE
University of Kentucky

MICHAEL T. NIETZEL
Missouri State University

THOMSON
™
WADSWORTH

Australia • Canada • Mexico • Singapore • Spain • United Kingdom • United States

THOMSON
™
WADSWORTH

Wrightsman's Psychology and the Legal System, Sixth Edition
Edie Greene, Kirk Heilbrun, William H. Fortune, Michael T. Nietzel

Executive Editor: *Michele Sordi*
Assistant Editor: *Dan Moneypenny*
Editorial Assistant: *Kara Warren*
Technology Project Manager: *Adrian Paz*
Marketing Assistant: *Natasha Coats*
Marketing Communications Manager: *Kelley McAllister*
Project Manager, Editorial Production: *Mary Noel*
Creative Director: *Rob Hugel*
Art Director: *Vernon Boes*
Print Buyer: *Karen Hunt*
Permissions Editor: *Sarah Harkrader*

Production Service: *Merrill Peterson, Matrix Productions*
Text Designer: *Terri Wright*
Photo Researcher: *Sarah Evertson, Image Quest*
Copy Editor: *Connie Day*
Illustrator: *Dartmouth*
Cover Designer: *Yvo Riezebos*
Cover Image: *Peter Samuels/Stone/Getty Images*
Cover Printer: *Coral Graphic Services*
Compositor: *Integra Software Services, Pvt. Ltd.*
Printer: *RR Donnelley/Crawfordsville*

Thomson Higher Education
10 Davis Drive
Belmont, CA 94002-3098
USA

Library of Congress Control Number: 2006920187

Student Edition: ISBN 0-534-52106-1

For more information about our products, contact us at:
Thomson Learning Academic Resource Center
1-800-423-0563

For permission to use material from this text or product, submit a request online at
http://www.thomsonrights.com.
Any additional questions about permissions can be submitted by e-mail to **thomsonrights@thomson.com.**

Dedicated, with gratitude,
to our mentors in psychology and law
Elizabeth Loftus (E.G.)
Ned Megargee (K.H.)
Robert Lawson (W. F.)
Douglas A. Bernstein (M.N.)

Brief Contents

Contents

2

The Legal System and Its Players   33

5

Crime Investigation: Witnesses   124

6 | *Identification and Evaluation of Criminal Suspects* 155

9 | *Forensic Assessment in Civil Cases* 250

12   *Jury Trials II: Concerns and Reforms*   328

13 *Psychology of Victims*   357

Preface

It has sometimes been said that the "law sharpens the mind by narrowing it." With this edition of *Wrightsman's Psychology and the Legal System*, we hope to reverse that trend and broaden our perspective by applying concepts, theories, and research findings from scientific psychology to the study of law. In doing so, we welcome the addition of a new author, Kirk Heilbrun, whose expertise in a variety of areas related to clinical psychology and law enhances that breadth of focus. His considerable knowledge and experience contribute to our coverage of several new topics and allow a fresh look at the content that has been updated from prior editions.

As authors, we bring varying and complementary backgrounds to this book, including training in social psychology, cognitive psychology, clinical psychology, and law. What we share are careers dedicated to studying and participating in the legal system, merging psychology and law in our research, teaching, and consulting.

We believe that the law is inherently psychological: forged by people with varying desires and ambitions, interpreted by individuals with different (sometimes contradictory) perspectives, and experienced (either directly or indirectly) by all of us. Both psychology and the law are about motivation and behavior. Indeed, for centuries the legal system has exerted a powerful influence on people's everyday activities. From the Supreme Court's school desegregation decision of 1954 to its recent decisions concerning forced medication of mentally ill offenders and constitutionally protected speech, the courts have had considerable impact on individual lives.

But here in the early years of the 21st century, we are experiencing the institution of the law from a different vantage point, as scholars from a wealth of disciplines have applied their concepts to analysis of the legal system. As one of these perspectives, psychology has much to offer. Indeed, matters of law and psychology have become standard fare in the media. Whether they involve allegations of police brutality, criminal trials of the rich and famous, multi-billion-dollar civil litigation, charges of racism in the criminal justice system, or debates about the utility and morality of capital punishment, headlines and lead stories are often about some aspect of psychology and law. Although this attention appears to cater to an almost insatiable curiosity about crime and other types of legal disputes, it also engenders a growing ambivalence about the law. Many citizens are suspicious of the police, but police are still the first responders in a crisis. Attorneys are often held up to ridicule, but the number of people entering the legal profession continues to grow. Juries are frequently criticized for their decisions, but most litigants would prefer to have their cases decided by juries rather than by judges.

The primary audience for *Wrightsman's Psychology and the Legal System* is made up of those students who are taking a course in psychology and the law or the criminal justice system, as well as others who seek to know more about the discoveries and practices of legal psychology. This book may also be used as a supplement in psychology courses that emphasize applied psychology, social issues, or policy analysis. In addition, it covers a number of topics relevant to law school courses that introduce law students to social science research findings and applications.

We have attempted to find the right mix of psychology and legal analysis in the text. The book's emphasis remains on psychological science and practice, but we also summarize the legal history of many key topics and present the current status of relevant legal theories and court decisions. Specific topics that are covered for the first time in this edition include drug courts, mental health courts, new forensic assessment measures, police responses to terrorist threats and mentally ill individuals, brain fingerprinting, forced medication to restore competence, the death penalty for mentally retarded and juvenile offenders, interrogation of suspected terrorists, juveniles' right to self-determination, death row exonerees, and legal issues surrounding children living in nontraditional families.

We continue to focus on the psychological dimensions of several topics that remain important in contemporary society, just as they were important when previous editions of this text were written. These topics include the social influence effects of interrogations (involving children in investigative interviews and adults in interrogation rooms), clinicians' assessments of competence in various domains, reforms to eyewitness identification procedures based on research in perception and memory, recovery from victimization in light of our understanding of posttraumatic stress disorder, and examination of adolescents' decisional abilities relevant to self-determination rights.

NEW FEATURES AND REVISIONS

We have made the following major changes from the last edition:

- The total number of chapters has been reduced from 17 to 15 to reflect more closely the realities of the college schedule.
- In each chapter, case summaries in boxes ("The case of . . .") describe real cases or trials that illustrate or explain an important legal concept or psychological principle covered in the chapter. Readers will be familiar with many of the recent cases, including those of Terri Schiavo, Scott Peterson, the Central Park jogger, former Roman Catholic priest Paul Shanley, Michael Jackson, and Abu Ghraib defendant Charles Graner. We also feature the historic cases of Ernest Miranda, Clarence Gideon, John Hinckley, Ted Bundy, and others.
- We have combined three chapters that had served as introduction to the previous edition and have now sharpened our coverage of the role of psychologists in the legal system and the ethical issues they face. Chapter 1 also introduces the conflicts that pervade a psychological analysis of the law: the rights of individuals versus the common good, equality versus discretion as ideals that can guide the legal system, discovering the truth and resolving conflicts as the goals that the legal system strives to accomplish, and science versus the law as a source of legal decisions.

- We have added a new chapter (Chapter 14) devoted exclusively to psychological issues pertaining to children, adolescents, and the law, including coverage of juvenile offenders, prevention of child maltreatment and child abuse, and the reliability of child witnesses.
- Coverage of the rights of victims and defendants is now distributed throughout the book.

This edition includes a thorough, authoritative revision of every chapter in light of research and professional literature published since the last edition appeared in 2002. Highlights include the following:

- Chapter 2, on players in the legal system, expands our discussion of therapeutic jurisprudence and includes coverage of problem-solving courts such as drug courts and family courts.
- Chapter 4, on the psychology of police, includes updates on crisis intervention and focuses on police interactions with the mentally ill (an increasingly common occurrence), police officers' roles in domestic disturbances and hostage negotiations, and their responses to terrorist threats.
- Chapter 5 describes reforms to lineup procedures in cases involving eyewitness identification. These modifications, which are based on the scientific study of eyewitness memory, have now been implemented in several jurisdictions.
- Chapter 6 includes details of proven false confessions and highlights the large body of recent research on social influence factors in interrogations.
- Chapter 8 on forensic assessment in criminal cases covers the controversial use of forced medications to restore competence and the role of amnesia in decisions regarding competence to stand trial. It also describes the development of important new forensic assessment tools.
- Chapter 9 on forensic assessment in civil cases includes updated coverage of competence to make treatment decisions and new material on competence to execute a will, another increasingly thorny subject at the intersection of psychology and law.
- Chapter 10 provides a newly published update of the classic study by Harry Kalven and Hans Zeisel comparing judges' decisions to juries' decisions. Perhaps the most striking finding is how closely the modern results mirror those of 50 years ago.
- Chapter 11 describes recent controversial cases involving the consideration of racial factors in jury selection, along with new and relevant psychological research.
- Chapter 12 includes the description of some findings from the Arizona Jury Project, a remarkable research effort that involved detailed analyses of actual jury deliberations. From those deliberations we have learned much about what jurors discuss as the trial is going on and at its conclusion.
- Chapter 13 on the psychology of victims features a new section entitled "Offenders as Victims."
- Chapter 15 on punishment and sentencing provides expanded coverage of sex offender sentencing and treatment options. It also describes the current status of laws requiring registration and community notification when sex offenders are released from correctional institutions. This chapter includes updated information

about capital punishment, a topic that has generated considerable psychological research, important judicial decision making, and fervent public debate.

Acknowledgements

We are grateful to the reviewers of this new edition for their helpful and constructive comments: Alfred E. Cohoe, Ohio Northern University; Donna Dahlgren, Indiana University Southeast; Deborah Davis, University of Nevada at Reno; Ann Dirks-Linhorst, Southern Illinois University; Ronald K. McLaughlin, Juniata College; Jerry I. Shaw, California State University at Northridge; Richard P. Wiebe, Fitchburg State College.

Michele Sordi, our editor at Wadsworth, provided support and prompting, wit and wisdom. It was a pleasure to have her on our team. Merrill Peterson coordinated the production in a careful and efficient way. Sarah Harkraker obtained the necessary permissions, and Dan Moneypenny oversaw production of the instructor's manual with test bank. Wendy P. Heath of Rider University wrote the instructor's manual with test bank. We are grateful to all of them.

For assistance closer to home, Edie Greene thanks Melanie Hazlehurst, and Kirk Heilbrun thanks Rachel Kalbeitzer, Michele Pich, and Anna Heilbrun. All of these assistants were prompt, tireless, knowledgeable, and extremely helpful, and each added immeasurably to the final product.

Edie Greene
Kirk Heilbrun
William H. Fortune
Michael T. Nietzel

About the Authors

Photo: Barry Kaplan

Edie Greene earned her Ph.D. in cognitive psychology and law at the University of Washington in 1983. She served as postdoctoral research associate at the University of Washington between 1983 and 1986 and joined the faculty at the University of Colorado, (Colorado Springs) in 1986. She is currently Professor of Psychology. From 1994–1995, Greene was a fellow in Law and Psychology at Harvard Law School. She received her college's award for Outstanding Research and Creative Works in 1999 and her university's award for Excellence in Research in 2001. She has been invited to lecture at the National Judicial College and at continuing legal education programs nation-wide. Greene has received several federally funded grants to support her research on legal decision making and eye-witness memory. She consults with lawyers on various trial-related issues including jury selection, trial strategies, and jury decisions and has, on numerous occasions, testified as an expert witness on jury behavior and eyewitness memory. Greene is the author of a number of articles, columns, and book chapters and co-author of *The adversary system* (with Frank Strier, 1990), and *Determining damages: The psychology of jury awards* (with Brian Bornstein, 2003). She has served as President of the American Psychology-Law Society/APA Division 41.

Anna Heilbrun

Kirk Heilbrun is currently Professor and Head, Department of Psychology, Drexel University. He received his doctorate in clinical psychology in 1980 from the University of Texas at Austin, and completed postdoctoral fellowship training from 1981–82 in psychology and criminal justice at Florida State University. His current research focuses on juvenile and adult offenders, legal decision making, and forensic evaluation associated with such decision making. He is the author of a number of articles on forensic assessment, violence risk assessment and risk communication, and the treatment of mentally disordered offenders, and has published three books (*Principles of Forensic Mental Health Assessment*, 2001, which won the AP-LS book award;

Forensic Mental Health Assessment: A Casebook, with Geff Marczyk and Dave DeMatteo, 2002; and *Juvenile Delinquency: Prevention, Assessment, and Intervention*, with Naomi Goldstein and Rich Redding, 2005). He is board certified in Clinical Psychology and Forensic Psychology, American Board of Professional Psychology, and has previously served as president of both the American Psychology-Law Psychology/APA Division 41 and the American Board of Forensic Psychology. He received the 2004 Distinguished Career Contribution to Forensic Psychology award from the American Academy of Forensic Psychology.

Bill Fortune

William H. Fortune (J.D., University of Kentucky, 1964) is Alumni Professor of Law at the University of Kentucky, Lexington. He formerly served as Academic Ombud for the University of Kentucky and Associate Dean of the College of Law. He is the author of five books and numerous journal articles. His most recent publications include *Kentucky Criminal Law* (with co-author Robert Lawson), published in 1998, and the second edition of the *Modern Litigation and Professional Responsibility Handbook* (with co-authors Richard Underwood and Edward Imwinkelried), published in 2001. Fortune has taught a number of law school courses, including criminal law, criminal procedure, evidence, and professional responsibility.

Fortune served as one of the drafters of the state of Kentucky's rules of evidence and rules of professional responsibility. He currently chairs the Kentucky Justice Council committee, which is charged with rewriting the Kentucky criminal laws. On three occasions he has taken academic leave to serve as a public defender in state and federal court. With Michael Nietzel, Fortune regularly teaches a course in law and psychology to undergraduate and graduate law students.

Lee P. THomas, Photography

Michael T. Nietzel earned his Ph.D. in clinical psychology at the University of Illinois at Urbana–Champaign in 1973 and joined the faculty at the University of Kentucky, Lexington, that same year. During most of the 1980s, Nietzel served as Director of the Clinical Psychology Program, Professor of Psychology (and Law), Dean of the Graduate School, and Provost at the University of Kentucky, and is currently at the University of Kentucky. He is currently President of Missouri State University. Nietzel's research and teaching interests are focused on forensic psychology, jury behavior, the origin of criminal behavior, abnormal psychology, and psychotherapy. He is a frequent consultant to attorneys, law enforcement agencies, and correctional facilities. Nietzel has assisted in jury selection for more than 50 death-penalty trials and regularly trains police officers on various topics involving mental illness. In addition to more than 75 articles, books, and book chapters, he is the co-author of various textbooks on clinical psychology and abnormal psychology.

Psychology and the Law: Impossible Choices

ORIENTING QUESTIONS

1. *Why do we have laws and what is the psychological approach to studying law?*
2. *What dilemmas are reflected in the psychological approach to the law?*
3. *How do recent laws reflect the contrast between the due process model and the crime control model of the criminal justice system?*

4. *What are four roles that psychologists may play in the legal system and what does each entail?*
5. *Is what society considers moral always the same as what it considers legal?*
6. *How do different models of justice explain people's level of satisfaction with the legal system?*
7. *What is commonsense justice?*

Consider the following stories, all of which were prominently featured in the news in the same one-month period:

◆ As students at Red Lake High School in northern Minnesota slowly filed back to class after the most deadly school shooting since Columbine, psychologists and educators cautioned that it would take years for these young people to heal. The trauma of a school shooting may manifest itself in several ways, including poor grades, absenteeism, alcohol and drug abuse, and high teacher turnover. Students are as rattled by the squad of counselors brought in to help them as they are by the extra guards in their hallways and the police cars patrolling outside the building.

◆ A drunken driver who killed a 10-year-old boy in suburban Dallas was sentenced to spend 180 days in jail over the next 10 years, including every Christmas Day, New Year's Day, and June 8, the child's birthday. The judge said he wanted to remind the defendant of the family's loss on these important family holidays.

◆ The Hamilton New Jersey Township Council unanimously approved an ordinance prohibiting sex offenders from moving within 2500 feet of any school, playground, or park, essentially making the township off-limits to registered sex offenders. Hamilton was the home of 7-year-old Megan Kanka, who was raped and murdered in 1994 by a sex offender who moved into her neighborhood. Her death inspired the creation of sex offender registries across the country.

◆ The U.S. Army released thousands of pages of documents describing instances of detainee abuse by American soldiers in Iraq. According to witness statements, one Army 2nd lieutenant was especially sadistic; he took a boy detainee out of a truck and fired his weapon next to the boy's head. Witnesses in the soldier's platoon report that he enjoyed administering "street justice" and felt good when he scared people.

These stories illustrate a few of the psycholegal issues that we consider in this book: the motivations of criminals, discretion in sentencing decisions, the nature of victimization, and the consequences of criminal behavior. They show the real flesh and blood of the major dilemmas we focus on throughout the book.

The Importance of Laws

Taken together, these incidents illustrate the pervasiveness of the law in our society. But just how does the law work? The purpose of this book is to help you understand how the legal system operates by applying psychological concepts, findings, and methods to its study.

Laws as Human Creations

Laws are everywhere. They entwine us; they bear on—often intrude upon—everything from birth to death. Laws regulate our private lives and our public actions. Laws dictate how long we must stay in school, how fast we can drive, when (and, to some extent, whom) we can marry, and whether we are allowed to enjoy many individualistic pleasures, such as playing our car stereos at full blast or letting our boisterous dog romp through the neighbors' yards and gardens. Given that the body of laws has such a widespread impact, we might expect that the law is a part of nature, that it was originally discovered by a set of archaeologists or explorers. Perhaps we summon the image of Moses carrying the Ten Commandments down from the mountain. But our laws are not chiseled in stone. Rather, laws are human creations that evolve out of the need to resolve human conflicts. All complex societies differ in what is considered acceptable behavior, and hence, there are disagreements among people. When these disagreements occur, society must have mechanisms to resolve them. Thus societies develop laws and other regulations as conflict resolution mechanisms.

Laws and the Resolution of Conflict

Conflict—disagreement, argument, and dispute— is not necessarily bad; nor is it always good. Mainly, conflict is inevitable. It cannot be avoided, any more than you can avoid sneezing when the urge to sneeze begins. But society can establish procedures to control your behavior when your sneezing intrudes on another's rights. We recognize the need for mechanisms—laws, rules, and habits—to discourage a person from sneezing in people's faces or on their food. Customs and rules of etiquette evolve partly to deal with the conflict between one person's impulses and other people's rights. Similarly, laws are developed to try to untangle and resolve those conflicts that cannot be prevented.

The Changing of Laws

Because our society is so technologically developed, it also is constantly changing. As society changes, so does our day-to-day existence. The basic raw material for the construction and the revision of laws is human experience. Laws need to be developed, interpreted, reinterpreted, and modified to keep up with the rapid changes in our lives. As George Will (1984) put it, "Fitting the law to a technologically dynamic society often is like fitting trousers to a 10-year-old: Adjustments are constantly needed" (p. 6).

Certainly the framers of the U.S. Constitution, and even the lawmakers of 25 years ago, never antic-

ipated the possibility that frozen embryos and in vitro fertilization procedures would lead a man to sue a fertility clinic for wrongfully impregnating his ex-wife with a frozen embryo created years before. Although Richard Gladu consented to in vitro fertilization while still married, he claims that he should have had a choice about what would happen to the embryos when his marriage was dissolved and accused his ex-wife of using the frozen embryos without his consent. Also, no one could have anticipated the ways that DNA testing would change the scope of criminal investigations. Some states, such as Virginia and Ohio, take DNA samples from all convicted felons, and anyone arrested for a crime in Louisiana is required to give a blood sample. (We describe the role of DNA analysis in the exoneration of convicted criminals in Chapter 5.)

Recently, the rapidly growing popularity of the Internet has caused legislators to consider what, if any, restrictions should be placed on its use. (Cyberlaw, virtually unheard of a couple decades ago, has become an important subfield in the law.) The Children's Internet Protection Act was passed by Congress in 2000. It required libraries that receive federal funding to use antipornography filtering software. Despite claims by the American Library Association that filters block access to constitutionally protected speech, the law was upheld by the U.S. Supreme Court (*United States v. American Library Association*, 2003).

Car accidents—even minor ones—also cause conflicts over basic rights. The technological development of the automobile produced several new adversaries—including pedestrians versus car drivers—and hence new laws. Consider a driver whose car strikes and injures a pedestrian. Does this driver have a legal responsiblity to report the incident to the police? Yes, of course. But look again. Doesn't this requirement violate the Fifth Amendment to the U.S.Constitution, which safeguards each of us against self-incrimination, against bearing witness in conflict with our own best interests?

Shortly after automobiles became popular in the first two decades of the 20th century, a man named Edward Rosenheimer was charged with violating the newly necessary hit-and-run regulation. He did not contest the charge that he had caused an accident that injured another person, but he claimed that the law requiring him to report it to the police was unconstitutional because it forced him to incriminate himself. Therefore, he argued, that law should be removed from the books, and he should be freed of the charge of leaving the scene of an accident. Surprisingly, the Court of General Sessions in New York State agreed with him and released him from custody.

Authorities in New York were, of course, unhappy with a court decision that permitted a person who had caused an injury to avoid being apprehended, so they appealed the decision to a higher court, the New York Court of Appeals. This court, recognizing that the Constitution and the recent law clashed with each other, ruled in favor of the state and overturned the previous decision. This appeals court concluded that rights to "constitutional privilege"—that is, to avoid self incrimination—must give way to the competing principle of the right of injured persons to seek redress for their sufferings (Post, 1963). This example illustrates once more that the law is an evolving human creation, designed to arbitrate between values in opposition to each other. Before the advent of automobiles, hit-and-run accidents seldom occurred. However, once cars became a part of society, many new laws had to be enacted, and the courts obliged by holding the new laws to be constitutional.

The Psychological Study of Law

Laws and legal systems are studied by several traditional disciplines. For example, anthropologists compare laws (and mechanisms for instituting and altering laws) in different societies and relate them to other characteristics of these societies. They may be interested in how frequently women are raped in different types of societies and in the relationship between rape and other factors, such as the extent of separation of the sexes during childhood or the degree to which males dominate females (Sanday, 1997).

Sociologists, in contrast, usually study a specific society and examine its institutions (e.g., the family, the church, or the subculture) to determine their role in developing adherence to the law. The sociologist might study the role that social class plays in criminal behavior. This approach tries to predict and explain social behavior by focusing on groups of people rather than on individuals.

A psychological approach to the law emphasizes its human determinants. The focus in the psychological approach is on the individual as the unit of analysis. Individuals are seen as responsible for their own conduct and as contributing to its causation. Psychology examines the impact of the police officer, the victim, the juror, the expert witness, the corporate lawyer, the judge, the defendant, the prison guard, and the parole officer on the legal system. Psychology assumes that characteristics of participants in the legal system affect how the system operates, and it also recognizes that the law can affect individuals' characteristics and behavior (Ogloff & Finkelman, 1999). By *characteristics*, we mean these persons' abilities, their perspectives, their values, their experience—all the factors that influence their behavior. Will a defendant and his attorney accept a plea bargain, or will they go to trial? Will a Hispanic juror be more sympathetic toward a Hispanic person on trial than toward a non-Hispanic defendant?

But the behavior of participants in the legal system is not just a result of their personal qualities; the setting in which they operate matters, too. Kurt Lewin, a founder of social psychology, proposed the equation $B = f(p, e)$; that is, behavior is a function of the person and the environment. Qualities of the external environment and pressures from the situation affect an individual's behavior. A prosecuting attorney may recommend a harsher sentence for a convicted felon if the case has been highly publicized, the community is outraged over the crime, and the prosecutor happens to be waging a reelection campaign. A juror holding out for a guilty verdict may yield if all the other jurors passionately proclaim the defendant's innocence.

This book concentrates on the behavior of participants in the legal system. As the examples at the beginning of this chapter indicate, we are all active participants in the system, even if we do not work in occupations directly tied to the administration of justice. We all face daily choices that are colored by the law—whether to speed through a school zone because we are late to class or whether to report the person who removes someone else's book bag from a table at the library. Hence, this book will devote some attention to the determinants of our conceptions of justice and the moral dilemmas we all face.

But we will pay more concentrated attention to the central participants in the legal system: defendants and witnesses, civil and criminal lawyers, judges and juries, convicts and parole boards. We will also focus on the activities of **forensic psychologists** who generate and communicate information to answer specific legal questions or to help resolve legal disputes (Grisso, 2003; Nicholson, 1999). Most forensic psychologists are trained as clinical psychologists, whose specialty involves the psychological evaluation and treatment of others. Forensic psychologists are often asked to evaluate a person and then prepare a report for a court or provide expert testimony in court. For example, they may evaluate adult criminal defendants or children involved with the juvenile justice system and offer the court information relevant to determining whether the defendant has a mental disorder that prevents him from going to trial, what the defendant's mental state was at the time of the offense, or what treatment might be appropriate for a particular defendant.

Basic Choices in the Psychological Study of the Law

Just as each of us has to make decisions, society must decide which values it wants its laws to reflect. Choices lead to conflict, and often the resulting dilemmas are unresolvable. Should the laws uphold the rights of specific individuals or protect society in general? For example, which should take precedence—your right to run a loud floor waxer at 3:00 A.M. or the right of everyone else in your apartment building to get a decent night's sleep? Is it better for ten murderers to go free than for one innocent person to be sentenced to death? The law constantly changes as it struggles to provide and ensure rights that, individually, are desirable but that, in combination, are incompatible.

What kind of a society do we want? What laws will best achieve our society's goals? What functions should the legal system serve in our society? These questions highlight four basic choices that pervade the law as it applies to each of us in the United States, Canada, and many other countries. Each choice creates a dilemma. No decision about these choices will be completely satisfactory because no decision can simultaneously attain two incompatible goals, both of which our society values. These four dilemmas (and the tension inherent in their competing values) are so basic that they surface time and again throughout this book.

For example, our society champions both freedom and equality, but it is hard to achieve both at the same time. A small-town civic organization that has always had a "males-only" policy at its Friday night dinners also is a vehicle by which prominent citizens transact their business. The men enjoy the "freedom" to act like "good ol' boys" in the company of their own gender. But what if a woman starts a new insurance agency in the town? Doesn't she have the right to "equality"—to full and equal participation in the civic organization that is influential in the success of any business in this community? It is hard to see how a resolution of this conflict could fully meet both of these goals (freedom of existing members and equality among all comers). The balance in such cases often shifts from one value to another, emphasizing the attainment of first one and then the other goal.

The First Dilemma: Rights of Individuals versus the Common Good

Consider the following:

◆ Smokers have long been restricted to smoky airport lounges and back sections of restaurants, and they often huddle together outside of workplace doors. But now employers are telling their workers that they can be fired for smoking *off* the job as well. Twenty states have no laws preventing employers from firing workers who smoke off the job. The president of Weyco, an insurance benefits administrator, set a deadline for employees to stop smoking and threatened to fire anyone who failed to quit. Should employers have such control over employees' choices away from the workplace, or should employees be able to smoke in the comfort of their own homes? Whose rights prevail?

◆ A Massachusetts state court decision in 2004 paved the way for same-sex couples who reside in that state to marry. But this decision came on the heels of laws and initiatives passed in several other states that ban same-sex marriages. Americans are clearly divided on this issue: According to a 2003 Gallup Poll, 49% favor civil unions (which grant gay and lesbian couples virtually the same rights and privileges as heterosexual couples), yet a Pew Poll conducted that same year showed that only about a third of Americans favor same-sex marriage. This issue, discussed further in Chapter 14, raises complex questions about individual rights versus traditional societal definitions of the family.

◆ In 2005, the Supreme Court decided a case that pitted the Bush administration against 130 New Mexicans who belong to the Christian church O Centro Espirita Beneficiente Uniao Do Vegetal. Founded in Brazil, this church advocates the drinking of hoasca, a sacred herbal tea that members believe connects them to God. But hoasca contains dimethyltryptamine, a substance banned under the federal Controlled Substances Act. The administration maintained that allowing use of the tea would open the nation's borders to

A lesbian couple celebrating their marriage.

the importation and circulation of a mind-altering hallucinogen and interfere with attempts to combat international drug trafficking. Church members pointed out that the Controlled Substances Act allows for some exceptions, including Native Americans' right to use a different hallucinogen—peyote—in their religious ceremonies and that the Religious Freedom Restoration Act protects them from governmental interference in the exercise of religion. The Supreme Court sided with church members.

Values in Conflict

The preceding vignettes share a common theme. On the one hand, individuals possess rights, and one function of the law is to ensure that these rights are protected. The United States is perhaps the most individualistic society in the world. People can deviate from the norm, or "do their own thing," to a greater degree here than virtually anywhere else. Freedom and personal autonomy are two of our most deeply desired values; "the right to liberty" is a key phrase in the U.S. Constitution.

On the other hand, society has expectations, too. People need to feel secure. They need to believe that potential lawbreakers are discouraged from breaking laws because they know they will be punished. All of us have rights to a peaceful, safe existence. Likewise, society claims a vested interest in restricting those who take risks that may injure themselves or others, because these actions can create burdens on society.

It is clear that two sets of rights and two goals for the law are often in conflict. The tension between what rights each individual possesses and what constraints society may place on the individual for its collective welfare is always present. We have seen it in the back-and-forth Supreme Court decisions since the 1960s with respect to the rights of criminal suspects and defendants versus the rights of crime victims and the power of the police. The Supreme Court in the 1960s, headed by Chief Justice Earl Warren, established a number of principles that provided or expanded explicit rights for those suspected of breaking the law. The *Miranda* rule (detailed in Chapter 6) was established in 1966. About the same time, the courts required that criminal defendants, in all cases in which incarceration is possible, have the right to an attorney, even if they can't pay for one themselves. These and other rights were established in an effort to redress a perceived imbalance in responding to important values.

The Supreme Court under Chief Justice Warren Burger, from 1969 to 1986, and Chief Justice William Rehnquist, from 1986 to 2005, trimmed the rights established by the Warren Court by frequently ruling in favor of the police. (For example, in the 1996 case of *Whren v. United States*, the Supreme Court ruled that the police can properly stop a motorist whom they believe has violated traffic laws even if their ulterior motive is to investigate

the possibility of illegal drug dealing. Because most motorists break the speed limit, most motorists are subject to being pulled over and questioned about drug trafficking.) Chief Justice John Roberts is widely expected to follow in the footsteps of his immediate predecessor and mentor, William Rehnquist.

Two Models of the Criminal Justice System

The conflict between the rights of individuals and the rights of society is related to a distinction between two models of the criminal justice system. This distinction is between the due process model and the crime control model (Packer, 1964).

The **due process model** places primary value on the protection of citizens, including criminal suspects, from possible abuses by the police and the law enforcement system generally. It assumes the innocence of suspects and requires that they be treated fairly (receive "due process") by the criminal justice system. It subscribes to the maxim that "it is better that ten guilty persons shall go free than that one innocent person should suffer." Thus the due process model emphasizes the rights of individuals, especially those suspected of crimes, over the temptation by society to assume suspects are guilty even before a trial.

In contrast, the **crime control model** seeks the punishment of lawbreakers. It emphasizes the efficient detection of suspects and the effective prosecution of defendants, so that society can be assured that criminal activity is being contained or reduced. The crime control model is exemplified by a statement by then-attorney general of the United States William P. Barr that with regard to career criminals, the goal is "incapacitation through incarceration" (Barr, 1992)—that is, removing them permanently from circulation. When the crime control model is dominant in society, laws may be passed that in other times would be seen as unacceptable violations of individual rights. The Racketeer Influenced and Corrupt Organizations laws (called RICO), passed by Congress in 1970, are an example. Although the original purpose of the RICO laws was to combat the growing influence of organized crime on legitimate business (Vise, 1989), they have been used to prosecute Wall Street executives for stock fraud and tax evasion charges, going beyond the usual definition of "racketeer."

Despite the drop in crime rates in recent years, the crime control model is clearly in ascendancy in the United States, more so than in Canada, Europe, and Australia. Currently, the United States incarcerates 492 of every 100,000 of its citizens, and the decade of the 1990s saw far more prisoners incarcerated than any decade in recorded history. According to the Center on Juvenile and Criminal Justice, the United States has only 5% of the world's population but 25% of its prisoners (www.cjcj.org/pubs/punishing/punishing.html).

Beginning with the state of Washington in 1993, several states and the federal government have passed laws that reflect the crime control model's goal of keeping lawbreakers off the streets. California's 1994 **three-strikes law** ("three strikes and you're out") is the most stringent. Under this law, criminals convicted of a third felony, no matter how minor, must be sentenced to either 25 years to life in prison or triple the regular sentence, whichever is greater, if their first and second offenses were serious or violent. Persons convicted a second time of a serious or violent felony have their sentences doubled. Although such laws have

the intent of increasing the punishments for habitual criminals, they sometimes lead to results that make it doubtful whether the punishment fits the specific crime. For example, a California man with multiple convictions was sentenced to 25 years to life in prison for stealing a slice of pizza; another received the same sentence for impersonating his dead brother in a routine traffic stop.

In fact, one study found that the vast majority of those receiving the stiff sentences had committed, as their third-and-out crime, a nonviolent offense. Almost 200 were sentenced for marijuana possession, compared to 40 who were convicted of murder, 25 of rape, and 24 of kidnapping. "We're worried about Willie Horton [a convicted sex offender], and we lock up the Three Stooges," said Professor Franklin Zimring of the University of California at Berkeley (quoted by Butterfield, 1996, p. A8). Another study found that seven years after it was enacted, the three-strikes law had contributed to the aging of the prison population but had had no effect on the state's crime rate. This study estimates that by 2026, California will have 30,000 inmates serving sentences of 25 years to life, at a cost to taxpayers of at least $750 million, and that more than 80% of them will be 40 or older (King & Mauer, 2001).

Psychology, as an approach to the law, provides methods for assessing public opinion about the desirability of these two models. In one survey, 72% approved of a three-strikes law. In another survey, 50% responded "true" to the following: "In a criminal trial, it is up to the person who is accused of the crime to prove his innocence." This is a false statement—the accused doesn't even have to offer a defense, other than to plead "not guilty"—but half the respondents answered incorrectly, implicitly advocating the crime control view.

Their error does not mean that the crime control model is wrong. The values underlying each of the contrasting models are legitimate, and the goal of our society is to achieve a balance between them. As you will see throughout this book, our government constantly struggles to offer a mix of laws that reasonably honors each set of values. For example, nearly all

Illinois Sex Offender Information

Illinois Sex Offender

Name:	EARL ABNEY
Alias Name(s):	ABNEY,LARRY HUNT,CHARLES
Date of Birth:	8/24/1943
Alias DOB(s):	7/24/1943
Height:	5 ft. 05 in.
Weight:	185 lbs.
Race:	W
Sex:	M
Address:	2301 BENTON UPSTAIRS
City:	GRANITE CITY
State:	IL
Zip Code:	62040

VICTIM UNDER THE AGE OF 18

Crimes:	
AGGRAVATED CRIMINAL SEXUAL ASSAULT	
CRIMINAL SEXUAL ABUSE FORCE	
INDECENT LIBERTIES WITH A CHILD/SEX	
County of Conviction:	MADISON

COMPLIANT

Back Print

Print options may also be found under the 'File' menu from the browser or hit CTRL+P.

Criminal history information may be available for sex offenders on parole or mandatory supervised release through the Illinois Department of Corrections link below. Click on the link, select 'inmate search' and type in the offender's name or other identifying information. Illinois Department of Corrections

Copyright © 2005 Illinois State Police

Illinois State Police

Sex-offender online registry.

states—as well as the U.S. Congress—have passed **notification laws** that require convicted sex offenders to register with police, indicating where they live. The laws also instruct law enforcement officials to notify neighbors when those sex offenders move into their neighborhoods. In addition, parents in some states can use these laws to protect their children from released sex offenders lurking in cyberspace, because convicted sex offenders in those states must report their Internet accounts and screen names to police.

The Second Dilemma: Equality versus Discretion

Kenneth Peacock was a long-distance trucker who was caught in an ice storm and came home at the wrong time. He walked in the door to find his wife Sandra in bed with another man. Peacock chased the man away and some four hours later, in the heat of an argument, shot his wife in the head with a hunting rifle. Peacock pled guilty to voluntary manslaughter and was sentenced to 18 months in prison. At the sentencing, Baltimore County Circuit Court Judge Robert E. Cahill said he wished he did not have to send Peacock to prison at all but knew that he must to "keep the system honest" (Lewin, 1994). He continued, "I seriously wonder how many men . . . would have the strength to walk away without inflicting some corporal punishment."

Move the clock ahead one day. A female defendant pleads guilty to voluntary manslaughter in a different Baltimore courtroom. She killed her husband after 11 years of abuse and was given a 3-year sentence, three times longer than what the prosecutors had sought (Lewin, 1994). Some people find no inconsistency in the severity of these punishments, believing that each case should be judged on its own merits. However, psychology analyzes these decisions as examples of a dilemma between the goals of equality and discretion.

What should be the underlying principle in response to persons accused of violating the law? Again, we discover that two equally desirable values are often incompatible and hence create conflict. And again, psychology provides concepts through which this conflict can be studied and better understood.

The principle of **equality** means that all people who commit the same crime should receive the same consequences. Fundamental to our legal system is the assumption advanced by the founders of the American republic that "all men are created equal." This statement is frequently interpreted to mean that no one should receive special treatment by the courts simply because he or she is rich, influential, or otherwise advantaged. We cherish the belief that in the United States, politically powerful or affluent people are brought before the courts and, if guilty, convicted and punished just like anyone else who commits similar offenses. For example, in 2005 former Connecticut Governor John Rowland was sentenced to a year in prison and 4 months of house arrest after he pleaded guilty to a corruption charge stemming from his use of state funds for lavish trips and a house remodel. He joined the ranks of more than a dozen former governors who have spent time in prison.

Protest against racial profiling.

But this value of equality before the law is not always implemented. The late 1990s saw a series of incidents that—at least on the surface—seemed to indicate unequal treatment of citizens by the legal system. A common practice among police and state patrols in the United States is *profiling*—viewing certain characteristics as indicators of criminal behavior. Black and Hispanic motorists have filed numerous lawsuits over the practice of profiling, alleging that police, in an effort to seize illegal drugs and weapons, apply a "race-based profile" and stop and search them more frequently than white drivers. The plaintiffs in a Maryland case assembled an impressive set of statistics: Although 75% of drivers on Interstate 95 are white, only 23% of the people stopped and searched between 1995 and 1997 were white. Conversely, although only 17% of drivers on the interstate are black, 70% of those pulled over were black. Says Michigan Congressman John Conyers, Jr., "There are virtually no African-American males—including Congressmen, actors, athletes and office workers—who have not been stopped at one time or another for . . . driving while black" (Barovick, 1998). (Indeed, State Senator Kevin Murray of California was pulled over and questioned by police as he drove through Beverly Hills on the very night he won his Senate primary in 1998.)

Many police agencies now gather statistics on the racial makeup of people targeted for traffic stops, border inspections, and other routine searches, and some courts have ruled that a person's appearance may not be the basis for such stops. Psychologists also have a role to play on this issue, gathering data on the psychological consequences to victims of racial profiling, improving police training so that cultural and racial awareness is enhanced, and examining how decision makers form implicit judgments of others on the basis of race.

In keeping with the laudable goal of equality in the law, the Supreme Court has, on occasion, applied a **principle of proportionality**; that is, the punishment should be consistently related to the magnitude of the offense. More serious crimes should earn more severe penalties. If a relatively minor crime leads to a harsh punishment, then the fundamental value of equality has been violated. Yet the Supreme Court has also upheld the constitutionality of California's three-strikes law, setting aside arguments that at least in some cases, the punishment is grossly disproportionate to the severity of the offense (*Ewing v. California*, 2003). Even the highest court in the land struggles with the meaning of equality and its application to diverse sets of facts.

Although equality often remains an overriding principle, society also believes that **discretion** is appropriate. Rigid application of the law can lead to injustices. By discretion, we mean the use of judgments about the circumstances of certain offenses that lead to appropriate *variations* in how the system responds to these offenses. Many players in the legal system have the opportunity to exercise

discretion, and most do so on a regular basis. Police officers show discretion when they decide not to arrest someone who technically has broken the law. Prosecutors exercise discretion when they decide which of many arrestees to charge and for what particular crime. Juries exercise discretion in not convicting defendants who have killed others but who did so under circumstances that may have justified their actions (e.g., self-defense, heat of passion).

Although not usually considered formal participants in the justice system, state governors also have the opportunity to exercise discretion when they decide whether to commute a death sentence to life imprisonment (a process called granting clemency) or to allow an execution to proceed as planned. George W. Bush faced that stark choice when he was governor of Texas in 1998 (see Box 1.1). He had to decide whether Karla Faye Tucker, an attractive, seemingly reformed, well-behaved death row inmate, should be executed by lethal injection or allowed to live. This case raises interesting questions about both discretion and the role of gender in the criminal justice system.

Discretion may be most obvious in the sentences administered by judges to convicted criminals. In many cases, judges are able to consider the particular circumstances of the defendant and of the crime itself when they determine the sentence. It would seem that this use of discretion is a good thing, yet it can also lead to **sentencing disparity**, the tendency of different judges to administer a variety of penalties for the same crime. The contrasting sentences meted out by judges in the Baltimore cases we described earlier offer an example of sentencing disparity.

Sentencing disparity also is manifest in the penalties given to African Americans and members of other minority groups. A thorough survey of the sentences given to convicted murderers in Philadelphia (Baldus, Woodworth, Zuckerman, Weiner, & Broffitt, 1998) found that blacks were significantly more likely than people of other races to receive the death penalty, even when the research design included controlling for the severity of the crime (see Chapter 15). But inequality in

BOX 1.1   Karla Faye Tucker and a governor's discretion

In 1983, Karla Faye Tucker was a drug addict and a prostitute. On June 13, she and her boyfriend, Daniel Ryan Garrett, hacked Tucker's former boyfriend and his female companion to death using a pickax. At her trial, Tucker even boasted of experiencing an orgasm with each plunge of the ax down upon her victims. Both perpetrators were convicted and sentenced to death. (Garrett subsequently died while in prison.)

But over the years she spent on death row, Tucker began to turn her life around. She converted to Christianity, had a spotless disciplinary record, and was, by all accounts, rehabilitated. In the months preceding her scheduled execution, she became something of a cause célèbre. Her supporters included the Reverend Pat Robertson; Dana Brown, a prison chaplain she married in 1996

during her imprisonment; a homicide detective who recommended the death penalty in the first place; thousands of citizens; and siblings of one of the victims. In various pleas to save her life, these advocates argued that Tucker was not the same person she had been 15 years earlier. But then-Governor George W. Bush was not convinced. He refused to intervene in Tucker's case, and she was executed by lethal injection in 1998.

One wonders about the role of Tucker's gender in this dispute and whether a male death row inmate could generate the same loud cries of protest. Tucker is one of only ten women to have been executed since the death penalty was reinstated in the United States in 1976. (Aileen Wuornos, whose crimes are depicted in the movie *Monster*, is another.) Surely some of the gender disparity in executions can be

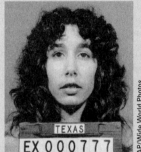

explained by the kinds of crimes that men and women typically commit (men tend to commit more violent crimes) and by the likelihood of receiving a death sentence for those crimes. But there have undoubtedly been male death row inmates who exhibited the same clean record and apparent atonement as Karla Faye Tucker. We usually hear little about their pleas for clemency.

punishment is not limited to the most serious crimes. A study of prison and jail incarceration rates (across *all* crime categories) for 2001 revealed that African Americans were more than six times as likely as whites to be imprisoned (Sentencing Project, 2004).

A simple explanation for this disparity is **racial bias**, whereby police officers, prosecutors, jurors, and judges use an individual's race as a basis for judgments of his or her behavior. But the situation may actually be a bit more complex; some studies have shown that once these decision makers are made aware of the potential for racial bias,

they can largely avoid it, and racial injustices in the criminal justice system have declined in recent years (Spohn, 2000). A subtler, more insidious form of race-based judgments may still be prevalent in the justice system, however. Social psychological research has shown that individuals of the same race may be stereotyped and discriminated against to different degrees, depending how "typical" of their group they look (Maddox & Gray, 2002). Thus, blacks who possess more Afrocentric facial features may be subjected to more prejudicial treatment. Indeed, an analysis of criminal sentencing in Florida showed that among black defendants, those with more Afrocentric features were given longer sentences than those with less distinctive Afrocentric features (Blair, Judd, & Chapleau, 2004).

To counteract sentencing disparity, many states have implemented what is known as **determinate sentencing**; the offense determines the sentence, and courts and parole commissions have little discretion. In 1987, the U.S. Sentencing Commission established strict guidelines to govern the sentences to be meted out for federal crimes. For every crime, the guidelines assigned a "Base Offense Level," which was adjusted up or down (usually up) on the basis of certain factors in the case (such as serious injury to the victim). But many judges have been frustrated by the severe limitation on their discretion. One federal judge who resigned his appointment in protest over mandatory sentencing rules said, "It's an unfair system that has been dehumanized. There are rarely two cases that are identical. Judges should always have discretion. That's why we're judges. But now we're being made to be robots. I cannot in good conscience play this game any longer."

The pendulum may now have begun to swing away from determinate sentencing and toward allowing judges more discretion. The Supreme Court ruled that both state (*Blakely v. Washington*, 2004) and federal sentencing guidelines (*United States v. Booker*, 2005) violate a defendant's right to a jury trial because the guidelines require judges to decide questions that are normally reserved for juries, such as the quantity of drugs involved in a narcotics case. Sentencing guidelines are now merely advisory. Permitting judges more leeway to consider factors such as the defendant's background, motivations for committing the crime, and any psychological disorders may strike a balance between the sentencing uniformity that the guidelines intended and the judicial discretion that some judges prefer.

The tension between equality and discretion is also apparent in cases where mitigating circumstances cry out for mercy as well as justice. In some cases, juries refuse to convict defendants even though there is clear evidence of their guilt. This preference to acquit legally guilty, but morally blameless, defendants is known as **jury nullification**; it is discussed more fully in Chapter 10. Psychology can play a role in determining the degree of public discontent (if any) over verdict options and sentencing disparities.

The Third Dilemma: To Discover the Truth or to Resolve Conflicts

What is the purpose of a trial or a hearing before a judge? Your first reaction may be "To find out the truth, of course!" Determining the truth means learning the facts of the case, including events, intentions, actions, and outcomes. All this assumes that "what really happened" between two parties can be ascertained.

Finding out the truth is a desirable goal, but it may also be a lofty, unattainable one. The truth often lies somewhere between competing versions of an event. Given that it is difficult for even well-meaning people to ascertain the true facts in certain cases, some observers have proposed that the real purpose of a hearing or trial is to provide social stability by resolving conflict. Supreme Court Justice Louis Brandeis once wrote that "it is more important that the applicable rule of law be settled than [that] it be settled right" (*Burnet v. Coronado Oil and Gas Co.*, 1932). In other words, there is a shift away from viewing the legal system's purpose as doing justice toward viewing its goal as "creating a sense that justice is being done" (Miller & Boster, 1977, p. 34).

Because truth is elusive, the most important priority of a hearing or a trial—whether it is to determine child custody or an alleged drug dealer's guilt—may be to provide a setting in which all interested parties have their "day in court." Justice for all parties replaces truth as the predominant goal. In fact, attorneys representing the opposing parties in a case do not necessarily seek "the truth." Nor do they represent themselves as "objective." They reflect a different value—the importance of giving their side the best representation possible, within the limits of the law. (The Code of Ethics of the

American Bar Association even instructs attorneys to defend their clients "zealously.") Because lawyers believe the purpose of a hearing or trial is to win disputes, they present arguments supporting their client's perspective and back up their arguments with the best available evidence.

Some psychologists note that one argument in favor of the adversary system, in which a different attorney represents each party, is that it encourages the attorneys to discover and introduce every bit of evidence that might induce the judge or jury to react favorably to their client's case. When both sides believe that they have had the chance to voice their case fully and their representatives have revealed all the relevant facts, participants are more likely to feel they have been treated fairly by the system, and the system is more likely to be considered an effective one.

"Conflict resolution" and "truth," as goals, are not always incompatible. When each participant sees to it that his or her concerns and supporting documentation are presented in court, the goal of knowing the truth often becomes more attainable. But a tension between these goals often exists. In some instances, the satisfactory resolution of a conflict may be socially and morally preferable to discovering an objectively established truth. But when conflict resolution compromises truth, the outcome can often be unsatisfactory.

This was the case for Richard Jewell, a security guard at the 1996 Summer Olympics in Atlanta. Shortly after a bombing that disrupted the Games, the FBI began to question Jewell, who discovered the bomb. Although at first the FBI denied that he was a suspect, they treated him like one, and his name and photograph were circulated to the entire world. The pressure to find the person who caused this terrifying act—and the desire to give people a sense that no more bombings would occur because the perpetrator had been caught—doubtless drove the focus on Richard Jewell. Despite relentless FBI investigation, no charges were brought against Jewell, and in 2005, Eric Rudolph, a fugitive who lived in the hills of North Carolina for years after the bombing, pleaded guilty to that charge.

Eric Rudolph, a North Carolina fugitive, who pled guilty in 2005 to a bombing at the 1996 Olympics in Atlanta.

Truth versus Conflict Resolution in Plea Bargaining and Settlement Negotiation

The legal system is a massive bureaucracy, and in every bureaucracy, there is a temptation to value pragmatic efficiency rather than correct or just outcomes. The heavy reliance on plea bargaining is often criticized because it appears to give priority to conflict resolution over truth seeking. From 80% to 95% of defendants never go to trial; they accept the offer of the prosecutor and plead guilty to a lesser charge. Even some innocent persons plea-bargain after being convinced that the evidence against them is overwhelming. Indeed, plea bargaining remains an integral part of the criminal justice system. The state benefits by escaping the expense and trouble of trial, by avoiding the possibility of an acquittal, and often by obtaining the testimony of the accused against others involved in the crime. The defendant benefits by receiving some kind of reduction in the penalty imposed. Many would argue that, in addition to these pragmatic benefits, justice is furthered by a system that rewards a show of contrition (which usually accompanies a guilty plea) and enables the prosecutor and defense counsel, often in concert with the judge, to negotiate a resolution appropriate to the degree of wrongdoing (Kamisar, LaFave, & Israel, 1999). Nonetheless, the process illustrates how the goal of maintaining stability and efficiency in the system is achieved at some sacrifice of the public's opportunity to determine the complete truth.

In civil cases, a procedure that parallels plea bargaining resolves about 90% of the conflicts between a plaintiff and a defendant. **Settlement negotiation** involves a sometimes lengthy pretrial process of give-and-take, offer-and-demand that ultimately ends with a plaintiff agreeing to accept what a defendant is willing to offer to end their legal disagreement.

Settlement negotiations also offer an opportunity for defendants to apologize for unforeseen outcomes experienced by the plaintiff. Although some defendants are loath to apologize because they fear that their apologies could be interpreted by judges and juries as admissions of responsibility, recent research shows that apologies may actually advance settlement negotiations and have other positive effects. In one study, people who were asked to take on the role of an injured person and evaluate a settlement offer were more likely to accept the offer when it was accompanied by an apology (Robbennolt, 2003). Apologies may also reduce plaintiffs' inclinations to sue (Gallagher et al., 2003), dissipate tension and antagonism in the settlement process (Shuman, 2000), and enhance jurors' perceptions of defendants (Bornstein, Rung, & Miller, 2002).

The Fourth Dilemma: Science versus the Law as a Source of Decisions

When one discipline (in our case, psychology) seeks to understand another (the law), a dilemma is likely to arise because each approaches knowledge in a different way. When asked, "How do you know whether that decision is the right one?" each relies on different methods, even though both share a general goal of understanding human experience.

As you will see on several occasions in this book, in its recent decisions, the U.S. Supreme Court has often considered data and conclusions presented by psychologists and other social scientists. In several recent cases, the American Psychological Association has prepared a supporting brief, called an ***amicus curiae*** ("friend of the court") **brief**, for an appellant whose appeal was being considered by the Court. In many of these decisions, the Court has incorporated input from the *amicus curiae* brief into its decision, although in other cases it has disregarded the social science data. Sometimes these decisions reflect the fact that the justices use different procedures and concepts from those of social science in forming their judicial opinions (Grisso & Saks, 1991).

In addition to employing different procedures, each profession may use idiosyncratic, or unique, concepts to describe the same phenomenon. An attorney and a social scientist will see the same event from different perspectives. Neither is necessarily more accurate than the other; the differences are the results of exposure to and training in different points of view. The following subsections illustrate such differences in more detail (see also Ogloff & Finkleman, 1999).

Law Is Doctrinal; Psychology Is Empirical

Psychology, in contrast to the law, is generally committed to the idea that there is an objective world of experience that can best be understood by adherence to the rules of science—systematic testing of hypotheses by observation and experimental methodology. As a scientist, the psychologist should be committed to a public, impersonal, objective pursuit of truth, using methods that can be repeated by others and interpreting results by predetermined standards. Although this traditional view of psychology's approach to truth is often challenged as naive and simplistic (Gergen, 1994) because it ignores the importance of the personal, political, and historical filters that are used just as much by scientists as by nonscientists, it still represents the values and methods in which most psychologists are trained. (It also represents our belief, as authors, that the scientific method and the research skills of psychologists are the most essential and reliable tools available for examining the many important legal questions we address throughout the book.)

By contrast, legal experts rely heavily on precedents in establishing new laws. When confronted with a case, judges and attorneys examine rulings in previous cases (as well as the Constitution and the statutes) for guidance. **Case law**, the law made by judges ruling in individual cases, is very influential; statutes and constitutional safeguards do not apply to every new situation, and so past cases often serve as precedents for deciding current ones. The principle of *stare decisis* ("let the decision stand") is important in this process. Judges typically are reluctant to make decisions that contradict earlier ones, as the history of the Supreme Court's school desegregation decision indicates.

When the U.S. Supreme Court voted unanimously in May 1954, in *Brown v. Board of Education*, that public school segregation was contrary to the law, many reports claimed that it "supplanted" or even "overturned" a previous ruling in the 1896 case of *Plessy v. Ferguson*. But intermediate decisions by the Court permitted this seemingly abrupt change to evolve more predictably.

A brief history of rulings that led up to the *Brown v. Board of Education* (1954) decision illustrates this phenomenon. During a train trip in Louisiana in the 1890s, Homer Plessy sat down in a railroad car labeled "Whites Only." Plessy's ancestry was mostly Caucasian, but he had one Negro great-grandparent. Therefore, according to

the laws of Louisiana at that time, Plessy was considered a black (or "colored," in the prevalent terminology at that time). Plessy refused to move to a car designated for "colored" passengers, as a recently passed state law required. He took his claim to court, but a New Orleans judge ruled that, contrary to Plessy's argument, the statute that segregated railroad cars by race did not violate the Fourteenth Amendment to the Constitution; that is, it did not fail to give Plessy "equal protection under the law." Plessy persisted in his appeal, and eventually, in 1896, the Supreme Court affirmed the decision of the judge and the lower courts. Judge Henry Billings Brown, speaking for the majority, declared that laws that had established separate facilities for the races did not necessarily imply that one race was inferior to the other.

Although this opinion was a far cry from the 1954 *Brown* decision, which highlighted the detrimental effects of segregation on the personality development of black children, cases subsequent to *Plessy* would foreshadow the Court's eventual leanings. One case was brought by George McLaurin, the first black student admitted to the University of Oklahoma's graduate school of education. Although McLaurin was allowed to enroll, he was segregated from all his classmates. His desk was separated from all the others by a rail, to which the sign "Reserved for Colored" was attached; he was given a separate desk at the library; and he was required to eat by himself in the cafeteria. In the 1950 case of *McLaurin v. Oklahoma State Regents*, the U.S. Supreme Court ruled unanimously that these procedures denied McLaurin the right to equal protection of the law; it concluded that such restrictions would "impair and inhibit his ability to study, to engage in discussion and exchange of views with other students." But again, the Court did not strike down *Plessy v. Ferguson*.

It was not until Earl Warren was appointed chief justice in 1953 that enough momentum built to reverse *Plessy v. Ferguson*. Justice Warren was not a precise legal scholar; he was less concerned with the fine points of the law than with whether the law was just. He liked to ask, "What is fair?" It was Warren who spearheaded the unanimous decision that finally overturned the idea that separate facilities can be "equal." He wrote that to separate black children "from others of similar age and qualifications solely because of their race generates a feeling of inferiority as to their status in the community that may affect their hearts and minds in a way unlikely to ever be undone." (*Brown v. Board of Education*, 1954).

Law Functions by the Case Method; Psychology, by the Experimental Method

Lawyers reason from case to case. They locate cases that are similar to the one at hand and then base their arguments on the rulings from these other cases, termed **legal precedence**. Psychologists, on the other hand, value the experimental method and prefer to gather data that are descriptive of large numbers of people. Just as psychologists are leery of findings based on very small samples, lawyers are hesitant to decide a person's fate on the basis of aggregate data drawn from other people (Ellsworth & Mauro, 1998).

Law Deals with Absolutes; Psychology Deals with Probabilities

Lawyers think in terms of "either–or": A person was either insane or not insane when he committed a particular act; a person is either fit or unfit to be a parent (Ellsworth & Mauro, 1998). Psychologists are not comfortable reasoning in absolutes; they prefer to think in terms of probabilities (e.g., that a white eyewitness to a crime is more likely to misidentify an African American perpetrator than a white perpetrator). When the law looks to psychologists for either–or answers to questions ("Was this person sane when he committed the crime?"), psychologists usually prefer to answer in terms of likelihoods or quantified "maybes." Lawyers have difficulty with such inconclusive responses because they need a final resolution to a dispute.

Law Supports Contrasting Views of Reality; Psychology Seeks to Clarify One Muddled View of Reality

As indicated earlier, judges and jurors must decide which of two conceptions of the truth is more acceptable in light of a mixed set of facts. Attorneys representing clients marshal all the facts that support their side and argue forcefully that their version of the facts is the correct one. Although this procedure is similar to some scientific activities (a psychologist may do a study that pits predictions from two theories against each other), the psychologist is trained to be objective and open to all perspectives and types of data. The psychologist's ultimate goal is to integrate or assimilate conflicting findings into one refined view of the truth, rather than choosing between alternative views.

Some observers have likened this difference between psychology and law to the difference between scaling a mountain and fighting in a boxing match. As psychologists gain increasingly clear understanding of a topic (e.g., the causes of domestic violence), they scale a figurative mountain, at the top of which lies true and complete understanding. Although they may never actually reach this pinnacle of knowledge, psychologists place high value on the accumulation of data, the development of psychological theory, and the quest for "truth." By contrast, lawyers are less interested in ascertaining the objective truth about a topic and more concerned with winning against their adversary. Of value to lawyers is the resolution of conflicts in favor of their clients (although the restorative justice movement that we describe in Chapter 15 strives for a win–win resolution of conflicts). Of course, for most lawyers, scoring a knockout would be even better.

The foregoing distinctions only scratch the surface of the differences between law and psychology. Later in this chapter we will consider differing notions of justice in the two fields, and in subsequent chapters we will encounter many implications of these differences. As with the previous choices, selecting one domain over the other is not a satisfactory response. The use of both approaches moves us closer to the goal of an adequate understanding than does reliance on one approach alone. We must remain aware of the limits of our own perspective and realize that other viewpoints are essential for a full understanding of complex behavioral issues in the law.

However, the contrast in knowledge-generating procedures does raise tough procedural questions. For example, given the differences in approach, how should a psychologist respond to the challenge of studying the law? What kind of role or roles should the psychologist play in the legal system? What are some of the ethical concerns associated with psychologists' involvement in the legal system?

Psychologists' Relationship to the Law

Most courses in psychology portray only two roles for psychologists: that of the scientist who conducts basic research about the causes and development of behavior and that of the applied psychologist (usually the clinical psychologist) who tries to understand and assist individuals or groups in confronting their problems. The possibilities are more elaborate, however, especially when the psychologist interfaces with the legal system. Four contrasting roles can be ordered on a continuum from isolated academic research in psychology and law, on one end, to collaboration with persons from other disciplines to provide services to the legal system, on the other end.

The Psychologist as a Basic Scientist of the Law

A **basic scientist** pursues knowledge for its own sake. Basic researchers study a phenomenon simply for the satisfaction and joy of understanding it. They do not seek to apply their findings; many have no concern with whether the knowledge they generate is ever put to any practical, problem-solving use. For example, laboratory research on visual perception helps us understand just how accurate eyewitness testimony about a crime or accident is. Psychologists who test different theories of memory promote a better understanding of whether repression can cause long-term forgetting of traumatic events. Basic research on the relationship of one's social attitudes to one's behavior can help us realize why people obey or disobey the law. Research in personality psychology can begin to illuminate what kind of person will become a follower in a terrorist group and what kind of person will be a leader. Finally, clinical research can assess whether psychologists' basic attitudes about the causes of crime affect their professional evaluations of criminal defendants.

The Psychologist as an Applied Scientist in the Law

Applied scientists are dedicated to applying knowledge to solve real-life problems. Most of the public's awareness of the psychologist's work reflects this role, whether this awareness comes from viewing TV's Dr. Phil or from watching a psychologist testify as an expert witness in a trial televised on Court TV. Indeed, an important role for psychologists who are interested in applying the findings of their profession is serving as an expert witness in legislative hearings or in a courtroom. Psychologists often testify as expert witnesses during a trial. Either side, as part of its presentation of the evidence, may ask the judge to allow expert witnesses to testify. Juries—and judges, too, for that matter—cannot be expected to be well versed in every topic from abscesses to zinfandel wine. An **expert witness** is someone who possesses special knowledge about a subject, knowledge that the average juror does not have. The judge must be convinced that the testimony any expert will present is of a kind that requires special knowledge, skill, or experience and that the testimony will help resolve the dispute and lead jurors toward the truth.

The psychological topics that call for expertise are almost limitless. And psychologists, as expert witnesses, have been called on to testify in many types of cases. For example, expert testimony may be useful in understanding issues such as the following:

◆ The mental state of a defendant at the time of an alleged offense and the mental competence of the defendant to stand trial
◆ The degree of emotional or brain damage suffered by a victim in an accident
◆ Employee discrimination through selection and promotion procedures
◆ The accuracy of identifications by eyewitnesses
◆ The effects of posting warning signs or safety instructions on potentially dangerous equipment
◆ The effects of alternative child custody arrangements after divorce
◆ The prospects for a convicted defendant's rehabilitation in prison or on probation
◆ The factors that may cause a suspect to make a false confession

Expert witnesses are usually proposed by one side in a trial, and the judge decides whether they will be allowed to testify. Many judges fear that an expert witness's testimony will be so powerful that it will usurp the jury as the fact finder in the case, and so judges sometimes refuse to let experts testify, especially if they are convinced that the topic is one that most laypeople are familiar with. On other occasions, judges have disallowed expert testimony as irrelevant or immaterial. Consider the case of unlucky Pedro Gil. On a night of wild abandon in the fall of 1993, Gil hoisted a bucket of plaster over the wall of a Manhattan rooftop. It dropped seven stories to the ground and hit and killed a police officer standing on the street below. Gil claimed that he expected the bucket to drop unceremoniously onto an unoccupied street directly below him, rather than to continue forward as it fell and land on the street where the police officer was positioned. To support his

naive belief that objects drop straight down, Gil's attorneys attempted to introduce the testimony of cognitive psychologist Michael McCloskey, an expert in intuitive physics, who was prepared to testify that people commonly misunderstand physical laws. The trial judge did not let McCloskey take the stand, claiming that intuitive physics was irrelevant to the issues under contention. The jury convicted Gil of second-degree manslaughter.

Judges have discretion about many kinds of decisions in their courtrooms, and whether to allow expert testimony is one of the most important, and often controversial, examples of this discretion. The Supreme Court has indicated (*Daubert v. Merrell Dow Pharmaceuticals, Inc.*, 1993) that judges' decisions about the admissibility of expert testimony based on "scientific" knowledge must turn on the validity of the science in question. In essence, judges are supposed to function as "gatekeepers" who must evaluate potential expert testimony by the standards of science. The *Daubert* decision listed four factors that should be considered in assessing the validity—and subsequent admissibility—of the expert's testimony: (1) whether the expert's theory or technique can be and has been tested, a concept known as falsifiability, (2) whether it has been evaluated by peer review, (3) the reliability and error rate of the claims, and (4) the extent to which the expert's techniques and claims have been generally accepted by the relevant scientific community. The Court has said that these criteria also apply to testimony based on technical or nonscientific knowledge (*Kumho Tire C. v. Carmichael*, 1999).

One clear implication of the *Daubert* decision is that judges must become savvy consumers of science if they are to decide which opinions qualify as "scientific." Unfortunately, judges are not trained in scientific methodology and, indeed, do not seem to understand some of the more technical aspects of the guidelines (such as falsifiability and error rates) (Gatowski et al., 2001). Thus, their decisions about the admissibility of expert testimony are based less on the *Daubert* criteria and more on nontechnical considerations such as whether the findings are generally accepted and whether the expert testimony is relevant to the case at hand (Dahir et al., 2005; Groscup et al., 2002).

Various groups of psychologists have provided resources for judges to use when faced with cases involving psychological issues, and others have sponsored workshops and training about psychological questions that arise in legal proceedings. The intent of these overtures is to educate judges about the methods of science so that they can make better-informed decisions about which psychological experts will be allowed to testify and which will be excluded.

The Psychologist as a Policy Evaluator in the Law

In addition to their knowledge of substantive problems, psychologists have methodological skills that they use in assessing how well an intervention has worked. Psychologists and other social scientists have been asked so frequently in the last several decades to conduct evaluation studies that a separate subfield called policy evaluation, or evaluation research, has emerged. The **policy evaluator** provides data to answer questions such as "I have instituted a change; how do I know whether it was effective? Or, more laudably, "I want to make a change in our organization's procedures, but before I do, how do I design it so I will be able to determine later whether it worked?" Psychologists working as policy evaluators might be asked whether changing the laws for teen drivers by restricting the number of passengers they can carry will reduce traffic accidents or whether the chemical castration of released rapists will reduce the rate of sexual violence.

The law enforcement and criminal justice systems frequently alter their operating procedures. For example, police departments may change from automobile patrols to foot patrols to increase surveillance and to improve relations between police and community. Often these innovations are introduced without adequate planning about how they can be evaluated; hence their outcomes, whether good or bad, cannot be determined (Reppucci &

Haugaard, 1989). The methodological skills of the psychologist as policy evaluator are essential in designing an innovation so that its effects can be tested.

Psychologists have been involved in evaluating changes in the federal law that governs special education. The Individuals with Disabilities Education Act (IDEA) guarantees children with disabilities the opportunity to receive a free and appropriate public education. Recent revisions in the law change the way that schools determine whether a child has a learning disability. The traditional method, in use since the 1970s, identified students as having a learning disability when their scores on achievement tests were significantly lower than their IQ would suggest they should be. But with the dramatic increase in the number of students identified as learning disabled in recent years, many people have begun to suspect that learning disabilities are overidentified. (Some conjecture that parents have pushed for this label so that schools will be forced to provide services for their academically struggling students.) When children struggle for reasons unrelated to a learning disability—poor instruction or speaking English as a second language, for example—shunting them into special education courses is of little value. Therefore, the new version of IDEA provides for alternative methods of identification, something that psychologists have been evaluating for some time (Bailey, 2003).

The Psychologist as an Advocate in the Law

The final role for psychologist, that of **advocate**, is the most controversial because it is the most "activist." Some people believe that psychologists should act only as neutral observers of behavior and not take sides in any partisan disputes. One early advocacy effort by social scientists was to challenge the "separate but equal" doctrine that undergirded the racial segregation of public schools in the first half of the 20th century. A group of prominent social scientists in the early 1950s prepared a statement titled "The Effect of Segregation and the Consequences of Desegregation: A Social Science

Statement," which became part of the legal brief submitted to the U.S. Supreme Court before its 1954 *Brown v. Board of Education* decision. The statement began with a review of the detrimental effects of segregation, prejudice, and discrimination on black children. The statement asserted that these children learned from their environment that they were members of what American society considered to be an inferior group. As Stuart Cook (1984), one of the authors of the report, noted, "They react to this knowledge with a sense of humiliation and feelings of inferiority, and come to entertain the possibility that they are, in fact, worthy of second-class treatment" (p. 3). It is uncertain whether the Supreme Court, in its decision overturning school segregation, was strongly influenced by this social science statement. But some commentators have noted a resemblance between parts of the statement and one famous passage in the Supreme Court's *Brown* opinion:

> Segregation of white and colored children in public schools has a detrimental effect upon the colored children. The impact is greater when it has the sanction of the law; for the policy of separating the races is usually interpreted as denoting the inferiority of the Negro group. A sense of inferiority affects the motivation of a child to learn. Segregation with the sanction of law, therefore, has a tendency to retard the educational and mental development of Negro children and to deprive them of some of the benefits they would receive in a racially integrated school system.

One major difference between an advocate and an expert witness is the fact that the former identifies strongly with one side. By contrast, even if an expert witness (or other kind of consultant) is paid by one side in a case, he or she is under oath to tell "the truth, the whole truth, and nothing but the truth." Advocates, although they use psychological methods and try to render an objective analysis of data, commit their skills to one side; they become partisans.

The field of trial consulting provides another example of an advocacy role for a psychologist working in the legal arena. Social scientists who

began this work in the 1970s used so-called scientific jury selection procedures (further described in Chapter 11) to assist defense lawyers in highly politicized trials resulting from antiwar activities in the United States. Since then, these techniques have been refined and expanded. Today the field of trial consulting is a booming business and involves far more than jury selection; **trial consultants** also conduct community attitude surveys, prepare witnesses to testify, advise lawyers on their presentation strategies, and conduct mock trials.

The national media devoted extensive coverage to the use of trial consultants in the celebrity-status trials of Martha Stewart and O. J. Simpson, and research on community attitudes was also influential in recent convictions of former Ku Klux Klansmen for the 1963 bombing of a Birmingham church. The jury consultant hired by the prosecution in one of the trials suggested that the case not be cast as an attack on the KKK, because research showed that the Klan has little relevance to jurors today. Rather, he urged prosecutors to emphasize that the bombing singled out children (four girls were killed in the attack) and a place of worship. The jury took only two hours to convict the defendant (Sack, 2001).

Critics have argued that these techniques essentially rig the jury (Kressel & Kressel, 2002), but at least in the realm of jury selection, there are few, if any, convincing demonstrations that scientific jury selection is more effective than routine jury selection (e.g., Fulero & Penrod, 1990). Consultants suggest that they are simply borrowing techniques commonly used in politics and bringing them into the courtroom. Politicians hire people to help them project a better image, so why shouldn't a lawyer do the same? They also argue that in an adversarial system, attorneys should be able to use every tool available to them.

A footnote on psychologists' relationship to the law: Students often wonder how they can become involved in this field as basic scientists, applied scientists, policy evaluators, or advocates. What career paths should one pursue, and what professional opportunities exist at the ends of those trails? How might a developmental psychologist, a cognitive neuropsychologist, or a clinician (for example) interact with the legal system? To answer these questions, the American Psychology-Law Society (a division of the American Psychological Association) has published a guide entitled *Careers in Psychology and Law*. It can be accessed from the Society's web page (www.ap-ls.org).

Ethical Considerations in Each Role

The four roles just presented vary in several respects. But whatever role a psychologist chooses, it carries standards about what is acceptable and unacceptable behavior. Professional people often develop explicit statements of ethical standards of behavior; for psychologists, those principles have been published by the American Psychological Association (www.apa.org/ethics). Recent modifications to the guidelines now specify, for example, what psychologists should tell their patients about treatments for which generally recognized procedures have not yet been established, when psychologists should terminate treatment and how to do it, and how to safeguard the privacy rights of graduate students enrolled in programs that require psychotherapy as part of their training.

Psychologists working directly with the legal system must also abide by guidelines drawn up by the American Psychology-Law Society (APA Division 41) and the American Board of Forensic Psychology. These rules provide guidance to forensic psychologists in monitoring their professional conduct when acting in assistance to courts, parties to legal proceedings, correctional and forensic mental health facilities, and legislative agencies. These guidelines amplify the APA principles in several areas, including confidentiality, methods of evaluation and reporting, and relationships between the psychologist and the contending party in litigation.

But making the right choice is complicated by the fact that the principles specified by the ethics codes may conflict with the psychologist's legal responsibilities. The most explicit illustration of this dilemma is the ethical obligation of confidentiality versus the legal duty to warn potential victims of clients' threats. This conflict was most apparent in the *Tarasoff* decision by the Supreme Court of California, described in Box 1.2.

Ethical dilemmas are common for all psychologists who work in the legal system, but they are felt most acutely by applied scientists/expert witnesses, policy evaluators, and advocates.

The Ethics of the Applied Scientist/Expert Witness

The psychologist as expert witness represents a profession that stands for objectivity and accuracy in its procedures. Even though expert witnesses are usually hired (and paid) by one side, they are responsible for reporting all their conclusions, whether or not these favor the side paying them. Furthermore, it violates the ethical standards of both psychologists and lawyers for expert witnesses to accept payment that is contingent on the outcome of the case.

But achieving objectivity is by no means easy. From the jury's perspective, the psychologist is often perceived as an advocate rather than as an unbiased scientist (Horgan, 1988). Regardless of this perception, a psychologist, when asked to testify, has an ethical responsibility to be candid and explicit with the court about his or her opinions. Still, psychologists may be tempted to sympathize with the side that has employed them. This sympathy may not even be conscious; instead, the psychologist may simply filter the facts of the case through perceptions motivated by a spirit of helpfulness to his or her client.

Another ethical dilemma arises whenever the adversary system forces an expert to make absolute "either–or" judgments. Has the pretrial publicity caused potential jurors to be biased against the defendant? In a custody case stemming from a divorce, which parent would be better for the child to live with? Does the evaluation of a defendant indicate that she is insane? In all of

THE CASE OF

BOX 1.2　　**Tanya Tarasoff and the duty to protect**

Few legal decisions have had as much impact on the practice of psychotherapy as the now-famous case of *Tarasoff v. Regents of the University of California*. The decision focuses on the duties required of psychotherapists.

Here are the facts of the case: Prosenjit Poddar was a graduate student at the University of California who became infatuated with Tatiana Tarasoff. Poddar was inexperienced in romantic relationships and was confused about Tatiana's on-again-off-again behavior; she was friendly toward him one day but avoided him completely the next night. After Poddar went to the university counseling center and became a client of a staff psychologist, he confided that he intended to kill a girl who had rebuffed him. The

psychologist told his supervisor of this threat and then called the campus police, requesting that they detain Poddar. They did so but soon released him, believing his promise that he would stay away from Tatiana, who was out of the country at the time. Poddar didn't keep his promise; two months later, he went to Tatiana's home and stabbed her to death. He was eventually convicted of murder.

Tatiana's parents sued the university, the psychologists, and the campus police. After a lower court decided in favor of the university, the parents appealed to the California Supreme Court, which ruled in the parents' favor by deciding that the university had been negligent. The court established a standard that therapists have a duty

to use "reasonable care" to protect identifiable potential victims from clients in psychotherapy who threaten violence. After the *Tarasoff* decision in 1976, courts in several other states extended this duty to the protection of property and the protection of all foreseeable victims, not just identifiable ones. The *Tarasoff* case still governs psychologists' conduct and still, even after 30 years, raises concerns about the nature of the psychotherapeutic relationship. Many psychologists feel caught in a no-win situation: They can be held responsible for their clients' violence if they do not warn potential victims, but they can also be held responsible for breaching their clients' confidentiality if they do.

these situations, the law requires the psychologist to reach a firm conclusion on the witness stand, regardless of ambiguity in the evidence (Sales & Shuman, 1993).

The Ethics of the Policy Evaluator

The psychologist who evaluates the impact of new or proposed legislation, court reforms, and other changes in the legal system faces ethical responsibilities similar to those of the expert witness. The standard canons of scientific procedure apply, but again, because of the source of payment, pressures exist to interpret results of evaluation studies in a certain way.

Consider, for example, a large state prison that wants to improve its parole system. Prison officials have identified a problem with convicts eligible for parole who are heavy drug users. If released into society, they are likely to commit further crimes to maintain their drug habit. Hence they will soon return to prison. Accordingly, the prison seeks to introduce and evaluate an innovative halfway house program for those parolees with a history of narcotics addiction. It hires a policy evaluator to design a study and evaluate the effects of this innovation. The prison provides money to carry out the study, and prison officials are sincerely committed to its goals. Assume the psychologist concludes that the halfway house does not significantly reduce drug use by parolees. The authorities are disappointed and may even attack the integrity of the policy evaluator. Yet, as scientists, program evaluators must "call 'em like they see 'em," regardless of the desirability of the outcome.

Even if the program is successful, the policy evaluator faces other ethical dilemmas. To assess such an innovative program, the researcher might have to deny some parolees access to the program and place them in a "status quo" control group. The ethical dilemma becomes more critical when some potentially lifesaving innovation is being evaluated. But often it is only through such research methods that a potentially helpful new program can be convincingly demonstrated to be effective.

The Ethics of the Advocate

As we noted earlier, when the psychologist becomes an advocate for one side in the selection of jurors, ethical problems emerge. Just how far should the selection procedures go? Should jurors have to answer consultants' intrusive questions about their private lives? Should their private lives be investigated? Should consultants be able to sculpt the jury to their client's advantage? Do these techniques simply constitute the latest tools in the attorney's arsenal of trial tactics? Or, instead, do they bias the proceedings and jeopardize the willingness of citizens to participate in the process? These questions deal with fairness, and systematic jury selection may be a situation in which social scientists and lawyers, in concert, are in conflict with the way most people interpret the intent of the law.

When psychologists become advocates as trial consultants, they also subscribe to the ethical code of the attorneys, who, after all, are in charge of the trial preparation. The Ethics Code of the American Bar Association admonishes its members to defend their clients to the best of their abilities, short of lying or encouraging lying. Every litigant—whether a defendant or a plaintiff—regardless of the heinousness of the crime or the mass of evidence presented, is entitled to the best legal representation possible, including the use of psychological techniques to assess the relative favorability of prospective jurors.

Are psychologists who work for an advertising agency unethical when they use professional knowledge to encourage consumers to buy one brand of dog food rather than another? Many of us would say no; the free-enterprise system permits any such procedures that do not falsify claims. Is this example analogous to jury selection? Probably, especially given that rival attorneys—whether they employ jury consultants or not—always try to select jurors who will sympathize with their version of the facts. The adversarial system rests on the expectation that each side will eliminate those jurors most favorable to the other side and that an unbiased jury will result. As long as the adversarial system permits attorneys from each side to eliminate some prospective jurors without giving reasons, it does not seem unethical for psychologists to assist these attorneys, as long as their advocacy is consistent with the law and the administration of justice.

Legality versus Morality

As we have seen, laws are designed to regulate the behavior of individuals—to specify precisely what conduct is illegal and what behaviors are unreasonable. But do these laws always comport with people's sense of what is right and wrong?

Consider the case of Lester Zygmanik. Lester was charged with murdering his own brother, George, but only because George had demanded that he do it. A motorcycle accident a few days earlier had left George, age 26, paralyzed from the neck down. He saw a future with nothing but pain, suffering, and invalidism; as he lay in agony, he insisted that his younger brother Lester, age 23, swear he would not let him continue in such a desperate state. "I want you to promise to kill me; I want you to swear to God," George said. (Other family members later verified that this had, in truth, been George's wish.) So, on the night of June 20, 1973, Lester slipped into his brother's hospital room and shot him in the head with a 20-gauge shotgun. Dropping the gun by the bed, he turned himself in moments later. There was no question about the cause of death; later, on the witness stand during his murder trial, Lester told the jury that he had done it as an act of love for his brother. Because New Jersey had no laws regarding mercy killing, the prosecution thought a case could be made for charging Lester with first-degree murder. And in New Jersey at that time, such a conviction would require that Lester be sentenced to life in prison.

The state believed it had a good case against Lester. His actions met every one of the elements that the law required for his guilt to be proved. There was, first of all, premeditation, or a plan to kill; there was deliberation (as defined in the New Jersey criminal code, "the weighing of the 'pros' and 'cons' of that plan); and there was willfulness ("the intentional carrying out of that plan"). Lester had even sawed off the shotgun before hiding it under his coat, and he had packed the bullets with candle wax, which compacted the explosion and made it more deadly. Lester forthrightly admitted to his lawyer: "I gave it a lot of thought. You don't know how much thinking I did on it. I had to do something I knew that would definitely put him away" (Mitchell, 1976, p. vii). At his trial, Lester took the stand and described his motivations. He did not fall back on the insanity plea; he simply explained that he did what his brother wanted.

If you had been a juror in this trial, how would you have voted? College students usually split just about evenly between verdicts of "guilty of first-degree murder" and "not guilty." Those who vote guilty often hope that the sentence will be seen as a humanitarian one, but they believe it is their duty to consider the evidence and apply the law. Certainly, this was an act of murder, they say, regardless of Lester's good intentions. But those who vote not guilty often feel that it is appropriate, on occasion, to disregard the law when mitigating circumstances are present or when community standards argue for forgiveness.

Both reactions are reasonable, and they illustrate the dilemma between treating similar defendants equally and showing discretion if circumstances warrant. They also demonstrate important differences between judgments based on **black letter law** and judgments based on one's conscience or personal sentiments about a given situation. By "black letter law" (sometimes referred to as the "law on the books"), we mean the law as set down by our founding fathers in the Constitution, as written by legislators, and as interpreted by judges (Finkel, 1995). By black letter law, Lester Zygmanik was guilty. But there is another way to judge his actions, namely by focusing on his altruistic motives and the desire to help his brother, rather than to harm him.

As Lester Zygmanik's trial began, the prosecutor was confident that he would be found guilty. The jury, composed of seven men and five women, was tough, conservative, blue-collar; all jurors were over age 30. And the judge had even ruled that the term *mercy killing* could not be used in the trial. But after deliberating for fewer than three hours, the jury found Lester Zygmanik not guilty. The jurors focused, apparently, on the relationship between Lester and his brother, and they concluded that Lester had been overcome by grief, love, and selflessness. Their decision implicitly acknowledged that moral considerations such as the commitment to care for others were more important to their decision than following the strict guidelines of the law.

Obviously, the Lester Zygmanik trial is not the only one in which the defendant claimed his act was a mercy killing. Helping terminally ill patients to commit suicide (so-called assisted suicide) is usually justified by the "offender" as an act of compassion or mercy, ending the "victim's" pain and suffering. Yet in all states except Oregon, helping someone to commit suicide is a crime. (Even in Oregon, assisted suicide is legal only if performed by a physician under narrowly defined circumstances.) Still, many people are loath to call the perpetrators of these acts criminals, and proponents of assisted suicide often hail them as heroes.

Mercy killings and assisted suicides are examples of **euthanasia**, the act of killing an individual for reasons that are considered merciful. They illustrate the often-tragic differences between what an individual feels is the morally right or just thing to do and what the law dictates is the legally proscribed act to avoid. Should someone who voluntarily, willfully, and with premeditation assists in killing another human being *always* be punished, or should that person, in some circumstances, be treated with compassion and forgiveness? Many people can imagine exceptional circumstances in which individuals who have technically broken the law should be exonerated. Often, these circumstances involve a lack of intention to harm another person and the desire to help a person who is suffering. The topic of euthanasia highlights the inconsistency between legality and people's perceptions of what is moral, ethical, and just.

Citizens' Sense of Morality and Legality

On first thought, we might assume that what is defined as "legal" and what is judged to be "morally right" would be synonymous. But in the Zygmanik example, the jury concluded that what they considered to be a moral action and what the system required as the proper legal resolution were inconsistent. Legislators and scholars have argued for centuries whether the law should be consistent with citizens' sense of morality. In fact, inconsistencies abound. For example, prostitution is universally condemned as immoral, yet it is legal in parts of Nevada and in some European countries. Acts of civil disobedience, whether performed in racially segregated buses in Montgomery, Alabama, five decades ago, or more recently to protest of the war in Iraq, are applauded by those who consider some laws and policies to be morally indefensible.

Psychologists have now conducted a number of studies that illustrate the differences between citizens' sense of morality and justice, on the one hand, and the legal system's set of formal rules and laws, on the other. At first glance, it may seem nearly impossible to study people's views about the legitimacy of formal laws because there are so many variations in laws and so many different penalties for violating those laws. (Because criminal penalties are decided on a state-by-state basis in the United States, there could be 50 different penalties for the same crime.) Fortunately, though, a large majority of states base their criminal laws on the Model Penal Code drafted by the influential American Law Institute in the 1960s. Thus we can ask whether the principles embodied in the Model Penal Code are compatible with citizens' intuitions about justice and legality. Do people tend to agree with the dictates of the Model Penal Code or does their sense of right and wrong diverge from this black letter law? One set of studies has examined the category of attempted crimes and the important role that intention plays in these cases.

Attempted crimes and the concept of intention in law and psychology. Consider the following fundamental question of criminal law: How should attempted (but not completed) crimes be punished? An attempt may be unsuccessful for one of three reasons: (1) the perpetrator tries to commit a crime but fails (e.g., he shoots but misses); (2) success is impossible because of something the perpetrator is unaware of (e.g., thinking it's the real thing, a hunter shoots a decoy deer out-of-season; or (3) the attempt falls short because it is interrupted or abandoned (e.g., robbers are about to enter a bank with guns drawn when they see a police officer inside).

The Model Penal Code says that attempts should be punished the same way as completed crimes. If the offender's conduct strongly corroborates his criminal **intention**—showing that he not merely thought about the crime but actually tried to accomplish it—the Model Penal Code holds that he should be punished to the same degree as the successful offender. In keeping with the central role of intent, the Model Penal Code assigns the same penalty to attempted crimes as to completed crimes. Thus, the inveterate pickpocket who thrusts his hand into another person's pocket, only to find it empty, is just as guilty (and just as deserving of punishment) as the pickpocket who makes off with a fat wallet. Regardless of the outcome of the heist, he tried to steal, and so, by definition, a crime was committed. A similar situation arose in the case of *State v. Damms* (1960), described in Box 1.3.

THE CASE OF

BOX 1.3   **Ralph Damms and the unloaded pistol**

Prior to the events in question, Marjory Damms had initiated divorce proceedings against her husband Ralph, and the two were living apart. On April 6, 1959, Ralph Damms drove to a location in Milwaukee where his estranged wife usually boarded a bus to go to work. He lured her into his car by falsely claiming that her mother was ill and dying. He then took his wife for a car ride, stopped the car, and brandished a gun. Marjory Damms ran away, but Ralph caught her and raised the pistol to her head. Slowly,

deliberately, he pulled the trigger. The gun did not fire. He had forgotten to load it! Two police officers witnessed the event and heard Damms exclaim, after he pulled the trigger of the unloaded gun, "It won't fire. It won't fire." (It was not clear whether the exclamation was made in a tone of assurance, disappointment, surprise, or desperation.) Damms was found guilty of attempted murder, but he appealed his conviction on the ground that it was impossible to kill his wife with an unloaded gun. The court upheld

his conviction, concluding that the mere fact that the gun was unloaded when Damms pulled the trigger did not absolve him of attempted murder if he actually believed the gun was loaded at the time. Intention is the central issue here; at least for the charge of attempted murder, it is more important than the consequences of the act. The judges concluded that Damms assumed he had put bullets in the gun. And if he had, his wife would have been dead.

According to the Model Penal Code, an offender who tries but fails is just as culpable as an offender who tries and succeeds. But do ordinary people think about intent and attempted crimes this way? Do they think that attempting to break into a store is as serious as actually breaking into the store?

Psychologist John Darley and his colleagues asked respondents to read short scenarios that described people who had taken one or more steps toward committing either robbery or murder and to assign punishment for those people (Darley, Sanderson, & LaMantha, 1996). They found that people's intuitions differed in predictable ways from the position of the Model Penal Code. In situations where the person depicted in the scenario had taken only preliminary action (e.g., examining the store he planned to burgle or telling a friend about his plan), few respondents thought he was guilty of any offense, and punishments were generally mild. (Yet, according to the Model Penal Code, this person is just as guilty as one who actually completed the burglary.) When the scenario described a person who had reached the point of "dangerous

proximity" to the crime, punishments increased, but they still were only half as severe as those assigned to the person who actually completed the crime. Apparently people do not accept the view that intent to do an action is the moral equivalent of actually doing the action. Their notions about criminality and the need for punishment were more nuanced, less "black and white" than what the Model Penal Code prescribed.

Psychology's focus on mental states also reflects more differentiations and less clear-cut distinctions than those of the legal system (and therefore might be perceived as more reasonable to most people). Psychology considers a spectrum of behavior, motivated by both conscious and unconscious processes, and ranging from pure accidents, to actions taken under stress, to actions that grow out of peer pressure and social suggestions, to actions directed by conscious intent (Marshall, 1968, p. 72).

Even this continuum may oversimplify variations in intention because it minimizes the importance of the environmental situations and cultural expectations that different persons face. The overall social context in which behavior occurs can strongly influence a person's intention to behave in different ways. Different contexts may make it all but impossible for an individual to conceive of certain behavioral options; therefore, one person's ability to intend a given behavior might be much more limited than that of another person who operates in a context in which more behavioral alternatives are possible.

Psychologists have also studied how people assign causes, including intentions, to the behavior of others and themselves. The well-established field of **attribution theory** has led to a number of discoveries, including these:

1. Attributions tend to vary along three dimensions: *internality*—whether we explain the cause of an event as due to something within ourselves or to something that exists in the environment; *stability*—whether we see the cause of a behavior as enduring or merely temporary; and *globalness*—whether we see the cause as specific to a limited situation or applicable to all situations.
2. An individual who makes internal, stable, global attributions about an act of misconduct ("He is so evil that he doesn't care what anyone thinks or feels about him") will see an offender as more culpable and more deserving of punishment than a person who offers external, unstable, specific explanations for the same act ("As a result of hanging out with a rough crowd, she was in the wrong place at the wrong time").
3. When making inferences about what caused another person's behavior—especially behavior that has negative consequences—we tend to attribute the cause to stable factors that are internal to the person; that is, we are inclined to believe that others are disposed to act the way they do.
4. But when our own actions lead to negative outcomes, we are more likely to blame the external environment for the outcome, suggesting an unstable cause for our behavior that will probably change in the future.

Consequences of citizen–code disagreements. What difference does it make if laws do not comport with people's sense of what is right and what is wrong? Can people simply ignore the laws that they believe to be immoral? Indeed, we can find many examples of situations in which people opt not to obey laws and legal authority. When parents fail to make child support payments or when people violate restraining orders, it is often because they do not accept the legitimacy of a judge's decision. When people use illegal drugs or cheat on their income tax returns, it is often because they do not believe that the laws regulating these behaviors are just or morally right. During the era of prohibition in the United States, when alcohol consumption was outlawed, honest citizens became "criminals," entire illicit industries were created, and gang membership and gang-related violence increased significantly.

But there may be more significant and more general consequences of discrepancies between citizens' sense of morality and the legal system's sense of legality. For the law to have any authority, it must be consistent with people's shared sense of morality. When that consistency is lacking, citizens may feel alienation from authority and become less likely to comply with laws they perceive as illegitimate (Darley, Fulero, Haney, & Tyler, 2002). Initial disagreement with one law can lead to contempt for the legal system as a whole, including the police who enforce laws and the judges who punish wrongdoers. If the law criminalizes behaviors that people do not think are immoral, it begins to lose its legitimacy (Darley et al., 2002). In the words of Oliver Wendell Holmes, "[The] first requirement of a sound body of law is that it should correspond with the actual feelings and demands of the community" (Holmes, 1881, pp. 41–42).

What Is Justice?

More than 2000 years ago, at the beginning of the *Republic*, Socrates posed that question, and we continue to ponder it today. Definitions of justice have changed throughout history; in the Old Testament and in Homer's *The Iliad*, justice meant something like revenge. By the time of the Golden Age of Athens in the fifth century B.C.E., the concept of justice became less preoccupied with vengeance and more concerned with achievement of the well-being of individuals (Solomon, 1990). The development of Christianity and Islam accentuated a conception of justice within religious traditions of morality. As a result, people began to see matters of social injustice (e.g., the suffering of the poor and the oppressed) as issues of concern, along with offenses against one's person or one's family (Solomon, 1990).

Distributive and Procedural Justice

Our discussion so far has assessed perceptions of legitimacy in the *outcomes* of legal disputes, such as whether the would-be pickpocket who came up empty-handed should be punished as severely as one who got the loot. This focus on the fairness of the outcome in a legal dispute is the main tenet of **distributive justice** models. According to the principles of distributive justice, a person will be more accepting of decisions and more likely to believe that disputes have been resolved appropriately if the outcomes seem just (or if the outcomes—in the same sense as salaries or promotions—seem distributed equitably, hence the term *distributive justice*).

A series of classic studies in psychology and law showed that although distributive justice theories were correct, there was clearly more to the story. This work, conducted by a psychologist and a law professor, suggests that disputants' perceptions of the fairness of the *procedures* are vitally important to the sense that "justice" was done (Thibaut & Walker, 1975). Such an orientation leads us to think of justice not only as punishment for wrongdoing, but also as a process by which people receive what they deserve or are due. **Procedural justice** models suggest that if individuals view the procedures of dispute resolution or decision making as fair, then they will view the outcome as just, regardless of whether it favors

them or not. According to this perspective, an important question in a contested divorce might involve the means by which each person was wronged. In a dispute with an insurance company over an accident claim, one might ask whether the injured party was treated unfairly.

Generally, individuals perceive a decision-making process as fair to the extent that they believe they have a voice in how the process unfolds, are treated with dignity and respect during the process, and trust the authorities in charge of the process to be motivated by concerns about fairness (Folger, Cropanzano, Timmerman, Howes, & Mitchell, 1996; Sydeman, Cascardi, Poythress, & Ritterband, 1997). A full opportunity to state one's viewpoint and to participate actively and personally in the decision makes a strong contribution to an assessment of fairness, probably because it allows people to feel that they retain some control over their affairs (Ebreo, Linn, & Vining, 1996).

Can we apply these findings to the real-world interactions that occur in police stations and courtrooms? Police officers and judges are not likely to generate warm feelings in the community when they give people less than what they feel is deserved or when they limit people's abilities to act as they wish. Do citizens have a better view of police officers and judges (and, by extension, of the entire legal system) if they perceive that they are being treated fairly? And will this enhance the chances that they will comply with the law?

To answer these questions Tom Tyler and Yuen Huo (2002) interviewed 1656 individuals in Oakland and Los Angeles, who were chosen because they indicated to an initial interviewer that they had had at least one recent experience with a police officer or a judge. The authors attempted to oversample members of minority groups and ended with approximately equal numbers of whites, African Americans, and Hispanics as participants in their study. The researchers asked about the fairness of the outcomes of those encounters with authorities, as well as about the fairness of the procedures that were used to achieve the outcomes. They also measured people's trust in the motives of a particular authority figure by asking participants whether they felt that their views had been considered, whether they could trust the authority, whether the authority tried to do the right thing, and whether the authority cared about their concerns.

As one might expect, the favorability of the outcomes that participants received shaped their responses to this encounter. (We feel better about situations and people when we get what we want from those situations and from those individuals). But importantly, the willingness to accept the decision of a police officer or judge was strongly influenced by perceptions of procedural fairness and trustworthiness: When people perceived that police officers and judges were treating them fairly and when they trusted the motives of these officials, they were more likely to accept their decisions and directives.

Commonsense Justice: Everyday Intuitions about Fairness

Another approach to the study of justice—one closely aligned with the analysis of citizens' agreement with the criminal code—is to learn about the untutored intuitions that average people hold about culpability, fairness, and justice. Psychologist Norman Finkel has examined the relationship between the "law on the books" as set out in statutes and judicial opinions and what he calls "**commonsense justice**"—ordinary citizens' basic notions of what is just and fair. This work has much to say about inconsistencies between the law and public sentiment in the types of cases we have examined in this chapter—assisted suicide and euthanasia—as well as in cases involving self-defense, the insanity defense, the death penalty, and felony murder (Finkel, 1995). Commonsense justice is also reflected in cases in which a jury refuses to convict a defendant who is legally guilty of the crime charged—the phenomenon known as jury nullification.

According to Finkel and others who have examined the contours of commonsense justice (e.g.,

Haney, 1997a; Olsen-Fulero & Fulero, 1997), there is mounting evidence that the "black letter law" on the books may be at odds with community sentiment. This work is an important contribution to the field of law because it explains *how* jurors' sentiments depart from legal concepts and procedures. There are three identifiable discrepancies.

1. *The commonsense context is typically wider than the law's.* Ordinary people tend to consider the bigger picture: Their assessment of the event in question extends backward and forward in time (including, for example, the defendant's conduct prior to the incident and behavior after the crime), whereas the law allows consideration of a more limited set of circumstances. For example, in a date rape case or other case in which the victim and defendant knew each other, jurors would be likely to consider the history of the individuals, both together and apart. Is the incident one in a series of troublesome encounters in a tumultuous relationship? Have these events been alleged by other partners?

Whereas jurors contemplate the wider context of the story, the law freezes the frame at the time of the act and then zooms in on that relatively finite moment. Reasoning that this narrower perspective will result in a cleaner and more precise judgment, the law then asks jurors to determine culpability on the basis of the defendant's actions and intentions within this narrow window. But jurors would often rather learn about the big picture; for many, viewing only the last act does little to reveal the entire drama (Finkel & Groscup, 1997).

2. *Jurors' perspectives on the actions of the defendant and the victim are more subjective than the law allows.* In cases that involve two people with a prior history, jurors construct a story about what happened, and why, by stepping into the shoes of the defendant and viewing the events through that person's eyes. The stories they construct typically describe the hidden motives of the defendant— considerations that can be discerned only by a "plunge into the subjective waters" (Finkel, 1995, p. 325). But, as Finkel further notes, "such a subjective, discretionary enterprise grounds the law not on

terra firma but on the unstable and invisible, where all we have are constructions, interpretations and stories constructed by jurors and judges" (p. 327).

The concern, of course, is that too much subjectivity will result in lawlessness, that jurors' judgments will be rooted in illusion rather than in the more objective premises of the law. But jurors do not yield indiscriminately to their imaginations. In fact, when the individuals in a case are strangers to each other (as is often the situation), jurors tend to judge the circumstances and the actors' intentions objectively rather than subjectively.

3. *Jurors take a proportional approach to punishment, whereas the law asks them to consider the defendant in isolation.* Imagine a situation in which an armed robber enters a convenience store while his female accomplice watches guard outside the store. Further imagine that things go awry—the robber ends up shooting the cashier, and the cashier dies. The robber has certainly committed a crime, but what about the accomplice?

According to the felony-murder doctrine (which applies in about half the states), the accomplice is as culpable as the triggerman. Yet, as Finkel points out, this egalitarian approach seems to contradict the notion of proportional justice, in which a defendant's actions and intentions are assessed in comparison to others and the more culpable defendants are dealt with more severely. Jurors make distinctions among types of crimes and criminals, and they usually want to punish most those criminals they find most blameworthy.

SUMMARY

1. *Why do we have laws and what is the psychological approach to studying law?* Laws are human creations that have as their major purpose the resolution of human conflict. As society changes, new conflicts surface, leading to expansion and revision of the legal system. A psychological approach focuses on individuals as agents within a legal system, asking how their internal qualities (personality, values, abilities, and experiences) and their environments, including the law itself, affect their behavior.

2. *What dilemmas are reflected in the psychological approach to the law?* Several basic choices must be made between pairs of options in the psychological study of the law. These options are often irreconcilable because each is attractive, but both usually cannot be attained at the same time. The choices are (1) whether the goal of law is achieving personal freedom or ensuring the common good, (2) whether equality or discretion should be the standard for our legal policies, (3) whether the purpose of a legal inquiry is to discover the truth or to provide a means of conflict resolution, and (4) whether it is better to apply the methods of law or those of science for making decisions.

3. *How do recent laws reflect the contrast between the due process model and the crime control model of the criminal justice system?* Recent laws in several states, including "three-strikes" laws, reflect the increased salience of a crime control model, which seeks to contain or reduce criminal activity.

4. *What are four roles that psychologists may play in the legal system and what does each entail?* Four possible roles are identified in this chapter: the psychologist as (1) a basic scientist, interested in knowledge related to psychology and law for its own sake; (2) an applied scientist (often, an expert witness) who seeks to apply basic research knowledge to a particular problem in the legal system; (3) a policy evaluator who capitalizes on methodological skills to design and conduct research that assesses the effects of innovations and program changes in the legal system; and (4) an advocate who works on behalf of a party or position in a legal case, sometimes combining a research function and a political function. Each role entails its own set of ethical dilemmas.

5. *Is what society considers moral always the same as what it considers legal?* What is considered moral is not always what is ruled legal, and vice versa. When determining right and wrong, some people rely on the law almost entirely, but many people have internalized principles of morality that may be inconsistent with the laws.

6. *How do different models of justice explain people's level of satisfaction with the legal system?* According to the distributive justice model, people's

acceptance of a legal decision is related to whether they think the outcome, or decision, is fair. According to the procedural justice model, fairness in the procedures is a more important determinant of satisfaction.

7. *What is commonsense justice?* Commonsense justice reflects the basic notions of everyday citizens about what is just and fair. In contrast to black letter law, commonsense justice emphasizes the overall context in which an act occurs, the subjective intent of the person committing the act, and the desirability of making the legal consequences of the fact proportionate to the perceived culpability of the actor.

KEY TERMS

advocate	crime control model	forensic psychologists	procedural justice
amicus curiae brief	determinate sentencing	intention	racial bias
applied scientist	discretion	jury nullification	sentencing disparity
attribution theory	distributive justice	legal precedence	settlement negotiation
basic scientist	due process model	notification laws	*stare decisis*
black letter law	equality	policy evaluator	three-strikes law
case law	euthanasia	principle of	trial consultants
commonsense justice	expert witness	proportionality	

The Legal System and Its Players

ORIENTING QUESTIONS

1. *What is the difference between the adversarial and inquisitorial models of trials?*
2. *What are the characteristics of courts, and how are judges selected?*
3. *What are some examples of problem-solving courts? How do they differ from traditional courts?*
4. *What is alternative dispute resolution? What are some types of ADR?*
5. *What different kinds of work do lawyers do?*
6. *What have been the experiences of women and minorities in the legal profession?*
7. *What are some of the common criticisms of lawyers?*

In Chapter 1, we described the different roles that psychologists can assume when they interact with the legal system. In this chapter, we describe the legal system itself and the roles played by participants in the legal system—judges and lawyers. We discuss courts, including juvenile courts, family courts, and drug courts; we describe alternative dispute resolution (arbitration and mediation), and we conclude with some thoughts about law schools and the legal profession. An understanding of the workings of the legal system will help make it clear how psychologists study and assist judges, lawyers, and ordinary citizens involved in the law.

The Adversarial System

American trial procedure—whether in criminal or civil cases—involves an **adversarial system** of justice. Exhibits, evidence, and witnesses are introduced by representatives of one side or the other for the purpose of convincing the fact finder that their side's viewpoint is the truthful one. The choice of what evidence to present is left, within broad limits, to the discretion of the parties in dispute and their attorneys (Lind, 1982). Judges rarely call witnesses or introduce evidence on their own. In bench trials (trials without a jury), judges often question witnesses, but in jury trials, judges hesitate to question witnesses because they do not want to appear to favor one side over the other. Although traditionally jurors have not been permitted to question witnesses (Heuer & Penrod, 1988), a majority of states now allow jurors to give written questions to the judge, who then decides whether the questions should be asked—either by the judge or by one of the attorneys (Munsterman and Hannaford-Agor, 2004). When the American College of Trial Lawyers, a prestigious organization of experienced trial lawyers, polled its members on this topic, 49% of those responding said juror questioning (by submitting questions to the judge) improved the quality of justice, whereas 33% viewed juror questioning negatively. We consider this issue in greater depth in Chapter 12.

The adversarial system is derived from English common law. This approach contrasts with the **inquisitorial approach** used on the continent of Europe (but not in Great Britain), in which the judge has more control over the proceedings.

Lind (1982) describes the procedure in France as follows: "The questioning of witnesses is conducted almost exclusively by the presiding judge. The judge interrogates the disputing parties and witnesses, referring frequently to a dossier that has been prepared by a court official who investigated the case. Although the parties probably have partisan attorneys present at the trial, it is evident that control over the presentation of evidence and arguments is—firmly in the hands of the judge" (p. 14). In the inquisitorial system, the two sides do not have separate witnesses; the witnesses testify for the court, and the opposing parties are not allowed to prepare the witnesses before the trial (Sheppard & Vidmar, 1980).

The adversarial model has been criticized for promoting a competitive atmosphere that can distort the truth surrounding a dispute (Lind, 1982). Jurors may have to choose between two versions of the truth, neither of which is completely accurate, because witnesses often shade their testimony to favor the side of the lawyer who interviews them first (Sheppard and Vidmar, 1980).

However, research on these contrasting approaches reveals several benefits of the adversarial model. A research team led by a social psychologist, John Thibaut, and a law professor, Laurens Walker (Thibaut & Walker, 1975; Thibaut, Walker, & Lind, 1972; Walker, La Tour, Lind, & Thibaut, 1974), carried out a program of research and concluded that the adversarial system led to less biased decisions that were more likely to be seen as fair by the parties in dispute. One possible explanation for this more favorable evaluation of the adversarial system is that it is the system with which American subjects are most familiar. But a study by Lind, Erickson, Friedland, and Dickenberger (1978) found that subjects who lived in countries with nonadversarial systems (France and West Germany) also rated the adversary procedure as fairer. Why? Perhaps because the adversarial system motivates attorneys to try harder to identify all the evidence favorable to their side. When law students, serving as experimental subjects, believed that the weight of the information and evidence favored the opposing side, they conducted more thorough investigations of the case. Thus, when the case was presented to the judge, the arguments appeared more balanced than the original distribution of facts would have warranted (Lind, 1975; Lind, Thibaut, & Walker, 1973).

The primary advantage of the adversarial system is that it gives participants plenty of opportunity to present their version of the facts so that they feel they have been treated fairly (Lind & Tyler, 1988); Sheppard and Vidmar (1983) point out that any method of dispute resolution that fosters this belief is more likely to be viewed favorably than alternatives that do not. This finding comports with the procedural justice perspective described in Chapter 1.

Courts

Federal courts have jurisdiction over cases arising under the Constitution or laws of the United States. Federal courts do not have jurisdiction over cases arising under state law, unless there is diversity of citizenship (the plaintiff and defendant are from different states). When Congress passes a law (for example, the statute making car-jacking a federal crime), the effect is to increase the case load of the federal courts.

Federal trial courts are called United States District Courts. There is at least one district in every state; some states (California, for example) have several districts. The number of judges per district varies according to the district's case load.

The federal appellate courts are called the United States Courts of Appeals. There are 13 federal courts of appeal, divided into geographical circuits; there is a circuit for appeals from federal agencies (the Federal Circuit), a circuit for the District of Columbia, and 11 circuits for the rest

of the country. In population, the largest circuit is the Ninth Circuit, which includes California, and the smallest is the First Circuit, which includes only a few New England states. The number of judges on each of the appellate courts depends on the case load of the particular court. Thus, there are 21 active judges on the Ninth Circuit and only 11 on the First Circuit.

Appeals are assigned to three-judge panels; the three judges assigned to a particular case examine the record (the papers, transcripts, and documents that the lawyers believe the judges need to read in order to decide the case), read the briefs (the lawyers' written arguments), and listen to the oral argument (the lawyers' debate about the case) before voting. The panel decides the case by majority vote (either 3–0 or 2–1), and one of the judges writes an opinion explaining why the court decided as it did. The opinion is sent to the parties and published in bound volumes (the Reporters). Opinions can be accessed through the Internet (for some courts) and through Westlaw and Lexis, computer-assisted legal research services. Very important cases are sometimes heard *en banc*, —meaning that all the judges on the particular court of appeals sit on the case. Decisions of a federal appellate court sitting *en banc* are nearly always published.

Nine justices make up the United States Supreme Court, which has the authority to review all cases decided by the federal appellate courts. The Supreme Court also has the authority to review state court decisions based on the Constitution or on laws of the United States. When a state court decision rests on the Constitution or laws of the United States, lawyers and judges refer to the decision as "raising a federal question." The Supreme Court reviews only those cases that the justices view as most significant. When the Court decides to review a case, the order granting review is called a **writ of *certiorari***. The Court reviews only a small percentage of the cases it is asked to consider.

Justices of the Supreme Court, like other federal judges, are appointed by the president and

THE CASE OF

BOX 2.1   **Terri Schiavo: A threat to judicial independence?**

For a few weeks in March 2005, headlines about Iraq, social security, and the economy were replaced by front-page stories chronicling the battle over the life and death of Terri Schiavo. In 1990, Schiavo had suffered a heart attack that caused permanent brain damage, described by her doctors as a "persistent vegetative state." She could breathe on her own, her eyes were open at times, but she could not eat or drink, and her responses were random. Michael Schiavo, Terri's husband, claimed she had said she would not want to live "like that," and he asked that the feeding tube keeping her alive be withdrawn. Terri's parents, Bob and Mary Schindler, argued that she wanted to live and objected to removal of the feeding tube. The Schindlers and Michael Schiavo fought over Terri for seven years—in state and federal court, the halls of the U.S. Congress, and the court of public opinion. Ultimately, the courts ruled that Michael Shiavo could decide for

A public demonstration held outside Terri Schiavo's nursing home prior to her death.

Terri, because she could not decide for herself. The tube was withdrawn on March 14, 2005, and she died two weeks later.

We learned two things from the Schiavo case. First, to avoid family fights, everyone should have a "living will" and should designate a surrogate for health care decisions. Second, we should treasure and support judges who refuse to yield to political pressure and conscientiously make decisions based on their view of the law and the facts.

The political pressure on the judiciary in the Schiavo case was extraordinary; indeed, the case raises important concerns about the independence of the judiciary from legislative "oversight." In 1998, Michael Schiavo filed suit to have the tube removed. The Schindlers opposed the request, but a Florida judge ruled that Terri would not have wanted to live in an "unconscious, reflexive state, totally dependent on others to feed her and care for her most private

---

confirmed by the Senate. Federal judges are appointed for life, and, like other federal officers, can be removed by the Congress for "treason, high crimes and misdemeanors." To remove a federal judge, the House impeaches the judge, and the Senate holds a trial on the articles of impeachment; a two-thirds vote is required for removal. Chief Justice William Rehnquist, who presided over the 1999 impeachment trial of President Clinton, wrote a fascinating book entitled *Grand*

Inquest, in which he described the 1805 impeachment and trial of Justice Samuel Chase, whose primary "sin" was to be a Federalist (the party of John Adams) at a time when Jeffersonian Republicans controlled the presidency and the Congress. Chase was acquitted by the Senate (although a majority of the Senators voted for two of the four impeachment articles). In Rehnquist's opinion, Chase's acquittal established the principle that disagreement with a judge's

needs." (in re Guardianship of Schiavo, 2004, p. 177) He ordered the tube removed, and the Florida appellate courts affirmed his decision. But the Schindlers didn't give up. They fought this decision in the Florida courts for five years, and when the last appeal was lost and the tube removed (for the first time) in October 2003, they took their cause to Governor Jeb Bush and the Florida legislature. A few days later, the legislature responded with an extraordinary statute ("Terri's law"), giving the governor the authority to reinsert the feeding tube. Governor Bush signed the law that same day, and the feeding tube was reinserted.

Michael Shiavo then sued the governor in state court, claiming that the legislature and governor had violated the principle of separation of powers as embodied in the Florida constitution and had encroached on the power and authority of the judiciary. The courts agreed. It is basic to the American system of government, in the words of the Florida Supreme Court, that legislatures pass laws and courts decide cases. By attempting to reverse the decision of the Florida courts in the Schiavo case, the legislature had exceeded its authority in violation of the state constitution. The Florida Supreme Court unanimously held the law to be unconstitutional (*Bush v. Schiavo*, 2004).

After further litigation in both state and federal courts, the tube was removed again in March 2005. But then the United States Congress did an extraordinary thing: The Congress passed a law, which President Bush signed, entitled "An Act for the relief of the parents of Theresa Marie Schiavo." The act directed the federal court in Florida to consider the Schindlers' request to have the feeding tube reinserted, notwithstanding the many opinions upholding the decision that the tube be removed.

It is clear that Congress was attempting to force a federal judge in Florida to order the tube reinserted. When the judge refused to do so, the Schindlers pressed on, buoyed at this point by throngs of supporters holding vigil outside the hospice where Terri lay. They filed several more appeals and suffered more defeats, including one the day before Terri died. In one of these opinions, a federal judge scolded Congress for telling the federal district court how to exercise its judicial functions:

> [W]hen the fervor of political passions moves the Executive and the Legislative branches to act in way inimical to basic constitutional principles, it is the duty of the judiciary to intervene. If sacrifices to the independence of the judiciary are permitted today, precedent is established for the constitutional transgressions of tomorrow. . . . Accordingly, we must conscientiously guard the independence of our judiciary and safeguard the Constitution, even in the face of the unfathomable human tragedy that has befallen Mrs. Schiavo and her family. . . ." (*Schindler ex rel Schiavo v. Schiavo*, 2005, at p. 713153)

decisions or judicial philosophy is not grounds for impeachment.

> The acquittal of Samuel Chase by the Senate had a profound effect on the American judiciary. First, it assured the independence of federal judges from congressional oversight of the decisions they made in cases that came before them. Second, by assuring that impeachment would not be used in the future as a method to remove federal judges for their judicial opinions, it helped to safeguard the independence of that body. (Rehnquist, 1992, p. 114)

A quite different event, many years later, again tested the independence of the judiciary. The case of Terri Schiavo is described in Box 2.1.

State court systems are typically divided as follows: (1) "lower" courts, which have jurisdiction only over specific matters, such as probate of wills (proving that a will was properly signed) and administration of estates (supervising the payment of the deceased's debts and the distribution of his or her assets); (2) courts of general jurisdiction, which might be called the superior court (California), the circuit court (Kentucky), or even the supreme court (New York). A court of general jurisdiction may hear any case that concerns state laws but may not try a person for a federal crime, because Congress has authorized only federal courts to try those accused of committing federal crimes.

In addition to lower courts and trial courts of general jurisdiction, state court systems typically include one or more courts of appeal, similar to the federal appellate courts, and a state supreme court. Like the United States Supreme Court, state supreme courts review only those cases that are deemed to be important, and they authorize publication only of significant opinions. Published opinions are found in state Reporters, and all opinions are accessible through Westlaw and Lexis.

"Problem-Solving Courts"

Fed up with "revolving door" justice, states and communities increasingly are creating "problem-solving" courts, combining the justice system with social work principles to address underlying causes of antisocial behavior (Post, 2004a). The premise of problem-solving courts is that the legal system should help troubled individuals cope with the problems that brought them to court. This approach, in which the law is used as a vehicle to improve the lives of those enmeshed in it, is called **therapeutic jurisprudence**. Examples of problem-solving courts include juvenile courts, women's courts (now an outdated concept), drug courts, mental health courts, homeless courts, and family courts.

In these settings, judges become social workers and cheerleaders as much as jurists, offering opportunities for people to deal with their addictions, violent tendencies, and squabbles with their landlords, rather than imposing punishment (Eaton & Kaufman, 2005). Judges are trained in their courts' specialty and may have a psychologist on their staff. Although some aspects of these courts are traditional—for instance, judges wear robes and employ court officials in uniform, just as in traditional courtrooms many characteristics of problem-solving courts are unconventional. For example, the people who appear in court are often called clients rather than defendants, and these "clients" are able to speak directly to the judge, rather than communicating through their attorneys. Judges are often given a great deal of information about the clients and may interact with them over a number of years. On occasion, a friendly relationship develops, as described in Box 2.2.

The oldest form of a problem-solving court is the **juvenile court**, an innovation that originated in Chicago in 1899 and rapidly spread across the country. Juvenile courts grew out of the progressive movement of the latter part of the 19th century, when social reformers advocated for a system in which misbehaving children would be corrected and reformed, rather than punished (Schwartz, Weiner, & Enosh, 1998). For many years, juvenile courts functioned to protect children from the rough-and-tumble world of adult criminal courts and to dispose of their cases in a supportive, nonadversarial way. Today, public opinion reflects a widespread belief that juvenile courts are "kiddy courts," and many clamor for "adult time for adult crimes." As a result, 40 states and the District of Columbia have passed laws in recent years making it easier for juveniles to be tried as adults. All states have provisions that allow juvenile courts to transfer certain serious cases to adult courts. We discuss this evolution in juvenile courts and juvenile justice in more detail in Chapter 14.

The progressive movement is also credited with the creation of **women's courts**. The first women's court was established in Los Angeles in 1914 as a branch of Los Angles Municipal Court, with the express purpose of protecting members of the "weaker sex" charged with minor crimes. Women, like juveniles, were thought to need

THE CASE OF

BOX 2.2 **a "client" of Justice Matthew D'Emic**

An immigrant from Barbados in his early twenties arrived in the New York courtroom of Justice Matthew D'Emic in 2003, facing a serious charge of arson after starting a fire that damaged a small public housing complex (Eaton & Kaufman, 2005). The man was delusional, believing that he was the son of God; he had been hospitalized nine times in five years. In a traditional courtroom, the case would have been disposed of by a guilty plea or verdict, and the defendant would have been shuffled off to prison. But in the mental health court over which Justice D'Emic presided, something very different happened. The judge decided that the young man could safely return to live with his mother, provided that he stayed on his medications. Later, when the man complained of stomach cramps and began to miss appointments, the judge suggested he change his medicine. The judge insisted that the man sign up for job training, allowing him to "graduate" from court with only a misdemeanor on his record. Most remarkably, Justice D'Emic gave the client his cell phone number and urged him to call if he got into a jam. The man said he used it just once, to ask the judge for advice about a woman he was considering marrying.

protection and guidance, and the mission of the Los Angeles Women's Court was to help wayward women who ran afoul of the law. Like juvenile court, Women's Court was closed to the public, "to exclude the male degenerates that cluster about our police courts, as they do in any large city, to prey upon the girls and women." (Cook, 1993, p. 144)

Georgia Bullock, a formidable woman who later became a judge of the Los Angeles Superior Court, served as the first judge of the Los Angeles Women's Court. Rehabilitation was her sentencing philosophy. She placed "good girls" on probation and worked closely with the social agencies of the time to find resources for women who came to her court. In 1927, she and her staff arranged to find jobs or send home about 150 girls "infected with the movie virus" who had run out of money and were committing petit larceny or worse.

Men came to Judge Bullock's courtroom on "failure to provide" petitions filed by their wives or girlfriends. She showed no mercy to men who didn't support their children. She gave first offenders 60 days and repeat offenders a year in jail. She lambasted child deserters and urged the legislature to increase the penalties for non support.

In the early 1930s, Los Angeles gave up its separate Women's Court. In retrospect, a separate court for women was condescending and reinforced the belief that women, like children, needed protection from the evils of the industrial age (Cook, 1993).

Drug Courts

The most common form of problem-solving court is **drug court**, created to deal with offenders whose crimes are related to addiction. The first drug court opened in Miami in 1989 (Lurigio, 2001), and according to the Office of National Drug Control Policy, in September 2004 there were 1212 drug courts in the 50 states and 476 more in the planning phase.

The mission of drug courts is to stop the abuse of alcohol and other drugs and the criminal activity that is related to addictions. Drug courts offer treatment programs and extensive supervision to drug-addicted offenders. In exchange for successful completion of the program, the court may dismiss the original charge, reduce or set aside a sentence, assign some lesser penalty, or make a combination of these adjustments.

Writing in 2001, a team of authors headed by Arthur Lurigio described drug courts' team approach, in which the prosecutor, defender, judge, and probation officers work as a team to monitor offenders and hold them accountable for rule infractions through a series of graduated sanctions. The five common elements of drug courts are "immediate intervention, a non-adversarial process, a hands-on judicial role, drug treatment with clearly defined rules and goals and a team approach" (Lurigio, Watson, Luchins, & Hanrahan, 2001, p. 186).

How successful are drug courts in reducing drug-related criminal activity? A 2003 study of drug courts in New York found that "graduates" were about a third less likely to be rearrested on subsequent drug charges than similar defendants in traditional court (Eaton & Kaufman, 2005). But a study of over 4000 drug court graduates, sponsored by the Department of Justice, found that 27.5% had been arrested for a felony offense within two years of their graduation dates (Roma, Townsend & Bhati, 2003). It is perhaps not surprising that a quarter of the graduates were arrested, given that addiction was a condition of participation in drug court.

Mental Health, Homeless, and Family Courts

Mental health courts, homeless (or community) courts, and other "problem-solving" courts have sprung up in the wake of the drug court movement. **Mental health courts** for offenders with serious mental illness were started in Marion County, Indiana, in 1996 (Post, 2004) and in Broward County, Florida, in 1997 (Lurigio et al., 2001). In the early 2000s, federal funds were available for these programs, and by 2004 there were 94 mental health courts across the country, and more in the planning stage (Post, 2004a). Following the drug court model, the first decision

is whether to divert the offender from the regular criminal courts to the mental health court. This decision, which usually requires the consent of both the offender and the victim, is made after an evaluation of the offender and the offense. If the offender is diverted, the mental health team prepares a treatment plan to lead to long-term psychiatric care and integration into society. The charges are dismissed if the offender follows the treatment plan (Lurigio et al., 2001). Close monitoring is essential. Defendants are often assigned to a probation officer who is trained in mental health and who carries a greatly reduced caseload in order to provide a more intensive level of supervision and expertise.

Homeless courts were started in San Diego and Los Angeles with much the same design as mental health courts, and New York has created a variant on this approach termed "community courts" in Times Square and the Red Hook area of Brooklyn (Post, 2004a). Meeting in a refurbished Catholic school, the judges, prosecutors, and defenders in the Red Hook community court see their jobs as bettering the quality of life in the community. They know the people of the community and make it a point to know the offenders and to make sure the offenders know them. "The clerk of court has been known to stop her car at street corners and tell defendants the judge has issued a warrant for them and they'd best get over to court" (Carter, 2004, p. 39). The result is a reduction in low-level crime and decreased recidivism by offenders. Some courts aim to reduce homelessness by dealing with landlord and tenant issues and addressing the underlying causes of homelessness—mental illness, poor job skills, and language barriers.

Finally, **family courts** are springing up across the country, some standing alone and some combined with juvenile courts. The premise of family court is "one family, one judge"—the idea that a given family's legal issues ought all to be handled by a single judge. In Kentucky the voters amended the state constitution to allow the creation of family courts, thereby consolidating matters that had been heard by different courts.

Like drug courts and mental health courts, the premise of family court is problem-solving: not only resolving legal issues but also trying to help the family deal with the underlying problems that brought the family to the courts. Judges in such courts must determine whether there was violence and, if there was, develop a remedy that will protect the victim without unduly penalizing the perpetrator. Terrible consequences may flow from an erroneous prediction about the perpetrator's future behavior (Eaton & Kaufman, 2005).

Criticisms of Problem-Solving Courts

Criticism has been directed at problem-solving courts because middle-class judges inevitably reflect their middle-class values and may become inappropriately paternalistic in what they require of those who come before them (Eaton & Kaufman, 2005). Some have argued that problem-solving courts lack legitimacy because threatening punishment to coerce rehabilitation is considered unfair and because guilt or innocence is not determined by a trial (Casey, 2004). Prosecutors and public defenders have expressed concern over the "social worker" roles inherent in drug court philosophy; prosecutors feel pressured to favor rehabilitation of the offender over protection of society, and defenders feel pressured to plead their clients guilty and to inform the court of client failure to comply with the terms of probation (Feinblatt, 2001). Despite these criticisms, problem-solving courts will continue to develop and evolve, focusing on the reasons why people end up in court in the first place.

Judges

Even though judges are still predominately white and male, there are signs that the times are changing. Before 1961, only two women and one African American male had been appointed to lifetime positions on federal courts. Although President Carter moved beyond tokenism by appointing a number of women and African-Americans, it was not until the Clinton presidency that judicial appointments began to mirror the county in an "emerging triumph of affirmative action" (Goldman & Saronson, 1994, p. 73). In President Clinton's eight-year tenure, he appointed more women and minorities to the federal bench than any of his predecessors; among the 370 judges appointed to the district courts and courts of appeal were 108 women, 61 African Americans, 25 Latinos, 5 Asian-Americans and 1 Native American (Spill & Bratton, 2001). Although minorities tended to replace minorities, 17 of 20 women appointed to the courts of appeal and 71 of 88 women appointed to the district court by President Clinton replaced men (Spill & Bratton, 2001). His record has not matched President Clinton's, but President George W. Bush has so far appointed a higher percentage of women and minorities to the bench than either his father or President Reagan did (Carp, 2004).

State courts are also increasingly diverse. As of 2000, only three states had all-male supreme courts and 26 state supreme courts included at least one minority justice (Bonneau, 2001). The percentage of women on state supreme courts increased from 16% in 1994 to 26% in 2000; the percentage of minorities increased from 9% to 12% in the same period (Bonneau, 2001). Using two states as examples, the Florida Supreme Court (which was the focus of attention in *Bush v. Gore* in 2000 and in the Terri Schiavo case in 2005) was composed of four white men, one Latino man, and two women, one of whom was African-American. The New Jersey Supreme Court was comprised of three white men, one African-American man, and three women.

Do male and female judges view cases differently? Davis, Haire, and Songer (1993) analyzed the decisions of federal courts of appeals cases between 1981 and 1990 in three areas: employment discrimination, criminal procedural rights, and obscenity. When controlled for political party affiliation, there were no differences in the attitudes of male and female judges toward criminal procedural rights and obscenity. In employment discrimination cases, however, female judges were more liberal than their male counterparts; they favored the plaintiff employee more often than did the male judges. For example, female southern Democratic judges favored the plaintiff 82% of the time, whereas while male southern Democrats favored the plaintiff 52% of the time. The authors cautiously concluded that female judges see employment cases differently than their male counterparts. The reason? Female judges are more likely to have experienced discrimination and are more sympathetic to victims of discrimination.

There is some evidence that female judges do not handle stress as well as male judges. In a 2001 study using the Occupational Stress Inventory—Revised (OSI-R), female judges' scores on nine out of ten stressors were higher than those of their male counterparts (the only stressor on which men scored higher was responsibility) and female judges' scores were lower than men's on coping mechanisms (recreation, self-care, and social support) (Bremer & Todd, 2004).

But for both male and female judges, the stresses of judgeship are considerable: Not only do most judges have sizable caseloads, but because they make unpopular decisions—at least in the eyes of some who appear in their courtrooms—they become objects of public scorn and even, on occasion, fear for their safety. Within a one-month period in 2005, the husband and mother of a Chicago judge were gunned down in their home (apparently in retaliation for the judge's handling of a case), and an Atlanta judge was shot to death in his courtroom. Both of the assailants were disgruntled defendants.

Other judges have felt the wrath of the public. One notable example is Penny White, formerly a justice of the Tennessee Supreme Court. Justice White was targeted in a retention election by the Republican Party, ostensibly because she had voted—along with other members of the Tennessee Supreme Court—to set aside a death penalty. A typical mailing sent to Tennessee voters opened as follows:

> 78-year-old Ethel Johnson lay dying in a pool of blood. Stabbed in the heart, lungs, and liver, she fought back as best she could. Her hands were sliced to ribbons as she tried to push the knife away. And then she was raped. Savagely. . . . But her murderer won't be getting the punishment he deserves. Thanks to Penny White.

Justice White was voted off the bench, and then-Governor Don Sundquist was quoted as saying, "Should a judge look over his shoulder [when making decisions] about whether they're going to be thrown out of office? I hope so." (Bright, 1997, pp. 166, 168).

How Are Judges Selected?

Federal judges are appointed by the president and confirmed by the Senate. They serve for life, subject to impeachment for "high crimes and misdemeanors." There are different methods for selection of state judges. The most common forms are by appointment and by election. In some states, as in the federal courts, judges are appointed. (In Massachusetts judges are appointed by the governor for life; in Vermont they're appointed by the governor for an initial six-year term and may be continued in office by the legislature.) In other states, judges are elected. (Texas judges run for elective office under party label. Because voters typically know very little about the judicial candidates, the effect of top-of-the-ticket candidates is very strong. In Kentucky, judges are elected in a non-partisan election and do not publicly identify themselves as Democrats or Republicans, although voters are often aware of the candidates' political affiliations.) In a number of states, the governor appoints judges from names submitted by a merit selection commission. After a period on the bench, the judges run for retention. The electorate votes the judge up or down on the basis of the judge's record (Penny White was defeated in such an election). If retained, the judge serves a term of years, after which he or she again runs for retention. With notable exceptions (Penny White, Chief Justice Rose Bird in California), most judges are retained in these elections (Sheldon, 1994).

In recent years judicial races in many states have been hotly contested, with special interests pouring money into advertising, often negative advertising, to elect judges thought to favor their positions. For example, in West Virginia, coal company executives spent $1.7 million to fund attack ads and automated phone calls to defeat an incumbent and seat the challenger in the 2004 election. That same election cycle, Illinois experienced what critics called "the race to the bottom": $10 million was spent on a race for the state supreme court, with attack ads featuring the opponents' alleged leniency toward violent offenders in such graphic terms as to almost "make you believe the candidate committed the crime" (Carter, 2005) A member of Judicial Watch, a non-partisan group tracking judicial elections, lamented, "when you have any interest group treating its candidates like trophies on the wall, we do have a risk to fairness and impartiality of the courts" (Heller, 2004, p. 6).

Attack ads cause the public to view judicial candidates in the same light as candidates for legislative or executive offices. In the 2000 race for the Ohio Supreme Court between Terrence O'Donnell and Alice Resnick, an anti-Resnick ad virtually accused her of taking a bribe: The ad showed Lady Justice peeking out of her blindfold as money was dumped on the scales of justice with a voice saying, "Resnick became the only justice to reverse herself in the case—Alice Resnick, is justice for sale?" (Thomas, Boyer, & Hrebenar, 2003, p. 142). The attack ads against Resnick were so extreme that they were renounced by her Republican challenger. They may have backfired, because she won the election anyway.

Until the last decade of the 20th century, judicial races were decorous affairs in which candidates rarely stated their positions or criticized their opponents. Those times are over. In *Republican Party v. White* (2002), the United States Supreme Court held that the First Amendment protects truthful statements made in the course of judicial campaigning so long as such statements do not amount to a promise to decide a prospective case in a particular way. The Court made it clear that a candidate has a right to make general statements (e.g. "pro-life," "strict constructionist") designed to resonate with the voting public. Although this was not at issue in the *White* case, it is implicit that candidates may criticize their opponents' decisions and thereby suggest they would vote differently if elected.

The politicization of judicial races is unfortunate. Judges are not accountable to the electorate in the same way as other elected officials. What is a virtue in a legislative office—keeping a campaign promise—is a vice in a judicial office. Judges who promise in a campaign not to probate offenders either break their promise to the voters by probating an offender who deserves probation, or violate their obligation as judge by denying probation. No judicial candidate should state or imply that he or she would favor one side over the other or decide an issue on anything other than the facts and the law.

There is no easy answer to the issue of judicial selection. Perhaps the balance between public accountability and judicial independence can best be struck by a system that combines merit appointments with retention elections in which voters are provided with an evaluation of the judge's entire tenure in office by a non-partisan judicial qualifications commission. Such a system is in place in Alaska and Colorado. Of judges surveyed in ten states, 86% favored retention elections. The judges said their behavior was improved by knowing that they would have to face the electorate; they were less likely to be arrogant to jurors and litigants and more likely to explain their decisions (Aspin & Hall, 1994).

Alternative Dispute Resolution

From watching television news and entertainment, one might get the impression that most lawsuits wind up in trial by jury. In fact, however, most cases are resolved through negotiation or by **alternative dispute resolution** (ADR). Fewer and fewer cases are being settled in trials. In a 2001 study of courts in 46 randomly selected counties in 22 states, the National Center for State Courts found that the number of cases tried had decreased by 50% in 10 years, a decrease of about 5% per year in a period when the number of cases filed increased by 1% a year (Post, 2004c).

The decrease in trials in the federal courts is even more dramatic. In 1962, 50,320 civil cases were disposed of in federal courts, and 11.5% of them were decided by trial. By 2002 the number of dispositions had climbed to 258,876, and the number of dispositions by trial had *decreased* to just 1.8% of the total (Galanter, 2004). On the criminal side, trials also decreased, though not as sharply as on the civil side. In 1962, when the cases of 33,110 defendants were disposed of, 15.39% were decided by trials; in 2002 the cases of 76,827 defendants were disposed of, yet only 4.65% were resolved by trial (Galanter, 2004).

The decline in cases tried is attributable to several factors, principally the perceived cost of litigation—the "transaction costs," in economists' language. Lawyers' fees to prepare for and try a case often make a trial economically unfeasible (Galanter, 2004). In addition, federal courts pressure litigants to settle or, in the case of criminal defendants, plead guilty. The federal sentencing guidelines gave criminal defendants an incentive to plead guilty rather than stand trial because judges could decrease the length of a sentence on the basis of "acceptance of responsibility" (which normally requires a guilty plea) (Galanter, 2004).

On the civil side, federal judges are required to attempt to resolve disputes through ADR, and in both state and federal courts, judges are empowered to require litigants to try to settle their cases through ADR. Increasingly, American courts assume that cases will be settled, not tried, to the point where a trial is viewed "as a failure of the system." (Sanborn, 2002, p. 25). Edmund Ludwig, a judge with over 30 years of experience, describes the role of judges as follows:

> Litigation represents a breakdown in communication, which consists in the civil area of the inability of the parties to work out a problem for themselves and in the criminal area, of ineffectively inculcating society's rules and the consequences for violating them. Trials are the method we have ultimately used to deal with

those breakdowns. However, the goal of our system is not to try cases. Rather, it is to achieve a fair, just, economical, and expeditious result by trial or otherwise, where communication has previously failed (Ludwig, 2002, p. 217).

Many cases are settled by **negotiation**, without the assistance of a third party. (Technically, ADR involves the use of a third person, or persons, to help resolve the controversy, so negotiation is actually not a method of ADR.) Negotiation might be formal, as happens when management and union representatives negotiate a labor contract, or informal, as when attorneys jockey back and forth in a series of phone calls to settle a personal injury claim.

Arbitration

One form of ADR, **binding arbitration**, bears the closest resemblance to a trial. When the parties agree to binding arbitration, they agree to be bound by the decision of an arbitrator. Binding arbitration settles the controversy, unless there has been a procedural error of some kind. Salary arbitration in major league baseball is a good example of binding arbitration. The contract between the owners and the players' union provides that players' salary disputes are to be settled by binding arbitration, and it further provides that the arbitrator must accept either the owner's offer or the player's offer but cannot split the difference. Much as on the television show "The Price is Right," the parties have an incentive to make an offer as close as possible to the player's "value" (their estimate of the arbitrator's valuation of the player's worth).

Arbitration provides a speedy, flexible, and informal alternative to litigation, and arbitration clauses are often made part of contracts (Cox, 1999). For example, a construction contract might provide that all disputes between the builder and owner be decided by an arbitrator selected by the parties. The owner and builder thus write into the contract a non-litigation means to settle controversies. Arbitration provisions are sometimes controversial because they are often attached to "take-it-or-leave-it" contracts, drafted by employers for their employees or merchants for their customers. "You want the product or the service, you're stuck with mandatory arbitration. And often the clause is in tiny print, tucked in stacks of paperwork" (Carter, 2003, p.15). Arbitration is generally perceived as a process that works to the advantage of merchants and employers and to the disadvantage of consumers and employees. A consumer dissatisfied with, for example, cell phone service, might be required by the fine print in the contract to travel a long distance to arbitrate and to pay the arbitrator as much as $500 a day (Neil, 2005, at p. 53). Although some cases require binding arbitration, other cases are resolved by **nonbinding arbitration**. If one of the parties is dissatisfied with the arbitrator's decision, that person may ask that the case be tried before a judge or jury.

Arbitration, whether binding or nonbinding, is trial-like. The parties present evidence and argue the case, and the arbitrator (or arbitrators) makes an award. Arbitration in Atlanta is described as follows:

> The arbitrators hear cases in panels of three attorneys (volunteers paid $100 a day). The hearing, which is presided over by the chairperson, begins with short presentations by each of the respective panel members. They explain the nature and purpose of the hearing, the legal effect of the hearing, and the hearing's ground rules. Additionally, they indicate where, when, and how the panel's decision will be made public. The hearing consists of case summaries by counsel for the plaintiff and the defense, the introduction of exhibits and witnesses, cross-examination, and closing statements by each side. Hearings last for two hours, followed by a half-hour deliberation by the panel. In their discussions, the arbitrators consider the facts and law presented to them and do not speculate on what a judge or jury might do if more evidence had been presented or better arguments had been made. (Boersema, Hanson, & Keilitz, 1991, p. 30).

Litigants are usually satisfied with the outcome of arbitration. In the Georgia survey, 90% of the attorneys said that the arbitrators on their cases were fair. Though many attorneys did not agree with the outcome (45% believed the damage award was at least somewhat unfair), attorneys were inclined to accept (not appeal) the arbitrators' decisions because the hearings were perceived as fair—another example of the importance of procedural justice. Litigants usually want to resolve their disputes, not protract them, and the arbitrator's decision serves that function.

Summary Jury Trial

The **summary jury trial** (SJT) is an interesting variation on arbitration. Developed by Judge Thomas Lambros in 1980, the summary jury trial is much like a conventional jury trial. A jury is empaneled, and the lawyers tell the jurors what the witnesses would say if they were present. The lawyers argue the case and try to answer the jurors' questions about the facts. The judge tells the jury what the law is and tries to answer the jurors' questions about the law. The jurors then deliberate and decide the case. Although the "verdict" does not bind the parties, the process educates the lawyers and clients on how a conventional jury might view the facts and the law. Once educated, the lawyers and their clients are more amenable to settling the case (Lambros, 1993). In 2004, the American Bar Journal reported favorable comments from lawyers and judges who had availed themselves of this form of ADR (McDonough, 2004). Commenting on the summary jury trial, federal judge William Bertelsman said:

> I believe that a summary jury trial is a useful device . . . to settle a complex case with one or two key issues, where the problem with settlement is that the parties differ in their views of how the jury will react to the key issues. I believe that substantial amounts of time can be saved by using summary jury trial in a few select cases. Also . . . the summary jury trial gives the parties a taste of the courtroom and satisfies their psychological need for a confrontation with each other. Any judge or attorney can tell you that

emotional issues play a large part in some cases. When emotions are high, whether between attorneys or parties, cases may not settle even when a cost-benefit analysis says they should. A summary jury trial can provide a therapeutic release of this emotion at the expenditure of three days of the court's time instead of three weeks. After the emotions have been released the parties are more likely rationally to do the cost-benefit analysis, and the case may then settle. (*McKay v. Ashland Oil Inc.*, 1988, p. 49)

Mediation

Mediation is the use of a neutral person (the mediator) to work with the litigants and their lawyers to achieve a settlement of the controversy. The mediator does not have authority to decide the controversy but, rather, acts as a facilitator. Mediation often involves "shuttle diplomacy," a term associated with former Secretary of State Henry Kissinger. Much as Kissinger would "shuttle" between the two sides in international diplomacy, the mediator goes back and forth between the parties, caucusing first with one side, then with the other, in an attempt to broker an agreement between the two.

Mediation can be either evaluative or nonevaluative. In an evaluative mediation, the mediator is most interested in the substance of the dispute; the mediator questions the litigants and their lawyers about the facts of the controversy and then evaluates the case. In the evaluation, the mediator summarizes the strengths and weaknesses on each side and might even predict how a judge or jury would decide the case. Evaluative mediators use their expertise to lead the parties to a settlement that approximates what the mediator thinks the case is "worth."

A nonevaluative mediator is primarily concerned with the process. The mediator strives to open lines of communication and to help the litigants reach an acceptable settlement. The mediator is more focused on the means by which the end is achieved than on the end itself. Thus, the mediator will be reluctant to state what

the case is "worth," because such an evaluation would impose the mediator's judgment on the process.

After observing judge-mediated settlement conferences in New Jersey, Hyman and Heumann (1996) described the two evaluative styles as the "minitrial" style and the "matchmaker" style. "Judge Jay" (a pseudonym) epitomizes the evaluative, or minitrial, style. The plaintiff claimed he had been permanently injured in an auto accident. Pointing to pictures that showed no damage to plaintiff's car, the defendant denied that the injuries were serious or permanent. In response to Judge Jay's question, the plaintiff admitted that he had gone to see his lawyer before going to the doctor. After pointing out the negative implications of seeing a lawyer first, Judge Jay said that $2500 to $3000 would be a good settlement because verdicts were getting lower and lower as juries increasingly saw a connection between verdicts and the cost of insurance. This evaluation must have shocked the parties because the defense counsel had already made a tentative offer of $9000. Obviously believing that defense counsel had been very generous (stupidly so), Judge Jay told the plaintiff to take the $9000 or risk the imposition of "reverse interest" if the jury verdict was less than $9000. It took the plaintiff all of 12 minutes to settle for $9000.

"Judge Ellsworth" epitomizes the nonevaluative, or matchmaker, style. After obtaining a brief description of the auto accident, he asked the attorneys whether they had attempted to settle the case. The plaintiff had demanded $12,500 and the defendant had offered $2500. Judge Ellsworth then began to work back and forth between the attorneys, nudging one up and the other down in a series of separate meetings (caucuses). When the plaintiff's lawyer said his bottom line was $6000, Judge Ellsworth asked the defense counsel whether he could get $5000 to $6000 for the plaintiff. The defense counsel replied that he thought he could get authority to settle for $3500 to $4000. Judge Ellsworth asked the defense lawyer to confer with the adjuster.

The lawyer did so and reported that he had authority to settle at $3500 but thought he could get the adjuster up to $4000. Judge Ellsworth then went back to the plaintiff and said he couldn't get $6000. After some discussion, the plaintiff's counsel told Judge Ellsworth he would settle for $4000, but he authorized Judge Ellsworth only to tell defense counsel he would settle at $5000. Judge Ellsworth attempted to induce defense counsel to offer more than $4000. When this effort was unsuccessful, plaintiff's counsel accepted the $4000 offer (Hyman & Heumann, 1996).

Most judges combine the minitrial and matchmaker styles. The attorneys who were surveyed liked elements of both styles. They liked caucusing, a necessary element of the matchmaker style, and they liked evaluation, the key element of the minitrial style (Hyman & Heumann, 1996).

One thinks of lawyers as eager to do battle—to slay their opponents with rhetorical swords. The facts, however, indicate otherwise: Lawyers prefer mediation over arbitration and trial by jury (Reuben, 1996). A 1999 study of court-ordered mediation in domestic relations cases found that most participants and lawyers were satisfied with both the process and the results (Gordon, 2002). Why do lawyers like mediation? One of the authors of this book has mediated over 50 cases since 1992. In his experience, most lawyers are **risk averse**; in other words, they work to avoid taking risks. They prefer that controversies be *settled* rather than *decided*. In a settlement, there is no winner and no loser. The parties reach an agreement and, having done so, are not in a position to criticize their lawyers' performances. In a decision made by arbitration or trial, however, there is a winner and a loser. The loser often blames the lawyer for the loss. In general, lawyers prefer the certainty of a settlement over the uncertainty of arbitration or trial.

Mediation facilitates settlement. Lawyers use the mediator to provide a "reality check" on their client's expectations. A client, after hearing the mediator's somewhat negative assessment of the claim, is more likely to accept a reasonable settlement offer. A skillful mediator can make both parties feel that they've gotten a good deal and that the lawyers for the parties have done an excellent job.

What form of ADR do people tend to favor? The answer to this question is important, because although courts can encourage the use of ADR procedures, they will be accepted and used only if they are respected and considered legitimate. A recent study investigated the preferences of role-playing participants for different dispute resolution features. People evaluated civil disputes and indicated their preferences for a particular process, set of the rules, and decision (Shestowsky, 2004). The most consistent finding was that participants favored options that offered them control (e.g., a neutral third party helping disputants to arrive at *their own* resolutions, processes that allow disputants to control *their own* presentation of evidence and their agreement in advance on the rules that govern the decision).

Should courts force litigants to try ADR (mediation, arbitration, summary jury trial, etc.) before setting a case for trial? The reports from courts that mandate ADR are generally positive. Atlanta's mandatory arbitration program is very successful, as measured by the percentage of cases settled and attorney satisfaction. Attorneys like the process, believing that the process is fair and saves clients time and money (Boersema, Hanson, & Keilitz, 1991). A survey of 600 attorneys whose cases in Pennsylvania federal court were referred to arbitration produced the same results: 93% approved of the program, and 61% said they preferred arbitration over trial (Broderick, 1991).

The counter argument is that litigants have a right to trial by judge or jury; judges are paid to effectuate that right; and mandating ADR undermines that right. Arkansas federal judge Thomas Eisele commented on this issue:

> Let us face the truth: from the court's point of view, coerced settlement is the primary objective of these compulsory ADRs, despite

protests to the contrary. The many rules requiring parties or persons with settlement authority to be present at ADR sessions should make this obvious—particularly when one realizes that in many cases the presence of such persons would not be required at the actual trial before a judge or jury (Eisele, 1991, p. 36).

According to Judge Eisele, mandatory ADR leads to an unintended effect: Lawyers ("piranhas" he calls them) file meritless claims, knowing that their claims will have "settlement value" in mediation. Recall Judge Ellsworth, the "matchmaker" mediator. He was primarily concerned with the process—with ascertaining the litigants' bottom lines and pushing them to offer more and accept less. It is easy to see that by emphasizing the "transaction costs" (the cost of defending a meritless case), a matchmaker mediator might encourage a blameless defendant to pay something to settle a case that substantively has no merit.

Lawyers

Lawyers are plentiful in the United States; over 70% of the world's lawyers live in the United States, three times as many per capita as in Great Britain and more than 25 times as many per capita as in Japan. The 2000 census reported 871,115 lawyers and 58,355 judges, so there may be as many as one million lawyers in the United States in 2005—enough lawyers to populate a fair-sized city (www.abanet.org). With law school enrollments stabilized at about 125,000, approximately 40,000 new lawyers are sworn in annually, more than are needed to replace those who leave the practice.

The National Association of Law Placement (www.nalp.org) provides statistical information on the employment of recent law graduates. A 2003 survey on information about 35,787 graduates showed that six months after graduation, 90% were employed, 2% were not seeking work, 2% were studying for the bar exam, 2%

were working on advanced degrees, and only 4% were seeking a job. About 60% of those employed were in private practice, with the balance spread out in government, business, and academic endeavors. The median reported beginning salaries were $52,500 for women and $60,000 for men.

What Kind of Work Do Lawyers Do?

Those in law firms work for the firm's clients; some lawyers specialize (e.g., labor law or intellectual property), and some are generalists, trying to handle most of their clients' legal matters. Some lawyers work for corporations and are called "house counsel." These lawyers have only one client, their corporate employers. Lawyers working for firms often seek house counsel positions with corporations that their firms represent. House counsel are generally well paid, have job security, work reasonable hours, and need not be concerned with drumming up business or keeping track of billable hours.

Many lawyers work for the government—on the federal, state, or local level. Like house counsel for corporations, government lawyers have only one client, the governmental unit for which they work. Although they are not so well paid as corporate counsel, government lawyers enjoy reasonable hours, job security, and freedom from the business aspects of law practice. Prosecutors are government lawyers with the responsibility of prosecuting individuals charged with crime. Whereas federal prosecutors (U.S. Attorneys) are appointed by the president, the head prosecutors for cities and counties, often called States' Attorneys, are elected, often in partisan elections.

Because few people accused of crime can afford to hire a lawyer, most defendants are represented by public defenders. The history of public defenders dates from the 1963 case of *Gideon v. Wainwright*, in which the Supreme Court held that the state of Florida was obligated to pay for a lawyer for Clarence Earl Gideon, a small-town thief who lived on the fringes of society. His story is detailed in Box 2.3.

States responded to the Gideon case by paying appointed lawyers on a case-by-case basis and by establishing public defender programs, with lawyers hired by the state to represent those who cannot afford to hire counsel. Even though they are typically over-worked and under-paid, public defenders generally represent their clients well. They know the law, they know the system and the other players in the system (the judge, the prosecutor, the probation officer), and they often obtain excellent results for their clients.

But heavy caseloads and low salaries sap the energy of all but the most dedicated public defenders. James Kunen, a former public defender, described his experience in a book whose title asks the question inevitably posed to every public defender: *How Can You Defend Those People?* (1983):

> [Y]ou get tired of the pressure—someone's freedom always riding on you. And you get tired of what the exertion and the pressure is all about; you're defending the Constitution; you're defending *everybody's* rights, but you're also, more often than not—defending a criminal. That needs to be done, but it doesn't need to be done *by you*, not all your life. After a while, it's somebody else's turn. (p. 142)

Public defenders might be young, inexperienced, and overworked, but they know the law. The same cannot always be said of "appointed counsel," lawyers appointed to handle often serious cases for little or no fee. Stephen Bright, director of the Southern Center for Human Rights, describes some of these lawyers in his aptly titled journal article "Counsel for the Poor: The Death Sentence Not for the Worst Crime But for the Worst Lawyer" (1994):

◆ a lawyer appointed in a Georgia capital case[,] who was paid $15 an hour, did not request funds to hire an expert to challenge the state's hair-identification evidence; his closing argument was only 225 words long

◆ a lawyer appointed in a Texas capital case, who was paid $11.84 an hour, failed to interview witnesses and misinterpreted the law

◆ a lawyer appointed to defend a capital case in Alabama[,] and given only $500 to investigate the case, later admitted that he had not properly investigated the facts

◆ a lawyer, who when asked to name some criminal cases, could name only *Miranda* and *Dred Scott* (the latter, of course, is not a criminal case) (pp. 1835–1838)

In many states, public defender systems (and appointed counsel systems as well) are improving, thanks to changing public opinion and litigation aimed at forcing states to increase funding. The Spangenberg Group, a nationally recognized criminal justice research and consulting firm, has worked with many states over the last 15 years to raise public defender salaries and reduce caseloads to manageable levels. In Connecticut, the state drastically increased funding for defender services in order to settle a lawsuit brought by the American Civil Liberties Union on behalf of indigent defendants. And in Mississippi, three counties sued the state in an attempt to force the state to create a statewide public defender system in order to relieve the counties of financial burdens, such as the one experienced by one small Mississippi county that was forced to raise taxes and borrow money to pay the cost of prosecuting two men for a quadruple homicide (Rovella, 2000b, p. A1).

Occasionally one reads of a public defender or appointed counsel who goes far beyond what can reasonably be expected of someone who is overworked and underpaid—a person such as Annette Lee of the Bronx (New York) Defenders. Appointed to defend a 15-year-old charged with selling drugs, Ms. Lee went to her client's home to find proof of his age in order to keep him out of adult court. On the basis of what she found during the home visit—a drug-addicted single mother—Lee persuaded the court to put the boy in a drug treatment program and then kept tabs on him while he was in the program, visiting him,

THE CASE OF

BOX 2.3

Clarence Gideon, his famous pauper's plea, and the right to an attorney

Clarence Earl Gideon, Petitioner
vs.
H.G. Cochran, Jr., Director, Division of Corrections. State of Florida,
Respondent

"Answer to respondent's response to petition for Writ of Certiorari."

Petitioner, Clarence Earl Gideon recieved a copy of the response of the respondent in the mail dated sixth day of April, 1962. Petitioner can not make any pretense of being able to answer the learned Attorney General of the State of Florida because the petitioner is not a attorney or versed in law nor does not have the law books to copy down the decisions of this Court. But the petitioner knows there is many of them. Nor would the petitioner be allowed to do so. According to the book of Revised Rules of the Supreme Court of the United States sent to me by Clerk of the same Court. The response of the respondent is out of time (Rule #24). Under this rule the respondent has thirty days in which to make a response. The respondent claims that a citizen can get a equal and fair trial without legal counsel. That the constitution of the United States does not apply to the State of Florida. Petitioner thinks that the fourteenth amend. makes this so. Petitioner will attempt to show this Court that a citizen of the State of Florida cannot get a just and fair trial without the aid of Counsel. Petitioner when he wrote his petition for Writ of Habeas Corpus to the Florida Supreme Court and his petition to this Court for a Writ of Certiorari and this brief was and is not allowed to send out a prepared petition. Petitioner is required to write his petition under duress or as the attorney General states, under physical restrain. If the petitioner had a attorney he could send out any kind of a petition he was so minded too, which shows he can not have *equal* rights to the law unless he does have a attorney. The same thing applies to the lower court. If the petitioner would of had a attorney there would not of been allowed such things as hear say perjury or Bill of attainer against him. Petitioner claims that there was never the crime of Breaking and Entering ever comitted. At that time he call to the The Federal Bureau of Investigation for help at Panama City, Fla., But was told they could not do nothing about it. Respondent claims that I have no right to file petition for a Writ of Habeas Corpus. Take away this right to a citizen and there is nothing left. It makes no difference how old I am or what color I am or what church I belong too if any. The question is I did not get a fair trial. The question is very simple. I requested the court to appoint me attorney and the court refused. All countrys try to give there Citizens a fair trial and see to it that they have counsel. Petitioner asks of this court to disregard the response of the respondent because it was out of Time and because the Attorney General did not have one of his many assistant attorney Generals to help me a citizen of the State of Florida to write my petition or this brief. But instead force me to write these petitions under duress. On this basis it is respectfully urged that the petition for a Writ of Certiorari shall be issue.

Clarence Earl Gideon
Petitioner

At age 51, Clarence Earl Gideon was tried for breaking into and entering the Bay Harbor Pool Room in Panama City, Florida, and stealing money from a cigarette machine and a jukebox. At his trial, Gideon asked the judge to appoint an attorney to defend him because he had no money to pay for one. The judge, following the laws in Florida, refused. Free attorneys were provided only if there were special circumstances in the case—if, for instance, the offense was a very serious one or if the defendant's mental abilities were limited.

Gideon did not have a lawyer during his trial, and although he was no stranger to a courtroom, having been convicted on four previous occasions, he lost this case, too. Eventually, from his prison cell, Gideon filed a pauper's appeal to the U.S. Supreme Court. His contention, laboriously printed in pencil, was that the U.S. Constitution guaranteed the right of every defendant in a criminal trial to have the services of a lawyer. Gideon's effort was a long shot; well over 1500 pauper's appeals are filed each term, and the Supreme Court agrees to consider only about 3% of them. Furthermore, 20 years earlier, in the case of *Betts v. Brady* (1942), the Supreme Court had rejected the very proposition that Gideon was making by holding that poor defendants had a right to free counsel only under "special circumstances" (e.g., if the defendant was very young, illiterate, or mentally ill).

Yet, ever since its adoption, the doctrine of *Betts v. Brady* has been criticized as inconsistent and unjust. The folly of requiring a poor person to represent himself is exemplified by Gideon's cross-examination of the most important witness for the prosecution:

Q. Do you know positively I was carrying a pint of wine?

A. Yes.

Q. How do you know that?

A. Because I seen it in your hand. (Lewis, 1964)

When the Supreme Court agreed to hear Gideon's appeal, four of the justices had already declared, in other cases, that they believed *Betts v. Brady* should be overturned. When Gideon's case was argued before the Supreme Court in January 1963, he was represented by Abe Fortas, a Washington attorney later named a Supreme Court justice. Fortas argued that it was impossible for defendants to have a fair trial unless they were represented by a lawyer. He also observed that the "special circumstances" rule was very hard to apply fairly.

On March 18, 1963, the Supreme Court ruled unanimously that Gideon had the right to be represented by an attorney, even if he could not afford one. As Justice Hugo Black put it, "[that] the government hires lawyers to prosecute and [that] defendants who have the money hire lawyers to defend are the strongest indications of the widespread belief that lawyers in criminal cases are necessities, not luxuries" (*Gideon v. Wainwright*, 1963, p. 344). Although *Gideon* applied only to defendants accused of felonies, nine years later the Supreme Court extended the right to counsel to persons accused of misdemeanors (*Argersinger v. Hamlin*, 1972).

Nearly two years after he was sentenced, Clarence Gideon was given a new trial. With the help of a free court-appointed attorney, he was found not guilty. The simple handwritten petition of a modest man had changed the procedures of criminal trials, perhaps permanently. Gideon lived the rest of his life almost free of legal tangles; his only subsequent difficulty came two years later, when he pleaded guilty to a charge of vagrancy in Kentucky. He died in 1972.

bringing him clothes, and ultimately helping him obtain a small grant to pay for technical college (Rovella, 2000b, p. A1).

Law Schools and Legal Education

American lawyers of the 18th and 19th centuries typically learned to be lawyers through the apprentice method: An enterprising young man (the first female lawyer graduated in 1869) would attach himself to an attorney for a period of time, until both he and the lawyer were satisfied that he was ready to be "admitted to the bar." He would then be questioned, often superficially, by a judge or lawyer and pronounced fit to practice (Stevens, 1983). In his prize-winning biography of Abraham Lincoln, Carl Sandburg (1926) described Lincoln as bar examiner:

> When Jonathon Birch came to the hotel in Bloomington to be examined by Lincoln for admission to the bar, Lincoln asked three or four questions about contracts and other law branches. And then, as Birch told it: "He asked nothing more. Sitting on the edge of the bed he began to entertain me with recollections, many of them vivid and racy, of his start in the profession." Birch couldn't figure out whether it was a real examination or a joke. But Lincoln gave him a note to Judge Logan, another member of the examining committee, and he took the note to Logan, and without any more questions was given a certificate to practice law. The note from Lincoln read:
>
> > My Dear Judge:
> > The bearer of this is a young man who thinks he can be a lawyer. Examine him if you want to. I have done so and am satisfied. He's a good deal smarter than he looks to be. Yours, Lincoln

Powerful forces shaped legal education as we know it today. States began to require those aspiring to be lawyers to pass meaningful examinations. Influenced by the American Bar Association (ABA), the states also gradually increased the educational requirements for admission to these exams, first requiring some college, then some law school, and finally graduation from an accredited law school. (Apprenticing still exists as an alternative—however seldom used—in a few states, notably California.) Because most states require graduation from an ABA-accredited law school as a condition of admission to the bar, a degree from an unaccredited school is almost worthless. In 2005, 189 schools were accredited by the ABA; students who graduate from an ABA-approved law school may sit for the bar exam in any state. Students from state-accredited schools (California has over 30 state-accredited schools) may sit only in the state of accreditation (ABA, 2005).

Women in Law School and the Legal Profession

In 1872, the Supreme Court of the United States upheld the denial of a law license to a Vermont woman named Myra Bradwell. Justice Bradley's opinion reflects the 19th-century view of a woman's place:

> Man is, or should be, woman's protector and defender. The natural and proper timidity and delicacy which belongs to the female sex evidently unfits it for many of the occupations of civil life. . . . The paramount destiny and mission of woman are to fulfill the noble and benign offices of wife and mother. This is the law of the Creator. And the rules of civil society must be adapted to the general constitution of things, and cannot be based upon exceptional cases. (*Bradwell v. State*, 1872)

Women were denied admission to elite law schools well into the 20th century. Yale did not admit women until 1918, and Harvard Law School did not become coeducational until 1947 (Stevens, 1983). As late as 1975, only 5% of American lawyers were women (Lentz & Laband, 1995). By 1980, however, women made up almost 40% of law students, a percentage that gradually increased to 49% in 2000 and then leveled off (American Bar Association, 2005). Because women came into the profession in large numbers only recently, the percentage of women lawyers trails the percentage of women law students. The 2000 census reports that 29% of attorneys are female.

Some of our most powerful female lawyers experienced discrimination in law school. When former Attorney General Janet Reno entered Harvard Law School in the fall of 1960, she was 1 of just 16 women in a pool of over 500 male students. Harvard had first admitted women only 13 years before, and some of the older professors evidently regarded legal coeducation as a failed experiment. Professors such as W. Barton Leach made little secret of their disdain for women. Leach, who taught property law, declared that "he wouldn't call on women in the big classrooms. He said their voices weren't powerful enough to be heard," recalled Charles Nesson, one of Reno's classmates who now teaches at the law school. So Leach scheduled Ladies' Day, and he made the women sit in front. Continued Nesson, "And we sat through that and laughed, without the thought ever occurring to us that something totally wrong was happening. It had to have had some powerful effects on Janet and the others."

Ladies' Day infuriated Elizabeth Hanford Dole, class of 1965, who served in the Reagan and Bush (senior) administrations and as U.S. senator from North Carolina. "Charles W. Kingsfield, the infamous law professor of the novel, movie, and television series *The Paper Chase*, at his most perverse could not have devised a more public humiliation," Dole later wrote.

What kind of work experiences do female attorneys encounter? Do they face discrimination on the job? Overt pay discrimination based on gender was largely ended by Title VII and the Supreme Court case of *Hishon v. King & Spaulding* (1984), and male and female attorneys are now paid about the same for equal work. However, in firms that have fewer than 15 employees and are not covered by Title VII, job satisfaction among men and women is not equal (Lentz & Laband, 1995). Women believe they are discriminated against "on intangible margins," involving factors such as work assignments, secretarial support, mentoring, invitations to social functions, and office camaraderie (Lentz & Laband, 1995).

A 1988 Stanford survey, however, found no significant differences between men and women in employment or job satisfaction. The sample of this study was 764 women (all the known living Stanford female graduates) and 764 randomly selected men. The return rate was 58%. The results indicated no statistically significant difference between female and male law students' or graduates' responses regarding their ultimate career goals or the setting in which they ultimately wanted to work. A gender difference was found for only one factor: 43% of the male graduates, but only 27% of the female graduates, considered the adversarial nature of the job important to job satisfaction. The survey also found that women (29%) were much more likely to interrupt a career than men (8%) and more likely to work part-time at some point in their careers (women 31%, men 9%) (Taber, 1988).

A survey of 1012 graduates of the University of New Mexico (with a return rate of 60%) indicated little difference between men and women in stress levels, job satisfaction, and hours worked. The study did reveal that women are more likely to be dissatisfied with a perceived lack of flexibility in their work schedules and with excessive time demands. The study indicated that women are somewhat more cooperative than men at work; they scored significantly higher on a "commitment to cooperation" question (Teitelbaum, 1991).

Although the New Mexico and Stanford studies indicate few gender differences in the professional lives of male and female lawyers, Lentz and Laband (1995) found that by most indicators, female attorneys are less happy professionally than male attorneys. A 2000 survey of Mississippi lawyers and judges revealed a "perception gap": Female respondents believed they were treated differently because of their gender by other lawyers (80%) and judges (53%). Male respondents, on the other hand, did not think gender makes a difference. Female respondents referred to patronizing references (e.g. "honey," "little lady") and sexual innuendos, and to a belief that engaging in appropriately aggressive behavior labeled them as "bitches" (Winkle & Wedeking, 2003, p.130).

A 1996 National Law Journal survey of 250 law firms revealed substantial gains in the number of women who had made partner between 1985 (6%) and 1995 (13.6%). In 2004, according to a similar survey, the percentage of female partners had increased to 17% (National Association of Law Placement, 2005). Although women are still under-represented at the partnership level, the fact that the percentage of partners continues to increase indicates that demographics (older lawyers are pre-dominately male) rather than discrimination might be the cause of this under-representation.

However, there may be lifestyle issues that affect the success of female attorneys. Like their male counterparts, female lawyers are often expected to work long hours. It is not uncommon for firms to expect the partners and associates to bill 2200 hours a year—about 45 hours a week—not including the hours spent commuting, eating lunch, or attending to matters that do not create billable hours. A study of 584 female lawyers revealed a positive correlation between hours worked and stress-related ailments. Women lawyers working more than 45 hours per week were three times as likely to miscarry as those working less than 35 hours (Gatland, 1997). Balancing motherhood with a busy law practice isn't easy. Mothers in many law firms succeed through hard work, organization, and the support of partners, friends and baby-sitters. One mother described her life as one "without sleep," in which she gave her clients tax advice by cell phone while watching her children swim at the beach (Brennan, 1998). Women are more likely than men to put their families first and, if need be, to quit the firm or work on a part-time basis—in any case to withdraw from the partnership track (Choo, 2001).

There is also a social barrier in some firms at the "equity partner" level; equity partners are the partners who own and control the firm. As described in a 1996 article:

> Often, however, women lawyers don't get a chance to build relationships in the firm or with the client. The days of institutional clients that are handed from one generation of partners to the next are over. Attaining new business, key to the coveted equity partnership, requires a fair amount of socializing. But social events tend to be male-centered: golf, ball games and "nights on

the town when everyone ends up in a room smoking cigars," as one woman lawyer who asked not to be identified put it. (Klein, 1996, p. 1)

Minorities in Law School and the Legal Profession

In 1930, there were only six black lawyers in Mississippi, a state with a black population of more than one million (Houston, 1935). By 1966, the number had grown only to nine (Gellhorn, 1968). This rate reflected national trends; in 1988, only about 1% of the nation's lawyers were black (McGee, 1971). Jim Crow laws and prac-tices barred blacks from southern law schools; Thurgood Marshall, who later became a justice on the U.S. Supreme Court, was denied admis-sion to the University of Maryland Law School and attended Howard University, a predomi-nantly black school in the District of Columbia (Rowan, 1993).

Not until 1951 did the Association of American Law Schools (AALS) take a position against racial discrimination in admissions (Cardozo, 1993), and not until 1964 could the AALS state that none of its member schools reported denying admission on the basis of race. Nonetheless, in that year only 433 out of more than 50,000 students in predominantly white law schools were black (ABA, 1992).

The number of minority lawyers in the United States has grown steadily since the mid-1960s, although the numbers still lag far behind the per-centage of minorities in the general population. In 1960, less than 1% of lawyers in the United States were African-American; in 1990, 3.3% of American attorneys were black. However, in the next decade, the percentage of African-American attorneys increased only from 3.3% to 3.9% (ABA Commission on Racial and Ethnic Diversity, 2005).

Minority admissions into law schools and the role of affirmative action programs were at the core of a case considered by the U.S. Supreme Court in 2003. The plaintiff was a white female applicant to the University of Michigan Law School by the name of Barbara Grutter (see Box 2.4).

THE CASE OF

BOX 2.4   **Barbara Grutter and her admission to law school**

Barbara Grutter, a white resident of the state of Michigan, applied in December 1996 for admission into the first-year class of the University of Michigan Law School for the fall of 1997. At the time of her application, Grutter was 43 years old and had graduated from college 18 years earlier. She applied with a 3.8 undergraduate grade point average and an LSAT score of 161, representing the 86th percentile nationally. In June 1997, her application was rejected. Grutter believed that she was the victim of reverse discrimination—that she would have been admitted if she had been African-American. The Center for Individual Rights, an organization opposed to affirmative action, agreed with her and sponsored a suit on her behalf against the University of Michigan in federal court.

The trial lasted 15 days, during which Grutter relied on statistical evidence that the University admitted African-American applicants with credentials inferior to hers, and the University defended its policy as one of diversity, not quotas (*Grutter v. Bollinger*, 2001).

The trial court ruled in favor of Grutter, the federal court of appeals ruled against her, and the case came to the Supreme Court in 2003. In a 5-4 opinion, the Court also ruled against her, holding that the Law School could, in the name of diversity, prefer minority students of inferior numerical credentials over white applicants. Justice O'Connor wrote the majority opinion, reasoning that diversity is a legitimate educational goal—that the Law School's admission policy, "promotes cross-racial understanding, helps to break down racial stereotypes, and enables students to better understand persons of different races," which in turn "better prepares students for an increasingly diverse workforce and society." (Interestingly, the Court ruled against the University in a companion case attacking a somewhat different policy for undergraduate admissions, *Grutter v. Bollinger*, 2003).

Turned away by the Court, the Center for Individual Rights has taken the fight to the voters, sponsoring a ballot initiative to amend the Michigan constitution to prohibit the state from extending preferential treatment to any group or individual based on race, gender, ethnicity, or national origin. Barbara Grutter has been a spokesperson for the initiative—not an easy task, for she is greeted with "boos, hisses, and picket signs" and "frequently interrupted by jeers and murmurs of disapproval" (www.adversity.net/michigan).

What will be the effect on minority admissions if Michigan voters amend the constitution to outlaw affirmative action? In California, passage of Proposition 209 in 1995 required state law schools to admit on a color-blind basis. At highly-rated Boalt Hall (the law school at the University of California at Berkeley), the number of African-Americans admitted dropped sharply in the wake of Proposition 209's passage but rebounded when Boalt changed the way it looked at students' records (grades from all undergraduate institutions are now weighted the same)(Ward, 1998).

Corporate America has made a commitment to diversity and might be minority lawyers' best friend. In choosing their lawyers, large corporations increasingly look for firms with women and minorities. Roderick Palmore, general counsel for Sara Lee, asked his counterparts in other corporations to use their positions to persuade the legal community not only to hire minorities and women but also to give them positions of responsibility. As of 2005, 73 large corporations had pledged to give work to diverse law firms and to freeze out firms that weren't making progress in that area (McDonough, 2005).

Trends in Lawyering

LEADING THE GOOD LIFE WHILE MAKING A GOOD LIVING

Whereas Andrew Struve, a San Diego attorney, works more than 60 hours a week (he billed 3060 hours in 2003) (Ward, 2005), Nancy Margolis works 15–20 hours a week for a Philadelphia firm so that she can spend time with her children (Ward, 2004b). Ms. Margolis is a member of an emerging class of lawyers who are unwilling to sacrifice family life to make partner and earn the salary that comes with partnership. Emery Bright practices law part-time while pursuing an acting career; Robert Byrnes practices 20–30 hours a week and oversees a small business he created (Ward, 2004a). Nina Kalle, a solo practitioner in Boston, works at home; not only does she save on rent, but she can play with her toddler daughter at any time (Tebo, 2004). John Sandberg took a six-month sabbatical from his St. Louis law firm to sail the East Coast with his family. Lori Gordon took a sabbatical from her Chicago firm and wrote a book (*Rest Assured: The Sabbatical Solution for Lawyers*) about the experience (Neil, 2003). Firms are aware that bright and productive lawyers will be attracted to lifestyle accommodations. For example, Arnold and Porter, a prestigious Washington firm, provides on-site child care, paid maternity leave for mothers *and fathers*, and part-time status if desired (Mandel, 2003).

One of the authors of this book teaches Professional Responsibility, an ethics class required of all law students. He routinely asks his classes what kind of practice and life they desire. Nearly all students say they want a balanced life, one in which they work a normal week and have time for family and fun. Rarely does a student say that he or she wants to work 80 hours a week, become partner, and earn a huge salary.

LAWYERS MUST BE BUSINESS-SAVVY

The practice of law is a profession, but it is also a business. Whether in a large firm, in a small firm, or in solo practice, 21st-century lawyers must market themselves and be technologically astute. They must strive to keep their clients satisfied, because clients today have little loyalty to their lawyers. They must keep expenses down and budget for lean times. Lawyers and clients alike are dissatisfied with billing by the hour, which leads to inefficiencies and claims of bill-padding. It can be expected that clients will increasingly insist on fee-for-service billing, similar to that employed by doctors and dentists.

WHAT MAKES A GOOD LAWYER?

Students decide to go to law school for many different reasons: Some want to do well in the world, others seek to make money, a few want to satisfy parental expectations, and others elect law school because at the time there seems to be nothing better to do with a degree in history (or political science or English or economics).

John Hunter, a general practitioner in Raleigh, North Carolina, describes his decision to attend law school as follows:

> In my own case, I became interested in the law as a profession largely as a result of two factors which touched me entirely by chance. First, I was born and grew up in a neighborhood in which my family lived across the street from a very good lawyer who often talked with me about his profession, and secondly, I happened to take a course in public speaking during my first year in high school which led to a great interest in it and developed in me a skill in speaking in public which could be nicely worked in with the practice of law. In addition, I discovered in connection with the work I did in some of my English courses that I liked to work with words and particularly to express ideas in written or spoken language. The result was that by the time I entered college, I knew definitely that I wanted to be a lawyer, even though I had virtually no experience that touched upon the law itself or the type of work a lawyer does. (Love & Childers, 1963, pp. 75–76)

Hunter is representative of those who went to law school because of a perceived aptitude for the

Two of America's most famous Lawyers: Janet Reno and Thurgood Marshall

study and practice of law. Alan Dershowitz, the youngest professor to attain tenure at Harvard Law School and a frequent defender of unpopular clients, studied the law out of a motivation to "argue and debate," a motive described as of great importance by 26% of the respondents in Stevens's (1983) survey. Dershowitz started talking about the law while growing up in a devout Jewish household in Brooklyn; he remembers his father and uncles spending hours discussing the Talmud, the basic treatise of Jewish law (Bayles, 1984). "The Jewish religion is a very argumentative religion," Dershowitz says. "You argue with everyone. You essentially put God on trial." The experience left him with "a problem with authority." He is quoted as saying, "Teachers were always telling me 'You're stupid, but you have a big mouth so you ought to be a lawyer' " (Bayles, 1984, p. 16).

As a young man, Clarence Darrow saw himself as a man of letters and sought the law as a medium in which he could express himself. He had also experienced farm work:

> I was brought up on a farm. When I was a young man, on a very hot day, I was engaged in distributing and packing down the hay which a horse-propelled stacker was constantly dumping on top of me. By noon, I was completely exhausted. That afternoon, I left the farm,

never to return, and I haven't done a day of hard work since. (quoted in Tierney, 1979, p. 21)

Supreme Court Justice Thurgood Marshall turned to the law after flunking anthropology, thus derailing his plans to be a dentist. Denied admission to the University of Maryland because he was black, Marshall attended Howard Law School in the District of Columbia. There Marshall came under the influence of Charles Houston, "who set a fire in Marshall's belly, a rage to go out into the legal profession immediately and reverse the myriad injustices of Maryland and America" (Rowan, 1993, p. 47).

Janet Reno's father was a crime reporter for the *Miami Herald*. "The courtrooms of the Dade County Courthouse, of that beautiful old federal building, were like magical places to me when I went with my father as he covered trials, both criminal and civil. And I thought that one of the most wonderful things anybody could do was to be a lawyer," Reno recalled (Anderson, 1994, p. 34). Her parents wanted her to be a doctor, and she graduated from Cornell University with a degree in chemistry. However, a summer job as a researcher convinced her she wasn't cut out for a medical career, and she took her leadership skills to Harvard Law School in 1960 (Anderson, 1994).

Johnnie Cochran, who masterminded the successful defense of O. J. Simpson, put himself through school by selling insurance and working for the U.S. Postal Service. After a few years as a prosecutor, he began a criminal defense practice, which blossomed after the 1965 riots turned the Watts area of Los Angeles into a war zone. Early in Cochran's career he came to believe that his mission as a lawyer was to vigorously represent citizens, usually African-Americans, who were the victims of police oppression or violence. Though paid handsomely for defending Simpson, Cochran saw himself as a champion of the downtrodden: "[M]y cases all have a component of official, under-color violence against a citizen who is usually poor, African-American, Haitian-American or some person of color." (Rovella, 1999, p. A1).

Lawyers and Ethics

Lawyers are human, and it is inevitable that some will behave unethically or even criminally. Every state attempts to protect the public against such behavior through a code of ethics (usually patterned after the ABA's Model Rules of Professional Conduct), enforced by a disciplinary body whose decisions are reviewed by the highest court of the state. The disciplinary body can censure, suspend, or even disbar unethical lawyers. In addition, most states have created "client security funds" to reimburse clients whose money has been embezzled by lawyers.

Public criticism of the disciplinary process for lawyers generally takes two forms: (1) an assumption that lawyers "get away with anything," based on the fact that disciplinary proceedings are often closed, and the disciplinary tribunal is composed primarily of lawyers, and (2) a perception that the ethical rules—the lawyers' code—do not provide any relief for those who are overcharged or poorly represented. Both criticisms are warranted. The public can never be expected to accept a disciplinary process that takes place behind closed doors, and the failure of bar associations and disciplinary tribunals to come to grips

with price gouging and/or inept lawyers explains in part why the public perception of lawyers is as negative as it is. Gradually, states are opening the disciplinary process and are adding non-lawyers to the disciplinary panels that hear cases against lawyers. However, states rarely discipline lawyers who overcharge or perform poorly.

ETHICAL TRAINING FOR LAWYERS

ABA standards state that law schools should teach law students "the history, goals, structure, and responsibilities of the legal profession and its members, including the ABA Model Rules of Professional Conduct." In addition, many states require lawyers to take continuing legal education courses, including ethics courses. Lawyers often face ethical dilemmas in which the answer is less than obvious. Suppose, for example, a client tells the lawyer in confidence that he intends to burn down his business to collect the insurance proceeds. One might expect that the lawyer should inform the police of the impending arson. Because of the importance assigned to client confidences, however, the Model Rules require the lawyer to keep silent unless he or she reasonably believes that the fire might endanger someone within the building. The lawyer may, of course, try to talk the client out of the planned crime, but ultimately, the lawyer is required to keep the information confidential.

Take another example: Suppose a couple planning on an amicable divorce decides to hire a lawyer who has helped the husband with his business over the years. The couple asks the lawyer to "help them with the divorce." Can the lawyer represent both? The Model Rules allow the lawyer to represent both only if the lawyer reasonably believes that the husband and wife are in total agreement and that there is little likelihood that they will fall into conflict during the course of the divorce proceedings. Even then, the lawyer must be careful, because the wife will need to know her husband's business transactions in order to enter into a fair property settlement. The lawyer cannot fairly represent the wife's interest unless the husband is willing to authorize the lawyer to tell the wife about matters earlier communicated to the lawyer in confidence.

Yet another example: Suppose a lawyer represents a client engaged in secret negotiations to buy a farm for development as a shopping center. Can the lawyer ethically buy the adjoining farm (which the client is not interested in buying) in anticipation of profiting when the shopping center is developed? The answer: only with the client's consent. As the client's agent, the lawyer cannot use confidential information to make a side profit unless the client consents.

There are, of course, many other ethical conundrums in the law, which have been debated in Legal Ethics courses, law journal articles, and TV talk shows. Some of these problems have no satisfactory answers, because the Model Rules do not resolve all questions and because sound arguments can be advanced for contrary positions. You might try to develop arguments for different solutions to some of the most difficult of these legal puzzles, such as the following:

◆   On examining his client's back tax returns, the lawyer tells the client that he probably will be charged with tax fraud. The client asks the lawyer for a list of countries that do not have extradition treaties with the United States. May the lawyer provide this information, knowing that the client may be planning to flee to escape prosecution?

◆   On being interviewed by his lawyer, the client tells a patently unbelievable story about the alleged crime. To what extent can a lawyer closely question the client in order to help the client develop an equally false, but more believable story?

◆   In a criminal case, the defense lawyer knows that his client robbed the victim. In cross-examining the victim, may the lawyer ethically suggest that she is mistaken in her identification of the defendant as the assailant? May the lawyer ethically suggest that the victim is lying?

Criticisms of Lawyers

The legal profession has been criticized for reasons other than its self-serving definition of ethics. Chief among these other criticisms are that the legal profession is relatively indifferent to the middle class, that it has a tendency to make the law overly complicated so that no one but a lawyer can understand it, that it tolerates or even encourages the practice of excessive billing, that it disregards the truth, and that it often indulges the filing of frivolous lawsuits. Lawyers, it is claimed, fail to adequately serve the "middle 70%" of the population. Rich criminal defendants can afford expensive law firms to represent them; corporations have the resources to pay for extensive legal research and preparation. At the other end of the economic scale, poor people are provided lawyers without cost if they are defendants in criminal trials, and they may rely on legal aid clinics, including volunteer private attorneys, if they are involved in civil suits. It is middle-income families who have the most difficulty obtaining legal assistance, because attorneys' fees of $100 to $500 an hour quickly become prohibitive.

Lawyers typically respond that such cases demonstrate the merits of the contingency fee procedure, which is used for civil plaintiffs. In a **contingency fee system**, a plaintiff pays a lawyer a fee only if the plaintiff wins the case. For example, if you believe your physician's negligence has caused you a serious illness or injury, you can ask an attorney to represent you in a civil suit against the physician. If the case is settled in your favor, your attorney receives a percentage (usually 25% to 40%) of whatever is awarded to you. But if you lose, you do not have to pay your attorney any fee. Contingency fees apply only to plaintiffs in civil cases; they are not ethical in criminal cases and are not used with defendants in civil cases.

According to his biographer, Abraham Lincoln would not charge more than his client could afford or more than he thought his services merited. He once teamed with another lawyer named Lamon to protect an incompetent woman from being swindled out of her life savings. The woman's brother had agreed to pay Lamon a fee of $250, but Lincoln gave half back to the woman.

> Judge Davis [a friend of Lincoln's] said, in the wheezing whisper of a man weighing 300 pounds, "Lincoln, you are impoverishing this bar by your picayune charges of fees, and the lawyers have reason to complain of you." Other lawyers murmured approval. Lincoln stuck to the point: "That money comes out of the pocket of a poor, demented girl, and I would rather starve than swindle her in this manner." In the evening at the hotel, the lawyers held a mock court and fined him; he paid the fine, rehearsed a new line of funny stories, and stuck to his original point that he wouldn't belong to a law firm that could be styled "Catch 'em and Cheat 'em." (Sandburg, 1926, p. 51)

On the other hand, Lincoln demanded what he felt he was owed when the client could pay. He handled a tax case for the Illinois Central Railroad in 1855, obtaining a favorable decision in the Illinois Supreme Court that saved the railroad millions. When the Illinois Central refused to pay his bill of $2000, Lincoln sued for the value of his services; he received a verdict of $5000, a very sizable fee in those days (Sandburg, 1926).

Lawyers are also charged with complicating the law unnecessarily so that consumers must hire an attorney to interpret the law for them. In apparent response to this criticism, the Florida Bar Association developed a procedure that allows childless couples who agree to divide their assets and debts to receive a divorce at a cost of less than $100 in filing fees, without the assistance of an attorney. In this example, a public institution arguably protected consumers from overly complicated legal maneuverings. Other institutions have done the same. Founded in 1978, HALT (not an acronym), an Organization of Americans for Legal Reform, claims to be "dedicated to the principle that all Americans should be able to handle their legal affairs simply, affordably and equitably." (www.halt.org)

Another frequent criticism of lawyers is that they abuse the system by filing frivolous suits. Horror stories abound: pro football fans suing a referee over a bad call, umpires suing baseball managers over name calling, an adult man suing his parents for lack of love and affection, a man suing his former girlfriend over injuries he received during consensual sex, one prisoner suing his guards for "allowing" him to escape, another inmate suing prison officials for denying him the chance to contribute to a sperm bank.

The reality, however, is that the extent of tort litigation involving claims of personal injury has been nearly constant since 1975 and has actually decreased since 1990. Most of the ten million cases that clog the courts each year are divorce cases and contract and property claims. At the same time, there is considerable evidence that some litigants and their lawyers seek compensation for nonexistent injuries. From 1980 to 1989, rates of motor vehicle accidents fell, and the number of claims made for property damages per million miles traveled also decreased 12%. With safer cars, the rate of claims for bodily injuries should have dropped even faster. Instead, the rate of bodily injury claims rose 15%.

Of course, much of the criticism of lawyers is attributable to lawyer advertising and solicitation. In Lincoln's day, lawyers advertised and solicited as did any other tradespeople. As Carl Sandburg (1926) describes it, when McLean County, Illinois, attempted to tax the Illinois Central Railroad, Lincoln offered his services to both sides, because "in justice to myself, I cannot afford it, if I can help it, to miss a fee altogether." Lincoln represented the Illinois Central, won the case, and sued the railroad for his fee.

In the 20th century, however, the organized bar deemed advertising and solicitation "unprofessional." The Canons of Ethics promulgated by the ABA in 1908 forbade advertising, solicitation, and any form of "stirring up strife and litigation." It was not until 1977 that lawyers became able to advertise, after the Supreme Court decided the case of *Bates v. State Bar of Arizona* (1977). The Court held that lawyers have a First Amendment right to truthfully advertise their services. The organized bar may require truth (or at least prohibit deception) in advertising, but the bar may not require advertising lawyers to do so with "dignity."

A final criticism of lawyers is the public's perception that lawyers, as a group, do not have the same regard for the truth as the public supposedly has. Sometimes the criticism focuses on some lawyers' willingness to hide behind legalisms to bend the truth. President Clinton (a skilled lawyer) amused us by contending that oral sex wasn't sex and by denying a sexual relationship with Monica Lewinsky because of the tense of the verb in the question. As noted by political scientist Austin Sarat, he "played into every stereotype of taking refuge in narrow legalisms. . . . He's a caricature of the overly prepared witness. As for the public view of lawyers, this does damage to the profession" (Carter, 1998, p. 42). President Clinton escaped being removed from office by the Senate following his impeachment in the House of Representatives. However, on May 22, 2000 a disciplinary committee of the Arkansas Supreme Court recommended that he lose his license to practice law because of his perjury in denying that he had a sexual relationship with Monica Lewinsky.

Often, lawyers are said to encourage falsity by consciously shaping a witness's recollection. Consider this description of famed lawyer Edward Bennett Williams's interviewing technique:

> As a rule, Williams didn't bother to take notes of the initial interview because he knew the client was lying. Slowly he'd probe for the truth . . . . The fact is, however, that Williams did not always want the truth—at least the whole truth. . . . He would . . . help the client come up with a plausible theory to explain away incriminating facts. This was done subtly, through leading questions and a certain amount of winking and nodding. (Thomas, 1991, p. 405)

As another example, the Dallas law firm of Baron & Budd sent clients allegedly suffering from asbestosis (a constellation of symptoms related to exposure to asbestos), instructions for depositions (pretrial questioning of a witness by an attorney hired by the other party). The instructions went beyond the usual "make sure you understand the question" advice and clearly were designed to tell the workers how to testify:

- It is important to emphasize that you had NO IDEA ASBESTOS WAS DANGEROUS when you were working around it.
- It is important to maintain that you NEVER saw any labels on asbestos products that said WARNING or DANGER (Rogers, 1998).

These examples are exceptions, not the rule, however. Most lawyers understand that their job is not to create the facts but, rather, to present the facts in the most favorable light to the client. The ethical lawyer might be compared to a poker player who plays the hand dealt as well as possible. The unethical lawyer might be compared to one playing draw poker who discards bad cards and draws better ones.

SUMMARY

1. What is the difference between the adversarial and inquisitorial models of trials? The trial process in the United States and several other countries is called the adversarial model because all the witnesses, evidence, and exhibits are presented by one side or the other. In contrast, in the inquisitorial model used in much of Europe, the judge does nearly all questioning of witnesses. Although the adversarial model has been criticized for instigating undesirable competition between sides, in empirical studies it has been judged to be fairer and to lead to less biased decisions.

2. *What are the characteristics of courts, and how are judges selected?* Federal crimes are prosecuted in federal courts, state crimes in state courts. Federal judges are appointed for life and may be removed only by the Senate on articles of impeachment brought by the House of Representatives. Some state judges are elected; in other states, judges are appointed and then run on their records in retention elections.

3. *What are some examples of problem-solving courts? How do they differ from traditional courts?* Juvenile courts, drug courts, and mental health courts are examples of problem-solving courts. They differ from traditional courts in their focus on the underlying causes of people's legal difficulties and in their attempt to assist people with these problems (e.g., drug addiction, mental illness), rather than to punish them.

4. *What is alternative dispute resolution? What are some types of ADR?* Alternative dispute resolution (ADR) is an umbrella term for alternatives to the court and jury as a means of resolving legal disputes. The most common forms are mediation, in which a third party tries to facilitate agreement between the disputants, and arbitration, in which a third party decides the controversy after hearing from both sides. The summary jury trial is another ADR mechanism.

5. *What various kinds of work do lawyers do?* Attorneys work in a variety of settings, including law firms and corporations, and in the employment of local, state, and federal governments. Prosecutors are government attorneys responsible for prosecuting alleged criminals, and many defense attorneys work for government-funded public defender agencies.

6. *What have been the experiences of women and minorities in the legal profession?* As we move into the 21st century, women are accepted in every facet of the legal profession, although many find that it is difficult to balance commitments to home and job. Women are not so adversarial in their approach to the practice of law as men. Minorities are underrepresented, and law schools' affirmative action programs are under attack, although the University of Michigan program was recently deemed constitutional by the U.S. Supreme Court.

7. *What are some common criticisms of lawyers?* Criticisms include lawyers' efforts to complicate legal matters unnecessarily in order to secure business, the proliferation of lawyers, lawyers' putative disregard for the truth, and frivolous lawsuits.

KEY TERMS

adversarial system	drug courts	mediation	summary jury trial
alternative dispute	family courts	mental health courts	therapeutic
resolution	homeless courts	negotiation	jurisprudence
binding arbitration	inquisitorial approach	nonbinding arbitration	women's courts
contingency fee system	juvenile courts	risk averse	writ of *certiorari*

Psychology of Crime

ORIENTING QUESTIONS

1. *Theories of crime can be grouped into four categories. What are they?*
2. *Among sociological explanations of crime, how does the subcultural explanation differ from the structural explanation?*
3. *What is emphasized in biological theories of crime?*
4. *What psychological factors have been advanced to explain crime?*
5. *How do social-psychological theories view crime?*

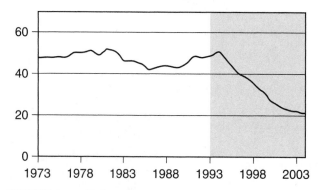

Adjusted victimization rate
per 1000 persons age 12 and over

FIGURE 3.1 *Violent crime rates, 1973–2004*
National Crime Victimization Survey Violent Crime Trends, 1973–2004
(http://www.oip.usdoj.gov/bjs/glance/viort.htm)

Rates of serious crime have been steadily declining in the United States. This decrease is confirmed by both victimization studies and official police statistics. According to the National Crime Victimization Survey (Bureau of Justice Statistics, 1999), the rate of violent crime has been steadily dropping since 1994, and in 2003, the total violent crime rate decreased to the lowest level recorded by the National Crime Victimization Survey since 1973 (http://www.ojp.usdoj.gov/ bjs/cvict.htm). There is a similar pattern for property crimes; however, 2003 statistics suggest these rates are beginning to level off (http://www. ojp.usdoj.gov/bjs/cvict.htm).

Despite this downturn in crime rates, many Americans continue to list crime and the fear of crime as one of their most serious concerns. Why, if the rate of crime is declining, do so many individuals continue to perceive crime as a major threat in their lives? One reason is that, despite recent decreases, the rate of violent crime is still relatively high: 22 out of every 1000 residents age 12 or older and living in an urban area were victimized by violent crime in 2003. The average citizen's fear of crime is also heightened by the highly publicized crimes of a few individuals that conjure up images of an epidemic of random violence beyond the control of a civilized society. For instance, in a span of only two years, the media blanketed the country with images and

'round-the-clock coverage of seemingly random heinous crimes, contributing to a shared state of public fear.

◆ In early 2004, Charles Allen McCoy, Jr., dubbed the Ohio Highway sniper, committed

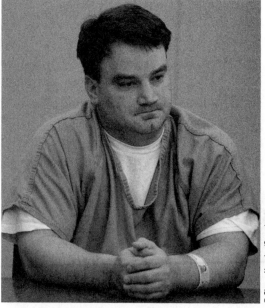

A defendant in jail garb

an estimated 24 acts involving firing at cars from an overpass, killing a woman, and terrorizing many more (http://search.cnn.com/pages/search.isp? query = highway%20 sniper).

♦ Beginning on October 2, 2002, John Allen Muhammed and John Lee Malvo paralyzed the Washington, D.C., area during a three-week shooting spree that left ten people dead and three more critically wounded (http://rchives.cnn.com/2002/US/South/10/15/shooting.victims/index.html).

Perhaps even more troubling than overall crime rates or highly publicized crime sprees is the frequency of serious criminal activity among young people. Although the number of serious violent offenses committed by persons ages 12 to 17 declined by 66% from 1993 to 2003, juveniles continue to be responsible for committing about 25% of violent crimes. Specifically, youths under 18 years old commit approximately 14% of sexual assaults, 30% of robberies, and 27% of aggravated assaults (http://www.ojp.usdoj.gov/bjs/glance/offage.htm; http://ojjdp.ncjrs.org/ojstatbb/offenders/qa03202.asp?qaDate = 19990930).

In 1997, juveniles were involved in approximately 12% of all homicides (Snyder & Sickmund, 1999, see http://www.ncjrs.org/html/ ojjdp/national-report99/toc.html Chapter 3, p. 53). Although the number of murders involving juveniles has steadily decreased since 1994 (Snyder & Sickmund, 1999), juveniles continued to be involved in several high-profile fatal events.

♦ In March of 2005, on Red Lake Indian Reservation, 16-year-old Jeff Weise shot and killed ten people at his high school (http:www.cnn.com/2005/LAW/03/28/school.shooting/index.html).

♦ In November of 2001, Christopher Puttnam, at the age of 12, shot and killed his grandparents in South Carolina (http://www.cnn.com/2005/LAW/02/08/Zoloft.trial/index.html).

♦ In April 1999, two students at Columbine High School in Littleton, Colorado, shot 12 of their classmates and a teacher before killing

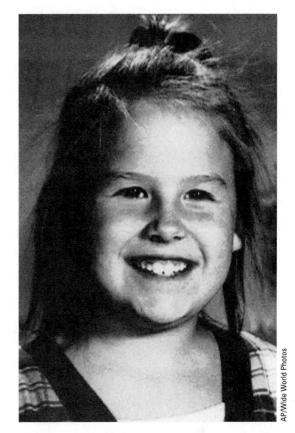

MEGAN KANKA
In May 1996, President Bill Clinton signed legislation that requires law enforcement authorities to notify communities when convicted sex offenders move into their neighborhoods. The law was known as Megan's Law, after seven-year-old Megan Kanka who was murdered in 1994. The man charged with Megan's murder was a twice-convicted child molester who had settled in her neighborhood.

AP/Wide World Photos

themselves (http:www.cnn.com/2005/ LAW/03/ 28/school.shooting/index.html).

Finally, the public becomes especially fearful about crime when they perceive it to be occurring in environments that they traditionally considered safe. In the 1990s, crime in the workplace and violence in our schools caused great national concern. Pearl, Mississippi. West Paducah, Kentucky. Jonesboro, Arkansas. Springfield, Oregon. Littleton, Colorado.

These five communities share something that sets them apart from the thousands of other American towns that they resemble in many other ways. In each, one or more students went to school one day, armed with guns, and proceeded to kill and wound their classmates. The grizzly totals from these five shootings—all of which occurred within a year of one another—were 30 dead and more than 60 wounded.

The spree of school shooting fatalities in the late 1990s has experts, parents, teachers, and youngsters themselves searching for answers about what motivates school shootings and what can be done to prevent them. Are school environments to blame? Is the ready availability of guns one explanation? Were the killers mentally ill or emotionally disturbed misfits? Were they driven by violent music and gory video games? Did their parents fail to support and supervise them adequately?

Statistics about school violence, and the case histories of those boys who have murdered their classmates at school, provide some possible answers. First, according to a national survey of public schools in 1999–2000, 71% of students reported experiencing one or more violent incidents, and 20% reported *serious* violent incidents, which include rape, sexual battery other than rape, physical fight with a weapon, and robbery with or without a weapon. However, only about 36% of these schools reported one or more of these incidents to the police (National Center for Education Statistics, 2004). These events occurred more often in high schools than in elementary or middle schools, and high schools reported these events to police more often than did elementary or middle schools (National Center for Education Statistics, 2004). One survey conducted in 2001 (National Center for Education Statistics, 2003) revealed that 17% of high school students had carried a weapon (a gun, knife, or club) at least once in the previous month, and about 6% of these students carried the weapon to school. These statistics are sobering, considering that one national survey found that 5.1% of students had been injured by a weapon at school during the previous 12 months and that 15% had been threatened by someone with a weapon (Bureau of Justice Statistics, 1995).

School-ground homicides remain very rare, but when they do occur, they attract a great deal of speculation about the motives of the shooters. Based on the small sample of cases, a few common characteristics have been identified in the backgrounds of the boys responsible for recent killings (Cloud, 1998; Verlinden, Hersen, & Thomas, 2000). Such boys tend to have

- had more than the usual experience with firearms, showing a persistent fascination with guns.
- felt isolated from, rejected by, or even tormented by classmates and to have had particular difficulty relating comfortably with girls.
- been preoccupied with various forms of graphically violent media, including music, Internet sites, and video games.
- suffered teasing because of their physical appearance—most of these assailants are either frail or somewhat obese;
- a history of angry brooding, often over their real or perceived status as social outcasts.
- developed a detailed plan for their aggression, which was often communicated to others in the days or weeks prior to the event.

Whether we will ever be able to explain this kind of crime is not clear. In retrospect, many of these individuals' classmates and teachers report that they now recognize there were warning signs about the danger to come. But how best to respond to these indicators *in time* remains the question. A number of reforms and programs have been attempted: requiring school uniforms, beefing up security measures, passing tougher gun laws, offering violence prevention programs, and restricting access to violent movies, among others. Another practice has involved "profiling" to predict which students are likely to commit violent crimes. However, this practice causes many students to be unjustly targeted, often on the basis of features not related to criminal behavior (e.g., clothing, music preferences). Furthermore, profiling in schools (even if it were very accurate in identifying those who are likely to commit homicides, which it is not) encounters the problem of "low base rates." That is, because school shootings are so rare, profiling would "overpredict," identifying many students who would actually not have committed a shooting. Instead, some researchers have proposed that increasing communication between students and school administrators may be a more productive approach to resolving the issues surrounding school violence and weapons (Mulvey & Cauffman, 2001). They note, "Students who are committed to school, feel that they belong, and trust the administration are less likely to commit violent acts than those who are uninvolved, alienated, and distrustful . . . Establishing school environments where students feel connected and trusted will build the critical link between those who often know when trouble is brewing and those who can act to prevent it" (http://www.drrobertbrooks.com/writings/articles/0504.html).

Highly publicized acts of violence at school or in the workplace threaten fundamental assumptions about personal security and the safety of our children and have a major effect on how individuals feel about their quality of life. For that reason, policymakers and social scientists have begun to pay particular attention to workplace and school violence, although neighborhood violence continues to be a concern.

Megan's Law is one example of how these highly publicized incidents bring about policy change in neighborhoods. In May 1996, President Bill Clinton signed legislation that requires law enforcement authorities to notify communities when convicted sex offenders move into their neighborhoods. The law is popularly known as Megan's Law and was named after a 7-year-old girl named Megan Kanka who was murdered in 1994. The man charged with Megan's murder was a twice-convicted child molester who had settled in her neighborhood.

The ups and downs of the crime rate give rise to much speculation about what factors are most responsible for causing and controlling crime. When crime is on the rise, the figures are used to justify requests for new policies and budget priorities. When the crime rate falls, the statistics are taken as an indication that one's favorite programs have been effective and need to be expanded.

The debate over the best means of crime control remains an impassioned social and political issue

in the United States. Should we hire more police, increase the number of courts, build more and bigger prisons, execute more violent criminals? Should we encourage more aggressive, "zero-tolerance" policing, aimed at apprehending individuals who commit even minor crimes such as vandalism and public intoxication? Should we impose curfews and school dress codes for adolescents? Is stricter gun control critical to curbing crimes of violence? Should parents be held legally liable for criminal assaults committed by their children?

Congress continues to pass anticrime bills that expand capital punishment to a wider spectrum of crimes, and, as noted in Chapter 1, many states have enacted so-called three-strikes legislation aimed at keeping repeat felons in prison for longer periods of time, sometimes for life. Other states have passed special anticrime measures that require a community to be notified whenever a former sex offender moves into its midst or that mandate the involuntary hospitalization of criminals still judged to be dangerous after they have completed their prison terms. The Supreme Court has issued a series of rulings that strengthen the powers of law enforcement officials in the areas of search and seizure, interrogation of criminal suspects, and the pretrial detention of persons who have been arrested. All these steps have been justified, in part, as remedies for America's crime problem.

But behavioral scientists argue that to ease the crime problem, we must first understand its causes. Why does crime happen? What motivates people to commit illegal acts? Bad genes? Inadequate parents? Failed schooling? Twisted impulses? Harsh environments? Delinquent friends? Social disadvantage? Drug addiction? Some combination of these factors? Can crime be predicted from knowledge of a person's early life? Or are many people capable of crime, given an unlucky mix of intoxication, anger, and unprotected victims, meeting, in the words of novelist Daniel Woodrell (1996), "like car wrecks that you knew would happen . . . almost nightly, at the same old crossroads of Hormones and Liquor" (p. 27)? Are some crimes, like those of Jeffrey Dahmer (see Box 3.1), so extreme that they defy scientific explanation?

THE CASE OF

BOX 3.1 **Jeffrey Dahmer: Can all crimes be explained?**

When police entered apartment 213 at the Oxford Plaza Apartments in Milwaukee, Wisconsin, on July 22, 1991, they encountered one of the most horrifying crime scenes in this country's history: severed human heads stacked in the refrigerator, photographs of dismembered bodies tacked to the walls, and human body parts immersed in a vat of acid. Ultimately, police uncovered the remains of 11 male victims in and around the grimy, stench-filled one-bedroom apartment.

Shortly after discovering these horrors, police arrested Jeffrey L. Dahmer, a 31-year-old chocolate factory worker who soon confessed to a total of 17 killings. Dahmer provided authorities with the details of his slayings, which typically involved luring men to his apartment, where he would have sex with them, kill them, dismem-

ber their bodies, and hoard the remains. He admitted to performing sex acts on his corpses and said that he cut one man's heart out and stored it in his freezer so he could eat it later.

Can any theory of crime offer a reasonable explanation of this gruesome carnage? Does Jeffrey Dahmer's history, even viewed now with the full knowledge of his terrifying crimes, offer any satisfying account of how a human being could engage repeatedly in such conduct? Or is Dahmer's behavior so extreme that social science explanations appear as shallow, pale excuses that fail to confront the fundamental evil that seems to lurk in someone like Dahmer?

A review of Dahmer's life has not revealed the trauma, prolonged mistreatment, or environmental deprivations that would sufficiently explain his serial murders, nor is

there convincing evidence that Dahmer suffered from a mental illness serious enough to compel this conduct. Dahmer was raised in a middle-class family in a prosperous suburb. Neighbors recalled him and his younger brother as "very polite children." In high school, Dahmer showed erratic behavior, became gradually isolated from friends, and earned a reputation as an outcast.

In 1978, Dahmer's parents went through a bitter divorce that led to a marked worsening of Dahmer's drinking problems, which had begun in junior high school. Dahmer attended Ohio State University briefly in 1978, but he did poorly and dropped out to join the army in 1979. He was released early from the army in 1981, because of his drinking problems, and went to live with his grandmother in West Allis, Wisconsin. In 1985, he started a laborer's job at the

---

These questions are the concern of **criminology**, which is the study of crime and criminal behavior. In this chapter, we summarize the major theories of crime, beginning with a brief review of the historical predecessors of 20th-century criminology.

Theories of Crime as Explanations of Criminal Behavior

Theories of crime are as old as crime itself. Aristotle claimed that "poverty is the parent of revolution and crime," but most ancient explanations of crime took

a religious tone; crime was either equivalent to or due to sin, a view that was popular throughout the Middle Ages and lives on today in many religious belief systems.

In the 17th century, Sir Francis Bacon argued that "opportunity makes a thief." During the 1700s, philosophers and social critics such as Voltaire and Rousseau emphasized concepts such as free will, hedonism, and flaws in the social contract to explain criminal conduct. These principles ultimately grew into the **classical school of criminology**.

The two leading proponents of classical criminology were the Italian intellectual Cesare Beccaria and the British philosopher Jeremy Bentham, who believed that lawbreaking occurred

Ambrosia Chocolate Factory, a job he held until shortly before his arrest.

In 1988, after moving out of his grandmother's house, Dahmer was arrested for molesting a 13-year-old boy and was sentenced to five years' probation. Some time later, he began his Milwaukee killing spree. Although Dahmer's acts seem beyond comprehension, a jury found that he was not insane during his crimes, and he was sentenced to life in prison (Wisconsin has no death penalty). A few years after he began serving his prison term, Dahmer was bludgeoned to death by another inmate.

There is no doubt that Jeffrey Dahmer's life began to unravel in the late 1980s. But as his troubles unfolded, they did not appear very different from the marginal existence of many lonely alcoholic men who, despite the tragedies of their lives, did not lure multiple victims into traps of violent death. Although social scientists may try to link Jeffrey Dahmer's crimes with several factors in his life, including the diagnosis that he had a personality or sexual disorder or that he was sexually abused as a child, we doubt that any scientific theory can adequately come to terms with the enormity of these murders.

Although few criminals can match the sheer horror of Dahmer's deeds, many commit acts of enormous cruelty. Their crimes are all the more alarming because they too defy any type of rational understanding. How can we comprehend juveniles such as Eric Harris and Dylan Klebold, the Columbine High School students whose well-planned Colorado massacre left 15 of their classmates dead, or Thomas Hamilton, a loner who stalked into a school in Dunblane, Scotland, with four handguns and slaughtered 16 first-graders and their teacher before killing himself? Have you read any really convincing explanation of why the so-called Unabomber carried out a 17-year string of bombings that killed 3 people and wounded 23 more? Attributing crimes like these to "evil" or Satan or basic moral failure is no more satisfying than most psychological theories because one must still explain why moral failure would be manifest in this extreme way. The Jeffrey Dahmers and Thomas Hamiltons of the world are so frightening not only because of what they did but also because of our inability to comprehend why they did it.

when people, faced with a choice between right and wrong, freely chose to behave wrongly. People chose crime when they believed that the gains to be had through crime outweighed the losses it entailed. Classical theorists were interested in reforming the harsh administration of justice in post-Renaissance Europe, and they believed that punishment of criminals should be proportionate to the crimes committed—that punishment should fit the crime.

Classical theory influenced several principles of justice in Western societies (e.g., the U.S. Constitution's Eighth Amendment ban against "cruel and unusual punishment"), and, as we shall see in Chapter 15, it still exerts an important effect on modern correctional philosophy.

Modern theories of crime developed from the **positivist school of criminology**. Rather than focusing on individuals' free will, as previous philosophers had done, positivists emphasized factors that they believed determined criminal behavior. They sought to understand crime through the scientific method and the analysis of empirical data; some stressed sociological factors, whereas others preferred biological, psychological, or environmental explanations. Additionally, some positivistic theories try to explain how people choose between criminal and noncriminal behaviors, thereby sharing some common ground with classical theories.

In practice, however, combinations of classical and positivist theories have been rare. Cesare

Lombroso, Enrico Ferri, and Raffaelo Garofalo were three early positivists. They were preceded by Adolphe Quetelet, a Belgian statistician who, nearly 50 years before Lombroso, studied crime data and concluded that crime occurred more often in certain geographic areas and under specific social conditions. For various reasons, however, these early **ecological theorists** were not as influential as the Italian positivists. Lombroso (1876) and Garofalo (1914) emphasized the physical characteristics of criminals and proposed a strong biological predisposition to crime. Ferri (1917) also acknowledged physical causes but stressed social and environmental factors. Although the early positivists thought of themselves as scientists, their science was crude by current standards and led to conclusions that are not taken seriously today. Positivists believed that punishment should fit the criminal rather than the crime, a position that foreshadowed rehabilitation as a correctional priority and the indeterminate sentence as a means for achieving it.

Most modern theories of criminal behavior—including those of biology, genetics, psychology, sociology, economics, anthropology, and religion—are a legacy of the positivist tradition. The validity of these theories varies greatly. Most can account reasonably well for certain types of crime, but none explains all forms of criminality and some explain very little. Empirical data, rational analyses, moral values, and political ideologies all play a role in shaping preferences for the leading theories in criminology.

For the most part, criminologists have concentrated on those crimes that frighten the average citizen—violent acts (e.g., robbery, rape, assault, and murder) or aggressive behavior against property (e.g., burglary, theft, and arson). But many other kinds of legally prohibited conduct—environmental plunder, price fixing, and business fraud, for example—cause great damage to individuals and society. However, these crimes are not the typical focus of criminologists, nor are they the type of conduct that the general public has in mind when it debates the "crime problem."

In addition, most theories of crime have concentrated on men. This focus is not unreasonable, given that about three-quarters of all arrests are of men and that almost 85% of violent crimes are committed by men. However, the factors that influence female criminality deserve more attention, at least in part because crime by females has increased relative to crime by males over the past decade; the number of male adults in the correctional population increased by two-thirds from 1986 to 1997, while the number of females doubled (http://www.ojp.usdoj.gov/bjs/gcorpop. htm). Women offenders make up nearly 12% of the prison population, an increase from 10% in 1996, and are being arrested more often for violent offenses. In 2001, about 17% of women were charged with a violent offense, compared to 15% in 1996 (James, 2004; http://www.ojp.usdoj. gov/bjs/crimoff.htm). Despite these increases in violent criminal behavior, women are most often arrested for larceny and theft; in most of these incidents, the woman was collaborating with a male partner. One implication of this pattern is that explanations of female crime need to carefully consider the role of coercion, especially as it is exerted in close relationships.

In this chapter, we review criminological theories that attempt to explain aggressive crimes. We define these crimes as legally proscribed behavior in which one or more persons deliberately inflict or attempt to inflict physical injury on others or intentionally take or destroy the property of others. We group these theories into four categories: sociological, biological, psychological, and social-psychological. What are the most important distinctions among these four approaches?

Crime may appear to result from an individual's experience with his or her environment. This belief is explained through **sociological theories**, which maintain that crime results from social or cultural forces that are external to any specific individual, exist prior to any criminal act, and emerge from social class, political, ecological, or physical structures affecting large groups of people (Nettler, 1974).

Alternatively, criminal behavior may appear to result from an individual's biological characteristics.

Biological theories stress genetic influences, neuropsychological abnormalities, and biochemical irregularities. However, as we shall see, there is little empirical evidence that either sociological or biological theories independently predict criminal behavior. Instead, current theories of crime incorporate a combination of environmental and biological factors to understand the etiology of offending behaviors.

Psychological theories emphasize that crime results from personality attributes that are uniquely possessed, or possessed to a special degree, by the potential criminal. For example, psychoanalysts have proposed several variations on the theme that crime is the result of an ego and superego that are too weak to control the sexual and aggressive instincts of the id. Other psychologists have painted a psychological portrait of the "criminal type." Although a number of traits distinguish delinquent persons from nonoffenders, these findings do not necessarily mean that the traits in question caused the crimes observed.

Social-psychological theories (or social process theories; Nettler, 1974; Reid, 1976) bridge the gap between the environmentalism of sociology and the individualism of psychological or biological theories. Social-psychological theories propose that crime is learned, but they differ about *what* is learned and *how* it is learned. **Control theory** assumes that people will behave antisocially unless they learn, through a combination of inner controls and external constraints on behavior, not to offend. **Learning theory** stresses how individuals directly acquire specific criminal behaviors through different forms of learning. **Social labeling theory** holds that the stigma of being branded deviant by society can engender or underscore that belief within the individual.

Sociological Theories of Crime

Sociocultural theories may be divided into **structural** and **subcultural explanations**. Structural theories emphasize that dysfunctional social arrangements (e.g., inadequate schooling, economic adversity, or community disorganization) thwart people's efforts toward legitimate attainments and result in their breaking the law. Subcultural theories hold that crime originates when various groups of people endorse cultural values that clash with the dominant, conventional rules of society. In this view, crime is the product of a subcultural deviation from the agreed-on norms that underlie the criminal law.

Structural Explanations

A key concept of structural approaches is that certain groups of people suffer fundamental inequalities in opportunities to achieve the goals valued by society. Differential opportunity, proposed by Cloward and Ohlin (1960) in their book *Delinquency and Opportunity*, is one example of a structural explanation of crime. This theory can be traced to Émile Durkheim's ideas about the need to maintain moral bonds between individuals in society. Durkheim thought that life without moral or social obligations becomes intolerable and results in **anomie**, a feeling of normlessness that often precedes suicide and crime. One implication of anomie theory was that unlimited aspirations pressure individuals to deviate from social norms.

According to Cloward and Ohlin, people in lower socioeconomic subcultures usually want to succeed through legal means, but society denies them legitimate opportunities to do so. Consider, for example, a person from Nicaragua who emigrates to the United States because of a sincere desire to make a better life for his family. He faces cultural and language differences, financial hardships, and limited access to the resources that are crucial for upward mobility. Poor people cannot, for example, afford advanced education. In addition, crowding in large cities makes class distinctions more apparent. When legal means of goal achievement are blocked, intense frustration results, and crime is more likely to ensue. Youthful crime, especially in gangs, is one outgrowth of this sequence. The theory of differential opportunity assumes that people who grow up in crowded, impoverished, deteriorating neighborhoods endorse conventional, middle-class goals.

Thus, crime is an illicit means to gain an understandable end.

Consistent with this view, Gottfredson (1986) and Gordon (1986), a sociologist team, attempted to explain the higher crime rate of lower-class black youth in terms of their less than satisfactory scholastic performance. Denied legitimate job opportunities because of low aptitude scores or grades, these youth discover that they can make several hundred dollars a week dealing crack cocaine. In fact, with the advent of crack cocaine, arrests of juveniles in New York City, Detroit, Washington, and other cities tripled in the mid- to late 1980s.

The theory of differential opportunity has several limitations (Lilly, Cullen, & Ball, 1989). First, a great deal of research indicates that seriously delinquent youth display many differences from their law-abiding counterparts other than differing educational opportunities, and they tend to show these differences as early as the beginning of elementary school. Second, there is no evidence that lower-class youth find limited success in school to be more frustrating than do middle-class youngsters. On the contrary, the exact opposite is likely to be true. The assumption that lower-class juveniles typically aspire to membership in the middle class is also unproved. Furthermore, the major terms in the theory, such as *aspiration, frustration*, and *opportunity*, are defined too vaguely; the theory does not explicitly explain what determines adaptation to blocked opportunities (Sheley, 1985). Last and most apparent, crimes are often committed by people who have never been denied opportunities; in fact, they may have basked in an abundance of good fortune. Think of Martha Stewart's conviction for insider trading or of the fraudulent activities by the executives of Enron. Many other examples come readily to mind: the head of a local charity who pockets donations for personal enrichment, the pharmacist who deals drugs under the counter, the politician who accepts bribes for votes.

Other structural explanations exist, but all have limitations, and there is little empirical support for the claim that they offer meaningful, comprehensive explanations of crime. For instance, the **rational crime theory** (Nettler, 1974) involves illegal behavior that "makes sense" because the person is rewarded for it and because it can be committed with a relatively low risk of detection. It is crime encouraged by some nearly irresistible "golden opportunity." Two major problems exist with rational crime theory. First, it does not explain repeated, violent crimes; second, it does not explain why, given the same "golden opportunities," some people offend whereas most do not.

Subcultural Explanations

The subcultural version of sociological theory maintains that a conflict of norms held by different groups causes criminal behavior. This conflict arises when various groups endorse subcultural norms that pressure its members to deviate from the norms underlying the criminal law (Nietzel, 1979). Gangs, for example, enforce unique norms about how to behave. For many youths, a gang replaces the young person's parents as the main source of norms, even when parents attempt to instill their own values.

This theme of cultural conflict is illustrated by Walter Miller's theory of **focal concerns**. Miller explains the criminal activities of lower-class adolescent gangs as an attempt to achieve the ends valued in their culture through behaviors that appear best suited to obtain those ends. Thus, youth must adhere to the traditions of the lower class. What are these characteristics? Miller (1958) lists six basic values: trouble, toughness, smartness, excitement, fate, and autonomy. For example, lower-class boys pick fights to show their toughness, and they steal to demonstrate their shrewdness and daring (Sheley, 1985). Hundreds of juvenile homicides occur each year; many are done for the sole purpose of demonstrating macho toughness or relieving sheer boredom (Heide, 1997). However, the theory of focal concerns does not explain crime by individuals who are not socially disadvantaged, such as the rich hotel owner, the television evangelist, or the Wall Street swindler. In addition, key concepts in the theory are vague.

Like structural theories of crime, subcultural explanations have not demonstrated a strong theoretical or empirical basis. Questions remain. How do cultural standards originate? How are they transmitted from one generation to the next? How do they control the behavior of any one individual? The most troublesome concept is the main one—subculture. Some critics reject the assumption that different socioeconomic groups embrace radically different values.

Biological Theories of Crime

Biological theories of crime search for genetic vulnerabilities, neuropsychological abnormalities, or biochemical irregularities that predispose people to criminal behavior. These dispositions, biological theorists believe, are then translated into specific criminal behavior through environments and social interactions. Research on biological theories commonly focuses on twin and adoption studies to distinguish genetic from environmental factors.

In twin studies, the researcher compares the **concordance rate** (the percentage of pairs of twins sharing the behavior of interest) for **monozygotic twins** (identical twins) and **dizygotic twins** (commonly called fraternal twins). If the monozygotic concordance rate is significantly higher, the investigator concludes that the behavior in question is genetically influenced, because monozygotic twins are genetically identical whereas dizygotic pairs share, on average, only 50% of their genetic material. This method assumes that the environments of the twins in a dizygotic pair are no more different from each other than are the environments of the monozygotic twins, an assumption that may not always be accurate.

In one study of 274 adult twin pairs, participants were asked to complete several questionnaires about past criminal behaviors, such as destroying property, fighting, carrying and using a weapon, and struggling with the police. Results reflected a finding of 50% heritability for such violent behaviors (Rushton, 1996, found at

http://www.eugenics.net/papers/rushton.html). These significant findings are supported by previous studies (Christiansen, 1977; Dilalla & Gottesman, 1991; Kranz, 1936; Kranz, 1937; Lang, 1929), suggesting that inherited tendencies may play a "preponderant part" in causing crime (Lange, 1929).

However, most twin studies lump violent and nonviolent criminals together, rather than calculating concordance rates separately for the two types of crime. Studies that distinguish between crimes against property and violent crimes against persons have found that heredity and environment play important roles in both types of crime, but the influence of heredity is higher for aggressive types of antisocial behavior (assaults, robberies, sexual predation) than for nonaggressive crimes such as drug taking, shoplifting, and truancy (Eley, 1997).

Adoption studies also support the contention that genetic factors play some role in the development of criminality. Cloninger, Sigvardsson, Bohman, and von Knorring (1982) studied the arrest records of adult males who had been adopted as children. They found that men whose biological parents had a criminal record were four times more likely to be criminal themselves (a prevalence rate of 12.1%) than those adoptees who had no adoptive or biological criminal background (2.9%) and twice as likely to be criminal as adoptees whose adoptive parents had a criminal history. More recently, researchers conducted a review of several twin and adoption studies in this area and found similar results (Tehrani & Mednick, 2000).

Research has focused on genetic influences for specific types of criminal behavior, such as bullying. A longitudinal study (Huesmann, Eron, & Yarmel, 1987) carried out over a 22-year period followed 870 children from Columbia County, New York, from the ages of 8 to 30. At age 8, the incipient bully was seen by other children as starting fights over nothing, being quick to anger, and taking things without asking (Goleman, 1987). He was often a social outcast who disliked school, expressing his defiance through tardiness and truancy.

By age 19, he was likely to have dropped out of school. At that point, he was three times more likely

than others to have been in trouble with the law (Goleman, 1987). At age 30, his wife saw him as aggressive, even abusive. His run-ins with the law ranged from drunken driving to crimes of violence. As a parent, he was uncaring and punitive; his children tended to follow his own earlier pattern of being a bully (Goleman, 1987).

Likewise, females who were aggressors as children were more likely to punish their own children severely. In fact, the bully's characteristics can be traced over three generations (Huesmann et al., 1987). The parents of incipient bullies discipline them severely, and when the younger generation become parents, their children also tend to be troublemakers, even in elementary school. The researchers found that bullies did not have lower IQ scores than other children but that as teenagers and adults, they performed below their expected level on achievement tests and often held jobs below their levels of ability.

A belief that crime is even partially determined by genetic factors still begs the obvious question: What, exactly, is inherited? There is a lengthy list of likely candidates (Brennan & Raine, 1997; Di Lalla & Gottesman, 1991; Moffitt & Mednick, 1988), but five possibilities are emphasized:

1. *Constitutional predisposition.* The data on this factor are inconclusive and do not carry us much beyond the finding that strong, athletic, muscular youth are more successful bullies than their portly or puny peers (Olweus, 1995). Physical stature is clearly influenced by genetic factors, and to the extent that a strong physique interacts with other variables to increase the likelihood of aggressive behavior early in life, genetics can contribute some risk of antisocial conduct.

2. *Neuropsychological abnormalities.* High rates of abnormal electroencephalogram (EEG) patterns have been reported in prison populations and in violent juvenile delinquents. These EEG irregularities may indicate neurological deficits that result in poor impulse control and impaired judgment. Unfortunately, a high percentage of persons in the general population have EEG abnormalities, and this limits the diagnostic utility of the EEG.

Furthermore, some studies have not found a significant relationship between EEG pathology and delinquent behavior (Loomis, 1965).

More promising results have been reported concerning abnormalities in four subcortical regions of the brain—the amygdala, hippocampus, thalamus, and midbrain—specifically in the right hemisphere of the brain, which has been linked to the experience of negative emotions. In one study (Raine, Meloy, & Buchshaum, 1998), brain scans of a group of homicide offenders showed that, compared with normal controls, the offenders experienced excessive activity in the four subcortical structures. Excessive subcortical activity may underlie a more aggressive temperament that could, in turn, predispose an individual to violent behavior.

A recent review of the neuropsychological literature supports a relationship between deficits in the prefrontal cortex, a region of the brain responsible for planning, monitoring, and controlling behavior, and antisocial behavior (see Raine, 2002). Damage to the prefrontal cortext may predispose individuals to criminal behavior in one of several ways. Patients with impairment in this region of the brain have decreased reasoning abilities that may lead to impulsive decision making in risky situations (Bechara, Damasio, Tranel, & Damasio, 1997). In addition, prefrontal impairment is associated with decreased levels of arousal, and individuals may engage in stimulation seeking and antisocial behaviors to compensate for these arousal deficits (Raine, Lencz, Bihrle, Lacasse, & Colletti, 2000),

Other lines of research suggest that impaired functioning in the prefrontal cortex contributes to aggressive behavior. Offenders, on average, have about an eight- to ten-point lower IQ (intelligence quotient) than nonoffenders. This difference is mainly due to verbal (as opposed to performance) IQ scores, feeding speculation that offenders are less able to (1) postpone impulsive actions, (2) use effective problem-solving strategies (Lynam, Moffitt, & Stouthamer-Loeber, 1993), and (3) achieve academic success in schools as a route to socially approved attainments (Binder, 1988).

A frequent criticism of these findings is that incarcerated delinquents are not representative

of delinquents at large. However, regardless of whether they are incarcerated or not, delinquent youth perform more poorly on IQ measures than their nondelinquent peers but do not differ among themselves (Moffitt & Silva, 1988). Using a meta-analysis (a statistical technique that combines effect sizes of many studies to yield a much larger and presumably more accurate estimate of effects) to consider the relationship between juveniles' IQ scores and delinquency, investigators found that low intelligence and attention problems significantly predict later delinquency (Maguin & Loeber, 1996). In addition, IQ deficits are reliably found before actual offending begins, which suggests that the causal relation runs from low IQ to antisocial behavior, not vice versa.

In one longitudinal study of 411 London boys, low IQ at ages 8 through 10 was linked to persistent criminality and more convictions for violent crimes up to age 32 (Farrington, 1995). This relationship persists even after controlling for the effects of social class, race, and motivation to do well on tests (Lynam et al., 1993).

Although there is support in the empirical literature for some neurobiological contribution to criminal behavior, environmental factors also play a large role. One study explored the potential of a childhood enrichment program to prevent later criminal behavior (Raine et al., 2003). Findings revealed that, compared to a matched control group, individuals who participated in the enrichment program for two years beginning at age 3 had lower scores on measures of antisocial behavior when they were 17 years old and on measures of criminal behavior when they were 23 years old. These findings implicate environmental factors in psychological and behavioral outcomes of individuals predisposed to engage in antisocial behavior.

3. *Autonomic nervous system differences.* The autonomic nervous system (ANS) carries information between the brain and all organs of the body. Because of these connections, emotions are associated with changes in the ANS. In fact, we can "see" the effects of emotional arousal on such ANS responses as heart rate, skin conductance, respiration, and blood pressure. Some criminals—those

most repetitively in trouble—are thought to differ from noncriminals in that they show chronically low levels of autonomic arousal and weaker physiological reactions to stimulation (Mednick & Christiansen, 1977). These differences, which might also involve hormonal irregularities (see the next section), could cause this group of criminals to have (1) difficulty learning how to inhibit behavior likely to lead to punishment and (2) a high need for extra stimulation that they gratify through aggressive thrill seeking. These difficulties are also considered an important predisposing factor by some social-psychological theorists that we discuss later.

4. *Physiological differences.* A number of physiological factors might lead to increased aggressiveness and delinquency (Berman, 1997). Among the variables receiving continuing attention are (1) abnormally high levels of testosterone, (2) increased secretion of insulin, and (3) lower levels of serotonin (DiLalla & Gottesman, 1991). Research on testosterone has yielded inconsistent results (Archer, 1991), but depleted or impaired action of serotonin has received considerable support as a factor underlying impulsive aggression (Coccaro, Kavoussi, & Lesser, 1992).

One study using animal models provides further support for the role of these physiological variables in aggressive behavior. Researchers found that rats with increased production of testosterone and lower levels of serotonin exhibited more aggressive behaviors; these rats displayed an increased number of attacks and inflicted a greater number of wounds on other rats compared to rats with lower testosterone and higher serotonin levels (Toot, Dunphy, Turner, & Ely, 2004). Such findings may be helpful in understanding the biological contributions to human aggression as well. Low levels of serotonin might be linked to aggressiveness and criminal conduct in any of several ways—for example, through greater impulsivity and irritability, impaired ability to regulate negative moods, excessive alcohol consumption, or hypersensitivity to provocative and threatening environmental cues (Berman, Tracy, & Coccaro, 1997).

5. *Personality and temperament differences.* Several dimensions of personality, known to be

heritable to a considerable degree, are related to antisocial behavior. Individuals with personalities marked by undercontrol, unfriendliness, irritability, low empathy, and a tendency to be easily frustrated are at greater risk for antisocial conduct (Nietzel, Hasemann, & Lynam, 1997). We discuss some of these characteristics more fully in the next section on psychological theories of crime.

Psychological Theories of Crime

Psychological explanations of crime emphasize individual differences in the way people think or feel about their behavior. These differences, which can take the form of subtle variations or more extreme personality disturbances, might make some people more prone to criminal conduct by increasing their anger, weakening their attachments to others, or fueling their desire to take risks and seek thrills.

Psychoanalytic Theories of Crime

Psychoanalysts believe that crime results from a weak ego and superego that cannot restrain the antisocial instincts of the id. Each individual's unique history should reveal the specific factors that produced a defective ego or superego, but the factor most commonly blamed is inadequate identification by a child with his or her parents. Freud believed that the criminal suffers from a compulsive need for punishment to alleviate feelings of guilt stemming from the unconscious, incestuous feelings of the Oedipal period. He wrote, "In many criminals, especially youthful ones, it is possible to detect a very powerful sense of guilt which existed before the crime, and is therefore not its result but its motive. It is as if it was a relief to be able to fasten this unconscious sense of guilt onto something real and immediate" (1961, p. 52).

Franz Alexander (Alexander & Healy, 1935) proposed that the criminal does not orient his

behavior with the **reality principle**, a task of the ego that requires a person to postpone immediate gratification to obtain greater rewards in the future. Alexander thought that family and general social forces also contributed to criminality. In *Roots of Crime*, written with William Healy in 1935, Alexander argued:

> Criminal acts are not always committed by certain individuals who can be defined and characterized psychologically or in terms of personality as specifically inclined to crime, but neither are criminal acts restricted to certain social groups which can be characterized and defined sociologically . . . . both personality and sociological factors are active at the same time; either of them may be predominant in one case, negligible in another. (p. 273)

Other psychoanalysts have suggested that criminal behavior is a means of obtaining substitute gratification of basic needs such as love, nurturance, and attention that have not been normally satisfied within the family. John Bowlby (1949, 1953; Bowlby & Salter-Ainsworth, 1965) believes that disruptions of the attachment between mother and infant or parental rejection of the developing child account for a majority of the more intractable cases of delinquency and repetitive crime (Bowlby, 1949, p. 37).

Psychoanalytic theories often trap their adherents in tautological circles, and, for the most part, they are no longer favored in modern criminology. What have been called "antisocial instincts" may simply be alternative names for the behaviors they are intended to explain. Another major problem with psychoanalytic interpretations of crime is that they are contradicted by patterns of real criminal conduct. Freud's idea that criminals commit crimes in order to be caught and punished, and thus to have their guilt expiated, ignores the obvious extremes to which most offenders go to avoid detection of their wrongdoing. Most offenders do not appear frustrated or guilt-ridden by the fact that their "crimes pay," at least some of the time. In fact, the success of their crimes seems to be a major source of gratification. Finally, psychoanalytic descriptions are at odds with the observation that many forms of crime are more calculated than compulsed, more orchestrated than overdetermined, and more devised than driven.

Criminal Thinking Patterns

In a controversial theory spawned from their frustration with traditional criminological theories, Samuel Yochelson and Stanton E. Samenow (1976; Samenow, 1984) have proposed that criminals engage in a fundamentally different way of thinking than noncriminals. They claim that the thinking of criminals, though internally logical and consistent, is erroneous and irresponsible. In short, consistent lawbreakers see themselves and the world differently from the rest of us.

Yochelson and Samenow reject sociological, environmental, and psychoanalytic explanations of criminality, such as a broken home, unloving parents, or unemployment. Rather, they argue that criminals become criminals as a result of choices they start making at an early age. These patterns, coupled with a pervasive sense of irresponsibility, mold lives of crime that are extremely difficult to change. Yochelson and Samenow describe the criminals they studied as very much in control of their own actions, rather than being victims of the environment or being "sick." These criminals are portrayed as master manipulators who assign the blame for their behavior to others. They are such inveterate liars that they can no longer separate fact from fiction. They use words to manipulate reality, not to represent it.

Yochelson and Samenow's conclusions are based on intensive interviews with a small number of offenders, most of whom were incarcerated "hard-core" criminals or men who were hospitalized after having been acquitted of major crimes by reason of insanity. No control groups of any sort were studied. Yochelson and Samenow portray one type of criminal, but their analysis does not accurately represent the majority of lawbreakers. Furthermore, the "criminal thinking pattern" theory does not explain how these choices are made in the beginning (Pfohl, 1985), although in other publications Samenow hints at genetic predispositions to crime. In fact, in this way and others, this theory is similar to the notion of the psychopathic personality, to which we now turn.

Personality Defect as an Explanation of Criminality

Many individuals attribute crime to personality defects, typically in the form of theories that posit the criminal's basic antisocial or psychopathic nature. The concept of **psychopathy** has a long history. Generally, this term refers to individuals who engage in frequent, repetitive criminal activity for which they feel little or no remorse. Such persons appear chronically deceitful and manipulative; they seem to have a nearly total lack of conscience that propels them into repeated conflict with society, often from a very early age. They are superficial, are arrogant, and do not seem to learn from experience; they lack empathy and loyalty to individuals, groups, or society (Hare, Hart, & Harpur, 1991). Psychopaths are selfish, callous, and irresponsible; they tend to blame others or to offer plausible rationalizations for their behavior.

The closest diagnostic label to psychopathy is **antisocial personality disorder**. The two disorders are similar in their emphasis on chronic antisocial behavior, but they differ in the role of personal characteristics, which are important in psychopathy but are not among the diagnostic criteria for antisocial personality disorder. About 80% of psychopaths are men, and their acts often garner massive publicity (see Box 3.2).

Research using a measure of psychopathy, the Psychopathy Checklist–Youth Version (PCL-YV), suggests that offenders who score higher on the dimension of psychopathy are more likely to commit a violent offense, and are likely to reoffend sooner after discharge from a secure facility, than those who score lower. Furthermore, whether the offender engaged in a violent reoffense or a nonviolent act was more strongly related to the interpersonal characteristics of the offender (e.g., callousness) than to behavioral characteristics (e.g., previous offending). (Gretton, Hare, & Catchpole, 2004). By some estimates, those with

THE CASE OF

BOX 3.2   Ted Bundy: Antisocial personality?

Born in 1946, Theodore Robert Bundy seemed destined for a charmed life; he was intelligent, attractive, and articulate (Holmes & DeBurger, 1988). A Boy Scout as a youth and then an honor student and psychology major at the University of Washington, he was at one time a work–study student at the Seattle Crisis Clinic. Later he became assistant to the chairman of the Washington State Republican Party. It is probably around this time that he claimed his first victim; a college-age woman was viciously attacked while sleeping, left alive but brain-damaged.

From 1974 through 1978, Bundy stalked, attacked, killed, and then sexually assaulted as many as 36 victims in Washington, Oregon, Utah, Colorado, and Florida. Apparently, some of the women were taken off guard when the good-looking, casual Bundy approached, seeming helpless walking with crutches or having an apparent broken arm. He usually choked them to death and then sexually abused and mutilated them before disposing of their bodies in remote areas (Nordheimer, 1989).

It is characteristic of many people with psychopathy to maintain a facade of charm; acquaintances often describe them (as they did Bundy) as "fascinating," "charismatic," and "compassionate." As a matter of fact, beneath his surface charm, Bundy was deceitful and dangerous. Embarrassed because he was an illegitimate child and that his mother was poor, he constantly

sought, as a youth, to give the impression of being an upper-class kid. He wore fake mustaches and used makeup to change his appearance. He faked a British accent and stole cars in high school to help maintain his image. He constantly sought out the company of attractive women, not because he was genuinely interested in them but because he wanted people to notice and admire him.

At his trial for the murder of two Chi Omega sorority sisters in their bedrooms at Florida State University, he served as his own attorney (Bundy had attended two law schools, although he did not graduate from either). He was convicted; he was also found guilty of the kidnapping, murder, and mutilation of a Lake City, Florida, girl who was 12 years old. Bundy was sentenced to death.

Shortly before he was executed on January 24, 1989, Bundy gave a television interview to California evangelist James Dobson in which he blamed his problems on pornography. He said, "Those of us who are . . . so much influenced by violence in the media, in particular pornographic violence, are not some kind of inherent monsters. We are your husbands, and we grew up in regular families" (quoted by Lamar, 1989, p. 34).

Bundy claimed that he spent his formative ages with a grandfather who had an insatiable craving for pornography. He told Dr. Dobson, "People will accuse me of being self-serving but I am

Serial killer Ted Bundy

just telling you how I feel. Through God's help, I have been able to come to the point where I, much too late, but better late than never, feel the hurt and the pain that I am responsible for" (quoted by Kleinberg, 1989, p. 5A).

The tape of Bundy's last interview, produced by Dobson and titled "Fatal Addiction," has been widely disseminated, especially by those who seek to eliminate all pornography. (Dr. Dobson served on a federal pornography commission during the Reagan administration.) But Bundy's claim that pornography was the "fuel for his fantasies" should be viewed skeptically. It may merely have been one last manipulative ploy to buy more time. In none of his previous interviews, including extensive conversations in 1986 with Dorothy Lewis, a psychiatrist he had come to trust, did he ever cite "a pornographic preamble to his grotesqueries" (Nobile, 1989, p. 41).

antisocial personality disorder account for two-thirds of violent crime in the United States.

There are a multitude of theories about what causes psychopathic behavior. One view is that psychopathic persons suffer a cortical immaturity that makes it difficult for them to inhibit behavior. Robert Hare (Hare & McPherson, 1984) has proposed that psychopaths may have a deficiency in the left hemisphere of their brains that impairs what psychologists call **executive function**, the ability to plan and regulate behavior carefully (Moffitt & Lynam, 1994). As previously discussed, considerable research supports a strong relationship between antisocial behavior and impaired executive functioning (Morgan & Lilienfeld, 2000).

Compared to normal controls, psychopathic persons experience less anxiety subsequent to aversive stimulation and are relatively underaroused in the resting state as well. This low autonomic arousal generates a high need for stimulation. Consequently, the psychopath prefers novel situations and tends to "shorten" stimuli, thereby being less controlled by them. One study demonstrated this by examining EEG readings of brain waves in 35 hospital patients who met diagnostic criteria for antisocial personality disorder and compared those readings with a matched control group of 35 hospital patients who met criteria for diagnoses other than antisocial personality disorder (Dewolf, Duran, & Loas, 2002). The neurophysiologist interpreting the readings was blind to the patients' diagnoses. Findings revealed that the patients with psychopathy showed significantly slower waves and more abnormalities than the controls, even during a state of excitement. The authors question, however, whether these brain abnormalities are a result of risky behaviors (i.e., head trauma) that are often associated with conduct disorder or are a result of brain development that leads to this type of personality disorder. To date, no studies have emerged that can answer this question.

Herbert Quay (1965) advanced the **stimulation-seeking theory**, which claims that the thrill seeking and disruptive behavior of the psychopath serve to increase sensory input and arousal to a more tolerable level. As a result of such thrill seeking, the psychopathic person seems "immune" to many social cues that govern behavior. Eysenck (1964) proposed a theory that emphasizes the slower rate of classical conditioning for persons classified as psychopaths. Eysenck argues that the development of a conscience depends on acquisition of classically conditioned fear and avoidance responses and that psychopathic individuals' conditioning deficiencies may account for their difficulties in normal socialization.

Another popular explanation for psychopathy involves being raised in a dysfunctional family (Loeber & Stouthamer-Loeber, 1986; Patterson, 1986). Arnold Buss (1966) identified two parental patterns that might foster psychopathy. The first is having parents who are cold and distant. The child who imitates these parents develops an unfeeling, detached interpersonal style that conveys a superficial appearance of social involvement but lacks the empathy required for stable, satisfying relationships. The second pattern is having parents who are inconsistent in their use of rewards and punishments, making it difficult for the child to imitate a stable role model and develop a consistent self-identity. A child in this situation learns to avoid blame and punishment but fails to learn the finer differences between appropriate and less appropriate behavior.

The major drawback of psychopathy as an explanation for crime is that it describes only a small percentage of offenders. It might be tempting to classify most offenders as psychopaths and feel content that their crimes had been explained with that terminology. In fact, however, most offenders are not psychopathic. One study found that only about 25% of a correctional sample could be classified as psychopathic, and this percentage was even smaller for women than for men (Salekin, Trobst, & Krioukova, 2001). In addition, several criticisms have been made about using the PCL and revised versions of the instrument (e.g., PCL-R, PCL:YV) as diagnostic tools on which legal decisions are based (Zinger & Forth, 1998). First, although the PCL-R has an excellent interrater reliability when carried out in accordance with manualized instructions, a lack of training and possible biases on the part of the clinician may contribute to disparities in scores. Slight differences in scores may account for differences in courts' dispositions of these cases. Evidence suggests that expert testimony about an offender's psychopathic traits is associated with an increase in severity of the court's disposition (Zinger and Forth, 1998). These instruments require significant training in administration and scoring, which some clinicians do not have. Given that scoring on these instruments is based, in part, on the administrator's subjective ratings, two raters should complete the PCL-R for each offender, and the average of the two scores should be used as the final score.

Furthermore, because the PCL is a self-report measure, the administrator is subject to relying on inaccurate information. As a safeguard against potentially erroneous information, the administrator must have access to collateral information to compare with information obtained from the examinee. Because the number of judicial decisions that rely on the PCL-R appears to be on the rise, ongoing efforts to ensure appropriate training are particularly important.

A second criticism of the use of these psychopathy assessment instruments in criminal proceedings revolves around their use in cases involving adolescent and female offenders. Although some evidence suggests that these instruments can be successfully used with women offenders (Loucks & Zamble 1994; Neary 1990; Salekin, Rogers, & Sewell 1997; Vitale & Newman, 2001) and male adolescent offenders (Chandler & Moran 1990; Forth 1995; Forth & Burke, 1998; Forth, Hart, & Hare 1990; Trevethan & Walker 1989), more research is needed. Nonetheless, it is fair to say that these psychopathy assessment tools offer a valuable way of assessing personal characteristics and history that are related to criminal offending. But there are other contributors as well, including social influences, to which we now turn.

Social-Psychological Theories of Crime

Social-psychological explanations view crime as being learned through social interaction. Sometimes called social-process theories in order to draw attention to the processes by which an individual becomes a criminal, social-psychological theories fall into two subcategories: control theories and direct learning theories.

Control Theories

Control theories assume that people will behave antisocially unless they are trained not to by others (Conger, 1980). Some people never form emotional bonds with significant others, so they never internalize necessary controls over antisocial behavior. For example, Hirschi's (1969, 1978) social control model stresses four control variables, each of which represents a major social bond: attachment, commitment, involvement, and belief. Young people are bonded to society at several levels. They differ in (1) the degree to which they are affected by the opinions and expectations of others, (2) the payoffs they receive for conventional behavior, and (3) the extent to which they subscribe to the prevailing norms.

Another example is Walter Reckless's (1967) **containment theory**. Reckless proposes that it is largely external containment (i.e., social pressure and institutionalized rules) that controls crime. If a society is well integrated, has well-defined limits on behavior, encourages family discipline and supervision, and provides reinforcers for positive accomplishments, crime will be contained. But if these external controls weaken, control of crime must depend on internal restraints, mainly an individual's conscience. Thus, a positive self-concept becomes a protective factor against delinquency. Strong inner containment involves the ability to tolerate frustration, be motivated by long-term goals, resist distractions, and find substitute satisfactions (Reckless, 1967).

Containment theory is a good "in-between" view, neither rigidly environmental nor entirely psychological. Containment accounts for the law-abiding individual in a high-crime environment. But this theory explains only a part of criminal behavior. It does not apply to crimes within groups that are organized around their commitment to deviant behavior.

The British psychologist Hans Eysenck (1964) proposes a related version of containment theory in which "heredity plays an important, and possibly a vital, part in predisposing a given individual to crime" (p. 55). Socialization practices then translate these innate tendencies into criminal acts. Socialization depends on two kinds of learning. First, **operant learning** explains how behavior is acquired and maintained by its consequences: Responses that are followed by rewards are strengthened, whereas responses followed by aversive events are weakened. Immediate consequences are more influential than delayed consequences. However, according to Eysenck (1964), in the real world the effects of punishment are usually "long delayed and uncertain [whereas] the acquisition of the desired object is immediate; therefore, although the acquisition and the pleasure derived from it may, on the whole, be less than the pain derived from the incarceration which ultimately follows, the time element very much favors the acquisition as compared with the deterrent effects of the incarceration" (p. 101).

Because of punishment's ineffectiveness, the restraint of antisocial behavior ultimately depends on a strong conscience, which develops through **classical conditioning**. Eysenck believes that conscience is conditioned through repeated, close pairings of a child's undesirable behaviors with the prompt punishment of these behaviors. The taboo act is the **conditioned stimulus**, which, when associated frequently enough with the **unconditioned stimulus** of punishment, produces unpleasant physiological and emotional responses. Conscience becomes an inner control that deters wrongdoing through the emotions of anxiety and guilt. Whether conditioning builds a strong conscience depends on the strength of the autonomic nervous system. According to Eysenck, conditioned responses have a genetically determined tendency in some people to develop slowly and extinguish quickly. In others, conditioning progresses rapidly and produces strong resistance to extinction.

Underlying these differences are three major personality dimensions: **extroversion, neuroticism**, and **psychoticism** (Eysenck & Gudjonsson, 1989). Extroverted people are active, aggressive, and impulsive. Persons high in neuroticism are restless, emotionally volatile, and hypersensitive. Persons high in psychoticism are troublesome, lacking in empathy, and insensitive to the point of cruelty.

Extroversion, neuroticism, and psychoticism are inherited to a substantial degree and also are associated with important physiological differences, some of which we described in our previous discussion of psychopathy. High extroverts have relatively low levels of arousal that slow their ability to be conditioned *and* render responses that are conditioned easier to extinguish. Conditioning is also impaired because physiological arousal dissipates more slowly in extroverted people and psychopaths. As a result, avoiding a previously punished act may be less reinforcing for such people because they experience less reduction in fear following their avoidance of the taboo behavior (Mednick, Gabriella, & Hutchings, 1984).

Persons high in neuroticism tend to overreact to stimuli. Therefore, high neuroticism interferes with efficient learning because of the irrelevant arousal that is evoked. In addition, high neuroticism leads to greater restlessness and drive to carry out behavior of all sorts, including crimes.

Eysenck believes that high extroversion and neuroticism result in poor conditioning and, consequently, inadequate socialization. Poor conditioning leads to a faulty conscience, which in turn produces a higher risk for criminality. Finally, if the person is high on psychoticism, he or she will be more of a primary, "tough-minded" psychopath.

Research on the links between criminal offending and personality supports a positive association between high levels of extroversion and increased offending. However, the role of neuroticism and psychopathy is less clear; in fact, neuroticism may be lower in most psychopaths than in normal controls (Doren, 1987). Another problem is that Eysenck has not clearly separated the predisposition to be conditioned from the different conditioning opportunities that children experience. Genetic differences are accompanied by different conditioning histories. A family of extroverts can transmit a potential for crime not only through inherited personality traits but also through laissez-faire discipline that is too scarce or inconsistent to be effective.

Learning Theories

Learning theory focuses on how criminal behavior is learned. According to Edwin H. Sutherland's (1947) differential association approach, criminal behavior requires socialization into a system of values conducive to violating the law; thus, the potential criminal develops definitions of behavior that make deviant conduct seem acceptable. If definitions of criminal acts as being acceptable are stronger and more frequent than definitions unfavorable to deviant behavior, then the person is more likely to commit crimes. It is not necessary to associate with criminals directly to acquire these definitions. Children might learn procriminal definitions from watching their father pocket too much change or hearing their mother brag about exceeding the speed limit.

Using the differential association approach, Sutherland and Cressey (1974, pp. 75–76) propose nine explanations of criminal behavior. Those explanations are as follows:

1. Criminal behavior is learned.
2. Criminal behavior is learned in interaction with other persons in a process of communication.
3. The influential aspect of the learning of criminal behavior occurs within intimate social groups.
4. When criminal behavior is learned, the learning includes (1) techniques of committing the crime, which are sometimes very complicated but at other times simple, and (2) the specific direction of motives, drives, rationalizations, and attitudes.
5. The specific direction of motives and drives is learned from definitions of the legal code as favorable or unfavorable.
6. A person becomes delinquent because of an excess of definitions favorable to violation of law over definitions unfavorable to violation of law.
7. Differential associations may vary in frequency, duration, intensity, and priority.
8. The process of learning criminal behavior by association with criminal and anticriminal patterns involves all the mechanisms that operate in any other learning.
9. Although criminal behavior is an expression of general needs and values, it is not explained by those general needs and values, because noncriminal behavior is an expression of the same needs and values.

Sutherland's theory has been translated into the language of operant learning theory as developed by B. F. Skinner. According to **differential association reinforcement theory** (Akers, Krohn, Lanz-Kaduce, & Radosevich, 1996; Burgess & Akers, 1966), criminal behavior is acquired through operant conditioning and modeling. A person behaves criminally when such behavior is favored by reinforcement contingencies that outweigh punishment contingencies. The major contingencies occur in families, peer groups, and schools, which control most sources of reinforcement and punishment and expose people to many behavioral models (Akers et al., 1996).

Differential association attempts to explain crime in places where it would not, on first blush, be expected (e.g., among lawbreakers who grew up in affluent settings). But it has difficulty explaining impulsive violence, and it does not explain why certain individuals, even in the same family, have the different associations they do. Why are some people more likely than others to form criminal associations?

SOCIAL LEARNING THEORY

Social learning theory acknowledges the importance of differential reinforcement for developing new behaviors, but it assigns more importance to cognitive factors and to observational or **vicarious learning**. Its chief proponent, Albert Bandura (1986), claims that "most human behavior is learned by observation through modeling" (p. 47). Learning through modeling is more efficient than learning through differential reinforcement. Sophisticated behaviors such as speech and complex chains of behavior such as driving a car require models from which to learn. In all likelihood, so does crime. Observational learning depends on (1) *attention* to the important features of modeled behavior, (2) *retention* of these features in memory to guide later performance, (3) *reproduction* of the observed behaviors, and (4) *reinforcement* of performed behaviors, which determines whether they will be performed again.

The most prominent attempt to apply social learning theory to criminal behavior is Bandura's (1973) book *Aggression: A Social Learning Analysis* (see also Platt & Prout, 1987; Ribes-Inesta & Bandura, 1976). The theory emphasizes modeling of aggression in three social contexts.

1. *Familial influences.* Familial aggression assumes many forms, from child abuse at one extreme to aggressive parental attitudes and language at the other. It is in the arena of discipline, however, where children are exposed most often to vivid examples of coercion and aggression as a preferred style for resolving conflicts and asserting desires.

2. *Subcultural influences.* Some environments and subcultures provide context that supports aggression and an abundance of rewards for their most combative members. "The highest rates of aggressive behavior are found in environments where aggressive models abound and where aggressiveness is regarded as a highly valued attribute" (Bandura, 1976, p. 207).

3. *Symbolic models.* The influence of symbolic models on aggression has been attributed to the mass media, particularly television. A large number of studies have investigated the effects of televised violence on viewers, especially on children.

Interpretations of this literature vary in terms of whether viewing televised violence is inferred to cause later aggression in viewers. The consensus is that TV violence does increase aggression for children and adolescents, that this influence is small but meaningful in magnitude, that short-term effects have been demonstrated more clearly than long-term effects, that TV violence might have a larger impact on children who are initially more

aggressive, and that children who watch a lot of televised violence are more likely to become fearful of the world around them at the same time as they become less sensitive to the feelings of others (Friedrich-Cofer & Huston, 1986; Huston et al., 1992; Pearl, Bouthilet, & Lazar, 1982; Surgeon General's Scientific Advisory Committee on Television and Social Behavior, 1972; for the dissenting view that TV violence has not been shown to increase aggression, see Freedman, 1984, 1986).

However, a more recent longitudinal study, conducted over a 15-year period, suggests that there are significant long-term effects from watching violent television in childhood (Huesmann, Moise-Titus, Podolski, & Eron, 2003). Results from this study revealed a significant relationship between watching violence on television as children and aggressive behavior in adulthood. This pattern held for male and female participants, although the types of aggressive behavior differed. Males engaged in more overt aggression (e.g., domestic violence, physical fights), whereas women engaged in more indirect aggression (e.g., traffic violations). Women who watched violent television as children were also four times more likely than other women to be victims of domestic violence. Furthermore, the study found that early exposure to violence on television significantly predicted aggression in adulthood regardless of the level of aggression the individual displayed in childhood.

Researchers also hypothesized that viewing television violence in childhood can lead to other potentially harmful effects. For instance, children may become desensitized to the effects of violence (e.g., may care less about others' feelings) or experience a heightened fear of victimization. Children younger than 8 years old may be especially vulnerable to the effects of viewing violence because of their cognitive limitations in distinguishing fantasy and cartoon violence from reality. (http://www.trivision.ca/documents/2003/TV_Violence.pdf). Of more recent interest is the question of whether movies, which often feature much more graphic depictions of violence than those allowed on TV, exert stronger modeling effects on aggression.

Social learning theory also points to several environmental cues that increase antisocial behavior. These "instigators" signal when it might be rewarding to behave antisocially (rather than risky to do so). Six instigators deserve special mention:

1. *Models.* Modeled aggression is effective in prompting others to behave aggressively, particularly when observers have been previously frustrated or when the modeled aggression is seen as justified.

2. *Prior aversive treatment.* Assaults, threats, reductions in available reinforcers, blocking of goal-directed behaviors, and perceptions of inequitable treatment can lead to increased aggression and can enhance the perceived rewards of aggression.

3. *Incentive inducements.* Antisocial behavior can be prompted by the anticipated rewards of misbehavior. Bandura (1976) suggests that aggression is sometimes stimulated and temporarily sustained by erroneously anticipated consequences. Habitual offenders often overestimate their chances of succeeding in criminal acts and ignore the consequences of failing.

4. *Instructions.* Milgram's (1963) famous experiment demonstrating widespread willingness to follow orders to inflict "pain" on another person suggests that antisocial behavior can be instigated by commands from authorities. The strength of instructional control is limited to certain conditions, and it is not a common source of instigation in most crimes. However, it may play a role in some hate crimes, in which the perpetrator believes he or she is doing the will of a religious or patriotic fanatic.

5. *Delusions.* Individuals occasionally respond aggressively to hallucinated commands or paranoid jealousies and suspicions. People who suffer delusional symptoms also tend to be socially isolated, a factor that sometimes minimizes the corrective influences that a reality-based environment could have on them.

6. *Alcohol and drug use.* Alcohol and drugs can be potent instigators to antisocial conduct. There is a strong, positive association between crime and alcohol use, especially for violent crime (Parker, 2004; Richardson & Budd, 2003). By depressing a person's responsiveness to other cues that could inhibit impulsive or aggressive behavior, alcohol often leads to an increase in antisocial behavior even though it is not a stimulant (Chermack & Giancola, 1997). Narcotics use, by virtue of its cost and deviant status, also acts as a catalyst to or amplifier of criminality, especially property crime.

According to social learning theorists, people also regulate their behavior through self-reinforcement. Individuals who derive pleasure, pride, revenge, or self-worth from an ability to harm or "con" others enjoy an almost sensual pleasure in the way criminal behavior "feels" (Katz, 1988). Conversely, people will discontinue conduct that results in self-criticism and self-contempt.

People can also learn to exempt themselves from their own conscience after behaving antisocially. These tactics of "self-exoneration" assume many forms: minimizing the seriousness of one's acts by pointing to more serious offenses by others, justifying aggression by appealing to higher values, displacing the responsibility for misbehavior onto a higher authority, blaming victims for their misfortune, diffusing responsibility for wrongdoing, dehumanizing victims so that they are stripped of sympathetic qualities, and underestimating the damage inflicted by one's actions.

The major strength of social learning theory is that it explains how specific patterns of criminality are developed by individual offenders. A second strength is that the theory applies to a wide range of crimes. The major limitation of social learning theory is that little empirical evidence indicates that real-life crime is learned according to behavioral principles. Most of the data come from laboratory research where the experimental setting nullifies all the legal and social sanctions that actual offenders must risk incurring. A second problem is that the theory does not explain why some people fall prey to "bad" learning experiences and others resist them. Learning might be a necessary ingredient for criminality, but it is probably not a sufficient one. Individual differences in the way people respond to reinforcement need to be considered. The theory we review next does so.

WILSON AND HERRNSTEIN'S CONSTITUTIONAL LEARNING THEORY

Some theorists have integrated several learning processes into comprehensive, learning-based explanations of criminality (e.g., Feldman, 1977). The most influential and controversial multiple-component learning theory is James Q. Wilson and the late Richard Herrnstein's (1985) book *Crime and Human Nature*. Wilson and Herrnstein begin by observing that criminal and noncriminal behavior have both gains and losses. Gains from committing crime include revenge, excitement, and peer approval. Gains associated with not committing crime include avoiding punishment and having a clear conscience. Whether a crime is committed depends, in part, on the net ratio of gains and losses for criminal and noncriminal behavior. If the ratio for committing a crime exceeds the ratio for not committing it, the likelihood of the crime being committed increases (a proposition similar to what Cornish & Clarke [1986] call **rational choice theory**).

Wilson and Herrnstein argue that several individual differences influence these ratios and determine whether an individual is likely to commit a crime. Like Eysenck, they propose that individuals differ in the ease with which they learn to associate, through classical conditioning, negative emotions with misbehaviors and positive emotions with proper behaviors. These conditioned responses are the building blocks of a strong conscience that increases the gains associated with noncrime and increases the losses associated with crime.

Another important personality factor is what Wilson and Herrnstein call *time discounting*. All reinforcers lose strength the more remote they are from a behavior, but people differ in their ability to delay gratification and obtain reinforcement from potential long-term gains. More impulsive persons have greater difficulty deriving benefits from distant reinforcers. Time discounting is important for understanding crime because the gains associated with crime (e.g., revenge, money) accrue immediately, whereas the losses from such behavior (e.g., punishment) occur later, if at all. Thus, for impulsive persons, the ratio of gains to losses shifts in a direction that favors criminal behavior.

Equity is another important influence on criminality. *Equity theory* states that people compare what they feel they deserve with what they observe other people receiving. Inequitable transactions are perceived when one's own ratio of gains to losses is less than that of others. Judgments of inequity change the reinforcing value of crime. If one perceives oneself as being unfairly treated by society, this sense of inequity increases the perceived gains associated with stealing because such behavior helps restore one's sense of equity. Another major component in Wilson and Herrnstein's theory is a set of constitutional factors, including gender, intelligence, variations in physiological arousal, and the aforementioned impulsivity, all of which conspire to make some persons more attracted to wrongdoing and less deterred by the potential aversive consequences of crime.

Of several social factors linked to criminal behavior, Wilson and Herrnstein believe that family influences and early school experiences are the most important. Families that foster (1) *attachment* of children to their parents, (2) *longer time horizons*, where children consider the distant consequences of their behavior, and (3) *strong consciences* about misbehavior will go far in counteracting criminal predispositions.

The work of Gerald Patterson and his colleagues is important here as well. On the basis of elaborate observations of families with and without aggressive and conduct-disordered children, Patterson (1982, 1986) has identified four family interaction patterns associated with later delinquency: (1) disciplinary techniques involving either excessive nagging or indifferent laxness, (2) lack of positive parenting and affection toward children, (3) ineffective parental monitoring of a child's behavior, and (4) failure to employ adequate problem-solving strategies, thereby increasing stress and irritability within a family.

Research on parenting practices and the quality of the parent–child relationship underscores the relevance of familial interaction to childhood delinquency. Findings from a qualitative study with juvenile offenders and their parents revealed that their familial interactions were characterized by poor communication and high levels of conflict between children and parents. These interactions were associated with children's perceptions of lack of parental concern and warmth (Madden-Derdich, Leonard, & Gunnell, 2002). In addition, an intergenerational study examining the effect of parenting styles on antisocial behavioral patterns across generations suggests that familial interactions have far-reaching implications; parental conflict and highly demanding, unresponsive parents were related to childhood behavioral problems in two successive generations (Smith & Farrington, 2004).

The remedies to these harmful patterns involve warm supportiveness combined with consistent enforcement of clear rules for proper behavior. Unfortunately, these methods are least likely to be practiced by parents whose own traits reflect the predispositions they have passed to their children. Therefore, many at-risk children face the double whammy of problematic predispositions coupled with inadequate parental control and support.

Biological factors interact with family problems and early school experiences to increase the risks of poorly controlled behavior even more. Not only are impulsive, poorly socialized children of lower intelligence more directly at risk for criminality, but their interactions with cold, indifferent schools that do not facilitate educational success can further discourage them from embracing traditional social conformity. Consistent with this part of the theory is a long line of research studies showing that children officially diagnosed with early conduct problems and/or attention deficit/hyperactivity disorder face a heightened likelihood of becoming adult offenders (Nietzel et al., 1997).

Because they took hereditary and biological factors seriously, Wilson and Herrnstein have come under heavy fire from critics who portray their ideas as a purely genetic theory. It is not. Instead, it is a theory that restores psychological factors (some inheritable, some not) and family interaction variables to a place of importance in criminology, which for decades was dominated by sociological concepts.

The Social Labeling Perspective

The most extreme version of a social-psychological theory of crime is the social labeling perspective. Its emergence as an explanation reflects (1) frustration about the inability of prior approaches to provide comprehensive explanations and (2) a shift in emphasis from why people commit crimes to why some people are labeled "criminals" (Sheley, 1985).

Some examples will illustrate this shift. In one study (Heussanstamm, 1975) during the turbulent 1970s, a group of college students in Los Angeles—all of whom had perfect driving records in the last year—had "Black Panther" bumper stickers put on their cars. Within hours, they began to get pulled over for traffic violations such as improper lane changes, implying that the Los Angeles police officers were labeling behavior differently on the basis of the presence of the bumper sticker.

A more contemporary illustration of this troubling phenomenon is the allegation that police use **racial profiling** as a basis for making a disproportionate number of traffic stops of minority motorists, particularly African Americans. As we noted in Chapter 1, this practice has often been justified by police as a tool for catching drug traffickers, but arresting motorists for "driving while black" as a pretext for additional criminal investigations clearly raises the risk of harmful and inappropriate labeling, to say nothing of its discriminatory impact. The outcry over racial profiling has resulted in a call for federal legislation that would prohibit the practice and has led to several lawsuits, including one in which the Maryland state police agreed to pay damages to four African American drivers who had been targets of profile stops.

The basic assumption of labeling theory is that deviance is created by the labels that society assigns to certain acts. Deviance is not simply based on the quality of the act; rather, it stems also from an act's consequences in the form of society's official reactions to it. Social labeling theory makes a distinction between **primary deviance**, or the criminal's actual behavior, and **secondary deviance**, or society's reaction to the offensive conduct (Lemert, 1951, 1972). With regard to primary deviance, offenders often rationalize their behavior as a temporary mistake, or they see it as part of a socially acceptable role (Lilly et al., 1989). Whether or not that self-assessment is accurate, secondary deviance serves to brand them with a more permanent "criminal" stigma.

However, this perspective assumes some basic principles (Sheley, 1985, pp. 233–234): (1) The individuals' behavior must be noticed, or at least assumed to be noticed, by society before they can be labeled as criminals. (2) Individuals cannot be labeled as criminals unless society reacts to, or attempts to give meaning to, their offense. (3) Society's attempt to label people as criminals may necessarily lead to the imposition of a label. (4) The outcome of the negotiation of a label between society and individuals involves more than just the qualities of alleged criminal acts; it also involves characteristics of the alleged violator, such as race, gender, or socioeconomic status, and the social or political climate in which the negotiation occurs. (5) Whether the effects of the labeling are long-lasting is also negotiable and depends on individuals' reactions to their labels, society's perceptions of those reactions, and society's willingness to negotiate.

Despite these assumptions, the main point of the social labeling theory is that the stigma of being branded a deviant can create a self-fulfilling prophecy (Merton, 1968). Even those ex-convicts who seek an honest life in a law-abiding society are spurned by prospective employers and by their families and are labeled "ex-cons." Frustrated in their efforts to make good, they may adopt this label and "live up to" its pejorative connotations by engaging in further lawbreaking (Irwin, 1970). According to this perspective, the criminal justice system produces much of the deviance it is intended to correct.

The social labeling approach raises our awareness about the difficulties offenders face in returning to society. Moreover, it reminds us that some lawbreakers (e.g., those who live in crime-ridden neighborhoods where the police patrol often) are more likely to be caught and "criminalized" than are others. But the social labeling approach does not explain most criminal behavior. Primary deviance (i.e., a law violation in the first place) usually has to occur before secondary deviance takes its toll, and many lawbreakers develop a life of crime before ever being apprehended (Mankoff, 1971). Behavioral differences between people exist and persist, despite the names we call them.

Integration of Theories of Crime

Where do all these theories leave us? Do any of them offer a convincing explanation of crime? Do they suggest how we should intervene to prevent or reduce crime? Although many commentators decry the lack of a convincing theory of crime, knowledge about the causes of serious crime has accumulated and now provides certain well-supported explanations for how repeated, violent criminality develops. Serious criminality is extraordinarily versatile, involving careers that include violent behavior, property offenses, vandalism, and substance abuse.

One implication of this diversity is that individuals travel several causal pathways to different brands of criminality. No single variable causes all crime, just as no one agent causes all fever or upset stomachs. However, several causal factors are associated reliably with many types of criminality. Any one of these factors may sometimes be a sufficient explanation for criminal behavior, but more often they act in concert to produce criminality. Our attempt to integrate these various factors (see Figure 3.2) emphasizes four contributors to crime that occur in a developmental sequence.

Our model emphasizes what we believe are the variables best supported by criminological research as causal factors in crime.

1. *Antecedent conditions.* Chances of repeated offending are increased by biological, psychological, and environmental antecedents that make it easier for certain individuals to learn to behave criminally and easier for this learning to occur in specific settings. The leading candidates

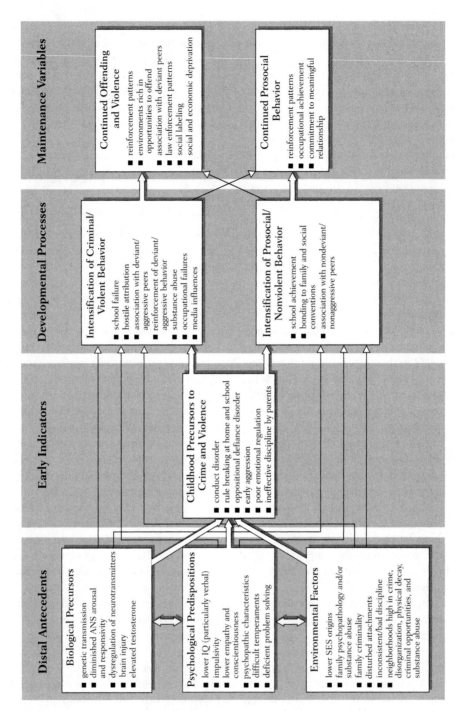

FIGURE 3.2 *An integrated model for explaining repeated crime*

NOTE: Thick arrows indicate probable paths; thin arrows indicate less likely paths.

for biological risk are genetic inheritance, neurochemical abnormalities, brain dysfunction, and autonomic nervous system irregularities.

Among psychological variables, poor social skills; lower verbal intelligence; the personality traits of irritability, impulsiveness, and low empathy; and deficiencies in inner restraint (or conscience) leave some people well stocked in attitudes, thinking, and motivations that encourage antisocial behavior and that also render them relatively immune to negative consequences for misconduct. These psychological factors may accompany biological risks or may convey their own independent vulnerability to crime.

Finally, certain environments are rife with opportunities and temptations for crime and help translate biological or psychological predispositions toward criminal behavior into ever-stronger antisocial tendencies. Such environments function this way because of social impoverishment and disorganization, fundamental economic inequalities, a tradition of tolerating if not encouraging crime, social dissension and strife, and an abundance of inviting targets and easy victims of crime (Heide, 1997; Patterson, 1986). Crime-causing environments encourage offending because they are replete with antagonists who provoke violence, easy targets to be victimized by violence, and high rates of alcohol and substance abuse that lower inhibitions against violence (Chermack & Giancola, 1997).

Within family environments, high levels of mental disorders, criminality, parental absenteeism, and substance abuse also lead to more violence. These links may be forged through any one of several factors: genetic influence, modeling, increased hostility against a constant backdrop of harsh living conditions, disturbed attachments with parents, or lax or overly punitive discipline that does not teach youngsters how to control behavior. Research suggests that early exposure to harsh family living conditions can aggravate some of the biological factors that contribute to aggression, such as a child's physical and emotional reactions to threat (Gallagher, 1996).

2. *Early indicators.* Repetitive antisocial conduct is disconcertingly stable over time. Aggressive children often grow up to be aggressive adults, and the precedents for adult violence and substance abuse are often seen as early indicators of aggressiveness in preschool and elementary school children (Lynam, 1998; Slutske et al., 1998). Although there are tools that can identify youth who are at elevated risk for behavioral problems, it remains difficult to predict whether these individuals will commit serious, violent acts later in life (Sprague & Walker, 2000). Relatively few at-risk youth commit serious, violent offenses, but many display major long-term adjustment problems. For instance, youth identified as at risk in childhood may experience drug and alcohol abuse, domestic and child abuse, divorce or multiple relationships, employment problems, mental health problems, dependence on social services, and involvement in less serious crimes (Obiakor, Merhing, & Schwenn, 1997).

Although not all chronic offenders were violent children, many repetitively aggressive adults began to exhibit that pattern early; in fact, most psychologists who study aggression believe that severe antisocial behavior in adulthood is nearly always preceded by antisocial behavior in childhood. These early indicators include officially diagnosed conduct disorder, oppositional defiant disorder, and attention deficit/hyperactivity disorder (Lynam, 1996; McGee, Feehan, Williams, & Anderson, 1992).

Developmental models have enhanced our understanding of the onset and maintenance of antisocial behavior. For instance, one model suggests two subtypes of adolescent offenders: those who display behavioral problems later in adolescence and desist in early adulthood, and the relatively smaller group who display conduct-disordered behaviors earlier in adolescence that persist into adulthood. Adolescent offenders in the latter group are more likely to develop antisocial personality disorder than those in the former group.

Another model suggests that early emergence of conduct-disordered behavior that is displayed across multiple and diverse settings may predict the development of antisocial personality disorder in adulthood. One study found that early indicators of a diagnosis of antisocial personality disorder included a formal diagnosis of conduct disorder by age 10, participation in frequent and varied conduct-disordered behavior at an early age, and significant drug use in childhood or early adolescence (Myers, Stewart, & Brown, 1998).

Long-term longitudinal studies have demonstrated that aggression in childhood predicts violence in adulthood. Huesmann, Eron, and Yarmel (1987) measured aggression in childhood and tracked the boys and girls for 22 years. They found that aggression began to crystalize around the age of 8 and remained stable across three generations (Eron, 1990; Huesmann, Eron, Lefkowitz, & Walder, 1984). Aggressive boys turned into men who were more likely to commit serious crimes, abuse their spouses, and drive while intoxicated. Aggressive girls turned into women who were more likely to punish their children harshly.

3. *Developmental processes*. Whether early indicators of criminal offending harden into patterns of repeated adult crime or soften into prosocial nonviolent conduct depends on several developmental processes. These processes occur in families, schools, peer groups, and the media—and in the thinking of the youth themselves.

Delinquency is often associated with poor school achievement. Grades in school begin to predict delinquency around age 15. As adolescent youth fall further and further behind in school, they have fewer and fewer opportunities or reasons to stay bonded to school and to strive for academic success (Cernkovich & Giordano, 1996). School failure seems to narrow the options for prosocial behavior because it decreases the chances of employability and job success.

Modeling and peer pressure also promote criminality. Crime increases when peers support it, as is sometimes the case in the criminal justice system itself when, by virtue of its official processing of offenders, "beginning" criminals are thrown together with more serious offenders. Furthermore, the more delinquent friends a youth has, the more likely he or she is to behave criminally (Elliott, Huizinga, & Ageton, 1985).

However, recent research suggests that the association between delinquency and negative peer influences may be more complex. One study found that poor parental monitoring and supervision, as well as increased social stress and poor social skills, affected the relationship between adolescents' delinquent behavior and negative peer affiliation (Kimonis, Frick, & Barry, 2004). On the basis of these findings, the authors concluded that intervening with training in parenting skills and social skills, specifically encouraging more parental involvement and monitoring of their child's behavior, may be especially important in reducing negative peer affiliation and decreasing delinquency.

Modeling influences can also be mediated through the media. In Leonard Eron's (1987) large-scale study of aggression, children's viewing of TV violence at age 8 had a correlation of 0.41 with several aggressive behaviors at age 30, even after controlling for baseline levels of aggressiveness, IQ, and socioeconomic status. TV and other media depictions of graphic violence could exert harmful effects by providing youngsters with opportunities to rehearse a lot of aggressive strategies. A steady diet of media violence might teach children to see their world as hostile and competitive. Repeated exposure to violence might also provide the "scripts" that youth elaborate into personal crime stories in which aggression and deceit are seen as necessary for surviving in a harsh world.

Another intensifier of aggression is alcohol and substance abuse (Murdoch, Pihl, & Ross, 1990). Numerous mechanisms could account for the tendency for substance abuse to lead to more crime. Alcohol is a depressant, so it might suppress the ability of certain areas of the brain to inhibit behavior effectively. The more time a youth spends abusing drugs and alcohol, the less time he or she has for prosocial, academic activities. Substance abuse typically results in more associations with deviant peers, thereby increasing the opportunities for antisocial behavior to be reinforced. Repeated substance abuse during adolescence serves as one more "trap" that shuts off many youngsters' options for prosocial behavior. These limits, in turn, increase the reinforcing potential of antisocial conduct.

Unfortunately, these developmental processes tend to compound one another. The impulsive, low-IQ child is more likely to fail at school. School dropouts increasingly associate with antisocial peers. Parents who fail to monitor and sanction their children when they misbehave tend not to show much concern about what movies their children watch. Finally, early conduct and academic problems are strongly related to later substance abuse. When it comes to crime, at-risk youth stay at risk.

4. *Maintenance factors.* Violent offending can become an entrenched way of life when one or more of the following maintenance factors are in place: The short-run positive payoffs for offending are stronger and more probable than the long-term risks of apprehension and punishment. The person lives in environments that are rich in opportunities for offending and low in the chances of being detected. As a result of the inevitable arrests and incarcerations that repeat offenders experience, their associations with aggressive peers increase, just as contacts with law-abiding citizens decrease. As the long-run consequence of many earlier estrangements from conventional norms and values, delinquents begin to feel growing resentment and contempt for social rules. These maintenance factors do not cause crime so much as they solidify it. Once they start to work their influence, the battle is often already lost, because criminal conduct has become a basic part of a person's identity.

An implication of our integrative model is that preventing crime might be a better way of fighting the "crime problem" than rehabilitating criminals. Certainly, with the help of treatment programs that strengthen their social skills, build better cognitive controls, model prosocial behavior, and reinforce law-abiding conduct, some people can "turn around" a life of violent offending (Andrews & Bonta, 1994). But however promising the rates of "success" in correctional rehabilitation might eventually become, it is still likely that some who are arrested and incarcerated will continue to offend throughout their lives.

This should not be surprising. After a protracted history of learning antisocial behavior, rejecting prosocial behavior, and facing closed doors to legitimate opportunity, repeat offenders will not yield easily to attempts to suppress criminal conduct. That is why prevention becomes so important. If most at-risk youth can be reliably identified, we can then intervene in multiple areas—with individuals, families, schools, peer groups, and neighborhoods—to interrupt those processes that eventually ensnare youth into antisocial lifestyles. Brought about by hostile environments and the decisions of youth themselves, these processes include experimenting with alcohol and drugs, dwelling on violent media and subcultures, dropping out of school, failing at legitimate employment, and associating with other lawbreakers. They are the pathways to deviance that must be blocked early before they become too well traveled for any change to occur.

SUMMARY

1. *Theories of crime can be grouped into four categories. What are they?* The most common theories can be classified into four groups: sociological, biological, psychological, and social-psychological.

2. *Among sociological explanations of crime, how does the subcultural explanation differ from*

the structural explanation? The structural explanation for crime emphasizes chronic barriers to conventional success that certain people face; these barriers include cultural and language differences, financial hardships, and limited access to those resources crucial to upward mobility. In contrast, the subcultural explanation proposes that certain groups, such as gangs, adhere to norms that conflict with the values of others in society and encourage criminal conduct.

3. *What is emphasized in biological theories of crime?* Both genetic and physiological factors are emphasized in biological explanations of criminal behavior. Hereditary factors influence criminal behavior, but the mechanisms through which this influence is exerted are unclear. The most likely candidates involve neurotransmitters, such as serotonin, and certain subcortical and cortical brain structures, particularly the prefrontal cortex, which is responsible for monitoring behavioral inhibition, planning, and decision making.

4. *What psychological factors have been advanced to explain crime?* Psychological theories of criminal behavior emphasize criminal thinking patterns or a personality defect, such as psychopathy.

5. *How do social-psychological theories view crime?* Social-psychological theories view criminal behavior as a learned response resulting from classical conditioning, reinforcement, observation or modeling, and social labeling.

KEY TERMS

anomie

antisocial personality disorder

biological theories of crime

classical conditioning

classical school of criminology

concordance rate

conditioned stimulus

containment theory

control theory

criminology

differential association reinforcement theory

dizygotic twins

ecological theorists

executive function

extroversion

focal concerns

learning theory

monozygotic twins

neuroticism

operant learning

positivist school of criminology

primary deviance

psychological theories of crime

psychopathy

psychoticism

racial profiling

rational choice theory

rational crime theory

reality principle

secondary deviance

social labeling theory

social learning theory

social-psychological theory of crime

sociological theories of crime

stimulation-seeking theory

structural explanations

subcultural explanations

unconditioned stimulus

vicarious learning

InfoTrac COLLEGE EDITION • For additional readings go to http://www.infotrac-college.com/wadsworth and enter a search term related to your interest. The key terms that have been marked with asterisks above will pull up several related articles.

Psychology of Police

ORIENTING QUESTIONS

1. *What is the role of the police in our society?*
2. *What procedures are used to select police?*
3. *How has the training of police officers expanded into new areas?*
4. *Describe the different activities of the police. Is law enforcement central?*
5. *What stressors do the police face?*
6. *Is there a police personality?*
7. *What is the relationship between the police and the communities they serve?*

In any survey of public concerns, "crime" is usually near the top. This ranking stems from the pervasiveness of crime in our country, as well as from the fear that crime typically instills. Despite the decreasing crime rate over the last 10 years, almost 20% of Americans were victims of either property or personal crime in 2002 (Bureau of Justice Statistics, 2003a). These figures also indicate that at least twice as many violent crimes and three times as many property crimes occur as are officially reported to the police. Only crimes that are detected and reported to the police find their way into the criminal justice system. But the physical, financial, and psychological effects of being a victim of crime persist even when the victimization is never reported to the police. Whether measured in lost cash, damaged property, medical expenses, emotional trauma, or lost income due to injuries, the annual economic impact of crime runs to the billions of dollars.

The road from reporting a crime to convicting and punishing an offender can be long and tortuous, but in most cases the police are the officials in the criminal justice system with whom citizens have the most contact. The police are the ones who confront criminal activities face-to-face, and we expect them to keep our streets safe and our homes secure. They are the "thin blue line" that stands between the law-abiding citizen and public disorder. The visibility of the police is heightened by the uniforms they wear, the weapons they carry, and the special powers they are given. This visibility makes the police convenient targets for the public's frustrations with the criminal justice system. At the same time, many people place enormous trust in the police, and they are the first people whom most citizens call in emergencies. Consequently, the public holds conflicting attitudes about the police. It demands protection from them at the same time that it resists interference from them.

The major purpose of this chapter is to describe the selection, training, and behavior of police officers. This chapter also serves as an introduction to the next two chapters, on crime investigation and detection.

Police perform a complex set of tasks in the criminal justice system. To succeed at their jobs, street officers must combine physical prowess, perceptual acuity, interpersonal sensitivity, and intelligent discretion. They need to make quick judgments about all sorts of human behavior, often under very stressful conditions. They should be well versed in the law and should have at least some familiarity with the social sciences. Despite the complexity of these demands, police are usually overworked and underappreciated. These factors, along with the job pressures they face, the criminal elements they encounter, and the isolation in which they often work, render the police subject to the lures of bribery, corruption, and abuses of power.

When we consider the police from a psychological perspective, we encounter each of the dilemmas introduced in Chapter 1. Many individuals see the police as intruding on their rights to privacy and freedom, yet they also recognize that such an institution is necessary to protect society. Police officers investigate crime—their job is to find out what happened—but they also must make arrests and maintain an image of stability in society. In their quest for arrests, convictions, and the truth as they see it, police officers sometimes go beyond the bounds of accepted legal procedures. In a dynamic society in which occasional injustices are inevitable, it is difficult to obtain efficient law enforcement and effective crime control from the police and, at the same time, ensure due process and equal justice (Chevigny, 1969).

Another conflict arises when social scientists question the validity of techniques that the police often use, such as lineup identifications and lie detector tests. Last, but of great importance to the police, is the dilemma of equality versus discretion. When should an arrest be made, and when should only a warning be issued? How much force can legitimately be used in an arrest? Should all suspects be treated the same way?

Selection of Police Officers

One purpose of this chapter is to examine the police officer from a psychological perspective. How are police officers selected? Do the selection criteria work? Is there a set of personality characteristics that police officers share? How are the police trained, and does training improve their actual performance on the job? Can the police officer's image in the community be improved?

These questions took on a special urgency in the 1990s as a result of several highly publicized cases in which police officers had brutally beaten suspects in their custody. Many of these cases involved white officers attacking black citizens, raising the possibility that racial bias was a motive.

Beginning with the prosecution of the Los Angeles police officers who were videotaped beating Rodney King (described in Box 4.2), which was followed by similar incidents more recently, concerns have grown over police brutality. For instance, in June 2004, videotapes showed Stanley Miller, a suspect in an auto theft, apparently trying to surrender while Los Angeles officers tackled him and began kicking and repeatedly hitting him in the head (CNN, 2004).

This kind of incident has been reported in several cities throughout the country, including Detroit, New York, Louisville, Pittsburgh, and Miami. Perhaps no case sparked such heated national debate over the relationship between minorities and the police as the assault against Abner Louima, the Haitian immigrant who was beaten and sodomized with a bathroom plunger by New York City police officer Justin Volpe, as a second officer, Charles Schwarz, held him down. After Volpe pled guilty, a federal jury convicted Schwarz of conspiracy to sodomize and of violating Louima's civil rights, but it acquitted three other officers who had also been charged in the beating. Although it is tempting to view this case as an isolated incident, similar cases have occurred often enough to raise the possibility that they reflect a pervasive problem. Are certain police officers prone to these kinds of attacks? If so, can they be identified in advance and screened out of police work?

Psychological evaluation of police personnel began in 1916 when Lewis Terman, the Stanford University psychologist who revised Alfred Binet's intelligence scales to produce the Stanford-Binet intelligence test, tested the intelligence of 30 applicants for police and firefighter jobs in San Jose,

The brutal police assault of Abner Louima by several New York City police officers led to their conviction on federal criminal charges.

California. Terman (1917) found that the average IQ among these applicants was 84 and recommended that no one with an IQ below 80 be accepted for these jobs. A few years later, L. L. Thurstone tested the intelligence of 358 Detroit policemen, using the Army Alpha Intelligence Examination. Like Terman, he reported below-average IQ scores, and he also found that police of higher ranks scored lower than entry-level patrolmen.

Throughout the years, psychologists continued to assess police candidates, although their work was often unsystematic and poorly evaluated. As late as 1955, only 14 American cities with populations greater than 100,000 formally tested police candidates; by 1965, 27% of local police agencies reported some psychological evaluation of applicants (Ostrov, 1986). In the 1960s and 1970s, the period when police psychology became an established specialty, several national commissions, including the 1967 President's Commission on Law Enforcement and the Administration of Justice and the 1973 National Advisory Committee on Criminal Justice Standards, called for formal psychological assessment of police personnel in all departments. By the mid-1980s, 11 states required psychological screening of police candidates, and more than 50% of the country's departments psychologically screened beginning police officers (Benner, 1986). By the 1990s, formal assessment of police candidates had become routine, partly because of attempts by municipal governments to prevent or defeat lawsuits claiming that they were liable for dangerous or improper conduct by their police employees.

Psychological evaluation of police applicants can focus on selecting those candidates who appear most psychologically fit or on eliminating individuals who appear least suited for police work. Most selection methods concentrate on screening out disturbed candidates, because it is very difficult to agree on the "ideal" police profile. Despite concerns about the validity of psychological evaluations in police selection (Kent & Eisenberg, 1972; Levy, 1967), many experts (Arrigo & Claussen, 2003; Bartol, 1983; Gowan & Gatewood, 1995; Ostrov, 1986; Reiser & Klyver, 1987; Scogin, Schmacher, Gardner, & Chaplin, 1995; Spielberger, 1979) believe that psychological screening is useful in the selection process and should be included. However, the current standards for screening may not be sufficient. Psychological tests are currently used to assess levels of psychopathology that may interfere with officers' abilities to perform their duties rather than focusing on risk assessment, situational testing, or job simulations that could detect potential problem behaviors or attitudes (such as racism) (Scrivner, 1994).

In general, the courts have upheld the legality of psychological screening of police candidates as long as the evaluation and testing involved do not violate the provisions of various civil rights acts or the Americans with Disabilities Act and are in compliance with federal guidelines.

If it were your task to select police officers from a pool of applicants, what psychological qualities would you look for? Your answers probably reflect your values, as well as your image of what police officers do. Among the psychological characteristics usually generated in such a list are the following:

◆ *Incorruptible*: A police officer should be of high moral character. Reports of officers taking bribes or framing innocent suspects are especially disturbing, because the police officer must treat all citizens fairly within the rules of law.

◆ *Well-adjusted*: A police officer should be able to carry out the stressful duties of the job without "cracking up." Officers are always in the public view. They need to be thick-skinned enough to operate without defensiveness, yet they must be sensitive to the needs of others. They also need to cope with the dangers of their jobs, including the constant awareness that death may lurk around the corner. Throughout the 1990s, about 100 to 150 American police officers were killed annually in the line of duty.

◆ *People-oriented*: A police officer's major duty is service to others. An officer needs to have a genuine interest in people and compassion for them. At a commencement program of the New York City Police Academy, new officers were told, "There is one thing we cannot teach you and that is about people. The bottom line is to treat people as people and you'll get by" (quoted by Nix, 1987, p. 15).

◆ *Free of emotional reactions*: Although a degree of chronic suspiciousness may be desirable for the job, the police officer should be free of impulsive, overly aggressive reactions and other responses in which emotions overcome careful, thoughtful reactions. Restraint is essential because officers are trained to take an active stance in crime detection and are even encouraged by their superiors to be wary of what is happening around them (Greenberg & Ruback, 1982). A new police officer, reflecting on the effect of his training, said, "I've always been suspicious. [But now] I find myself looking up at the roofs of buildings to see if people are going to throw anything off" (quoted by Nix, 1987, p. 15). A study of police officers by Ruby and Brigham (1996) supports this police officer's reaction; they found that, compared to laypersons, police are more attentive toward indications that people's actions might be criminal.

◆ *Logical*: Police officers should be able to examine a crime scene and extract hypotheses about what happened and what characteristics might be present in the lawbreaker. This deductive ability is apparent in the actions of Al Seedman, whose work is described in Box 4.1.

Keep these characteristics in mind as we now discuss particular approaches to evaluating police candidates. To what extent can each of these characteristics be accurately assessed?

Psychologists who evaluate police candidates rely on three tools: (1) personal interviews, (2) observations of candidates performing in special situations contrived to reflect real-world characteristics of police work, and (3) psychological tests. How much emphasis different psychologists place on these tools depends on several factors, including their professional background and training, the resources available for the evaluation, and the focus of the assessment (e.g., different strategies will be used for assessing mental disorders than for predicting what type of person will do best in which kind of position).

The Interview

Personal interviews are the most widely employed tool, despite evidence that interviews are subject to distortion, low reliability, and questionable validity. The extent to which an interview yields the same information on different occasions or with different interviewers (*reliability*) and the degree to which that information is accurately related to important criteria (*validity*) have not been clearly established for most police selection interviews.

However, there is good evidence that reliability, at least, is increased by the use of **structured interviews**—those in which the wording, order, and content of the interview are standardized (Rogers, 1995). Work is under way on the Law Enforcement Candidate Interview—a structured interview for the psychological screening of law enforcement personnel—and preliminary research suggests that it is a modest predictor of performance in the training academy (Varela, Scogin, & Vipperman, 1999).

Interviews are a necessary part of an evaluation, according to guidelines recommended by police psychologists (Blau, 1994). They are also valuable as a rapport-building introduction to the evaluation process. They increase applicants' cooperation at the same time that they reduce apprehension. Interviews are also popular because they are flexible and economical. However, because they are subject to distortions and impression management by candidates, interviews are still more useful for orienting candidates to the evaluation than for predicting subsequent performance.

Situational Tests

Situational tests have been used from time to time in police selection. For example, Mills, McDevitt, and Tonkin (1966) administered three tests that simulated various police abilities to a group of Cincinnati police candidates. The Foot Patrol Observation Test required candidates to walk a six-block downtown route and then answer questions about what they remembered having just observed. In the Clues Test, candidates were given ten minutes to investigate a set of planted clues about the disappearance of a city worker from his office. They were observed as they performed this task and were graded on the information they assembled. The Bull Session was a two-hour group discussion of several topics important in police work. Performance on the Clues Test correlated significantly with class ranking in the police academy, but scores from the Foot Patrol Observation Test did not. Although "grades" for the Bull Session were not derived, it was viewed as an important measure of emotional and motivational qualities.

Despite the fact that situational tests have an intuitive appeal as selection devices, they have not proved to be better predictors of performance

THE CASE OF

BOX 4.1   the unidentified skeleton

Al Seedman, former chief detective of the New York City Police Department, once explained to an interviewer that he had been helping some detectives from a small Connecticut town investigate a case:

In the woods just outside town they found the skeleton of a man who'd been dead for three months or so. They figured they'd find out who he was as soon as his family reported him missing, but it's been three months since he was found—which makes six months since he died—and nobody has claimed him. They don't know what to do . . . . Once I got the answer to one question I was able to give them a method.

I asked whether this skeleton showed signs of any dental work, which usually can be identified by a dentist. But according to the local cops, they said no, although the skeleton had crummy teeth. No dental work at all. Now, if he'd been wealthy, he could have afforded to have his teeth fixed. If he'd been poor, welfare would have paid. If he was a union member, their medical plan would have covered it. So this fellow was probably working at a low-paying non-unionized job, but making enough to keep off public assistance. Also, since he didn't match up to any family's missing-person report, he was probably single, living alone in an apartment

or hotel. His landlord had never reported him missing, either, so most likely he was also behind on his rent and the landlord probably figured he had just skipped. But even if he had escaped his landlord, he would never have escaped the tax man. The rest was simple. I told these cops to wait until the year is up. They can go to the IRS and get a printout of all single males making less than $10,000 a year but more than the welfare ceiling who paid withholding tax in the first three quarters but not the fourth. Chances are the name of their skeleton would be on that printout (quoted in Seedman & Hellman 1974, pp. 4–5).

than standardized tests. Because they are time-consuming and expensive, they are used mainly to supplement psychological tests.

Psychological Tests

Many standardized psychological tests have good reliability and can be objectively scored and administered to large groups of subjects at the same time; as a result, they are the backbone of police screening methods. Two types of tests are included in most selection batteries: tests of cognitive or intellectual ability and tests of personality traits, integrity, or emotional stability.

Police officers tend to score in the average to above-average range on intelligence tests (Brewster & Stoloff, 2003; Poland, 1978), and intelligence tends to correlate fairly strongly with the performance of police recruits in their training programs. However, intelligence scores are only weakly related to actual police performance in the

field (Bartol, 1983; Brewster & Stoloff, 2003). These results point to the problem of predictive validity, which is a pervasive difficulty that we discuss in the next section.

The Minnesota Multiphasic Personality Inventory (MMPI; the 1989 revision of this test is called the MMPI-2) is the test of personality most often used in police screening; it is followed by the California Psychological Inventory (CPI) and the Sixteen Personality Factor Questionnaire (16PF). Evidence for the validity of these tests in screening out candidates unsuitable for police work is mixed. Several investigations support the validity of the MMPI (Bartol, 1991; Beutler, Storm, Kirkish, Scogin, & Gaines, 1985; Blau, Super, & Brady, 1993), the MMPI-2 (Detrick, Chibnall, & Rosso, 2001; Kornfeld, 2000), and the CPI (Hiatt & Hargrave, 1988; Hogan, 1971; Spielberger, Spaulding, & Ward, 1978), but others (Hogg & Wilson, 1995; Lester, Babcock, Cassissi, & Brunetta, 1980; Mills & Stratton, 1982) have questioned the general value of psychological testing of police recruits.

One personality test designed specifically to identify psychologically unsuitable law enforcement candidates is the Inwald Personality Inventory (Detrick & Chibnall, 2002; Inwald, 1992; Inwald, Knatz, & Shusman, 1983). It consists of 26 scales that tap past and present behaviors presumed to have special relevance for law enforcement applicants; examples include Lack of Assertiveness, Trouble with Law and Society, Undue Suspiciousness, and Driving Violations. This instrument demonstrates good reliability, and some research suggests that its predictive validity is significantly better than that of the MMPI (Scogin, Schumacher, Gardner, & Chaplin, 1995).

Another new test developed to screen criminal justice employees is the 50-item National Criminal Justice Officer Selection Inventory (NCJOSI). The test has several components, including problem solving, reading comprehension, writing, mathematics, and a personality screening. Although the NCJOSI is advertised as having adequate psychometric properties (http://www.iosolutions.org/examinations.html), we were not able to find published norms or measures of validity for this instrument.

An excellent study of psychological test validity was conducted by Beutler and colleagues (1985), who examined the relationship between several tests (including the MMPI and five other standardized tests) and various measures of performance for 65 subjects who had been accepted for police work. Of these officers, 22 were employed in an urban police department, 27 worked in a department associated with a major state university, and 16 were from a community college police department. The researchers gathered an extensive list of criteria on how well each officer performed on the job. Ratings were obtained from supervisors, and seven indicators of performance (e.g., different kinds of reprimands, commendations, grievances, and suspensions) were collected from each officer's personnel record. The results suggest that performance on the different criteria was predictable by psychological tests, and these predictions even generalized across different types of police departments. The MMPI profile was particularly effective in predicting reprimands, grievances, and suspensions. However, another discovery points out a difficulty in measuring police performance: Supervisors' ratings were not strongly related to criteria obtained from the personnel records (e.g., suspensions and reprimands). Beutler and colleagues (1985) suggested that supervisor bias might account for this result, and they cautioned against relying too heavily on supervisor ratings as measures of police job performance.

The Validity of Police Screening

Although experts disagree on the usefulness of psychological screening of police, they all agree that good empirical research on this topic is difficult to conduct (Gaines & Falkenberg, 1998; Inwald, 1986). Studies of **predictive validity** using actual police performance in the field as the criterion are so time-consuming and expensive that most departments cannot afford them. Instead, they settle for research that examines the relationship between screening results and performance by police recruits in police academies or training schools. This relationship is usually positive, but success or failure in training is not the criterion of real interest. One fairly inexpensive form of assessment is to gather peer ratings from trainees as they progress through their training classes together; these ratings have been shown to correlate with job retention of police officers, but not with most other measures of job performance or with supervisor ratings (Gardner, Scogin, Vipperman, & Varela, 1998).

Another problem with studies of validity is that the police candidates who do poorly on screening evaluations are eliminated from the pool of trainees and potential employees. Although this decision is reasonable, it makes it impossible to study whether predictions of poor performance by these individuals were valid.

In addition, applicants for police work, like applicants for most jobs, are likely to try to present an unrealistically positive image of themselves. They may deny or underreport symptoms of mental illness, answer questions to convey a socially desirable impression, and respond as they believe a psychologically healthy individual generally would. If evaluators fail to detect such "fake good" test-taking strategies, they may mistakenly identify some psychologically disturbed candidates as well-adjusted applicants. For these reasons, tests such as the MMPI-2 and the Inwald include various **validity scales** intended to detect test takers who are trying to fake good scores (Baer, Wetter, Nichols, Greene, & Berry, 1995). Research on these scales has shown that they are useful in detecting defensiveness and deception by some candidates for police positions (Borum & Stock, 1993).

Finally, selecting adequate criteria to measure effective police performance is notoriously difficult. Supervisor ratings are often inflated or biased by factors that are irrelevant to actual achievements or problems. In some departments, especially smaller ones, the individual police officer will be expected to perform so many diverse functions that it becomes unreasonable to expect specific cognitive abilities or psychological traits to be related in the same way to the multiple facets of performance. In addition, if we are interested in predicting which officers will act in risky, dangerous, or inappropriate ways, our predictions will be complicated by the fact that such behaviors occur only rarely in any group of people. As a consequence, these assessments will result in many erroneous predictions in which predicted events do not take place.

Fitness-for-Duty Evaluations

Another type of psychological assessment of police officers is the **fitness-for-duty evaluation**. As a result of stress, a life-threatening incident, a series of problems, injuries, or other indicators that an officer is psychologically impaired, police administrators can order an officer to undergo an evaluation of fitness to continue performing his or her duties.

These evaluations pose difficulties for everyone involved. Administrators must balance the need to protect the public from a potentially dangerous officer against the legal right of the officer to privacy and fair employment. Clinicians have to navigate a narrow path between a department's need to know the results of such an evaluation and the officer's expectation that the results will be kept confidential. Finally, the officers themselves face a dilemma: They can be honest and reveal problems that could disqualify them from service, or they can distort their responses to protect their jobs and consequently miss the opportunity for potentially beneficial treatment.

Two different models of fitness-for-duty evaluations have been used. In the first, departments use the same psychologist to perform the evaluation and to provide whatever treatment is necessary for the officer. In other departments, the psychologist who evaluates the officer does not provide any treatment; this avoids an ethical conflict between keeping the therapy confidential and disclosing an officer's psychological functioning to supervisors. The second approach is endorsed in the "Guidelines for Fitness-for-Duty Evaluations" distributed by the Police Psychological Services Section of the International Association for Chiefs of Police (Psychological Fitness-for-Duty Evaluation Guidelines, 2004). This is the closest thing to an official position on this question that is available. In-depth discussions of ethical dilemmas facing police psychologists are also provided by Dietz and Reese (1986) and Super (1997).

Training of Police Officers

Once candidates have been selected, they participate in a course of police training that usually lasts several months. Many major American cities require 24 weeks of training, with 40 hours of training per week. Smaller jurisdictions have training programs averaging 14 to 16 weeks. An increasing number of departments are now requiring that police officers complete some amount of college education.

Two types of criticism of police training programs are common. One is that after rigorous selection procedures, few trainees fail the training. For example, of 1091 recruits who began the training program in New York City in 1987, only about 6% dropped out or were dismissed for a variety of reasons, including physical or academic inadequacies (Nix, 1987). In a smaller sample of 93 cadets who began training in 2003, only about 10% either dropped out or failed mandatory academic or physical endurance exercises (Phillips, 2004). Advocates count this rate of success as an indication that the initial selection procedures were valid, but critics complain that graduation is too easy, especially given the burnout rate of on-the-job police officers.

A second criticism is that there is insufficient training in the field, as well as a lack of close supervision of trainees during the time they spend on patrol. The limited time that trainees spend with veteran training officers on patrol may give them a false sense of security (Beck, 1987) and deprive them of opportunities to learn different ways of responding to citizens from various cultural backgrounds or ways to resolve disputes other than through arrests.

However, another side to this story, which we discuss later, argues against the benefits of extensive supervision by senior officers. It is possible that such contacts teach new officers to be cynical about law enforcement, to "cut corners" in their duties, and, above all, to identify almost exclusively with the norms of police organizations rather than with the values of the larger and more diverse society (Tuohy, Wrennal, McQueen, & Stradling, 1993).

Training in Crisis Intervention

The police are often asked to maintain public order and defuse volatile situations involving persons who are mentally ill, intoxicated, angry, or motivated by politically extreme views. Because of the instability of the participants in such disputes, they pose great risks to the police as well as to bystanders. In this section, we examine three types of crisis situations to which police are often called: incidents involving mentally ill citizens, family disturbances, and the taking of hostages. Psychologists have made important contributions to each of these areas by conducting research, designing interventions, and training the police in crisis intervention skills.

Interactions with Mentally Ill Citizens

For the past two decades, several factors have forced mentally ill persons from residential mental health facilities where they formerly lived into a variety of noninstitutional settings, including halfway houses, community mental health centers, hospital emergency rooms, "flophouses," the streets, and local jails. Deinstitutionalization itself is an admirable goal; spending much of one's life in an institution breeds dependency, despair, and hopelessness. People with mental illness should receive treatment in the least restrictive environment possible, allowing them to function in and contribute to their local communities. However, the evidence on how people with mental illness have fared suggests that deinstitutionalization in the United States has not achieved its lofty goals. The problems stem from two fundamental difficulties.

First, even under ideal conditions, severe mental illness is difficult to treat effectively. The impairments associated with disorders such as schizophrenia, chronic substance abuse, and serious mood disorders can be profound, and relapses are common. For example, fewer than a third of nonhospitalized persons with schizophrenia are employed at any given time. Second, sufficient funding for alternative, noninstitutional care has not been provided in the United States. As a result, community-based treatment of severely mentally ill persons seldom takes place under proper circumstances, despite the fact that the economic costs of severe mental disorders rival those of diseases such as cancer and heart disease and could be reduced considerably if proper care were provided.

The deinstitutionalization movement resulted from four historical forces: (1) advances in antipsychotic medications, which first became available in the 1950s, that enabled persons to function better outside of hospitals; (2) increased legal restrictions on the involuntary commitment of the mentally ill to hospitals; (3) reductions in the length of the average psychiatric hospitalization; and (4) decreased public funding for mental health programs throughout the 1980s and 1990s (Kiesler, 1982; Teplin, 1984). The rise of the homeless population, among whom problems of substance abuse and mental illness are frequent and severe (Fischer & Breakey, 1991; McNiel & Binder, 2005), is also linked to declining availability of publicly supported mental health treatment.

One consequence of deinstitutionalization is that supervising people with mental illness has become a primary responsibility for the police. In medium-size to large police departments, about 7% of all police contacts involve citizens with mental illness, and it is estimated that the police are responsible for up to one-third of all mental health referrals to hospital emergency rooms. In one survey, nine out of ten police officers had responded to a call involving a mentally ill individual in the past month, and eight out of ten had responded to two or more such calls in the same time period (Borum, Deane, Steadman, & Morrissey, 1998). Another survey found that 33% of all calls made to a police district in a one-year period were for mental-health-related situations (Steadman, Deane, Borum, & Morrissey, 2000). Research on how the police handle mentally ill persons has concentrated on the discretion that officers use in crisis incidents. Will they arrest the citizen, or will they have the person hospitalized? Will they offer on-the-spot counseling, refer the citizen to a mental health agency, or return the person to a safe place, to relatives, or to friends?

Early research on these questions suggested that the police were reluctant to arrest the mentally ill or to require their emergency hospitalization unless their behavior presented an obvious danger to themselves or others (Bittner, 1967; Lamb, Weinberger, & DeCuir, 2002). These findings are consistent with research on the use of discretion by police in general, which suggests that they tend to avoid an arrest in minor incidents unless the suspect is disrespectful to the officer, the complaining party prefers that an arrest be made, or the officer perceives the benefits of arresting the subject to outweigh the perceived costs.

Other studies, however, have shown that the police find the handling of mentally ill citizens to be among the most difficult cases they encounter. As a result, many may prefer arrest over hospitalization when dealing with mentally ill persons (Matthews, 1970), especially if they believe there will be less red tape in completing an arrest than in finalizing a hospitalization.

The best research on the question of how frequently mentally ill persons are arrested by the police has been conducted by Linda Teplin, a sociologist at Northwestern University. Teplin (1984) assembled a team of psychology graduate students and trained them to observe and code the interactions of police officers with citizens over a 14-month period in two precincts in a large U.S. city. Observers used a symptom checklist and a global rating of mental disorder to assess mental illness in the citizens observed. Teplin studied 884 nontraffic encounters involving a total of 1798 citizens, of whom 506 were considered suspects for arrest by the police. Arrest was relatively infrequent, occurring in only 12.4% of the encounters; in terms of individuals (some incidents involved several suspects), 29.2% were arrested. The observers classified only 30 (5.9%) of the 506 suspects as mentally ill. The arrest rate for these 30 persons was 46.7%, compared to an arrest rate of 27.9% for suspects who were not rated as having mental disorders. Mentally ill suspects were more likely to be arrested regardless of the type or seriousness of the incident involved.

Teplin concluded that the mentally ill were being "criminalized" and that this outcome was the result not only of the provocative nature of their psychological symptoms but also of the inadequacies of the mental health system in treating such persons. As a result, the criminal justice system has become a "default option" for patients whom hospitals refuse to accept for treatment because they are too dangerous, are not dangerous enough, or suffer a disorder that the hospital does not treat.

Not surprisingly, the rate of severe mental disorders in jail populations, often combined with diagnoses of substance abuse and personality disorder in the same individuals, is alarmingly high (Teplin, 1994; Teplin, Abram, & McClelland, 1996).

Another study examined police responses to incidents involving individuals with mental illness in three jurisdictions differing in the level of mental health training that police received. Findings suggested that the jurisdictions with specialized mental health training were especially effective in crisis intervention and made fewer arrests. However, the officers' decisions about how to handle the situation depended on the overall resources available; jurisdictions with mobile crisis units were able to transport mentally ill individuals to treatment locations to ensure that they obtained treatment, whereas all that those without crisis units could do was refer individuals for treatment (Steadman, Deane, Borum, & Morrissey, 2000).

The importance of evaluating how police interact with individuals with mental illness is underscored by the prevalence of mentally ill offenders in prisons and jails. Estimates suggest that 16% of state prison inmates, 7% of federal prison inmates, and 16% of those in local jails suffer from mental illness. Offenders in this survey were identified as mentally ill if they reported either a mental condition or an overnight stay in a mental hospital. In addition, about 16% of individuals on probation cited symptoms of a mental condition or reported a history of hospitalization due to a mental illness at some point in their lifetime (Ditton, 1999).

The jailing of mentally ill persons does not reflect improper behavior by the police as much as a failure of public policy regarding the treatment and protection of people with chronic mental illness. More and better training of police officers in the recognition and short-term management of mentally ill persons is necessary, but an adequate resolution of this problem requires better organization and funding of special services for those with serious mental illness (Abram & Teplin, 1991).

One possibility is to increase the use of **jail diversion programs**, in which mentally ill individuals who have been arrested and jailed are considered for supervised release to the community, where they will presumably have better access to treatment and support services. One evaluation of a jail diversion program found that two months after arrest, approximately one in five diverted participants (20%) had been rearrested. In the same time period, about 50% of nondiverted subjects either had been arrested or had never been released from jail (Steadman, Cocozza, & Veysey, 1999). More recently, an evaluation of a jail diversion program for offenders with mental illness found that diverting the individuals to crisis stabilization units rather than incarcerating them reduced recidivism 59%, down from 70% to 11%. Although recidivism was slightly higher a year later (18%), the program appeared to be significantly effective in maintaining reduced rates of reoffending (Buchan, 2005).

Domestic Disturbances

When violence erupts in a family or between a couple, the police are often the first people called to the scene. What will they encounter when they arrive? Are the participants armed? Are they intoxicated or psychologically disturbed? How much violence has already taken place? What is certain is that responding to family disturbances is one of the most dangerous activities that police perform. The level of danger involved when intervening in a domestic dispute is not surprising, considering that people "are more likely to be killed, physically assaulted, hit, beat up, slapped, or spanked in their own homes by other family members than anywhere else, or by anyone else, in our society" (Gelles & Cornell, 1985, p. 12).

The amount of time police devote to domestic disturbances exceeds the time they spend investigating murders, rapes, and aggravated assaults combined (Wilt, Bannon, Breedlove, Sandker, & Michaelson, 1977), and about 25% of police deaths and assaults on officers occur during police intervention in family disturbances (Ketterman & Kravitz, 1978). Because of the risks and limited rewards for involvement (e.g., victims may decline to cooperate or to prosecute and may even be antagonistic toward police officers), police officers are often reluctant to get involved in "domestic disturbances." Not only are there personal risks to the officers, but many police officers—like many citizens—accept certain myths about the nature of family violence. Empirical research is shedding new light on the following five false assumptions, which were first described by Gelles and Cornell (1985).

MYTH 1: FAMILY VIOLENCE IS RARE

It is difficult to obtain accurate statistics on child abuse and other forms of family violence because no agency systematically gathers such data. But family violence is not a rare phenomenon; it is estimated that 14% of children in the United States are abused within their families each year and that the lifetime prevalence of spouse abuse may be as high as 50% of married couples. Nor is family violence exclusively or even largely restricted to male perpetrators. Recent surveys in both the United States and New Zealand suggest that women are as likely as men to be violent toward their partners (Magdol, Moffit, Caspi, Newman, Fagan, & Silva, 1997). (We discuss spousal abuse in Chapter 13 and child abuse in Chapter 14.)

The question of how gender affects partner violence reveals an important aspect of the approaches used in researching such problems: The answers will vary—sometimes to a great extent—depending on the types of individuals who participate in the research. The initial studies of family violence relied on *clinical samples* of women who sought physical or psychological help for the injuries they suffered, or male batterers who had been ordered into treatment or arrested because of their violence. Not surprisingly, these studies suggested that male perpetrators far outnumbered females.

More recent studies have used *community surveys* of large cohorts of people, selected at random rather than because they have been referred for assistance or charged with an offense. These studies suggest that the rates of partner violence are substantial among both male and female abusers. Each of these approaches addresses a slightly different question (Magdol et al., 1997). If one is

interested in studying the consequences of especially severe partner violence, clinical samples are to be preferred. If one is trying to outline the epidemiological patterns and general risk factors for partner violence, then community surveys are likely to yield the more trustworthy answers.

MYTH 2: FAMILY VIOLENCE IS CONFINED TO MENTALLY DISTURBED OR SICK PEOPLE

When we hear or read that a woman has plunged her 2-year-old son into a tub of boiling water or that a man has had sexual intercourse with his 6-year-old daughter, our first reaction might be, "That person is terribly sick!" The portrayal of family violence in the mass media often suggests that "normal people" do not harm family members. In reality, however, family violence is too widespread to be adequately explained by mental illness, although perpetrators of serious domestic violence often experience depression or personality disorder (Andrews, Foster, Capaldi, & Hops, 2000).

MYTH 3: FAMILY VIOLENCE IS CONFINED TO POOR PEOPLE

Violence and abuse are more common among families of lower socioeconomic status, but they are by no means limited to such families. Among middle-class couples seeking a divorce, 23% cited violence as one of the reasons for wanting to end the marriage (Levinger, 1966). Nonetheless, unemployment, inadequate education, and sparse social support remain substantial risk factors for family violence (Magdol et al., 1997).

MYTH 4: BATTERED WOMEN LIKE BEING HIT; OTHERWISE, THEY WOULD LEAVE

This belief reflects two myths in one. First, as noted earlier, family violence is perpetuated by both males and females, although violence by men against women tends to produce more serious injuries. But faced with the fact that many female victims of partner violence do not leave even the most serious of abusers, people seek some type of rational explanation.

A common belief is that women who remain in violent relationships must somehow provoke or even enjoy the violence. This form of "blaming the victim" (see Chapter 13) is not a useful explanation. The concept of **learned helplessness** better explains why so many women endure such extreme violence for so long (Walker, 1979). Psychologist Lenore Walker observed that women who suffer continued physical violence at the hands of their partners have a more negative self-concept than women whose marriages are free from violence. She proposed that the repeated beatings leave these women feeling that they won't be able to protect themselves from further assaults and that they are incapable of controlling the events that go on around them (Gelles & Cornell, 1985). Under such circumstances, they give in to the belief that there is nothing they can do to change their circumstances and that any effort at starting a new life not only will be futile but also will lead to even more violence against them.

MYTH 5: ALCOHOL AND DRUG ABUSE ARE THE REAL CAUSES OF VIOLENCE IN THE HOME

"He beat up his children because he was drunk" is another popular explanation of domestic violence, and most studies do find a considerable relationship between drinking and violence (Gerber, Ganz, Lichter, Williams, & McCloskey, 2005; Magdol et al., 1997; Wolfgang, 1958), especially among male perpetrators. Perhaps as many as half of the incidents of domestic violence in the past have involved alcohol or drugs (Gelles & Cornell, 1985); in the case of violence directed toward a spouse, both the offender and the victim may have been drinking copiously before the violence.

This observation appears to be as accurate today as it was 20 years ago. In a recent longitudinal study considering the relationships among drinking, alcohol-related problems, and recurring incidences of partner violence over a 5-year period (Caetano, McGrath, Ramisetty-Mikler, & Field, 2005), investigators found that the rate of domestic violence among men who drink more than four drinks at a time at least once per month was three times higher than that among men who abstain or drink less often and less frequently. This pattern also held for women. But does the substance cause the violence?

Some assume that alcohol is a disinhibitor of behavior and that it therefore facilitates the expression of violence. There is certainly some truth to this. However, reactions in those who have been drinking are also a function of social expectations and "blaming the bottle" ("I was drunk and didn't know what I was doing"). Furthermore, those who have trouble controlling their aggressive behavior while drinking can certainly anticipate this and take steps to manage their risk (e.g., drinking in moderation or not at all).

Because of their danger and frequency, family disturbances pose a difficult challenge for the police. Can these encounters be handled in a manner that protects potential victims, reduces repeat offenses, and limits the risk of injury to responding officers?

The first project on crisis intervention with domestic disputes was developed by Morton Bard, a psychologist in New York City. Bard (1969; Bard & Berkowitz, 1967) trained a special group of New York City police officers (nine black and nine white volunteers) in family disturbance intervention skills for a project located in West Harlem. The month-long training program focused on teaching officers how to intervene in family disputes without making arrests. The training emphasized the psychology of family conflict and sensitivity to cross-racial differences. Role playing was used to acquaint officers with techniques for calming antagonists, lowering tensions, reducing hostilities, and preventing physical violence.

For two years after the training, all family crisis calls in the experimental precinct were answered by the specially trained officers. They performed 1375 interventions with 962 families. Evaluation of the project concentrated on six desired outcomes: (1) a decrease in family disturbance calls, (2) a drop in repeat calls from the same families, (3) a reduction of homicides in the precinct, (4) a decline in homicides among family members, (5) a reduction of assaults in the precinct, and (6) a decrease in injuries to police officers. But results indicated that the intervention affected only two of these outcomes. Fewer assaults occurred in the precinct, and none of the trained officers was injured (compared with three police officers who were not part of the program but were injured while responding to family disturbances).

Evaluations of similar domestic crisis units in other cities have yielded mixed results (Pearce & Snortum, 1983). Specially trained officers typically rate their resolutions of disturbance calls more favorably than do officers without special training. However, the long-term effects of the special interventions are less positive; sometimes they lead to an increase in repeat callers, but in other cases this effect is not observed.

In recent years, as more is learned about domestic violence, crisis intervention and other nonarrest alternatives for resolving family disturbances have come in for increased criticism. Women's rights groups have filed lawsuits against law enforcement agencies that have not arrested seriously assaultive domestic batterers. These critics maintain that when actual assaults have taken place in a family, arrest is the most appropriate response to protect victims and reduce future violence (Dutton, 1987).

In response to these concerns and to their own evaluation of the problem of domestic assaults, many police departments have shifted policies and now advocate the arrest and prosecution of domestic batterers. Is this a better alternative than crisis intervention or counseling?

The first well-controlled evaluation of the effects of arresting domestic batterers was the Minneapolis Domestic Violence Experiment (Sherman & Berk, 1984). In this experiment, police officers' responses to domestic violence were randomly assigned to be (1) arresting the suspected batterer, (2) ordering one of the parties to leave the residence, or (3) giving the couple immediate advice on reducing their violence. Judging on the basis of official police records and interviews with victims, subsequent offending was reduced by almost 50% when the suspect was arrested, a significantly better outcome than that achieved by the two nonarrest alternatives. These findings quickly changed public and expert opinion about the value of arresting domestic batterers, and soon many cities had replaced informal counseling with immediate arrest as their response to domestic violence cases.

Since the initial Minneapolis experiment, at least five other jurisdictions—Charlotte, Colorado Springs, Miami, Omaha, and Milwaukee—have conducted experiments designed to test whether arresting batterers is the best deterrent to repeated domestic violence. The results of these projects, collectively known as the Spouse Assault Replication Program, have been mixed. In some cases, arrests reduced recidivism; in other cases, they increased recidivism; and in a few instances, the effect was different depending on whether official arrest records or victim interviews were considered (Brame, 2000; Garner, Fagan, & Maxwell, 1995). These inconsistencies may be attributed to differences in methodologies and analyses across the various sites. However, a more comprehensive analysis integrating the data from all five sites revealed that arresting the violent partner significantly reduced future victimization independent of other criminal justice sanctions or individual factors (Maxwell, Garner, & Fagan, 2002). Thus, even though one large-scale study supports the conclusion that arrests reduce recidivism, the search continues for factors that could resolve the inconsistent results. Another caveat to those interpreting these findings is that deterrent effects associated with arrest tend to diminish over time (Mills, 1998).

What conclusion should we reach about the value of arrest as a deterrent to future spouse abuse? At this point, the jury is still out. Deterrence is achieved in some cases but is too inconsistent an outcome to justify the enthusiastic claims that are often made for arrest programs.

Questions about how best to quell domestic violence illustrate an interesting phenomenon often encountered with social reforms. Social problems and well-intentioned efforts to modify them tend to revolve in cycles rather than moving in a straight line toward progress and increased sophistication. A reform in vogue today, aimed at correcting some social evil, often fosters its own difficulties or inequities and ultimately becomes itself a problem in need of reformation.

Crisis intervention was originally preferred over arrest as a more psychologically sophisticated response by police to family disturbances. However, this intervention fell out of favor and was criticized as an inadequate response to serious domestic violence. Official arrest was then championed as the most effective intervention, but as additional data are gathered about its effectiveness, new questions are raised about whether arrest and prosecution are the best answers for domestic violence.

Hostage Negotiation

Although hostage incidents are at least as old as the description in Genesis of the abduction and rescue of Abraham's nephew Lot, most experts agree that the massacre of 11 Israeli athletes taken hostage and murdered by Palestinian terrorists at the 1972 Munich Olympic Games spurred the creation of new law enforcement techniques for resolving hostage incidents. Developed through extensive collaboration among military, law enforcement, and behavioral science experts, these hostage negotiation techniques are still being refined as more is learned about the conditions that lead to effective negotiations.

One study of 120 hostage-related incidents found that the perpetrator used a barricade to separate himself and his hostage from police in over half of the incidents (55.8%) (Feldmann, 2001), creating a complicated situation for negotiation strategies because police could not be fully aware of the perpetrator's activities and intentions. Soskis and Van Zandt (1986) have identified four types of hostage incidents that differ in their psychological dynamics and techniques for resolution (see also Gist & Perry, 1985; Hatcher, Mohandie, Turner, & Gelles, 1998).

More than half of hostage incidents involve *persons suffering a mental disorder* or experiencing serious personal or family problems (Feldmann, 2001). In these situations, the hostage takers often have a history of depression, schizophrenia, or other serious mental illness, or they harbor feelings of chronic powerlessness, anger, or despondency that

compel a desperate act. Disturbed hostage takers pose a high risk of suicide, which they sometimes accomplish by killing their hostage(s) and then themselves. In other situations, they try to force the police to kill them; such victim-precipitated deaths are termed **suicide by cop**. This underscores the importance of incorporating mental health consultants' expertise into the effort to peacefully negotiate and resolve these hostage situations.

A second common type of hostage situation involves the *trapped criminal*. Here, a person who is trapped by the police while committing a crime takes, as a hostage, anyone who is available and then uses the hostage to bargain for freedom. Because these incidents are unplanned and driven by panic, they tend to be, especially at their early stages, very dangerous to the victims and the police.

The third type of hostage situation, also involving criminals, is the *takeover of prisons* by inmates who capture prison guards or take other inmates as hostages. In these incidents, the passage of time tends to work against nonviolent resolution because the hostage takers are violent people, working as an undisciplined group with volatile leadership.

The fourth type of hostage taking, and the one that is most widely publicized, is **terrorism**. Terrorists use violence or the threat of violence "to achieve a social, political, or religious aim in a way that does not obey the traditional rules of war" (Soskis & Van Zandt, 1986, p. 424; see also Lake, 2002).

Terrorists usually make careful plans for the kidnapping of hostages or the taking of property, and they are typically motivated by extremist political or religious goals. These goals may require their own deaths as a necessary but "honorable" sacrifice for a higher cause. For this reason, terrorists are less responsive to negotiation techniques that appeal to rational themes of self-preservation. Therefore, new ways of responding to this type of terrorism must be sought. One terrorism specialist suggested that a country has three options in responding. At the lowest level of response, it may increase its internal security to prevent further attacks. A slightly more proactive response may be to attempt to capture or eliminate the terrorists in a limited operation targeting the leaders of the terrorist organizations. Lastly, a country may implement a military retaliation with the aims of eradicating the terrorists and their organizations and deterring future attacks from other groups (Lake, 2002).

The 1990s saw an outbreak of right-wing domestic terrorism and sieges in the United States. In the most visible of these incidents (e.g., the mass death of the Branch Davidian sect under the leadership of David Koresh; the three-month standoff between the FBI and the antigovernment Freemen group in Montana), conventional negotiation techniques did not prove effective. The reasons why negotiations were not successful are not clear; the American public seems divided between those who believe the government was too aggressive and those who think officials were too restrained in their handling of these incidents. This remains true for the U.S. government's response to the more recent attacks on the World Trade Towers and the Pentagon on September 11, 2001; again, the nation is divided between support for the war on terror and opposition to it.

The new millennium has brought additional forms of terrorism that redefine what it means to be "taken hostage." For example, **bioterrorism**, in which biological "weapons" such as viruses and bacteria are released or threatened, could hold far larger populations hostage than conventional guns or bombs. One study examined public distress following the anthrax-related incidents that occurred shortly after the September 11, 2001, attacks. Findings suggested that even for individuals not actually exposed to the anthrax, initial media exposure to the anthrax attacks was a significant predictor of distress. Levels of distress were especially high when the attacks were first detected (Dougall, Hayward, & Baum, 2005). Effective countermeasures to such threats require new collaborations among law enforcement officials, public health experts, and behavioral scientists.

Successful hostage negotiation requires an understanding of the dynamics of hostage incidents so that these dynamics can be manipulated by the negotiator to contain and ultimately end the incident with a minimum of violence (Schlossberg &

Freeman, 1974). For example, in many hostage situations, a strong sense of psychological togetherness and mutual dependency develops between the hostages and their kidnappers. These feelings emerge from (1) the close, constant contact between the participants, (2) their shared feelings of fear and danger, and (3) the strong feelings of powerlessness induced by prolonged captivity. This relationship, dubbed the **Stockholm syndrome**, involves positive feelings by the hostages toward their kidnappers as well as reciprocated positive feelings by the kidnappers toward their hostages. Hostage negotiators try to take advantage of this dynamic by becoming a part of it themselves. First attempting to become a psychological member of the hostage group who nevertheless maintains important ties to the outside world, negotiators will then try to use their outside contacts to persuade terrorists to bring the crisis to a peaceful end.

Successful negotiators make contact with hostage takers in as nonthreatening a manner as possible and then maintain communication with them for as long as necessary. Generally, the negotiator attempts to isolate the hostage takers from any "outside" communication in order to foster their dependency on the negotiator as the crucial link with other people. Once communication is established, the negotiator tries to reduce the hostage takers' fear and tension so that they will be more willing to agree to a reasonable solution. Negotiators structure the situation in ways that maximize predictability and calm. For example, they may offer help with any medical needs the hostage group has, thereby fostering positive components of the Stockholm syndrome. Finally, through gradual prompting and reinforcement, the negotiator tries to encourage behaviors that promote negotiation progress. Examples of such behaviors include increased conversation between the negotiator and the hostage taker, the passage of deadlines without threatened violence taking place, and less violent content and fewer threats in the speech of hostage takers.

The term *Stockholm syndrome* derives from a 1973 event in which hostages held in a Swedish bank developed a close emotional attachment to their captors (Eckholm, 1985). Hostages may come to sympathize with the lawbreakers and even adopt, at least temporarily, their captors' ideological views. The behavior of Patricia Hearst, a newspaper heiress who was kidnapped in 1974 and later helped her captors rob a bank, has been explained through this syndrome. It was also seen in 1985, when 39 passengers from TWA Flight 847 were detained as hostages for 17 days by hijackers in Beirut. Allyn Conwell, the spokesperson for the hostages in the hijacking, was criticized for his statements expressing "profound sympathy" for his captors' Shiite position, but he explicitly denied that he was influenced by the Stockholm syndrome (Eckholm, 1985).

According to Martin Symonds, a New York psychiatrist and expert on terrorism, the Stockholm syndrome (which is one of several that is known to form among hostages, hostage takers, and negotiators) is more likely to emerge when the hostages are purely "instrumental" victims of no genuine concern to the terrorists except as means to obtain leverage over a third party. In such situations, the captors say, "We'll let you go if our demands are met," and the captives begin "to misperceive the terrorist as the person who is trying to keep you alive" (Symonds, quoted in Eckholm, 1985, p. 6). For this reason, it is especially important for the police to determine the motivations of any hostage takers, as well as their specific goals.

Increasingly, police departments have developed special crisis/hostage negotiation teams that usually include a psychologist as a consultant or adviser (Hatcher et al., 1998). In this capacity, the psychologist helps select officers for the team, provides on-the-scene advice during hostage incidents, profiles the hostage taker's personality, and assesses the behavior of the hostages themselves.

Do psychologist-consultants make a difference? In the one study evaluating the effects of psychological consultation in hostage incidents, Butler, Leitenberg, and Fuselier (1993) found that using a psychologist resulted in fewer injuries and deaths to hostages and more peaceful surrenders by hostage takers.

The Police Officer's Job

In the eyes of most citizens, the job of the police officer is to catch criminals and enforce the law, just as the officers on *America's Most Wanted* and *Law and Order* do weekly on TV. But the police are responsible for more functions than these. The major duties of the police are divided into three general areas:

- *Enforcing the law*, which includes investigating complaints, arresting suspects, and attempting to prevent crime. Although most citizens perceive law enforcement to be the most important function of the police, it accounts for only about 10% of police activity.
- *Maintaining order*, which includes intervening in family and neighborhood disputes and keeping traffic moving, noise levels down, rowdy persons off the streets, and disturbances of the peace to a minimum. It is estimated that three out of every ten requests for police officers involve this type of activity.
- *Providing services*, such as giving assistance in medical and psychological emergencies, finding missing persons, helping stranded motorists, escorting funerals, and rescuing cats from trees.

Most studies indicate that the largest percentage of police activities fall into the third category. According to one review (Klockars, 1985), the typical day's duty for a police officer in the high-crime areas of three of the nation's largest cities (Boston, Chicago, and Washington, D.C.) did not see the arrest of a single person!

Should the police spend so much time on community services? The major objections to community services are that they waste police resources and distract the police from the crucial roles of law enforcement and public protection for which they are specially trained. In the 1990s, special initiatives were taken to increase the time police commit to crime-fighting activities. Federal legislation providing funds for cities to hire thousands of new police officers was justified with the promise that additional police would lead to more arrests of criminals. And urban police forces have found that concentrating more police officers in high-crime areas and instructing them to arrest all lawbreakers (even for relatively minor offenses such as loitering and public drunkenness) have resulted in lowered crime rates. This **zero tolerance** policy demands that police officers concentrate more time on apprehension and arrest activities. Although it has been credited with bringing about reductions in crime, the zero tolerance policy has also been linked to increases in citizen complaints and lawsuits against the police (Greene, 1999). For instance, a 12-year-old boy in Florida was hand-cuffed after he stomped in a puddle and splashed his classmates, and a 13-year-old boy in Viriginia was suspended and required to attend drug aware-ness classes after accepting a breath mint from a classmate (Koch, 2000).

There are two advantages to the police continuing to provide an array of social services. First, short of spending massive amounts of money to train and employ a new cadre of community service workers, no feasible alternative to using the police in this capacity exists. Second, by providing these services, the police create a positive identity in the community that carries goodwill, respect, and cooperation over to their crime-fighting tasks.

These "side effects" also serve as a buffer that gives the police opportunities to interact with people who are not behaving criminally, thereby reducing the tendency of police to develop cynical, suspicious attitudes toward others. They also may encourage citizens to perceive the police in a less threatening and less hostile manner.

Stress and the Police

Not only is the police officer's job composed of mul-tiple duties, but the requirements of these duties may lead to feelings of stress, to personal conflicts, and eventually to psychological problems. Scores of books, technical reports, and journal articles have been written on the causes and treatment of police

stress (e.g., Alkus & Padesky, 1983; Ford, 1998; Harpold & Feemster, 2002; Kirschman, 1997; White, Lawrence, Biggerstaff, & Grubb, 1985), and entire Web sites (e.g., the Police Stressline: www.stressline.com, http://www.geocities.com/ stressline_com/police_stressline.html) are now devoted to this topic.

All of this begs the question: Is police work more stressful than other occupations? Although the stereotype of police work is that it must be extremely stressful because it entails a constant threat of danger and exposure to criminals, surpris-ingly little is known about whether policing is inherently stressful. The National Institute on Workers' Compensation lists police work among the "ten toughest jobs" (Miller, 1988, p. 43), but one large-scale survey of Australian police officers indicated that police felt no more stress as a group than the average citizen or college student (Hart, Wearing, & Headey, 1995). Whether this same finding would characterize American police offi-cers is not certain. Also, the reasons for the rela-tively high level of psychological well-being reported by these officers are not clear. It might be because most of them were males, and males report fewer stressful feelings than females. It might be due to a reluctance of police officers to admit to feeling stressed. Or it could reflect the fact that pre-employment screening of police can-didates eliminated easily stressed individuals.

Regardless of this survey's findings, no one would suggest that a police officer's job is easy. Certain factors make the occupation particularly difficult. One problem that comes with being a police officer is the "life in a fishbowl" phenome-non. Officers are constantly on public view, and they realize that their every act is being evaluated. Often they perform their job differently than the public wants, and they are then likely to hear an outcry of protest and condemnation (Lefkowitz, 1975). Police are sensitive to public criticism, and this criticism also leads their spouses and children to feel isolated and segregated.

Several investigators have divided the stress of police work into different categories according to the sources of the stress or the type of problem involved

(Harpold & Feemster, 2002; Ostrov, 1986; Spielberger, Westberry, Grier, & Greenfield, 1980). Project Shield, a large-scale study conducted by the National Institute of Justice, asked police officers to respond to a series of questions about the negative effects of stress in several different categories, including psychological, physical, behavioral, and organizational public health (Harpold & Feemster, 2002). Results from the surveys showed that officers reported an increased vulnerability to alcohol abuse and heightened levels of anxiety within the first 5 years of employment. In addition, approximately one percent of officers in the study reported having contemplated suicide at some point. Compared to the general population, officers reported more experiences of physical and medical problems over their lifetime, including cancer, heart disease, hypertension, acute migraine headaches, reproductive problems, chronic back problems, foot problems, and insomnia. They also reported increased behavioral problems in their personal lives, such as physical abuse of their spouses and children, as a result of job-related stress. Officers reported the highest levels of organizational, or job-related, stress when faced with making split-second decisions with serious consequences, when hearing media reports of police wrongdoing, when working with administrators who did not support the officers, and when not having enough time for personal or family responsibilities.

Another study (Solomon and Horn, 1986) examined the effects of shooting incidents in the line of duty with 86 police officers. These officers, 53% of whom had been involved in a shooting in which a person was killed, were attending a three-day workshop on post-shooting-incident trauma at the time. Participants were asked to report whether they experienced 18 different postincident reactions. More than half reported a heightened sense of danger (58%) after the incident, many reported feeling angry (49%), feeling isolated or withdrawn (45%), having difficulty sleeping (46%), experiencing flashbacks or intruding thoughts about the incident (44%), emotional numbing (43%), depression (42%), and alienation (40%). Other common reactions after an incident included

guilt or remorse (37%), nightmares (34%), family problems (27%), substance abuse (14%), and suicidal thoughts (11%). In addition, participants reported several perceptual distortions, including perceiving the event to occur in slow motion (67%), perceiving the event to occur in rapid motion (15%), and tunnel vision during the event (37%).

The leading example of a questionnaire designed to measure police stress is the Police Stress Survey (PSS; Spielberger et al., 1980), which in its original form consisted of 60 items. Then the PSS was revised to include an additional 25 items derived from open-ended interviews with police officers (White, Lawrence, Biggerstaff, & Grubb, 1985). The Police Daily Hassles Scale (PDHS) is another measure used to assess police stress levels. It is divided into the Organizational Hassles and the Operational Hassles subscales to detect stress stemming from different sources (Hart, Wearing, & Headey, 1993). The following three categories of stress are most commonly encountered by the police:

1. *Physical and psychological threats.* Included here are events related to the unique demands of police work, such as using force, being physically attacked, confronting aggressive people or grisly crime scenes, and engaging in high-speed chases. Danger can emerge from even apparently innocuous circumstances. Three police officers in Inkster, Michigan, made a routine call at a motel to serve a warrant for writing a bad check. They were met with a fusillade of gunfire; all three were killed. Patrolman Gary Lorenzen was one of the first officers to discover the bodies. "I haven't had anyone here I could talk to—I'm hurting like a son of a bitch inside but I have to be strong for the other officers," he said (Clancy, 1987, p. 1A).

2. *Evaluation systems.* These stressors include the ineffectiveness of the judicial system, court leniency with criminals, negative press accounts of the police, the public's rejection of the police, and put-downs and mistreatment of police officers in the courts. This source of stress is a major problem in countries other than the United States. For example, in France, where the public is

particularly contemptuous of the police, the rate of suicide is 35 for every 100,000 officers, a rate exceeding that in most major U.S. cities. However, even in the United States, many more police officers die as a result of suicide than of homicide.

3. *Organizational problems and lack of support.* Examples of these stressors include bureaucratic hassles, inadequate leadership by police administrators, weak support and confused feedback from supervisors, lack of clarity about job responsibilities, and poor job performance by fellow officers. In the survey of Australian police cited earlier (Hart et al., 1995), as well as in other studies (Violanti & Aron, 1994; Brown & Campbell, 1990), organizational problems proved to be one of the most important sources of stress—more influential even than physical danger, bloody crime scenes, and public scrutiny.

Arresting a high-risk suspect after a car chase

A certain degree of stress is inevitable, given the demands placed on the police. Yet police officers often find it hard to admit that the stressful nature of their job is affecting them. A stigma exists about admitting a need for professional help. Too often, police officers believe that if they acknowledge personal problems or ask for assistance, they will be judged unprofessional or inadequate.

These fears are not entirely unreasonable. Officers found to have psychological problems are sometimes belittled by other officers or are relieved of their weapons and badges and assigned to limited-duty tasks. Fear of these consequences induces some officers to hide the fact that they are suffering from job-related stress.

Stressful working conditions also lead to **burnout**, which has been defined as "a syndrome of emotional exhaustion, depersonalization, and reduced personal accomplishment that can occur among individuals who work with people in some capacity" (Maslach & Jackson, 1984, p. 134). Emotional exhaustion reflects feelings of being emotionally overextended and "drained" by one's contact with other people. Depersonalization frequently takes the form of a callous or insensitive response to other people, particularly crime victims and others requesting police assistance.

Reduced personal accomplishment is manifested in a decline in one's feeling of competence at the end of a day's work with other people (Maslach & Jackson, 1984). Burnout also affects behavior off the job. In Jackson and Maslach's (1982) study of police officers and their families, emotional exhaustion was found more likely than any other factor to affect behavior at home. Police officers were described by their wives as coming home upset, angry, tense, and anxious. No wonder that high rates of substance abuse, domestic battering, and divorce are regarded as occupational hazards of police work.

Burnout may also result from working many years at the same job. Patrol officers sometimes speak of the "seven-year syndrome." Initially, officers are eager and anxious about their job performance. The tasks are interesting and challenging at first. But after several years, some officers lose interest; the job feels stale. Enthusiasm plummets.

What can be done to reduce stress and burnout in police officers? From their analysis of the research on organizational behavior, Jackson and Schuler (1983) have hypothesized four organizational qualities that increase employee burnout: (1) lack of rewards (especially positive feedback),

(2) lack of control over job demands, (3) lack of clear job expectations, and (4) lack of support from supervisors. Although each of these is especially problematic for police officers, certain interventions can reduce the likelihood of burnout. For example, the police officer seldom hears when things go well but often hears of the complaints of enraged citizens. Police officials could create opportunities for citizens to express their appreciation of what police officers are doing daily. Officers often feel a lack of control in their jobs. They must react to calls; they cannot change the flow of demands. Furthermore, citizens expect them to respond immediately.

Although the level of demands cannot be changed, officers can be given greater flexibility in how they respond to these demands. Their daily duties can be restructured so as to increase their sense of choice among activities. The importance of discretion can be emphasized to the officers, because they must exhibit a great deal of it when dealing with suspected offenders. Officers do not always make an arrest, even when they catch a suspect breaking the law. In one study, police officers did not make an arrest in 52% of the misdemeanors and 43% of the felonies, even when they had probable cause to believe that the suspect had committed a crime (Reiss, 1971). LaFave (1965) provides one illustration:

> A traffic officer stopped a car that had been going 15 m.p.h. over the speed limit. The driver was a youth, but he had a valid driver's license. Although the 15 m.p.h. excess was beyond the ordinary toleration limit for speeding violations, the officer only gave the youth a severe warning. The officer knew that the law required suspension of the license of a juvenile driver for any moving violation. (p. 138)

One strategy for decreasing burnout among police is the use of **team policing**. Team policing involves a partial shift of decision making from a centralized authority to front-line officers and their immediate supervisors, who share the responsibility of setting policing priorities and making management decisions. Teams are often organized around neighborhoods, where they focus their efforts for extended periods of time. Within a neighborhood team, members perform several different functions so that they come to realize how important each team member is to the overall success of the group. In addition, because the team stays in the neighborhood, citizens should come to know the officers more closely and develop a better understanding of them.

In addition to team policing, many police agencies have developed their own stress management programs or referred their officers to other agencies for counseling to reduce burnout. These programs emphasize the prevention of stress through various techniques, including relaxation training, stress inoculation, detection of the early signs of stress, and effective problem solving (Reiser & Geiger, 1984). As useful as these types of techniques may be, the stigma associated with obtaining mental health treatment may be strong enough to discourage officers from going to these agencies. Perhaps one way to reduce the stigma and offer mental health services to officers is through peer counseling programs in which counselors within the policing profession, who have an understanding of the role, responsibilities, and problems of law enforcement officers, provide the intervention (Madonna & Kelly, 2002). Providing treatment through a peer counseling program can have a "dramatic effect on the successful resolution of problems experienced by law enforcement officers" (Sewell, 2005, p.7).

Despite attempts to prevent stress and to change organizations in positive ways, some officers will experience stress-related problems that require counseling. Psychological treatment of police officers is complicated because police officers are often reluctant to become involved in therapy or counseling, for several reasons. First, they tend to believe that capable officers should be able to withstand hardships and that failure to do so signals a lack of professionalism or emotional control. Second, police fear that counseling will brand them with the stigma of mental disorder and thus undercut respect from their peers. Finally, officers are justifiably concerned that the department's need to know their psychological status with respect to their fitness for continuing duty will override their rights of confidentiality and lead to embarrassing disclosures of personal information.

Police departments have developed several alternatives for providing psychological counseling to their officers. Although none of these options solves all the problems mentioned earlier, each attempts to address the more common obstacles that arise in police counseling programs. As we have noted, peer counseling, involving the delivery of services by police officers, has the potential to overcome the stigma of being involved in treatment with a psychiatrist or psychologist. Describing their experiences with peer counseling in the Los Angeles Police Department, Reiser and Klyver (1987) reported that 200 trained peer counselors conducted about 5000 hours of counseling with their fellow officers in one year alone. Most of this counseling was aimed at relationship problems and job dissatisfaction.

A second method is to provide counseling targeted at problems specific to police officers. The most noteworthy example of these focused interventions is its application with officers who have been involved in the use of deadly force (see Blau, 1986). The emotional aftermath of shooting incidents is among the most traumatic experiences the police encounter and can often lead to symptoms of posttraumatic stress disorder (Reiser & Geiger, 1984; Solomon & Horn, 1986). Providing postincident counseling is a common service of police psychologists; in many departments, counseling for officers involved in shooting incidents is mandatory (McManis, 1986). The goals of this counseling, which also often relies on peer support, are to reassure officers that their emotional reactions to incidents are normal, to give them a supportive place to express these emotions, to help them reduce stress, and to promote a well-paced return to duty. Many departments also try to make counseling services available to the family of officers who have been involved in traumatic incidents.

There are several ethical considerations involved in psychological counseling for police officers (D'Agostino, 1986), and some of the most difficult concern confidentiality. Police counseling services are usually offered in one of two ways: by an "in-house" psychologist who is a full-time employee of the police department, or by an "outside" psychologist who consults with the department on a part-time basis. In-house professionals are more readily available and more knowledgeable about police issues. Outside consultants, because of their independence from the department, may be better able to protect the confidentiality of their clients' disclosures.

Is There a Police Personality?

Given that the work of a police officer entails a number of challenging tasks and that the job is highly visible, the public has a tendency to label police officers as having a certain set of qualities. Is there a distinct "police personality"? Do police officers share a cluster of personality characteristics that differentiates them from other people? If there is a police personality, how does it come about? Are police officers, by nature, a homogeneous group? Do they differ from other occupational groups and from the general population in terms of inherited personality traits? Or is the personality of police officers shaped gradually over their careers as a result of common occupational demands and experiences?

Different answers have been given to these questions, but the consensus is that career socialization is a stronger influence than preexisting differences in temperament. Among the most influential conceptions of a police personality is Joel Lefkowitz's description of the psychology of the police. After studying a host of variables, Lefkowitz concludes that the police do not differ from other groups in terms of psychological disorders or intelligence, but he also suggests that there were other important differences. According to Lefkowitz (1975):

> There exists a constellation of traits and attitudes or a general perspective on the world which particularly characterizes the policeman. This constellation ... presumably [comprises]

such interrelated traits as authoritarianism, suspiciousness, physical courage, cynicism, conservatism, loyalty, secretiveness, and self-assertiveness (p. 6).

Lefkowitz and others (Charles, 1986; Muir, 1977) have identified two clusters of personality traits that have been viewed as characteristic of police officers, but not in any pathological way. Cluster 1 includes the traits of isolation and secrecy, defensiveness and suspiciousness, and cynicism. These traits suggest a close-knit group of people whose occupational isolation and accompanying secrecy lead to strong feelings of being misunderstood by outsiders, who are in turn viewed with suspiciousness and cynicism by the police. Feelings of insecurity develop in response to this isolation and sense of being different; such feelings underlie the officers' desire for a uniform and badge as symbols to bolster their limited sense of personal adequacy to meet the extraordinary challenges of their jobs. In fact, being misunderstood by the public is one of the three most frequent problems reported by police officers. The segregation that results from wearing a uniform daily and from their role in the community leads to what Lefkowitz (1975) calls socio-occupational isolation, which only intensifies the individual's solidarity with other police officers.

Another manifestation of this cluster is what has been called the "blue wall of silence," the tendency for police officers to cover up the wrongdoings of fellow officers. The extent of this problem is unknown, but increased attention has been paid to it ever since Alan Dershowitz, one of O. J. Simpson's attorneys, charged that officers are routinely trained at the police academy to lie on the witness stand. This charge is easier to make than to verify, but it may be that some police officers shade the truth or ignore it all together to protect themselves and obtain convictions. In fact, allegations of police misconduct, including the planting of evidence, have become a mainstay argument among criminal defense attorneys. Moreover, this argument works; many convictions have been overturned because the police either faked or suppressed evidence. For instance, in 2004 Laurence Adams, who was convicted of killing a

Protesting for justice

transit worker during an attempted robbery, was released on his own reconnaissance after 30 years on death row. Mr. Adams's attorney presented evidence that Boston police withheld key documents in the case, including reports of other individuals' confessions of their involvement in the murder (Lindsay, 2004).

Lefkowitz's second cluster includes the qualities of **authoritarianism**, status concerns, and violence. This cluster is much more controversial than cluster 1 and includes a penchant for violence and several dimensions of authoritarianism. Authoritarianism, as conceived by Adorno, Frenkel-Brunswik, Levinson, and Sanford (1950), is a set of beliefs that reflect identification with and submissiveness to authorities, an endorsement of power and toughness, intolerance of outgroups and minorities, pressure for conformity to group norms, and rejection of anything unconventional as "deviant" or "sick." Although the police appear submissive to authority and tend to be politically conservative, they do not as a group score as particularly authoritarian on the California F Scale of Authoritarianism or as particularly rigid on Rokeach's Dogmatism Scale (Carlson, Thayer, & Germann, 1971; Fenster & Locke, 1973). In some studies, they score lower on these dimensions than college students and teachers. If police officers are authoritarian, it is primarily in the sense of exhibiting middle-class conventionality.

Police may also become more aggressive when they perceive their personal authority to be questioned and when they work at a job that justifies (and sometimes overjustifies) the use of force. Police also appear to be more responsive to politically powerful figures than to powerless ones. In a provocative investigation, Wilson (1978) asked police officers how they would respond if they saw a car with a very low license number (such as NY-2) speeding. Such low-number plates are offered to politicians in many states. Police officers in two New York communities, Amsterdam and Newburgh, responded without hesitation that they would "mind our own business."

Several studies provide evidence of police discrimination against persons of lower socioeconomic status and members of minority groups (Cochran, 1971; Cureton, 2000; Skolnick, 1975; Westley, 1970; Wilson, 1978). Another study examining the effect of race and class on attitudes about police found a more complicated pattern; class moderated the effect that race had on attitudes about police discrimination, and middle-class blacks sometimes felt more police discrimination than lower-class blacks (Weitzer & Tuch, 1999). Chambliss and Seidman (1971), among others, contend that suspects of lower socioeconomic status are discriminated against by the police because they wield less political power than middle-class suspects, adding that because the police associate minority-group membership with lower socioeconomic status, minority-group members have become the objects of police discrimination (p. 82).

The labels *authoritarian* and *violent* may be justified for police officers, but in a narrower sense than is usually applied. Police officers do tend to be a politically conservative, conventional group, very loyal to one another, and concerned with assertively maintaining the status quo. They are authoritarian, primarily in the sense of respecting the higher authority of the law, the nation, and the government they serve.

A primary psychological motivation to become a police officer appears to be the preference for order and security, which probably reflects the working-class backgrounds from which many police officers come (Gorer, 1955; Niederhoffer, 1967). A second important motive is a desire to provide social services to others. Police officers also report a desire for a job that allows them to exercise independent thought, to be creative, and to learn new things (Lurigio & Skogan, 1994).

Research indicates that police officers do not possess pathological extremes of personality. Most studies indicate that as a group, they are "normal" or "healthy" in their adjustment.

Police–Community Relations

Police officers are justified in feeling that they live in a fishbowl. Their performance is constantly being reviewed by the courts and evaluated by the public. Several amendments to the U.S. Constitution impose limits on law enforcement officers; such limits are part of the first ten amendments, known as the Bill of Rights. The Fourth Amendment protects against unreasonable search and seizure of persons or property. The Fifth Amendment provides guarantees for persons accused of a crime; for example, no such person "shall be compelled in any criminal case to be a witness against himself, nor be deprived of life, liberty, or property, without due process of law." As we discuss in other chapters, limits on police activities are frequently reevaluated on the basis of current court interpretations of these amendments. The Sixth Amendment guarantees the accused "the right to a speedy and public trial" and "the assistance of counsel for his defense"; the way these provisions are interpreted also has implications for police procedures. Protection against "cruel and unusual punishment" is promised by the Eighth Amendment, and the Fourteenth Amendment guarantees all citizens "due process." These amendments also govern and constrain several police activities.

During the last 25 years, citizens' groups have become increasingly critical of the police. Two types of concerns can be identified. The first deals with the manner in which the police perform certain duties (e.g., arrests and interrogations); the second concerns the increasing prevalence of police brutality.

Historically, the interrogation practices used by the police to elicit confessions from suspects have been a major focus of concern, and we discuss coercion of confessions extensively in Chapter 6. Briefly, the police are often criticized for using manipulative tactics to induce confessions from suspects. The most common approach is "to overwhelm the suspect with damaging evidence, to assert a firm belief in his or her guilt, and then to suggest that it would be easier for all concerned if the suspect admitted to his or her role in the crime" (Kassin & Wrightsman, 1985, p. 75). Along with this tactic, police often express concern for the suspect's welfare. Undue physical force is used far less than in the past, but promises of lowered bail, reduced charges, and leniency by the judge, as well as vague threats about harsher treatment, are common. These techniques are sometimes supplemented with exaggerated or trumped-up evidence to scare suspects into confessing (Kassin & Kiechel, 1996).

A police technique that has caused widespread concern and condemnation more recently is racial profiling—the practice of making traffic arrests of an illegitimately larger percentage of minority than non-minority motorists. Although some law enforcement officials have defended this procedure as a reasonable crime control tool, the public outcry over its potential for abuse has led several states to abandon it.

The second major concern of community groups is excessive force or brutality by the police (Fyfe, 1988). During the protests of the 1960s that took place in Watts (a section of Los Angeles), in Detroit, and throughout the South, massive demonstrations were held by American citizens, mostly African Americans, against what they believed was racially motivated harassment by the police.

The police officer has come to be viewed in predominantly African American neighborhoods as a representative of an overwhelmingly white male power structure that exerts economic, political, and social control over the citizenry and lies when it is expedient to do so. Although law enforcement officers are trained to act within legally prescribed boundaries and to do so equally toward all citizens, charges of "police brutality" have once again become all too frequent in the United States. It is estimated that during the late 1980s, approximately 2500 cases of police brutality were reported and investigated annually. In the past 15 years, the beating or killing of suspects by the police again commanded national attention. For example, the spotlight shone on three New Orleans police officers who, in the aftermath of Hurricane Katrina, were captured on film beating a black man in the French Quarter. Another particularly vivid case—also involving police brutality filmed by a bystander—is described in Box 4.2.

More recent events suggest that the King case was not an isolated incident; minority citizens can point to many cases justifying their concerns that they are often not treated fairly by the police (Weitzer & Tuch, 1999). In 2001, the shooting and killing of Timothy Thomas by Cincinnati police officers sparked riots in the streets, followed by days of civil unrest (Larson, 2004). In a two-month period prior to the shooting, Thomas, a 19-year-old African American man, was pulled over a total of 21 times and ticketed for either not wearing a seatbelt or driving without a license. Then, in the early morning hours of April 7, 2001, a police officer who reportedly recognized Thomas from having ticketed him, spotted him outside a local nightclub. When the officer approached Thomas, he ran. The officer called for backup, stating that he was engaged in a chase with a suspect who had approximately 14 warrants. Thomas ran into a dark alley and the officer followed, shooting a single gunshot that killed Thomas. The officer reported shooting because Thomas was reaching for a gun, but no gun was ever found.

Other cases publicized in the national media include the sodomy and torture of Abner Louima, which we described earlier; the shooting and killing of Amadou Diallo, an innocent West African immigrant, by four plainclothes New York City police officers; and the shooting of Javier

THE CASE OF

BOX 4.2

Rodney King: Videotaped police brutality?

In March 1991, police chased a black motorist who they alleged was speeding through a Los Angeles suburb in his 1988 Hyundai. As the unarmed man emerged from his car, a police officer felled him with a blast from a 50,000-volt stun gun, and three patrolmen proceeded to beat and kick him while a police helicopter hovered overhead. As a result of this attack, which was witnessed by at least 11 other police onlookers, Rodney King—a 25-year-old man who, it was later learned, was on parole—lay seriously injured with multiple skull fractures, a broken ankle, a cracked cheekbone, and several internal injuries.

One special feature of this attack was that a nearby citizen captured the entire episode on his video camera; within hours, the tape of this terrifying beating was played across the country on network news programs. Soon thereafter, local, state, and federal agencies launched investigations into the beating and into the entire Los Angeles Police Department. Three of the four officers who were charged with beating King were initially acquitted of all criminal charges, an outcome that shocked millions of Americans. But in a second trial, brought in federal court, two of the officers were found guilty of depriving

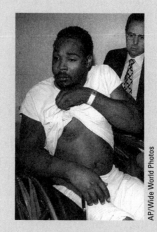

Claims of personal injury

King of his civil rights and were sentenced to prison.

Franciso Ovando by two Los Angeles police officers, who then planted a gun on the paralyzed victim to frame him for a crime he did not commit.

Even the U.S. Supreme Court has found it necessary to restrict the use of deadly force by police (see Box 4.3).

What causes the police to act brutally? How can we explain incidents in which officers clearly have used excessive force? One popular explanation is that police excesses stem from the personality problems of a "few bad apples." In this view, brutality reflects the sadistic extreme of the aggressive, tough pole of the authoritarian personality that we have already discussed. A contrasting explanation is that brutality is the unfortunate price occasionally paid for situations in which rising numbers of violent, even deadly, criminals demand forceful responses from the police. A third alternative is that police brutality reflects a fundamental sociological

pathology—that the deep strains of racism are still endemic in society. Which view is correct?

Police brutality is another example of a problem for which psychology seeks explanations not in individual personalities or in environmental situations but in the interactions between persons and the situations in which they function. From this perspective, we begin with police officers who, on average, are strongly committed to maintaining the conventional order and to protecting society. We repeatedly put them into potentially dangerous situations, we arm them well, we urge them to be "tough on crime," and we train and authorize them to use appropriate force. The result of mixing this type of person with these types of situations is predictable: In some encounters, the police will use excessive force against citizens who are suspected of wrongdoing that threatens public safety. Even more disturbing, however, is that the suspicions on

THE CASE OF

BOX 4.3   **Edward Garner and limits on the use of deadly force**

In the 1985 case of *Tennessee v. Garner*, the United States Supreme Court struck down a Tennessee law that allowed police to shoot to kill, even when an unarmed suspect fleeing a crime scene posed no apparent threat (Duning & Hanchette, 1985; Fyfe, 1982). In October 1974, Edward Garner, then 15, fled when the police arrived just after he had broken the window of an unoccupied house. He was pursued by Officer Elton Hymon.

As Garner scaled a 6-foot chain-link fence at the back of the property, Officer Hymon yelled, "Police— halt!" Garner didn't halt, and Officer Hymon, knowing that he was in no shape to catch the fleeing youth, shot and killed him with a bullet to the back of the head.

Garner's father sued public officials and the city of Memphis, alleging that the police had violated his son's civil rights by the use of excessive force. The city defended itself on the basis of a state statute giving peace officers the right to use deadly force if necessary to stop a fleeing felon. The lower courts agreed with the city, but 11 years later the United States Supreme Court struck down the statute in a 6–3 decision (*Tennessee v. Garner*, 1985).

The majority held that shooting a person, even one suspected of a felony, violates that person's Fourth Amendment right to be free from unreasonable searches and seizures. The majority opinion added, however, that deadly force would be justified if the officer had reason to believe that the suspect posed an immediate threat to him or others. Three justices (Sandra Day O'Connor, Warren Burger, and William Rehnquist) dissented from the majority opinion, stating that it would give suspects a constitutional right "to flee unimpeded" from the police.

---

which police force is based are sometimes motivated by stereotypes, mistaken information, and the mutual mistrust that can develop between individuals from different cultural and ethnic backgrounds.

As it turns out, many episodes of police brutality occur following high-speed chases, when (as with Rodney King) police lose control of their behavior after pursuing a suspect they think is belligerent or threatening. In a 2000 incident that has been compared to the Rodney King beating, three Philadelphia police officers punched and kicked one man 59 times in 28 seconds while trying to arrest him (Associated Press, 2000). In such tension-charged situations, police are prone to let their emotions dictate their actions. Some police departments are now concentrating on the problem of high-speed pursuits as triggers for what they call "mad cop disease." They try to teach police to "keep their cool" during these incidents and not be overwhelmed by their own fear and anger.

Since the 1970s, but particularly since the Rodney King episode, a number of attempts have been made to improve police relations with people in the community, especially in neighborhoods with large numbers of ethnic minorities. We have already described team policing as one effort to make the police officer's job less stressful and to respond to some community concerns about the way police perform. Evaluations of this type of innovation are inconsistent. In some cities, only minor changes were made, such as stenciling "Neighborhood Police Team" on several radio cars; it is unlikely that such trivial actions will improve police–community relations. In other cities, proposed changes were thwarted by higher levels of police administration. But after team policing was introduced in Newark, New Jersey, crime rates decreased dramatically and officer morale was reported to be high.

Structural changes such as team policing must be accompanied by changes in operating philosophy (Skolnick & Bayley, 1986). Traditionally, police have been only reactive; they have responded to crime incidents. But now, police officials are asking whether they can reduce crime by managing—or even preventing—the problem rather than just responding to manifestations of it (Wilson & Kelling, 1989).

"Managing the problem" includes, for example, preventive maintenance. The philosophy behind this approach is that "if the first broken window in a building is not repaired, soon all the windows will be broken; likewise, when disorderly behavior is left unchallenged or neighborhood decay is left unattended, the disorder escalates and the decay spreads" (Wilson & Kelling, 1989, p. 23). To counteract neighborhood decay, police departments have organized local citizens' groups to paint out graffiti and have convinced city agencies to tow away abandoned cars. The goals of such interventions are twofold. They involve (1) "hardening the target" so that criminals have reduced opportunities to commit crime, and (2) preventing physical deterioration so that citizens feel a larger stake in preserving order in their communities.

Another example of the community problem-solving orientation occurred when the city of Houston opened up storefront police stations. In this approach, known as **community-based policing**, police officers develop a proactive, problem-solving approach with active collaboration from local citizens who support the police in the effort to combat crime, promote safety, and enhance the overall quality of neighborhoods. This type of policing was designed to enhance the working relationship between the police and the public (Zhao, Lovrich, & Thurman, 1999). Residents of small to midsize cities were questioned about the effects of community-oriented policing. Findings revealed that awareness of this type of policing, compared to more conventional policing focused on arresting offenders, was associated with greater self-protection efforts (e.g., putting bars on windows), lower fear of crime, and stronger feelings of attachment to the community (Adams, Rohe, & Arcury, 2005). This finding held regardless of the respondents' history of victimization; participants associated community-oriented policing with a

© Koolvoord/The Image Works

Community policing is a philosophy designed to increase the amount and quality of specific police officers' contact with citizens and to involve police more in crime prevention and community maintenence activities.

lower fear of crime even when they had previously been a victim of crime.

Another recent study examined the relationships between these policing practices and the public's confidence in the police. Results revealed that individuals involved with this type of community crime prevention collaboration with the police showed increased confidence in the police overall (Ren, Cao, Loyrich, & Gaffney, 2005). However, some opponents of the practice have criticized community policing as expensive and as seeking to turn police officers into "social workers with guns" (Worsnop, 1993). Nonetheless, as of June 30, 2000, two-thirds of all local police departments and over half of the sheriffs' offices across the country had full-time officers engaging in community-based policing activities (Bureau of Justice Statistics, 2005c).

From a community-based policing perspective, officers combine their law enforcement techniques with the skills of a community organizer. Rather than nightly busting drunks who congregate in an empty lot, the police might elicit the help of business owners to convert the lot into a vest-pocket park (Anderson, 1988; Press, 1988).

In most versions of community policing, greater use is made of foot patrols by officers who stay in the same neighborhoods. As a result, community-based policing seeks to humanize police and citizens in one another's eyes and to broaden the roles that police play in a community. For example, Chicago's version of community policing, known as the Chicago Alternative Policing Strategy (CAPS), contains six basic features (Lurigio & Skogan, 1994):

1. *A neighborhood orientation*, in which officers forge friendships with individual residents in a community, know where the "hot spots" for crime are, and develop partnerships with community organizations for fighting crime

2. *Increased geographic responsibility*, which means that officers regularly walk a given neighborhood "beat" and become highly visible, well-known experts about problems in that area

3. *A structured response to calls for police service*, in which emergency calls are handled by a special-response team, thereby permitting beat officers to stay available for routine calls and maintain a high-profile presence

4. *A proactive, problem-oriented approach*, whereby more effort is devoted to crime prevention (e.g., closing down drug houses, breaking up groups of loitering youth) rather than responding to discrete disturbances or criminal activities

5. *Brokering more community resources for crime prevention*, such that police enlist the help of other city agencies to identify and respond to local community problems

6. *Analysis of crime problems*, which enables officers to focus their attention on the highest-risk areas by using computer technology to keep accurate track of crime patterns.

Does community policing work, or is it just a fad, long on rhetoric but short on success? As with most social reform projects, the results have been mixed. Some cities that have introduced community-policing initiatives report large improvements in the public's attitude toward their police departments (Adams et al., 2005; Peak, Bradshaw, & Glensor, 1992) and sizable reductions in rates of serious crimes. For instance, a community-policing project in New Haven, Connecticut, has shown promising results, including a 10.3% decrease in crime from 1991 to the first six months of 1992, com-

pared to only a 2% decrease in crime nationally (Worsnop, 1993).

Other evaluations indicate that police officers themselves remain skeptical about community policing. In Chicago's program, police officers initially doubted that community-based policing would reduce crime or improve relationships with racial minorities, and they believed it would require more work on their part and possibly undercut their authority in the community (Lurigio & Skogan, 1994). In general, police administrators endorse the value of community policing and believe that its advantages (improved physical environment, more positive attitudes toward police, fewer citizen complaints) outweigh its disadvantages (displacement of crime to a non-community-policing area, more opportunities for officer corruption, resistance from rank-and-file officers). Currently, about three-quarters of police departments have some level of community policing in place.

Police administrators are also beginning to acknowledge the need for changes in attitudes on the part of individual officers as well as in overall policing patterns. Recognizing the absence of dialogue between the police and the African American community in many cities, Teahan (1975a) used role playing and interpersonal feedback during police academy training to improve communication and relationships between black and white police officers. (Black police officers are especially vulnerable to miscommunication problems because some white officers assume that a black person with a weapon must be a criminal, not an undercover cop [Lewis, 1996].)

Here is an example of the role-playing situations that Ethan used to improve black–white relations:

> Two officers representing scout car partners were chosen (or volunteered) from the group. A third officer was then assigned the role of citizen. The scout car men were given a card stating: "You are cruising in your scout car at 12 P.M. in the 13th precinct when you receive information over the car radio that an armed robbery has just been committed a few blocks away. The suspect is described as a young adult male in his early twenties, dressed in

a dark overcoat. Suddenly, you notice a young man fitting that description ahead of you. You pull up beside him and . . . ." The officer designated as the citizen received a similar card reading: "You are a black university student who has just finished seeing a movie a few blocks away. It is 12 P.M. and you are hurrying home to your apartment when a police squad car pulls up beside you." (Teahan, 1975a, p. 38)

The results were mixed. The black officers believed workshops were beneficial; these officers showed greater concern over racial issues and felt that relationships between black and white officers were better than they had been at the beginning of training. But white officers became more prejudiced toward blacks. (White officers in control groups who did not participate in the workshops became less prejudiced.) Furthermore, they reported less contact with blacks at the end of the project.

Results were even more disappointing to Teahan when, in a second study, he followed up police officers 18 months after their participation in police academy workshops (Teahan, 1975b). He found that racial animosity between black and white officers had increased radically over the 18 months. All officers seemed to become more impersonal and detached; they also more easily developed feelings of hostility toward authority figures. As black officers progressed through the academy and on to regular police work, they became increasingly negative toward whites and disillusioned with the department; they began to feel a greater sense of black unity against whites. Blacks saw greater preference being given to whites, but white officers perceived things to be the opposite. The result was that both groups became more ethnocentric and polarized.

Similar results have been reported for police in other countries. One study assessed racial attitudes toward Aborigines by Australian police at the time of recruitment, after the completion of training, and after one year of service. Although the training resulted in decreased authoritarianism and ethnocentrism, the police became more ethnocentric and prejudiced after a year in the field, and this effect was greatest for those officers working in districts that contained more Aborigines (Wortley & Homel, 1995).

One partial solution to the problem of race relations is greater representation of minorities on police forces. Many cities are now actively recruiting minorities, and the results are encouraging. According to the most recent estimates, about one in every five police officers represents a racial minority, and in cities with populations of 25,000 or more, about one in ten is African American (Zhao & Lovrich, 1998).

SUMMARY

1. *What is the role of the police in our society?* Policing is necessary in any society concerned with maintaining public order, even though some people in our society see police activity as restricting individual freedom. Police officers daily face the dilemma of equality versus discretion: whether to treat all suspects or lawbreakers equally or to temper justice with mercy.

2. *What procedures are used to select police?* Selection of police officers usually includes the completion of psychological tests and a clinical interview. Another assessment device is the use of situational tests, in which the candidate role-plays responses to real-life challenges that would face a police officer, such as intervening in a dispute between a wife and her husband or aiding an injured child in a public place. Although responses to these situational tasks are valuable supplements to psychological testing and interviewing, carrying them out is costly and time-consuming.

3. *How has the training of police officers expanded into new areas?* Training of police officers usually involves a variety of activities, including criminal law, human relations training, self-defense, and the use of firearms. Most training programs last at least six months. Police officers are now frequently trained in crisis intervention, including handling the mentally ill, resolving family disputes, and responding to hostage-taking situations.

4. *Describe the different activities of the police. Is law enforcement central?* The police officer's job is multifaceted. Law enforcement (including investigation of complaints, arrest and prosecution of suspects, and efforts at crime prevention) accounts for only about 10% of police activity. Maintaining order (intervening in family and neighborhood disputes, keeping traffic moving, responding to disturbances of the peace) accounts for about 30% of police activity. Providing social services to the community is even more time-consuming.

5. *What stressors do the police face?* Three problems are especially significant: the "life in a fishbowl" phenomenon, job-related stress, and burnout. Job duties and perceptions of police work can be modified to reduce burnout. Special psychological interventions are also available to counteract stress reactions suffered by the police.

6. *Is there a police personality?* Whether a specific "police personality" exists is controversial, but research suggests that there are two clusters of relevant traits: (1) isolation and secrecy, defensiveness and suspiciousness, and cynicism; and (2) authoritarianism, status concerns, and aggression. The evidence for the existence or strength of the second cluster is less convincing than for the first, and there is no indication that police officers as a group exhibit pathological personalities.

7. *What is the relationship between the police and the communities they serve?* In recent years, community groups have been very critical of police behavior. Manipulative tactics used to coerce confessions from criminal suspects have been documented. Brutal treatment of innocent citizens, especially those of racial minorities, has been highly publicized. Efforts to improve police–community relations include team policing, reorganization of the police department that restructures the traditional chain of command, community-based policing, interracial human relations workshops, and the hiring of more minority officers. These interventions have had a mixed degree of success.

KEY TERMS

authoritarianism	fitness-for-duty	predictive validity	team policing
bioterrorism	evaluations	Stockholm syndrome	terrorism
burnout	jail diversion	structured	validity scales
community-based	program	interviews	zero tolerance
policing	learned helplessness	suicide by cop	

ORIENTING QUESTIONS

1. *What psychological factors contribute to the risk of mistaken identifications in the legal system?*
2. *How do courts regard the use of hypnotically refreshed memory? What procedures should be followed when hypnosis is used in a forensic setting?*

3. *How do jurors evaluate the testimony of eyewitnesses, and can psychologists help jurors understand the potential problems of eyewitness testimony?*

4. *Can memories for trauma be repressed, and if so, can these memories be recovered accurately?*

As we saw in Chapter 4, the tasks facing the police include investigating crimes and accumulating evidence so that suspects can be identified and arrested. Particularly at the early stages of an investigation, eyewitnesses to those crimes provide important information to police. In fact, sometimes they provide the only solid leads. According to a report from the National Institute of Justice (Department of Justice, 1999), approximately 75,000 defendants are implicated by eyewitnesses in the United States every year.

But in their attempts to solve crimes—and especially in their reliance on eyewitness observers — police and prosecutors face a number of challenges. Witnesses sometimes make mistakes in their reports to police. The police may pressure them to point the finger at a suspect; sometimes the desire to get a case "nailed down" overshadows the goal of discovering the truth. Hence, the reports of eyewitnesses can lead the police down blind alleys or cause them to arrest the wrong suspect, and the testimony of mistaken observers can lead to wrong verdicts by judges and juries.

The extent to which eyewitness errors create problems for the justice system (and for the people mistakenly identified!) has become increasingly apparent. Of the first 150 people who were exonerated on the basis of analysis of DNA found at the crime scene, approximately 70% had been identified incorrectly by seemingly honest, but mistaken eyewitnesses (Innocence Project, 2005). (The introduction of DNA testing procedures in the 1980s made it possible to take a new look at previously decided cases in which DNA-rich evidence such as blood and semen had been - preserved. Unfortunately, only a small fraction of crimes have physical evidence left behind by perpetrators, and even when present, it often is not tested or is destroyed. Furthermore, on occasion, prosecutors have failed to release people from prison even when DNA tests confirmed that they were innocent.) Inaccurate eyewitness identifications account for more wrongful convictions than do false confessions, problems with snitches, and defective or fraudulent science combined (Innocence Project, 2005).

Concern about eyewitnesses' accuracy is not restricted to criminal cases or to the identification of persons (Wells & Loftus, 1984). The results of civil lawsuits are also often affected by the reports of eyewitnesses, and law enforcement officials know that eyewitness descriptions of unusual events cannot always be trusted. The potential unreliability of eyewitness accounts was a major reason why the FBI discounted the theory that the July 1996 explosion of TWA Flight 800 was caused by a missile fired from the ground. Agents doubted the accuracy of at least 20 eyewitness reports of a streak of light shooting skyward seconds before the plane exploded into pieces over the Atlantic Ocean, killing all 230 passengers. In similar fashion, investigators from the National Transportation Safety Board discounted eyewitness reports on the crash of American Airlines Flight 587 over Rockaway Beach, New York, a few months after 9/11 because those reports clashed with the results of the Board's investigation.

Many crimes have only one eyewitness. A rape, for example, is usually witnessed only by the victim, and the same is true for the sexual abuse of children. But eyewitness testimony, even from one person, can still be very convincing to a judge or jury. In fact, eyewitness testimony may be the least reliable but most persuasive form of evidence presented in court (Wells, Small, Penrod, Malpass, Fulero, & Brimacombe, 1998).

Examples of Mistaken Eyewitness Identification

Cases of proven wrongful convictions based on faulty eyewitness testimony abound. The ordeal of Calvin C. Johnson, Jr., is a good example. Johnson, a college graduate with a degree in communications, a job with Delta Air Lines, and some petty crimes under his belt, spent 16 years behind bars for a rape he did not commit. And he is not alone. In fact, Johnson was the 61st person in the United States to be exonerated through the use of DNA testing. Tests in Johnson's case proved definitively that he could not have been the man who raped and sodomized a College Park, Georgia, woman in 1983. Yet the victim had picked Johnson out of a photographic lineup two weeks after her attack and identified him as the rapist at trial. The all-white jury convicted Johnson, who is black, despite the fact that forensic tests excluded him as the source of a pubic hair recovered from the victim's bed, and serology tests conducted on blood found at the scene were inconclusive. The jury also apparently chose to disregard the testimony of four alibi witnesses, including Johnson's fiancée, the fiancée's mother, his employer, and his mother, who claimed that Johnson was home asleep at the time. One of the jurors later stated that the victim's eyewitness testimony had been the most compelling evidence in the case.

One reason why such mistakes are so common is that when eyewitnesses make a tentative identification, police often stop investigating other leads and seek out further evidence that implicates the chosen suspect. This is an example of **confirmation bias**, whereby people look for, interpret, and create information that verifies an existing belief. In terms of eyewitness identification, the goal of finding the truth is submerged, often unintentionally, in the rush to find the cause of a crime. In Johnson's case, police pushed ahead with the case even after the victim picked someone else at a live lineup (conducted after the photographic lineup). She testified at trial that she had picked the wrong person at the lineup because looking at Johnson was too much for her: "I just pushed my eyes away and picked

© Davis Designs

James Newsome, the victim of mistaken identification, spent 15 years in prison for a crime he did not commit.

someone else," she reported (Boyer, 2000). (Calvin Johnson's book—entitled *Exit to Freedom*—chronicling his wrongful arrest, conviction, imprisonment, and eventual exoneration, was published by the University of Georgia Press in 2003.)

The Johnson case illustrates one type of eyewitness error—choosing the wrong person from a photographic lineup—but other sources of error also exist. Richard M. Nance (notice the middle initial *M*) was arrested in Los Angeles. His was not a very serious charge, but he was found guilty and sentenced to a brief jail term. In the midst of his ten-day sentence, a nationwide computerized crime network spat out the information that a Richard Lee Nance was being sought in Sonoma County, in northern California, on a burglary charge.

The Sonoma County Sheriff's Department warrant for Richard Lee Nance said he was born on July 3, 1946, was 5 feet 10 inches tall, and had brown hair and brown eyes. The L.A. prisoner's middle name was Marion, not Lee; he was born on July 6, 1946, not July 3; and his eyes were blue, not brown. Yet he was flown to Sonoma County and put in jail, with bail set at $5000. During the pretrial hearing, the burglary victim even pointed to Richard M. Nance and identified him as the man who had stolen a valuable ring and $100 from his farmhouse. Because Richard M. Nance was at the hearing, labeled as the defendant, the victim was quick to assume that Nance was the robber, even though his fingerprints differed from those left at

THE CASE OF

BOX 5.1   **Thomas Lee Goldstein: How to value 24 years lost to prison**

Thomas Lee Goldstein emerged from the black hell of the California Department of Corrections in April 2004 as a homeless, white-haired man of 55, clad only in a jail jump-suit and cheap slippers, without a cent to his name. He had spent the previous 24 years in prison for a murder he did not commit, sent there through the false testimony of a supposed eyewitness to a 1979 murder in Long Beach and by a jury convinced of his guilt.

Over the years he was impris-oned, Goldstein slowly lost his sense of disbelief, bitterness, and even revenge fantasies until all he was left with was a sense of numbness (Broder, 2004). Sadly, even his exit from prison was numbing: His first stop was a Veteran's Administration office where he hoped to get a few clothes, some money, and a place to

live. But the office computers were down, and officials could locate no record of his three years of service as a Marine. He drove away with his attorney, still homeless and penni-less. When asked the next day how he spent his first night of freedom after nearly a quarter-century, Goldstein replied that he "called up an old girlfriend hoping for a day of wild sex. Of course, she wasn't home so I went to the law library instead."

Indeed, Goldstein had become quite a legal scholar in the years he spent behind bars, filing many petitions for his release and eventually earning a paralegal cer-tificate. Those petitions caught the attention of a federal judge in 1996, and in 2002 a federal magis-trate determined that Goldstein had been wrongly convicted and

ordered him released. He now spends his days as a paralegal in a small Pasadena law firm, working with his attorney on a claim of wrongful imprisonment. In pon-dering the size of the claim, his attorney, Ronald Kaye, asks, "How do you really evaluate in financial terms what 24 years of life are worth? He was locked up from age 30–55. He didn't get a chance to find a wife, have children, build a career. I ask you, is $25 million enough? Is $50 million enough?" As for Goldstein, his "sustaining fantasy" is of a farm in Kansas: "I dream of owning a large plot of land in the Midwest with a house and a dog and a huge field of flowers and a grassy area. I want to just sit back there and look at the fields and fields of nothing, the antiprison" (Broder, 2004).

the scene of the crime. As Nance said later, "I can laugh about it now but can you believe me sitting there in the bright orange jail jumpsuit. Who else is the guy going to point to? The judge?" Despite the inconsistencies in name, appearance, and fingerprints, it took an investigator from the public defender's office almost a month to unravel the case and get Nance released from jail.

Nance asked rhetorically, "Who else is the witness going to point to?" but witnesses *have* sometimes pointed to the wrong person. In a trial in Washington, D.C., two different U.S. park police officers, on the witness stand, pointed to the defense attorney rather than the defendant when asked to identify the protester charged with assaulting a police officer. After the first witness

erred, the defense attorney moved his note pad and papers in front of his client, who began to scribble furiously, thus contributing to the impression that the defendant was the attorney, and vice versa. After the second misidentification, the govern-ment dropped the charges (Strasser, 1989).

You might suppose that people like Calvin Johnson and Richard M. Nance, who had been mistakenly identified and wrongly imprisoned, would have some recourse—that they could get something back for the time they lost in prison. (One wrongly convicted man, James Newsome, was awarded $15 million by a Chicago jury in 2001, $1 million for each of the 15 years Newsome was imprisoned for a 1979 slaying that he did not commit.) But Calvin Johnson received nothing for

An example of a sketch drawn by a police artist

his years behind bars; Georgia does not have a law providing compensation for people who are wrongly imprisoned. In fact, the majority of people who are wrongly incarcerated get either nothing or a token sum from state compensation funds. One commentator has suggested that the new crime is how little these lost lives are worth (Higgins, 1999). The case of Thomas Lee Goldstein is illustrative (see Box 5.1)

Points at Which a Mistaken Eyewitness Identification Can Occur

Jurors in a criminal trial see a victim take the witness stand and confidently identify the defendant as his or her attacker. Not only may the jurors assume that this identification is accurate, but they are also likely to believe that the victim was just as confident about the initial description or identification. These assumptions fail to recognize the

many problems that can undermine the accuracy of a criminal identification (Wells & Olson, 2003).

Mistakes in the process of identification can occur the moment the crime is committed. It may be too dark, events may move too swiftly, or the encounter may be too brief for the victim to perceive the incident accurately. Yet when they are questioned by police, victims are forced to rely on their impressions about the criminal's height, hair color, voice, and other identifying features. These impressions are sometimes translated into sketches of suspects, usually drawn by police artists

Mistakes can also occur during the investigation of a crime. In cases that involve eyewitnesses, police often ask these witnesses to examine a series of photos (called a photo spread) or a physical lineup of suspects and decide whether the perpetrator is present. During this process, the police may coax reactions from eyewitnesses. At this point, eyewitnesses want to help the police solve the crime; they may feel implicit pressure to identify someone, even if the police do not explicitly encourage them to do so.

© Rhodes John F./DMN/Corbis SYGMA

Facial composites prepared by eyewitnesses to a crime

The study of eyewitness identification grew out of our understanding of the basic principles involved in perception and memory. All of us, as observers, are prone to making errors in perceiving and remembering events that we experience. But because eyewitnesses must remember experiences that are typically brief, complicated, and sometimes very frightening, they are especially prone to error. To illustrate these errors, we next consider the steps involved in acquiring information from the outside world and recalling it; the very steps that an eyewitness must take to record a moment in time.

Basis Information Processing: Perception and Memory

We have all had the experience of greeting someone we recognize, only to realize that we are mistaken—that the person is actually a stranger. Similar mistakes can be made when crime is observed. To process information about a crime, we must first perceive a stimulus and then retain it in our minds at least momentarily. Failures and errors can emerge at any step along the way.

Perception

Although our perceptual abilities are impressive (Penrod, Loftus, & Winkler, 1982), we do make

errors. We tend to overestimate the height of criminals. We also overestimate the duration of brief events, although we underestimate the duration of prolonged incidents. When watching a short film, we notice more about the actions than about the persons doing the acting. Studies of **change blindness** suggest that our mental representations of visual scenes are sparse or incomplete and that people often fail to notice large changes in their visual worlds. For example, 50% of observers failed to notice when the person they were talking to was surreptitiously replaced by a different person as a doorframe was carried between them (Grimes, 1996; Simons & Ambinder, 2005).

Many factors affect our perceptual abilities. For example, if a weapon is present when a crime is committed, we may devote more attention to it than to the facial features or other physical aspects of the person who has the weapon. This **weapon focus effect** has been demonstrated even when people watch a film of a crime (Tooley, Brigham, Maass, & Bothwell, 1987). It appears to be caused not so much by emotional arousal as by the fact that witnesses narrow their attention to the weapon. This limits the amount of attention they can pay to other aspects of the situation, such as physical features of the perpetrator (Shaw & Skolnick, 1999). The weapon focus effect is particularly likely to occur in situations in which the weapon is surprising and unexpected (Pickel, 1999).

The presence of a weapon can do more than interfere with the perception of visual information; it can affect the processing of auditory information, as well. Kerri Pickel and colleagues showed a film that depicted a man holding either a weapon (e.g., a gun, a switchblade knife) or a neutral object (e.g., a soda pop bottle; a retractable ballpoint pen) and speaking to a woman in such a way that his words were either easy or difficult to understand (Pickel, French, & Betts, 2003). Witnesses had difficulty understanding the man's speech in the latter condition, and the presence of a weapon worsened their comprehension. A reasonable explanation is that their focus on the weapon and their attempt at language comprehension competed for limited perceptual processing time. They had a hard time doing both things at once.

Memory

Experimental psychologists subdivide the building of a memory into three processes: encoding, storage, and retrieval. We describe the memory of eyewitnesses in each of these three stages.

ENCODING

Encoding refers to the acquisition of information. Many aspects of a stimulus can affect how it is encoded; stimuli that are only briefly seen or heard cannot be encoded fully, of course. The complexity of a stimulus also affects its encoding, but the relationship is not a straightforward one. As the complexity of an event increases (consider an earthquake, explosion, or tsunami), some aspects of the event probably will be misremembered, while others will be accurately recalled.

Contrary to what many people believe, a stressful situation does not necessarily enhance the encoding of events. Although mild stress or arousal may indeed heighten alertness and interest in the task at hand, extreme stress usually causes the person to encode the information incompletely or inaccurately. Thus if a person is facing an excessively stressful situation, perception is narrowed, encoding is impaired, and less learning occurs than under mild levels of stress. Performance on many tasks is best when the level of arousal is sufficient to ensure adequate attention but not so high as to disrupt accuracy.

Although a number of studies have investigated what people remember about traumatic events, the studies are often criticized for their lack of intensity and real-world applicability. But a recent meta-analysis examined only those studies that involved actual differences in stress level as a function of the experimental manipulations (Deffenbacher, Bornstein, Penrod, & McGorty, 2004). This study combined the results of 27 tests of the effects of heightened stress on eyewitness identification and found support for the idea that high levels of stress negatively affect eyewitnesses' accuracy.

A recent study on the accuracy of eyewitness memory in highly stressful military survival school interrogations provides good evidence of the effects of stress on memory (Morgan et al., 2004). Survival school interrogations are one of the greatest training challenges that active duty military personnel ever experience. (These interrogations are intended to test one's ability to withstand exploitation by the enemy, and to train people to hold up under the physical and mental stresses of capture.)

Participants in this study were 500 soldiers, sailors, and pilots who were placed in mock POW camps and deprived of food and sleep for approximately 48 hours prior to interrogation. During 40 minutes of intense questioning, half of them were physically threatened and all participants were presented with the challenge of being tricked into giving away information. One day later, they were asked to identify their interrogators from an 8-picture photo spread (chance accuracy is therefore 1/8, or 12.5%). The results were startling. Among soldiers who experienced low stress (without the threat of physical injury), 76% were correct in identifying the target from among the photographs shown. By contrast, only 34% of participants who experienced the high stress of a physically threatening situation were correct; the majority incorrectly chose another person.

Characteristics of the witness also affect encoding. We all differ in visual acuity and hearing ability. When we have more experience perceiving a given kind of stimulus, we usually notice its details better than when perceiving it is a novel experience. This is why experienced judges notice flaws in a gymnast's performance that the rest of us can detect only in a slow-motion replay. Different expectancies about upcoming events also influence how they are subsequently perceived; in general, we have a tendency to see what we expect to see.

STORAGE

The second step in building a memory is the **storage** of stimulus information. How well do we retain what we encode? Many years ago, the experimental psychologist Hermann Ebbinghaus showed that early memory loss is rapid. Lipton

(1977) illustrated this phenomenon in a setting relevant to the concerns of this chapter. Participants were shown a film of an armed robbery and shooting without any prior knowledge that they would be serving as eyewitnesses. Those who were questioned after one week dredged up 18% less memory information than those who were questioned immediately after viewing the film.

A second phenomenon—a surprising and potentially disturbing one—also occurs during the storage phase. Activities that eyewitnesses carry out or information they learn after they observe an event, which is termed **postevent information**, can alter their memory of the event. For example, viewing mug shots or photographs of suspects can alter an eyewitness's capacity to recognize faces that he or she viewed before seeing the mug shots (Memon, Hope, Bartlett, & Bull, 2002). Attempting to reconstruct a perpetrator's face using a computer face-composite program (these programs permit eyewitnesses to select various facial features and combine them into an intact face) can also affect a witness' ability to later identify that perpetrator from a lineup (Wells, Charman, & Olson, 2005). In both of these examples, the new activity interferes with memory of the old. In similar fashion, simply providing an eyewitness with information about what other witnesses have already said influences the first witness's recollection (Shaw, Garven, & Wood, 1997).

A similar conclusion derives from the now-classic studies of Elizabeth Loftus (1975, 1979; reviewed in Loftus, 1992, 1993). In one of her projects, participants viewed a one-minute film of an automobile accident and were later asked a series of questions about it. The first question asked either how fast the car was going "when it ran the stop sign" or how fast it was going "when it turned right." Then, on the last question, all subjects were asked whether they had seen a stop sign in the film. In the first group, which had earlier been asked about the speed of the car "when it ran the stop sign," 53% said they had seen a stop sign, whereas only 35% of the second group said they had seen the sign. The effect of the initial question was to "prompt," or refresh, the memory for this part of the film. In a second study, Loftus included a misleading follow-up question that mentioned a nonexistent barn. When questioned one week later, 17% of the subjects reported seeing the barn in the original film! In essence, the new information that was conveyed simply as part of a question was added to the same memory store as the original stimulus.

RETRIEVAL

The third and final step in establishing memory is the **retrieval** of information. This process is not as straightforward as you might think. For example, we all have experienced the "tip of the tongue" phenomenon, when we know an answer or a movie title or a person's name but can't dredge it out of our memory store. Once again, the wording of questions can influence output at the retrieval phase (Wells, Wright, & Bradfield, 1999). For example, consider the question "What was the man with the mustache doing with the young boy?" Assume that the man in question had no mustache. This form of the question may not affect the eyewitness's report of the man's actions, but it may influence memory of the man's appearance. Later, if asked to describe the man, eyewitnesses may incorporate the detail (in this case, the mustache) that was embedded in the original question (Loftus & Greene, 1980).

In recalling information from our memory store, we often generate memories that are, in a sense, accurate but are not relevant to the task at hand. For instance, victims sometimes pick from a lineup or a photo spread the face of a person whom they have seen before but who is not the actual criminal. For example, a clerk at a convenience store who is the victim of a late-night robbery may mistakenly identify an innocent shopper who frequents the store. In an actual case, a Los Angeles judge who was kidnapped and attacked while she was jogging picked a suspect's picture from the police mug book after the attack, and on that basis, he was charged with the crimes. She later stated that she had not remembered at first that he had appeared before her in court four years earlier, for similar offenses, and that she had sentenced him to unsupervised probation (Associated Press, 1988).

This phenomenon, called **unconscious transference**, was demonstrated experimentally by David Ross and his colleagues, who showed two versions of a filmed robbery to college student witnesses (Ross, Ceci, Dunning, & Toglia, 1994). Half of the witnesses saw the film with an innocent bystander in the background, and the other half saw the same film without the bystander. When witnesses were asked whether they could identify the robber from a lineup (in this particular lineup, the bystander was present but the assailant was missing), eyewitnesses in the first group were three times more likely to misidentify the bystander than eyewitnesses in the latter group. The majority of people who selected the bystander thought that the assailant and the bystander were the same person. This is one means by which innocent persons are sometimes charged with a crime and eventually convicted.

In summary, as Hall, Loftus, and Tousignant (1984) conclude, testing one's memory for an original event can alter the memory for that event; indeed, "the witness reacts as if original memory and post event information had been inextricably integrated" (p. 127).

Distinguishing System and Estimator Variables

Expanding from this research on basic information processing, psychologists have identified several other variables that can influence the validity of identifications. Professor Gary Wells, a prolific researcher in the area of eyewitness identification, introduced a useful dichotomy to categorize these variables (Wells, 1978). He coined the term **system variable** to refer to those factors that are under the control of the criminal justice system (for example, the instructions given to eyewitnesses when they consider a lineup or photo spread, and the composition of that lineup or photo spread). The term **estimator variable** refers to factors that are beyond the control of the justice system and whose impact on the reliability of the eyewitness can only be

estimated (examples include the lighting conditions at the time of the crime and whether the culprit was wearing a disguise). Because system variables hold more promise for preventing errors in eyewitness identification (they are, after all, controllable), many psychologists have focused their research efforts on those variables. But research on estimator variables is important, too; it can help us understand the situations in which eyewitnesses may experience problems in perception and memory.

Assessing the Impact of Estimator Variables on Eyewitness Accuracy

We have already described in detail two estimator variables—the witness's stress level at the time of the crime and the presence of a weapon. We will discuss a few other factors here.

RACE OF THE EYEWITNESS

Eyewitnesses are usually better at recognizing and identifying members of their own race or ethnic group than members of another race or ethnic group. In fact, the chances of a mistaken identification are 1.56 times greater when the witness and suspect are of different races than when they are of the same race (Meissner & Brigham, 2001). This phenomenon, which is termed the **other-race effect**, has been examined extensively in laboratory studies, and analysis of DNA exoneration cases show that it is a significant problem in actual cases, as well. In their analysis of 77 known cases of mistaken identification, Scheck, Neufeld, and Dwyer (2000) reported that 35% of these cases involved white victims or witnesses who misidentified black suspects, whereas only 28% of cases involved white victims or witnesses who misidentified white suspects. These figures are even more troubling when one considers that most criminal victimizations happen *within* race (that is, whites are more likely to be victimized by other whites, and blacks are more likely to be victimized by other blacks). Because white-victim/white-perpetrator crimes happen more often than white-victim/black-perpetrator crimes, we would expect that white victims would make more mistakes with white suspects than with black suspects (Wells & Olson, 2001). But that's not what happens.

Understanding the reasons for the other-race effect has vexed psychologists for some time. Racial attitudes are apparently not related to this phenomenon (people with prejudicial attitudes are not more likely to fall victim to the other-race effect than are people with unbiased attitudes). Recent explanations of the other-race effect have tended to involve both cognitive and social processes.

Cognitive interpretations hold that there are differences between faces of one race and faces of another race in terms of the variability in those features, something psychologists refer to as **physiognomic variability**. Faces of one race differ from faces of another race in terms of the *type* of physiognomic variability. For example, white faces show more variability in hair color, and black faces show more variability in skin tone. For eyewitnesses to correctly identify members of other races, they must focus on the characteristics that distinguish that person from other people of the same race. Thus, black eyewitnesses would be better off noticing and encoding a white perpetrator's hair color than her or his skin tone, whereas white eyewitnesses could more profitably pay more attention to a black assailant's skin tone. But because most of us have more experience with members of our own race, our natural instinct is to focus on the features that distinguish members of *our own group*; we have less practice distinguishing one member of another race from other people of that race.

Social psychologists have also tried to explain the other race effect. One reasonable hypothesis is based on social perception and **in-group/out-group differences** (Sporer, 2001). When we encounter the face of a person from another race or ethnic group (the out-group), our first job is to categorize the face as a member of that group (e.g., "That person is Asian"). Attentional resources that are directed toward categorization come at the expense of attention to facial features that would distinguish that person from other members of the out-group. On the other hand, when we encounter the face of a person from our in-group, the categorization step is eliminated, and we immediately devote our attention to distinguishing that person from other members of the in-group. In the end, because identifying people of other races involves both a cognitive and a social process, both explanations may well be right; there probably will never be one all-encompassing theory to explain why it is difficult to do (Wells & Olson, 2001).

AGE AND GENDER OF THE EYEWITNESS

The age and gender of an eyewitness are also estimator variables; we can't control their influence on the justice system, but we can estimate them. Less attention has been focused on understanding the effects of age and gender than on understanding the effects of race. But we can ask whether males make better eyewitnesses than females and whether young people make better eyewitnesses than older people.

The evidence for gender effects is not overwhelming; a meta-analysis of several studies (Shapiro & Penrod, 1986) showed that although women are slightly more likely to make accurate identifications, they also make slightly more errors than men (because they are more likely to choose someone from a lineup or photo spread). Thus, there is no clear evidence that one gender is superior to the other in ability to identify people from lineups.

There is stronger evidence that the age of the eyewitness matters: Older eyewitnesses and young children make more errors than younger and middle-aged adults (Brimacombe, Jung, Garrioch, & Allison, 2003; Pozzulo & Lindsay, 1998). In addition, the errors of older adults and young children are fairly predictable: They are more likely to choose someone from a lineup in which the culprit is absent and, hence, make more mistaken identifications than young and middle-aged adults (Memon, Bartlett, Rose, & Gray, 2003). But when the lineup contains the culprit, young children and elderly people perform as well as younger adults. (We describe the issues associated with children as witnesses in Chapter 14.)

SPEED OF IDENTIFICATION

One other estimator variable—the speed with which an eyewitness makes an identification from a lineup—has intrigued psychologists recently. Witnesses who make accurate identifications generally take less time to look at a lineup than witnesses who make mistaken identifications, although there is some controversy about what time frame can differentiate accurate from inaccurate identifications (Dunning & Perretta, 2002; Weber, Brewer, Wells, Semmler, & Keast, 2004). Is it 5 seconds, 10 seconds, or 30 seconds? Unfortunately, we don't yet know the answer. Even if we did, the speed of identification could never be a foolproof method of assessing accuracy, but it may hold some promise as an estimator.

Controlling the Impact of System Variables on Eyewitness Accuracy

System variables are those factors in an identification over which the justice system has some control. In general, system variables tend to come into play after the crime or accident, usually during the investigation. In the criminal justice realm, they tend to be associated with how the lineup or photo spread is put together and shown to the eyewitness. We have already touched on two system variables: the influence of postevent information on witnesses' memory, and the effects of questions posed to eyewitnesses. In the next section, we describe other system variables and the important role they have played in suggesting changes to procedures that investigators use with eyewitnesses.

But first, it may helpful to draw an analogy between the procedures employed in criminal investigations and the steps used by researchers when doing an experiment (Wells & Luus, 1990). Like scientists, crime investigators begin with a hypothesis (that the suspect actually committed the crime), test the hypothesis (by placing the suspect in a lineup and instructing the eyewitness about what to do when looking at the lineup), observe and record the eyewitness's decision, and draw conclusions from the results (e.g., that the suspect was the assailant).

There are certain principles that are essential to good experimental design (e.g., that observers should be unbiased), and violation of those principles affects the usefulness of the experiment's findings. In similar fashion, violating the principles of good criminal investigation affects the results of the investigation. For example, if the instructions to the eyewitness are biased, if the suspect appears to be different from the other people in the lineup in some obvious way, or if the person conducting the lineup conveys his or her suspicions to the eyewitness, then the results of that identification procedure can be misleading. Applying the analogy of an experiment to criminal investigations enables us to evaluate critically the steps involved in these investigations.

Recommendations for Reforming Identification Procedures

One important aspect of a system variable is that because it is controllable, it can be modified. For example, we know that instructions given to eyewitnesses at a lineup affect the likelihood of correct identifications. Thus, we can suggest that people conducting lineups use only unbiased instructions.

As psychological research findings have accumulated and been disseminated to prosecutors and police officers, some departments have changed the procedures they use with eyewitnesses. In fact, studies showing the impact of system variables on eyewitness accuracy formed the basis for a set of guidelines issued by the U.S. Department of Justice in 1999 on recommended procedures for collecting eyewitness evidence. In her introduction to these guidelines, then-Attorney General Janet Reno wrote, "Eyewitnesses frequently play a vital role in uncovering the truth about a crime. The evidence they provide can be critical in identifying, charging, and ultimately convicting suspected criminals. That is why it is absolutely essential that eyewitness evidence be accurate and reliable. One way of ensuring we, as investigators, obtain the most accurate and reliable evidence from eyewitnesses is to follow sound protocols in our investigations" (U.S. Department of Justice, 1999, p. iii). Reno also cited the "growing body of research in the field of eyewitness identification" as support for the guidelines.

The guidelines issued by the Justice Department are recommended for use in conducting lineups and photo spreads. These guidelines have two important goals: to maximize accurate identifications and minimize the rate of eyewitness errors. Because police officers want to catch the real culprits and avoid mistaken identifications, we expect that police departments will eventually incorporate many of these recommendations as routine procedure. Already, police in New Jersey, Boston, Madison, the District of Columbia, Chicago, Minneapolis, and most of North Carolina have embraced these principles, and others are being trained in their use (Turtle & Steblay, 2005).

In this section, we describe what is known about four system variables: instructions to eyewitnesses, selection of filler photos, the lineup presentation method, and the influence of feedback. On the basis of this research, psychologists have made suggestions about how these variables should be factored into identification procedures so that those procedures will be fair and unbiased. Many of their recommendations are included in the federal guidelines.

Instructions to the Eyewitness

There is ample research showing that the investigator conducting the photo spread or lineup should instruct the witness that the offender *may or may not be* present in the spread or lineup (Malpass & Devine, 1981). Without this instruction, eyewitnesses may assume that their task is to pick *someone*, so they choose the person who looks most like the perpetrator. Based on her analysis of all the studies that examined the presence of a "might or might not be present" instruction, Professor Nancy Steblay found that use of this instruction reduced the rate of mistaken identifications (i.e., saying that the offender was present in the lineup when he was not) by 42% and did not significantly reduce the rate of correct identifications (i.e., choosing the

offender from a lineup in which he was present) (Steblay, 1997).

Selection of Fillers

If the suspect stands out from other people in the lineup or photo spread (the fillers), then he or she can be easily picked out, even by people who did not witness the crime. For example, if the victim of a robbery recalled that the robber had acne and the photo spread or lineup showed only one person (namely, the suspect) with acne, a nonwitness who was simply given the description of the culprit would be able to pick out the suspect. Suspects can stand out from other people in the lineup in a number of different ways: They might be the only person in the lineup with a prominent facial feature; their pictures might be a different size than the others or use a different background; or the suspect might be shown in jail clothes whereas the fillers might appear in street clothes. Defense attorneys who suspect that their clients would stand out from the fillers can now perform a do-it-yourself test on the fairness of a lineup or photo spread. On-line instructions are provided by Professor Roy Malpass from the Eyewitness Identification Research Laboratory at the University of Texas at El Paso (http://eyewitness.utep.edu/diy.html).

Police departments differ in the care they give to creating photo spreads and lineups. To their credit, most police officers try to have all members of a lineup look fairly similar. But others may place the suspect in a lineup of people who differ from that suspect in height, weight, physique, hair style, and other significant features mentioned in the witness's description of the offender. Here are some examples:

> In one case . . . the defendant had been picked out of a line-up of six men, of which he was the only Oriental. In other cases, a black-haired suspect was placed among a group of light-haired persons, tall suspects have been made to stand with short suspects, and, in a case where the perpetrator of the crime was known to be a youth, a suspect under twenty was placed in a line-up with five other persons, all of whom were forty or over. (*United States v. Wade*, 1967)

As the recommended procedures become more widely used, we hope that these miscues will diminish.

Lineup Presentation Method

In a typical lineup or photo spread, the eyewitness sees the suspect and the foils simultaneously. (In a photo spread, six photos are typically arrayed on a single page. In a live lineup, the suspect and foils are shown together, standing in a line.) This procedure is termed **simultaneous presentation**. An alternative procedure is to show suspects and foils sequentially—one at a time (Lindsay & Wells, 1985)—in a procedure called **sequential presentation**. The manner in which a lineup or photo spread is presented can affect the accuracy of identification. For example, Cutler and Penrod (1988) showed a one-minute videotape of a staged liquor store robbery and varied the way in which the lineup was constructed. When the six members of the lineup were shown simultaneously, witnesses falsely accused an innocent person 39% of the time. However, when suspects were shown sequentially, witnesses picked the wrong individual only 19% of the time.

A compilation of 25 studies that compared simultaneous and sequential presentation showed that the chances of mistaken identifications were reduced by nearly half when presentations were sequential (Steblay, Dysart, Fulero, & Lindsay, 2001). However, that good news must be balanced against another concern: whether the identification of actual perpetrators is *also* reduced when lineups and photo spreads are shown sequentially. According to Professor Nancy Steblay and her colleagues, under real-world conditions involving crimes with only one perpetrator and cautionary instructions to the eyewitness, there will be few differences in witnesses' ability to correctly identify a perpetrator as a function of presentation format. Thus, we can be reasonably confident that in most situations, sequential presentation is preferable.

Why are there more mistaken identifications in the traditional lineup (i.e., with simultaneous presentation)? In the simultaneous presentation of individuals in a lineup or photo spread, eyewitnesses tend to identify the person who, in their opinion, looks most like the culprit *relative to* other members of the group. In other words, they make a **relative judgment**. But what happens when the actual culprit is not shown? Under this condition, the relative-judgment process will still yield a positive identification because someone in the group will always look *most* like the culprit (Wells et al., 1998).

Contrast this situation with a lineup or photo spread in which the members are presented sequentially, one at a time. Here, the eyewitness compares each member in turn to his or her memory of the perpetrator and, on that basis, decides whether any person in the lineup is the individual who committed the crime. In other words, they make an **absolute judgment**. The value of sequential presentation is that it decreases the likelihood that an eyewitness will make a relative judgment in choosing someone from the lineup or photo spread.

Professor Gary Wells, a vocal advocate of reforming eyewitness evidence procedures, cleverly demonstrated the use of relative-judgment processes in his "removal without replacement" study (Wells, 1993). In this procedure, all eyewitnesses watched a staged crime. Some were shown a photo spread that included the actual culprit and five foils; their identifications were recorded. Another group saw the same photo spread with one exception: The culprit's photo was removed and was not replaced with another photo. If identifications of the culprit by the culprit-present group are based solely on their recognition of him, then the percentage of people in that group who identified him *plus* the percentage who said "not there" should be exactly the same as the percentage in the culprit-absent group who said "not there." Wells tested this idea by showing 200 eyewitnesses to a staged crime either a culprit-present lineup or a lineup in which the culprit was absent but was not replaced by anyone else (see Table 5.1). When the culprit was present in the lineup, 54% of eyewitnesses selected him, and 21% said "not there." Did 75% of

TABLE 5.1 ◆ **Rates of choosing lineup members when a culprit is present versus removed without replacement**

	LINEUP MEMBER						
	1	2	3 (CULPRIT)	4	5	6	NO CHOICE
Culprit present	3%	13%	54%	3%	3%	3%	21%
Culprit removed (without replacement)	6%	38%	—	12%	7%	5%	32%

SOURCE: "What do we know from witness identification?" from G. Wells, *American Psychologist, 48*, 553–571.

eyewitnesses in the "target-absent" lineup say "not there"? Unfortunately, no. The "not there" response was given by only 32% of people in that group; the others all mistakenly identified someone else from the lineup. Why? Through a process of relative judgment, eyewitnesses apparently select whoever looks most like the perpetrator.

The Influence of Feedback

Recall our analogy between a criminal investigation and a scientific experiment. One of the cardinal rules of a good experiment is that the person conducting the experiment should not influence the results, a situation referred to as **experimenter bias**. To avoid this problem, experimenters should know little about the study's hypotheses and less about which experimental condition any participant is in. Nearly all clinical drug trials adhere to these rules in that neither the patient taking the pills nor the doctor assessing the patient's health knows whether the pills are actually a new drug or a placebo. These so-called **double-blind testing procedures**, commonplace in medicine and other scientific fields, have gone largely unheeded in criminal investigations (although some jurisdictions are now beginning to adopt them [Post, 2005]).

What happens if the officer conducting the lineup knows who the suspect is? Does that knowledge affect the eyewitness in any way? The answer, based on several recent studies, is yes. A lineup administrator's knowledge of the suspect can affect both the likelihood that an eyewitness will choose

someone from the lineup (Phillips, McAuliff, Kovera, & Cutler, 1999) and the confidence that the eyewitness attaches to that choice (Garrioch & Brimacombe, 2001; Semmler, Brewer, & Wells, 2004). Furthermore, eyewitnesses who have a lot of contact with the administrator—either because they are in close physical contact or because they have extensive interactions—are likely to make decisions consistent with the administrator's expectations (Haw & Fisher, 2004). An obvious solution to this situation is to have the lineup administered by someone who does not know which person in the lineup or photo spread is the suspect.

As we have seen, eyewitnesses sometimes express increased certainty in their identifications as a result of events that happen after they choose someone from the lineup. For example, if eyewitnesses get confirming feedback from the lineup administrator ("Good, you identified the suspect"), they inflate the certainty they had in their initial identifications, compared to eyewitnesses who received no such feedback. This inflation of confidence is actually greater for eyewitnesses who are mistaken in their identifications than for eyewitnesses who are correct (Bradfield, Wells, & Olson, 2002). Remarkably, confirming feedback also bolsters eyewitnesses' retrospective confidence in how good a view they had of the perpetrator, how well they could make out details of his face, and how readily they made the identification (Wells, Olson, & Charman, 2003). Even *without* confirming feedback, eyewitnesses infer from the facts of an ongoing investigation and eventual prosecution that they must have picked the suspect from the lineup.

Hence, their confidence increases. This enhanced confidence is troubling because of the repeated finding that the confidence expressed by eyewitnesses during their trial testimony is one of the most compelling reasons why jurors believe such identifications are accurate (Brewer & Burke, 2002).

The problem with witness confidence and its great influence on juries is that many studies have shown that witness confidence is not a very strong predictor of whether the witness's identification is accurate (Sporer, Penrod, Read, & Cutler, 1995). Another problem with eyewitness'es confidence is its apparent malleability: After making a false-identification from a photo spread, witnesses who were told that another witness identified the same person became highly confident in their false identifications (Luus & Wells, 1994). One result of feedback from the lineup administrator—whether it subtly conveys to the witness that he or she picked the suspect or tells the witness that another person picked the same suspect—is a sense of false confidence.

Can the development of false confidence be prevented? Wells and Bradfield (1998) hypothesized that confidence inflation occurs because at the time that feedback is delivered by the investigator, the eyewitness has not yet formed an independent opinion about his or her confidence. Therefore, asking witnesses to provide a statement of their degree of certainty before giving any feedback can be an effective way to eliminate the problem of false confidence. This recommendation, along with suggestions to use unbiased instructions, similar-looking fillers, and sequential lineups, is included in the Justice Department guidelines.

Use of Hypnosis with Eyewitnesses

Most eyewitnesses cannot remember everything that happened during the crime; their memories are often fragmented and vague. Are there ways to enhance the memories of eyewitnesses—to help them accurately remember facts and details?

Law enforcement officials are eager to use techniques that will increase the detail, accuracy, and usefulness of recollections by victims and other witnesses. Hypnosis has been investigated as an aid to memory and has been credited with helping solve some notorious crimes. Hypnosis was used in the Sam Sheppard murder case, the trial of the Boston Strangler, and the investigation of the assassination of Robert Kennedy. Probably the most notorious example of its use was the 1976 Chowchilla, California, kidnapping case, in which a busload of 26 schoolchildren and their driver were abducted by three masked kidnappers and buried underground in a large tomb, from which they later escaped. The driver had seen the license plate on one of the kidnappers' vans and had tried to memorize the numbers. However, he was unable to recall the numbers until he was hypnotized. At one point during the hypnotic session, he suddenly called out a license plate number he remembered seeing. The number was correct except for one digit, and this information expedited the capture of the three culprits, who were later convicted and sentenced to life in prison.

What Is Hypnosis?

Everyone is aware of hypnosis, and perhaps you have been hypnotized yourself. During the past two centuries, hypnotism has been used to treat a range of psychological and physical disorders, including obesity, smoking, addictions, pain, fears, asthma, and stress disorders (Flammer & Bongartz, 2003; Montgomery, DuHamel, & Redd, 2000). Many different explanations exist for what occurs during a hypnotized state, as well as for the essential ingredients of hypnosis.

Explanations of hypnosis fall into one of two categories. Some investigators think of hypnosis as a procedure delivered by a skilled practitioner who induces in subjects a special mental state known as a *trance*, which endows them with unique mental abilities. The second perspective focuses on subjects' *suggestibility*, which is maximized during hypnotic inductions. We define hypnosis as a state of *extreme suggestibility*, in which the hypnotized subject is very relaxed, attentive to incoming stimuli, and responsive to suggestions from the hypnotist. In effect, the subject agrees to reduce logical judgment and yield to the hypnotist's instruction. Hypnosis often heightens subjects' attention and imagination, but it also sometimes leads to confusion between imagined memories and memories of real events.

In the past, hypnosis was used extensively by law enforcement officials and government agencies for two main purposes: (1) generating investigative leads that can then be pursued through other means and (2) refreshing the memories of witnesses, victims, or defendants who have forgotten important details of events about which they might testify in court. The methods used to reach these two goals are basically identical, but their legal and professional status is different, as we describe below.

Effects of Hypnosis on Memory: Memory Aid or Altered Memory?

Few professionals find fault with forensic hypnosis when it is restricted to its first purpose: generating new leads for the police. However, the situation is different when hypnosis is used to help a witness recall details that may later be included in court testimony or to help witnesses choose between conflicting versions of events that they have provided on different occasions. In these situations, many observers contend, the technique is fraught with so many problems that it raises risks for criminal defendants and should be allowed only under the strictest of safeguards or banned altogether (e.g., Newman, 2001; Webert, 2003). As a result of these concerns, many U.S. jurisdictions have, in the past decade, abandoned their use of hypnosis, although police in other countries continue to use hypnosis for memory enhancement purposes (Wagstaff, 1999).

What are the dangers of hypnotically enhanced memory? Critics point to five concerns, all consistent with the commonly held theory that memories are malleable and reconstructed, rather than facsimile recordings of prior experiences. The concerns are as follows:

1. Subjects often remember more material when hypnotized than when they are in a nonhypnotized state, an effect known as **hyperamnesia**. This additional material consists of a mixture of accurate and inaccurate recollections (Dywan & Bowers, 1983). False "recollections" can be implanted through suggestions from the hypnotist, or they can originate in other ways that are not yet completely understood. The addition of false information to accurate recollections is called **confabulation**. For example, an Illinois man was charged with first-degree murder after an eyewitness, under hypnosis, described his license plate. The witness claimed to have seen the car from 230 feet away, at night, with lights shining directly in his eyes. The charges were dropped, however, after an ophthalmologist testified that a person could not see more than 30 feet under such conditions. The net conclusion appears to be that hypnotized subjects do not show a reliable increase in accurate recall compared to nonhypnotized subjects (Steblay & Bothwell, 1994).

2. One reason why confabulation occurs under hypnosis is that subjects relax their standards for reporting information. They become less critical and accept approximations of memory as "accurate enough." These approximations are then added to accurate memories to yield a version of events that is part fact and part fabrication. A second factor that contributes to confabulation is that hypnotized subjects are extremely suggestible and want to please the hypnotist by giving as full a report as possible. This motive encourages subjects to fill in the gaps in their memory with plausible details or with information they believe the hypnotist is expecting.

3. The greatest danger of confabulation is that persons who have been hypnotized find it difficult to separate actual memories from those generated under hypnosis. This problem can be compared to that of the basketball fan who watches a controversial play at an arena and then later watches TV replays of the same play. This fan develops a clear "picture" of the play in

memory but is unable to tell which parts of the picture are from the actual game and which come from the TV replay.

4. Not only do hypnotized witnesses find it difficult to distinguish their original memories from those brought out under hypnosis, but they also tend to become more confident about their recall despite the fact that it might contain false recollections (Scoboria, Mazzoni, Kirsch, & Milling, 2002). This confidence can persist long after the hypnosis session has ended. Hypnosis thus translates beliefs or expectations into "memories," a process called **memory hardening**.

5. Several studies have shown that hypnotized subjects are more responsive to the biasing influence of leading questions. For example, Scoboria et al. (2002) played an audiotape story for research participants who then recalled as much as they could about the narrative. At this point, half the participants were hypnotized, and the researchers then asked questions of all participants; some were misleading questions (e.g., "Did the woman have one child or two?") and others were neutral (e.g., "Did the woman have any children?"). Misleading questions produced significantly more memory errors than hypnosis, but the two effects compounded each other, so the combination of misleading questions and hypnosis produced significantly more errors than either manipulation alone. What's interesting about this finding is that leading questions are allowed (and expected) in court, despite the effect that they seem to have on the accuracy of the respondent's memory. However, as you will learn in the next section, witnesses are often not allowed to testify about memories that are enhanced through hypnosis.

Legal Status of Hypnosis

What if, as a result of being hypnotized, a victim claims to be able to identify her attacker—for example, by remembering his name or the license plate of his car? Can such information be introduced at a trial? Courts sharply differ in their responses to the question of whether hypnotically refreshed testimony can be admitted at trial. The decisions cluster into one of three camps.

Up until about 1980, the majority view was that hypnotically assisted testimony was admissible (Diamond, 1980). Today, only five states allow the admission of hypnotically assisted testimony in all circumstances (Webert, 2003). According to this position, identified with the Maryland case of *Harding v. State* (1968), the fact that a witness has been hypnotized has a bearing on how much weight a jury should give that person's testimony, but not on whether the testimony is admissible at trial. Courts that allow hypnotically enhanced testimony reason that cross-examination of the eyewitness and testimony of an expert witness can assist jurors and judges in deciding whether the hypnotically refreshed testimony is credible.

The second camp takes the position that the admissibility of hypnotically refreshed testimony depends on the circumstances of the case. Some states have adopted the view that such testimony is admissible only if certain safeguards were taken during the hypnosis session. The lead opinion in this category is *State v. Hurd* (1981), decided by the New Jersey Supreme Court, which set out the following guidelines: (1) The hypnosis should be conducted by a specially trained psychiatrist or psychologist. (2) The hypnotist should be independent of the prosecution, the police, and the defense. (3) Information learned prior to the hypnosis should be written and retained so that it can be examined by other parties in the case. (4) The entire hypnosis session should be recorded, preferably on videotape. (5) Only the hypnotist and the subject should be present during any phase of the hypnosis, including the posthypnosis interview. (6) All of the subject's prehypnosis memories for the events in question should be recorded and preserved. Other states and most federal courts consider procedural safeguards only one factor to consider in determining the admissibility of this evidence (Webert, 2003). They follow a more flexible approach, often involving a pretrial hearing, to assess whether, given the circumstances of the case, the testimony is sufficiently reliable and useful to the jury.

The third camp takes a position diametrically opposed to the first. Their position, adopted by the majority of states, is that hypnotically enhanced testimony is inadmissible in court. Many states prohibit a witness who has been hypnotized from testifying about either posthypnotic *or prehypnotic* recollections in the prosecution of that case. (The rationale is that witnesses will be unable to distinguish memories they recalled prior to hypnosis from those that may have been implanted during the hypnotic interview.) This view became increasingly popular in the 1980s, beginning with the case of *State of Minnesota v. Mack* (1980), in which the Supreme Court of Minnesota ruled that hypnosis had not been generally accepted by the scientific community as a reliable method for enhancing accurate recall and that hypnotically refreshed recall was to be excluded from the trial.

This topic was revisited in the 1987 U.S. Supreme Court decision of *Rock v. Arkansas* (see Box 5.2 for a summary of the facts of this case), in which the Court held that an automatic ban against hypnotically refreshed testimony violated previously hypnotized defendants' rights to testify on their own behalf. By deciding that hypnotically aided testimony cannot be automatically excluded, the *Rock* court reached a conclusion that is similar to the *Hurd* approach, in which each case is examined on the merits of how the hypnosis is conducted.

Law enforcement officials and victims of crime argue that it is unfair to permit defendants to have their memories refreshed by hypnosis but to deny this opportunity to prosecution witnesses. At the same time, the evidence about the potentially biasing effects of hypnosis is becoming more and more persuasive, so we would not expect a large swing in the direction of relaxing the admissibility standards for hypnotically aided testimony.

In summary, although it generates additional information that the police can check out, hypnosis also increases the risks of inaccurate recall. Given the inconsistent court rulings, what can we say about the wisdom of relying on hypnotically aided memory?

The best use of hypnosis is during the early stages of a criminal investigation. Hypnosis can help witnesses provide clues: a license number, a piece of clothing, a description of a gun. These leads, even if they don't pan out, are better than no clues at all. Inaccurate "facts" are not as damaging at the first stage of a criminal investigation as they are at a trial.

Less desirable is the use of hypnosis by the police to *verify* previously obtained information, especially if such verification involves leading questions. It is even riskier—in fact, undesirable—to hypnotize a witness who has given several different stories in order to learn the "true" story. This step will simply fix in the witness's mind one particular version of the testimony, which he or she then will faithfully produce on demand. The American Medical Association has expressed the opinion that hypnotically induced memories are not accurate enough to be allowed on the witness stand. This seems a wise conclusion.

A potential substitute for hypnosis is the **cognitive interview** (Fisher & Geiselman, 1992), which uses some of the techniques of hypnosis, including rapport building, instructions to "report everything," and focused attention. Instead of a standard interview ("Tell me what happened"), witnesses participating in a cognitive interview are encouraged to recreate the scene mentally and report everything they can remember. (This process is sometimes referred to as **context reinstatement**.) The interviewer may ask them to think about the surroundings, the smells and sound, the temperature, the location of the furniture, or anything else that may elicit new memories. The interviewer may suggest that they recall events in reverse order or that they try to reexperience the moods they originally felt. All these activities help reinstate the context in which the crime occurred in the hope that additional memories will appear spontaneously.

Most of the evidence suggests that the cognitive interview has the potential to enhance recall. Furthermore, this enhancement comes without the problems of susceptibility to leading questions and exaggerated confidence that are associated with hypnosis (Geiselman, Fisher, MacKinnon, & Holland, 1985; Kebbell & Wagstaff, 1998).

THE CASE OF

BOX 5.2 · **Vicki Rock: Hypnosis and defendants**

All the court decisions and changes in state laws described in the text refer to the hypnosis of witnesses, usually victims of a crime. What if a defendant who is charged with a crime claims that he or she cannot remember what happened at a crucial time? Then, if the defendant is hypnotized before the trial and "remembers" facts that would help prove his or her innocence, should this testimony be admitted into evidence?

The U.S. Supreme Court faced this question in the case of *Rock v. Arkansas* (1987). Vicki Lorene Rock had been convicted of manslaughter in the shooting of her husband, Frank, in 1983 and was sentenced to ten years in prison. After the shooting, she could remember that she and her husband had been arguing, that he pushed her against a wall, and that she wanted to leave the house but he wouldn't let her. She recalled clutching the gun because she thought it would keep him from hitting her again. She also recalled phoning the police, who arrived to

find Frank lying on the floor, a bullet in his chest.

Only after Mrs. Rock had been hypnotized was she able to recall that she had not put her finger on the gun's trigger, that her husband had grabbed her from behind, that they struggled, and that the gun went off by accident. As a result of this new information, Rock's attorney hired a gun expert to examine the handgun. This investigation revealed that the weapon was defective and prone to fire when hit, even without the trigger being pulled.

The judge at Mrs. Rock's trial, following the law in Arkansas, refused to let jurors hear anything the defendant remembered as a result of being hypnotized. In her appeal, Mrs. Rock contended that this ruling denied her the opportunity to present evidence crucial to her defense.

Note the dilemma facing the U.S. Supreme Court: On the one hand, hypnosis "is not generally regarded by the scientific community as reliable" (to quote the

Arkansas attorney general), and recent rulings had restricted its application. On the other hand, a defendant has a Fourteenth Amendment constitutional right to due process; in this case, the defendant's defense depended on the recollection of events that she could not remember before she was hypnotized.

The Supreme Court ruled 5–4 in favor of Mrs. Rock and struck down the Arkansas law prohibiting all hypnotically refreshed testimony. Mrs. Rock was granted a new trial. In the majority opinion, Justice Harry Blackmun acknowledged that hypnosis may produce "incorrect recollections" but said that the Arkansas court decision excluding all hypnotically refreshed testimony per se was "arbitrary." However, the decision did not open the door to all types of hypnotically enhanced testimony. Blackmun wrote, "We express no opinion on the admissibility of previously hypnotized witnesses other than criminal defendants."

The Eyewitness in the Courtroom

Despite limitations on the reliability of their identifications, eyewitnesses are one of the prosecution's most influential resources to convict defendants in criminal trials. Jurors put a great deal of weight on testimony from an eyewitness. In a study showing this influence, Loftus (1974) gave

subjects a description of an armed robbery that had resulted in two deaths. Of mock jurors who heard a version of the case that contained only circumstantial evidence against the defendant, 18% convicted him. But when an eyewitness's identification of the defendant was presented as well, 72% of the mock jurors convicted him. It is hard to overestimate the power of confident eyewitnesses to convince a jury of the correctness of their testimony.

Psychological research shows that jurors overestimate the accuracy of eyewitnesses. In one study, Wells, Lindsay, and Ferguson (1979) staged a "theft" under viewing conditions that were good, moderate, or poor for witnesses. As you might expect, eyewitnesses did a better job when the viewing conditions were good: 74% of them were accurate, compared with 50% in the moderate viewing conditions and 33% in the poor viewing conditions. Then some mock jurors watched these eyewitnesses being cross-examined, after which the jurors indicated whether they believed the eyewitnesses. Belief rates for the good, the moderate, and the poor witnessing conditions were, respectively, 69%, 57%, and 58%. Thus, when the viewing conditions are only so-so or poor, jurors tend to overestimate the witnesses' accuracy.

Jurors overestimate the validity of eyewitnesses' testimony because they appear to be unaware of several of the factors that compromise eyewitness accuracy. For example:

◆ Jurors have little awareness of the factors that interfere with accurate retention, such as weapon focus, amount of violence in a criminal event, effects of prior exposures (Cutler, Penrod, & Dexter, 1990), and the other-race effect (Abshire & Bornstein, 2003).

◆ Jurors show a lack of sophistication about the problems inherent in typical lineups and photo spreads used by the police to test witness recognition (Cutler et al., 1990; Loftus & Wagenaar, 1990).

◆ Jurors are usually not told about those eyewitnesses who could not identify a suspect; even the defendant's attorney may not be aware of these misses (Wells & Lindsay, 1980).

We also know that jurors pay attention to factors that may not help them distinguish accurate from inaccurate eyewitness testimony. One of these factors is the confidence with which an eyewitness testifies. We have already shown that confident testimony can distort jurors' perceptions of other testimony-relevant criteria, such as the eyewitness's opportunity to view the crime. In a study of the effects of eyewitness confidence on mock jurors' verdicts, Brewer and Burke (2002) found that witness confidence had a strong effect on jurors' judgments, regardless of whether the witness gave consistent testimony (i.e., similar responses to questions from prosecutor and defense attorney) or inconsistent testimony (i.e., different responses to prosecutor and defense attorney). This creates a dangerous situation for an innocent defendant because it means that a confident eyewitness can be persuasive to jurors, even when he or she is wrong (Wells, Olson, & Charman, 2002).

Safeguards against Mistaken Identification

Much of the eyewitness research is motivated by a desire to increase the accuracy of eyewitnesses. If the validity of eyewitness testimony can be improved (careful adherence to the Department of Justice guidelines would certainly help), then there would be no need to caution jurors and judges about the potential fallibility of eyewitnesses (Seelau & Wells, 1995). Until that time, though, it would seem that truth would be better served if there were a means by which jurors and judges could be alerted to and educated about some of the problems inherent in eyewitness reports. There are three ways in which this might be done.

Evaluating the Effectiveness of Cross-Examination

First, eyewitnesses can be cross-examined in an attempt to reveal factors that might compromise their identification. But cross-examination may not be especially effective in increasing juror sensitivity to the factors that can affect eyewitness performance (Devenport, Stinson, Cutler, & Kravitz, 2002). For cross-examination to be effective, the following conditions must all be met:

1. Attorneys must have access to the information necessary to cross-examine the eyewitness

effectively, including the conditions under which the crime was committed. Unfortunately, like everyone else, attorneys are forced to rely on the witness's memory of the crime, the perpetrator, and the conditions under which the crime was committed. The quality of the information available to attorneys depends on the witness's memory and willingness to cooperate (Penrod & Cutler, 1999).

2. Attorneys must have knowledge of the factors that potentially influence eyewitnesses' performance. Do they have this knowledge? One study has shown that attorneys are generally insensitive to factors that influence the suggestiveness of lineups and are not aware that jurors overestimate the accuracy of eyewitnesses (Stinson, Devenport, Cutler, & Kravitz, 1996). If attorneys lack knowledge of these issues, they may simply ask the wrong questions.

3. Judges must also be aware of the factors that influence the accuracy of an eyewitness's memory because they decide to what extent cross-examination (and other remedies) can be used to guard against erroneous eyewitness testimony. Are judges knowledgeable about concerns related to eyewitness evidence? A recent survey of 160 U.S. judges showed that they were correct on some issues (e.g., that eyewitness testimony about an event often reflects not only what a witness actually saw but also information obtained later from other sources, and that an eyewitness's perception and memory may be affected by attitudes and expectations) but lack knowledge that eyewitness confidence is not a good indicator of accuracy and that jurors are often unable to distinguish accurate from inaccurate eyewitnesses (Wise & Safer, 2004). Judges also decide whether jurors will receive guidance in order to be better informed about the factors that influence eyewitness performance, so there is serious concern that they may be making these decisions on the basis of biased expectations of eyewitnesses and jurors alike.

How, then, can jurors become better informed about the factors that influence eyewitness performance? Two further remedies have been proposed. One solution would be to allow psychologists who are knowledgeable about the relevant research on perception and memory to testify to juries about their findings. As a second remedy, judges could instruct juries about the potential weaknesses of eyewitness identifications and suggest how to interpret this testimony. (Of course, both solutions require judges to be aware of the vagaries of eyewitness testimony and of jurors' need for instruction!) We describe these two alternatives next.

Evaluating the Expert Testimony of Psychologists

Psychologists could have much to say to jurors about experimental research on eyewitness testimony: that eyewitnesses are sometimes inaccurate, that extreme stress usually inhibits accurate and complete encoding, that feedback from a lineup administrator can increase an eyewitness's confidence, that extremely confident eyewitnesses are not necessarily accurate, and that differences in the way lineups are constructed and presented to witnesses affect eyewitness accuracy. Note that the expert witness does not tell the jury what to believe about a particular eyewitness or whether the eyewitness is accurate. Even the eyewitness cannot always know this with certainty. Rather, the expert's task is to provide the jury with a scientifically based frame of reference within which to evaluate the eyewitness's evidence.

But psychologists are sometimes not allowed to testify about these matters, and appellate courts have generally upheld such decisions. In most states, the decision about whether an expert psychologist can testify is left to the presiding judge— an example of the breadth of discretion that the legal system grants to judges. Recently, federal courts have become more receptive to expert testimony about eyewitness identification. For example, the courts are more likely to allow such testimony when a prosecutor's case against a defendant relies almost entirely on an eyewitness's identification (*United States v. Jordan*, 1996).

Why have judges sometimes been reluctant to let psychological experts testify? First, some judges believe that scientific research on eyewitness identification is not sufficiently established to yield valid research findings. In the past, a few psychologists have agreed with this opinion (e.g., Egeth, 1995; Elliott, 1993; Konecni & Ebbesen, 1986), but most psychologists disagree (Tubb, Kassin, Memon, & Hosch, 2000). Second, judges may believe that such expert testimony would not provide facts that are beyond the common knowledge of most jury members and would therefore invade the province of the jury as finders and triers of fact. Third, judges fear that admitting such expert testimony would open the gates to conflicting expert testimony, setting the scene for a confusing and uninformative "battle of the experts." (Such battles have occurred in some highly publicized trials involving a criminal defendant's claim of insanity; see Chapter 8.) Finally, judges worry that this type of testimony might lead jurors to give insufficient weight to eyewitness evidence, making them too skeptical of all eyewitnesses (Woocher, 1986), even those who witnessed a crime or accident under good viewing conditions and who were not subjected to suggestive identification procedures. Indeed, expert testimony would be most useful if it could sensitize jurors to variations in witnessing and identification procedures that might threaten the reliability of the identifications. But can it serve this limited function, or does it instead make jurors generally skeptical of all eyewitnesses? Research studies have addressed that question.

Some early studies (e.g., Fox & Walters, 1986; Hosch, Beck, & McIntyre, 1980) manipulated the presence of expert testimony about eyewitnesses in a simulated jury study. Participants in those studies heard testimony from an eyewitness, and some also heard from a defense expert witness about the potential unreliability of eyewitness memory. What effect did the expert have? Generally, the expert testimony resulted in reduced belief in the eyewitness. Unfortunately, because of the design of those early studies, it is hard to know whether the expert sensitized jurors to the factors that might impair the witness's ability to make a correct identification or caused them to become skeptical of all eyewitnesses. Because these studies did not *independently* vary the presence of expert testimony, evidence about the witness's viewing conditions, and identification procedures, sensitivity, and skepticism were confounded. The question remained: Would jurors who heard an expert become distrustful of *all* witnesses (indicating general skepticism) or of only those witnesses whose viewing and identification conditions were poor (indicating sensitivity to the importance of these factors)?

Brian Cutler and his colleagues were eventually able to answer that question (Cutler, Penrod, and Dexter, 1989; Devenport et al., 2002). They showed subjects realistic videotaped trials that focused on the accuracy of an eyewitness's identification from a lineup. Some subjects heard an expert testify about the effects of identification conditions on accuracy, whereas other jurors heard no expert testimony on these matters. In addition, some mock jurors heard evidence that the identification conditions were good (e.g., that the lineup was presented in an unbiased manner), and others heard that they were poor. In other words, the researchers varied the presence of expert testimony and evidence about identification factors *independently*. What do the results say about sensitivity and skepticism? They suggest that the effect of expert testimony was to generally sensitize jurors to the importance of witnessing and identification conditions. There was no evidence that mock jurors became more skeptical about the eyewitness when they heard an expert.

A report of one actual crime also lends anecdotal support to the conclusion that the testimony of an expert witness has impact. Loftus (1984) described the trial of two Arizona brothers charged with the torture of three Mexicans. Two juries were in the courtroom at the same time, one deciding the verdict for Patrick Hanigan, the other deciding the fate of his brother, Thomas. Most of the evidence was from eyewitnesses, and it was virtually identical for the two defendants. However, expert testimony about the inaccuracy of eyewitnesses was introduced in Thomas's trial only. (The jury hearing Patrick Hanigan's case waited in the jury room while this evidence was presented.) Patrick Hanigan was convicted by one jury; his brother was acquitted by the other. This is as close to a "natural experiment" as the legal system has happened to offer for assessing the influence of a psychologist in the courtroom.

To summarize, the bulk of research examining the effects of expert testimony about eyewitness identifications suggests that mock jurors who are exposed to expert testimony about the vagaries of eyewitness identifications do not reject all or even most such identifications, but they do tend to view them a bit more critically. Unfortunately, even when allowed, expert testimony is an expensive safeguard that is available in only a small fraction of the cases that come to trial each year (Wells et al., 1998). Are there other, more readily available remedies?

Evaluating the Effectiveness of Cautionary Jury Instructions

The other major alternative for alerting jurors to the limitations of eyewitnesses is through a judge's instructions. Since the 1970s, both the federal courts and many state courts have encouraged trial judges to alert jurors to the possible mistakes and misinterpretations of eyewitnesses. In *Neil v. Biggers* (1972), the U.S. Supreme Court specified five conditions that jurors should consider in evaluating identification evidence:

1. The opportunity for witnesses to view the criminal at the time of the crime
2. The length of time between the crime and the later identification
3. The level of certainty shown by the witnesses at the identification
4. The witnesses' degree of attention during the crime
5. The accuracy of the witnesses' prior description of the criminal.

The Court reasoned that satisfactory reports on these conditions would suggest that an eyewitness's report was accurate. These conditions were restated and reaffirmed five years later in *Manson v. Braithwaite* (1977).

Although psychologists were pleased to see the Supreme Court take this action, they did not agree

with all its strictures. Research supports consideration of the first two guidelines and the fourth and fifth conditions are plausible. It is recommendation 3—to take into account the witnesses' level of certainty—that is most questionable as a factor in evaluating identification evidence. We have already mentioned two problems related to witness confidence: It is not a strong predictor of accuracy, and it is malleable in the face of feedback. Therefore, advising jurors to assess a witness's level of certainty may be misleading. As some consolation, a study that examined how people combine these five criteria in an overall judgment of a witness's accuracy showed that certainty does not carry more weight than the other criteria (Bradfield & Wells, 2000). Instead, people used all five criteria to assess identification accuracy.

Many states have followed the Supreme Court's lead in using a cautionary instruction similar to that from *Neil v. Biggers*. The instructions typically mention the eyewitness's degree of certainty as one of the factors that jurors should use to assess accuracy.

But even these less-than-perfect cautionary instructions have not been universally accepted in the courts. Some individual judges are reluctant to use such instructions. The defense typically requests that the instruction be given, but judges sometimes refuse. One reason is their concern that these instructions intrude on the jury's task. When asked whether they would use a cautionary instruction on eyewitness reliability in their courts, 78% of the judges polled said that it was improper to give such an instruction to the jury; only 12% approved (Greene, 1988).

What effects do cautionary instructions have on jurors' beliefs about eyewitness accuracy? One study compared the effectiveness of the so-called *Telfaire* instruction, a frequently used instruction based on the case of *U.S. v. Telfaire* (1972), and a set of instructions modeled after typical expert testimony regarding eyewitness reliability (Ramirez, Zemba, & Geiselman, 1996). The researchers were interested in the "sensitivity versus skepticism" concerns that we mentioned with regard to expert psychological testimony. The *Telfaire* instruction reduced mock jurors' sensitivity to eyewitness evidence (probably because that instruction mentions only vague directives and gives little indication how jurors should evaluate the evidence) and produced either skepticism or overbelief in the eyewitness, depending on the timing of the instruction. However, an instruction that incorporated information likely to be delivered by an expert preserved jurors' sensitivity to the factors that influence eyewitness reliability.

One might think that judges should be willing to issue an instruction that apparently increases sensitivity to witnessing conditions and that does not simultaneously cause jurors to question the truthfulness of *all* eyewitnesses. In general, though, judges will not deliver an instruction that provides the kind of detail that is inherent in expert testimony on eyewitness reliability. In a recent survey, judges were asked whether they would deliver jury instructions on issues for which jurors may lack knowledge (e.g., confidence malleability, weapon focus, and lineup presentation format). Only approximately one-quarter of the judges said that they would (Wise & Safer, 2004). As a result, most jurors are not informed about the possibility of suggestive lineup procedures, the debilitating effects of stress on eyewitness memory, and a host of other factors that reduce the accuracy of eyewitness reports.

Repressed and Recovered Memories

Although the retrieval of memories over short time periods is a complex task, these complications pale in comparison to those involved in retrieving memories that have been forgotten over long time periods. Two basic processes need to be distinguished in discussing and understanding long-lost memories. The first is natural forgetting, which tends to occur when people simply do not think about events that happened years earlier. Just as you might have trouble remembering the names of your third- and fourth-grade teachers (or at least

remembering which teacher taught which grade), witnesses to crimes, accidents, and business transactions are likely to forget the details of these events, if not the entire event, after the passage of months or years. Such forgetting or misremembering is even more likely when the target event is confused with prior or subsequent events that bear some resemblance to it.

No one disputes the reality of natural forgetting. However, much more controversy exists about a second type of lost memory: memories that are presumed to have been repressed over long time periods. These scenarios involve events that are thought to be so traumatizing that after they are experienced, individuals bury them deeply in their unconscious through a process of emotionally motivated forgetting called **repression**. For example, soldiers exposed to the brutal horrors of combat and citizens who experienced a natural disaster such as an earthquake are sometimes unable to remember the traumas they obviously suffered. In such cases, repression is thought to serve a protective function by sparing the individual from having to remember and relive horrifying scenes. Furthermore, it is often reported that these repressed memories stay unconscious, and hence forgotten, unless and until they either are spontaneously recalled or are retriggered by exposure to some aspect of the original experience. (The smell of gasoline might remind a soldier of the battlefield, or the sight of an unusual cloud formation might remind an earthquake victim of the sky's appearance on the day of the disaster.)

A related unconscious process is **dissociation**, in which victims of abuse or other traumas are thought to escape the full impact of an event by psychologically detaching themselves from it. This process is thought to be particularly strong in children, who, because they are still forming integrated personalities, find it easier to escape from the pain of abuse by fantasizing about made-up individuals and imagining that the abuse is happening to those others. Many clinical psychologists believe that such early episodes of dissociation, involving unique ideas, feelings, and behavior, form the beginning of the altered personalities that are found in dissociative identity disorder (formerly called multiple personality disorder).

Repressed Memories and Memory Recovery Therapy

In legal circles, the memory issue that has received the most attention involves a set of claims by adults that they (1) suffered sexual/physical abuse as children (often at the hands of parents or other trusted adults), (2) repressed or dissociated any memory of these horrors for many years as a form of unconscious protection, and (3) eventually recovered their long-lost memories of the abuse. Some of the allegations of priest abuse that came to light and plagued the Roman Catholic Church in the 1990s and early 2000s, including the case of Father Paul Shanley, followed this pattern (Box 5.3).

Sometimes, repressed memories are recovered only after a person participates in "memory-focused" psychotherapy that applies techniques such as hypnosis, age regression, sodium amytal ("truth serum"), guided visualization, diary writing, or therapist instructions to help clients remember past abuse (Lindsay & Read, 1995). Such "de-repression" techniques have been advocated by popular books on incest (e.g., Bass & Davis, 1988) and by therapists who believe that unless severe childhood traumas are recalled, confronted, and defused, they will cause mental problems (Blume, 1990). Some therapists who suspect clients of harboring repressed memories of abuse may ask the clients highly suggestive questions, such as "You sound like you might have been abused; what can you tell me about that?" or "You show many of the signs of childhood sexual abuse; can you tell me some of the things you think might have happened to you when you were a very young child?" One book explicitly encouraged women to believe that they were abused as infants by several perpetrators: "How old do you think you were when you were first abused? Write down the very first number that pops into your head, no matter how improbable it seems to you. . . . Does it seem too young to be true? I assure you it is not" (Fredrickson, 1992, pp. 59–66). In addition to

being asked to dredge up memories of traumatic incidents, clients are often encouraged by therapists to join special support groups, such as Survivors of Incest Anonymous, that urge their members to search aggressively for buried memories of abuse.

Many researchers and therapists question the empirical and clinical validity of repressed-memory techniques, especially when apparent memories of trauma resurface many years after the alleged incidents and then only after the individual has been in therapy that first presumes and then finds such memories (Gerrie, Garry, & Loftus, 2005; Holmes, 1995). These skeptics point out that most people who suffer severe trauma do not forget the event; in fact, many of them suffer intrusive recollections of it for years afterward. Skepticism is also fueled by the fact that some alleged victims claim to have recalled traumas that happened when they were less than 1 year old, a feat that nearly all research on childhood memory and amnesia shows is not possible, for reasons related to neurological development.

One of the most widely cited studies on this topic confirms that it is possible for people to forget horrible events that happened to them in childhood, but it does not answer the question of how this forgetting occurs or how memories are usually recovered. Linda Williams (1994) interviewed 129 women who had experienced well-documented cases of childhood sexual abuse. She asked these women detailed questions about their childhood abuse histories, which had occurred an average of 17 years earlier. More than one-third of the women did not report the abuse they had experienced in childhood. But this figure does not prove that the forgetting was due to repression. It is possible that when the abuse occurred, the women were too young to be fully aware of it; in addition, some of the women might have been unwilling to report sexual abuse to an interviewer, who was a relative stranger, even if they did remember it.

However, what should we make of the sudden recall of events that a person claims to have repressed for years? If recollections of past abuse do not stem from actual traumatic events, where else

BOX 5.3   Recovered memories and the case against Father Paul Shanley

On February 11, 2002, Paul Busa, the man who would eventually accuse Father Paul Shanley—a controversial and charismatic Roman Catholic priest—of child sexual abuse years before, was working as an Air Force police officer in Colorado. That day, he received a phone call from his girlfriend in Boston, telling him of a newspaper article citing accusations against Mr. Shanley by a childhood friend of Busa's. The sex abuse scandal that rocked the Roman Catholic Church had just broken, and allegations against Father Shanley and other priests were coming to light. In this context, Busa began to recall his own abuse at the hands of Father Shanley, although these memories had apparently been repressed for years. The accuser then began to speak openly about his abuse. Busa eventually received $500,000 from the Boston archdiocese to settle

a civil lawsuit against Shanley, and he agreed to proceed to trial in the criminal case against the now-defrocked former priest. Father Shanley, 74, was accused of molesting Busa, who was between the ages of 6 and 12, by pulling him out of Sunday school classes and orally and digitally raping him.

At the trial, the alleged victim, now a barrel-chested firefighter who lives in Massachusetts, gave emotional—even teary—testimony about the multiple incidents of abuse in the church bathroom, the pews, the rectory, and even the confession booth. Busa testified that he was so traumatized by the memories that surfaced years later that he was unable to continue to function in the Air Force. "I felt like my world was coming to an end," he said (Belluck, 2005). Despite some inconsistencies in his recollections and testimony from a defense expert witness who

Father Paul Shanley being taken into custody shortly after his conviction on charges of raping an alter boy years before.

explained how false memories can be created in susceptible minds, the jury was apparently convinced by Busa's seemingly heartfelt testimony. They convicted Father Shanley on two counts of rape and two counts of indecent assault on a child. He was sentenced to 12 to 15 years in prison.

could they originate? Several sources are possible, including fantasies, distorted recollections, and even the unintentional planting of memories by therapists who try (perhaps too hard) to find reasons for clients' psychological problems.

The possibility that therapy clients can recover memories of childhood abuse that have been long repressed has led many states to pass legislation that allows victims of childhood sexual abuse to bring suit against their attackers long after the alleged abuse occurred. (Typically, all lawsuits must be filed within a prescribed "limitations period" dating from the occurrence of the act that

caused harm. The defendant can bar a plaintiff's claim if the complaint was filed too late.) These **delayed-reporting statutes** suspend the statute of limitations and grant abuse survivors who claim to have repressed their memory of abuse, and were therefore unaware that it occurred, the right to bring a lawsuit within three years from the date of *recovering* the memory.

The fundamental questions are these: Are recovered memories true memories, consisting of vivid, albeit delayed, recall of past horrors? Or are they pseudomemories, created by needy and suggestible clients responding to overzealous therapists who are trying to find a convincing explanation for their clients' current problems? Even psychologists are deeply divided on these questions. In fact, the Working Group on Investi-gation of Memories of Childhood Abuse, appointed by the American Psychological Association, was so deeply divided that the group was forced to issue two reports. One report, written by clinical psychologists (Alpert, Brown, & Courtois, 1998), suggests that intolerable emotional and physical arousal can lead a child victim to use numbing and/or dissociative coping strategies; that these strategies may interfere with or impair encoding, storage, and retrieval of memories; and that numbing responses may lead to delayed recall. A second report, authored by experimental research psychologists (Ornstein, Ceci, & Loftus, 1998), pointed out that suggestibility, memory distortions, and misleading informa-tion can work to degrade memory performance; that memory for traumatic experiences can be highly malleable; and that it is relatively easy to create pseudomemories for events that never occurred.

We are not, of course, suggesting that child abuse does not occur. Not only does it occur, but it is a serious problem both in the United States and throughout the world. It appears that children who were abused are at increased risk to suffer mental disorders in adulthood. The real question is whether allegations of childhood abuse that first surface only after intensive searching for them in therapy are trustworthy (Bottoms, Shaver, & Goodman, 1996; Loftus, 1997b).

Can we really be sure that these alleged abuses took place? Is it possible that some memories, especially those that appear to have been repressed for years, only then to be recovered through aggressive "memory work" therapy, are imagined or made up? Although it is always difficult to assess the authenticity of any one individual's memories, evidence is accumulating that false memories can be implanted, that people can be led through suggestion and misinformation to believe such memories are real, and that third parties such as therapists may find it difficult to distinguish authentic from unauthentic recollections (Lindsay, Hagen, Read, Wade, & Garry,

2004; Porter, Yuille, & Lehman, 1999). One wonders, for example, about the authenticity of Paul Ingram's memories (see Box 5.4).

Creating Pseudomemories

In recent years, many psychologists have studied claims of repressed memories and the techniques used to retrieve them. They have used laboratory research and real-life cases to document how memories can be built from the suggestions of others.

One way that psychologists have been able to implant false memories is by enlisting the help of family members, who suggest to adult research participants that these relatives recall a fabricated event. For example, with help from participants' relatives, Loftus and Pickrell (1995) constructed a false story that the participant had been lost during a shopping trip at the age of 5, was found crying by an elderly person, and was eventually reunited with family members. After reading this story, participants wrote what they remembered about the event. Nearly 30% of participants either partially or fully remembered the made-up event, and 25% claimed in subsequent interviews that they remembered the fictitious situation. Other efforts to implant childhood memories have produced similar results, leading subjects to believe such fictitious experiences as being attacked by a vicious animal, being saved from drowning by a lifeguard, and attending a wedding reception and accidentally spilling punch on the parents of the bride (Heaps & Nash, 2001; Hyman, Husband, & Billings, 1995; Porter et al., 1999). People with higher dissociative capacity and hypnotizability are apparently more susceptible to these suggestions than others (Loftus, 1997a).

Still other experimental procedures have been used to examine the malleable nature of **autobiographical memory** (memory for one's past experiences). These include guided memory techniques to plant "impossible" memories about experiences that occurred shortly after birth (Spanos, Burgess, Burgess, Samuels, & Blois, 1999) and interpretation of participants' dreams to suggest that they had experienced a critical childhood event such as being

THE CASE OF

BOX 5.4   Paul Ingram: Real memories or fabricated memories?

The case of Paul Ingram provides one chilling example of how false memories might be created (Ofshe, 1992). Ingram, a sheriff's deputy in Olympia, Washington, was arrested for child abuse in 1988. He steadfastly denied the allegations, but the police continued to question and pressure him over the next five months, despite the lack of much evidence to support the allegations of sexual abuse that two of Ingram's children had lodged against him. To spur Ingram's memory, a psychologist or a detective would repeatedly describe to him an act of abuse, such as Ingram and other men raping his daughter. At first, Ingram would have no memory for such incidents, but after concerted effort, including praying and being hypnotized to strengthen his memory, he started "recalling" some

details. Ultimately, Paul Ingram confessed not just to the charges of incest but also to rapes, assaults, and participation in a satanic cult that was believed to have killed 25 babies (Wright, 1994).

To check the accuracy of Ingram's memory, sociologist Richard Ofshe, hired as a consultant to the prosecution, asked Ingram to recall an event that Ofshe totally fabricated—that Ingram had forced his son and daughter to have sex with each other in front of him. Just as with the police interrogation, Ingram could not remember anything at first, but after thinking and praying about it, he gradually formed images of the event and, within a matter of hours, endorsed a three-page confession to the events Ofshe fabricated. Ofshe concluded that Paul Ingram was not a

sex offender or satanic cult member, but a vulnerable man with a strong need to please authorities and a highly suggestible nature that made him fall easily into a trance.

Ultimately, Paul Ingram decided to plead guilty to six counts of third-degree rape. Throughout many years of incarceration, he insisted that he never abused his children, and he was eventually released, in April 2003. He was required to register as a sex offender in Washington State. Was Paul Ingram duped into confessing on the basis of false memories, or was he a guilt-ridden abuser who finally admitted his guilt? Questions such as these are at the heart of the controversy over whether therapists should aggressively try to help clients recover memories of abuse that they suspect have been repressed.

---

harassed by a bully before the age of 3 (Mazzoni, Loftus, Seitz, & Lynn, 1999). Simply imagining an event from one's past can affect the belief that it actually occurred (Mazzoni & Memon, 2003), even when the event is completely implausible—for example, shaking hands with Bugs Bunny at a Disney theme park (Braun, Ellis, & Loftus, 2002). (The Bugs Bunny character was created by Warner Brothers, not Disney.)

How can we account for this "imagination inflation" effect? One possibility stems from the notion of **source confusion**. The act of imagining may make the event seem more familiar, but that familiarity is mistakenly related to childhood memories rather than to the act of imagination

itself. Other studies suggest that the frequency of imagining is important: The more times participants imagine a nonexistent event, the more likely they are to report having experienced it (Thomas, Bulevich, & Loftus, 2003). The creation of false memories is most likely to occur when people who are having trouble remembering are explicitly encouraged to imagine events and discouraged from thinking about whether their constructions are real.

Recent neuroscientific data have shown that there are changes in brain activity as a result of visual imaging (Gonsalves, Reber, Gitelman, Parrish, Mesulam, & Paller, 2004). This may help explain how imagination can lead to false remembering. But

THE CASE OF

BOX 5.5   **Gary Ramona, his daughter's false memories, and the therapists who suggested them**

The first case in which a parent successfully sued a therapist for implanting a false memory of abuse was brought by Gary Ramona, once a highly paid executive at a large winery in Napa County, California. Ramona accused family counselor Marche Isabella and psychiatrist Richard Rose of planting false memories of trauma in his daughter, Holly, while she was their 19-year-old patient. In his suit, Ramona claimed that the therapists told Holly that her bulimia and depression were caused by having been repeatedly raped by her father when she was a child. They also told her, he claimed, that the memory of this molestation was so traumatic that she had repressed it for years. According to Ramona, Dr. Rose then gave Holly sodium amytal to confirm the validity of her "recovered memory." Finally, Isabella was said to have told Holly's mother that up to 80% of all bulimics had been sexually abused (a statistic for which no scientific support exists).

At their trial, the therapists claimed that Holly suffered flashbacks of what seemed to be real sexual abuse. She also became increasingly depressed and bulimic after reporting these frightening images. In addition, Holly's mother, Stephanie, who had divorced her husband after Holly's allegations came to light, testified that she suspected her husband might have abused Holly. She listed several pieces of supposedly corroborating evidence: that Holly had

complained of vaginal pains during childhood, that she always feared gynecological exams and disliked her father touching her; and that Gary had seemed overly eager to baby-sit Holly and their two other daughters when they were young. She also recalled once coming home to find young Holly wandering around the house wearing no underwear; she said she found the underwear, along with bed sheets, in the clothes dryer. During his testimony, Gary Ramona emotionally denied ever sexually abusing his daughter.

The scientific experts who testified on Ramona's behalf criticized the therapists for using risky and dangerous techniques. Elizabeth Loftus (1993), an expert called by Gary Ramona and a leading critic of therapists who aggressively pursue the recovery of long-buried traumatic memories, charged that these therapists often either suggest the idea of trauma to their clients or are too uncritical in accepting clients' reports of trauma. Another defense witness, Martin Orne, a renowned authority on hypnosis, condemned the use of sodium amytal interviews as "inherently untrustworthy and unreliable" and concluded that Holly's memory had been so distorted by her therapists that she no longer knew what the truth was.

The jury decided that Holly's therapists had indeed acted improperly and, in May 1994, awarded Gary Ramona damages in the amount of $500,000. Since then,

there has been other false memory litigation against therapists. In its first two years of operation, the False Memory Syndrome Foundation received more than 13,000 reports from people who said they were victims of false accusations; most were parents whose grown children had charged them with long-past abuse. This organization has also received reports from scores of former therapy patients who admit that their original charges of abuse were false and resulted from therapists encouraging them to "remember" events that never happened.

The threat of false-memory lawsuits adds to the already difficult challenges faced by therapists trying to help adult clients cope with a traumatic childhood. It is obvious that recovered-memory therapy has led to very real damage to some clients and their families (Ofshe & Watters, 1994). It is also clear that the trauma of child abuse does occur and can leave deep and long-lasting emotional scars. Accordingly, therapists must be sympathetic listeners for clients who remember the real horrors of their childhood. At the same time, therapists must be careful to avoid suggesting that clients' problems come from traumas that may never have been inflicted. In the words of Gary Ramona's attorney, Richard Harrington, "If [therapists] use nonsensical theories about so-called repressed memories to destroy people's lives, they will be held accountable."

bear in mind that even though false childhood memories can be implanted in some people, the memories that result from suggestions are not always false. Unfortunately, without corroboration, it is very hard to know which distant memories are true and which were implanted via suggestion.

False Memories in Court

Evidence that false memories are a significant problem for the law comes in two basic forms. First, several accusers have ultimately retracted their claims of repressed memories for abuse. One of the most highly publicized retractions involved another case of alleged priest abuse—this one filed in 1993 by Stephen Cook, who claimed that he had been sexually abused as a teenager 17 years earlier by the late Joseph Bernardin, when Bernardin had been archbishop of the Catholic archdiocese in Cincinnati. Cook reported that he had repressed these memories for years, only to recover them while hypnotized as part of therapy. The allegations were forcefully denied by Cardinal Bernardin, who at the time of the lawsuit was the head of Chicago's archdiocese and the senior-ranking Roman Catholic

official in the United States. Ironically, Bernardin was well known nationally for his work helping children who had been sexually abused by priests. Cook ultimately dropped the lawsuit after admitting that his charges were based on false memories. He and Bernardin reconciled shortly before Cook died of AIDS in 1995.

A second source of information about false memories comes from court cases in which parents sue therapists who have used aggressive memory recovery techniques to help the adult children of these parents recover supposedly repressed memories of childhood sexual abuse. The claims in these malpractice lawsuits usually take the following form: (1) the abuse never occurred, (2) the therapists created and implanted false memories of abuse through their uncritical use of memory retrieval techniques, and (3) the clients ultimately came to believe the false memories and accused their parents of the abuse, sometimes suing them under delayed-reporting statutes or even filing criminal charges against them. These cases have sometimes resulted in large financial settlements to those who were falsely accused, including Gary Ramona (see Box 5.5).

SUMMARY

1. *What psychological factors contribute to the risk of mistaken identifications in the legal system?* Evidence produced by eyewitnesses often makes the difference between an unsolved crime and a conviction. In the early stages of a crime investigation, eyewitness accounts can provide important clues and permit suspects to be identified. But witnesses often make mistakes, and mistaken identifications have led to the conviction of numerous innocent people. Errors can occur at the moment the crime is committed or at any of the three phases of the memory process: encoding, storage, and retrieval. Furthermore, subsequent questioning and new experiences can alter what has been remembered from the past. In describing the factors that affect the reliability of eyewitness memory, psychologists

distinguish estimator variables—variables whose impact on an identification can only be estimated and not controlled—from system variables—variables that are under the control of the justice system. Much recent research has focused on a particular set of system variables related to the way lineups are conducted.

2. *How do courts regard the use of hypnotically refreshed memory? What procedures should be followed when hypnosis is used in a forensic setting?* The courts have taken different positions on the admissibility of hypnotically induced testimony. Three cautions seem paramount: (1) The hypnosis should be carried out by a psychiatrist or a psychologist who is unaware of the facts of the case, not by a police officer, (2) the procedures should be recorded so that they can be scrutinized by others, and (3) the products of such hypnosis during the investigation of a crime either should not be used as evidence during the trial or should be admitted only under exceptional circumstances. A context reinstatement technique has recently been suggested as a substitute for forensic hypnosis.

3. *How do jurors evaluate the testimony of eyewitnesses, and can psychologists help jurors understand the potential problems of eyewitness testimony?* Psychological tests of eyewitnesses' accuracy conclude that eyewitnesses can be mistaken, although rates of accuracy depend on many factors—some environmental, some personal, and some related to the interval between the crime and the recall. Despite these limitations, jurors are heavily influenced by the testimony of eyewitnesses, and they tend to overestimate the accuracy of such witnesses, relying to a great extent on the confidence of the eyewitness. To alert jurors to these problems, two types of special interventions have been tried (in addition to the routine use of cross-examination of witnesses). Some trial judges permit psychologists to testify as expert witnesses about the problems in being an accurate eyewitness. Laboratory evaluations of mock juries find that such testimony generally sensitizes jurors to factors that affect an eyewitness's reliability. The other intervention, encouraged by the U.S. Supreme Court and several state courts, is for the judge to give the jurors a "cautionary instruction," sensitizing them to aspects of the testimony of eyewitnesses that they should especially consider.

4. *Can memories for trauma be repressed, and if so, can these memories be recovered accurately?* The problems that threaten accurate memories are compounded in cases in which an individual claims to have recovered memories for traumatic childhood events that have been repressed or dissociated for long periods. The accuracy of repressed and then recovered memories is particularly suspect when the recollections occur in the context of therapies that use suggestive memory retrieval techniques such as hypnosis. Recent research shows that people can "remember" events that never happened, sometimes simply by imagining them. Litigation involving the recovery of repressed memories involves lawsuits brought by victims claiming that therapists led them to believe that they were abused in the past and lawsuits brought by the accused claiming that therapists promoting such false recollections are guilty of malpractice.

KEY TERMS

absolute judgment	dissociation	other-race effect	simultaneous
autobiographical	double-blind testing	physiognomic	presentation
memory	procedure	variability	source confusion
change blindness	encoding	postevent	storage
cognitive interview	estimator variable	information	system variable
confabulation	experimenter bias	relative judgment	unconscious
confirmation bias	hyperamnesia	repression	transference
context reinstatement	in-group/out-group	retrieval	weapon focus
delayed-reporting	differences	sequential	effect
statutes	memory hardening	presentation	

Identification and Evaluation of Criminal Suspects

ORIENTING QUESTIONS

1. *What are some psychological investigative techniques used by the police?*
2. *What is criminal profiling?*
3. *Is the polygraph a valid instrument for lie detection? What are some problems associated with it?*
4. *How valid is confession evidence? What kinds of interrogation procedures can lead to false confessions?*
5. *What are some of the reforms proposed to prevent false confessions?*
6. *What are the main legal definitions of entrapment?*

In Chapter 5, we discussed how psychological findings and techniques have contributed to assessments of the accuracy of eyewitness reports and claims of repressed memory. In this chapter, we discuss three other activities in which psychology can assist law enforcement: the profiling of criminal suspects, the use of polygraphy in evaluating the truthfulness of suspects, and the evaluation of confessions from suspects. The common thread that ties these topics together is the assumption that psychological theory and techniques can be used to improve police officers' identification or evaluation of criminal suspects.

These contributions occur in a logical sequence. Psychological profiling is usually performed at the beginning of a criminal investigation, when the police need help focusing their investigation on certain types of people who might be the most likely suspects. Once suspects have been identified, law enforcement officials use other procedures to determine whether any of these suspects should be charged. The police often encourage suspects to confess, because confessions make it more likely that suspects will be successfully prosecuted (and eventually convicted). But confessions can be coerced, and as a result, individual rights may be submerged in the quest for conviction. Courts have tried to clarify when a confession is truly voluntary, but (as you will see in this chapter) psychological findings often conflict with the courts' evaluations of confessions—again reflecting the final dilemma described in Chapter 1.

The police may also suspect specific persons of criminal behavior but lack firm evidence of their lawbreaking. Hence, the police may create situations in which these suspicious persons have the opportunity to commit crimes. Often, when lawbreakers are caught in such actions, they claim entrapment as a defense. There are questions in the legal world about the meaning of this term; further problems become evident when entrapment is examined from a psychological perspective, as we do later in this chapter.

Suspects are often given so-called lie detection tests to provide more information about their guilt or innocence and, sometimes, to encourage them to confess. Here again, the legal system's belief about the efficacy of lie detection procedures conflicts with some psychological findings about their accuracy. Although some states permit the results of a lie detection test to be admitted into evidence under limited circumstances, many psychologists question the objectivity of the procedure as it is usually administered and, hence, the validity of its results. Thus, a consistent theme throughout this chapter is the conflict between the legal system and psychological science regarding ways of gaining knowledge and evaluating truth. A related conflict is subordination of the goal of truth to the desire to resolve conflict and maintain the stability of the system.

Profiling of Criminal Suspects

Do criminals commit their crimes or choose their victims in distinctive ways that leave clues to their psychological makeup, much as fingerprints point to their physical identity or ballistics tests reveal the kind of gun they used? Evidence is accumulating that psychological characteristics are linked to behavioral patterns and that these links can be detected by a psychological analysis of crime scenes. Behavioral scientists and police use **criminal profiling** to narrow criminal investigations to suspects who possess certain behavioral and personality features that were revealed by the way the crime was committed. Profiling, also termed criminal investigative analysis, does not identify a specific suspect. Instead, profilers sketch a general psychological description of the most likely type of suspect, including personality and behavioral characteristics identified via a thorough analysis of the crimes committed, so that the police can concentrate their investigation of difficult cases in the most profitable directions. (Profiles also help investigators search for persons who fit descriptions known to characterize hijackers, drug couriers, and undocumented aliens; Monahan & Walker, 1990). The result of a careful profile may provide specific information about suspects, including psychopathology, characteristics of their family history, educational and legal history, and habits and social interests (Woodworth & Porter, 2000). Although profiling can be used in diverse contexts, it is considered most helpful in crimes in which the offender has demonstrated some form of repetitive behavior with unusual aspects, such as sadistic torture, ritualistic or bizarre behavior, evisceration, or staging or acting out a fantasy (Woodworth & Porter, 2000).

A successful profiler should possess several key attributes, including both an understanding of human psychology and investigative experience (Hazelwood, Ressler, Depue, & Douglas, 1995). There is some controversy regarding who should be considered a successful profiler. Because of the importance of investigative experience in criminal profiling, some have suggested that mental health professionals may not be fully qualified to engage in profiling (Hazelwood et al., 1995). However, others maintain that clinical (forensic) psychologists possess a level of expertise that incomparably contributes to the effectiveness of criminal profiling (Copson, Badcock, Boon, & Britton, 1997; Gudjonsson & Copson, 1997).

Many famous fictional detectives have been portrayed as excellent profilers because they could interpret the meaning of a small detail or find a common theme among seemingly unrelated features of a crime. Lew Archer, the hero in Ross MacDonald's popular series of detective novels, frequently began his search for a missing person (usually a wayward wife or a troubled daughter) by looking at the person's bedroom, examining her reading material, and rummaging through her closet to discover where her lifestyle might have misdirected her. Helen McCloy's Dr. Basil Willing, the psychiatrist/detective featured in novels such as *The One That Got Away*, boasts, "Every criminal leaves psychic fingerprints and he can't wear gloves to hide them." Profiling has even infiltrated popular culture through TV programs such as *Law and Order* and its offspring (*Criminal Intent* and *Special Victims Unit*).

One of the earliest cases of criminal profiling involved the 1957 arrest of George Metesky, otherwise known as the Mad Bomber of New York City.

Over an eight-year period, police had tried to solve a series of more than 30 bombings in the New York area. They finally consulted Dr. James Brussel, a Greenwich Village psychiatrist, who, after examining pictures of the bomb scenes and analyzing letters that the bomber had sent, advised the police to look for a heavyset, middle-aged, Eastern European, Catholic man who was single and lived with a sibling or aunt in Connecticut. Brussel also concluded that the man was very neat and that, when found, he would be wearing a buttoned double-breasted suit. When the police finally arrested Matesky, this composite turned out to be uncannily accurate—even down to the right type of suit.

Not all early profiles were so useful, however. For example, the committee of experts charged with the task of profiling the Boston Strangler predicted that the killer was not one man but two, each of whom lived alone and worked as a schoolteacher. They also suggested that one of the men would be homosexual. When Albert De Salvo ultimately confessed to these killings, police discovered that he was a married construction worker who lived with his wife and two sons and was not homosexual (Porter, 1983).

The major source of research and development on criminal profiling has been the FBI's Behavioral Science Unit (the BSU), which has been working on criminal profiles since the 1970s and currently analyzes about 1000 cases per year (Homant & Kennedy, 1998). The National Center for the Analysis of Violent Crime (NCAVC), which was housed within BSU, was created in 1985 to continue these efforts. In 1995, the NCAVC was moved into the Critical Incident Response Group (CIRG) so that it could be housed in a more multidisciplinary environment. The NCAVC now has separate units that focus on crimes against adults, crimes against children, apprehension of violent criminals, and counterterrorism and threat assessment.

Following September 11, 2001, the FBI prioritized counterterrorism more highly (FBI Academy, 2002). Profiling terrorist suspects in the United States has proved challenging, and no reliable profile has been developed. Initial profiles of suspected suicide bombers include Arab males between 18 and 40 years old, wearing baggy clothing or clothing inappropriate to the weather (cited in Nunn, 2004). However, focusing only on individuals who match this vague description not only violates Americans' civil liberties, but would produce an overwhelmingly large number of "false positives" (those who are predicted to present a threat but who, in fact, do not).

Much of the historical focus of the BSU was on violent offenders, especially those who commit bizarre or repeated crimes (Jeffers, 1991). Special attention has been given to rapists (Ressler, Burgess, & Douglas, 1988), arsonists (Rider, 1980), sexual homicides (Hazelwood & Douglas, 1980), and mass and serial murderers (Porter, 1983). These types of violent offenses against persons remain a focus of the BSU's criminal profiling efforts (Woodworth & Porter, 2000). A key to this research has involved interviewing those who have committed a specific type of offense in order to learn how they select and approach their victims, how they react to their crimes, what demographic or family characteristics they share, and what personality features might predominate among them. For example, as part of its study of mass and serial killers, the FBI conducted detailed interviews with some of this country's most notorious killers— among them Charles Manson, Richard Speck, and David Berkowitz—to determine the similarities among them.

Classifying Mass Murderers

On the basis of this research, behavioral scientists have been able to classify mass murderers and show that the portrait of contemporary American murderers is changing. Historically, most murders were committed by killers who were well acquainted with their victim, had a personal but rational motive, killed once, and were then arrested. In the past two decades, however, increased attention is being paid to patterns of homicide involving killers who attack multiple victims, sometimes with irrational or bizarre motives, and who are much less likely to be apprehended

than in former days. The criminal trail of these murderers may center on one locale and period of time or cross through different locations and stretch over a longer period of time.

Mass murderers have become a favorite subject of lurid "true crime" books such as *The Only Living Witness* (Ted Bundy), *The Co-Ed Killer* (Edmund Kemper), and *Killer Clown* (John Gacy), as well as of more scholarly, comparative studies of multiple homicides (Meloy, Hempel, Gray, Mohandie, Shiva, & Richards, 2004; Fox & Levin, 1998; Levin & Fox, 1985). Although experts differ on what precise number of victims to use in defining multiple homicides, Fox and Levin's (1998) criterion of "the slaying of four or more victims, simultaneously or sequentially, by one or a few individuals" is probably the most widely accepted opinion. It is difficult to estimate how many double homicides are committed each year, but the consensus is that they are increasing, and this increase does not reflect merely greater media attention or police apprehension rates.

Mass murders remain relatively rare, however, which makes it more difficult to formulate predictive statistical models that are accurate. In this absence of large data sets, current research aimed at understanding factors related to these behaviors has focused on identifying esoteric characteristics of these murderers and examining patterns between individuals. One study comparing 30 adult with 34 adolescent mass murderers found striking similarities between the two groups (Meloy et al., 2004). Three-quarters of the entire sample were Caucasian (75%), the majority of both the adolescents (70%) and adults (94%) were described as "loners," almost half of the adolescent sample (48%) and almost two-thirds of the adult sample (63%) demonstrated a preoccupation with weapons and violence, and about 43% of both groups had a violent history. Several differences existed between the adolescent and adult murderers. Adolescents were significantly more likely to abuse substances than their adult counterparts (62% compared to 10%), and nearly twice as many adults (50%) as adolescents (23%) had a psychiatric history.

Two types of multiple homicides have been identified: mass murders and serial murders, which share some similarities but are marked by several differences (Meloy & Felthous, 2004). The **mass murderer** kills four or more victims in one location during a period of time that lasts anywhere from a few minutes to several hours. It is estimated that about two mass murders are committed every month in the United States, resulting in the deaths of 100 victims annually (Fox & Levin, 1998). Although most mass murderers are not severely mentally ill, they do tend to harbor strong feelings of resentment and are often motivated by revenge against their victims. Contrary to popular myth, the majority of mass murderers do not attack strangers at random; in almost 80% of studied mass murders, the assailant was related to or well acquainted with the victims, and in many cases, the attack was a carefully planned assault rather than an impulsive rampage. For every Charles Whitman, who shot and killed 16 people and wounded more than 30 other strangers from a tower on the University of Texas campus, there are many more people like Thomas McIlvane, who shot four co-workers in Royal Oak, Michigan, before killing himself. Most mass murders are solved by law enforcement; the typical assailant is killed at the location of the crime, commits suicide, or surrenders to police. **Spree killers** are a special form of mass murderer in which the attacker kills victims at two or more different locations with no "cooling-off'" interval between the murders. The killing constitutes a single event, but it can either last only a short time or go on for a day or more.

Serial murderers kill four or more victims, each on separate occasions. Unlike mass murderers, **serial killers** usually select a certain type of victim who fulfills a role in the killer's fantasies. There are cooling-off periods between serial murders, which are usually better planned than mass or spree killings. Some serial killers (such as Angel Maturino Resendiz, called the Railway Killer because the murders he was charged with took place by railroad tracks) travel frequently and murder in several locations. Others (such as Gary Ridgway, the so-called

Dennis Rader, the "BTK Killer"

Green River Killer who confessed to killing 48 women, mostly prostitutes, and dumping their bodies along the Green River in Washington State) are geographically stable and kill within the same area. The Unabomber, who apparently remained in one place but chose victims who lived in different parts of the country to receive his carefully constructed mail bombs, reflected an unusual combination of serial killer characteristics.

Because they are clever in the way they plan their murders, capable of presenting themselves as normal members of the community, kill for idiosyncratic reasons, and frequently wait months between killings, serial murderers are difficult to apprehend. It took 30 years for Wichita police to figure out that Dennis Rader, a boy scout leader and president of Christ Lutheran Church, was a brutal serial killer who used the moniker "BTK"— bind, torture, kill. He confessed to ten counts of first-degree murder in 2005.

Social scientists have gained some knowledge about these criminals, who may number as many as 100 in the United States. One study compiled a list of characteristics from 157 serial offenders and found that most were white males in their early thirties (Kraemer, Lord, & Heilbrun, 2004). More than half of the offenders were employed at the time of the offense, and approximately one-third were married. The average offender had an eleventh-grade education. Victims of these offenders were most often white females in their early to mid-thirties who were strangers to their killers. More than half of the murders were sexually motivated. These characteristics differ from single-homicide offenders who more often know their victims and kill for emotional reasons such as anger or sexual jealousy (Kraemer et al., 2004).

Serial killers tend to select vulnerable victims of some specific type who gratify their need to control people. Consistent with the motive of wanting to dominate people, they prefer to kill with "hands-on" methods such as strangulation and stabbing, rather than with guns, which is the preferred weapon for mass murderers. They are often preoccupied with sadistic fantasies involving capture and control of their victims; these fantasies are frequently sexualized, as was the case with Jeffrey Dahmer. Many serial killers use pornography and violent sexual fantasies intensively as "rehearsals" for and "replays" of their crimes, and they often keep souvenirs (sometimes in the form of body parts from victims) to commemorate their savage attacks. Despite the apparent "craziness" of their behavior, serial killers are not typically psychotic individuals. Most of them have personality disorders with deficits in their capacities to experience empathy and remorse, however. In fact, serial killers often revel in the publicity that their crimes receive. Over the course of their criminal careers, serial killers may become less organized in how they plan and commit their murders.

Ronald Holmes, a criminologist at the University of Louisville who specializes in the study of serial murder, has identified four subtypes of serial killers (Holmes & De Burger, 1988). The *visionary* type feels compelled to murder because he hears voices or sees visions ordering him to kill certain kinds of people. An exception to the typical profile of serial killers, the visionary type is often psychotic. The *mission-oriented* type seeks to kill a specific group of people (prostitutes are often targeted) who he believes are unworthy to live and without whom the world would be a better place.

His everyday acquaintances frequently will describe him as a fine citizen. The *hedonistic* type kills for the thrill of it. Such killers enjoy the physical sensations and sadistic gratification of killing. Sexual arousal is commonly associated with this type of murder. Finally, the *power-oriented* type kills because he enjoys exerting ultimate control over his victims. These murderers are obsessed with capturing and controlling their victims and forcing them to obey their every command.

Steps Involved in Criminal Profiling

Douglas, Ressler, Burgess, and Hartman (1986) divided the FBI's profiling strategy into five stages, with a final, sixth stage being the arrest of the correct suspect. The six phases, as they evolve in a murder investigation, are as follows:

1. *Profiling inputs*. The first stage involves collecting all information available about the crime, including physical evidence, photographs of the crime scene, autopsy reports and pictures, complete background information on the victim, and police reports. The profiler does not want to be told about possible suspects at this stage, because such data might prejudice or prematurely direct the profile.

2. *Decision process models*. In this stage the profiler organizes the input into meaningful questions and patterns along several dimensions of criminal activity. What type of homicide has been committed? What is the primary impetus for the crime—sexual, financial, personal, or emotional disturbance? What level of risk did the victim experience, and what level of risk did the murderer take in killing the victim? What was the sequence of acts before and after the killing, and how long did these acts take to commit? Where was the crime committed? Was the body moved, or was it found where the murder was committed?

3. *Crime assessment*. On the basis of the findings in the previous phase, the profiler attempts to reconstruct the behavior of the offender and the victim. Was the murder *organized* (suggesting an intelligent killer who carefully selects victims against whom to act out a well-rehearsed fantasy) or

disorganized (indicating an impulsive, less socially competent, possibly even psychotic killer)? Was the crime staged to mislead the police? What motivation is revealed by such details as cause of death, location of wounds, and position of the body? Criminal profilers are often guided by the following hypotheses: (1) Brutal facial injuries point to killers who knew their victims. (2) Murders committed with whatever weapon happens to be available are more impulsive than murders committed with a gun and may reveal a killer who lives fairly near the victim. (3) Murders committed early in the morning seldom involve alcohol or drugs.

4. *Criminal profile.* In this stage, profilers formulate an initial description of the most likely suspects. This profile includes the perpetrator's race, sex, age, marital status, living arrangements, and employment history; psychological characteristics, beliefs, and values; probable reactions to the police; and past criminal record, including the possibility of similar offenses in the past. This stage also contains a feedback loop whereby profilers check their predictions against stage 2 information to make sure that the profile fits the original data.

5. *Investigation.* A written report is given to investigators, who concentrate on suspects matching the profile. If new evidence is discovered in this investigation, a second feedback process is initiated, and the profile can be revised.

6. *Apprehension.* The intended result of these procedures, arrest of a suspect, allows profilers to evaluate the validity of their predictions. The key element in this validation is a thorough interview of the suspect to assess the influences of background and psychological variables.

The Validity of Criminal Profiles

Is there any evidence that psychological profiling is valid? Are profilers more accurate than other groups in their descriptions of suspects, or is this activity little more than a reading of forensic tea leaves? Do profilers use a different process in evaluating information than other investigators?

In a review of criminal profiling, Homant and Kennedy (1998) concluded that different kinds of crime scenes can be classified with reasonable reliability and that differences in these crimes do correlate with certain offender characteristics, such as murderers' prior relationships and interactions with victims (Salfati & Canter, 1999), organized versus disorganized approaches, and serial versus single offenders (e.g., Knight, Warren, Reboussin, & Soley, 1998). At the same time, this research suggests several reasons for caution: (1) Inaccurate profiles are quite common, (2) many of the studies have been conducted in-house by FBI profilers studying a fairly small number of offenders, and (3) the concepts and approaches actually used by profilers have often not been objectively and systematically defined.

One study (Pinizzotto & Finkel, 1990) investigated the effectiveness of criminal profiling as practiced by real-life experts. In this investigation, four different groups of participants evaluated two criminal cases—a homicide and a sex offense—that had already been solved but were completely unknown to the subjects. The first group consisted of four experienced criminal profilers who had a total of 42 years of profiling experience and six police detectives who had recently been trained by the FBI to be profilers. The second group consisted of six police detectives with 57 years of total experience in criminal investigations but with no profiling experience or training. The third group was composed of six clinical psychologists who had no profiling or criminal investigation experience. The final group consisted of six undergraduates drawn from psychology classes.

All participants were given, for each case, an array of materials that profilers typically use. These materials included crime scene photographs, crime scene descriptions by uniformed officers, autopsy and toxicology reports (in the murder case), and descriptions of the victims. After studying these materials, participants were asked to write all the details they could recall for each crime and to indicate the importance of these details to completing a profile. Three tests of profiling quality were used: All subjects prepared a profile of a suspect in each case, answered 15 questions about the identity (e.g., gender, age, employment) of the suspects, and were asked to rank-order a written "lineup" of five suspects, from most to least likely to have committed each of the crimes.

The results indicated that, compared with the other three groups, the profiler group wrote longer profiles that contained more specific predictions about suspects, included more accurate predictions, and were rated as more helpful by other police detectives. Although they did not differ substantially in the way they thought about the evidence, profilers were more accurate than the other groups in answering specific questions about the sex offense suspect. The groups did not differ in their accuracy about the homicide suspect. Similar results were found with the "lineup" identification: Profilers were the most accurate for the sex offense, whereas there were no differences for the homicide case.

This study suggests that profilers can produce more useful and valid criminal profiles, even when compared to experienced crime investigators. This advantage may be limited, however, to certain kinds of cases or to the types of information made available to investigators. One study found that individuals (i.e., senior police officers and forensic professionals) perceive ambiguous statements, when presented as an "offender profile," as being accurate descriptions of suspects (Alison, Smith, & Morgan, 2003).

How do psychologists themselves view criminal profiling? In a survey of 152 police psychologists, 70% questioned the validity of crime scene profiling (Bartol, 1996). Nonetheless, despite such reservations, profiling is gaining popularity among law enforcement officials and is now practiced, in some form or other, in several countries (Woodworth & Porter, 2000; Homant & Kennedy, 1998).

"Lie Detection" via the Polygraph

Throughout history, many societies have assumed that criminals can be detected by the physical manifestations of their denials. Ever since King Solomon tried to discover which of two women who claimed to be the mother of an infant was lying by watching their emotions when he threatened to cut the baby in half and divide it between them, people have believed that the body will reveal in some way that the mind is lying when the liar's mouth protests innocence. Who knows how many children have been scared into truthfulness by the prospect that their noses, like Pinocchio's, will give away their deceit?

Suspects in India were once required to submit to "trial by sacred ass." After mud had been put on the tail of an ass in a tent, the potential suspects were required to enter the tent one by one and pull the ass's tail; they were told they would be judged innocent if it didn't bray. The logic of this method was that the innocent man, having nothing to hide, would immediately yank the tail and get mud on his hands. A guilty suspect, however, would try to shield guilt by not pulling the tail. In the end, the guilty suspect was the one with the clean hands. The ancient Hindus forced suspects to chew rice and spit it out on a leaf from a sacred tree. If the rice was dry, the suspect was considered guilty. The Bedouins of Arabia required conflicting witnesses to lick a hot iron; the one whose tongue was burned was thought to be lying (Kleinmuntz & Szucko, 1984). Both of these procedures reflect activity of the sympathetic nervous system (under emotional states, salivation usually decreases) and thus are crude measures of emotion, though not necessarily of lying. But emotion and lying are not the same, even if they are correlated to some extent (Saxe, 1991). The failure to appreciate this distinction is at the root of many mistaken ideas about the polygraph and affects its unacceptably high rate of misclassifying persons as honest or deceitful.

Emergence of the Polygraph

Despite this long history, the **polygraph**, or lie detector, was not developed until around 1917 with the work of William Moulton Marston, a complex and colorful figure who originated the term *lie detector*. Marston had studied at Harvard University with Hugo Munsterberg, who directed

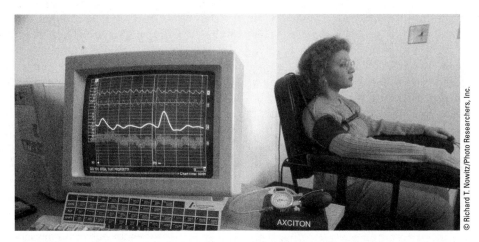

A polygraph examination

the university's experimental psychology laboratory. Marston claimed that he could detect lying by noting increases in systolic blood pressure when subjects told untruths. He was an avid publicist for his new technique; he even tried to get permission to test Bruno Hauptmann, the alleged kidnapper of the Lindbergh baby, on his new lie detector machine (Lykken, 1981).

Marston's technique was called into question in the landmark U.S. Supreme Court case *Frye v. United States* (1923). In this case, James Frye appealed his murder conviction on the ground that the trial judge did not allow a polygrapher to testify about the results of a physiological deception test that supported Frye's claim of innocence. Because of his extravagant claims, Marston was repudiated not only by the courts but also by serious investigators. (Marston was a man of many talents; for instance, using the name "Charles Moulton," he created the comic strip *Wonder Woman*.)

John A. Larson (1932) of the Berkeley, California, Police Department took a solid step forward in the use of the polygraph. He built a forerunner of the modern polygraph that could measure pulse rate, blood pressure, and respiratory changes during questioning. Here we see the origins of the polygraph concept (*poly-* means "many"). What is commonly called the lie detector does not measure lies as such; it measures *emotion*. It is more properly

called a polygraph because it employs several physiological measures—usually blood pressure, heart rate, breathing rate, and the galvanic skin response (or skin resistance to an electric current). Unfortunately for Marston, Larson, and others who sought a specific "lie response," the physiological manifestations of various negative emotions (e.g., fear, guilt, anger) are all very similar (physiological differences between positive and negative emotions are more apparent; Zajonc & McIntosh, 1992).

Larson also developed the first systematic method of questioning suspects. The R/I procedure (**relevant/irrelevant procedure**) intersperses relevant questions about the crime under investigation ("Did you steal Mrs. Riley's cow?") with irrelevant questions that are unrelated to the crime and are not stressful ("What did you do on your last birthday?"). Larson compared suspects' physiological reactions on these two types of questions to determine whether the subjects showed greater emotion in response to the relevant questions. He assumed that truthful subjects would respond with equivalent reactions to all questions, whereas guilty, and dishonest, subjects would have stronger reactions to the relevant questions.

Because one negative emotion can't be reliably distinguished from another on physiological grounds, Larson was forced to infer lying. But such an inference is often inaccurate. Simply being suspected of committing a crime, even if you are innocent, may generate a great deal of surplus emotion, but that should not be taken as a sign of guilt. Regardless of whether you are guilty or innocent, you are more likely to be aroused by relevant questions; these questions are obviously related to the crime being investigated, whereas the irrelevant questions are just as obviously unrelated to it. Despite these problems, law enforcement officials used the polygraph procedure during the 1930s and beyond without recognizing these limitations. In fact, from 1915 to 1965, Larson himself was the only investigator to report an objective study of the diagnosis of deception using polygraph recordings obtained from criminal suspects (Lykken, 1985). "Larson's honest scientific bent compelled him to subject his own theories to rigorous testing and he wound up rejecting polygraphy as a racket and psychological third degree" (Underwood, 1996, p. 629). Although largely discredited as unreliable, the relevant/irrelevant test is still used in some federal employee security screening programs— for instance, at the National Security Agency (National Research Council, 2003).

THE CONTROL QUESTION TEST

A further refinement was made by criminologists associated with the Northwestern University Law School. In the 1930s, the Keeler polygraph (the prototype of current instruments) was developed by Leonard Keeler, a student of Larson's, and his colleagues. During the mid-20th century, lie detectors were quite the topic of interest. In the movie *Northside 777*, it was Keeler himself who administered the R/I test to Richard Conte in Joliet Prison, proving what reporter Jimmy Stewart had suspected all along: that Conte was innocent of the crime for which he had been imprisoned. Such media portrayals contributed to the public's belief that lie detectors could infallibly distinguish between honesty and dishonesty.

While at Northwestern University, Keeler met Fred Inbau and John Reid. Reid had also developed a polygraph, and they established schools to train investigators to use polygraph techniques. Most present examiners have been trained through offshoots of these schools.

In the 1940s, John Reid pioneered the **Control Question Test**, which became the most popular approach to polygraphic examinations. This exam begins with an interview in which the examiner gathers biographical information from the subject and attempts to impress on the subject that he or she must be honest at all times during the test. The examiner tries to convince the subject that the polygraph is an infallible instrument; this strategy is meant to threaten guilty subjects at the same time that it reassures the innocent. Reid and Inbau (1966), leading experts in the development of the procedure, advise:

> After the subject's questions, if any, about the instrument and test procedure have been answered . . . he should be told something like the following: "You know, of course, that we're checking on the death of John Jones at First and Main Street the other night. . . . If you did do this thing . . . I'm going to know about it as soon as this investigation is over. If you did do this, therefore, I suggest you tell me about it now, before the test" (p. 13).

Examiners will also use tricks to intimidate suspects and to convince them that the machine is infallible. A favorite is the "stim test." The subject is shown seven playing cards and told to take one, look at it, and put it back in the deck without showing it to the examiner. Reid and Inbau (1966) write, "After the selection is made, the examiner proceeds to shuffle the cards and instructs the subject to answer 'no' to each question concerning the cards, even when asked the number of the card he selected. In other words, the subject's answer to one of the questions will be a lie" (p. 27).

At the end of this exercise, the examiner tells the subject which card he or she picked, leaving the implication that the apparatus detected lying. But Reid and Inbau (1966) advise examiners that "the cards are arranged and shown to the subject in such a way that the examiner will immediately know which card has been picked by the subject" (p. 27). Another variant of this shoddy procedure is to use a deck of 52 replications of the same playing card (Lykken, 1981). Reid and Inbau (1966) even acknowledge that the polygraph is not completely accurate; one of the reasons for the card trick deception is that "the polygraph record itself may not actually disclose the card 'lie'" (p. 27).

When the test finally begins, the subject is asked a series of two kinds of questions. *Relevant questions* inquire about the crime under investigation (e.g., "Did you steal the law school's TV set?"). *Control questions* are not directly concerned with the crime under investigation but are calculated to induce an emotional reaction because they cover common misdeeds that nearly all of us have committed at some point (e.g., "Have you ever stolen anything?" or "Prior to the age of 21, did you ever try to hurt someone you disliked?"). Most polygraphers consider these "known lies." They are assumed to have occurred, but subjects will deny them, thereby providing a characteristic physiological response to a lie. Guilty subjects should be more aroused by the relevant questions (to which they must respond with a lie in order to maintain their innocence), whereas innocent subjects should be more aroused by the control questions (because they will worry that admitting to a past misdeed might make them look more like a criminal at the present time). Therefore, this procedure works best when innocent subjects lie in response to the control questions (or at least show greater emotional turmoil over them) and the guilty subject lies (and becomes more emotionally aroused) in response to the relevant questions.

Reid also introduced "guilt complex" questions. In this procedure, the examiner pretends to be equally interested in whether the suspect is also guilty of some fictitious crime. Because this other crime is imaginary, the examiner knows that the suspect's denial is truthful and therefore can compare the subject's physiological responses to the guilt complex questions with the responses to the questions about the actual crime. However, the "measurement" of lying still rests here on a shaky assumption that differences in intensity of physiological reactions are based on guilt.

The final step in the Control Question Test is to interpret the polygraphic charts. Most polygraphers reach a conclusion about the subject's honesty on subjective grounds that include the physiological record as well as the interviewers' observations of the subject's behavior throughout

the test (Gale, 1988). A second approach, known as the *zone of comparison* method (Backster, 1974), involves a quantified comparison of physiological reactions to the relevant and control questions.

THE GUILTY KNOWLEDGE TEST

The **Guilty Knowledge Test** (GKT) was developed by David Lykken (1981), a University of Minnesota psychologist who has also been one of the staunchest critics of standard procedures such as the Control Question Test. Both the procedure and the purposes of this method are fundamentally different from the control question approach. The goal is to detect the presence of guilty knowledge in the suspect's mind, not to detect lying. The procedure relies on the accumulation of facts that are known only by the police, the criminal, and any surviving victims. For example: In what room was the victim's body found? What was the murder weapon? What strange garment was the victim wearing? What was clutched in the victim's hand?

A series of multiple-choice questions is created on the basis of this information, and the suspect is presented with each question in order and asked to respond to each choice. Was it the bedroom? Was it the kitchen? Was it the living room? Although each alternative would appear equally plausible to an innocent person, the true criminal will be revealed by physiological reactions that accompany recognition of guilty knowledge. Imagine that the suspect has been asked five questions about the crime, each of which has five choices, and that on question 1 his physiological reaction is much stronger to the "correct" response than to any of the others. Just by coincidence, that would happen 20% of the time (i.e., one time out of five choices), so we can't make any strong inference about his knowledge of the crime from his responses to just one question. But let us say further that for each of the five questions, his emotional reaction to the correct response is much greater than his reaction to the other choices. By coincidence, this latter set of reactions would be unlikely; its probability is $1/5 \times 1/5 \times 1/5 \times 1/5 \times 1/5$, or $1/3125$. One in 3125 is a probability of .0003, or very, very unlikely by chance. If this pattern of reactions occurs, we can be confident that the suspect has detailed and accurate knowledge of the crime. That in itself is suggestive, but not direct, evidence that the suspect committed the crime.

Note that the goal of the Guilty Knowledge Test is not to detect emotions that might accompany deception; rather, it is to detect knowledge possessed by subjects. The underlying assumption is that people are more physiologically aroused when they perceive a meaningful stimulus. This well-established pattern is known as the *orienting response* (Ben-Shakhar, Bar-Hillel, & Lieblich, 1986).

Obviously, this technique can be used only when the details of the crime have been kept from the public. Even then, it is conceivable that the suspect is not the perpetrator but, rather, was told about the crime by the true criminal and therefore possesses "guilty" knowledge. Moreover, it is possible that some guilty subjects are so distraught or pay so little attention to the details of their crimes that they actually lack the requisite knowledge that this method relies on. Some skeptics of the GKT suggest that it can be conducted properly in only a small percentage of real-life cases.

Validity of Polygraph Procedures

Advocates of polygraph procedures claim very high rates of accuracy. Reid and Inbau (1966) asserted that their success rate was 99%. F. Lee Bailey proposed on national television that out of every 100 polygraph tests administered, 96 are accurate, 3 are inconclusive, and only 1 will be in error (quoted in Lykken, 1985, p. 96). However, in its 2003 review of the research on polygraph examinations, the National Research Council found only 57 of 192 studies that met minimal standards of scientific adequacy and, of those 57, only a handful that met the quality standards necessary for National Science Foundation funding (National Research Council, 2003). The Council expressed concern over the quality of the research and the exaggerated claims of accuracy made by polygraph proponents. The report offers the following explanation for the substandard research:

> More intensive efforts to develop the basic science in the 1920s would have produced a more favorable assessment in the 1950s; more intensive efforts in the 1950s would have produced a more favorable assessment in the 1980s; more intensive efforts in the 1980s would have produced a more favorable assessment now. A research strategy with better grounding in basic science might have led to answers to some of the key validity questions raised by earlier generations of scientists. Polygraph techniques might have been modified to incorporate new knowledge, or the polygraph might have been abandoned in favor of more valid techniques for detecting deception. As we have suggested, the failure to make progress seems to be structural, rather than a failure of individuals (National Research Council, 2003, p. 100).

The Council reviewed polygraph research at the request of the U.S. Department of Energy, which wanted an objective assessment of the research in order to decide how to use polygraphs in personnel security screening. The Council noted that if the "guilty" are a small percentage of the tested population (a low base rate), then, depending on the assumed accuracy, the polygraph will either create an unacceptable number of false positives (those innocent but falsely identified) or an unacceptable number of false negatives (those guilty but not identified). The Council therefore recommended that the polygraph be used sparingly, if at all, by the Department of Energy (National Research Council, 2003).

Let's examine the "base rate problem" further. In the context of criminal investigations, detecting a liar is a *true positive*, and believing a truthful suspect is *a true negative*. Believing a liar is truthful is *a false negative*, whereas disbelieving a truthful subject is *a false positive*. The frequency of these errors depends on both the accuracy of the technique and the **base rate** (how often something happens) of liars and honest subjects among a tested sample. The following example illustrates this relationship. Assume that the overall accuracy of the polygraph is 80%; also assume that the base rate of guilt and accompanying deception among criminal suspects is 75% (a reasonable figure if we grant that the police usually arrest and charge the right suspects). If 1000 people are arrested, 750 will be guilty in our example. The polygraph will catch 600 (750 × 0.80), but it will yield 150 false negatives. Of the 250 innocent suspects, the polygraph will exonerate 200 (250 × . 0.80), but it will falsely implicate 50 persons (false positives). Given a constant level of polygraphic accuracy, as the base rate of liars increases, false negatives also increase. More false positives will occur when the base rate of lying by suspects is low.

The problem of base rates also indicates how a claim of "96% correct" can be misleading. Let us say that a major theft has occurred in a factory with 50 employees. One is the thief; 49 are honest. The polygrapher gives a lie detection test to each of the employees, and each denies being the thief. The polygrapher misclassifies one of the innocent people as the thief (false positive). He also fails to detect lying by the true thief (false negative). Thus he has erred in two cases, but he has been correct in classifying the 48 others as truthful. His accuracy rate is 48 of 50, or 96%. But he has still erred on the crucial determination; despite the 96% overall "accuracy rate," his answer to the referral question (Who stole?) is wrong.

There are other problems that should cause concern. A vexing problem in evaluating polygraph results is the difficulty of finding a decisive criterion of accuracy, sometimes known as **ground truth**. In some studies, ground truth is defined by a panel of judges who review all the evidence in a case and conclude who is the culprit. In other studies, ground truth is established through subsequent confessions. A third choice is to use the official judicial outcome (e.g., jury verdict) as the criterion. All three alternatives have some methodological limitations.

Field studies of the polygraph are based on real-life investigations of subjects who have a large stake in being cleared of suspicion. **Analog studies** involve investigations of mock crimes staged, usually in the laboratory, by an experimenter who also arranges for some subjects (often college students) to be "guilty" and others to be "innocent." Field studies face the problem of locating ground truth, although their use of subjects who are motivated to avoid detection is a methodological

advantage (Kircher, Horowitz, & Raskin, 1988). Some data show that physiological responses from participants tested "in the field" are of greater amplitude than those of participants tested in a laboratory setting. Despite these differences, classification accuracy (correctly identifying deceptive and nondeceptive individuals) is comparable in the two settings, suggesting that data from analog studies can be useful to polygraphers (Pollina, Dollins, Senter, Krapohl, & Ryan, 2004).

Finally, deceptive subjects may "beat" the test by taking countermeasures to avoid detection (Honts, Raskin, Kircher & Hodes, 1984). Deliberate physical movements (e.g. tightening leg muscles), drugs, and controlled breathing are among the countermeasures freely discussed on the Internet. Effective countermeasures should increase false negatives, but they should have negligible effects on false positives. In fact, the evidence does not strongly support the fear that countermeasures can consistently distort polygraph results (Raskin, 1989).

Even severe critics of the polygraph acknowledge that the technique has overall accuracy rates of 65% or better. But is this figure high enough to justify permitting polygraphic data as evidence at a trial or high enough to base the prosecution of a suspect on it as the primary evidence? We think not. Polygraph tests are most valuable at the investigatory stages of a criminal prosecution and as a means to encourage confessions from suspects against whom other incriminating evidence has been gathered. A recent FBI report found that of 2641 deceptive criminal polygraph reports they reviewed, half (1325 reports) resulted in the acquisition of information valuable to the investigations for which they were used (Warner, 2005).

Other "Lie Detection" Methods

As controversy about the polygraph has continued, other "lie detection" procedures have been advocated. The **psychological stress evaluator** (PSE) uses the speaking voice as the determinant of lying. Advocates of the PSE claim that it can measure variations in emotional stress and can distinguish words and phrases spoken in periods of high and low stress. Despite claims of accuracy by its users, no evidence that the psychological stress evaluator is effective has been published in any scientific journal (Lykken, 1985).

A second approach is to judge lying on the basis of facial, bodily, nonverbal, and vocal cues. For example, when subjects lie, their voice pitch tends to increase, they illustrate their language with gestures less frequently, and they may attempt to prolong the time they gaze at persons to whom they lie (Ekman, 1985). In one study, professionals who had training and experience in deception and demeanor (including law enforcement officers and clinical psychologists) were reasonably (though not overwhelmingly) accurate in judging whether people were lying or telling the truth about their opinions (Ekman, O'Sullivan, & Frank, 1999).

Several systems have been developed for differentiating the verbal content of truthful accounts from nontruthful reports. For example, because it is difficult to fabricate details that do not exist in memory, a large amount of reported detail should be indicative of truthful reports. Likewise, reports of sensory impressions (e.g., "the smell of freshly cut hay was in the air") are more common in truthful accounts, whereas hedging (e.g., "it seems to me") is more typical of fabrications. In a test of how well these cues discriminated between honest and deceptive alibis given by subjects who were told that they were trying to fool an interrogator investigating a theft, only three cues (of a possible 17) proved useful: truthful subjects (1) gave more detailed descriptions of their actions, (2) provided more coherent accounts of their behavior, and (3) were more likely to admit that they could not remember certain aspects of the event in question (Porter & Yuille, 1996).

A third approach to lie detection involves measuring cortical activity rather than physiological responses. Based on findings in the field of **cognitive psychophysiology**, these techniques, which have only recently been applied to lie detection, analyze the brain waves that are evoked when a subject attends to a stimulus (Bashore & Rapp, 1993). Certain components of these brain waves, called **event-related brain potentials**, vary depending on whether the person is confronted with a familiar, meaningful stimulus or a novel, nonmeaningful stimulus. Different components of evoked potentials also can be elicited if a subject is exposed to a stimulus that is inconsistent with the subject's expectations or personal knowledge. The logic of these findings is that electroencephalogram (EEG) measures could serve as an index of the brain activity that occurs specifically when people are attempting to conceal information; therefore, these brain activity measures might be used to identify people who are denying guilty knowledge. The idea that brain waves can serve as a valid physiological index of deceptive behavior is still not widely accepted, in part because of uncertainty about exactly what is indexed by different types of brain activity.

Using other cognitive neuroscience methods, such as the fMRI, studies have found some evidence that different parts of the brain are implicated when one engages in deception compared to when one tells the truth (Ganis, Kosslyn, Stose, Thompson, & Yurgelun-Todd, 2003). Findings further revealed that distinct neural networks support different types of deception; different components of the brain were activated during well-rehearsed lies compared to spontaneous lies.

A novel and controversial idea, **brain fingerprinting**, is the "brainchild" of Dr. Lawrence Farwell, director of the Human Brain Research Laboratory in Fairfield, Iowa. The theory of brain fingerprinting builds on two premises: that the brain houses information about experienced events and that it emits electric charges in response to stimuli. Dr. Farwell's premise is that a certain kind of electrical activity in the brain, termed the P300 wave, reflects whether the brain recognizes a stimulus or not. The P300 wave is larger when the stimulus is relevant and familiar than when it is irrelevant and unfamiliar.

In terms of the test's forensic applications, Farwell suggests that examining the pattern of brain activity related to the P300 wave can help investigators assess whether a suspect has specific information that only the criminal would know. In essence, brain fingerprinting evaluates neural activity in order to compare the facts from a crime scene (for example, the use of a specific murder weapon) with memory evidence involuntarily stored in the brain of a suspect by analyzing brain activity in response to those facts.

To test these ideas, suspects view words, phrases, or pictures on a computer screen. During the viewing, the suspect wears a sensor-equipped headband attached to the scalp that measures electrical responses to both neutral and crime-related images. The signals are then transmitted to a computer and analyzed. The analysis determines whether a particular electrical response has occurred and provides the statistical likelihood that the crime-relevant details are present in the suspect's memory (Denno, 2002).

Because Dr. Farwell's ideas have not yet been sufficiently tested, brain fingerprinting is not generally accepted by the scientific community, nor is the process admissible in court. However, the process has great potential. Studies attesting to the reliability of brain fingerprinting are posted to Dr. Farwell's website (www.brainwavescience.com), and a leading authority on forensic evidence—Andre Moenssens—believes the process is scientifically sound. Unlike the polygraph, brain fingerprinting does not depend on the subject's fear of detection. Because the reaction of the brain to encoded memory is involuntary, the subject cannot manipulate the test with drugs, tacks in the shoe, or other methods of deception (Moenssens, 2002).

Admissibility of Polygraph Records

New Mexico stands alone as the only state in which polygraph evidence is routinely admitted in court. (Other states allow its admission, but only under limited circumstances that we describe later.) In 1975, the New Mexico Supreme Court held that polygraph evidence should be admitted if the operator was qualified and followed testing procedures designed to produce reliable results (*State v. Dorsey*, 1975). In 1983, the court specified that those procedures must include polygraph examiners who have at least five years of experience in administration or interpretation of tests, scoring in a manner that is generally accepted as reliable by polygraph experts, and recording of both the pretest interview and the test itself.

In *Lee v. Martinez* (2004), the New Mexico Supreme Court heard an argument that expert testimony from a polygraph examiner based on the control question test does not meet the standards of admissibility established in *Daubert v. Merrell Dow Pharmaceuticals* (1993), a case we described in Chapter 1. The Court reviewed data from the 2003 report of the National Research Council and concluded that the Control Question Test satisfies the *Daubert* requirements of falsifiability, peer review and publication, and known rate of error. With regard to the final factor of "general acceptance in the relevant scientific community," the court equivocated, stating that the scientific community disagrees about the reliability of the Control Question Test—that there is no consensus that the test is reliable *and* no consensus that it is unreliable. Ultimately, the court resolved the controversy in favor of admissibility.

But in a contrary ruling, the United States Supreme Court declared that polygraph results and opinions shall not be admitted into evidence (*United States v. Scheffer*, 1998). Though binding only on military courts (because the case involved a Military Rule of Evidence), the Supreme Court's decision in *Scheffer* reinforces the general reluctance of courts to admit polygraph results and opinions. Indeed, most courts do not admit this type of evidence. Another example is provided in Box 6.1.

How do juries react to such polygraph evidence? Do they blindly accept polygraph evidence? Bryan Myers and his colleagues conducted a simulation study of a sexual assault trial that included, for some mock jurors, results of a polygraph examination indicating that the defendant had been deceptive (Myers, Rosol, & Boelter, 2003). These jurors put little stock in the results of the polygraph examination; knowing that the defendant had failed the polygraph affected neither jurors' verdicts nor their estimates of the probability that the defendant committed the crime. Their decisions were affected by an eyewitness whose testimony corroborated the defendant's guilt, however.

Recently, the legality of the polygraph has been challenged in another way. In response to complaints about false positives in employee screening, the United States Congress prohibited polygraph

THE CASE OF

BOX 6.1 | **Brian Lea and his rival's contaminated animals**

Brian Lea, an entrepreneur, was accused of dumping pesticides on a former business partner's dead farm animals that were sold as food by the partner's company, National By-Products ("NBP") (*U.S. v. Lea*, 2001). Following notification that NBP had sold contaminated animal food, the business was ordered to close one of its plants and order a recall of the contaminated food. Lea was indicted and charged for the offense. Lea maintained that a

former employee of NBP, Barry Werch, was the actual culprit and, in his defense, requested that a polygraph examination that Werch had "failed," as well as "incriminating" statements made by Werch, be allowed into evidence. The district court denied the request, and this evidence was not admitted. Lea was found guilty of contaminating NBP's animal stock and was sentenced to serve three years imprisonment, followed by a year of supervised

release, and to pay over $2 million in restitution. Lea appealed, asserting that his Sixth Amendment right (to present a defense) had been violated by excluding Werch's polygraph examination. The Court of Appeals affirmed the lower court's decision to exclude the polygraph evidence on the basis of the polygrapher's inability to provide statistics on the accuracy rate of the polygraph and on the accuracy of the results specific to this case.

---

examinations as part of an employment application for most jobs. The federal Employee Polygraph Protection Act of 1988 prohibits most private employers from using polygraphs (as well as PSE machines) to screen employees for honesty or past offenses. Ironically, many firms that previously used polygraph examinations are now using other devices, especially "integrity tests," to detect potentially dishonest employees. These paper-and-pencil tests are intended to measure employees' attitudes toward thefts or other crimes, but the evidence to date indicates that such tests are probably inferior to the polygraph as "honesty tests." They appear to be easily faked and only minimally related to actual honest or dishonest behavior (Guastello & Rieke, 1991).

Use of Confessions

Throughout history, confessions have been accorded enormous importance. Confession is valued as an indicator of truth and also as an act that benefits confessors because it relieves them of guilt and earns them forgiveness from their fellow citizens. Many

religions maintain that confession is the first step toward redemption and have evolved special rituals to encourage it. Interrogations and confessions play a role in military matters, also. People detained as terrorist threats in military jails in Afghanistan, Iraq, Guantanomo Bay, and elsewhere are interrogated by harsh methods (described in Box 6.2) that are unacceptable in United States criminal courts, although some tactics that are used in criminal interrogations (and that we describe in this chapter) are applied as well.

When the police capture suspects, one of their first acts is to encourage them to confess to the crime. A confession will, of course, permit a district attorney or grand jury to bring charges. Even if the suspect later denies the confession and pleads not guilty to charges, the confession can be introduced into evidence at the trial (Gudjonsson, 1988).

Although disputed "confessions" by defendants occur surprisingly often, and many false confessions have been documented (e.g., Drizin & Leo, 2004; Dwyer, Neufeld, & Scheck, 2000), the number of false confessions is actually a matter of contention (Cassell, 1999; Leo & Ofshe, 1998).

THE CASE OF

BOX 6.2   **Charles Graner: Interrogation, the war on terror, and torture**

In 2003, military interrogators at the Abu Ghraib prison in Baghdad threatened naked prisoners with attack dogs, held detainees in awkward, painful positions, deprived them of sleep for up to 24 hours, subjected them to sexual humiliation, and threatened some with extradition to countries with a reputation for brutality (Addicott, 2004). These acts led to the conviction of Specialist Charles Graner, one of the interrogators and the chief architect of the abuse. Although it is widely accepted that extraordinary measures are necessary to detect and prevent terrorist acts, we do not condone torture. International treaties and federal statutes prohibit torture, and Western democracies smugly state that torture is unacceptable under any circumstances.

We know that many regimes, ancient and modern, have employed torture to get information or to punish. Those interested can visit Europe's torture museums to marvel at instruments of pain such as the rack, the iron maiden, and the thumbscrew—testaments

to human ingenuity for inflicting suffering. But one need not travel long distances to find examples of inhumane treatment. In Mississippi less than 80 years ago, sheriff's deputies whipped two black suspects with a leather strap and a buckle until they confessed in the very manner demanded by those present (*Brown v. Mississippi*, 1936).

What is torture? The federal government's 2002 "torture memo" authored by Assistant Attorney General Jay Bybee defines torture as "an act specifically intended to inflict severe pain and suffering, mental or physical." In this context, "severe" means "of such a high level of intensity that the pain is difficult to endure." The examples in the memo—drawn from the federal Torture Victims Protection Act— are (1) severe beatings with clubs, (2) threat of imminent death, (3) threat of amputation, (4) burning, (5) administering electric shock or threats to do so, (6) rape or threats of rape, and (7) forcing the prisoner to watch the torture of others (Zernike, 2004).

Specialist Charles Graner during a recess in his court martial. In 2005, a military jury convicted Graner on nine charges stemming from his abuse of prisoners at the Abu Ghraib prison in Iraq.

The implication of the Bybee memo is that the following "stress and duress" tactics are permissible if done in accordance with standard procedures: sleep deprivation, extreme cold, stripping detainees, loud music and lights, and forcing detainees to maintain uncomfortable positions. The moral question is whether and to what extent we as a society condone such methods in the name of national security.

Prosecutors observe that defendants can easily recant confessions by alleging that police had coerced them, but defense attorneys say that false confessions happen more often than prosecutors acknowledge. It is undisputed, for example, that false confessions led to the wrongful conviction and imprisonment of five young men in the infamous case known by the identity of the victim, the Central Park Jogger (see Box 6.3)

Historical Background and Current Legal Standing

Many "confessions" do not come spontaneously from the defendant; rather, they result from intense questioning by the police—interrogations that may involve promises, threats, harassment, or even brutality (Wrightsman & Kassin, 1993). Until 1966, the traditional test for

THE CASE OF

BOX 6.3   the Central Park Jogger and five innocent suspects who confessed

One of the most notorious crimes in New York City history occurred in April of 1989, when a young woman was attacked while she jogged through Central Park. During the attack, she was beaten, raped, and sodomized and, in the process, lost nearly 80% of her blood. (She has since recovered and written about her ordeal in a book entitled *I am the Central Park Jogger: A Story of Hope and Possibility*.) That same evening, a group of teenage boys harassed and beat joggers and cyclists in Central Park. Because the woman's body was found near the location of these other assaults, six of the boys were taken in for questioning; all were between the ages of 14 and 16. Throughout the night and into the next day, the interrogations went on. Eventually, detectives obtained five confessions to the rape of the so-called Central Park Jogger. But there is significant controversy about what transpired during those hours: The boys and their

parents, some of whom were present during the questioning, claimed that the interrogations were highly coercive; police denied using high-pressure tactics. Unfortunately, only the final moments of the interrogations, featuring the confessions, were captured on videotape. No recordings were made of the hours of questioning that led up to those admissions of guilt.

Over the objections of the defendants, the videotaped confessions were admitted at their trials. All five defendants were convicted on charges related to the rape of the jogger and were sentenced to between 5 and 15 years in prison. Then, in January 2002, Matias Reyes, a convicted serial rapist, contacted the police to tell them that he, acting alone, had raped the Central Park Jogger. Eventually, DNA tests confirmed that semen stains found on the jogger's sock came from Reyes, and additional evidence emerged that tended to exonerate the boys. In December

One of the defendants in the Central Park jogger rape case, Yusef Salaam, arriving at the State Supreme Court in New York City in 1990. Salaam and four co-defendants were wrongly convicted and imprisoned for the crime.

2002, a New York judge vacated all the convictions of the original defendants. This case provided a startling example of the reality of false confessions and the role that interrogations play in securing those confessions.

admissibility of a confession was voluntariness: A voluntary confession was given without overt inducements, threats, promises, or physical harm. The trustworthiness of a confession was believed to be lost when it was obtained through one or more of those means (*Hopt v. Utah*, 1884).

Assessing the voluntariness of confessions proved difficult for many reasons, however. The task

was highly subjective, and it resulted in countless "swearing contests" between police and suspects about what went on behind the closed door of interrogation rooms. Therefore, in *Miranda v. Arizona* (1966), the Supreme Court held that a confession resulting from in-custody interrogation was admissible only if, in addition to meeting the standards for voluntariness, it had been obtained after the police had taken steps to ensure the suspect's protection from self-incrimination by delivering the so-called *Miranda* warnings (see Box 6.4). Whereas courts had previously been concerned with the potential untrustworthiness of coerced confessions, this case signaled an emphasis on protection of the dignity of the accused person.

The *Miranda* case did not solve all problems associated with the validity of confessions. Although the warnings add a new element to the interrogation, intense and secretive interrogations continue to this day, with the interrogator intent upon persuading the suspect to confess. Furthermore, many suspects waive their *Miranda* rights, and after a suspect voluntarily enters the interrogation room, investigators can use any number of tactics to obtain a confession (we describe some of them later in this chapter). Finally, some suspects (those who are young or mentally disabled) are especially vulnerable to the tactics of a skillful interrogator, and yet the Supreme Court has stated, in *Colorado v. Connelly* (1986), that a suspect's mental limitations or psychological problems alone do not necessarily lead to the conclusion that a confession was involuntary.

A defendant often makes and then withdraws an out-of-court confession. The Supreme Court, in *Jackson v. Denno* (1964), held that criminal defendants are entitled to a pretrial hearing that determines whether any confession they have made to officials was voluntarily given and not the outcome of physical or psychological coercion, which the U.S. Constitution forbids. Only if the fact finder (usually the judge) at this hearing determines that the confession was voluntary may it then be introduced to the jury at the trial. The *Jackson v. Denno* decision explicitly acknowledged the possibility of coerced confessions.

Whittling Away at Miranda

Miranda v. Arizona was one of the most controversial criminal procedure decisions of the past half-century. The chief justice at the time, Earl Warren, was castigated in congressional committees and on the floor of Congress (Warren, 1977), and "Impeach Earl Warren" billboards were widely seen.

Although *Miranda* has survived for 40 years, the case remains controversial to this day.

Miranda faced a major challenge from University of Utah law professor Paul Cassell through the case of *Dickerson v. United States* (2000). For many years Professor Cassell claimed that *Miranda* was an illegitimate exercise of judicial power that freed thousands of guilty defendants on technicalities. He railed at the Department of Justice for refusing to rely on 18 U.S.C. 3501, a statute Congress had passed in 1968 in an attempt to overrule *Miranda*. In 1999, the Court of Appeals for the Fourth Circuit responded to Professor Cassell's call and used the statute to admit a confession that had been taken in violation of *Miranda*. The defendant sought a review by the United States Supreme Court. To the surprise of many, however, the Supreme Court emphatically reaffirmed *Miranda*. In a 7–2 decision striking down 18 U.S.C. 3501 as unconstitutional, Chief Justice Rehnquist pointed out that *Miranda* warnings do not significantly deter people from confessing and that *Miranda* has become part of the national culture (*Dickerson v. United States*, 2000, p. 2336). This case is a good example of **stare decisis**—the court's preference for maintaining stability in its decisions whenever possible. Given *Miranda's* longtime acceptance in the United States, the Court opted against outright change in the law of confessions.

The Supreme Court has weakened *Miranda* through a series of subsequent decisions, however. (Ironically, these decisions were a factor in saving *Miranda* when the case was challenged by Professor Cassell. The police are able to live with *Miranda*, in large part because the following decisions have weakened its impact.)

1. *Confessions that violate Miranda may be used to impeach a defendant.* Suppose a person confesses when arrested, and the confession is taken in violation of the *Miranda* warnings. If the defendant testifies to his or her innocence at trial, the prosecutor may use the confession to show that the defendant should not be believed (*Harris v. New York*, 1971).

THE CASE OF

BOX 6.4

Ernest Miranda and the right to remain silent: Forever changing the face of police work

One of the best-known U.S. Supreme Court cases decided during the 1960s, *Miranda v. Arizona*, dealt with the problem of coerced confessions. The case started in an all too typical fashion with an all too disturbing outcome. Late on a Saturday night, May 2, 1963, an 18-year-old woman left her job at the refreshment stand at the Paramount Theater in downtown Phoenix, Arizona. After riding the bus to a stop near her home, she started walking the remaining distance. But a man grabbed her, dragged her to a parked car, tied her hands behind her, laid her down in the back seat, tied her ankles together, and told her to lie still. She felt a cold, sharp object—she was never sure what it was—at her neck. Her abductor drove her to the desert, where he raped her. Then, as he waited for her to get dressed, he demanded whatever money she had. She gave him the four $1 bills in her purse.

The Phoenix police had the victim look at a lineup on Sunday morning. She had described her attacker as a Hispanic American male; 27 or 28 years old; 5 feet, 11 inches tall; and weighing 175 pounds. He was slender, she said, and had a medium complexion, with short black hair. She remembered him as having a tattoo and as wearing Levis, a white T-shirt, and

dark-rimmed glasses. The police composed a lineup of likely-looking choices, but the victim failed to identify anyone. She was very shy; apparently of limited intelligence, she had dropped out of school after failing for several years.

But a week after the rape, the victim's brother-in-law spotted a car like the one she had described. He pointed it out, and she said yes, it did look like her assailant's car. As the car sped away, they were able to remember enough of the license plate for the police to trace the registration to a young woman who had a friend named Ernest Miranda, a Mexican American in his early twenties.

When the police located the car, they saw a rope strung along the back of the front seat, just as the young woman had described. Police records also confirmed that Miranda had several previous criminal convictions, including one for assault with intent to commit rape. A man with a long criminal history going back to age 14, he had been charged with attempted rape at the age of 15. So the police put together a new lineup, selecting three Hispanic Americans, all about the same height and build, to stand with Miranda. But he was the only person wearing a short-sleeved

AP/Wide World Photos

T-shirt, the only one with eyeglasses, and the only tattooed man in the lineup. Still, the young woman couldn't identify her assailant, although she felt that number 1—Miranda—had a similar build and features.

Frustrated, the police then took Miranda to an interrogation room for what they thought was routine questioning. But the exchanges that occurred in that tiny chamber forever changed the way police interact with citizens. Miranda asked about the lineup: "How did I do?" "You flunked," a police officer replied, and he began to question Miranda about the rape of the young woman. No attorneys, witnesses, or tape recorders were present. The police later reported that Miranda voluntarily confessed, that he "admitted not only that he was the person who had raped this girl but that he had attempted to rape another woman and to rob still another" (Baker, 1983, p. 13).

Miranda described the interrogation differently:

> Once they get you in a little room and they start badgering you one way or the other, "You better tell us . . . or we're going to throw the book at you." . . . They would try to give me all the time they could. They thought there was even a possibility that there was something wrong with me. They would try to help me, get me medical care if I needed it . . . . And I haven't had any sleep since the day before. I'm tired. I just got off my work, and they have me and they are interrogating me. They mention first one crime, then another one; they are certain I am the person . . . . Knowing what a penitentiary is like, a person has to be frightened, scared. And not knowing if he'll be able to get back up and go home. (Quoted in Baker, 1983, p. 13)

Whichever story one believes, Ernest Miranda emerged from the questioning a confessed rapist. Because the young woman had been unsure of her identification, the police summoned her to the interrogation room to hear Miranda's voice. As she entered, one of the officers asked Miranda, "Is that the girl?" "That's the girl," he replied, believing that she had already identified him in the lineup. In June of 1963, Miranda was convicted of rape and kidnapping, and he was sentenced to 20 to 30 years for each charge. But Miranda appealed his conviction all the way to the U.S. Supreme Court, and the Court—by a 5–4 vote—concluded that his right against self-incrimination had been violated. Henceforth, they stated, the police must warn suspects of certain rights before starting a custodial interrogation. If these procedures are not followed, any damaging admissions made by suspects cannot be used by the prosecution in a trial.

By unintentionally giving his name to the warning that police officers must give suspects, Ernest Miranda became a footnote to history. But his own history took an ironic twist. Miranda was given a new trial as a result of the Supreme Court's ruling. Even though his confession was excluded from the 1966 retrial, he was convicted again because the prosecution had uncovered new evidence against him. Between then and 1976, Miranda served some prison time, was released, but had several run-ins with the law. By the age of 34, he had been an ex-con, an appliance store delivery man, and probably a drug dealer.

On the night of January 31, 1976, he was playing poker in a flophouse section of Phoenix. A drunken fight broke out involving two undocumented Mexican immigrants. As he tried to take a knife away from one of them, Miranda was stabbed in the stomach and again in the chest. He was dead on arrival at the hospital. Miranda's killer fled, but his accomplice was caught. Before taking him to police headquarters, two Phoenix police officers read to him—one in English, one in Spanish—from a card:

- ◆ You have the right to remain silent.
- ◆ Anything you say can be used against you in a court of law.
- ◆ You have the right to the presence of an attorney to assist you prior to questioning and to be with you during questioning, if you so desire.
- ◆ If you cannot afford an attorney, you have the right to have an attorney appointed for you prior to questioning.
- ◆ Do you understand these rights?
- ◆ Will you voluntarily answer my questions?

Thus ended the life, but not the legacy, of Ernest Miranda.

2. *Confessions by defendants who don't fully understand the warnings may still be admissible.* There are suspects whose age, intellectual disability, or psychological instability renders them especially vulnerable to certain tactics of interrogation (Drizin & Colgan, 2004; Fulero & Everington, 2004). These individuals may have difficulty understanding the warnings and the meaning of a waiver. Nonetheless, if the police give the warnings and the defendant responds affirmatively when asked whether he or she wishes to make a statement, that statement is usually admissible.

3. *To stop an interrogation, a request for a lawyer must be unequivocal.* In *Davis v. United States* (1994), the Court held that the police were not obligated to stop the questioning or clarify an equivocal request by a suspect ("Maybe I should get a lawyer").

4. *Miranda does not apply unless the suspect is in the custody of the police.* The Supreme Court has treated *custody* in various ways. Thus, the Court held that roadside questioning of a motorist stopped for drunk driving is noncustodial, even though the motorist is not free to go (*Berkemer v. McCarty*, 1984). Warnings are not required in this circumstance. "Stop and frisk" questioning is also usually viewed as noncustodial because such questioning merely accompanies temporary detentions in public places.

5. *Miranda does not apply unless the defendant is being interrogated.* A volunteered confession is always admissible. Suppose the police arrest a robbery suspect and decide, for whatever reason, not to interrogate him. On the way to the station, the accused person volunteers that he wouldn't have been caught if he'd kept his mask on. This confession is admissible because it was not in response to police questioning (*Rhode Island v. Innis*, 1980).

6. *The police are not required to tell the defendant anything more than what is contained in the Miranda warnings.* They are not required to tell the defendant what he is suspected of doing (*Colorado v. Spring*, 1987). They are not required to tell him that a lawyer hired by his family wants to see him (*Moran v. Burbine*, 1986). They are not required to tell him that his silence cannot be used against him.

7. *The police can mislead defendants about the evidence in order to get them to confess* (Frazier v. Cupp, *1969*). Trickery is permissible so long as the police do not lie about the *Miranda* warnings themselves.

8. *Miranda warnings are not required in situations in which public safety might be endangered by giving the warnings.* In *New York v. Quarles* (1984), a woman told the police that she had been raped by an armed man who had just run into a supermarket. An officer entered the market and spotted Quarles running to the rear of the store. The officer gave chase and caught him in the storage area. After frisking Quarles and finding no gun, the officer asked where the gun was. Quarles nodded in the direction of some empty cartons and said, "The gun is over there." The police found the gun, and Quarles was prosecuted for criminal possession of the weapon (the rape charge was not pursued). The New York courts suppressed the defendant's statement (and the gun) because Quarles had not been given the *Miranda* warnings. The Supreme Court, however, used the case to create a "public safety" exception to *Miranda*; warnings do not have to be given when police questioning is reasonably motivated by a concern for public safety.

The Validity of Confession Evidence

How valid is confession evidence? In a perfect world, guilty people would always confess, and innocent people would never do so. Unfortunately, reality is far from perfect. We know that two kinds of erroneous outcomes are possible: false negatives (when guilty suspects fail to confess) and false positives (when innocent suspects confess) (Kassin & Gudjonsson, 2004). Although false negatives occur more often than false positives, the latter outcome has captured the attention of psychologists, lawyers, judges, and the public alike, reflecting widespread agreement that innocent people should not be convicted of crimes they did not commit.

Why, one might ask, would a truly innocent person confess to a crime that he or she did not commit? How often does this really happen? And what are the circumstances that would lead someone to confess falsely? Although it is difficult to gauge the frequency of false confessions, we do know that they occur. Drizin and Leo (2004) identified and analyzed 125 such cases, and Kassin (2005) noted that 25% of people who were exonerated by DNA evidence after serving time in prison had falsely confessed. Now we are beginning to understand the circumstances that give rise to false confessions. But before we detail those circumstances, we must ask how we can know, for certain, that a confession is false. Do we simply take the suspect or defendant at his word when he alleges that his admission of guilt was wrong? Alternatively, do we need some kind of evidence that proves, unequivocally, that the defendant could not have committed the crime to which he confessed?

PROVING THAT A CONFESSION IS FALSE

There are four ways in which we can be certain that a disputed confession is false (Drizin & Leo, 2004). First, a suspect could confess to a crime that did not occur. For example, three mentally retarded defendants (including Victoria Banks) were convicted by an Alabama jury of killing Ms. Banks's newborn child. Only after the three had served time in prison was it determined that Ms. Banks was incapable of giving birth to a child because she had had a tubal ligation operation that prevented her from getting pregnant.

Confessions can be proved to be false in situations where it was physically impossible for a suspect to commit the crime, as, for example, when jail records prove that the defendant was incarcerated at the time the crime was committed (S. Mills, 1998). When Charles Lindbergh's baby was kidnapped in 1932, more than 200 people confessed (Note, 1953).

A third way in which a disputed confession can be proved false is that the actual perpetrator is identified and his guilt is objectively established. This happened in the case of Christopher Ochoa, a high school honor student, who confessed to raping and murdering a woman in an Austin, Texas, Pizza Hut in 1988. Ochoa, who served 12 years in prison, claims that he confessed in order to avoid the possibility of a death sentence. He was released and

exonerated only after Achim Marino, the real perpetrator, confessed to killing the woman. Marino then led authorities to the weapon and the bag in which he had placed the money, and other evidence found at the crime scene was connected to him (Drizin & Leo, 2004).

Finally, a confession is known to be false when there is scientific evidence—most commonly DNA, that definitively establishes the defendant's innocence. For example, three teenagers—Michael Crowe, Joshua Treadway, and Aaron Houser—all falsely confessed to the 1998 murder of Michael's 12-year old sister Stephanie in Escondido, California. Charges against the boys were dropped only after DNA testing proved that blood found on the sweatshirt of a mentally ill drifter who had been in the neighborhood on the night of the murder was Stephanie's (Drizin & Colgan, 2004).

What would cause a person to confess to a crime he or she did not commit? Following up on recent interest in examining the role of police interrogations in confessions, social scientists are now beginning to understand the different coercive influences of those interrogations (Lassiter, 2004). New studies have documented the role that psychologically oriented coercion can have in inducing suspects to confess, especially when those suspects are vulnerable to begin with (e.g., children, adolescents, and those with mental limitations). In fact, what we are learning from these studies points to the mutually compounding effects of an interrogator's coercive tactics and a suspect's vulnerable state at the time of questioning.

Inside the Interrogation Room: Common Interrogation Techniques and the Likelihood of False Confessions

At earlier times in our history, torture and other "third-degree" tactics were used to get suspects to incriminate themselves. Because these techniques were considered by many to be morally offensive, and because they often yielded statements of questionable veracity, physical intimidation is virtually nonexistent today. In its place, however, interrogators now use psychologically oriented coercion that, because it is less blatant, may actually be more insidious (Leo, 2004).

Many police departments rely on a training manual entitled *Criminal Interrogation and Confessions*, currently in its fourth edition (Inbau, Reid, Buckley, & Jayne, 2004). This manual (and others like it, such as Gordon & Fleisher, 2002) outlines an interviewing and interrogation protocol that can be used to elicit statements from witnesses. The recommendations range from how to set up an interrogation room to enhance the likelihood that a suspect will talk, to a description of actual interrogative tactics that will force a suspect to confess. To fully understand why someone would confess falsely, one must be aware of the techniques of social influence that are recommended by this manual and characterize most interrogation rooms.

The training manual (Inbau et al., 2004) recommends that a small, bare, soundproof room be used for interrogations; preferably one that is devoid of sensory stimulation and distractions. In order to compound this social isolation and sensory deprivation, the interrogator is advised to use armless, straight-backed chairs, to keep all light switches, thermostats, and other controls away from the suspect, and to invade the suspect's personal space during questioning (Kassin & Gudjonsson, 2004).

The interrogator is instructed to use a carefully orchestrated procedure that will eventually overwhelm even the most reluctant suspects and get them to talk. The interview should begin with the interrogator confronting the suspect with the suspicion of his or her guilt: "If the suspect perceives that the investigator is not certain of his guilt, he is unlikely to confess. Consequently, [it is recommended that] the investigator initiate the interrogation with a direct statement indicating absolute certainty in the suspect's guilt" (Inbau et al., 2004, pp. 218–219). In addition, interrogators are advised to interrupt any statements of innocence or denial made by the suspect; to elicit suspects' trust by minimizing their responsibility for the alleged act and sympathizing with them; to help suspects to recall

"the truth" about the crime by having them imagine what would have transpired if a hypothetical third person had engaged in the alleged crime; to provide details about the victim's injuries and the perpetrator's actions; to emphasize or exaggerate the strength of the evidence against them; and to offer moral or psychological justification for the suspects' alleged behaviors. Suspects who offer verbal statements are instructed to write and/or sign confessions that assert their guilt (Gordon & Fleisher, 2002; Inbau et al., 2004).

Psychologists have begun to examine these interrogation tactics experimentally and have observed various results, some of them surprising. Sometimes, suspects confess in order to escape or avoid continuing aversive interrogation or to gain some sort of promised reward. These confessions—termed **coerced-compliant false confessions** by Kassin and Wrightsman (1985)—occur when a suspect knows that he is innocent but comes to believe that the short-term benefits of confessing (e.g., being left alone, being allowed to leave) outweigh the long-term costs (e.g., being charged with a crime, being convicted) (Kassin & Gudjonsson, 2004). Other times, suspects confess because they actually come to believe that they have committed the crime. These so-called **coerced-internalized false confessions** (Kassin & Wrightsman, 1985) can be directly related to the manipulative techniques that were used during the interrogation. Recent psychological studies have begun to show how interrogation techniques can lead some suspects to create false beliefs and illusory memories for crimes they did not commit.

Recall that many interrogations begin with the interrogator issuing an unequivocal statement of belief in the suspect's guilt. This presumption of guilt can apparently influence the way a detective conducts the questioning, causing the suspect to become defensive or confused and thereby increasing the chances of a false confession. This phenomenon—variably referred to as a self-fulfilling prophecy or **behavioral confirmation** (Meissner & Kassin, 2004) has been demonstrated in a wide range of settings (Rosenthal & Jacobson, 1968; McNatt, 2000). After people form a particular belief (e.g., in the guilt of a suspect), they unwittingly tend to seek out information that verifies that belief, overlook data that are contradictory, and behave in a manner that conforms to the belief. In turn, the target person (here, the suspect) behaves in ways that support the initial belief.

The effects of an implicit assumption of guilt on the conduct of interrogators and suspects and on judgments of the interrogation made by neutral observers were examined by Kassin, Goldstein, and Savitsky (2003). In the first phase of a two-part study, "suspects" were instructed either to steal $100 from a locked cabinet as part of a mock theft or to engage in a related but innocent act (approaching the locked cabinet but not stealing any money). Other participants acted as interrogators and were led to believe either that most suspects in the study were truly guilty of the mock theft or that most were truly innocent. These interviewing sessions were taped and then, in the second phase of the study, played for observers whose task was to judge whether the suspect was guilty or innocent.

Interrogators who assumed that suspects were guilty used more guilt-based interrogative techniques (e.g., presenting false evidence, trying harder to elicit a confession, making innocent suspects sound more defensive), and suspects toward whom these techniques were directed acted more defensively and were more likely to be identified as being guilty of the mock crime. In fact, the most pressure-filled interrogation sessions occurred when innocent suspects were questioned by interrogators who presumed guilt. The presumption of guilt apparently ushers in a process of behavioral confirmation by which the expectations of interrogators affect their questioning style, the suspects' behavior, and, ultimately, judgments of the guilt of the suspect. These findings may actually *underestimate* the risks of behavioral confirmation in actual interrogations, where the questioning can go on for hours rather than minutes, interrogators have often garnered years of experience in questioning suspects, and these same interrogators are trained to have confidence in their ability to divine guilt from a suspect's behavior (Meissner & Kassin, 2004).

Other common tactics of interrogation involve encouraging the suspect to imagine a hypothetical third person committing the crime and to visualize the events that allegedly occurred during the crime. By these processes, innocent suspects can create vivid images that they may later falsely interpret as recollections of the crime itself (Henkel & Coffman, 2004). This can occur through a phenomenon called **source misattribution**: mistaking memories that arise primarily from one's thoughts and images for memories that come from actual, experienced events. We know, for example, that people can be led to believe that they have performed actions that they really only imagined (Anderson, 1984), that imagining events in their life can increase people's belief in the occurrence of events that did not actually occur (Garry & Polaschek, 2000,) and that imagining an event can cause people to create "memories" of this event's occurrence, even when the event could not possibly have happened (Mazzoni & Memon, 2003). Thus, if interrogators ask people to imagine the crime scene, and if people confuse information derived from their imaginations with actual experiences, it seems likely that suspects could misattribute their recollections to actual perceptions (Henkel & Coffman, 2004).

So far, we have considered the effects of interrogation on adults accused of committing crimes. Although most children who interact with the law do so as witnesses or victims (we describe the particular problems of child witnesses in Chapter 14), a substantial number of juveniles come into contact with the police and legal system as suspects. Like adults, these juvenile suspects are interrogated by police. In fact, the training manual (Inbau et al., 2004) suggests that the principles of adult interrogation "are just as applicable to the young ones" (p. 298), and interviews with juveniles who were questioned by police showed that police used many of the same ploys on them, including the implied promise that the suspect can go home if he tells the police what they want to hear (Redlich, Silverman, Chen, & Steiner, 2004). Thus, like adults, these juveniles sometimes confess falsely (as did the defendants in the Central

Park Jogger case). How often does this happen? Of the 125 proven false confession cases compiled by Drizin and Leo (2004), fully 33% involved juveniles.

Inside the Courtroom: How Jurors Evaluate Confession Evidence

If a defendant confesses while under severe threat during an interrogation, that confession may be viewed either as a reflection of the defendant's true guilt or as a means of avoiding the negative consequences of silence. Ideally, jurors would employ what a leading attribution theorist (Kelley, 1971) has called the **discounting principle**: They would have more doubts about the truth and reliability of a confession elicited by threat than about one made in the absence of threat. In other words, they would "discount," or give less weight to, the confession—and perhaps even disregard it— because it was generated by threat of force. If jurors are good at identifying and discounting problematic confessions, then we have less need for concern about the manipulative tactics that were used to elicit those confessions in the first place.

Unfortunately, discounting doesn't always occur. A number of social psychological studies have reported that, when making attributions about the causes of another's behavior, people often commit the **fundamental attribution error**: They do not give sufficient importance to the external situation as a determinant; instead, they believe the behavior is caused by stable, internal factors unique to the actor (Jones, 1990). Thus, in the present situation, they would conclude, "He confessed, so he must be guilty."

Does the fundamental attribution error apply to situations in which jurors must judge the validity of a confession? Apparently, yes. In a series of jury simulation studies, Wrightsman and Kassin (1993; see also Kassin & Wrightsman, 1980, 1981) showed that when mock jurors read transcripts of a trial in which the defendant had confessed in response to a threat of punishment, they judged the confession to be involuntary and disregarded it in their verdict decisions. When the confession

was induced by a promise of leniency or favored treatment, however, mock jurors responded inconsistently: They conceded that the defendant had confessed involuntarily, but they judged him to be guilty anyway. These subjects accepted the defendant's confession as probative (i.e., as useful evidence) despite acknowledging that it had been induced through a promise of leniency.

More subtle forms of obtaining confessions show similar effects. When confessions are "noncoercively" encouraged by interrogators who sympathetically attempt to minimize the severity of the charges or the culpability of suspects during questioning, subjects show the same strong **positive coercion bias**: They are willing to vote guilty even when they see the confessions as being involuntary (Kassin & McNall, 1991).

On occasion, involuntary confessions are admitted into evidence erroneously (and the Supreme Court, in *Arizona v. Fulminante* [1991], held that admission of an involuntary confession does not automatically taint a conviction). Although jurors are not particularly attuned to the voluntariness of a confession, they might be skeptical about one that was admitted erroneously. But according to some evidence (Kassin & Sukel, 1997), they are not. In this study, mock jurors read a murder trial transcript that described a suspect who confessed in either a high-pressure interrogation (in which he was handcuffed and verbally abused and in which the detective brandished his weapon) or a low-pressure interrogation (no handcuffs, threats, intimidation, or weapons). In each of these confession conditions, half of the jurors learned that the judge admitted the confession into evidence, and half learned that the judge excluded it. Mock jurors did well at distinguishing between high-pressure and low-pressure interrogations and judged the confession to be significantly less voluntary in the former situation than in the latter. But jurors did *not* discount the coerced confession; in fact, they put significant weight on the confession, even when they believed it was coerced and when it was ruled inadmissible. As the authors stated, "The mere presence of a confession was thus sufficient to turn acquittal into conviction, irrespective of the contexts in which it was elicited and presented" (p. 42).

Reforming the System to Prevent False Confessions

Many people have advocated the recording of all police interrogations as a way to provide a complete, objective, and reviewable record of the interrogation itself. Recording has the potential to improve the quality of interrogations and deter police misconduct during questioning. More than half of all law enforcement agencies now record at least some of their interrogations, and recording is mandated in Alaska, Illinois, and Minnesota. But recording may not be a surefire preventive against the conviction of innocent people. Daniel Lassiter and his colleagues have shown that when the camera is focused on the suspect, as is usually done in order to allow observers to see what the suspect said and did, observers are more likely to judge the confession as voluntary, compared with the same confession recorded from a different camera perspective (i.e., focused equally on the suspect and the interrogator or solely on the interrogator (Lassiter & Geers, 2004). Lassiter concludes that filming can be an effective tool for recording interrogations but that it must be used judiciously. In particular, an equal-focus perspective can reduce any bias inherent in the use of recording to document interrogations.

Entrapment

In their efforts to catch criminals, the police may induce law-abiding people to commit crimes they otherwise would not have committed. This practice is called **entrapment**. Defendants who claim they were entrapped offer two explanations: (1) They were induced to break the law by a person or persons working for the police (often an informant), and (2) they were not predisposed to break that law—the police created a crime that otherwise would not have occurred.

Proactive law enforcement often necessitates deception. As citizens, we understand that the police must sometimes pose as drug buyers (or sellers) to catch those dealing in illegal drugs. We want the police to infiltrate conspiracies to prevent criminal activity and terrorism. We expect the police to "troll the net" to identify pedophiles who might use the Internet to perpetrate sex crimes. But we do not want the police to induce law-abiding people to commit crimes. The important distinction, as the Supreme Court stated in *Sherman v. United States*, is between a "trap for the unwary innocent and the trap for the unwary criminal" (*Sherman v. United States*, 1958, p. 372).

The defense of entrapment is recognized in all states. There are two general approaches to the defense. In a minority of states, the question is whether police methods would have induced an otherwise law-abiding citizen to commit the offense. This "objective approach" focuses on situational factors that may have prompted commission of a crime.

In the majority of states and in federal courts, the issue is whether the defendant was ready to commit the offense even in the absence of inducement or encouragement (i.e., was "otherwise disposed to engage in the conduct"). This "subjective approach" focuses on the offender's subjective state of mind, rather than on the objective facts of the police methods. In jurisdictions that use the subjective approach, defendants must prove that they were induced or persuaded to commit the crime. If the defendant is successful in meeting this burden, the prosecution then has the burden of responding to the claim of entrapment. The prosecution may respond by proving one or both of the following: (1) The police didn't induce the defendant to commit the offense but, rather, just provided an opportunity. (2) Even though police induced the defendant to commit the offense, he or she was predisposed to commit it anyway.

Consider the following situation: The police put an officer dressed like a prostitute on the corner and wait for would-be "johns" to take the bait. In such a case, the court and jury will probably say that there is no inducement—the police simply provided an opportunity for criminal activity.

THE CASE OF

BOX 6.5   Billy Burgess: Entrapment on the Internet?

When Billy Burgess (computer name "LandofAhz") logged onto an America Online chat room for men interested in "barely legal females," he might have thought "Maggie284," his cyberpal's computer persona, was a 13-year-old girl—a female of an age not "legal" in any state. After all, Maggie284 repeatedly referred to "Mom," misspelled words, and mentioned not only her age but also her weight (92 pounds) and her inexperience in sexual matters. Intrigued by Maggie284's responses to his sexually explicit messages, LandofAhz told Maggie284 that he would be coming to Orlando, where Maggie284 purported to live and would meet her in a limousine with lingerie, champagne, and other gifts. Maggie284 asked him to "e-mail me," and LandofAhz promised to do so before logging off.

Did Billy Burgess really believe he was corresponding with a 13-year-old girl, or was he merely engaged in fantasy play? In the world of Internet chat rooms, reasonable people should assume that their cyber pen pals might not be what they purport to be (Sheetz, 2000). Even if Burgess did believe he was corresponding with a 13-year-old, little evidence indicates that he intended to pursue the matter by going to Orlando—until Maggie284 contacted him two weeks later. Of course, Maggie284 was not a budding teenager. Maggie284 was a 26-year-old man named Randall Sluder, on probation for the felony of attempting to evade a police officer, who had created Maggie284 to identify and apprehend individuals who use the Internet to engage in cybersex with underage teenagers.

Sluder printed out the salacious e-mails and took them to the police in Kissimmee, Florida, who assumed the identity of Maggie284 and e-mailed LandofAhz to ask him to come to Orlando for a meeting. He promised to do so. Maggie284 then e-mailed a phone number, LandofAhz called, and a female police officer successfully simulated the voice of a 13-year-old girl. Two days later, LandofAhz, aka Billy Burgess, arrived at the Enterprise Hotel in a Lincoln Town Car (though without gifts) and was arrested. He was charged in federal court with attempting, through the Internet, to induce a minor to have sex and with traveling in interstate commerce to have sex with a minor.

Burgess claimed that he was entrapped—that he was induced to come to Orlando by Maggie284's e-mail to him two weeks after the initial correspondence, that he

---

Now consider the case described in Box 6.5, which involved deliberate inducement and persuasion to commit a crime. The crucial question in such a case is whether the defendant was predisposed to commit the offense and, if so, whether that predisposition originated before or after police contacts.

The leading case on the issue of inducing criminal behavior is *Jacobson v. United States* (1992). The defendant had ordered child pornography through the mail after a lengthy cultivation of his prurient interest by the postal and customs services. Before such acts were illegal, the defendant had obtained nude photos of young boys from a mail-order bookstore. After such acts were made criminal, postal authorities found Jacobson's name on the bookstore's mailing list and started a campaign of phony surveys, circulars, and letters designed to pique the defendant's interest in preteen sex. Responding to this lengthy cultivation (some of the come-ons flaunted the First Amendment), Jacobson placed an order for child pornography from a brochure mailed to him by the postal authorities.

had no intention of trying to meet Maggie284, and that he would not have come to Orlando had the Kissimmee police not contacted him.

At his trial, the jury seriously considered the entrapment defense, as evidenced by the following question it sent to the judge: "Need clarification on entrapment, the jury instruction seems contradictory. There is some reasonable doubt that the Defendant would have pursued this further if the police did not send the first E-mail. . . . [I]s this nothing more than the Govt. offering an opportunity?"(*United States v. Burgess*, 1999, p. 1268).

After being reinstructed, the jury convicted Burgess on all counts. Did the jury believe he was "merely offered an opportunity"? Or did the jury think he was predisposed to commit the offense?

We don't know, although clearly Maggie284's reopening of the correspondence went beyond "offering an opportunity." On appeal, the federal court of appeals reversed the conviction on other grounds (the trial judge had failed to instruct the jury not to draw an "adverse inference" from Burgess's failure to testify in his own behalf).

Is it fair for the police to assume that one who responds to sexually oriented chatter from purportedly underage correspondents is predisposed to engage in illegal sexual activity? As Michael Sheetz describes, a police investigator will assume a suggestive name (e.g., Rachel-12) and wait for hits. "It has been my experience as an investigator that when using a female sounding name and a youthful persona, so many requests for private chat occur within five minutes that immediate response to all would be

impossible" (Sheetz, 2000, p. 410). Although acknowledging that some of the correspondents are "offending pedophiles," Sheetz contends that most of those who would want to chat with "Rachel-12" are merely curious or are "nonoffending pedophiles" (who fantasize about sexual contact with children but do not act on those fantasies). The police might influence a nonoffending pedophile through the apparent eagerness of "Rachel-12" to engage in real sexual activity. In such a case, the police have created a crime that otherwise would never have occurred (Sheetz, 2000). A Santa Monica jury "bought" the fantasy defense in a 2000 prosecution in which the defendant claimed that he thought he was dealing with an adult woman playing the part of a young girl—a cyberspace fantasy game played by two (Yamagami, 2001).

Jacobson was convicted, but the Supreme Court reversed the conviction because the government had failed to show that Jacobson was predisposed to engage in illegal activity before the postal authorities started their campaign to induce him to order child pornography. His interest in child pornography at a time when it was not illegal did not give the authorities legitimate reason to believe that he would break the law in this regard. The decision furthers the goal of deterring police from the kind of overreaching that might induce law-abiding citizens to break the law.

Some Internet sting operations to snare men trolling for underage sex partners can fairly be said to be nothing more than "standing on a cyberspace street corner which could be frequented by [underage] females looking to have sex with older men" (*State v. Cunningham*, 2004, p. 492). In other operations, however, the "bait" appears to be an adult woman looking for sex partners; when the "fish" shows interest, the nature of the "bait" is gradually switched through an exchange of letters or e-mails. If the "fish" responds to the switch in bait, he is reeled in and arrested. In *United States v. Poehlman* (2000) and *State v. Canady* (2002), appellate courts reversed convictions arising out of such tactics, holding that there was nothing to show the defendants had an interest in underage sex before they were snared by the bait and switch. In *Poehlman*, Judge Alex Kozinski commented on the government's tactics:

> Prior to his unfortunate encounter with Sharon, he was on a quest for an adult relationship with a woman who would understand and accept his proclivities, which did not include sex with children. There is surely enough real crime in our society that it is unnecessary for our law enforcement officials to spend months luring an obviously lonely and confused individual to cross the line between fantasy and criminality. (*United States v. Poehlman*, 2000, p. 705)

The goal of these decisions is to deter police misconduct. Can governmental conduct ever be so outrageous that an admittedly predisposed defendant is entitled to be acquitted as a matter of due process? *United States v. Twigg* (1978) is the case most often cited as authority for the due process defense. In this case, an informant contacted Neville, an old friend, and proposed they set up a "speed" laboratory. Neville agreed and assumed responsibility for the capital and the distribution of the product. With the government's financial backing, the informant supplied the chemicals, apparatus, and expertise required to make the drug. Twigg, one of Neville's creditors, was drawn into the operation, and both were eventually convicted of conspiracy to sell drugs. But the federal court of appeals reversed their convictions because of the government's extraordinary level of involvement—the government had, in fact, manufactured the drug the defendants were accused of conspiring to sell.

Although not decided on due process grounds, an old Kentucky case shows that convictions obtained by unfair police practices will not be allowed to stand. In *Scott v. Commonwealth* (1946), the police trapped a bootlegger after they returned whiskey they had seized in an illegal search. The police gave the

whiskey back to the bootlegger and then obtained a search warrant for the very same whiskey. The Kentucky court reversed the resulting conviction because of the police conduct, even though the defendant clearly was predisposed to commit the offense.

In cases in which the police create the crime, courts may be inclined to find that the defendant was entrapped as a matter of law. The case of *United States v. Twigg* is one example: Supplying a person who harbors general criminal tendencies with the means and opportunity to commit a crime that he or she otherwise could not have committed is not acceptable. Another example is the offer that is "too good to refuse." Suppose the police advertise a willingness to pay $1000 for a basketball ticket in a jurisdiction where "ticket scalping" is illegal. Here, a judge might dismiss the charges without regard to the predisposition of the one who took the bait, on the ground that the nature of the offer is such that normal law-abiding citizens would be inclined to accept, and such an offer therefore serves no legitimate law enforcement goal.

How do average citizens react to the defense of entrapment? First, they have difficulty understanding the judge's instructions about the definition of entrapment (Morier, Borgida, & Park, 1996). Second, when the evidence indicates that the defendant may have been ready to commit the offense in the absence of inducement and when he has a prior conviction, he is more likely to be convicted (Borgida & Park, 1988).

To further assess citizen reactions to entrapment, Edkins and Wrightsman (2004) presented respondents with scenarios that varied along three dimensions: (1) whether the government was actively involved in inducement, (2) whether the evidence suggested predisposition to commit a crime, and (3) whether the "offender" was a public official or a private citizen. As might be expected, respondents were most likely to acquit the defendant in the scenario that described low predisposition and high inducement and were most likely to convict when they had evidence of high predisposition and low inducement. Surprisingly, only about half of respondents convicted when the evidence for both predisposition and inducement was high—suggesting that they were offended by overly aggressive solicitation, even though the defendant's predisposition showed he would have committed the crime anyway. Finally, respondents were much more likely to convict a public official (in a bribery case) than a private citizen.

SUMMARY

1. *What are some psychological investigative techniques used by the police?* The police use a variety of devices to increase the likelihood that suspects will be prosecuted and convicted. Among these are criminal profiling, the so-called lie detector (technically, the polygraph technique), and procedures to induce confessions. Police may even create crime situations to tempt suspects to commit new crimes. When the latter is done, the accused may claim entrapment as a defense against the charge.

2. *What is criminal profiling?* Criminal profiling is an attempt to use what is known about how a crime was committed to infer what type of person might have committed it. Preliminary evidence about profiling suggests that it may have some validity as a means of narrowing police investigations to the most likely suspects.

3. *Is the polygraph a valid instrument for lie detection? What are some problems associated with it?* Early attempts to be rigorous still confused "lying" with the display of any emotion. No measure of physiological reactions can precisely distinguish between guilt and other negative emotions, such as fear, anger, or embarrassment. Nevertheless, examiners using the Keeler polygraph (which measures pulse rate, breathing rate, and electrical resistance of the skin) claim high rates of accuracy in distinguishing between subjects who are lying and those who are not. There are several problems with such claims, including the lack of real follow-up, the question of adequate criteria, and the misleading nature of "accuracy rates." There is also the problem of lack of consistency between the conclusions of different examiners. New approaches to "lie detec-

tion" or the concealment of guilty knowledge are being developed and tested.

4. *How valid is confession evidence? What kinds of interrogation procedures can lead to false confessions?* Two kinds of errors arise in the context of confessions: when guilty suspects fail to confess, and when innocent suspects do confess. Among the interrogation techniques that can lead to false confessions are prolonged social isolation and interrogators who confront a suspect and express their belief in his or her guilt, emphasize or exaggerate evidence against the suspect, offer psychological and moral justification for the offence, and ask the suspect to imagine a hypothetical person committing the crime.

5. *What are some of the reforms proposed to prevent false confessions?* Critics of police interrogations suggest that these interrogations should be recorded in order to improve the quality of questioning and to deter police misconduct. In addition, filming of interrogations can preserve a record that can be evaluated at a later date to assess the possibility of coercive influences. Interrogators could benefit from training on the consequences of suggestive questioning techniques, especially with juvenile suspects.

6. *What are the main legal definitions of entrapment?* The objective test of entrapment focuses entirely on the propriety of investigative methods. It asks whether the actions of the authorities were so compelling that they elicited a criminal act in a person not otherwise ready and willing to commit it. In contrast, the subjective standard (used in most states and by the federal government) emphasizes the defendant's state of mind—whether he or she was predisposed to commit an offense.

KEY TERMS

analog studies

base rate

behavioral confirmation

brain fingerprinting

coerced-compliant false
  confession

coerced-internalized
  false confession

cognitive psycho-
  physiology

Control Question Test

criminal profiling

discounting principle

entrapment

event-related brain
  potentials

field studies

fundamental attribution
  error

ground truth

Guilty Knowledge Test

mass murderer

polygraph

positive coercion bias

psychological stress
  evaluator

relevant/irrelevant
  procedure

serial killer

source misattribution

spree killer

stare decisis

Between Arrest and Trial

ORIENTING QUESTIONS

1. *What are the major legal proceedings between arrest and trial in the criminal
   justice system?*
2. *What is bail, and what factors influence the amount of bail set?*
3. *Why do defendants and prosecutors agree to plea-bargain?*
4. *In what ways does pretrial publicity pose a danger to fair trials? How can
   these dangers be reduced?*

Previous chapters presented psychological perspectives on the actions of law enforcement officials as they investigate crimes and make arrests. Between these events and the eventual trial of a suspect are several other steps with psychological implications.

The grand finale in our adversary system of justice is the trial, a public battle waged by two combatants (prosecution versus defense in a criminal trial, or plaintiff versus defendant in a civil trial), each fighting for a favorable outcome. To the victors go the spoils of this contest; criminal defendants seek their freedom through an acquittal, and civil plaintiffs seek compensation for wrongs they have suffered. Although the trial may be the most dramatic conflict in our system, many other skirmishes play large—and often decisive—roles in determining victors. In the adversarial system, both sides seek tactical advantages to achieve favorable settlement or lay the groundwork for success at trial.

In this chapter we focus on pretrial proceedings in criminal cases, including (1) pretrial motions, (2) bail setting, (3) plea bargaining, and (4) requests to change venue to minimize the effect of pretrial publicity. All of these issues raise important psychological questions that have been examined by experimentation, observation, or empirical analysis.

In the next chapter, we discuss the legal concept of competence, emphasizing its assessment by psychiatrists and psychologists. In the criminal justice system, the term *competence* refers to a defendant's capacity to understand and participate meaningfully in legal proceedings; it covers mental and psychological abilities that the criminal justice system requires that defendants have in order for court actions to be applied to them. Like the topics we cover in this chapter, questions of competence are usually raised between the time of arrest and the formal trial. They typically concern two issues: competence to plead guilty and competence to stand trial.

Before we discuss pretrial motions, bail, plea bargaining, and change of venue in detail, it will be useful to provide a framework for these topics by describing the customary sequence of pretrial activities in the criminal justice system.

Steps between Arrest and Trial

If the police believe that a suspect committed a crime, they will in all likelihood arrest the suspect. However, being arrested for a crime and being charged with a crime are two different events. A person may be arrested without being charged; for example, the police may arrest drunks to detain them and sober them up, but formal charges might never be filed. Charging implies a formal decision to continue with the prosecution, and that decision is made by the prosecuting attorney rather than the police.

The Initial Appearance

The initial appearance is an important step in the criminal process that must be taken soon after arrest. Key players—the judge and the defense counsel—become participants in a process in which the defendant has previously been in the control of the police and prosecutor. The Fourth Amendment to the United States Constitution requires that the arrestee be brought before a judge within 48 hours of his or her arrest (*County of Riverside v. McLaughlin*, 1991). This is one of the most important protections of the Bill of Rights. In many countries the police arrest (or "detain," as arrest is euphemistically called) people and hold them without charge for extended periods—or indefinitely. In the United States, however, we inherited from England the requirement that anyone who is arrested be taken without delay before a magistrate (a judge), an important protection against abuse of power by the police. The primary purpose of the initial appearance is for the judge to review the evidence summarized by the prosecutor to determine whether probable cause exists for believing that the suspects committed the crimes charged. In addition, the judge will inform the defendants of the charges against them, inform them of their constitutional rights, review the issue of bail, and appoint counsel for those that cannot afford to hire counsel.

The Preliminary Hearing

The next step after the initial appearance is the preliminary hearing; one of its purposes is to filter out those cases in which the prosecution's proof is insufficient. At a preliminary hearing, the prosecution must offer some evidence on every element of the crime charged. **Hearsay** is admissible at this hearing, which means that one witness may summarize what another said earlier. Thus, a victim's account of a crime may be presented through the testimony of the investigating officer. The judge must decide whether the prosecutor has presented evidence sufficient to support a finding of probable cause on all elements of the crime. Cross-examination by defense lawyers is limited to the issue of probable cause. No jury is present, and the judge has no authority to choose between competing versions of the events.

For these reasons, the defendant rarely testifies or offers any evidence at a preliminary hearing. Furthermore, defense attorneys often waive the preliminary hearing because they are afraid that the publicity in newspapers or on television will harden community attitudes against their clients and make it more difficult to seat an impartial jury. At times, however, the preliminary hearing serves as an opportunity for defense attorneys to glimpse the prosecution's case and size up its chief witnesses.

At the preliminary hearing, the judge will bind the defendant over to the grand jury if the judge finds probable cause exists to believe that the defendant committed the crimes charged. It is also possible that the judge will reduce the charges, either because he or she believes the evidence does not support the level of crime charged by the prosecutor or because of a plea bargain between the prosecutor and the defense attorney. Generally, if the defendant is still being held in custody, the judge also reviews the amount of bail originally set.

The Grand Jury

Consisting of citizens drawn from the community, the **grand jury** meets in private with the prosecutor to investigate criminal activity and return indictments (a complaint prepared and signed by the prosecutor describing the crime charged). In theory, the grand jury functions both as a "sword," issuing subpoenas and compelling reluctant witnesses to testify, and as a "shield," protecting those accused of crime from unjust prosecution. In about one-third of the states, a criminal defendant cannot be prosecuted unless a grand jury has found grounds to do so. The remaining states permit the prosecutor to proceed either by grand jury indictment or by information presented to the court.

As we have said, the grand jury meets privately and listens to the witnesses called by the prosecutor (who may relate what other witnesses said) and votes whether to indict and, if so, for what offenses. The grand jury may call witnesses on its own initiative if it is dissatisfied with the witnesses presented by the prosecutor. In some states the defendant has a right to testify, and in all states the defendant may testify with the consent of the grand jury. Grand jurors are often interested in both sides of the story and may reward testifying defendants by refusing to indict. For example, in 2004, 14% of Brooklyn felony suspects testified, and half of the grand juries before whom they testified did not indict them (Glaberson, 2004).

If the grand jury decides that sufficient evidence exists to justify the defendant being tried, it issues an indictment signed by the foreperson of the grand jury. The indictment is a written statement by the grand jury accusing one or more persons of one or more crimes. Its function is to inform defendants clearly of the nature of the charges against them so that they will have the opportunity to prepare a defense. After hearing evidence about an inferno that killed 97 people and injured nearly 200 at a Rhode Island nightclub in 2003, a grand jury issued indictments of the club owners and the tour manager of Great White, the band whose pyrotechnic display ignited highly flammable foam used as soundproofing in the club.

Arraignment

A grand jury gives its indictments to a judge, who brings those indicted to court for arraignment

Remnants of Rhode Island nightclub after being destroyed by fire

on the indictment. At the arraignment, the judge makes sure that the defendant has an attorney and appoints one if necessary. The indictment is then read to the defendant, and the defendant is asked to plead guilty or not guilty. It is customary for defendants to plead not guilty at this time, even if they contemplate ultimately pleading guilty. The reason is to provide opportunities both for **discovery** (which means that the defendant's attorney gets to examine some of the evidence against the defendant) and for plea bargaining. At arraignment, the judge again reviews the issue of pretrial release (bail) and sets a date for the trial. Often the judge also fixes a date by which pretrial motions must be filed.

Discovery and Pretrial Motions

Defendants and their attorneys want to be aware of the materials the prosecution will use to prove its case. In civil trials, each side is entitled to *discovery*—that is, each side has a right to depose (ask questions of) the witnesses on the other side and to look at and copy documents that the other side might use at trial. In criminal trials, however, just how much the prosecution has to reveal to the defense is controversial.

Some states require prosecutors to turn over to the defense all reports, statements by witnesses, and physical evidence. Most states, however, require only that the prosecutor share certain evidence (e.g., laboratory reports) and evidence that is **exculpatory** (i.e., that tends to show the defendant to be not guilty or suggests that prosecution witnesses are not credible). In the case of *Brady v. Maryland* (1963), the U.S. Supreme Court ruled that the prosecution must disclose to the defense evidence in its possession favorable to the defendant. Beyond the constitutional obligation to disclose exculpatory evidence (called *Brady* material), however, the extent to which discovery occurs in criminal cases is determined by local statutes, not constitutional right.

In many cases, prosecutors provide "open file" discovery to defense attorneys even though they are not obligated to do so; one reason is to encourage a guilty plea and avoid a trial. A prosecutor, knowing that defense counsel will find it difficult to recommend a guilty plea without knowing the strength of the prosecution's case, will turn over most evidence, expecting that defense counsel, having been made aware of the prosecutor's firepower, will talk sense to the defendant and encourage a quick plea. At the same time, prosecutors must remain sensitive to witnesses who may not want their identities or statements given to defense counsel.

Discovery is a two-way street. In general, states require the defense to turn over whatever types of materials the prosecution is required to turn over. If the prosecution is required to reveal laboratory reports, the defense will likewise be required to share such reports. In many states, the defense is required to notify the prosecution if it intends to rely on certain defenses, notably insanity and alibi defenses. The reason for requiring such pretrial notice is to give the state an opportunity to investigate the claim and avoid being surprised at trial. The Supreme Court has upheld the constitutionality of pretrial notice requirements, provided that the state is required to notify the defendant of witnesses it would call to refute the defense (*Williams v. Florida*, 1970).

During the discovery phase of the case, pretrial motions are filed by both sides. The defense will often move for dismissal of the charges. Both sides will seek favorable rulings on the admissibility of evidence. Both sides will explore the possibility of a negotiated plea—a plea bargain.

Although it is impossible to list all pretrial motions, the following are the most common:

1. *Defense motion for separate trials.* When two or more defendants are jointly indicted, one of them can be counted on to move for a separate trial, claiming that to be tried together would be prejudicial. When some of the prosecution's evidence is admissible against one defendant but not against the other, the motion is often granted, as in the case of Timothy McVeigh and Terry Nichols, who were convicted in separate trials of bombing the federal building in Oklahoma City, killing 168 people. McVeigh was convicted of murder and sentenced to death, but Nichols was convicted of a lesser charge (conspiracy) and sentenced to life imprisonment.

2. *Defense motion to sever counts.* Suppose the indictment charges the defendant with robbing a convenience store on April 13 and burglarizing a house on April 15. The defendant may move for separate trials on these offenses. A defendant will argue that it is prejudicial for the same jury to hear

evidence about separate crimes because the jury will be tempted to combine the evidence introduced on the separate crimes to find the defendant guilty of each crime. There is good reason for defendants to be concerned about how a jury would react to multiple charges. Psychological research studies that simulate jury decision making have shown that jurors are more likely to convict a defendant on any charge (e.g., robbery) when it is combined with another (e.g., burglary) than when it is tried alone (e.g., Greene & Loftus, 1985).

3. *Defense motion for change of venue.* The defendant may move for a **change of venue** on the ground that community opinion, usually the product of prejudicial pretrial publicity, makes it impossible to seat a fair-minded jury. We discuss the involvement of psychologists in such motions later in this chapter.

4. *Defense motion to dismiss on speedy trial grounds.* The Sixth Amendment to the U.S. Constitution guarantees defendants a right to a "speedy trial." A delay in trial is cause for dismissal if the prosecutor was attempting to obtain an unfair advantage and the defendant was harmed by the delay, as would happen if a crucial defense witness died (*Barker v. Wingo*, 1972). Dismissals **with prejudice** are rarely granted. The term *with prejudice* refers to a dismissal that bars any subsequent attempt to reinstate the prosecution; a dismissal without prejudice allows the state to prosecute the defendant at a later time, if it chooses to do so.

5. *Defense motion to dismiss on grounds of selective prosecution.* Sometimes, a crime involves many participants, but only a few of them are charged. Generally speaking, indictments will not be dismissed simply because the defendants were selected for prosecution. Effective use of limited resources often requires that police and prosecutors direct their efforts toward the most culpable offenders or those whose convictions will best deter others (*Wayte v. United States*, 1985), as, for example, in drug-trafficking crimes. Selective enforcement and prosecution are unconstitutional, however, when the selection is made on racial or gender grounds or when the selection impermissibly interferes with First Amendment rights. For example, it would be

unconstitutional for the police to give speeding citations only to out-of-state motorists, because such a selection would interfere with the First Amendment right to travel freely within the United States. Dismissal on this ground is rare because the defense must prove that others similarly situated were not prosecuted, that the selection was purposeful, and that the selection was for an impermissible reason.

One lingering controversy concerning allegations of selective prosecution involves the fact that although African Americans make up only about 12% of the U.S. population, 90% of the defendants prosecuted in federal courts for trafficking in crack cocaine are African American. These defendants face much longer prison sentences than offenders trafficking in the same amount of powdered cocaine, for which about equal percentages of white and black defendants are prosecuted. Is this a case of racial discrimination in which prosecutors are treating black defendants more severely than whites, or is it, as prosecutors claim, a case of zeroing in on crime problems where they exist: inner-city gangs made up predominantly of minorities? In 1996, the Supreme Court rejected a claim by black defendants that the U.S. attorney had selectively prosecuted them for crack cocaine offenses (*United States v. Armstrong*, 1996). The Court held that a mere disparity does not support a claim that defendants were selected for prosecution on the basis of race.

6. *Defense motion to dismiss on double-jeopardy grounds.* The Fifth Amendment to the U.S. Constitution states that no person shall be "subject for the same offense to be twice put in jeopardy of life or limb." The Court has interpreted this clause to mean that the state is entitled to one, but only one, "fair chance" to convict the defendant. If the state loses—or if the trial is aborted without reason—the defendant cannot be retried. Most litigation over the double-jeopardy clause involves the question of whether the second charge is for the "same offense" for which the defendant previously was tried (*United States v. Dixon*, 1993). The issue reflects the first dilemma described in Chapter 1. Does society's right to be protected supersede the rights of individuals to be free from extended harassment by the state?

Los Angeles police officers Stacey Koon and Laurence Powell were found not guilty in a California state court of beating Rodney King after they stopped King for speeding. Koon and Powell were later tried a second time—this time in a federal court—on charges of violating King's civil rights. Much of the same evidence was used. In the second trial, the two police officers were found guilty and sentenced to several years in prison. Double jeopardy did not bar the second prosecution because it took place in federal court, rather than in a California state court, and the Supreme Court has held that the double-jeopardy clause does not protect against second prosecutions for the same crime by another state—or by the federal government after a state prosecution (*Abbate v. United States*, 1959).

7. *Defense motion to suppress evidence on Fourth Amendment grounds.* What if the police exceed the limits of the law in their law enforcement activities and yet, in doing so, discover evidence of criminal behavior? Should evidence, such as a murder weapon or stolen property, obtained during an illegal search and seizure be admitted in court? The **exclusionary rule** requires courts to suppress evidence obtained in violation of a defendant's right under the Fourth Amendment to be free from unreasonable searches and seizures (*Mapp v. Ohio*, 1961). Suppression motions are often filed to test the prosecution's case and to obtain information with which to plea-bargain.

8. *Defense motion to suppress a confession or other statement by the defendant.* The Fifth Amendment protects against self-incrimination, the due process clauses of the Fifth and Fourteenth Amendments protect against the use of confessions extracted by duress or promise, and the Sixth Amendment forbids the use of a statement taken in violation of the right to counsel. One or more of these constitutional provisions potentially become relevant any time the prosecution offers a confession or other statement by a defendant as evidence of guilt. Typically, defense counsel files a motion alleging that the confession was obtained in violation of the defendant's constitutional rights, the prosecutor files a written response, and the court holds a hearing at which the defendant and police give their versions of the circumstances under

which the confession was obtained. The judge hears the testimony without a jury and decides the issue on the basis of what was said and the credibility of the witnesses. Questions of who is telling the truth are usually resolved in favor of the police. Criminal defendants who believe that their confessions were coerced or made involuntarily have good reason to try to suppress them because, as we noted in Chapter 6, juries tend to accept a defendant's confession without careful evaluation of the circumstances that led to the confession.

9. *Discovery motions.* When disputes arise in the discovery process, either side can ask the trial court for assistance. The typical dispute involves a sweeping defense request (e.g., a request for the names of all persons who saw the robbery) and a prosecutor who interprets the *Brady* rule (the obligation to turn over exculpatory information) narrowly.

10. *Motions in limine.* Perhaps the most common pretrial motions are those that seek advance rulings on evidentiary issues that will arise at trial. Suppose, for example, that the defendant was previously convicted of burglary; the judge must decide whether to allow the prosecution to introduce that conviction into evidence in order to discredit the defendant if he chooses to testify. The defendant obviously wants a pretrial ruling on this issue in order to plan the questioning of the jurors and to decide whether to testify. Similarly, the prosecutor may want a pretrial ruling on the admissibility of a certain piece of evidence in order to plan the opening statement (a cardinal sin of trial practice is to refer, in the opening statement, to a matter that is later deemed inadmissible). A **motion *in limine*** is simply a request for a pretrial ruling. Although judges are not constitutionally required to grant such a request, most trial judges will cooperate with attorneys who are trying to avoid mid-trial problems.

The Decision to Set Bail

As we have already discussed, judges routinely decide whether to keep defendants in custody during the often lengthy process between arrest and trial. Judges have many options. In some cases (capital cases and cases in which the defendant poses a serious risk to flee or commit other crimes), they can deny bail altogether. Short of denying bail, judges can require that money (or a bail bondsman's pledge) be deposited with the court or that a third person agree to be responsible for the defendant's future appearances and to forfeit money in the amount of the defendant's bail if "he or she" does not appear. Minor offenders are often **released on** [their own] **recognizance (ROR)**—that is, on their promise to appear). Bail setting evolved in the American legal system as an attempt to resolve the basic conflict between individual and societal rights (as discussed in Chapter 1).

The Purposes of Bail

The bail decision determines whether defendants are detained or released before trial. When bail is higher than defendants can afford, they have no choice but to remain in jail. And often, bail can be quite high. In the case of John Emil List, who was arrested after his crimes of 17 years before were portrayed on the TV program *America's Most Wanted*, the judge set bail at $5 million. A similar amount was set for Imelda Marcos's bail after she was charged with fraud and with embezzling $100 million from the Philippine government.

The Eighth Amendment to the U.S. Constitution says that excessive bail shall not be required, but the Supreme Court has ruled that this provision does not guarantee a right to bail; it simply requires that bail, if any, should not be excessive (*United States v. Salerno*, 1987).

What Considerations Affect the Decision to Set Bail?

Traditionally, the justification for requiring bail has been the degree of risk that the defendant will not appear for his or her trial. Defendants who are believed not to pose this risk are often released on their own recognizance, those for whom some doubt exists are allowed to post a bail bond as a kind of insurance that they will appear, and those who are considered very high risks are kept in custody.

THE CASE OF

BOX 7.1   "Little Randy" Withers and the cybersearch
for defendants on the run

Bail bond agents are renowned for their diligence in tracking down defendants who have skipped bail and failed to return to court as required. Bonding agents stand to lose the value of the bond posted if the defendant cannot be located, so their financial incentive for locating and returning the defendant to custody is considerable. Although bonding agents have been criticized in the past for strong-arm search-and-return tactics, they increasingly are turning to modern technology to catch defendants on the run. One of those fugitive defendants was "Little Randy" Withers, who was charged

with possession of a firearm by a felon and whose picture was included on the website entitled "The World's Most Wanted—Bail Jumpers" (www. mostwanted.org). The 21st century's counterpart to the old "Wanted Dead or Alive" posters of the western frontier, this website describes Withers as a black male, born on April 28, 1975, 5 feet 7 inches tall, 175 pounds, black hair and brown eyes, residing in Charlotte, North Carolina. Warning that these defendants have "Nowhere to Run! Nowhere to Hide!" the subscribing companies typically offer $1000 and $2000

Cybersearch for a wanted suspect

cash rewards for information that leads to the apprehension of the most wanted bail fugitives. They also caution would-be bounty hunters that most of the suspects are armed and should be considered dangerous.

Studies of jurisdictions where defendants are given ROR reveal that very few defendants fail to appear (Ares, Rankin, & Sturz, 1963; Feeley, 1983). Whether bail bonds actually reduce the risk of nonappearance is not clear. Box 7.1 describes techniques that bail bond agents employ to ensure that defendants who post bail will show up for court.

Should the likelihood of committing other crimes in the interim also be a consideration? Around 1970, a push began for legislation that would increase the use of preventive detention— the detention of arrested persons who pose a risk of flight or dangerousness. Most citizens approve of preventive detention, valuing society's need to be protected from possible future harm over the rights of individual suspects to be free until proven guilty—an aspect of the presumption of innocence guaranteed by the Constitution.

The Bail Reform Act of 1984 was introduced by Congress in part to ensure that judges consider community safety when they set bail for criminal

defendants. Despite challenges to the constitutionality of the preventive detention authorized by this act, it was upheld by the U.S. Supreme Court. In the 1987 case of *United States v. Salerno*, the Court upheld the provision in this law permitting the detention of defendants charged with serious crimes if prosecutors could establish probable cause that the defendants committed the crimes charged and could convince the judge that "the safety of any other person and the community" would be jeopardized if the defendants were released on bail (Taylor, 1987). (The standard to be used was "clear and convincing evidence.") Thus, preventive detention on the grounds of perceived dangerousness is not only a federal law but is on the books (in some form) in many states as well. Reflecting the dilemma in Chapter 1 between individual rights and society's needs, Former Chief Justice Rehnquist wrote, "We have repeatedly held that the Government's regulatory interest in community safety can, in appropriate circumstances, outweigh an individual's liberty interest" (quoted in Taylor, 1987, p. 9). Crucial to the Court's opinion, however, was the assumption that the defendant would be tried promptly in accordance with the Federal Speedy Trial Act.

Although pretrial detention is intended to reflect concerns about an arrested person's risk of flight and likelihood of committing further offenses, other characteristics of offenders—namely, their race and gender—apparently also influence the pretrial release process. Data gathered on felony defendants from the 75 most populous counties in the United States between 1990 and 1996 showed that after controlling for prior record and conduct of the offense, Hispanic and African American defendants were more likely to be detained than similarly situated white defendants (Demuth & Steffensmeier, 2004). A major factor in securing pretrial release is the ability to post bail, which minority defendants are less able to do. Female defendants were more likely to be released than their male counterparts with similar records and charges.

Other variables that, in theory, should have little impact on bail decisions also seem to matter. Evidence from Canadian bail hearings suggests that personality assessments of arrestees made by the police can affect decisions about release before trial. Accused people who received negative assessments were more likely to be detained than those who received neutral assessments (Kellough & Wortley, 2002).

Psychologists and other social scientists can play a helpful role in this area by conducting research on the determinants and fairness of bail-setting decisions (Dhami, 2003; Goldkamp, Gottfredson, Jones, & Weiland, 1995). Psychologists have evaluated the following topics: (1) What factors most strongly influence whether defendants released from pretrial custody appear when they are required (e.g., which is more important: ties to the local community or the amount of money posted as bond?)? (2) Can defendants who pose a high risk of fleeing (or committing criminal acts) if they are released from pretrial custody be identified? (3) What effect does pretrial detention have on defendants' trials? (4) What criteria influence a judge's decision to set bail?

A research team housed at Temple University (Goldkamp et al., 1995) developed a set of guidelines to help courts decide between detention and release of defendants prior to trial. Such guidelines presume that judges will look at all the factors and make reasoned decisions that respect the presumption of innocence while protecting society and guaranteeing the defendant's presence. However, judges may not be looking at all the factors they *could* evaluate. In fact, the best predictor of judicial behavior on the bail question is what the prosecutor asks for. Mandeep Dhami (2003) analyzed bail-setting decisions in two London courts and found that a model based on only three cues—the prosecutor's request, the position of the police, and actions of the previous court—was a better predictor of judicial behavior than a model incorporating the various factors thought to be relevant to the bail-setting decision (e.g., defendant's record, seriousness of offense) (Dhami, 2003).

Can High-Risk Defendants Be Identified?

Preventive detention assumes that valid assessments of risk and accurate predictions of future dangerous conduct can be made, an assumption that is uncertain (Douglas & Webster, 1999). Thus, judges have difficulty knowing which defendants are dangerous and which can be trusted. In Shepherd, Texas, Patrick Dale Walker tried to kill his girlfriend by putting a gun to her head and pulling the trigger. The loaded gun failed to fire. Walker's original bail was set at $1 million, but after he had sat in jail for four days, the presiding judge lowered his bail to $25,000. This permitted Walker to be released; four months later, he fired three bullets at close range and killed the same woman. Afterward, the judge did not think he was wrong in lowering the bail, even though, since 1993, Texas has had a law that permits judges to consider the safety of the victim and of the community in determining the amount of bail. In fact, Patrick Walker had no previous record, was valedictorian of his class, and was a college graduate. Would a psychologist have done any better in predicting Walker's behavior?

The answer to this question is uncertain. Although psychologists have some modest ability to predict violent behavior in some situations (McNiel et al., 2002), a few scholars have argued that mental health professionals should not make such predictions because they lack adequate scientific validity (e.g., Ewing, 1991). We will return to this issue in the next chapter on forensic assessment, but for now we simply note that assessing risks and predicting violent behavior are very difficult tasks and that even the best clinicians have trouble making accurate long-term predictions.

If those defendants who pose the greatest risk for committing new offenses after their release could be accurately identified, guidelines could be developed for judges to use in their bail-setting decisions. In one extensive study (Goldkamp & Gottfredson, 1988), the researchers followed the status of 2200 persons who had been arrested for felonies and were then released from custody prior to their trials. Within 90 days of their release, 17% of these defendants had been arrested either for a new crime or for failing to appear as required in court. Among the factors that predicted new offenses or failure to appear were the following: the defendant lived alone, the original criminal charge was for robbery or a property offense, the defendant previously had failed to show up for a required court appearance, and the arresting police officer noted factors at the time of arrest suggesting a risk of fleeing. On the basis of these factors, defendants were classified into four groups representing increasing levels of risk. The failure rates (*failure* being defined as a new offense or a failure to appear) of these four groups were 6%, 12%, 23% and 30%. Many courts have created guidelines based on empirical studies to guide the bail-setting decision. Note, however, the large number of false positives among the highest-risk group; 70% of the persons in this group did not commit a new crime or fail to appear.

Does Pretrial Release Affect Trial Outcome?

What if the defendant cannot provide bail and remains in jail until the time of trial? Does this pretrial incarceration affect the trial's outcome? Clearly, yes. Defendants who are detained in jail are more likely to plead guilty or be convicted and to receive higher sentences than those who can afford bail, even when the seriousness of their offenses and the evidence against them are the same (Goldfarb, 1965; Kellough & Wortley, 2002). Some data suggest that prosecutors use pretrial detention as a "resource" to encourage (or coerce) guilty pleas. Pretrial detention is likely to cost defendants their jobs, making it harder for them to pay attorneys—so the threat of it may make them more likely to plead guilty. Among defendants who actually go to trial, an accused person who is free on bail finds it easier to gather witnesses and prepare a defense. Jailed defendants cannot meet with their attorneys in the latter's office, have less time with their attorneys to prepare for trial, and have less access to records and witnesses. Detention also corrodes family and community ties. Casper's (1972) interviews with convicted defendants who were serving prison sentences revealed that for many of them, the time spent in local jails prior to trial was worse than the time in prison; the conditions were terrible, there was nothing to do, and the guards were hostile.

Civil libertarians oppose pretrial detention because it conflicts with our society's fundamental assumption that a defendant is innocent until proven guilty. The Supreme Court has taken a somewhat different view—that the "presumption of innocence" refers to the rule of trial procedure that places the burden of demonstrating a defendant's guilt on the government, and that pretrial detention is not a punishment but rather a regulation (like a quarantine) for the public's protection. In other words, the presumption of innocence allows a judge to consider evidence that a defendant is dangerous. However, numerous surveys (reported in Goldfarb, 1965) have shown that defendants who are detained because they could not pay bail are frequently found not guilty (or have their charges dismissed). In Philadelphia, of 1000 people detained an average of 33 days, 67% were later acquitted or, if convicted, were not given any prison sentences. Another survey of 114,653 people in pretrial detention reported that

73% were later acquitted or not given jail or prison sentences. A partial explanation for these outcomes is that charges are sometimes dismissed (or the defendant is credited with time already served in jail) when the prosecutor believes that the pretrial incarceration has been sufficient punishment for the crime.

Plea Bargaining

Sometimes, pretrial detention of an accused person is used as a bargaining chip to encourage (or coerce) a guilty plea from that person (Kellough & Wortley, 2002). No better example exists of the dilemma between truth and conflict resolution as goals of our legal system than the extensive use of **plea bargaining** in the U.S. criminal justice system. Most criminal cases—at least 85%—end between arrest and trial, primarily when the defendant pleads guilty to some charge, usually in exchange for a concession by the prosecutor. In 2002, the cases of 76,827 defendants were resolved in United States district courts; of that number, only 3754 (4.65%) were resolved by trial (Galanter, 2004).

Both mundane and serious cases are resolved by plea bargains. In a routine case that would never have been publicized had the defendant not been a judge, Darke County, Ohio, judge Roger Hurley pled guilty in a domestic violence case. He was accused of grabbing his estranged wife by the neck during an argument and threatening her with a bread knife. According to Hurley, he accepted a plea bargain in order to get on with his life and end the hurt and friction that this incident caused in his family. In more notorious cases, Ted Kaczynski, the "Unabomber," accepted life imprisonment without possibility of parole to avoid facing the death penalty, and James Earl Ray, the assassin of Martin Luther King, died in prison while serving a life sentence as a result of a plea bargain with state prosecutors. In Kaczynski's case, the plea bargain satisfactorily resolved the controversy. Kaczynski had acted alone, the victims agreed to the resolution, and Kaczynski received what the public accepted as

a fair disposition for one who was mentally ill. In the case of James Earl Ray, however, the plea bargain was not well received. Many thought Ray had not acted alone, and the plea bargain meant that the facts would never be aired in a public forum. Years after Martin Luther King's death, the King family was still searching for answers, going so far as to visit with James Earl Ray in the hope that he would reveal what lay behind the assassination. After Ray's death in 1998, the King family released a statement expressing regret that Ray had never had his day in court and stating, "The American people have a right to the truth about this tragedy and we intend to do everything we can to bring it to light" (www.cnn.com, April 23, 1998).

Not all guilty pleas are reached through bargaining, of course; some defendants plead guilty with no promise of leniency because they choose to end the process as quickly as possible and get on with serving their sentences. However, most defendants plead guilty as a result of a negotiation process that leads them to expect some concession or benefit from the prosecutor in exchange for not contesting guilt. The defendant's part of the bargain requires an admission of guilt. This admission relieves the prosecutor of any obligation to prove that the defendant committed the crimes charged. It is usually a formal plea of guilty to a judge, who, if he or she accepts the plea, imposes a sentence. On occasion, prosecutors offer plea deals because they worry that they might have trouble with their evidence at trial. The case of American Taliban soldier John Walker Lindh is an example (Box 7.2).

Many states allow **deferred prosecution** for minor crimes, in which first-time offenders who admit guilt are placed on probation and have the charges against them dismissed if they stay out of trouble during probation. By admitting guilt—through either a guilty plea or a deferred-prosecution agreement—the defendant saves the prosecution the time, expense, and uncertainty of a trial. The prosecutor's part of the bargain may involve an agreement to allow the defendant to plead guilty to a charge less serious than the evidence supports. For example, manslaughter is a lesser charge than murder, and many murder prosecutions are resolved by a

THE CASE OF

BOX 7.2 | "American Taliban" John Walker Lindh, and his guilty plea

One morning in late November 2001, a few months after 9/11 and in the early days of the war on terror, CIA agent Mike Spann was sorting through approximately 300 Taliban prisoners held in a military garrison near Mazar-e Sharif, Afghanistan. One prisoner had been separated from the others; he gave his name as Abdul Hamil, but his real name was John Walker Lindh, and he was a 20-year old American who, until 2000, had lived with his family in Marin County, California. After escaping during a violent uprising later that day, getting shot in the thigh, starving for a week in a basement bunker, and being flushed out of the basement, Lindh eventually talked to his captors. During extensive questioning, he

explained how he had trained with the Taliban in Osama bin Laden's camps, and he signed confession documents acknowledging that he was not merely fighting for the Taliban but also was a member of al-Qaeda. In February 2002, he was indicted on ten charges, including conspiracy to support terrorist organizations and conspiracy to murder American citizens.

The prosecution might have had an easier case had the conditions of Lindh's confession been different. During his interrogation, Lindh was stripped of his clothes, blindfolded, duct-taped to a stretcher, and placed in a metal shipping container for transportation. Despite several requests, he was denied the assistance of a lawyer, and he was

threatened with denial of medical assistance if he opted not to cooperate. Fearing that the confession might be excluded from evidence as having been coerced, Michael Chertoff, head of the criminal division of the Department of Justice, eventually authorized prosecutors to offer Walker a plea bargain: If he pled guilty to just two charges—serving with the Taliban and carrying illegal weapons—the remaining eight counts would be dropped. According to some commentators (e.g., Babb, 2003), the government would not have been able to sustain a treason charge against Lindh. John Walker Lindh pled guilty in July 2002 and was sentenced to 20 years without parole.

plea of guilty to manslaughter. In one year in Brooklyn, of 6621 people charged with narcotics felonies, 2983 charges were ultimately reduced to misdemeanors (Kurtz, 1988).

In a common procedure known as **charge bargaining**, the prosecutor drops some charges in return for a plea of guilty. Laboratory research using role-playing procedures (Gregory, Mowen, & Linder, 1978) indicates that "overcharging" is effective; subjects were more likely to accept a plea bargain when relatively many charges had been filed against them. Charge bargaining may lead prosecutors to charge the defendant with more crimes or with a more serious crime than they could prove at trial as a strategy for motivating guilty pleas. The defendants who engage in this type of bargaining may win only hollow victories. Cases in which prosecutors offer to drop charges

are likely to be ones for which judges would have imposed concurrent sentences for the multiple convictions anyway. Judges and parole boards also tend to pay more attention to the criminal act itself than to the formal charge when making sentencing decisions.

Plea bargaining may also take the form of **sentence bargaining**, in which prosecutors recommend reduced sentences in return for guilty pleas. Sentencing is the judges' prerogative, and judges vary in their willingness to follow prosecutors' recommendations. Judges can rubber-stamp prosecutorial sentencing recommendations, and some judges do just that. On the other hand, judges should consider many factors when imposing a sentence—seriousness of the crime, harm to the victim, background of the offender, to name a few—and some judges believe that simply going along with every recommendation from the prosecutor compromises their duty to take these factors into account. In general, most defendants can expect that judges will usually follow the sentences that have been recommended by a prosecutor. Prosecutors can promote this expectation and earn the trust of judges by recommending sentences that are reasonable and fair.

Defendants try to negotiate a plea to obtain less severe punishment than they would receive if they went to trial and were convicted. But why do prosecutors plea-bargain? What advantages do they seek, given that they hold the more powerful position in this bargaining situation? Prosecutors are motivated to plea-bargain for one or more of the following reasons: (1) to dispose of cases in which the evidence against the defendant is weak or the defense attorney is a formidable foe, (2) to obtain the testimony of one defendant against a more culpable or infamous codefendant, (3) to expedite the flow of cases for an overworked staff and a clogged court docket, (4) to maintain a cordial working relationship with defense attorneys from whom the prosecutor may want certain favors in the future, or (5) to avoid trials that might be unpopular because the defendant is a well-liked figure in the community or the crime charged might be seen as morally justified.

Created by federal legislation in 1984, the United States Sentencing Commission's Sentencing Guidelines go a long way toward forcing defendants to plea-bargain. The guidelines assign an "offense level" to each offense, adjusting the offenses up or down according to what happened. For example, if the defendant endangered someone while fleeing from law enforcement, the offense level is raised by two levels. The defendant is then assigned a "criminal history category" from "no record" to "extensive record." The probation officer then looks at the sentencing table, which plots offense level on the vertical axis and criminal history category on the horizontal axis. Reading across the table yields a "presumptive sentence range." However, if the defendant "clearly accepted responsibility for his offense," he would be entitled to a two-level decrease in the offense level. The obvious way to "accept

responsibility for the offense" is to plead guilty, and in the federal courts, prior to *United States v. Booker*, a plea of guilty was often the only way a defendant could obtain a less severe sentence.

However, the court may opt out of the guidelines when sentencing a defendant who has "provided substantial assistance in the investigation or prosecution of another person who has committed an offense." Defendants thus are encouraged to testify against co-defendants or provide reliable information about others—in other words, to become snitches. Along with the "acceptance of responsibility" departure, the "substantial assistance" provision gives defendants a powerful incentive to plead guilty and provide whatever help they can in the prosecution of others.

In *United States v. Booker* (2005), described in Chapter 1, the Supreme Court held that these sentencing guidelines violated defendants' right to trial by jury by allowing judges to increase the sentencing range on the basis of facts not submitted to the jury (for example, that the defendant had endangered others in flight). However, the Court also opined that the guidelines could continue to be referred to, and it is anticipated that most judges will adhere fairly closely to the guidelines in the future.

Evaluations of Plea Bargaining

Plea bargaining has been practiced in the United States since the middle of the 19th century, although some states purport to forbid (Alaska) or restrict (California) the practice. The Supreme Court has upheld plea bargaining, calling it "an essential component of the administration of justice" (*Santobello v. New York*, 1971).

Guilty pleas must be voluntary, intelligent, and knowing. A plea of guilty is voluntary even if it is induced by a promise of leniency, so long as the defendant is represented by an attorney (*Brady v. United States*, 1970). Likewise, a plea can be voluntary even if encouraged by the threat of additional charges should the defendant insist on trial. In *Bordenkircher v. Hayes* (1978), the Court held that forcing a defendant to choose between unpleasant alternatives (e.g., pleading guilty or facing a trial in which a more severe sentence would be sought) does not mean that the choice is involuntary. However, some pressures will not be tolerated. In *Bordenkircher*, for example, the Court expressed reservations about offers not to prosecute third parties in exchange for a guilty plea from a defendant. Also, prosecutors cannot renege on their "deals" and require a more severe sentence than their original negotiated offer (*Santobello v. New York*, 1971).

Plea bargaining remains a controversial procedure. It has been defended as a necessary and useful part of the criminal justice system (American Bar Association, 1993b), and it has been condemned as a practice that should be abolished from our courts (Alschuler, 1968; Kipnis, 1979; Langbein, 1978; National Advisory Commission on Criminal Justice Standards and Goals, 1973). Advocates cite the following justifications for the procedure: (1) the defendant's admission of guilt is an important first step in rehabilitation; (2) guilty pleas relieve the backlog of cases that would otherwise engulf the courts; (3) outcomes are reached promptly and with a sense of finality; (4) other criminal justice participants benefit from the process—from the police officer who doesn't have to spend hours in court testifying, to the victim who is spared the trauma of a trial; and (5) the defendant's cooperation may facilitate prosecution of others.

Critics urge the abolition of plea bargaining on the following grounds: (1) improper sentences—sometimes too harsh but more often too lenient—are likely, (2) the process encourages defendants to surrender their constitutional rights, (3) prosecutors exert too much power in negotiating guilty pleas, (4) the process is private and encourages "shady" deals not available to all defendants, and (5) innocent defendants might feel coerced to plead guilty because they fear the more severe consequences of being convicted by a jury.

Data on these contentions are limited, but what evidence exists suggests that plea bargaining is not as evil as the abolitionists claim or as essential as its defenders believe. Rates of plea bargaining are surprisingly consistent across rural and urban jurisdictions, as well as across understaffed and well-funded prosecutors' offices (Heumann, 1978; Silberman, 1978). After Alaska ended plea bargaining in 1975, defendants continued to plead guilty at about the same rate, court proceedings did not slow down, and a modest increase in the number of trials occurred—though not so great an increase as had been feared (Rubinstein, Clarke, & White, 1980). On the other hand, when El Paso, Texas, abolished plea bargaining in 1975, it experienced a serious backup of cases. This result occurred largely because defendants perceived no benefit of pleading in comparison to waiting for their trials in the hope that witnesses would not be available or other weaknesses in the prosecution's case would develop, making acquittal more likely (Greenberg & Ruback, 1984). The risk of innocent parties pleading guilty is uncertain; however, data from laboratory simulation experiments suggest that guilty parties are more likely to plea-bargain than are the innocent (Gregory, Mowen, & Linder, 1978). Experimental research also suggests that "defendants" (college students or prisoners asked to imagine themselves plea-bargaining) prefer to participate in the bargaining process and perceive it as fairer when they do (e.g., Houlden, 1981).

Plea bargaining serves the need of the defense attorney to appear to gain something for his or her client and the need of the prosecutor to appear fair and reasonable. Both prosecutors and defense attorneys believe they are making the "punishment fit the crime" by individualizing the law to fit the circumstances of the case, and both are comfortable with a system in which most cases are resolved without a clear winner or clear loser. Experienced prosecutors and defense attorneys teach plea bargaining to the rookies in their offices, and lawyers from both sides engage in a ritual of give and take, with changing facts and personalities but with the same posturing and rationalizations.

In fact, the procedures are so well known that in some cases no formal bargaining even takes place; everyone involved—prosecutor, defense attorney, defendant, and judge—knows the prevailing "rate" for a given crime, and if the defendant pleads guilty to that crime, the rate is the price that will be paid.

Defense attorneys appeal to prosecutors' inclination to bargain through two approaches. First, they try to offer something of benefit to the prosecutor, enhancing the value of the benefit as much as possible without misstating facts. Benefits for prosecutors have already been described, but one constant advantage of guilty pleas is that they eliminate the uncertainty of a trial's outcome (a benefit whenever the prosecutor believes an acquittal is possible because of weak evidence). The second strategy is to offer the prosecutor the chance to "do the right thing" for a client who deserves a break. The duty of prosecutors is to "seek justice, not merely to convict" (ABA, 1993a, 3–1.2). Many prosecutors are open to alternatives to incarceration and will look for opportunities to mitigate the harshness of punishments that could be imposed if a defendant stood trial and was convicted. Community service and restitution to victims are attractive dispositions, particularly when related meaningfully to the offense. When the crime results from mental illness, supervised probation coupled with therapy for the offender can be an appropriate resolution.

Because plea bargaining is typically conducted "behind closed doors" and out of public view (and because little "bargaining" may actually occur), psychologists have paid relatively little attention to this issue. However, there are some interesting psychological data on what personal attributes a good plea negotiator possesses. This question was put to chief prosecutors across the United States, who were asked to think about an exceptionally effective defense attorney and to list this person's personality traits and negotiation style. Virtually all of the esteemed defense attorneys showed emotional stability, and most used a cooperative, rather than a competitive, negotiation style (Lynch & Evans, 2002). Obviously, possession of these character traits will enhance the chances for successful plea negotiations.

Of course, there is a "dark side" to plea bargaining when dispositions are not commensurate with the gravity of the offense. When these "errors" are in the direction of sentencing leniency, they often are attributed to a perceived overload in the prosecutor's office or the courts. It is wrong for a defendant to be able to plead to a greatly reduced charge simply because the criminal justice system lacks the resources to handle the case.

However, the answer to problems of unwarranted leniency is not the abolition of plea bargaining; rather, adequate funding must be provided for the court system, as well as for the correctional system, so that when severe penalties are necessary, severe penalties can be given. In the long run, if plea bargaining serves primarily as a method for balancing the underfunded budgets of our courts and correctional systems, it will cease to be a bargain in the larger sense and will become, instead, too great a price for our society to pay.

Ethical Issues in Plea Bargaining

Plea bargaining may work against the long-range goal of achieving justice. When some lawbreakers bargain a guilty plea, the agreement may permit other lawbreakers to escape prosecution. Sidney Biddle Barrows, a 33-year-old New York socialite, was arrested on charges of running a 20-woman prostitution ring from a brownstone house on Manhattan's Upper West Side. In 1985, she pled guilty to promoting prostitution. Her penalty: a $5000 fine and no prison sentence. As a result of the plea bargain, she was not required to reveal the names of the 3000 clients of her "escort service." If, in fact, Barrows was operating a house of prostitution, her customers were breaking the law, too. Plea bargaining also may prevent the families of victims from seeing the defendants "get justice" or hearing them acknowledge full responsibility for their offenses. In the so-called Preppie Murder Case, Robert Chambers agreed to plead guilty to a lesser charge of manslaughter *while the jury was deliberating* whether to convict him of the 1986 murder of Jennifer Levin (Taubman, 1988). The family of Ms. Levin was not consulted, although victims' rights legislation increasingly ensures that the victim or his or her family has a say in plea bargaining and some states now involve victims in the plea-bargaining process.

Another problem in plea bargaining involves the use of criminals as prosecution witnesses, which occurs when lawbreakers turn state's evidence to avoid prosecution or to reduce their own penalties. The federal sentencing guidelines reward the snitch—and in a sense reward the lawbreaker for a breach of trust. At times, the process creates inequitable results. Take for example, two defendants charged with trafficking in cocaine.

The courier—the "mule"—has no information of value, does not receive a downward departure (a more lenient sentence), and is sentenced to five years with no parole. The supplier, charged with the same crime, has valuable information for sale, receives a substantial downward departure, and serves six months in a halfway house. Law enforcement officials defend such results as a matter of necessity and argue that we need to reward informants in order to find and convict the perpetrators of more heinous crimes.

Pretrial Publicity

Conflicting Rights

Two cherished rights guaranteed by the U.S. Constitution are freedom of speech (the First Amendment) and the right to a speedy, public trial before an impartial jury (the Sixth Amendment). The right to free speech applies to the written as well as the spoken word. It also applies to the institution of the press, not just to individuals. The press is expected to be the government watchdog, a role encouraged by constitutional protection. The right to an impartial jury and a fair trial is also a fundamental expectation of Americans. The fairness of our adversarial system of justice rests in large part on the decision making of an unbiased group of jurors.

In the vast majority of cases, the liberties ensured by the First and Sixth Amendments are compatible and even complementary. The press informs the public about criminal investigations and trials, and the public not only learns the outcomes of these proceedings but often gains increased appreciation for both the justness and the foibles of our system of justice.

For a few trials, however, the First and Sixth Amendments clash. The press publishes information that, when disseminated among the public, threatens a defendant's right to a trial by impartial jurors. These problem cases can involve defendants and/or victims who, because of their fame or infamous acts, gain a national reputation. The trials of Michael Jackson, Martha Stewart, and Catholic priests charged with sexual abuse are examples. In one case, an unknown fertilizer salesman named Scott Peterson, charged with killing his pregnant wife Laci, became a household name as the details of his case were splashed across the airwaves. Because of this intense publicity, his trial was moved to a new location (although one wonders how, in this age of 24-hour news networks, widespread access to cable and satellite programming, and specialized channels such as Court TV, *any* location was immune to the heavy coverage of this story.) Peterson's case is described in Box 7.3.

A more common problem occurs when local media release incriminating information about a defendant that is later ruled inadmissible at trial. Once made public, this information can bias opinion about the defendant. Examples include publication of details about a prior criminal record, a confession made by the accused, and unfavorable statements regarding the defendant's character. Indeed, it is exceedingly difficult to disregard previously acquired information. As Studebaker and Penrod (2005) point out,

> When making social judgments (such as those involved in deciding whether a defendant is guilty), it is natural for people to process information in an integrative manner. That is to say, people make connections between various pieces of information and base decisions on overall impressions rather than on specific pieces of information. . . . To set aside preconceived notions requires someone to identify previously received information as biasing, to know how that information was eventually processed and stored in memory, and to reverse or control for any biasing effects the information has had. The integrative nature of human information processing makes it very difficult for people to do this successfully (p. 257).

In general, local news coverage of trials has a greater impact in small towns than in large cities because a larger percentage of the population in small towns knows the parties; also, serious crimes occur less frequently in smaller towns, thereby increasing attention and rumor when they do

THE CASE OF

BOX 7.3 **Scott Peterson: The "cliff-hanger that hooked the nation"**

People of the State of California v. Scott Lee Peterson was the "stuff of crime novels;" a "cliff-hanger that hooked the nation;" a "whodunit with a torrid plot" (Finz & Walsh, 2004). The plot involved Peterson, a handsome, 30-something salesman and his beautiful, pregnant wife who disappeared from their Modesto, California, home on Christmas Eve, 2002. It also involved Peterson's girlfriend, a massage therapist who, unbeknownst to Peterson, was secretly taping their telephone conversations.

As Peterson's alibi began to unravel in the months following his wife's disappearance and the discovery of her body, as his affair became very public, and as it became clear that he lied to his girlfriend, to the police, and even to Diane Sawyer, who interviewed him on ABC's "Good Morning America," the press had a field day. Reports of the ongoing investigation and of Peterson's

alleged role in the murders were staple fare for news organizations, on-line message boards, and bloggers for months.

Because of this extensive pretrial publicity, the trial was moved from Stanislaus County, where Peterson had been charged with murder, to nearby San Mateo County. But that move was not enough to satisfy Peterson's attorney, Mark Geragos, who argued in the midst of jury selection that the sensational case should be moved again: "The idea that moving this case 90 miles from Modesto would somehow solve the problem of the unremitting local television and print coverage has been rebutted by the eight weeks of jury selection and the questionnaires themselves" wrote Geragos. "In spite of this court's Herculean effort to try to seat an impartial jury it is time to transfer venue to the most populous county in the state, Los Angeles." (Finz & Walsh, 2004).

Laci and Scott Peterson, who married in 1997, in an undated family photo

Even though half of the prospective jurors who were questioned said they thought Peterson was guilty, a jury was eventually selected in San Mateo County. In late 2004, after months of testimony, jurors convicted Peterson on two counts of first degree murder and sentenced him to death. He is now awaiting execution at San Quentin.

---

occur. But as Scott Peterson's case illustrates, potentially biasing information can also be released by a national organization and, hence, create a nationwide problem. When Theodore Kaczynski was identified as the Unabomber in 1996, the FBI leaked to the media detailed information about the contents of his cabin, including a potentially incriminating typewriter, a partially assembled bomb, and lists of potential victims.

In cases with such extensive pretrial publicity, the courts must answer two basic questions. First, does the publicity threaten the fairness of a

defendant's trial? Second, if the answer to this question is yes, what steps should be taken to remedy the situation? Psychologists have conducted research on both queries and can offer guidance to judges who are willing to listen. We describe that work later in this chapter.

Court Decisions on Pretrial Publicity

The history of the "free press/fair trial" controversy includes several phases, which differ in the ways in which the courts assessed pretrial publicity and the steps they favored to remedy any prejudice that was created (Loh, 1984). Phase 1 began with the famous trial in 1807 of Aaron Burr, third vice president of the United States, who was charged with treason. Burr claimed that he could not get a fair trial because inflammatory newspaper articles had prejudiced the public against him. Chief Justice Marshall ruled that the law did not require a jury "without any prepossessions whatever respecting the guilt or innocence of the accused" and that finding such a jury would be impossible anyway. However, the Court did consider "those who have deliberately formed and delivered an opinion on the guilt of the prisoner as not being in a state of mind to fairly weigh the testimony, and therefore as being disqualified to serve as jurors in the case" (*United States v. Burr*, 1807). In phase 1, therefore, the question of pretrial publicity was evaluated in terms of the effects jurors reported it to have on their minds.

In phase 2, the Supreme Court began to question whether jurors' own assurances of impartiality in the face of massive amounts of prejudicial publicity constituted a sufficient protection for defendants subjected to this publicity. *Irvin v. Dowd* (1961) was the first case in which the U.S. Supreme Court struck down a state conviction on the ground of prejudicial pretrial publicity. In this case, six murders had been committed around Evansville, Indiana, between December 1954 and March 1955. Shortly after the defendant, Leslie Irwin, was arrested, the prosecutor and local police issued extensively publicized press releases saying that Irvin had confessed to the present crimes as well as to 24 other burglaries; that he had been previously convicted of arson, burglary, and AWOL charges; and that he was a parole violator, a bad check artist, and a remorseless and conscienceless person. Irvin's attorney obtained a change of venue to adjoining Gibson County, which was saturated by the same publicity that tainted the original venue. He petitioned to have the trial moved again, but this motion was denied. At Irvin's trial, 430 prospective jurors were examined; 268 were excused because they were convinced of Irvin's guilt. Eight members of the jury that was seated

admitted that they thought he was guilty prior to his trial. At the trial, Irvin was convicted of murder and sentenced to death.

Following *Irvin*, the Supreme Court considered several cases in which defendants claimed that their right to an impartial jury had been destroyed by inflammatory pretrial publicity. For example, in *Rideau v. Louisiana* (1963), the Court decided that exposure to news that included information strongly pointing to the defendant's guilt was a violation of due process. A local TV station broadcast at three different times a 20-minute clip of Rideau, surrounded by law enforcement officials, confessing in detail to charges of robbery, kidnapping, and murder. A request for a change of venue was denied, and Rideau was convicted and sentenced to death by a jury, of which at least three members had seen the televised confession. The Supreme Court reversed this decision, Rideau was granted a new trial, and he was eventually convicted of manslaughter, rather than murder. In the 43 years he spent in prison (he was released in 2005), Rideau transformed himself from an illiterate eighth-grade dropout to a national advocate for prison reform, a filmmaker, and an award-winning editor of Angola State Prison's renowned *Angolite* magazine. Perhaps most important, he acknowledged responsibility for his crime and apologized for the hurt he caused (Green, 2005).

In *Sheppard v. Maxwell* (1966), the Court reviewed the famous trial of Dr. Sam Sheppard, a prominent Cleveland physician charged with the murder of his wife. News coverage of this trial was unrestrained and turned the proceeding into a media carnival. The Court overturned Sheppard's conviction, concluding that "where there is a reasonable likelihood that prejudicial news prior to a trial will prevent a fair trial, the judge should continue the case until the threat abates, or transfer it to another county not so permeated with publicity" (p. 363). The Court also discussed several options to prevent a trial where "bedlam reigned at the courthouse." This attention to remedies for adverse publicity heralded the beginning of phase 3.

Phase 3, spanning the 1970s and 1980s, was concerned with various preventive or remedial techniques for adverse pretrial publicity. It is important to recognize at the outset that these methods are usually rejected by the courts. One such measure is for a judge to order the press not to publish pretrial information likely to be prejudicial, a procedure known as prior restraint or a **gag order**. The leading case is *Nebraska Press Association v. Stuart* (1976), in which the Supreme Court ruled that a trial judge could not order the press to refrain from publishing information likely to be prejudicial to a defendant unless it could be shown that a fair trial would be denied the defendant without such prior restraint. In most cases, gag orders are quickly overturned on appeal.

Likewise, the press cannot be barred from attending and reporting a trial because the First Amendment guarantees public access to criminal trials (*Richmond Newspapers, Inc. v. Virginia*, 1980). However, the press can be excluded from pretrial hearings in which potentially prejudicial material might be at issue (*Gannett Co. v. De Pasquale*, 1979). The press can also volunteer to defer publishing incriminating information, and responsible members of the media often limit their disclosures, especially when the police are investigating possible suspects in unsolved crimes.

We would prefer that the history of the free press/fair trial debate had ended with phase 3. However, there is a phase 4, initiated by the 1984 Supreme Court case of *Patton v. Yount*, that represents a return to the standards of *Burr* or even something less than this standard. In 1966, Jon Yount confessed that he had killed a high school student. His confession was published in two local papers and was admitted into evidence at trial. Yount actually had two trials; his conviction in the first trial was overturned because his confession had been obtained in violation of his *Miranda* rights. Prior to the second trial, Yount moved for a change of venue, citing continuing publicity about the case. The motion was denied, despite the fact that 77% of prospective jurors admitted they had an opinion about Yount's guilt. After his second conviction, Yount appealed again, claiming that the publicity had made a fair trial impossible. Nonetheless, the Supreme Court reasoned that a "presumption of correctness" should be given to

the trial judge's opinion because, being present at the trial, the judge was in a better position to evaluate the demeanor, the credibility, and, ultimately, the competence of prospective jurors. Unless the record shows that the judge made a "manifest error," reviewing courts should defer to the trial judge.

From a psychological standpoint, an obvious problem with this decision was the Court's willingness to accept, at face value, what jurors say about their own opinions. The problem is not that jurors lie about their beliefs (although some probably do). The issue is that there are many reasons why people might not admit the full measure of their prejudice in public. People might not recognize the extent of their biases; even if completely aware, they might not disclose them in an open courtroom before a judge who encourages them to be fair and open-minded. Finally, they might experience **evaluation apprehension**, whereby they provide the answers that they perceive the judge wants to hear, regardless of whether their responses are truthful (Vidmar, 2002).

Finally, in its more recent look at the potentially prejudicial effects of pretrial publicity (*Mu'Min v. Virginia*, 1991), the Supreme Court compounded the problem of jurors promising impartiality. In this case, the Court held that defendants do not have a constitutional right to ask prospective jurors about the specifics of the pretrial publicity to which they have been exposed. Under such circumstances, it is difficult to know how much trust to place in jurors' assurances that they are impartial, but the Supreme Court concluded that such assurances are all that the Constitution requires. (Frankly, we think there are better remedies for ensuring fair trials in light of heavy pretrial publicity; we discuss these remedies later in this chapter.)

Effects of Pretrial Publicity

Does pretrial publicity influence public opinion? Does adverse publicity produce negative opinions about defendants? If so, do these negative opinions continue despite efforts to control them? Several studies have been conducted that measure the effects of various kinds of pretrial publicity presented in different media. The studies are of two types. In experimental studies, participants are first exposed (or not exposed) to some form of publicity and then are asked to assume the role of juror in a simulated trial. Researchers measure the impact of the publicity on these subjects' decision making. In field studies, respondents are surveyed to assess the effects of publicity about a particular real-life case. Taken together, these studies fairly convincingly point to the conclusion that jurors may be adversely affected by pretrial publicity and that the publicity can prejudice them in some surprising ways.

EXPERIMENTAL STUDIES OF THE EFFECTS OF PRETRIAL PUBLICITY

Experimental procedures, in which the researcher manipulates the presence of pretrial publicity and measures its impact on jurors' decisions, ensure that the only differences between the two sets of jurors (i.e., those who have seen pretrial publicity and those who have not) involve the nature and extent of the publicity. Thus, researchers can be fairly confident that differences in responding are related to the impact of the pretrial information.

Early studies using this methodology studied the impact of pretrial information that would have been inadmissible at trial (e.g., confessions [Padawer-Singer & Barton, 1975] and prior criminal records [Hvistendahl, 1979]). More recent studies have looked at the effects of varying amounts of negative information included in the pretrial publicity, pretrial publicity effects in different types of crimes, and whether the interval between exposure to the pretrial information and the juror's judgment affects the impact of that information (Steblay, Besirevic, Fulero, & Jiminez-Lorente, 1999). These studies generally show that pretrial publicity can affect jurors' evaluations of the defendant's character, their feelings of liking and sympathy for him, their pretrial sentiments about his guilt, and their final verdicts. The publicity has greater impact as the interval between exposure and jurors' judgment lengthens. Pretrial publicity has also been shown to affect jurors in

a civil case, increasing the likelihood that a defendant will be found liable in the aftermath of negative pretrial information (Bornstein, Whisenhunt, Nemeth, & Dunaway, 2002).

An interesting question, given the pervasiveness of cable and satellite TV and the declining readership of newspapers, is whether pretrial information conveyed by television has a different impact than information conveyed in print. In an experiment designed to test this question, participants were randomly assigned to one of three conditions that varied the format by which pretrial media information was presented about the Mount Cashel orphanage case, a highly publicized case in Canada concerning alleged sexual abuse by a group of Roman Catholic men who ran an orphanage in Newfoundland (Ogloff & Vidmar, 1994). The damaging pretrial material was presented to subjects through (1) television, (2) newspaper articles, or (3) both TV and newspapers; a fourth control group received only minimal information about the case. Presentation of publicity via television had a greater biasing impact than the same information presented in print, but the combined effects of TV and newspaper publicity had the greatest impact of all. Of additional interest was the finding that the subjects were generally unaware that their opinions had been biased by this material; subjects who had formed opinions about the trial were just as likely to say that they could be fair as were those who had not formed opinions.

To this point, we have considered the effects of **specific pretrial publicity**, showing that case-specific information made available prior to trial can affect the sentiments of jurors in that trial. Other studies have shown that mock jurors can also be influenced by **general pretrial publicity**— that is, media coverage of issues not specifically related to a particular case but thematically relevant to the issues at hand. For example, Greene and Wade (1988) showed that subjects who read the inflammatory facts about a series of heinous crimes were more likely to judge a defendant guilty in an unrelated case than were subjects who instead first read about a miscarriage of justice. Similarly, Polvi, Jack, Lyon, Laird, and Ogloff (1996) showed that subjects previously exposed to inflammatory publicity about a sexual abuse case rendered more guilty verdicts, were more likely to believe the complainants, and assigned longer prison sentences to a defendant in an unrelated case than did subjects who had not been exposed to the general publicity. In a test of the effects of general pretrial publicity in a rape case, Kovera (2002) showed that media exposure and preexisting attitudes interact: Exposure to a story about a rape case influenced participants' appraisals of the witnesses and verdicts in a different acquaintance rape case, but preexisting attitudes also moderated the influence of the media on mock jurors' judgments.

General pretrial publicity probably works by transferring preexisting prejudices and stereotypes about categories of people to a particular defendant in a trial setting (Vidmar, 2002). As a result, the facts of the case and the personal characteristics of the defendant go relatively unheeded. Racial and ethnic stereotypes are the most common forms of generic prejudice; for example, some people believe that an African American defendant is more likely to be guilty of a crime than a white defendant, all other things being equal. Any Arab Americans on trial in the United States in the aftermath of 9/11 might have experienced some generic prejudice of their own.

FIELD STUDIES OF THE EFFECTS OF NATURALLY OCCURRING PUBLICITY

Serious crimes attract extensive news coverage, typically from the prosecutor's view of the case. A number of studies have examined effects of pretrial publicity by polling samples of people exposed to varying media coverage about actual crimes. These studies, whether surveying opinions about notorious crimes (Studebaker et al., 2002) or cases of only local interest (Moran & Cutler, 1991; Nietzel & Dillehay, 1982; Vidmar, 2002), consistently find that persons exposed to pretrial publicity possess more knowledge about the events in question, are more likely to have prejudged the case, and are more knowledgeable of incriminating facts that would be inadmissible at the trial. On rare occasions, when a field study demonstrates

that the volume of publicity has been overwhelming and when a crime has touched the lives of large numbers of local residents, a judge will have no option but to move the trial. The Oklahoma City bombing case described in Box 7.4 is a good example.

In field studies, participants are typically asked about their knowledge of the crime in question, their perceptions of the defendant's culpability, and their ability to be impartial in light of their knowledge. Surveys have revealed both specific prejudice stemming from media coverage of a particular case, and more generic prejudice that derives from mass media reports of social and cultural issues. Law professor Neil Vidmar provides an example of the effects of specific pretrial publicity in a Canadian case, *R. v. Reynolds* (Vidmar, 2002).

The crime occurred in Kingston, Ontario, a city of 160,000 people, in 1997. Louise Reynolds was charged with killing her 7-year old daughter. In the two-year period following the incident, the local newspaper, the *Kingston Whig Standard*, published 48 articles about the case, including many lengthy feature stories, but none that reported the defendant's side of the case. Instead, media reports detailed the prosecution's belief that the victim had been stabbed 84 times in the head, described her life of tragedy and abuse, and included the allegation that the mother had borne all five of her children to different men. The defense put forward an alternative theory that the child had been killed by a pitbull dog that was found near the crime scene covered in blood. Two years after the killing, the child's body was exhumed for examination, and two forensic scientists issued reports that were consistent with the alternative theory. Their conclusions were never reported by the local paper.

The following year, in preparation for trial, the defense hired Professor Vidmar to assess whether community attitudes were still highly inflamed or whether passions had cooled over the intervening months. Most survey respondents said they had heard about the case, and more than a third said that an acquittal would be unacceptable to them.

THE CASE OF

BOX 7.4   **Timothy McVeigh: Data on the prejudicial effects
of massive pretrial publicity**

At 9:02 A.M. on April 19, 1995, a massive explosion destroyed the Murrah Federal Building in Oklahoma City. The bombing killed 163 people in the building (including 15 children in the building's day care center visible from the street) as well as 5 people outside. The explosion trapped hundreds of people in the rubble and spewed glass, chunks of concrete, and debris over several blocks of downtown Oklahoma City. It was the country's most deadly act of domestic terrorism.

Approximately 75 minutes after the blast, Timothy McVeigh was pulled over while driving north from Oklahoma City because his car lacked license tags. After the state trooper discovered a concealed, loaded gun in his car, McVeigh was arrested and incarcerated for transporting a firearm. Two days later,

the federal government filed a complaint against McVeigh on federal bombing charges. By August 1995, McVeigh and co-defendant Terry Nichols had been charged with conspiracy, use of a weapon of mass destruction, destruction by explosives, and eight counts of first-degree murder in connection with the deaths of eight federal law enforcement officials who had been killed in the blast.

The bombing, the heroic actions of rescue workers, and the arrest of McVeigh all generated a tremendous amount of publicity. The image of an exhausted and despondent rescue worker, emerging from the wreckage with a dead baby in his arms, was flashed across the country. Millions of Americans saw images of McVeigh wearing orange jail garb and a bulletproof vest, being

led through an angry crowd outside the Noble County Jail in Perry, Oklahoma. One wondered, at that time, whether any location in the country was not saturated with news of the bombing. Predictably, McVeigh requested a change of venue from Oklahoma City to a more neutral (or at least a less emotionally charged) locale.

As part of a motion to change venue, McVeigh enlisted the help of a team of psychologists to provide information to the court about the extent and type of publicity in the Oklahoma City newspaper and in the papers from three other communities (Lawton, Oklahoma, a small town 90 miles from Oklahoma City; Tulsa; and Denver) (Studebaker & Penrod, 1997). The psychologists identified all articles pertaining to the bombing in these

It would probably have been difficult to find an impartial jury in this case, but the charges against Reynolds were eventually dropped when a forensic scientist hired by the prosecution admitted errors and changed his opinion (Vidmar, 2002).

Survey studies have also documented generic prejudice that can arise from exposure to the media portrayals of certain kinds of crime. Moran and Cutler (1991) showed that media accounts of drug crimes influenced attitudes toward defendants who were charged with drug distribution. Cases involving sexual abuse also engender strong sentiments, fed in part by media coverage. Sizeable percentages of Canadian jurors who were asked in

court whether they could be impartial in a case involving sexual abuse of children said they could not be (Vidmar, 1997). Among the responses were these: "If I were to answer this question honestly, I do have somewhat of a problem with this [given that I am] a teacher"; "I'm very prejudiced against child molesters, rapists and wife beaters and I think they should be lashed in my opinion."

Generic prejudices can also be engendered by publicity about jury damage awards and the controversy over tort reform in civil cases. Nearly half of prospective jurors awaiting jury selection in Seattle said that their attitudes about tort reform were informed by the media, and the more that four papers between April 20, 1995, and January 8, 1996, and coded the content of the text including negative characterizations of the defendant, reports of a confession, and emotionally laden publicity. They also measured the number of articles printed in each paper and the amount of space allotted to text and pictures (*U.S. v. McVeigh*, 1996).

The data were compelling: During the collection period, 939 articles about the bombing had appeared in the Oklahoma City newspaper and 174 in the *Denver Post*. By a whopping 6312-to-558 margin, the *Daily Oklahoman* had printed more statements of an emotional nature (e.g., emotional suffering, goriness of the scene) than the *Denver Post* (Studebaker & Penrod, 1997). On the basis of this analysis

and other evidence presented at the hearing, Judge Richard Matsch moved the trial to Denver. In support of his decision, Matsch cited the development of differences in both the volume and the focus of media coverage in Oklahoma compared with national coverage, the demonization of the defendant versus the humanization of the victims in the local pretrial publicity, and the frequency of televised interviews of Oklahoma citizens who implied that McVeigh's death would be the appropriate resolution (Studebaker & Penrod, 1997). In June 1997, McVeigh was convicted on all 11 counts and sentenced to death. He was executed in June 2001.

Critics have long suggested that studies of pretrial publicity lack usefulness because they do not measure the public's reactions

to naturally occurring publicity (as we pointed out, researchers often "expose" participants to news reports in the context of an experiment). To address these concerns, Christina Studebaker and her colleagues conducted a study using the Internet to examine how differences in naturally occurring exposure to pretrial publicity affected public attitudes, evidence evaluation, and verdict and sentencing preferences in the *McVeigh* case (Studebaker et al., 2002). They found, among other things, that the closer people were to the bombing site, the more they knew about it and the more they believed that McVeigh was guilty. This study employs a novel methodology to explore important real-world effects of pretrial information.

these individuals supported tort reform, the more negatively disposed they were to the plaintiff (Greene, Goodman, & Loftus, 1991).

Survey studies have several strengths. For example, they use large and representative samples of prospective jurors, and they rely on naturally occurring publicity about actual cases. They also have a weakness: The data are correlational in nature. As such, they cannot indicate the direction of the relationship between exposure to publicity and prejudice. For example, does exposure to publicity lead to prejudicial sentiments about the defendant, or, alternatively, are people with an antidefendant bias likely to expose themselves to

such publicity? Reasoning from Kovera's study on the interactive effects of the media and preexisting attitudes in a rape case, we suspect that both alternatives are possible.

Some scholars (e.g., Carroll et al., 1986) have suggested another weakness in these field surveys. They argue that courts should not conclude that pretrial publicity biases jurors just because it affects their attitudes; to be truly prejudicial, it must also affect their verdicts. According to this logic, we need to know whether pretrial publicity effects persist through the presentation of trial evidence. But some evidence suggests that antidefendant biases held at the beginning of the trial may persist through the presentation of evidence and may even color the way the evidence is remembered (Moran & Cutler, 1991).

Finally, it is important to acknowledge case studies showing that in addition to the effects of mass media publicity, prospective jurors are influenced by other sources of prejudice, including those that arise when a juror has a direct or indirect interest in the outcome of the trial or perceives that there is strong community sentiment in favor of a particular outcome in the case (Vidmar, 2002).

Remedies for the Effects of Pretrial Publicity

If pretrial publicity adversely affects juror impartiality, the next question is what procedures should be used to restore the likelihood of a fair trial for the defendant. Five alternatives are available.

1. *Continuance*. The trial can be postponed until a later date with the expectation that the passage of time will lessen the effects of the prejudicial material. This view remains in vogue with the current Supreme Court. However, research indicates that although continuances may decrease jurors' recall of factual evidence (and hence their reliance on factual pretrial publicity), they do not dampen jurors' recall or use of emotionally biasing information (Kramer, Kerr, & Carroll, 1990).

2. *Expanded voir dire*. The most popular method for rooting out pretrial prejudice is to conduct a thorough *voir dire* (questioning) of potential jurors. The American Bar Association recommends that in cases in which jurors have been exposed to prejudicial publicity, an intensive, thorough questioning of each prospective juror be conducted outside the presence of other chosen and prospective jurors.

Although thorough *voir dire* can be a valuable protection against partiality, it may not always be adequate. As we have noted, jurors may not recognize their own biases, and they can hide their true feelings from an examiner if they so choose. There is some evidence that jurors may be hesitant to

self-disclose in a public courtroom. Nietzel and Dillehay (1982) evaluated different types of questioning procedures in the jury selection process of 13 Kentucky death penalty trials. (As we explain in Chapter 11, one purpose of jury selection is to elicit responses from prospective jurors that allow an attorney to make informed decisions about which jurors to excuse.) The questioning of jurors in these cases was directed either to an individual or to the entire group, and individual questioning was either in open court with other jurors present or in the judge's chambers. More jurors were excused in cases that involved individual questioning in seclusion than in cases that involved other procedures. Jurors probably feel more comfortable sharing their true feelings when they can do so privately.

3. *Judicial instructions*. A fairly simple remedy for the bias that can result from pretrial publicity involves an instruction from the judge to the jury, admonishing members to base their decision on the evidence rather than on nonevidentiary information. However, a judicial instruction is often unable to reduce the biasing effect of exposure to either factual or emotional pretrial publicity (Nietzel, McCarthy, & Kern, 1999). An instruction to disregard certain information may have the unintended consequence of drawing jurors' attention to it, a so-called boomerang effect.

Some work by Steven Fein and his colleagues (Fein, McCloskey, & Tomlinson, 1997) may help us understand the role of judicial instructions in this context. Participants in this study read the transcript of a case in which the defendant was charged with killing his estranged wife and a neighbor who was in her home. Before trial, half of the mock jurors read a series of articles about the murders and the evidence. Some of these subjects also read an article that called into question the motives of the media covering the case. In this article, the defense attorney complained about the negative publicity: "The coverage of this case serves as another fine example of how the media manipulates information to sell papers, and knowingly ignores acts which would point toward a defendant's innocence" (p. 1219).

Despite judicial instructions to ignore the pretrial information, jurors' verdicts were significantly influenced by it, unless they had been made suspicious of the media's motives. Thus, although judicial instructions had no effect on conviction rates per se, mock jurors could follow the instruction when they were given some reason to suspect the source of the pretrial information.

4. *Imported jurors*. Prospective jurors can be imported to the venue from another county "whenever it is determined that potentially prejudicial news coverage of a given criminal matter has been intense and has been concentrated primarily in a given locality in a state" (ABA, 1993b). This remedy allows the trial to be conducted in the original venue but before a group of jurors presumably less affected by prejudicial material than local jurors would be. Judges are often reluctant to exercise this alternative because of the inconvenience to jurors and the expense.

Of the four previous remedies, the first three alternatives appear, on the basis of existing research, to be largely ineffective, and the fourth— importing jurors from another area—is seldom used because of its perceived impracticality. Why do the methods most commonly relied on tend to fail as safeguards? The answer probably lies in several basic features of the way that human beings remember and use information to form impressions and overall judgments (Studebaker & Penrod, 2005). Unless they have some reason to discount or ignore pretrial publicity when it is first encountered, most people will use it to help them interpret subsequent information and to make various pieces of information "fit" together in a coherent theme. Therefore, once the idea of a guilty perpetrator is established, it may become an organizing principle for the processing of additional information about the person. Furthermore, if people try to suppress forbidden thoughts, they often find that the thoughts actually become stronger or more frequent (Wegner & Erber, 1992).

For these reasons, safeguards that attempt to remove an existing bias may never work as well as trying to seat jurors who never had a bias to start with. The value of achieving this goal is why most social scientists prefer changes of venue.

5. *Change of venue*. A change of venue is the most extreme remedy for pretrial prejudice. Changing venue requires that the trial be conducted in another geographic jurisdiction altogether and that jurors for the trial be drawn from this new jurisdiction. Because venue changes are expensive, inconvenient, and time-consuming, courts are reluctant to use them.

Venue changes can result in significant variations in characteristics of the communities involved, as was illustrated by the case of William Lozano, a Hispanic police officer who was convicted of killing an African American motorist in Miami. After his conviction was reversed because of pretrial publicity, the case was moved to Tallahassee (which has a much smaller Hispanic population than Miami) and finally to Orlando (where the Hispanic population is more sizeable). The Florida appellate court reasoned that in cases in which race may be a factor and changes of venue are appropriate, trials should be moved to locations where the demographic characteristics are similar to those of the original venue (*State v. Lozano*, 1993).

Psychologists can be enlisted to support a lawyer's motion for one or more of these protections against pretrial prejudices. When pretrial contamination is extensive, a professionally conducted public opinion survey is the technique of choice for evaluating the degree of prejudice in a community. Public opinion surveys gauge how many people have read or heard about a case, what they have read or heard, whether they have formed opinions, what these opinions are, and how their opinions affect the way the case is perceived.

Change-of-Venue Surveys

A growing body of literature exists on ways to conduct venue surveys, as well as on the practical, methodological, legal, and ethical issues that they raise (Moran & Cutler, 1997; Posey & Dahl, 2002). In this section, we briefly outline the steps involved in these surveys.

1. *Planning the survey and designing the questionnaire*. Scripts for the survey questionnaires are

written for telephone interviews. The content is based on an analysis of the media to which the community has been exposed.

2. *Training the interviewers.* The persons who conduct the telephone interviews are trained to administer the questionnaire in a standardized fashion. Insofar as possible, interviewers should be "blind" to the purpose of the survey. Therefore, the callers do not construct the questionnaire or interpret the results.

3. *Drawing the sample.* Respondents to venue surveys must be drawn at random for the results to be valid. Usually, persons are surveyed in at least two jurisdictions: the original venue county and at least one other "comparison" county. Data about the differences between the surveyed counties are then presented to show the relative levels and effects of pretrial influence in the different jurisdictions.

4. *Presenting the results.* Survey results are presented in one of two ways. The expert can prepare an **affidavit**, which is a written report sworn to be truthful. A stronger presentation results when the expert testifies in person about the design, results, and meaning of the survey at a change-of-venue hearing.

Public opinion surveys are time-consuming, hectic activities that often demand more resources than the typical client can afford. However, they usually yield valuable information. Obtaining a change of venue for a highly publicized case is probably the most effective procedure available for improving the chances for a fair trial. Moreover, even if the venue is not changed, the results of the survey can often be used in jury selection. Because of the multiple purposes for which they can be used, public opinion surveys are a popular tool among litigation consultants. We discuss some of these additional uses in Chapter 11.

SUMMARY

1. *What are the major legal proceedings between arrest and trial in the criminal justice system?* (1) An initial appearance, at which defendants are informed of the charges, of their constitutional rights, and of future proceedings, (2) a preliminary hearing, in which the judge determines whether there is enough evidence to hold the defendant for processing by the grand jury, (3) action by the grand jury, which decides whether sufficient evidence exists for the defendant to be tried, (4) an arraignment, involving a formal statement of charges and an initial plea by the defendant to these charges, (5) a process of discovery, requiring that the prosecutor reveal to the defense certain evidence, and pretrial motions, or attempts by both sides to win favorable ground rules for the subsequent trial.

2. *What is bail, and what factors influence the amount of bail set?* Bail is the provision, by a defendant, of money or other assets that are forfeited if the defendant fails to appear at trial. In determining whether to release a defendant between the indictment and trial, the judge should consider the risk that the defendant will not show up for his or her trial. Most judges also consider the potential danger to the community if the defendant is released. Predictions of dangerousness, however, are often unreliable.

3. *Why do defendants and prosecutors agree to plea-bargain?* Plea bargaining is an excellent example of the dilemma between truth and conflict resolution as goals of our legal system. At least 85% of criminal cases end between arrest and trial with the defendant pleading guilty to some (often reduced) charges. Plea bargaining benefits both defendants and prosecutors. Defendants who plead guilty often receive reductions in the charges or in their sentences; prosecutors secure a "conviction" without expending their time at trial.

4. *In what ways does pretrial publicity pose a danger to fair trials? How can these dangers be* *reduced?* The right to a free press and the right to a fair trial are usually complementary, but some criminal trials (and some civil trials) generate so much publicity that the defendant's right to an impartial jury is jeopardized. In addition, publicity about other cases or about social or cultural issues can create generic prejudice that can also influence jurors' reasoning in a particular case. Psychologists have studied the effects of pretrial publicity on potential fact-finders and have also evaluated different mechanisms for curbing or curing the negative effects of pretrial publicity.

KEY TERMS

affidavit

change of venue

charge bargaining

deferred prosecution

discovery

evaluation apprehension

exclusionary rule

exculpatory

gag order

general pretrial publicity

grand jury

hearsay

indictment

motion *in limine*

plea bargaining

released on
   recognizance (ROR)

sentence bargaining

specific pretrial publicity

with prejudice

Forensic Assessment in Criminal Cases: Competence and Insanity

ORIENTING QUESTIONS

1. *What is the scope of forensic psychology?*
2. *What is meant by competence in the criminal justice process?*
3. *How do clinicians assess competence?*
4. *What are the consequences of being found incompetent to proceed in the criminal justice process?*
5. *What is the legal definition of insanity?*
6. *How frequently is the insanity defense used, and how successful is it?*
7. *What are the major criticisms of the insanity defense, and what attempts have been made to reform it?*

On the morning of June 20, 2001, Andrea Yates, a 37-year-old wife and mother of five, said goodbye to her husband as he left for work. Before her mother-in-law arrived to help care for the children, who ranged in age from six months to seven years old, Yates filled the bathtub of her Texas home with water. Beginning with her middle son, Paul, she drowned each of her children in turn. She laid the four youngest children in the bed, covering them with a sheet. Her oldest boy was left floating lifelessly in the bathtub. She then called the police and her husband to tell them what she had done.

Prior to the killing of her children, Yates had a long psychiatric history. She reportedly suffered numerous psychotic episodes and had been diagnosed with schizophrenia and postpartum depression. These episodes resulted in several hospitalizations, including one just a month prior to the killings, and required psychotropic medications to help stabilize her ("The Andrea Yates Case," 2005).

Yates pled not guilty by reason of insanity to drowning three of her children. She was not charged in the other two deaths. Her insanity plea was based on her claim that she had no choice but to kill them because her children were not "righteous" and "they would burn in hell if she did not kill them while they were still innocents" (Wordsworth, 2005). No one disputed that Yates systematically killed each of her children, but the question remained whether she was so disturbed by the symptoms of her severe mental illness that she could not be held criminally responsible for the murders.

At the conclusion of her trial, Yates was found guilty and sentenced to life in prison. After she had served three years of her sentence, however, the court declared a mistrial and Yates's conviction was overturned. During the trial, one of the psychiatric experts mistakenly testified that the television show "Law and Order" had aired an episode in which a defendant had been acquitted by reason of insanity after drowning her children in the bathtub. Although the expert himself did not link this observation to Andrea Yates's thinking or motivation, the prosecutor did so in closing arguments. In fact, there had never been an episode of "Law and Order" with this specific story line. Yates now

Andrea Yates with her family

remains in a psychiatric prison in Texas awaiting her new trial (Wordsworth, 2005).

The question of whether Andrea Yates—or any criminal defendant—was insane at the time of a criminal offense is one of the most controversial questions that forensic psychologists and psychiatrists are called upon to help the court decide. It is also a question that has attracted extensive research by forensic specialists. In this chapter, we survey how insanity is defined, how claims of insanity are assessed by mental health professionals, and some of the implications of the insanity defense. We also discuss one other concept—competence to stand trial—which is often confused with insanity. We cover trial competence and insanity together in this chapter because these issues are raised together in some cases, because they occur fairly close to one another within the sequence of criminal adjudication, and because they are sometimes assessed at the same time and documented in the same report (Heilbrun & Collins, 1995). In the next chapter, we explore several other forensic questions that clinicians assess. These questions arise in criminal trials, civil litigation, divorce and child custody disputes, commitment hearings, and many other types of legal proceedings.

The Scope of Forensic Psychology

Forensic psychologists use knowledge and techniques from psychology, psychiatry, and other behavioral sciences to answer questions about individuals involved in legal proceedings. In most cases, forensic assessment activities are performed by clinical psychologists, and the field of forensic psychology has prospered and matured considerably in the last 30 years (Nicholson, 1999; Nicholson & Norwood, 2000). For example, forensic psychology is officially recognized as a specialty by the American Board of Professional Psychology and by the American Psychological Association, specialty guidelines for the practice of forensic psychology have been approved (Committee on Ethical Guidelines for Forensic Psychologists, 1991), forensic psychology training programs have been developed, and the research and clinical literature on forensic practice has increased dramatically.

Despite both public concerns and professional skepticism about whether forensic psychology should be afforded as much credibility and stature as it now appears to enjoy, the field continues to expand. According to one survey, the use of expert witnesses increased from an average of three experts per case in 1991 to more than four in 1998. Of these expert witnesses called, about 40% were in the medical or mental health professions (Ivkovic & Hans, 2003). Other estimates suggest that psychologists and psychiatrists testify in about 8% of all federal civil trials, and mental health professionals participate as experts in as many as a million cases per year (O'Connor, Sales, & Shuman, 1996). If anything, this level of participation will continue to increase because of three forces at work that encourage forensic activities.

First, mental health experts may have expertise in a variety of areas relevant to litigation. As scientists learn more about human behavior, attorneys will find new ways to use this information in various legal proceedings; in this chapter and Chapter 9, we focus on several topics that mental health professionals are called on to assess for individuals involved in court proceedings.

Second, forensic psychology is flourishing because the law permits, and even encourages, the use of expert testimony in a host of areas, including psychology, anthropology, criminology, engineering, toxicology, genetics, and medicine. Expert testimony of all types is used increasingly often, but psychological topics have enjoyed an especially large increase in prominence.

In general, a qualified expert can testify about a topic if such testimony is relevant to an issue in dispute and if the usefulness of the testimony outweighs whatever prejudicial impact it might have. If these two conditions are satisfied—as they must be for any kind of testimony to be admitted—an expert will be permitted to give opinion testimony if the judge believes that "scientific, technical, or other specialized knowledge will assist the trier of fact to understand the evidence or to determine a fact in issue" (Federal Rule of Evidence 702). As we noted in Chapter 1, the U.S. Supreme Court ruled in the 1993 case of *Daubert v. Merrell Dow* that federal judges are allowed to decide when expert testimony is based on sufficiently relevant and reliable scientific evidence to be admitted into evidence. This opinion, which applies to all federal courts and to any state courts that have adopted it, encourages the consideration of innovative opinions, and many critics, including experts themselves, fear that some judges—especially those who cannot accurately distinguish valid from invalid research—will allow jurors to hear "expert" testimony that is based on little more than "junk science" (Goodman-Delahunty, 1997; Saks, 2000; Shuman & Sales, 1999). This idea found empirical support in a survey of judges that found the majority lacked the "scientific literacy" necessary to comprehend and evaluate the evidence effectively under *Daubert* (Gatowski et al., 2001, p. 454).

In the case of opinions offered by behavioral scientists and mental health experts, the *Daubert* standard suggests that for expert testimony to be admitted, the expert should have relied on methods and knowledge that are scientifically based (Penrod, Fulero, & Cutler, 1995; Rotgers & Barrett, 1996). The Supreme Court has decided that this requirement also applies to opinions that are tied to the technical or professional skills of practitioners and clinicians (*Kumho Tire Co., Ltd v. Carmichael*, 1999).

Finally, forensic assessment and expert testimony by forensic psychologists thrive because they can be very lucrative. At an hourly rate of anywhere between $200 and $500, forensic experts can earn thousands of dollars per case. If one party in a lawsuit or criminal trial hires an expert, the other side usually feels compelled to match that expert. Consequently, the use of psychological experts feeds on itself, and it has become a significant source of income for many professionals.

Competence

The Andrea Yates case discussed earlier highlights the importance of evaluating a defendant's competence to stand trial. Did Yates understand the nature of her charges and the possible consequences of those charges? This question is particularly salient, given that during an interview with Yates's mother, she recalled that Andrea Yates, while in prison for the murders of her children, asked her mother who would be watching them (Gibson, 2005). Questions were also raised about whether Yates was taking her antipsychotic medication at the time of the murders as well as during her trial. As we will see later in the chapter, knowing her history of medication compliance helps the court assess her ability to become competent with the use of medication, if she is found incompetent to stand trial on the initial assessment.

What do we mean by competence to stand trial? How do clinicians assess competence? What legal standards should be applied? The question of a

defendant's competence is the psychological issue most frequently assessed in the criminal justice system. Basically, **competence** refers to a defendant's capacity to function meaningfully and knowingly in a legal proceeding; defendants are typically declared incompetent if they are seriously deficient in one or more abilities, such as understanding the legal proceedings, communicating with their attorneys, appreciating their role in the proceedings, and making legally relevant decisions. Concerns about a defendant's competence are tied to one fundamental principle: Criminal proceedings should not continue against someone who cannot understand their nature and purpose. This rule applies at every stage of the criminal justice process, but it is raised most often at pretrial hearings concerned with two topics: competence to plead guilty and competence to stand trial.

Why is competence an important doctrine in our system? The law requires defendants to be competent for several reasons (Melton, Petrila, Poythress, & Slobogin, 1997). First, competent defendants must be able to understand the charges against them so that they can participate in the criminal justice system in a meaningful way and make it more likely that legal proceedings will arrive at accurate and just results. Second, punishment of convicted defendants is morally acceptable only if they understand the reasons why they are being punished. Finally, the perceived fairness and dignity of our adversary system of justice requires participation by defendants who have the capacity to defend themselves against the charges of the state. As Grisso and Siegel (1986) observed, "there is no honor in entering a battle in full armor with the intention of striking down an adversary who is without shield or sword" (p. 146).

Adjudicative Competence

When defendants plead guilty, they waive several constitutional rights: the right to a jury trial, the right to confront their accusers, the right to call favorable witnesses, and the right to remain silent. The Supreme Court has held that waiving such important rights must be done knowingly, intelligently, and voluntarily (*Johnson v. Zerbst*, 1938), and trial judges are required to question defendants about their pleas in order to establish clearly that they understand that they are waiving their constitutional rights by pleading guilty. A knowing, intelligent, and voluntary guilty plea also includes understanding the charges and the possible penalties that can be imposed, and it requires the judge to examine any plea bargain to ensure that it is "voluntary" in the sense that it represents a considered choice between constitutionally permissible alternatives. For example, prosecutors can offer lighter sentences to a defendant in exchange for a guilty plea, but they cannot offer the defendant money to encourage a guilty plea.

The accepted national standard for **competence to stand trial**, as we discuss next, is a "sufficient present ability to consult with [one's] attorney with a reasonable degree of rational understanding, and . . . a rational, as well as factual understanding of the proceedings against [one]" (*Dusky v. United States*, 1960). Logically, **competence to plead guilty** would require that defendants understand the alternatives they face and have the ability to make a reasoned choice among them. Such a test, theoretically at least, is more exacting than competence to stand trial. Defendants standing trial need only be aware of the nature of the proceedings and be able to cooperate with counsel in presenting the defense. Defendants pleading guilty, on the other hand, must understand the possible consequences of pleading guilty instead of going to trial and must be able to make a rational choice between the alternatives.

In the past, even though several courts recognized a difference between competence to stand trial and competence to plead guilty (*United States v. Masthers*, 1976), the majority used the *Dusky* standard (cited earlier) for both competencies. There were two reasons for this practice. First, a separate standard for competence to plead guilty cuts too fine a distinction between different types of legal understanding; it is doubtful that this decision could be made meaningfully in practice. Second, a separate standard could create the difficult situation of having a class of defendants who are competent to stand trial but incompetent to plead guilty and who thereby could not participate in the possibly advantageous plea-bargaining process.

The American Bar Association has suggested a compromise between those who say that the tests for competence to stand trial and competence to plead guilty should be the same and those who would require a separate finding of competence to plead guilty. Criminal Justice Mental Health Standard 7–5.1 (ABA, 1989) reads in part:

a) No plea of guilty or **nolo contendere** (no contest) should be accepted from a defendant who is mentally incompetent to enter a plea of guilty.

   i) Ordinarily, absent additional information bearing on defendant's competence, a finding that the defendant is competent to stand trial should be sufficient to establish the defendant's competence to plead guilty.
   ii) The test for determining mental competence to plead guilty should be whether the defendant has sufficient present ability to consult with the defendant's lawyer with a reasonable degree of rational understanding and whether, given the nature and complexity of the charges and the potential consequences of a conviction, the defendant has a rational as well as factual understanding of the proceedings relating to a plea of guilty.

Despite these recommendations and the belief by many psychologists that competence cannot be separated from the specific decisions a defendant must make, the Supreme Court resolved this debate in its 1993 decision of *Godinez v. Moran*. In this opinion, the Court ruled that the standard for competence to stand trial will be used in federal courts for assessing other competence questions that arise in the criminal justice process. In so doing, it rejected the idea that competence to plead guilty involves a higher standard than competence to stand trial.

As a result of this decision, the terms *competence to plead guilty* and *competence to stand trial* have become somewhat misleading. Instead, many scholars are now suggesting that **adjudicative competence** is a better concept for describing the multiple abilities that criminal defendants are expected to exercise in different legal contexts (Bonnie, 1993; Hoge et al., 1997). The ABA Standards also require prosecutors and defense attorneys to alert the court if

TABLE 8.1 ◆ **Foundational and Decisional Components of Adjudicative Competence**

FOUNDATIONAL COMPETENCE

1. Can the defendant *understand* the basic elements (e.g., prosecutor, defense attorney, judge, jury, guilty plea) of the adversarial process?
2. Can the defendant use *reasoning* to relate relevant information to his or her attorney?
3. Can the defendant *appreciate* his or her legal predicament?

DECISIONAL COMPETENCE

1. Can the defendant *understand* information that is relevant to decisions, such as pleading guilty or waiving a jury trial?
2. Can the defendant use *reasoning* about alternative courses of action in making decisions about his or her defense?
3. Can the defendant *appreciate* the decisions that need to be made in his or her own best interest?
4. Can the defendant make a *choice* among the alternative defense strategies available?

they have information that bears on a defendant's adjudicative competence. Imposing this requirement on defense attorneys may work to the defendant's detriment, but the ABA Standards reflect the reasoning that attorneys have an obligation of candor to the court that overrides loyalty to the client. Thus, lawyers must inform a trial judge that their clients might not be competent to plead guilty, even though the client does not want to raise the issue and even though a lengthy incarceration could result from a competence evaluation. This principle has led to the censure of a defense attorney who hid evidence of his client's mental illness because neither the client nor the lawyer wanted a competence evaluation (*State v. Johnson*, 1986).

In evaluating adjudicative competence, the mental health professional focuses on two basic components. First, there is the *foundational* question of whether the defendant has the capacity to assist counsel. As Table 8.1 summarizes, this foundational component has three requirements: (1) the ability to understand the basic elements of the adversary system, (2) the ability to relate to one's attorney information that is relevant to the case, and (3) the ability to understand one's situation as a criminal defendant. The second component of adjudicative competence is *decisional competence*, which consists of four interrelated abilities: (1) understanding the information relevant to decisions the defendant must make, (2) thinking rationally about the alternatives involved in these decisions, (3) appreciating the specific legal questions one must resolve as a defendant, and

(4) making and expressing a choice about one's legal alternatives.

If an evaluator believes a defendant has the capacities to be competent, the evaluator will prepare a report that states this opinion and the reasons for it (see Box 8.1). However, if the evaluator believes the defendant does not have the relevant capacities to be competent, the report will also discuss possible treatments that might render the defendant competent. The evaluator's report should not be changed at the request of an attorney, although it may be supplemented in response to questions from an attorney. In the real world of the criminal justice system, attempts by attorneys to influence the content, style, or conclusions of these reports are not uncommon.

As noted earlier, the standard for competence to stand trial was defined by the U.S. Supreme Court in *Dusky v. United States* (1960): "whether [the defendant] has sufficient present ability to consult with [his] attorney with a reasonable degree of rational understanding—and whether he has a rational as well as factual understanding of the proceedings against him."

With minor differences across jurisdictions, this is the standard for competence to stand trial in all American courts. It establishes the basic criteria for competence as the capacities for having a factual and rational understanding of the court proceedings and for consulting with one's attorney in a rational way. These criteria refer to *present* abilities rather than to the mental state of the defendant at the time of the

THE CASE OF

BOX 8.1 Jamie Sullivan: Assessing competence

Jamie Sullivan was a 24-year-old clerk charged with arson, burglary, and murder in connection with a fire he had set at a small grocery store in Kentucky. The evidence in the case was that after closing hours, Sullivan had returned to the store where he worked and forced the night manager, Ricky Ford, to open the safe and hand over the $800 in cash that was in it. Sullivan then locked Ford in a backroom office, doused the room in gasoline, and set the store on fire. Ford was killed in the blaze. On the basis of a lead from a motorist who saw Sullivan running from the scene, police arrested him at his grandmother's apartment a few hours later. If convicted on all charges, Sullivan faced a possible death sentence.

Jamie Sullivan was mentally retarded. He had dropped out of school in the eighth grade, and a psychologist's evaluation of him at that time reported his IQ to be 68. He could read and write his name and a few simple phrases, but nothing more. He had a history of drug abuse and had spent several months in a juvenile correctional camp at the age of 15 after vandalizing five homes in his neighborhood. The army rejected his attempt to volunteer for service because of his limited intelligence and drug habit. His attorney believed that Sullivan's mental problems might render him incompetent to stand trial and therefore asked a psychologist to

evaluate him. After interviewing and testing Sullivan and reviewing the evidence the police had collected, the psychologist found the following: Sullivan's current IQ was 65, which fell in the mentally retarded range; he did not suffer any hallucinations or delusions, but he expressed strong religious beliefs that "God watches over his children and won't let nothing happen to them." The psychologist asked Sullivan a series of questions about his upcoming trial, to which he gave the following answers:

Q. What are you charged with?
A. Burning down that store and stealing from Ricky.

Q. Anything else?
A. They say I killed Ricky too.

Q. What could happen to you if a jury found you guilty?
A. Electric chair, but God will watch over me.

Q. What does the judge do at a trial?
A. He tells everybody what to do.

Q. If somebody told a lie about you in court, what would you do?
A. Get mad at him.

Q. Anything else?
A. Tell my lawyer the truth.

Q. What does your lawyer do if you have a trial?
A. Show the jury I'm innocent.

Q. How could he do that best?
A. Ask questions and have me tell them I wouldn't hurt Ricky. I liked Ricky.

Q. What does the prosecutor do in your trial?
A. Try to get me found guilty.

Q. Who decides if you are guilty or not?
A. That jury.

At a hearing to determine whether Jamie Sullivan was competent to stand trial, the psychologist testified that Sullivan was mentally retarded and that, as a result, his understanding of the proceedings was not as accurate or thorough as it might otherwise be. However, the psychologist also testified that Sullivan could assist his attorney and that he did understand the charges against him, as well as the general purpose and nature of his trial. The judge ruled that Jamie Sullivan was competent. A jury convicted him on all the charges and sentenced him to life in prison.

It is estimated that, much like Jamie Sullivan, as many as 60,000 defendants are evaluated annually to determine their competence (Bonnie & Grisso, 1998). Among those mentally disordered offenders who are committed to nonfederal hospitals, the single largest category is made up of defendants being evaluated for competence or already judged to be incompetent to stand trial (IST) (Steadman, Rosenstein, MacAskill, & Manderscheid, 1988).

alleged offense, which, as we will discuss later, is the focus of evaluations of a defendant's sanity.

A problem with the *Dusky* standard is that it does not specify how the evaluator assessing competence should judge the sufficiency of rational understanding, ability to consult, or factual understanding. A number of courts and mental health groups have expanded on *Dusky* by listing more specific criteria related to competence. For example, evaluators are sometimes urged to consider these 21 factors concerning a defendant's abilities (Group for the Advancement of Psychiatry, 1974):

1. To understand his current legal situation.
2. To understand the charges against him.
3. To understand the facts relevant to his case.
4. To understand the legal issues and procedures in his case.
5. To understand legal defenses available in his behalf.
6. To understand the dispositions, pleas, and penalties possible.
7. To appraise the likely outcomes.
8. To appraise the roles of defense counsel, the prosecuting attorney, the judge, the jury, the witnesses, and the defendant.
9. To identify and locate witnesses.
10. To relate to defense counsel.
11. To trust and to communicate relevantly with his counsel.
12. To comprehend instructions and advice.
13. To make decisions after receiving advice.
14. To maintain a collaborative relationship with his attorney and to help plan legal strategy.
15. To follow testimony for contradictions or errors.
16. To testify relevantly and be cross-examined if necessary.
17. To challenge prosecution witnesses.
18. To tolerate stress at the trial and while awaiting trial.
19. To refrain from irrational and unmanageable behavior during the trial.
20. To disclose pertinent facts surrounding the alleged offense.
21. To protect himself and to utilize the legal safeguards available to him.

Raising the Issue of Competence

The question of a defendant's competence can be raised at any point in the criminal process, and it can be raised by the prosecutor, the defense attorney, or the presiding judge. The issue is typically raised by the defense attorney, but prior to the 1970s, it was common for prosecutors to question a defendant's competence, because up until that time, defendants found incompetent were often confined in mental hospitals for excessive periods of time. (Sometimes such confinements were even longer than their sentences would have been had they stood trial and been convicted.) However, this practice was stopped, at least in theory, in 1972 when the U.S. Supreme Court decided the case of *Jackson v. Indiana*. This decision ordered that defendants who had been committed because they were incompetent to stand trial could not be held "more than a reasonable period of time necessary to determine whether there is a substantial probability that [they] will attain that capacity in the foreseeable future." As a result of this decision, the length of time a defendant who is found incompetent can be confined is now limited, although such limitations are often still exceeded.

Once the question of incompetence is raised, the judge will order an evaluation of the defendant if a "bona fide doubt" exists that the defendant is competent. Judges consider the circumstances of each case and the behavior of each defendant when making this determination. However, if the question of competence is raised, an examination will usually be conducted. Because it is relatively easy to obtain such evaluations, attorneys often seek them for reasons other than a determination of competence. Competence evaluations are used for several tactical reasons: to discover information about a possible insanity defense, to guarantee the temporary incarceration of a potentially dangerous person without going through the cumbersome procedures of involuntary civil commitment (see Chapter 9), to deny bail, and to delay the trial as one side tries to gain an advantage over the other (Berman & Osborne, 1987; Winick, 1996). Defense attorneys have questions about their clients' competence in up to 15% of felony cases (approximately twice the rate for defendants charged with misdemeanors); in many of these cases, however, the attorney does not seek a formal evaluation (Hoge et al., 1997; Poythress, Bonnie, Hoge, Monahan, & Oberlander, 1994).

Evaluating Competence

After a judge orders a competence examination, arrangements are made for the defendant to be evaluated by one or more mental health professionals. Although these evaluations were traditionally conducted in a special hospital or inpatient forensic facility, research suggests that most evaluations are now conducted in the community on an outpatient basis (Grisso, Cocozza, Steadman, Fisher, & Greer, 1994; Nicholson & Norwood, 2000). The transition from inpatient to outpatient facility has occurred because inpatient exams are more costly and require more time and because local, outpatient evaluations are usually sufficient (Winick, 1985, 1996).

Physicians, psychiatrists, psychologists, and social workers are authorized by most states to conduct competence examinations, but psychologists are the professional group responsible for the largest number of reports (Nicholson & Norwood, 2000). Some data suggest that nonmedical professionals with relevant forensic specialty knowledge prepare reports of trial competence evaluations that are equivalent, if not superior, to those prepared by physicians (Petrella & Poythress, 1983).

Prior to 1970, the usual evaluation of competence involved a standard psychiatric or psychological examination of a defendant and consisted of assessing current mental status, administering psychological tests, and taking a social history. If the examiner diagnosed a serious disorder such as schizophrenia or a paranoid state, or if the defendant was seriously mentally retarded, the expert would often conclude that the defendant was incompetent to stand trial. The problem with this approach was that it ignored the legal definition of competence as the capacity to understand and function as a defendant, and it often neglected crucial information that was available in existing records or could be obtained by interviewing third parties who had recently interacted with the defendant.

Under the current standard, the presence of mental illness or mental retardation does not guarantee that a defendant will be found incompetent to stand trial. The crucial question is whether the disorder impairs a defendant's ability to participate knowingly and meaningfully in the proceedings and to work with the defense attorney. A psychotic defendant might be competent to stand trial in a relatively straightforward case but incompetent to participate in a complex trial that would demand more skill and understanding. Consider the case of John Salvi, who, despite an apparent psychotic disorder, was found competent to stand trial and was convicted of murdering two people and wounding five others during a shooting spree at two Massachusetts medical clinics that performed abortions. Salvi later committed suicide in prison. In addition, just as we saw with Jamie Sullivan, his mental retardation did not substantially compromise his ability to understand the charges against him and the basic nature of his trial. Thus, he was found competent to stand trial. In contrast, Todd Hall was found incompetent to stand trial on charges that he murdered nine people after starting a fire in an Ohio fireworks store. Hall displayed serious cognitive impairments as a result of severe brain damage that occurred earlier in his life, which rendered him unable to meet the *Dusky* standard required for a finding of competent to stand trial.

Current competence evaluations focus on the defendant's present ability to function adequately in the legal process. This focus has been sharpened by the development of several structured tests or instruments specifically aimed at assessing competence to stand trial. Psychological testing remains a common ingredient in competence evaluations, and although clinicians have begun to use one or more of these specially designed competence assessment instruments in their practice, their use is not as widespread as it should be (Skeem, Golding, Cohn, & Berge, 1998). Examples of these instruments are described in the following paragraphs.

COMPETENCY SCREENING TEST (CST)

Developed by A. Louis McGarry, Paul Lipsitt, and their colleagues at the Harvard Laboratory of Community Psychiatry, the CST is a 22-item sentence completion task designed as an initial screening test for incompetence (Lipsitt, Lelos, & McGarry, 1971). Because the majority of defendants referred for competence evaluations are later determined to be competent (Nicholson & Kugler, 1991; Roesch & Golding, 1987), an instrument that can quickly identify those referred defendants who *are* competent is especially useful because it can save the time and expense of many unnecessary full evaluations.

In the CST, the defendant answers each of the 22 sentence stems, and each response is then scored as 2 (a competent answer), 1 (a questionably competent answer), or 0 (an incompetent answer). Total scores can range from 0 to 66; generally, a score of 20 or less suggests possible incompetence to stand trial.

Despite its widespread use, the CST has several weaknesses. First, the scoring of the sentence completions reflects what some observers (Roesch & Golding, 1987) suggest is a naively positive view of the legal process. For example, on the item "Jack felt that the judge . . . ," the answer "would be fair to him" would be scored 2, whereas a response of "would screw him over" would be scored 0. Yet some defendants have encountered judges for whom the second answer was more accurate than the first, so such a response should not be regarded as a sign of incompetence.

A second difficulty is that the CST produces a large number of false positives (defendants called incompetent who, with fuller evaluations, are judged to be competent). Although a false positive is less troubling than mistakenly forcing to trial a defendant who is incompetent (a false negative), too many false positives discredit the CST's claim to be an effective screening instrument. Finally, despite evidence for excellent interrater reliability and internal consistency (Lipsitt et al., 1971; Randolph, Hicks, & Mason, 1981, Melton et al., 1997), the high levels of agreement between raters appear to require extensive training and experience with the instrument.

COMPETENCY ASSESSMENT INSTRUMENT (CAI)

Also developed by the Harvard group as a more in-depth instrument for assessing competence, the CAI is a structured, one-hour interview that covers 13 functions relevant to competent functioning at trial (Laboratory for Community Psychiatry, 1974) including appraisal of available legal defenses, unmanageable behavior, quality of relating to attorney, and planning of legal strategy.

INTERDISCIPLINARY FITNESS INTERVIEW (IFI)

Golding and Roesch's IFI is a semistructured interview that evaluates a defendant's abilities in specific legal areas (five items). It also assesses 11 categories of psychopathological symptoms. Evaluators rate the weight they attached to each item in reaching their decision about competence. These weights vary depending on the nature of the defendant's case; for example, hallucinations might impair a defendant's ability to participate in some trials, but they would have minor effects in others and would therefore be given slight weight. The IFI is designed to be administered jointly by a mental health professional and an attorney, although it is probably administered by a mental health professional only in most cases. A related instrument, the *Fitness Interview Test* (FIT; Roesch, Zapf, Eaves, & Webster, 1998), is a 30-minute screening test and is the only instrument designed to assess competence as defined in Canadian law.

Golding, Roesch, and Schreiber (1984) found that interviewers using the IFI agreed on final judgments of competence in 75 of 77 cases evaluated. These judgments agreed 76% of the time with independent decisions about competence made later at a state hospital. Preliminary research on the FIT (e.g., Zapf & Roesch, 1997) suggests that it is a promising screening tool.

GEORGIA COURT COMPETENCY TEST (GCCT)

Consisting of 21 questions, the GCCT has been found to be a highly reliable instrument that taps three dimensions: general legal knowledge (e.g., the jobs of the judge, the lawyer, etc.), courtroom layout (e.g., where the judge or the jury is located in the courtroom), and specific legal knowledge (e.g., how to interact with defense counsel) (Bagby, Nicholson, Rogers, & Nussbaum, 1992). The GCCT does not do as good a job of measuring the less cognitive aspects of competence, such as defendants' ability to cooperate with counsel and assist in their own defense, but it shows significant correlations with a variety of independent criteria of competence (Nicholson, 1999).

THE MACARTHUR MEASURES OF COMPETENCE

Growing out of the concept of adjudicative competence, which describes several interrelated components that need to be considered in the evaluation of competence, the *MacArthur Structured Assessment of the Competence of Criminal Defendants* (MacSAC-CD; Hoge et al., 1997) is a highly regarded research instrument. Most of the 82 items in the MacSAC-CD rely on a hypothetical vignette about which the defendant is asked questions that tap foundational and decisional abilities. Defendants are asked the questions in a sequence: Open-ended questions come first; in the event of a wrong answer, correct information is provided to the defendant; defendants are then asked additional open-ended questions to determine whether they now have the necessary understanding based on this disclosure; a series of true–false questions concludes each area of assessment. This format has several advantages. It offers a more standardized evaluation across different defendants, and it is possible to assess separately defendants' preexisting abilities as well as their capacity to learn and apply new information.

One major disadvantage of the MacSAC-CD is that it was developed as a research instrument and takes about two hours to complete, far too long to be used in clinical practice. To overcome this limitation, a 22-item clinical version of this measure, called the *MacArthur Competence Assessment Tool—Criminal Adjudication* (MacCAT-CA) was developed (Poythress et al., 1999). This instrument begins with a hypothetical vignette about a crime, upon which the first 16 items are based. These items assess the defendant's general understanding of the legal system and adjudicative process and his or her reasoning abilities in legal situations. The remaining six items are specific to the defendant's own legal situation. This instrument has demonstrated satisfactory psychometric properties in a large-scale study that was funded by NIMH (Otto et al., 1998).

THE EVALUATION OF COMPETENCE TO STAND TRIAL–REVISED (ECST-R)

This tool is a semistructured interview that was developed using the *Dusky* criteria (Rogers, Tillbrook, & Sewell, 2004). It has three factors (factual understanding of proceedings, rational understanding of proceedings, and consultation with counsel) that have been empirically tested using a statistical technique known as confirmatory factor analysis. It focuses on case-specific information (unlike the MacCAT-CA, which uses a general vignette involving two individuals who fight in a bar), and it specifically addresses the question of whether a defendant being evaluated is trying to exaggerate or fake deficits that might make that person appear incompetent to stand trial.

Several additional specialized competence tests have been developed in the past decade and are finding their way into forensic practice. For example, the *Computer-Assisted Determination of Competence to Proceed* (CADCOMP; Barnard et al., 1991) is a 272-item instrument that uses interactive computer technology to simulate a competence assessment by a clinician. Studies of this instrument's reliability and validity suggest its potential value (e.g., Nicholson, Robertson, Johnson, & Jensen, 1988), but a number of questions still remain about several of this test's subscales. At present, most evaluators who use a specialized instrument rely on the CST, CAI, IFI, GCCT, or some local variation of one of them, or they utilize one of the newer tools such as the MacCAT-CA or the ECST-R. These different tests of competence show moderate agreement in how they classify defendants; in other words, a defendant classified as competent with one test is usually—but not always—similarly classified with another of the tests (Ustad, Rogers, Sewell, & Guarnaccia, 1996).

COMPETENCE ASSESSMENT FOR STANDING TRIAL FOR DEFENDANTS WITH MENTAL RETARDATION

This measure was developed specifically for assessing defendants with mild to moderate mental retardation (CAST-MR; Everington & Luckasson, 1992). Preliminary studies have indicated its potential usefulness, but it has not been employed with a large enough sample of mentally retarded defendants to assess its overall effectiveness (Nicholson, 1999).

One other issue being studied by forensic clinicians is the extent to which defendants can successfully fake incompetence on these tests. Some research suggests that although offenders can simulate incompetence, they often take such simulations to extremes, scoring much more poorly on competence tests than their truly incompetent counterparts (Gothard, Rogers, & Sewell, 1995; Gothard, Viglione, Meloy, & Sherman, 1995). Therefore, very low scores should make evaluators suspicious that a defendant might be exaggerating her or his deficiencies.

With estimates of malingering (faking or grossly exaggerating) mental illness in competence evaluations nearing 18% (Rogers, Salekin, Sewell, Goldstein, & Leonard, 1998), this issue has gained a great deal of attention. Therefore, screening tools have been developed to offer a more scientific method of detecting malingering in patients who are being evaluated for their competence to stand trial. One of these instruments is the Miller Forensic Assessment of Symptoms Test (M-FAST; Miller, 2001). The M-FAST is a brief, 25-item structured interview that is divided into seven subareas that have demonstrated accurate identification of individuals who are attempting to feign mental disorders (see Miller, 2004). Empirical evidence thus far supports the use of the M-FAST in detecting malingering (Jackson, Rogers, & Sewell, 2005), but it is a screening instrument and should be used in conjunction with a wider array of assessments to form a conclusive opinion about whether the defendant is actually malingering.

Following the collection of assessment data, evaluators communicate their findings to the judge. Often, a written report is submitted that summarizes the evidence on capacities related to competence to stand trial, as well as the likelihood of appropriate treatment being able to restore competence. In controversial or strongly contested cases, such as the Jamie Sullivan case described earlier in this chapter, it is more likely that there will be a formal competence hearing where the evaluating experts testify and are questioned by attorneys from both sides. The proper content of such testimony and written reports has been debated in the field. Some (Heilbrun, 2001; Melton, Petrila, Poythress, & Slobogin, 1997; Morse, 1978) believe that experts should restrict themselves to a description of the referral questions and the techniques used to answer these questions, followed by a thorough summary of the findings and a discussion of the defendant's mental difficulties and the possible consequences of these impairments. They recommend that the expert not offer an opinion on the ultimate question of whether the defendant is competent to stand trial, because it is the court's responsibility to make that legal decision. On the other hand, many judges require the expert to state just such a conclusion, believing, along with many mental health experts, that no one is better suited to make such a judgment than a qualified mental health professional (see Poythress, 1982; Rogers & Ewing, 1989).

In formal competence hearings, who bears the burden of proof? Do prosecutors have to prove that defendants are incompetent, or do defendants have to overcome a presumption of competence? In the 1992 case of *Medina v. California*, the U.S. Supreme Court held that a state can require a criminal defendant to shoulder the burden of proving that he or she is incompetent. But how stringent should that burden be? Most states established the criterion to be a "preponderance of the evidence," meaning that the defendant had to show that it was more likely than not that he or she was incompetent. But four states—Oklahoma, Pennsylvania, Connecticut, and Rhode Island— required a higher standard of proof that was "clear and convincing."

In 1996, in the case of *Cooper v. Oklahoma*, the Supreme Court held that this standard was too stringent. The Court reasoned that it could lead to situations in which a defendant proved that he or she was probably incompetent (using the lowest of the three burden-of-proof standards, "preponderance of the evidence") but failed to prove incompetence by the intermediate "clear and convincing evidence" standard and was therefore forced to proceed to disposition of charges. (The highest standard, "beyond a reasonable doubt," is applied when deciding a criminal defendant's guilt.) The Court thought that although the "clear and convincing" standard might prevent some instances of defendants faking their incompetence, the risks of forcing a certain number of incompetent defendants to trial were constitutionally unacceptable.

Results of Competence Evaluations

About 70% of the defendants referred for evaluation are ultimately found competent to stand trial (Nicholson & Kugler, 1991; Melton et al., 1997); when very rigorous examinations are conducted, the rate of defendants found competent approaches 90%. Judges seldom disagree with clinicians' decisions about competence (Steadman, 1979), and opposing attorneys often will **stipulate** (agree without further examination) to clinicians' findings (Melton et al., 1997). One study asked judges, prosecutors, and defense attorneys to rank in order of importance eight items typically offered by expert witnesses in competence evaluations (e.g., clinical diagnosis of the defendant, weighing different motives and explanations, providing an ultimate opinion on the legal issue) (Redding, Floyd, & Hawk, 2001). The results revealed that judges and prosecutors agreed that the expert's ultimate opinion on the legal issue was in the top three most important pieces of information the expert could provide. This suggests that mental health professionals exert great—perhaps excessive—influence on this legal decision.

What sort of person is most often judged to be incompetent? In his study of more than 500 defendants found incompetent to stand trial, Steadman (1979) described them as often "marginal" men who were undereducated and deficient in job skills, with long histories of involvement in both the legal and the mental health systems (see also Williams & Miller, 1981). Problems of substance abuse were common. Minorities were overrepresented. Others report relatively high percentages of psychosis,

lower intelligence, and more problems with certain aspects of memory among IST defendants (Nestor, Daggett, Haycock, & Price, 1999; Nicholson, Briggs, & Robertson, 1988; Roesch & Golding, 1980; Ustad et al., 1996). One other consistent finding is that IST defendants are charged with more serious crimes than defendants in general. After an extensive review of competence research, Nicholson and Kugler (1991) described the typical defendant found IST to (1) have a history of psychosis for which previous treatment had been received; (2) exhibit symptoms of current serious mental disorder; (3) be single, unemployed, and poorly educated; and (4) score poorly on specific competence assessment instruments.

If a defendant referred for a competence evaluation is found competent to stand trial, the legal process resumes, and the defendant again faces the possibility of trial or disposition of charges through plea bargaining. If the defendant is found IST, however, the picture becomes more complicated. For crimes that are not serious, the charges are occasionally dropped, sometimes in exchange for requiring the defendant to receive treatment. In other cases, however, the defendant is hospitalized to be treated for restoration of competence, which, if successful, will result in the defendant proceeding with disposition of charges. Outpatient treatment of incompetent defendants is used less often, even though it might often be justified.

How successful are efforts to restore defendants' competence? One study evaluated an experimental group treatment for a sample of incompetent defendants sent to one of three Philadelphia facilities (Siegel & Elwork, 1990). In addition to receiving the psychiatric medication, defendants assigned to these special treatment groups watched videotapes and received special instructions on courtroom procedures. They also discussed different ways of resolving problems that a defendant might face during a trial. A matched control group received treatment for their general psychiatric needs, but no specific treatment relevant to incompetence. Following their treatment, defendants participating in the special competence restoration group showed significant increases in their CAI scores compared to the controls. In addition, hospital staff judged 43% of the experimental subjects competent to stand trial after treatment compared to 15% of the control subjects. In general, most defendants have their adjudicative competence restored, usually with about six months of treatment (Melton et al., 1997).

The real dilemma for IST defendants occurs when treatment is not successful in restoring competence and holds little promise of success in the future. At this point, all options are problematic. Theoretically, the previously described *Jackson* ruling bars the indefinite confinement of an individual judged incompetent to stand trial. The law varies across states as to how long such involuntary hospitalization is allowed, but many states permit the defendant to be hospitalized for a period up to the maximum sentence that he or she could have received if convicted of the charges. When such defendants have been hospitalized for this period, however, they can be found "unrestorably incompetent" in a hearing held before the committing court.

Typically, unrestorably incompetent defendants are committed to a hospital through involuntary civil commitment proceedings (see Chapter 9). Standards for this type of commitment are narrower than for being found IST, however. The state must show that the person is mentally ill and either imminently dangerous to self or others or so gravely disabled as to be unable to care for himself or herself. Should an incompetent defendant not meet the criteria for a civil commitment, what happens? One possibility is that unrestorable incompetence might immunize this person from standing trial for future crimes. It appears that in response to this fear, and despite the ruling in the *Jackson* case, some states simply continue to confine incompetent defendants for indefinite periods. Although this "solution" might appease the public, we believe it jeopardizes defendants' due process rights and results in lengthy periods of punishment (disguised as treatment) without a conviction.

Several alternative procedures have been proposed to solve this catch-22, including proposals to abolish the IST concept altogether (Burt & Morris, 1972), to allow defendants to seek trial continuances without going through an elaborate evaluation, or to waive their right to be competent under certain circumstances (Fentiman, 1986; Winick, 1996). One additional proposal (American Bar Association, 1989) is that a provisional trial be held for a defendant who is likely to be found unrestorably incompetent. This hearing would decide the question of guilt or innocence. If the defendant is found not guilty, he or she is formally acquitted and can be further confined only through civil commitment. If proven guilty, the defendant would be subject to a special form of commitment that would recognize society's needs for secure handling of these persons.

Amnesia and Competence to Stand Trial

Are defendants with amnesia incompetent to stand trial? Not necessarily. Loss of memory might render a defendant incompetent, but the law does not presume that amnesia per se is incapacitating. Most courts believe this question should be answered on a case-by-case basis, with consideration given to the severity of the amnesia and the extent to which it interferes with preparation of a defense.

A leading decision in this area, *Wilson v. United States* (1968), lists six factors to be considered when deciding whether amnesia produces IST:

1. The extent to which the amnesia affected the defendant's ability to consult with and assist counsel.
2. The extent to which the amnesia affected the defendant's ability to testify at trial.
3. The extent to which evidence concerning the crime could be reconstructed by others.
4. The extent to which the prosecution assisted the defendant and counsel in that reconstruction.
5. The strength of the prosecution's case; if there is a substantial possibility that the accused could, but for the amnesia, establish an alibi or other defense, it should be presumed that she or he would have been able to do so.
6. Any other facts and circumstances that would indicate whether the defendant had a fair trial.

THE CASE OF

BOX 8.2 **Charles Sell: Involuntary medication to restore competence?**

Charles Sell, once a practicing dentist, suffered an extensive history of severe mental illness and several hospitalizations. He was accused of fraud after he allegedly submitted fictitious insurance claims for payment. His competence to stand trial was evaluated, and he was found competent and was released on bail. Subsequently, a grand jury indicted Sell on 13 additional counts of fraud and, later, attempted murder. During his bail revocation hearing, Sell's mental illness was markedly worse, and his behavior was "totally out of control" and included "spitting in the judge's face" (p. 2). His competence was again evaluated, at which time he was found incompetent to stand trial. He was hospitalized for treatment to help restore his competence to proceed. Hospital staff recommended antipsychotic medication, which Sell declined to take. The facility

chose to administer these medications to him involuntarily. Sell challenged this in court, arguing that involuntary medication violates the Fifth Amendment Constitutional right to "liberty to reject medical treatment" (p. 10). The lower court found that Sell was a danger to himself and others, that medication was the only way to render him less dangerous, that the benefits to Sell outweighed the risks, and that the drugs were substantially likely to return Sell to competence. The court further held that medication was the only viable hope of rendering Sell competent to stand trial and was necessary to serve the Government's interest in obtaining an adjudication of his guilt or innocence. Sell appealed and this case was granted *certiorari* by the United States Supreme Court.

At the heart of this case is the issue of whether it is a violation of a defendant's rights to be forcibly

medicated in order to become competent to proceed to trial, with the associated possibility of conviction and incarceration in prison. On the other hand, if the defendant cannot be restored to competence without medication, he or she may remain hospitalized, and thus also deprived of his or her liberty, for a period that may be longer than the prison sentence that could have been imposed upon conviction. In this decision, the Court weighed these considerations and outlined the conditions under which the government may forcibly administer psychotropic medication to render a mentally ill defendant competent to stand trial. The treatment must be (1) medically appropriate, (2) substantially unlikely to have side effects that may undermine the trial's fairness, and (3) necessary to significantly further important government trial-related interests.

Most judges are skeptical about claims of amnesia, believing that it can be easily faked. Consequently, claims of amnesia do not usually lead to a finding of incompetence, but they might result in the prosecution having to cooperate more with the defense attorney in reconstructing the facts and exploring possible defenses.

Competent with Medication, Incompetent Without

For most defendants found IST, psychoactive medication has been the treatment of choice because it is assumed to be the best intervention for restoring

defendants to competence in a reasonable period of time. Can incompetent defendants refuse this treatment? If medicated, will defendants be found competent to stand trial even though the medication, through its temporarily tranquilizing effects, might undercut a defense such as insanity? The case *Sell v. U.S.* (2003), concerns questions of competence and forced medication (Box 8.2).

Other Competence Issues

Because questions about competence can be raised at any point in the criminal process, several other competences are at issue in deciding whether a defendant can participate knowingly in different functions. Competence for any legal function involves (1) determining what functional abilities are necessary, (2) assessing the context where these abilities must be demonstrated, (3) evaluating the implication of any deficiencies in the required abilities, and (4) deciding whether the deficiencies warrant a conclusion that the defendant is incompetent (Grisso, 1986). Mental health professionals are asked, on occasion, to evaluate each of the following competences (see also Melton et al., 1997). Other questions about competencies arising in civil law are discussed in Chapter 9.

CAPACITIES TO WAIVE MIRANDA RIGHTS

One aspect of the waiver of *Miranda* rights requires that defendants, once in police custody, make a confession only after having waived these rights knowingly, intelligently, and voluntarily. A clinician's assessment of these abilities is challenging because, in most cases, the waiver and confession occur months before the professional's evaluation, requiring many assumptions about the defendant's psychological condition at the time.

Another aspect of a defendant's rights guaranteed by *Miranda* involves the Sixth Amendment right to be represented by counsel when he or she is in police custody. The same standard to waive this right—knowing, intelligent, and voluntary—is applied to the question of whether an individual had the capacity to waive the right to counsel before providing police with a confession.

A slightly different twist on the right to be represented by counsel involves the question of whether defendants can decide that they do not want a lawyer to represent them at trial. The Supreme Court has held that defendants have a constitutional right to waive counsel and represent themselves at trial, providing that this decision is made competently (*Faretta v. California*, 1975). Theoretically, the standard for this competence is the same as for competence to stand trial. In addition, the presiding judge must be convinced that the waiver of counsel is both voluntary (uncoerced) and intelligent (with understanding). Defendants do not have to convince the court that they possess a high level of legal knowledge, although some legal knowledge is probably important.

Competence to waive the right to counsel was at issue in the trial of Colin Ferguson, charged with murdering 6 passengers and wounding 19 more when he went on a killing rampage aboard a Long Island Railroad train in December 1993. Ferguson insisted on serving as his own attorney, after rejecting the "black rage" defense suggested by his two lawyers, Ron Kuby and the late William Kunstler. At first, Ferguson proved effective enough to have several of his objections to the prosecutor's case sustained. But then, giving new meaning to the old saying that a defendant who argues his own case has a fool for a client, Ferguson opened his case by claiming that, "There were 93 counts to that indictment, 93 counts only because it matches the year 1993. If it had been 1925, it would be a 25-count indictment." This was a prelude to Ferguson's attempt at cross-examining a series of eyewitnesses, who, in response to his preposterous suggestion that someone else had been the murderer, answered time after time to the effect that "No, I saw the murderer clearly. It was you."

COMPETENCE TO REFUSE THE INSANITY DEFENSE

In cases in which it is likely that the defendant was insane at the time of the offense, can the defendant refuse to plead insanity? If there is evidence that a defendant was not mentally responsible for criminal acts, do courts have a duty to require that the defendant plead insanity when the defendant does not want to do so? Courts are divided on this question. In some cases, they have suggested that society's stake in punishing only mentally responsible persons requires the imposition of an insanity plea even on unwilling defendants (*Whalen v. United States*, 1965). Other decisions (*Frendak v. United States*, 1979) use the framework of competence to answer this question—if the defendant understands the alternative pleas available and the consequences of those pleas, the defendant should be permitted to reject an insanity plea. This latter approach, which is followed in most courts, recognizes that an acquittal on grounds of insanity is not always a "better" outcome for a defendant than a conviction and criminal sentence.

This question was at the heart of the prosecution of Theodore Kaczynski for his two-decade-long "Unabomber" attacks. Although the consensus of several experts was that Kaczynski suffered from paranoid schizophrenia, he adamantly refused to let his attorneys use an insanity or diminished-capacity defense, arguing that he did not want to be stigmatized, in his words, as a "sickie." Was Kaczynski competent to make this decision, or was Judge Garland E. Burrell, Jr. correct in ruling that Kaczynski's lawyers could control his defense, even over the defendant's persistent objections? It is doubtful that either an insanity or a diminished-capacity defense would have been successful—Kaczynski's own diary proved that he understood and intended to commit his crimes—but we will never know for sure. Ultimately, to avoid the possibility of the death penalty, Kaczynski pled guilty to murder and was sentenced to life in prison.

COMPETENCE TO BE SENTENCED

For legal and humanitarian reasons, convicted defendants are not to be sentenced to punishment unless they are competent. In general, the standard for this competence is that the defendant can understand the punishment and the reasons why it is being imposed. Competence to be sentenced is often a more straightforward question for the clinician to evaluate than adjudicative competence, which involves issues of whether the accused can interact effectively with counsel and appreciate alternative courses of action.

COMPETENCE TO BE EXECUTED

A particularly controversial and related aspect of this area is determining whether a defendant is competent to be executed. The U.S. Supreme Court decided, in the case of *Ford v. Wainwright* (1986), that the Eighth Amendment ban against cruel and unusual punishments prohibits the execution of defendants while they are incompetent. Therefore, mental health professionals are at times called on to evaluate inmates waiting to be executed to determine whether they are competent to be put to death. The practical problems and ethical dilemmas involved in these evaluations are enormous (Heilbrun, 1987; Heilbrun & McClaren, 1988; Mossman, 1987; Susman, 1992) and have led some psychologists to recommend that clinicians not perform such evaluations.

The Insanity Defense

The issue of insanity intensifies each of the dilemmas of Chapter 1. Any society that respects the rights of individuals recognizes the possibility that some of its citizens cannot comprehend the consequences or the wrongfulness of their actions. Yet the highly publicized "success" of defendants who claimed insanity as an explanation for their actions (e.g., John Hinckley) has caused lawmakers to introduce new legislation intended to make it more difficult for jurors to acquit defendants by reason of insanity.

The quest for equality is also threatened by great discretion in how the insanity defense is used. It is much harder to find a defendant not guilty by reason of insanity in some states than in others because of differing definitions of insanity held by different jurisdictions. Four states (Idaho, Kansas, Montana, and Utah) have abolished the insanity defense (Bard, 2005), even though they do allow defendants to introduce evidence about their mental condition at the time of an offense. In addition, the federal government has revised its definition of the insanity standard three times since 1950.

Likewise, truth is an ideal that is very hard to implement when a defendant uses insanity as an explanation for his or her actions. The jury or judge must answer the question "Why did he fire the gun?" rather than "Did he fire the gun?" How can we determine whether a defendant is truly insane? Can we know a person's state of mind when he or she committed an antisocial act? The task of truth finding becomes even more formidable when we acknowledge that the fact finders—juries and judges—must determine not whether the person is currently insane but, rather, whether he or she was insane at the time of the crime, possibly months or years before.

" *Paying my fee will also help as evidence for our insanity defense.* "

Reprinted by permission of Artizans

This problem is further complicated by the fact that there are far fewer instruments specifically designed to assess insanity than to assess competence. One brief screening instrument—the Mental Status Examination at the Time of the Offense (Slobogin, Melton, & Showalter, 1984)— has been developed, but research on its reliability and validity is limited to one study. More research has been conducted on the Rogers Criminal Responsibility Scales (RCRAS; Rogers, 1986), a set of 25 scales that organize the many factors and points of decision that clinicians need to consider when assessing criminal responsibility. Although the RCRAS has clear limitations, it is the only formal instrument with some proven reliability and validity for guiding clinicians' decision-making process in insanity evaluations (Nicholson, 1999).

Another reason why truth is so elusive in cases of alleged insanity stems from the conflict between law and behavioral sciences as alternative pathways to knowledge. Insanity is a legal concept, not a medical or psychological one. In many states, a defendant could be hallucinating, delusional, and diagnosed as schizophrenic, but if the individual knew the difference between right and wrong, he or she would be legally sane. Thus, psychiatrists and clinical psychologists are called on as forensic experts to provide information regarding a decision that is ultimately outside their professional/ scientific framework. The therapeutic goals of psychiatry and clinical psychology—diagnosis and assessment that are probabilistic and complex— compete with the legal system's demand for a straightforward "yes or no" answer (Heilbrun, 2001). Furthermore, although psychiatrists and other mental health experts can give names to disorders, the diagnostic label is less important than the specific symptoms and their impact on the functional legal demands associated with the insanity standard (whether the defendant "knew" the behavior was wrong; in some states, additionally, whether the defendant could conform his or her conduct to the requirements of the law).

Some mental health professionals even argue that the law and the behavioral sciences are incompatible (Winslade & Ross, 1983). Certainly they hold competing assumptions on the important question of personal responsibility for one's behavior. The law assumes that we are free agents (with a few exceptions) and that when we act illegally, we should be punished. The behavioral sciences assume that behavior is caused both by conditions within the person and by the environment acting on the person. Under the latter assumption, the concept of "responsibility" and the associated justification for punishment are both diluted.

Rationale for the Insanity Defense

Why do we have laws about insanity at all? Wouldn't it be simpler to do away with insanity in the legal system? Allowing a criminal defendant to plead not guilty by reason of **insanity** reflects a fundamental belief that a civilized society should not punish people who do not know what they are doing or are incapable of controlling their conduct. Thus, on occasion, the state must tell the victim's friends and family that even though it abhors the defendant's acts, some offenders do not deserve punishment. Before it can do that, however, a judgment about whether such persons were responsible for their actions must be made.

As we have already discussed, in many cases in which an insanity defense is used, a decision about a defendant's competence to stand trial must be reached first. If the defendant is declared incompetent to stand trial, there is a delay in the disposition of charges until the defendant is found competent to proceed. Therefore, a judgment that a defendant is not competent does not relieve the

individual of responsibility for an illegal act; it only delays the determination of whether the individual is guilty. Furthermore, *competence* refers exclusively to the defendant's relevant legal capacities at the time of the proceeding, whereas *insanity* refers to the defendant's mental state at the time the offense was committed.

In the 1700s, the law defined insanity using phrases such as "did not know what he did" and "[did not know more] than an infant, than a brute, or a wild beast." By the 1800s, "knowing the difference between right and wrong" was the predominant legal definition. At that time, it was assumed that judges and juries could decide whether a defendant was insane without the help of professional witnesses. But the more we learn about psychological disorders, the more difficult we find the task to be.

What is the legal standard for insanity? There is no single answer. The following sections describe several definitions currently in use. The legal standards that define criminal responsibility vary from state to state, but in all states, the defendant is initially presumed to be responsible for his or her alleged act. Therefore, if pleading insanity, defendants have the duty to present evidence that would disprove the presumption of criminal responsibility in their case—a requirement known as an **affirmative defense**. A related legal issue is the assessment of ***mens rea***, or the mental state of knowing the nature and quality of a forbidden act. To be a criminal offense, an act not only must be illegal but also must be accompanied by the necessary *mens rea*, or guilty mind.

The M'Naghten Rule: An Early Attempt to Define Insanity

In 1843, an Englishman named Daniel M'Naghten shot and killed the private secretary of the British prime minister. Plagued by paranoid delusions, M'Naghten believed that the prime minister, Sir Robert Peel, was part of a conspiracy hatched by the Tory party against him. At first, M'Naghten sought to escape his imagined tormentors by traveling through Europe. When that didn't work, he stalked the prime minister and, after waiting in front of the prime minister's residence at No. 10 Downing Street, shot the man he thought was Peel.

M'Naghten was charged with murder, and his defense was to plead not guilty by reason of insanity. Nine medical experts, including the American psychiatrist Isaac Ray, testified for two days about his mental state, and all agreed that he was insane. On instructions from the lord chief justice, the jury brought down a verdict of not guilty by reason of insanity, without even leaving the jury box to deliberate. M'Naghten was committed to the Broadmoor asylum for the insane, where he remained for the rest of his life.

The public was infuriated, as was Queen Victoria, who had been the target of several attempts on her life. She demanded a tougher test of insanity. Subsequent debate in the House of Lords led to five questions, presented to 15 high court judges. Their replies constitute what has come to be called the **M'Naghten rule**, which was announced in 1843, long before psychiatry became a household word. The M'Naghten rule defines insanity as follows:

> The jury ought to be told in all cases that every man is to be presumed to be sane, and to possess a sufficient degree of reason to be responsible for his crimes, until the contrary be proved to their satisfaction; and that to establish a defense on the grounds of insanity it must be clearly proved that, at the time of committing the act, the accused was laboring under such a defect of reason, from disease of the mind, as not to know the nature and quality of the act he was doing, or, if he did know it, that he did not know what he was doing was wrong. (quoted in Post, 1963, p. 113)

The M'Naghten rule, which became the standard for defining insanity in Great Britain and the United States, thus "excuses" criminal conduct if the defendant, as a result of a "disease of the mind": (1) did not know what he was doing (e.g., believed he was shooting an animal rather than a human) or (2) did not know that what he was doing was wrong (e.g., believed killing unarmed strangers was "right"). In some jurisdictions, an *irresistible*

impulse test was added to try to deal with individuals who might have known that an act was wrong but lacked the capacity to avoid performing it. However, it has proved very difficult to distinguish between an irresistible impulse and an impulse that simply is not resisted. The American Psychiatric Association describes the line between an irresistible impulse and an impulse not resisted as "no sharper than that between twilight and dusk" (APA, 1982). One proposed solution is known as the "police at the elbow test": Was the impulse so overwhelming that the individual would have committed the crime even if a police officer had been standing at his or her elbow, thereby ensuring that he or she would be caught? Neither legal experts nor forensic clinicians are satisfied with the concept, and it is now used rarely.

Although the M'Naghten rule (or a close variation) is used in half the states (Bard, 2005), it has often been criticized by mental health professionals, who contend that the definition is too restrictive and that the relevant issue is more a motivational question of being able to control wrongful actions than a cognitive one of distinguishing right from wrong. Thus, modifications were inevitable.

The Brawner Rule, Stemming from the Model Penal Code

In 1954, in *Durham v. United States*, Judge David Bazelon wrote an opinion that established a new standard of insanity. It held that a defendant can be found insane, and thus not criminally responsible, if his criminal act was the product of mental disease or mental defect. However, this standard was soon found to be unworkable, because it allowed a wide range of problems (including personality disorders, which certainly influence behavior but do not profoundly alter it) to serve as the basis for an insanity defense. Only one state, New Hampshire, currently retains this standard for insanity.

In response to problems with the Durham rule, a committee of legal scholars sponsored by the American Law Institute (ALI) developed the Model Penal Code, which led to what is now called the

Brawner rule (or ALI rule). This rule states that a defendant is not responsible for criminal conduct if he, "at the time of such conduct as a result of mental disease or defect, [lacks] substantial capacity either to appreciate the criminality [wrongfulness] of his conduct or to conform his conduct to the requirements of the law." This standard, or a variation, allows judges and juries to consider whether mentally ill defendants have the capacity to understand the nature of their acts or to behave in a lawful way. It is used in about 20 states plus the District of Columbia (Reisner, Slobogin, & Rai, 1999). Federal courts have also adopted the ALI rule in a drastically altered form (which we will describe later). It may be the best solution yet, because the key concepts are general enough to allow the jury some latitude and yet solid enough to provide ground for the testimony of expert witnesses. It differs from the M'Naghten rule in three substantial respects. First, by using the term *appreciate*, it incorporates the emotional as well as the cognitive determinants of criminal actions. Second, it does not require that offenders exhibit a total lack of appreciation for the nature of their conduct, but only a lack of "substantial capacity." Finally, it includes both a cognitive element and a volitional element, making defendants' inability to control their actions a sufficient criterion by itself for insanity.

THE INSANITY DEFENSE REFORM ACT

In the wake of the trial of John Hinckley, Jr., who attempted to assassinate President Ronald Reagan, the U.S. Congress enacted the Insanity Defense Reform Act (IDRA) in 1984. The law modified the existing insanity defense (eliminating the "volitional" prong and retaining the "cognitive" prong), with the expectation that fewer defendants would be able to use it successfully. The law did not abolish the insanity defense. However, it changed it substantially. In addition to eliminating the volitional prong, it also changed the insanity defense process as follows:

1. It prohibited experts from giving ultimate opinions about insanity. The rule states, "[N]o expert witness testifying with respect to the mental state or condition of a defendant in a criminal case may state an opinion or inference as to whether the defendant did or did not have the mental state or condition constituting an element of the crime charged or of a defense thereto. Such ultimate issues are matters for the trier of fact alone." Although this prohibition may have little effect on jurors, reformers believed it would prevent expert witnesses from usurping the province of the jury.

2. It placed on the defendant the burden to prove insanity by clear and convincing evidence, replacing the previous requirement that the prosecution prove a defendant's sanity beyond a reasonable doubt.

What little research has been conducted on the Insanity Defense Reform Act suggests that it does not accomplish either what its proponents envisioned or what its critics feared. At least in mock jury studies, verdicts do not significantly differ regardless of whether the jurors have heard IDRA instructions, ALI (Brawner) instructions, or no instructions (Finkel, 1989).

EMPIRICAL RESEARCH RELEVANT TO THE INSANITY DEFENSE

In theory, varying rules for insanity should influence jurors to reach different verdicts, but psychologists have questioned whether the typical juror can comprehend the legal language of these definitions and then apply them as intended by the courts. (Further evaluation of the effectiveness of the judge's instructions to the jury can be found in Chapter 9.) Elwork, Sales, and Suggs (1981) found jurors only 51% correct on a series of questions testing their comprehension of instructions regarding the M'Naghten rule. Arens, Granfield, and Susman (1965) and Ogloff (1991) obtained similar results: Regardless of what insanity rule was used, college students showed very low rates of accurate recall and comprehension of crucial components in various insanity definitions.

The limited empirical evidence indicates that different standards of insanity make little difference in verdicts. Simon (1967) presented mock juries with re-creations of two actual trials in which the insanity defense had been used; in one the charge was housebreaking, in the other incest. A third of the juries received the M'Naghten rule, a third the Durham rule, and a third no instructions about how to define insanity (although they knew the defendant was using this as his defense). In both trials, jurors operating with the M'Naghten rule were less likely to vote for acquittal (although the differences between conditions were not large). The Durham rule seemed to produce verdicts more in keeping with the jurors' "natural sense of equity," as reflected in their judgments without any instructions at all. Interestingly, at least half of the uninstructed and Durham juries brought up the defendant's ability to distinguish between right and wrong—the M'Naghten standard—during their deliberations. This latter finding suggests that although instructions have some effect on jury decision making in insanity cases, they tell only part of the story—and perhaps a minor part at that (Finkel, 1989, 1991; Finkel & Slobogin, 1995; Ogloff, 1991; Roberts & Golding, 1991; Roberts, Golding, & Fincham, 1987).

Probably more important than formal instructions are jurors' own views, or schemata, through which they interpret and filter the evidence and then reach verdicts that are compatible with their own personal sense of justice. This decision process is yet another example of how jurors are prone to interpret "facts" in the context of a personal story or narrative that "makes the most sense" to each of them subjectively. Differences among jurors in the individual narratives they weave about the same set of trial "facts" may be related, in turn, to the different attitudes they hold about the morality of the insanity defense and the punishment of mentally ill offenders (Roberts & Golding, 1991). For instance, one study found that jurors conceptualized the prototypical insanity defendant in one of three ways: (1) severely mentally disordered (SMD), characterized by extreme, chronic, uncontrollable mental illness and retardation that impaired the defendant's ability to function in society; (2) morally insane (MI), typified by symptoms of psychosis and psychopathy, a categorization used to represent a malevolent, detached, and unpredictably violent offender; and (3) mental-state-centered (MSC), descriptions of a defendant who suffered from varied, but clearly supported, impairments in his mental state at the time of his offense (Skeem & Golding, 2001). The MSC group emphasized the most legally relevant characteristics for a defendant pleading insanity. Findings revealed that jurors who held SMD- or MI-like prototypes made up the vast majority of the sample (79%), and they tended to believe that the insanity defense was frequently raised, was easily abused, and jeopardized public safety. By contrast, those jurors who held MSC-like prototypes (21%) were less likely to perceive the insanity defense as unjust and tended to believe that the constitutional rights ascribed to defendants were necessary components of the legal process.

In general, it appears that jurors are more likely to find a defendant not guilty by reason of insanity when they (1) believe the defendant is seriously mentally ill, to the point of lacking the capacity to plan and control his or her behavior; (2) hear expert testimony, uncontested by a prosecution expert, about the defendant's mental illness; and (3) find no logical or evil motive for the defendant's actions (see, for example, Bailis, Darley, Waxman, & Robinson, 1995). In addition, jurors are flexible in how they use such personal constructs, emphasizing different variables in different cases rather than seeing all insanity cases in the same way. As an example, jurors appear more likely to believe that defendants are insane if they hear evidence that an offense was committed in a particularly unusual or bizarre manner (Pickel, 1998).

Famous Trials and the Use of the Insanity Plea

Is the insanity plea a frequent problem in the American criminal justice system? Are many defendants getting off without punishment by using it?

One reason for the congressional action to alter the federal standard was the public perception, generated largely by the verdict in John Hinckley's trial, that too many criminals were escaping punishment through this defense. Several surveys have concluded that most U.S. citizens view the insanity defense as a legal loophole through which many guilty people escape conviction (Skeem & Golding, 2001; Bower, 1984; Hans & Slater, 1983). One study explored the effects of jury instruction on the verdict (Wheatman & Shaffer, 2001). Results revealed that instruction mediated the verdict outcome; juries who were instructed about the implications of rendering an insanity verdict (i.e., the defendant would not be released but, rather, would be sent to a psychiatric hospital for treatment) were more likely to render such a verdict than uninstructed juries, because those who were not instructed believed that a defendant acquitted by reason of insanity would be free to return to the community and to engage in criminal behavior again. Before reporting on the actual frequency and effectiveness of attempts to use the plea, we review the results of several highly publicized trials that have molded public opinion about insanity pleas.

JEFFREY DAHMER

TRIALS IN WHICH THE INSANITY PLEA FAILED.

Among murder defendants who have pleaded insanity as a defense were Jack Ruby, whom millions saw kill Lee Harvey Oswald, President John F. Kennedy's alleged assassin, on television; Sirhan Sirhan, charged with the assassination of Robert F. Kennedy; John Wayne Gacy, who was convicted of killing 33 boys in Chicago; and Andrea Yates, charged with drowning her children in the bathtub. All these defendants were convicted of murder despite their pleas of insanity.

In the sensational case of Jeffrey Dahmer (described in Chapter 3), jurors rejected a plea of insanity as a defense against murder charges. Dahmer admitted killing and dismembering 15 young men over about a ten-year period, but his attorney, Gerald Boyle, argued that Dahmer was insane at the time: "This is not an evil man, this is a sick man." Prosecutor Michael McCann disagreed, arguing that Dahmer "knew at all times that what he was doing was wrong." After listening to two weeks of evidence and expert testimony about Dahmer's mental condition, the jury ruled, by a 10–2 margin, that Jeffrey Dahmer was sane. He was subsequently sentenced to life in prison for his crimes, only to be beaten to death in prison by a fellow inmate.

Wisconsin defines insanity with the ALI rule; consequently, to have found Dahmer insane, the jury would have had to conclude that he suffered a mental disorder or defect that made him unable either to appreciate the wrongfulness of his conduct or to control his conduct as required by the law. The jury rejected both conclusions, perhaps because of evidence that Dahmer was careful to kill his victims in a manner that minimized his chances of being caught. This cautiousness suggested that he appreciated the wrongfulness of his behavior *and* could control it when it was opportune to do so.

In the case of Herbert Mullin, there seemed to be a basis for an acquittal on the ground of insanity, but the jury convicted him nonetheless (Lunde & Morgan, 1980). Between October 1972 and February 1973, Mullin killed 13 persons around the area of Santa Cruz, California. There was no apparent pattern among the victims: a derelict, a hitchhiking young woman, a priest in a church, four teenaged campers, a family. Mullin reported hearing voices. For example, on the day he was caught, before delivering a load of wood to his parents, he was "instructed" to kill a man he had never seen before.

Mullin also had a history of hospitalizations (one in 1969, another in 1970) and diagnoses of schizophrenia. A psychologist, David Marlowe, had administered the Minnesota Multiphasic Personality Inventory and found that Mullin scored at very high levels on six out of ten clinical scales, suggesting a severe mental disorder. Marlowe concluded that Mullin suffered a "schizophrenic reaction, paranoid type." But at Mullin's trial, a psychiatrist, Joel Fort, testified for the prosecution that Mullin was legally sane at the time of the killings. Fort stated, "He knew the nature and quality of his actions and did specifically know that they were wrong" (quoted in Lunde & Morgan, 1980).

On the third day of deliberations, the jury found Mullin guilty of two counts of first-degree murder and eight counts of second-degree murder. The judge sentenced him to concurrent life terms for the first-degree murders and imposed consecutive sentences of five years to life for the eight second-degree murder convictions. He will be eligible for parole in the year 2020.

Another defendant who claimed insanity was Richard Herrin, the Yale graduate who brutally murdered his college sweetheart, Bonnie Garland, by splitting her head open with a hammer as she slept at her parents' home. Herrin claimed a "transient situational reaction," which his psychiatrist said was so different from his otherwise normal personality that the jury should not hold him responsible for murder (Gaylin, 1982). Although the jury rejected his plea, it found him guilty of manslaughter, not of murder—a verdict that left people on both sides frustrated with the outcome (Meyer, 1982).

Richard Herrin's trial points up a key dilemma of the insanity defense. Herrin was a good person—modest, tolerant, and good humored. He had risen above his illegitimate birth and his upbringing in an East Los Angeles barrio to graduate from Yale University. When Bonnie Garland, his sweetheart for almost three years, told him that she wanted to date other men, he suddenly decided to kill her and then commit suicide. Afterward, he could describe the act with amazing precision, but he reported experiencing no emotion while committing it and no understanding of why he had done it.

To many people, Herrin's behavior was incomprehensible; "he must have been crazy" was their gut reaction to the bludgeoning. Some kind of psychiatric explanation for this type of behavior is almost inevitable. But in succumbing to the temptation always to define extreme behavior in psychological terms, we lose sight of the jury's legal responsibility to assess criminality and provide justice (Robinson, 1982). Thousands of seriously mentally ill people live disoriented and disrupted lives, but they never murder anyone. Yet, when we think of their behavior exclusively in psychological terms, we are tempted to sympathize and perhaps overlook the fact that psychological problems do not usually rob individuals of responsibility for their actions.

Several other famous defendants who might have attempted to escape conviction through use of the insanity plea did not do so. Among these are Son of Sam serial murderer David Berkowitz, cult leader Charles Manson, and Mark David Chapman, who killed John Lennon.

TRIALS IN WHICH THE INSANITY PLEA "SUCCEEDED"

Occasionally, when a judge or jury concludes that the defendant is not guilty by reason of insanity, the defendant spends only a short period of time in a treatment program. After being acquitted on charges of malicious wounding (for cutting off her husband's penis), Lorena Bobbitt was released from the mental hospital following only several weeks of evaluation to determine whether she met criteria for involuntary hospitalization as not guilty by reason of insanity (she did not).

But sometimes when the insanity plea "works," the defendant spends more time in an institution than he or she would have spent in prison if found guilty. In fact, this outcome has led defense attorneys to request that judges be required to instruct jurors that if the defendant is found not guilty by reason of insanity, he or she will probably be committed to a mental hospital (Whittemore & Ogloff, 1995). The Supreme Court, however, has refused to require such an instruction (*Shannon v. United States*, 1994).

Ed Gein, another serial killer from Wisconsin, was acquitted by reason of insanity on multiple charges involving the mutilation, skinning, and murder of at least two women in the 1950s around Plainfield, Wisconsin. Gein admitted to other atrocious crimes, including robbing bodies from graves; he later made the corpse parts into ornaments and clothes that he wore to re-create the image of his dead mother. Gein, who was the real-life inspiration for several Hollywood films (including *Psycho* and *Silence of the Lambs*), was committed to a state psychiatric hospital, where he remained until his death in 1984.

The case of John W. Hinckley, Jr. has had the greatest single influence, perhaps, of all those discussed in this chapter, triggering much of the court reform and legislative revision regarding the insanity plea since 1982. Television replays show his March 30, 1981, attempt to kill President Ronald Reagan. When Hinckley came to trial 15 months later, his lawyers didn't dispute the evidence that he had planned the attack, bought special bullets, tracked the president, and fired from a shooter's crouch. But he couldn't help it, they claimed; he was only responding to the driving forces of a diseased mind. (Box 8.3 summarizes the key points of the defense's case.) Dr. William Carpenter, one of the defense psychiatrists, testified that Hinckley did not "appreciate" what he was doing; he had lost the ability to control himself.

Even though the Hinckley case is one in which the insanity defense was successful in the narrow sense of the word, that outcome was largely a result of a decision by the presiding judge regarding the burden of proof. Judge Barrington Parker instructed the jury in accordance with then-existing federal law, which required the prosecution to prove the defendant sane beyond a reasonable doubt, rather than with the law of the District of Columbia (which has its own penal code), which would have placed on the defendant the burden of proving his insanity. After listening to two months of testimony, the Hinckley jury deliberated for four days before finding the defendant not guilty by reason of insanity. Afterward, several jurors said that, given the instruction that it was up to the government prosecutors to prove Hinckley sane, the evidence was too conflicting for them to agree. They thought his travel meanderings raised a question about his sanity, and both sides' expert psychiatric witnesses had testified that he suffered from some form of mental disorder.

What types of defendants use the insanity plea successfully? The public tends to assume that such people are of three types: "mad killers" who attack victims without provocation; "crafty cons" who fake symptoms to escape conviction; or "desperate defendants," aware of the strength of the evidence against them, who use the insanity defense as a last resort (Sales & Hafemeister, 1984). The empirical data do not support these assumptions. The insanity defense is not used only for murder or attempted murder charges, as assumed (Pasewark & Pantle, 1981); one study noted that in Oregon and Missouri, only one of ten such pleas was for the crime of murder (Sales & Hafemeister, 1984).

Usually, the charges do involve violent felonies, however. In the largest study to date of insanity acquittees, data from NGRI acquittees from four states ($N = 1099$) were obtained (Steadman et al., 1993). These investigators found that 22.5% of the insanity acquittees had been charged with murder and that a total of 64% had been charged with crimes against persons (murder, rape, robbery, or aggravated assault).

The "crafty con" charge is also questionable. Available research consistently suggests that the majority of defendants found not guilty by reason of insanity (NGRI) have been diagnosed as psychotic,

THE CASE OF

BOX 8.3 **John W. Hinckley, Jr. and the attempted assassination of President Reagan**

The defense in John Hinckley's trial made several claims:

1. Hinckley's actions had reflected his pathological obsession with the movie *Taxi Driver*, in which Jodie Foster starred as a 12-year-old prostitute. The title character, Travis Bickle, is a loner who befriends Foster after he is rejected by the character played by Cybill Shepherd; he stalks a political candidate but eventually engages in a bloody shootout to rescue the Foster character. It was reported that Hinckley had seen the movie 15 times and that he so identified with the hero that he had been driven to reenact the fictional events in his own life (Winslade & Ross, 1983).

2. Although there appeared to be planning on Hinckley's part, it was really the movie script that provided the planning force. The defense argued, "A mind that is so influenced by the outside world is a mind out of control and beyond responsibility" (Winslade & Ross, 1983, p. 188).

3. The defense tried to introduce the results of a CAT scan—an X ray of Hinckley's brain using computerized axial tomography—to support its contention that he was schizophrenic. The admissibility of this evidence became a controversy at the trial. The prosecution objected, claiming that all the apparent scientific rigor of this procedure—the physical evidence, the numerical responses—would cause the jury to place undue importance on it. The prosecution also contended that there are no grounds for

Attempted presidential assassin John Hinckley

concluding that the presence of abnormal brain tissue necessarily denotes schizophrenia. Initially, the judge rejected the request to admit this testimony, but he later reversed the decision on the ground that it might be relevant.

suggesting severe and probably chronic mental impairments (Melton et al., 1997). Steadman and colleagues (1993) reported that 67.4% of the insanity acquittees described in their study were diagnosed with a schizophrenic disorder and that another 14.9% were diagnosed with another major mental illness. Insanity acquittees also do not appear to be especially "crafty"; in fact, one study revealed that defendants who were found NGRI had significantly lower IQ scores than men who pleaded insanity but were convicted (Boehnert, 1989).

Another approach to the "crafty con" question is to study how often criminal defendants being

assessed for insanity try to fake a mental disorder. On the basis of his research, Rogers (1986, 1988) estimates that about one of four or five defendants being assessed for insanity engages in at least moderate malingering of mental disorders. This figure suggests that crafty conning is not rampant but is frequent enough to cause concern. As a result, psychologists have developed a number of assessment methods to detect persons who are trying to fake a mental disorder. These methods include special structured interviews (Rogers, Gillis, Dickens, & Bagby, 1991), individual psychological tests (Wetter, Baer, Berry, Smith, & Larsen, 1992), and batteries of different tests (Schretlen, Wilkins, Van Gorp, & Bobholz, 1992).

In several laboratory studies, these techniques have shown promising results in distinguishing between subjects who were trying to simulate mental illness (to win monetary incentives for being the "best" fakers) and those who were reporting symptoms truthfully. In a careful study that was limited to the court records of a single county, Steadman, Keitner, Braff, and Arvanites (1983) were able to compare defendants who were successful and those who were unsuccessful in their pleas of insanity. The factor most strongly associated with success was the outcome of a court-authorized mental examination conducted before the trial. When the conclusion of this evaluation was that the defendant was insane, in 83% of cases the charges were dismissed or the defendant was later found at a trial to be not guilty by reason of insanity. If the mental examination concluded that the offender was sane in only 2% of the trials, did the insanity defense "work"? In their larger, four-state study, Steadman et al. (1993) observed that the decision to acquit by reason of insanity was most strongly influenced by clinical factors. They compared those who successfully employed the insanity defense with others who entered this plea but were nevertheless found guilty, and they reported that 82.3% of the former group but only 37.8% of the latter group had been diagnosed with a major mental illness.

On the basis of research studies, we are beginning to replace misconceptions about defendants found NGRI (not guilty by reason of insanity) with more accurate portrayals of these defendants. The following research can help us understand more about insanity acquittees:

1. Most NGRI defendants have a record of prior arrests or convictions, but this rate of previous criminality does not exceed that of other felons (Boehnert, 1989; Cohen, Spodak, Silver, & Williams, 1988).
2. Most NGRI defendants come from lower socioeconomic backgrounds (Nicholson, Norwood, & Enyart, 1991).
3. Most NGRI defendants have a prior history of psychiatric hospitalizations and have been diagnosed with serious forms of mental illness, usually psychoses (Nicholson et al., 1991; Steadman et al., 1993).
4. Most NGRI defendants have previously been found incompetent to stand trial (Boehnert, 1989).
5. Although most studies have concentrated on males, female defendants found NGRI have socioeconomic, psychiatric, and criminal backgrounds similar to those of their male NGRI counterparts (Heilbrun, Heilbrun, & Griffin, 1988).

Facts about the Insanity Plea

The American public has repeatedly expressed its dissatisfaction with the insanity defense. After John Hinckley was found NGRI for the shooting of President Reagan and four other men in 1982, a public opinion poll conducted by ABC News showed that 67% of Americans believed that justice had not been done in the case; 90% thought Hinckley should be confined for life, but 78% believed he would eventually be released back into society.

The public's disapproval of the insanity defense appears to be stimulated by trials such as Hinckley's that receive massive publicity. Melton et al. (1997) report the following four beliefs to be prevalent among the public: (1) A large number of criminal defendants use the insanity defense. (2) Most of those defendants who use the insanity defense are acquitted by juries who are too gullible about it. (3) Those defendants found NGRI are released back into society shortly after their NGRI acquittals. (4) Persons found insane are extremely dangerous.

How accurate are these views? Are they myths or realities? Given the interest and debate that swirls around the insanity defense, it is surprising that so few empirical studies have been conducted to investigate its actual outcomes. But we have some data concerning each of these questions.

TABLE 8.2   ◆   Insanity Acquittals per 100,000 People

◆   The median number of insanity acquittals per state per year was 17.7.
◆   California and Florida had the highest annual averages (134 and 111, respectively)
◆   New Mexico (0.0) and South Dakota (0.1) had the lowest.
◆   Most of the acquittals were for felonies rather than misdemeanors.

HOW OFTEN IS THE PLEA USED, AND HOW OFTEN IS IT SUCCESSFUL?

The plea is used much less often than people assume. A study in Wyoming showed that people assumed that the insanity plea was a ploy used in nearly half of all criminal cases and that it was successful in one of five cases (Pasewark & Pantle, 1981). The actual figures: It was pleaded by only 102 of 22,102 felony defendants (about 1 in every 200 cases) in a one-year period and was successful only once in those 102 times. A survey of the use of the insanity defense in eight states between 1976 and 1985 found that although the public estimated that the insanity defense was used in 37% of the cases, the actual rate was only 0.9% (Silver, Cirincione, & Steadman, 1994). Consistent with these figures, the data reported from the states of California, Georgia, Montana, and New York (Steadman et al., 1993) indicate that defendants in those states, over a ten-year period (beginning January 1976 for Georgia and Montana, October 1977 for New York, and July 1978 for California), entered an insanity plea in 0.9% of felony cases and were successfully acquitted as NGRI in 22.7% of these cases.

Studies such as these are particularly valuable because few individual states keep complete records on the use of the insanity plea and its relative success. The findings reported in these two studies suggest that of the nine insanity pleas raised in every 1000 criminal felony cases, about two will be successful.

To answer the question of how many people are acquitted by reason of insanity each year, Carmen Cirincione and Charles Jacobs (1999) contacted officials in all 50 states and asked for the number of insanity acquittals statewide between the years 1970 and 1995. After dogged attempts to collect these data from a variety of sources, they received at least partial data from 36 states. Few states could provide information for the entire 25-year period, but the results shown in Table 8.2 were obtained.

Of greatest interest is whether there has been any trend in the frequency of insanity acquittals. Are they becoming more common, or is the volume decreasing? Judging on the basis of these data, there appeared to be a steady increase from 1970 to 1981, followed by a gradual decline. Might this finding point to a "Hinckley effect"—a decrease in insanity acquittals that can be traced to reforms in insanity defense laws and the public outcry that followed John Hinckley's insanity acquittal in 1982? Whatever the interpretation, we can safely conclude that the number of insanity acquittals represents an extremely small percentage of the dispositions of criminal charges.

WHAT HAPPENS TO DEFENDANTS WHO ARE FOUND NGRI?

Many mistakenly assume that defendants who are found NGRI go free. Steadman and Braff (1983) found that defendants acquitted on the basis of the insanity plea in New York had an average hospital stay of three years in a secure hospital. During the period studied, the average length of hospitalization was increasing. These researchers also found a clear trend for longer detentions of defendants who had committed more serious offenses. Also, the average length of involuntary hospitalization was greater for those who had been charged with violent offenses (34.1 months) than for individuals with other categories of offenses (Steadman et al., 1993). The average length of confinement for all NGRI individuals was 28.7 months. But this figure undoubtedly underestimates the "true" average period of confinement. Why? These data describe only individuals who were hospitalized and released—they cannot tell us about individuals who were hospitalized but not released (even if they were hospitalized for a long period of time). This points to one of the important differences between a criminal sentence, which is determinate (of fixed length), and the hospital commitment following acquittal by reason of insanity, which is indeterminate (depending on the individual's no longer meeting criteria for hospitalization, rather than on how long that individual has been confined).

In general, researchers have been interested in finding answers to two basic questions: Are defendants who are acquitted of crimes on the basis of insanity released from confinement more often than those who are convicted? Are defendants found not guilty by reason of insanity confined for shorter periods than defendants who are found guilty of similar crimes? The previously described survey of the use of the insanity defense across several states, covering nearly one million felony indictments between 1976 and 1985, sought answers to these two questions (Silver, 1995). On the basis of more than 8000 defendants who pleaded insanity during this period, Silver (1995) found that

◆   defendants found guilty were actually more likely to be released from confinement than were defendants acquitted on the grounds of insanity.

◆   compared to convicted defendants, insanity acquittees spent less time in confinement in four states and more time in confinement in three states.

◆   in all seven states, the more serious the crime, the longer the confinement for those found not guilty by reason of insanity.

One reason why insanity acquittees sometimes are not confined for shorter periods than those convicted of comparable crimes is that many states follow a procedure of automatically committing persons found NGRI to a mental institution and then releasing them only when a judge is convinced that they can be released safely. These criteria for release are typically broader than those for civil commitment, thus intentionally promoting longer confinements.

In the 1983 case of *Jones v. United States*, the U.S. Supreme Court held that the additional duration of hospitalization for insanity acquittees (when compared with that of those who have been civilly committed) is justifiable because of the greater threat to public safety presented by NGRI acquittees. Further, the Court held that Mr. Jones, an insanity acquittee at St. Elizabeth's Hospital in Washington, D.C., did not have the right to be evaluated for continuing hospital commitment, even though he had been hospitalized for a period that exceeded the maximum sentence he could have received had he been convicted of his criminal charge (shoplifting a jacket). Research does not show that NGRI acquittees present a greater risk to public safety (particularly when they are discharged under conditional release, discussed below) than individuals who are civilly committed. However, the *Jones* decision underscores the *perception* by the general public and the legal community that this is so, a perception undoubtedly fueled by the reality that NGRI acquittees have both committed a criminal act in the past *and* have serious mental illness.

Some states use a procedure known as *conditional release*, in which persons found NGRI are released to the community (following a period of hospital confinement) and are monitored and supervised by mental health personnel. Conditional release is the mental health system's counterpart to parole; it functions essentially like a form of outpatient commitment. According to one four-state follow-up of 529 persons found NGRI, about 60% of these individuals were conditionally released within five years of their confinement (Callahan & Silver, 1998). Of those released, the median period of hospital confinement was 3.6 years for violent offenders and 1.3 years for those charged with less serious offenses. Other research has focused on factors related to maintaining conditional release. According to one recent study of 125 NGRI acquittees, minority status, a substance abuse diagnosis, and a prior criminal history significantly predicted revocation of conditional release (Monson, Gunnin, Fogel, & Kyle, 2001).

HOW DANGEROUS ARE DEFENDANTS FOUND NGRI?

Because most defendants who are found NGRI are quickly committed to an institution following their acquittal, it is difficult to assess the risk they pose to public safety at that time. In addition, they are likely to receive treatment in the hospital to which they are committed, further complicating the question of their risk of reoffending without this treatment. The meager evidence available on this question points either to no difference in recidivism rates between NGRI defendants and "regular" felons or to slightly lower recidivism rates among the NGRI group (Cohen, Spodak, Silver, & Williams, 1988; Melton et al., 1997). For instance, in a year-long study examining rehospitalization and criminal recidivism in 43 NGRI acquittees, the majority (47%) were rehospitalized, a minority of the patients (19%) were rearrested or had committed a new crime, and nearly a fourth of the patients (24%) were reintegrated into the community without difficulty (Kravitz & Kelly, 1999),

Nicholson, Norwood, and Enyart (1991) collected data on 61 defendants found NGRI in Oklahoma; this group constituted the entire population of NGRI defendants over a five-year period who had been treated in the state forensic hospital. Follow-up of persons released from custody indicated that within two years, half of the discharged patients had been either rearrested or rehospitalized. Thus, insanity acquittees continue to have legal and/or psychiatric problems, but their overall rate of criminal recidivism falls in the range found for criminals in general.

Whether the period of hospital commitment and treatment following an acquittal has any benefits for persons found NGRI is not certain; some studies show that individuals who complete a treatment program do better than those who go AWOL from the institution (Nicholson et al., 1991), but another study reported no differences between regularly discharged acquittees and those who escaped

from the institution (Pasewark, Bieber, Bosten, Kiser, & Steadman, 1982).

Current Criticisms of the Insanity Defense

Even if the insanity defense is not successful as often as presumed, legitimate concerns remain about its continued use. Several of these will now be evaluated.

IT SENDS CRIMINALS AND TROUBLEMAKERS TO HOSPITALS AND THEN FREES THEM

For example, E. E. Kemper III murdered his grandparents and then spent five years in a California hospital for the criminally insane. He was released in 1970; three years later, he petitioned to have his psychiatric records sealed. After psychiatrists examined Kemper and found him sane, the judge agreed to the request. The authorities were not aware that since his release, he had murdered his mother and seven other women—one of them only three days before the court decision. Most of the bodies had been dismembered. Kemper, it was later claimed, had memorized the responses to 28 standardized psychological tests so that he could appear to give "well-adjusted" answers (Gleick, 1978, p. 23).

Psychopathic killers can try to capitalize on the insanity plea to escape prison and eventually get released from the hospital. How often this happens is unknown, but as we have already discussed, some data indicate that persons found NGRI are confined more frequently and for longer periods than defendants convicted of similar crimes (Perlin, 1996; but compare Steadman et al., 1993). Certainly such confinement is indeterminate for NGRI acquittees, whereas sentences for criminal convictions are determinate. After such confinement, acquittees also may undergo an additional period of conditional release. Furthermore, NGRI defendants tend not to differ from non-NGRI felons in their reoffense risk (although NGRI persons who escape from the hospital may pose a higher risk of danger to the community).

The biggest problem with such incidents is that they are often highly publicized, contributing to the public's perception that these outcomes "happen all the time" and that the insanity defense is therefore a constant threat to justice. Such incidents do not happen all the time; in fact, they are rare. Furthermore, in the interest of protecting society, if all NGRI defendants were kept hospitalized until they no longer showed symptoms of mental illness, then society would have to be willing to violate the rights of many mentally ill persons to protect against the violence of a few.

IT IS A DEFENSE ONLY FOR THE RICH

The parents of John W. Hinckley, Jr. spent between $500,000 and $1,000,000 on psychiatric examinations and expert psychiatric testimony in their son's trial—an amount that contributes to the perception of the insanity defense as a jail dodge for the rich. Of all the criticisms leveled at the insanity defense, this one is perhaps the most definitively contradicted by the data. A long line of studies have failed to find socioeconomic or racial bias in the use or the success of the insanity defense (Boehnert, 1989; Howard & Clark, 1985; Nicholson et al., 1991; Pasewark & Pantle, 1981; Steadman et al., 1983).

In addition, this criticism is further weakened by the Supreme Court's 1985 ruling, in the case of *Ake v. Oklahoma*, that poor defendants who plead insanity are entitled to psychiatric assistance at state expense in pursuing this defense. Although defendants who can afford to hire their own experts might be more likely to benefit from raising the issue of insanity, this is not a problem unique to the insanity defense. Defendants who can afford ballistics experts, chemists, and their own private detectives also have an advantage over poor defendants, but no one suggests that a defense relying on ballistics evidence, blood analyses, or mistaken identity should be prohibited because of the expense.

IT RELIES TOO MUCH ON PSYCHIATRIC EXPERTS

Several issues are pertinent here. One criticism is that testifying about insanity forces psychiatrists and clinical psychologists to give opinions about things they are not competent or trained to do—for example, to express certainty rather than probability about a person's mental condition, and to claim greater knowledge about the relationship between psychological knowledge and legal questions than is justified.

Within the field of psychology, there is debate on these matters. The debate centers on three related questions: (1) Can clinicians reliably and validly assess mental illness, mental retardation, neuropsychological disorders, and disorders occurring in childhood and adolescence? (2) Will this assessment permit the formulation of accurate opinions about a defendant's criminal responsibility for acts committed in the past? (3) Assuming that the answers to the first two questions are yes, are psychologists any more expert or capable of answering these questions than nonprofessionals? A number of respected psychologists are skeptical about psychology's expertise on these issues and have challenged their forensic colleagues to provide whatever supporting evidence they have (Dawes, 1994; Dawes, Faust, & Meehl, 1989; Ziskin & Faust, 1988). However, in a recent literature review, researchers found some support for the reliability and validity of psychologists' evaluations of criminal responsibility. Results from several studies revealed strong agreement (88% to 93%) between evaluators' recommendations and court decisions about a defendant's criminal responsibility (see Viljoen, Roesch, Ogloff, & Zapf, 2003).

Additionally, critics are concerned over the intrusion of psychology and psychiatry into the decision-making process. They want to reserve the decision for the judge or jury, the fact finder in the trial. This criticism is an example of the general concern (discussed in Chapter 1) over the use and willingness of experts to answer legal questions for which they possess limited scientific evidence. Again, some psychologists vigorously oppose the courts' reliance on mental health experts' opinions about a defendant's status as insane or sane (Bonnie & Slobogin, 1980; Morse, 1978; Tillbrook, Mumley, & Grisso, 2003). In general, this opposition is grounded in the belief that psychology has not established that it can bring scientific findings to the courtroom on legally relevant questions; if one cannot show expertise as a scientifically grounded clinician, one should not testify as an expert. But even if we were to grant special expertise to psychologists, critics raise the additional objection that questions about a defendant's criminal responsibility for an act are properly answered only by jurors, not by expert witnesses, because such answers invariably involve matters such as "how much" is needed (symptoms, deficits, lack of understanding or control) in order to fairly conclude that the defendant is not guilty by reason of insanity. However, there is disagreement with this position; some argue that there is little harm in testifying about the ultimate issue and that courts are often interested in hearing such testimony (Rogers & Ewing, 2003).

One remedy proposed to solve this problem is to prevent experts from giving what is often called **ultimate opinion testimony**; that is, they could describe a defendant's mental condition and the effects it could have had on his or her thinking and behavioral control, but they could not state conclusions about whether the defendant was sane or insane. As we discuss next, the federal courts, as part of their reforms of the insanity defense, now prohibit mental health experts from offering ultimate opinion testimony about a defendant's insanity. But does this prohibition solve any problems, or is it, in the words of Rogers and Ewing (1989), merely a "cosmetic fix" that has few effects?

In a study of whether prohibiting ultimate opinion testimony affects jury decisions (Fulero & Finkel, 1991), subjects were randomly assigned to read one of ten different versions of a trial, all of which involved a defendant charged with murdering his boss and pleading insanity as a defense. For our purposes, the comparisons among three different versions of the trial are of greatest interest. Some subjects read transcripts in which the mental health experts for both sides gave only *diagnostic testimony* (that the defendant suffered a mental disorder at the time of the offense); a second group read a version in which the experts gave a diagnosis and then also offered differing *penultimate opinions* about the effects this disorder had on the defendant's understanding of the wrongfulness of his act;

a final group read a transcript in which the experts offered differing diagnoses, penultimate opinions, and *ultimate opinion testimony* about whether the defendant was sane or insane at the time of the killing. Did ultimate opinion testimony affect the subjects' verdicts? Not in this study; subjects' verdicts were not significantly different regardless of the type of testimony they read. The lack of difference could be interpreted as evidence that the prohibition of ultimate opinion testimony is unnecessary, or it could indicate that the ban streamlines the trial process without sacrificing any essential information.

Finally, there is the feeling that the process of assessing sanity in criminal defendants holds mental health professionals up to ridicule. When the jury sees and the public reads about a parade of mental health experts representing one side and then the other, their confidence in the behavioral sciences is jeopardized (Slater & Hans, 1984). Further, some experts, in an effort to help the side that has retained them, offer explanations of such an untestable nature that their profession loses its credibility with jurors and the public. However, in many cases involving claims of insanity, the experts retained by each side basically agree on the question of insanity. These cases receive less publicity because they often end in a plea agreement.

Revisions and Reforms of the Insanity Defense

Several reforms in the rules and procedures for implementing the insanity defense have been introduced, but they have led to mixed outcomes. Proposals have ranged from abolition of the insanity defense (as has already been done in four states), to provision of a "guilty but mentally ill" verdict, to reform of insanity statutes, to maintenance of the present procedures. We review three reforms in this section.

THE GUILTY BUT MENTALLY ILL (GBMI) VERDICT

Since 1976, about a quarter of the states have passed laws allowing juries to reach a verdict of guilty but mentally ill (GBMI) in cases in which a defendant pleads insanity. These GBMI rules differ from state to state, but generally they give a jury the following verdict alternatives for a defendant who is pleading insanity: (1) guilty of the crime, (2) not guilty of the crime, (3) NGRI, or (4) GBMI. Typically, a judge will sentence a defendant found GBMI exactly as he or she would the same defendant found guilty of the same offense. The intent is for the prisoner to start his or her term in a hospital and then be transferred to prison after treatment is completed.

Proponents of GBMI verdicts hoped that this compromise verdict would decrease the number of defendants found NGRI. Whether insanity acquittals have actually decreased as a result of GBMI legislation is highly questionable. Mock jury research consistently suggests that adding the GBMI option decreases NGRI verdicts (Roberts & Golding, 1991; Roberts, Sargent, & Chan, 1993). However, actual GBMI statutes have not produced decreases in NGRI verdicts in South Carolina or Michigan, although decreases were noted after GBMI laws were enacted in Georgia (Callahan, McGreevey, Cirincione, & Steadman, 1992) and Pennsylvania (see Roberts & Golding, 1991, for a discussion of the effects of this legislation on jury decisions). One possible explanation for the lack of change in NGRI verdicts in states with GBMI statutes is that jurors do not understand the differences between the verdicts. One study examined jurors' knowledge about the two verdicts and found that only 4.2% of 101 potential jurors correctly identified meanings and outcomes of both NGRI and GMBI verdicts (Sloat & Frierson, 2005).

Other problems have provoked a "second look" at the GBMI reform, leading to growing skepticism about its value (Borum & Fulero, 1999). If regular insanity instructions are confusing to jurors, the GBMI verdict only adds to the confusion by introducing the very difficult distinction for juries to make between mental illness that results in insanity and mental illness that does not. One possible effect of the GBMI verdict is that it raises jurors' threshold for what constitutes insanity, leading to a more stringent standard for acquitting defendants who use this defense (Roberts et al., 1993). Also, the claim that the GBMI option will make it more

likely that mentally ill offenders will receive treatment is largely a false promise. Overcrowding at hospitals in most states has impeded implementation of this part of the GBMI option. In one Michigan study, 75% of GBMI offenders went straight to prison with no treatment (Sales & Hafemeister, 1984).

In Kentucky, in spite of a statute that appears to promise treatment to those found GBMI, the chair of the parole board filed an affidavit in 1991 stating that "from psychological evaluations and treatment summaries, the Board can detect no difference in treatment or outcome for inmates who have been adjudicated as 'Guilty But Mentally Ill,' from those who have been adjudicated as simply 'guilty'" (Runda, 1991).

Finally, the opportunity to be found GBMI and then treated (in states where there is a difference in treatment opportunities) is available only to defendants who themselves first raise an insanity defense. An equally disturbed defendant who does not claim insanity cannot be found GBMI. Somewhat similar to the GBMI concept is the diminished-capacity defense.

THE DEFENSE OF DIMINISHED CAPACITY

Several states allow a defense of **diminished capacity**, which is a legal doctrine that applies to defendants who lack the ability to commit a crime purposely and knowingly. Like the insanity defense, diminished capacity often involves evidence that the defendant suffers a mental disorder. It differs from insanity in that it focuses on whether defendants had the state of mind to act with the purpose and intent to commit a crime—that is, to think through the consequences of their contemplated actions—not on whether they knew the crime was wrong or whether they could control their behavior. Suppose M'Naghten knew that murder was wrong but, because of his mental condition, wasn't thinking clearly enough to intend to kill Peel's secretary. Under these conditions, he would not be insane, but he would lack the *mens rea* for first-degree murder, so he probably would have been convicted of second-degree murder or manslaughter.

The rationale for this defense is simple: Offenders should be convicted of the crime that matches their mental state, and expert testimony should be offered on the issue of their mental state. Even when the diminished-capacity defense "works," it usually leads to a prison sentence.

In June 1982, a proposition to abolish the diminished-capacity defense was overwhelmingly passed by the voters of California (that state still permits defendants to use a M'Naghten-based insanity defense), and several other states either have outlawed the diminished-capacity defense or do not allow expert testimony about it. In general, however, the majority of states permit expert testimony about a defendant's *mens rea*, thereby allowing clinicians to present testimony that could be used in support of a diminished-capacity defense (Melton et al., 1997). As long as proof of a defendant's *mens rea* is required, defendants are likely to put forward expert evidence about it, especially in those states that have abolished an affirmative insanity defense.

ELIMINATION OF THE INSANITY PLEA

Winslade and Ross (1983) reviewed seven trials (mostly for murder) in which the insanity defense was used and psychiatric testimony was introduced to justify it. They conclude that the possibility of an insanity defense often leads to injustice for the following reasons:

1. Juries are asked to decide questions that predispose them to make arbitrary and emotional judgments because of either over-identification with or alienation from the defendant;
2. Psychiatrists and other mental health professionals are encouraged to parade their opinions, guesses, and speculations under the banner of scientific expertise; and
3. Society's views about criminality and craziness are so intertwined that an insanity defense to a crime does not make much sense. (p. 198)

On the basis of their analysis of the outcomes of these trials, Winslade and Ross recommend that the insanity defense be eliminated:

A workable solution would require the elimination of the insanity plea; the elimination of any testimony by psychiatrists about the actual or theoretical state of the defendant's mind at the time of the crime; the elimination of psychiatric expert witnesses in the guilt phase of the trial; and the requirement of a two-phase trial that would, in its first phase, establish guilt or innocence of the commission of the crime with no concern for the individual's state of mind in terms of mental illness at the time the crime was committed. The second phase of the trial, if guilt were found, would address itself to the appropriate disposition of the defendant. (p. 219)

In the second part of the trial, if a defendant claimed mental illness, he or she would be required to testify. The judge would permit psychiatrists to testify as expert witnesses, but only to report on previous clinical assessments, not to predict the defendant's future behavior. Psychiatrists representing state institutions would also be required to testify about the likelihood of rehabilitating the defendant; they would be asked to specify at least a minimum duration of treatment. Combinations of hospitalization and incarceration, in Winslade and Ross's proposal, would be based on the defendant's amenability to treatment.

ARGUMENTS AGAINST ELIMINATING THE PLEA

Winslade and Ross (1983) advocate an initial phase of a trial to "establish guilt or innocence of the commission of the crime with no concern for the individual's state of mind" (p. 219).

James Kunen (1983), a former public defender, challenges this idea, noting that "Anglo-American legal tradition . . . has required that to convict someone of a crime, the prosecution must prove not only that he did a particular act—such as pulling a trigger—but that he did it with a particular state of mind" (p. 157). Kunen argues that we cannot talk about guilt without bringing in the person's state of mind. If a defendant slashes his victim's throat, thinking that he is slicing a cucumber, we say that he committed an act but not that he was guilty of the intent to commit a crime. This is why, even in those few states that have abolished the insanity defense, defendants may still introduce evidence that they lacked the mental state required for the crime.

Some offenders are truly "not guilty by reason of insanity"; they do not know the "nature and quality of their acts"—they literally do not know what they are doing. Harvard law professor Alan Dershowitz has said, "I almost would be in favor of abolishing the insanity defense, except there really are a few genuinely crazy people who believe they're squeezing lemons when they're actually squeezing throats" (quoted in Footlick, 1978, p. 108). Of course, the actual number of such people is much smaller than the number of defendants who raise the NGRI defense.

We believe that the NGRI plea should be maintained as an option, and modifications of the system should be restricted to those that clarify the rule and later evaluate those for whom it is successful. For example, the federal government

has already acted to change the law that gave the prosecution the burden of proving beyond a reasonable doubt that John Hinckley was not insane. If an act similar to Hinckley's were committed today in a federal jurisdiction and in the vast majority of states, the defendant, not the prosecution, would bear the responsibility of proving his plea; otherwise, he would be found guilty. States should carefully monitor people committed after NGRI verdicts to ensure that they are not released while still mentally ill and dangerous. All indications are that this precaution is being taken. In fact, it is likely that some NGRI defendants are now confined even though they are not both mentally ill *and* dangerous (as required by the U.S. Supreme Court's holding in *Foucha v. Louisiana*, 1992).

SUMMARY

1. *What is the scope of forensic psychology?* Forensic psychology is a specialty that involves the application of knowledge and techniques from the behavioral sciences to answer questions about individuals involved in legal proceedings. The range of topics about which psychological and psychiatric experts are asked to testify continues to grow, despite both professional concerns and public skepticism about the validity of such testimony.

2. *What is meant by competence in the criminal justice process?* Adjudicative competence entails having a sufficient present ability to consult with one's attorney with a reasonable degree of rational understanding and with a rational, as well as factual, understanding of the proceedings. This same standard is applied to the questions of whether a defendant is competent to plead guilty and whether a defendant is competent to stand trial, so the phrase "competence to stand trial" is often used to refer to the entire process of disposition of charges, not merely the trial.

3. *How do clinicians assess competence?* When mental health professionals assess a defendant's

competence, they should use one of several special instruments designed specifically for the purpose of evaluating how well a defendant understands the charges and potential proceedings. These specific tests and structured interviews have made competence assessments more reliable, valid, and useful. Competence evaluations are sometimes complicated by such factors as malingering, amnesia, and the problem of whether incompetent defendants can be treated against their will. Other competence issues (e.g., competence to refuse the insanity defense and competence to be sentenced) can arise at different points in the criminal process.

4. *What are the consequences of being found incompetent to proceed in the criminal justice process?* When defendants are found incompetent to stand trial, they can be committed for a period of treatment designed to restore their competence. If later found competent, they will stand trial or dispose of their charges through the plea-bargaining process. If treatment is not successful in restoring competence, the state will usually attempt to commit the person to a mental hospital for a period of time. The alternatives that have been proposed for dealing with the unrestorably incompetent criminal defendant include her or his waiving the right to be found incompetent to proceed to trial and using a special form of commitment for incompetent defendants who are judged at a provisional trial to be guilty of the crimes with which they are charged.

5. *What is the legal definition of insanity?* Two major definitions of insanity are used currently. The M'Naghten rule defines insanity as not knowing the difference between right and wrong: "To establish a defense on the grounds of insanity it must be clearly proved that, at the time of committing the act, the accused was laboring under such a defect of reason, from disease of the mind, as not to know the nature and quality of the act he was doing, or, if he did know it, that he did not know what he was doing was wrong." In some jurisdictions, an "irresistible impulse" test has been added to the M'Naghten rule.

The Brawner rule states that a person is not responsible for a criminal act if, as a result of mental disease or defect, the person lacked "substantial capacity either to appreciate the criminality of his conduct or to conform his conduct to the requirements of the law." This rule or a variation of it is the standard in about half of the states. Until 1984, it was also the federal standard, but the federal system now requires the defense to show that, as a result of a severe mental disease or defect, the defendant was unable to appreciate the nature and quality or the wrongfulness of his or her acts.

Five states have outlawed insanity as a defense, although these states still allow the defendant to introduce evidence about his or her mental condition that is relevant to determining *mens rea*. Some highly publicized trials have led to "successful" use of the insanity defense. But many others who used this defense were found guilty.

6. *How frequently is the insanity defense used, and how successful is it?* The insanity plea is used much less frequently than people assume; it is tried in only about 9 of every 1000 cases, and it succeeds in only about 25% of these cases. When it does succeed, there is no guarantee that the defendant will be released from the hospital any sooner than he or she would have been paroled from prison.

7. *What are the major criticisms of the insanity defense, and what reforms have been attempted?* Some examples of early release of NGRI defendants have led to justified criticism of the procedure. Other criticisms are that insanity cannot be reliably and validly assessed and that the insanity defense relies too much on psychiatric testimony. Reforms include the Insanity Defense Reform Act and the adoption in several states of a "guilty but mentally ill" verdict, resulting (at least in theory) in the defendant's being treated in a state hospital until releasable and then serving the rest of the sentence in prison. A number of states also allow the diminished-capacity plea, a partial defense based on mental condition. But it also has been controversial, and at least one state (California) that formerly allowed the defense no longer does so.

KEY TERMS

adjudicative competence	competence	diminished capacity	*nolo contendere*
affirmative defense	competence to plead guilty	insanity	stipulate
Brawner rule	competence to stand trial	M'Naghten rule	ultimate opinion testimony
		mens rea	

Forensic Assessment in Civil Cases

ORIENTING QUESTIONS

1. *What problems are associated with expert testimony, and what reforms have been proposed?*
2. *Under what conditions can a plaintiff be compensated for psychological damages?*
3. *What is workers' compensation, and how do mental health professionals participate in such cases?*
4. *What capacities are involved in civil competence?*
5. *What criteria are used for decisions about disputes involving child custody or parental fitness?*
6. *How well can clinicians assess the risk of dangerousness, or violent behavior, a key criterion for civil commitments?*

Whether a defendant is mentally competent to stand trial (which is often called *adjudicative competence*, because it refers to a defendant's capacities to dispose of charges either through a trial or via plea bargaining) and whether a defendant was insane at the time of an alleged criminal offense are perhaps the best-known legal questions that mental health professionals are asked to help courts decide, but they are by no means the only questions. Throughout earlier chapters, we have examined other questions arising in the legal system that psychologists are often asked to comment on. Is a given individual a good candidate for police work? Will a person who is suffering from mental illness be violent in the future? How accurate is one's memory for, and testimony about, highly traumatic events likely to be? These questions—like those of competence and insanity—are often asked of forensic psychologists and psychiatrists, and they are usually answered on the basis of a combination of research knowledge and the results of individual assessments performed by forensic clinicians.

Litigation of all sorts is making increased use of scientific knowledge and expert opinion. Psychology and psychiatry are two fields in which the use of experts has proliferated. Nietzel and Dillehay (1986) provide a list of circumstances in which psychological testimony has been permitted in civil cases. This list continues to grow, as attorneys and forensic experts create new opportunities to apply behavioral science knowledge to litigation issues. In addition to the legal questions discussed in previous chapters, mental health experts are involved in hearings or trials in the areas of civil commitment, psychological damages in civil cases, psychological autopsies (i.e., to what extent psychological problems are attributable to a preexisting condition), negligence and product liability, trademark litigation, discrimination, guardianship and conservatorship (a guardianship-like arrangement for financial assets), child custody, adoption and termination of parental rights, professional malpractice, and other social issues such as sexual harassment in the workplace. Therefore, judges now often find themselves in the position of having to decide whether the expert testimony that an attorney seeks to introduce at trial meets the criteria that the *Daubert* and *Kumho* cases (discussed in Chapters 1 and 8) have established as the modern standard for admitting scientific evidence and expert testimony.

In general, a qualified expert can testify about a topic if such testimony is relevant to an issue in dispute and if the usefulness of the testimony outweighs whatever prejudicial impact it might have. If these two conditions are met, an expert will be permitted to testify if the judge believes that the testimony is based on sufficiently relevant and reliable scientific evidence. In other words, under the *Daubert/Kumho* criteria, the judge serves as a "gatekeeper" who must determine whether the theory, methodology, and analysis that are the basis of the expert's opinion measure up to scientific standards. If they meet this standard, the judge will probably admit relevant expert testimony; if they do not, the judge should not allow the testimony.

As we pointed out in Chapter 1, judges generally do not perform this gatekeeper function well (Gatowski et al., 2001). Many (if not most) judges lack the scientific training that *Daubert/Kumho* appears to require; even with such training, the range of expert topics about which judges will need to be informed is staggering. As a result, many critics, including experts and judges themselves, believe that the difficulty of distinguishing valid from invalid scientific evidence will result in jurors too often being exposed to "expert" testimony that is based on little more than "junk science" (Grove & Barden, 1999; see also Box 9.1).

In this chapter, we introduce some points about expert testimony in civil cases, and we describe six areas of forensic assessment in which forensic psychologists and psychiatrists are increasingly involved: (1) psychological damages to civil plaintiffs, (2) workers' compensation claims, (3) the assessment of civil competence, (4) psychological autopsies, (5) child custody and parental fitness and (6) civil commitment and risk assessment. Although these areas do not rival the publicity commanded by adjudicative competence or insanity at the time of the offense, which were discussed in Chapter 8, they illustrate several ways in which

BOX 9.1   The Judas Priest trial: Expert opinion or junk science?

Can subliminal messages cause someone to commit suicide? This was the question at the center of a widely publicized 1990 trial involving the British heavy metal rock band Judas Priest. Two teenage boys, James Vance and Ray Belknap, had attempted suicide by shooting themselves. Belknap died immediately from the gunshot wounds he inflicted, but Vance survived, only to die three years later as a result of drug complications. The boys' parents sued the band and its record company, claiming that the band had embedded provocative lyrics—below the conscious threshold of recognition—in its 1978 album *Stained Class* and that these lyrics had led to their sons' suicidal impulses. The specific phrase in question consisted of only two words—"do it"—which were alleged to be hidden in the song "Better by You, Better Than Me."

Among the plaintiffs' witnesses was Dr. Howard Shevrin, a well-known and well-respected psychologist on the faculty at the University of Michigan. Dr. Shevrin had published a number of scholarly articles on unconscious learning and subliminal influence. He testified that subliminal messages are

particularly powerful because their hidden nature makes them seem to reflect the individual's own motivation and they are therefore harder to resist. He stated his opinion that the subliminal "do it" message had triggered the boys' suicidal actions.

Although Dr. Shevrin's claims seem logical, empirical support for the notion that subliminal messages can compel behavior or influence motivation is lacking. In fact, when asked by defense attorneys to cite a single study that supported his theory that subliminal messages could motivate impulsive or harmful behavior, Dr. Shevrin cited a handful of references, none of which actually involved evidence that subliminal communications motivated behavior.

In addition to denying that any subliminal messages were planted on the album, the defense presented evidence that both boys had personal histories marked by petty crime, drug abuse, learning disabilities, and family difficulties and that these factors were much more likely to have contributed to the shootings than any rock music lyrics. The defense also countered Dr. Shevrin with three experts of its own—Drs. Timothy Moore, Anthony Pratkanis, and Don

Judas Priest band members

Read—who testified that although subliminal stimuli had been demonstrated to have small and fleeting effects on perception and memory, there was no scientific evidence that they could influence intentional behavior, such as suicide. The judge ultimately rejected the plaintiffs' claims and rendered a verdict in favor of the defendants. He stated that there was little scientific evidence establishing that subliminal stimuli were a strong influence on behavior, a conclusion that is close to what most experimental psychologists believe. However, perhaps the more important questions growing out of this case are these: (1) Was there any credible scientific basis for Dr. Shevrin's opinions? and (2) Should he have been permitted to express his opinion on this matter without being able to document a stronger scientific foundation for it?

psychological expertise can be brought to bear on important legal questions. For each of the six areas, we will:

◆ Discuss the basic psycho-legal questions that experts are expected to address

◆ Describe the techniques typically used by forensic clinicians to evaluate these questions

◆ Summarize the empirical evidence and legal status associated with the forensic activity

Experts in the Adversarial System

Some of the advantages of having mental health professionals provide expert testimony are clear. Mental health professionals are equipped with specialized knowledge and training that can provide the court with valuable information in a variety of cases. For example, some psychologists are trained to administer tools to determine malingering mental health or neuropsychological problems in workers' compensation cases or are experienced in conducting clinical interviews to assess civil competence. However, judges, lawyers, and mental health professionals themselves have expressed great concern about the reliability, validity, propriety, and usefulness of expert testimony and the forensic assessment on which it is based. Former federal appellate judge David T. Bazelon (1974) once complained that "psychiatry . . . is the ultimate wizardry . . . in no case is it more difficult to elicit productive and reliable testimony than in cases that call on the knowledge and practice of psychiatry." This view was echoed by Warren Burger (Burger, 1975), a former chief justice of the United States Supreme Court, who chided experts for the

"uncertainties of psychiatric diagnosis." Critiques of psychologists' expert testimony in this area can be found in several sources (Tillbrook, Mumley, Grisso, 2003; Bonnie & Slobogin, 1980; Ennis & Litwack, 1974; Morse, 1978), and one well-known guidebook in multiple editions (see, for example, Ziskin and Faust, 1988) has been devoted entirely to the subject of how to cross-examine mental health professionals who are giving expert testimony. This resource is so well known that experts who have been cross-examined according to its recommendations are often said to have been "Ziskinized."

What are the main problems with or objections to testimony by psychological or psychiatric experts? Smith (1989) lists the following eight concerns:

1. The scientific foundation for much of the testimony offered in court is often less than adequate, leading to unreliable information and therefore potentially incorrect verdicts.
2. Much of the testimony is of limited relevance, therefore wasting court time and burdening an already crowded docket.
3. Experts are too often permitted to testify about "ultimate issues" (Is the defendant insane? Was the plaintiff emotionally damaged?), which should be left to juries to decide.
4. Expert testimony is frequently used to introduce information that would otherwise be prohibited because it is hearsay. (Experts are permitted to share this information with juries if it is the kind of information they routinely rely on in reaching expert opinions.)
5. The adversarial system compromises experts' objectivity. Experts readily testify to opinions that favor the side that retained them.
6. Expert testimony is very expensive, and relying on experts gives an advantage to the side with more money.
7. Testing the reliability and validity of expert opinions through cross-examination is inadequate because attorneys are usually not well equipped to conduct such cross-examination, and juries often fail to understand the significance of the information that is uncovered during the cross-examination.

8. The spectacle of experts disagreeing with one another in trial after trial ultimately reduces the public's esteem for mental health professionals.

In response to these concerns, some of which are also supported by empirical research (which will be discussed later in this chapter), several reforms of expert testimony have been proposed. Most of these suggestions are aimed at reducing the undue influence or excessive partisanship that can adversely affect expert testimony. As a result, federal courts and some state courts do not allow experts to testify about the "ultimate issue" (Is a person competent? Would the best custody arrangement be shared custody?) in forensic cases. As you will recall from Chapter 8, this change was part of the overall reform of federal law concerning insanity that occurred in the 1980s. There is little evidence that limiting experts' testimony in this way has had much impact on the use or

success of the insanity defense (Borum & Fulero, 1999), and it is even less likely to have an impact on the kinds of cases we will discuss in this chapter.

Other suggestions have involved reducing the overly adversarial nature of expert testimony by limiting the number of experts on a given topic, requiring that the experts be chosen from an approved panel of individuals reputed to be objective and highly competent, and allowing testimony only from experts who have been appointed by a judge rather than hired by one of the opposing attorneys. Although these changes would appear to reduce the "hired gun" problem, it is not clear that consensus could be easily reached on which experts belong on an approved list, or on whether being appointed by a judge ensures an expert's impartiality. Furthermore, recent research suggests that jurors might already be inclined to discount the testimony of experts whom they perceive to be "hired guns" because of the high fees such experts are paid and their history of testifying frequently (Cooper & Neuhaus, 2000).

Several scholars have suggested that courts not permit clinical opinion testimony unless it can be shown that it satisfies standards of scientific reliability. The standard required by the *Daubert/ Kumho* decisions has made this recommendation more feasible (Faust & Ziskin, 1988; Imwinkelried, 1994). Such a requirement might reduce the frequency of testimony by forensic psychologists and psychiatrists, but unless lawyers and judges are educated more thoroughly about scientific methodology, it is not clear that they can make informed distinctions between "good" and "bad" science (Gless, 1995).

A more modest reform would involve simply banning any reference to witnesses as providing *expert* testimony, a term that suggests that jurors should give it extra credence. Instead, judges would always refer—in the presence of juries—to *opinion* testimony or witnesses.

In addition to deleting any mention of expert testimony, federal judge Charles R. Richey (1994) recommended that juries be read a special instruction before hearing any opinion testimony in order to reduce its possible prejudicial impact. Here ia an example of his recommended instruction:

> Ladies and Gentlemen, please note that the Rules of Evidence ordinarily do not permit witnesses to testify as to their opinions or conclusions. Two exceptions to this rule exist. The first exception allows an ordinary citizen to give his or her opinion as to matters that he or she observed or of which he or she has firsthand knowledge. The second exception allows witnesses who, by education, training and experience, have acquired a certain specialized knowledge in some art, science, profession or calling to state an opinion as to relevant and material matters. The purpose of opinion witness testimony is to assist you in understanding the evidence and deciding the facts in this case. You are not bound by this testimony and, in weighing it, you may consider his or her qualifications, opinions and reasons for testifying, as well as all other considerations that apply when you evaluate the credibility of any witness. In other words, you should give it such weight as you think it fairly deserves and consider it in light of all the evidence in this case.

Psychological Damages to Civil Plaintiffs

When one party is injured by the actions of a second party, the injured individual can sue the second party to recover monetary damages as compensation for the injury. This action is covered by an area of civil law known as torts. A **tort** is a wrongful act that causes harm to an individual. The criminal law also exacts compensation for wrongful acts, but it does so on behalf of society as a whole; by punishing an offender, the criminal law attempts to maintain society's overall sense of justice. Tort law, on the other hand, provides a mechanism to redress the harms that individuals have suffered from wrongful acts by another party.

As illustrated by the O. J. Simpson case, both criminal punishment and civil remedies can be sought for the same act. Simpson was prosecuted by the state, under the criminal law, for murder; he was also sued for money damages by the surviving relatives of the victims, who alleged that he caused the wrongful deaths of Nicole Brown Simpson and Ronald Goldman.

Many kinds of behavior can constitute a tort. Slander and libel are torts, as are cases of professional malpractice, invasion of privacy, the manufacture of defective products that result in a personal injury, and intentional or negligent behavior producing harm to another person.

Four elements are involved in proving a tort in a court of law. First, torts occur in situations in which one individual owes a **duty**, or has an obligation, to another; a physician has a duty to treat patients in accordance with accepted professional standards, and individuals have a duty not to harm others physically or psychologically. Second, a tort typically requires proving that one party breached or violated a duty that was owed to other parties. The **breached duty** can be due to negligence or intentional wrongdoing. **Negligence** is behavior that falls below a standard for protecting others from unreasonable risks; it is often measured by asking whether a "reasonable person" would have acted as the civil defendant acted in similar circumstances. **Intentional behavior** is conduct in which a person meant the outcome of a given act to occur. A party can be held strictly liable even without acting negligently or intentionally. This standard is often used in product liability cases. For example, if a company manufactures a product that harms an innocent user, it can be held liable for the harm even though the company was without fault. Third, the violation of the duty must have been the proximate cause of the harm suffered by a plaintiff. A **proximate cause** is one that constitutes an obvious or substantial reason why a given harm occurred. It is sometimes equated with producing an outcome that is "foreseeable"—that is, a given event would be expected to cause a given outcome. Fourth, a **harm**, or loss, must occur, and the harm has to involve a legally protected right or interest for which the person can seek to recover damages that have been suffered. If it can be established that (1) there was a duty that (2) was breached, which (3) proximally caused the (4) harm resulting, then a tort can be compensable in a civil lawsuit.

The damages a person suffers from a tort can involve destruction of personal property, physical injuries, and/or emotional distress (sometimes called "pain and suffering"). Historically, the law has always sought to compensate victims who are physically hurt or sustain property losses, but it was reluctant to allow compensation for emotional distress, largely out of concern that such damages are too easy to fake and too difficult to measure. In cases in which recovery for emotional damages was allowed, the courts often required that a physical injury have accompanied the psychological harm or that a plaintiff who was not physically injured was at least in a "zone of danger" (for example, even if the plaintiff was not injured by the attack of an escaped wild animal, she was standing next to her children when they were attacked) (Weissman, 1985).

One case that received extensive international coverage illustrates this historical approach to emotional damages. On the afternoon of March 22, 1990, the *Aleutian Enterprise*, a large fishing boat, capsized in the Bering Sea. Within ten minutes, the boat sank, killing nine crew members. Twenty-two sailors survived the disaster; of these men, two returned to work in a short time, but the other 20 filed a lawsuit against the company that owned the ship. Of the 20 plaintiffs, 19 consulted a psychologist or psychiatrist, and every one of these 19 individuals was subsequently diagnosed with posttraumatic stress disorder (PTSD) by his mental health professional (Rosen, 1995). (The defendant company hired its own psychologist, who evaluated the plaintiffs and diagnosed PTSD in only five of them and some other postincident disorder in three others.) The surviving sailors were entitled to recover for their psychological injuries because they had been in the "zone of danger."

In recent years, the courts have progressed to a view in which psychological symptoms and mental distress are more likely to be compensated regardless of whether the plaintiff suffered physical injuries. Two types of "purely" psychological injuries are now claimed in civil lawsuits: those arising from "extreme and outrageous" conduct that is intended to cause distress, and those arising from "negligent" behavior. In the latter type of case, plaintiffs are often allowed to sue for psychological damages if they are bystanders to an incident in which a loved one is injured (for example, a parent sees her child crushed to death when a defective roller coaster on which the child was riding derails).

In the case of intentional torts causing psychological distress, a plaintiff must prove that a defendant intentionally or recklessly acted in an extreme and outrageous fashion (sometimes defined as "beyond all bounds of decency") to cause emotional distress. In addition, the plaintiff must prove that the distress is severe; in other words, the effects must be something more than merely annoying or temporarily upsetting (Merrick, 1985). What kinds of behavior might qualify? Courts have found that a debt collector who was trying to locate a debtor acted outrageously when he posed as a hospital employee and told the debtor's mother that her grandchildren had been seriously injured in a wreck and that he needed to find the debtor to inform him of this fact (*Ford Motor Credit Co. v. Sheehan*, 1979).

THE CASE OF

BOX 9.2 **"Lyle" and the goosing salesmen: Psychological injury in the workplace**

The plaintiff, whom we will call Lyle, had been disabled since his teenage years with a left leg that was four inches shorter than the right leg and a left hip that had about 30% of the usual range of motion. Consequently, Lyle walked slowly and with a severe limp. It was a regular practice of the sales personnel at the dealership where Lyle worked to amuse themselves during slow business hours by goosing one another. They took special pleasure in goosing Lyle, particularly after discovering that he could not easily avoid them and that he would shriek loudly each time he was goosed. Lyle testified that he was goosed several times an hour and estimated that it had happened as many as 1500 times during his employment. His co-workers even gave him the nickname "Oops" because of the sound he would

make each time he was the recipient of a surprise attack. On one occasion, Lyle was goosed by a co-worker while talking with a couple to whom he was selling a car. Soon, the other sales personnel began making $2 bets on who could goose him in the presence of other customers. On another occasion, Lyle was goosed while he was standing next to a vehicle in the showroom, causing him to bang his left knee against the vehicle and miss two weeks of work because of the subsequent injury. After returning to work, he was chided by his colleagues for drawing "gooseman's compensation."

Lyle attempted several strategies to deal with the harassment. For a time, he joined in the goosing, hoping the other men would stop picking on him. He would stay seated in his chair or with his back to a wall to reduce the opportunities

for goosing, but this resulted in a severe loss of sales commissions. He repeatedly complained to his sales manager but obtained no relief. After learning that his prosthesis had been fractured—as a result of his goose-propelled bump into the showroom vehicle—Lyle quit his job and sued his employer for outrageous conduct causing physical and psychological damages.

At trial, Lyle testified how angry and humiliated he felt over the treatment and admitted that he often felt suicidal and fantasized about getting revenge against his protagonists. A clinical psychologist testified that Lyle suffered a mixed anxiety and mood disorder brought on by the repeated harassment. The jury returned a verdict for Lyle and awarded him $795,000 for his physical and psychological injuries.

In recent years, an increasing number of cases have dealt with the tort of sexual harassment, usually in the workplace. (We discuss sexual harassment in more detail in Chapter 13.) A plaintiff who claims to have been sexually harassed at work can sue the workers responsible for the harassment and can also sue the company itself, if the plaintiff can show that the company knew (or should have known) about the harassment and failed to stop it. These cases can be filed either in state courts or in federal courts, where Title VII of the federal Civil Rights Act of 1991 applies to companies with at least 15 employees. Plaintiffs can seek both **compensatory damages**

(payment for emotional harm and damages suffered) and **punitive damages** (punishing the company for its failure to respond properly to the misconduct).

Of course, the tort of harassment is not always based on gender. In one case, a car salesman sued his employer for permitting—and even participating in—the repeated "goosing" of the salesman at work. This case is described in Box 9.2.

When a mental health professional assesses a plaintiff, the clinician will typically conduct an evaluation that, like most evaluations, includes a social history, a clinical interview, and a number of psychological tests (Boccaccini & Brodsky, 1999).

One major difference, however, between standard clinical evaluations and forensic assessments is the much greater use of third-party interviews and review of available records in forensic examinations. This practice is based on two basic considerations (Heilbrun, 2001; Melton, Petrila, Poythress, & Slobogin, 1997). First, forensic experts must be sure that their opinions are based on accurate information, and self-reported information in the context of litigation is not necessarily accurate. Second, forensic experts are often asked to evaluate an individual's psychological condition at some specific moment or in some particular situation in the past. Therefore, clinicians are obligated to use independent sources of information, when possible, to verify their descriptions and judgments about such matters.

On the basis of the data gleaned from these sources, the clinician arrives at an opinion about the psychological condition of the person in question. With the exception of greater reliance on third-party interviews and records, this part of the evaluation is not much different from how a clinician would assess any client, regardless of whether the person was involved in a lawsuit. The more difficult question the clinician must answer in litigation is whether the psychological problems were caused by the tort, were aggravated by the tort, or existed before the tort. In fact, given that some research suggests that psychological problems make people more prone to accidents, the clinician even needs to consider whether certain psychological conditions might have contributed to the plaintiff's being injured in the first place.

There is no established procedure for answering these questions, although most clinicians will try to locate records and other sources of data that will help them date the development of any disorder that is diagnosed. In some situations, a plaintiff might allege that he or she was targeted for harassment precisely because the defendants knew of some prior difficulty that made the plaintiff vulnerable to a particular kind of harassment. In such cases, the clinician must factor in this additional piece of information before reaching a conclusion about the significance of the prior psychological problem.

One other complication affects many evaluations of individuals who claim to have suffered psychological harm: Plaintiffs may be motivated to exaggerate their claims in order to improve their chances of winning large awards. In some cases, the distortion is so large as to constitute outright lying. In other, more subtle instances of **malingering**, a real psychological disturbance is present, but the plaintiff exaggerates its seriousness. In some cases, no deception is intended at all; the plaintiff has simply become convinced that he or she is suffering from a disorder and responds to the evaluation in a way that is meant to convince the examiner to reach the same conclusion. One meta-analysis found that the possibility for receiving compensation for an injury increased subjects' reports of pain (Rohling, Binder, & Langhinrichsen-Rohling, 1995). Another study examined the effects of compensation on self-reported changes in levels of pain after rehabilitative efforts (Rainville, Sobel, Hartigan, & Wright, 1997). Results revealed differences between patients who were not seeking financial compensation through litigation and patients who were. Individuals seeking compensation reported no changes in pain symptoms at the 12-month follow-up, whereas those not seeking compensation did report improvement. Significant differences between the two groups remained even after controlling for initial differences in self-reported levels of pain. These findings are particularly interesting in that the groups did not differ on measures of treatment compliance and satisfaction with the rehabilitative efforts.

In a recent literature review exploring the ethics of attorneys "coaching" their clients on how to "beat" psychological tests in civil litigation cases, Victor and Abeles (2004) argued that these techniques are well within the ethical boundaries of legal practice and that attorneys often view such coaching as an important part of advocating for their clients. Another study found that some attorneys believe it to be malpractice *not* to coach their clients on the malingering scales of psychological assessments (e.g., the MMPI-2) often used in civil litigation (Youngjohn, 1995). These coaching strategies are often very effective. One study revealed that the *F* scale on the MMPI-2 (one of the instrument's validity scales designed to detect possible malingering) was not as effective at identifying coached malingerers as at identifying non-coached malingerers (Storm & Graham, 2000).

Spurred by results like these and by estimates of experienced clinicians that malingering and self-serving presentations are not at all uncommon in forensic evaluations (Rogers, Sewell, & Goldstein, 1994), some commentators have recommended that clinicians be vigilant in forensic contexts to consider the particular motivation of litigants and take extra steps to scrutinize their claims (Williams, Lees-Haley, & Djanogly, 1999).

Workers' Compensation

When a worker is injured in the course of his or her job, the law provides for the worker to be compensated through a streamlined system that avoids the necessity of proving a tort. This system is known as *workers' compensation law*; all 50 states and the federal government have some type of workers' compensation system in place. Prior to workers' compensation, a person who was injured at work had to prove that the employer was responsible for a tort in order to receive compensation. This was difficult because employers had several possible defenses they could use to defeat the worker's claim. They often blamed the employee's negligence or the negligence of another worker for the injury. In other cases, employers said that a worker's injuries were simply the unavoidable risks of particular jobs and that the worker was well aware of these risks at the time of employment. As a result, up to the early part of the 20th century, many seriously injured workers and their families were denied any compensation for their work-related injuries.

Workers' compensation systems were developed around the beginning of the 20th century to provide an alternative to the tort system. In workers' compensation systems, employers contribute to a large fund that insures workers who are injured at work, and employers also waive their right to

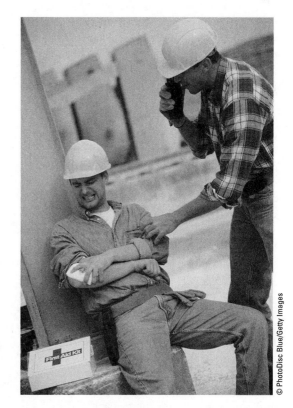

Injured on the job

blame the worker or some other individual for the injury. For their part, workers give up their right to pursue a tort case against their employers, and if they are compensated, the size of the award they receive is determined by (1) the type and duration of the injury and (2) their salary at the time of the injury. Workers can seek compensation for

- physical and psychological injuries suffered at work,
- the cost of whatever treatment is given,
- lost wages, and
- the loss of future earning capacity.

Determining how much impairment in future earning capacity a given mental disorder or psychological condition might produce is very difficult. Physicians can assess the degree of impairment from a ruptured disc or a paralyzed arm, but how can we measure the degree or permanence of a mental disability? To bring some uniformity to these determinations, many states require evaluators to use the American Medical Association's *Guide to the Evaluation of Permanent Impairment*. The latest edition of the *Guide* does not provide an objective rating system for quantifying psychological impairments, but it does include five categories of impairment, ranging from "no impairment" to "extreme impairment," that clinicians can use to organize their descriptions of a claimant (Spaulding, 1990). In general, however, ratings of psychological impairments are hard to quantify reliably.

Both employers and employees should benefit from a process in which workers' claims can be resolved fairly quickly, which is a major goal of the workers' compensation system. Formal trials are not held, and juries do not resolve these cases; they are heard and decided by a hearing officer or commissioner. (These decisions can be appealed.) In theory, workers' compensation cases should be handled expeditiously, but they often drag on for years as both sides go through a process of hiring one or more experts to examine the worker and give opinions about the injuries and any disability suffered.

How do mental health professionals become involved in workers' compensation claims? Because psychological injuries or mental disorders arising from employment can be compensated, clinicians are often asked to evaluate workers and render an opinion about the existence, cause, and implications of any mental disorders. Claims for mental disability usually arise in one of two ways. First, a physical injury can lead to a mental disorder and psychological disability. A common pattern in these *physical–mental* cases is for a worker to sustain a serious physical injury (e.g., a broken back or severe burns) that leaves the worker suffering chronic pain. As the pain and the disability associated with it continue, the worker begins to experience an overlay of psychological problems, usually depression and anxiety. These problems worsen until they become full-fledged mental disorders, resulting in further impairments in the worker's overall functioning.

The second work-related pathway to mental disability is for an individual either to suffer a traumatic incident at work or to undergo a long period of continuing stress that leads to substantial psychological difficulties. A night clerk at a convenience store who is the victim of an armed robbery and subsequently develops posttraumatic stress disorder is an example of such *mental–mental* cases. Another example is the clerical worker who, following years of overwork and pressure from a boss, experiences an anxiety disorder. In a third kind of case, known as *mental–physical*, work-related stress leads to the onset of a physical disorder such as high blood pressure. Many states have placed restrictions on these types of claims, and psychologists are seldom asked to evaluate them.

In recent years, the number of psychological claims in workers' compensation litigation has increased dramatically, and much of the increase can be attributed to a surge in mental–mental cases (Barth, 1990). In the 1980s, stress-related mental disorders became the fastest-growing category of occupational disease in the United States (Hersch & Alexander, 1990). More recently, according to one study, these claims account for only about 2% of all nonfatal workplace violence claims; however, their average cost is nearly three times higher than the average cost for other nonfatal workplace violence claims (Hashemi & Webster, 1998).

Although it is not clear what accounts for the increase in psychological claims, at least three explanations have been proposed. First, because more women have entered the workforce, and because women are more often diagnosed with anxiety and depression disorders than men, the rise in psychological claims might be due to the growing percentage of female workers (Sparr, 1995). A second possibility is that a shift in the job market from manufacturing and industrial jobs to service-oriented jobs has produced corresponding increases in job-related interpersonal stressors and decreases in physical injuries. A third possibility is that claims of psychological impairments are motivated primarily by financial incentives, generating a range of cases in which genuine impairments are mixed in with exaggerated or false claims of disability.

Very few empirical studies have been conducted on the assessment of psychological damages in workers' compensation cases. The little research that does exist has usually addressed one of the following questions:

◆ How do workers' compensation claimants score on standard psychological tests such as the Minnesota Multiphasic Personality Inventory (MMPI)?

◆ Are certain injuries or stressors associated with a particular pattern of psychological test scores?

◆ Can psychological tests distinguish claimants who are suffering from a bona fide disorder from those who are faking or exaggerating their problems?

One study investigated the most common pattern of scores on the MMPI for 200 individuals who filed worker compensation claims (Repko & Cooper, 1983). Seventeen percent of the profiles did not show any significant elevations, but over one-third of the MMPIs involved elevated scores on one or more of the scales measuring depression, fatigue and physical complaints, worrying, and a general lack of insight into psychological symptoms. These results have been replicated in other studies that have found, in addition to these psychological test patterns, a tendency for claimants to receive elevated scores on the MMPI scale measuring feelings of disorientation, isolation, alienation, and confusion (Hersch & Alexander, 1990). Of course, these high scores do not prove that the psychological distress was caused by a work-related difficulty; it is possible that already-existing psychological problems make it more likely that a person will suffer stressful or harmful experiences at work.

The research does not suggest that particular injuries or claims are reliably linked with different patterns of test scores (e.g., Snibbe, Peterson, & Sosner, 1980). One reason for the lack of distinguishing patterns might be that regardless of the injury or the stressor, most people manifest psychological distress through a mixture of physical complaints and negative emotions such as anxiety, depression, and feelings of isolation.

The objectivity of psychological evaluations performed in workers' compensation cases is threatened by several factors (Tsushima, Foote, Merrill, & Lehrke, 1996). Chief among these problems is that attorneys often retain the same expert over and over again to conduct evaluations. An expert who is repeatedly hired by the same attorney, whether it be a plaintiff or defense attorney, may risk merely advocating the opinions the expert knows is desired by the attorney, rather than rendering impartial opinions about each case.

One study investigated this issue by examining whether psychological assessments of workers' compensation claimants were related to the side that had retained the expert. Hasemann (1997) collected and compared 385 reports that had been prepared by various mental health professionals. Of these reports, 194 had been conducted by defense-hired experts, 182 were completed by plaintiff-hired experts, and 9 evaluations could not be classified. Did plaintiff and defense experts differ in their opinions in these cases? Several results indicate that they did and that they might have been unduly influenced by the adversarial system.

Consider these three results: (1) Plaintiff experts gave impairment ratings to claimants that were nearly four times larger than the impairment ratings assigned by defense experts. (2) Defense experts concluded that MMPIs completed by claimants were invalid or malingered in 72% of their evaluations, whereas plaintiff experts reached this conclusion in 31% of their evaluations. (3) Of the 19 experts who had conducted three or more evaluations, 17 tended to do so almost exclusively for one side. Ten showed partiality toward plaintiffs, conducting a total of 107 plaintiff evaluations and only 8 defense evaluations. Seven experts completed 147 assessments for the defense and only 36 for the plaintiffs.

Although these data do not prove that forensic experts cannot be impartial, they clearly raise concerns that experts are influenced by the adversarial nature of the legal process. It is conceivable that the experts were accurately describing claimants who behaved differently depending on the evaluator. One study suggests that plaintiffs who were referred for evaluations by their attorneys or who sought evaluations on their own tended to exaggerate their symptoms or respond inconsistently on the MMPI more often than did plaintiffs who were evaluated at the request of defense attorneys (Fox, Gerson, & Lees-Haley, 1995). Alternatively, it might be that the experts are reasonably impartial but the attorneys selectively introduce expert opinions depending on whether those opinions support their side. In order to consider the latter possibility, investigators such as Haseman would need to acquire the results of evaluations requested by attorneys but not subsequently presented as evidence. This is comparable to the "file drawer problem" encountered by investigators performing meta-analysis: Because research not reporting significant differences is often not accepted for publication, such results tend to languish, unpublished, in a file drawer, which limits the accuracy of the investigator's ability to determine an overall "effect" of a research phenomenon based on all the evidence. Even if forensic evaluators can be reasonably impartial, they still conduct such evaluations in the context of an adversarial system, and decisions about whether to introduce such reports as evidence are often made by attorneys who are advocates for their clients.

In addition, comparing the numbers of evaluations conducted for plaintiffs with the number conducted for defendants can be misleading, because these numbers depend on the number of referrals from each side. A better measure of evaluator impartiality involves the proportion of "useful" opinions (that is, opinions helpful to the referring attorney) relative to the overall number of referrals. For example, an evaluator who has conducted 90 evaluations for the defense and 10 for the plaintiffs might appear less impartial than the evaluator who has done 50 for the defense and another 50 for the plaintiffs. However, looking more closely at the "usefulness" proportion (termed the "contrary quotient" by Colbach, 1981) might reveal that the first evaluator has reached a conclusion favorable to the referring attorney in 50% of the defense cases and 45% of the plaintiff cases, whereas the second evaluator has favored the referring attorney in 98% and

100% of defense and plaintiff cases, respectively. Which evaluator appears less impartial? We discuss this "hired gun" problem more fully in the last section of the chapter.

Can psychological tests distinguish between claimants with bona fide disorders and those who are exaggerating? As we discussed in Chapter 4, the MMPI contains sets of items that are sometimes used to assess the test-taking attitudes of a respondent. These **validity scales** can be examined to determine whether respondents might have tried to fool the examiner by exaggerating or denying psychological problems. In workers' compensation cases, a main concern is that some plaintiffs might "fake bad" by exaggerating or inventing symptoms to improve their chances for an award.

A growing body of research focuses on whether existing or new validity scales on the MMPI-2 can distinguish respondents who have bona fide problems from those who are malingering. Tests such as the Validity Indicator Profile (Frederick, 1997, 2000; Frederick & Crosby, 2000) and the Test of Memory Malingering (Tombaugh, 1997) have been developed to detect malingering on cognitive and neuropsychological measures.

The typical case of a person trying to exaggerate or fake mental disorder involves the individual answering many items in the "bad" direction, thereby attempting to look as disturbed as possible. However, the strategy might be more complicated in the case of a person who is faking or exaggerating a disorder in a workers' compensation case. These individuals usually want to appear honest, virtuous, and free of any psychological problems that might have existed prior to the injury, while at the same time endorsing many symptoms and complaints that would establish that they had been harmed by a work-related incident. In other words, their motivation involves a combination of faking good and faking bad. A special validity scale composed of MMPI-2 items that tap this simultaneous fake-good/fake-bad strategy has been developed and has had some success in distinguishing between genuine and faked psychological injury claims (Lees-Haley, 1991, 1992).

Civil Competencies

The concept of legal competence extends to many kinds of decisions that individuals are called on to make throughout their lives. When we discussed competence to stand trial in Chapter 8, we focused on the knowledge that criminal defendants must have and the decisions they are required to make. However, the question of mental competence is raised in several noncriminal contexts as well; we refer to these other situations with the general term **civil competencies**.

The question of civil competence focuses on whether an individual has the capacity to understand information that is relevant to decision making in a given situation and then make an informed choice about what to do in that situation. Here are some questions that address issues of civil competence:

◆ Is a person competent to manage his or her financial affairs?

◆ Can an individual make competent decisions about his or her medical or psychiatric treatment?

◆ Is a person competent to execute a will and decide how to distribute property to heirs or other beneficiaries?

◆ Can a person make advance decisions about the kind of medical treatment he or she wants or does not want to receive if terminally ill or seriously injured?

The legal standards used to define competence have evolved over many years. Scholars who have studied this issue usually point to four abilities that contribute to competent decision making (Appelbaum & Grisso, 1995, Grisso, 2003). A competent individual is expected to be able to (1) understand basic information that is relevant to making a decision, (2) apply that information to a specific situation in order to anticipate the consequences of various choices, (3) use logical—or rational—thinking to evaluate the pros and cons of various strategies and decisions, and (4) communi-cate a personal decision or choice about the matter under consideration.

The specific abilities associated with each of these general criteria depend on the decision that a person must make. Deciding whether to have risky surgery demands different information and thinking processes than deciding whether to leave property to children or to a charitable organization.

Decisions about medical treatment that one might receive in the future, including the desire to have life-sustaining medical treatments discontinued, involve a special level of planning that has been encouraged by a 1990 federal statute known as the Patient Self-Determination Act. Planning about future medical treatments is formalized through what are known as **advance medical directives**, in which patients indicate what kinds of treatment they want should they later become incapacitated and incompetent to make treatment decisions. The most controversial of these advance directives is the "living will," in which a patient essentially asserts that he or she prefers to die rather than to be kept alive on a ventilator or feed-ing tubes. (In Chapter 2, we described the case of Terri Schiavo, the brain-damaged woman who died after her feeding tube was removed in 2005. Her case was controversial precisely because she had no living will; her husband vowed that she would have preferred death over life by artificial means. As a result of the intense publicity that surrounded that case, many more Americans now have advance medical directives.) The ethical and practical issues involved in determining patients' competence to issue advance medical directives are enormous, but the trend, revealed in Supreme Court decisions such as *Cruzan v. Director, Missouri Department of Health* (1990), is to recog-nize that patients have great autonomy in accept-ing or rejecting a variety of treatments and health care provisions (Cantor, 1998; Rich, 1998).

Advance medical directives seem like a sim-ple and direct way to communicate end-of-life decisions. But for living wills to be effective, indi-viduals must be able to generate preferences that are stable over time and across changes in health. Unfortunately, individuals' predictions about what kind of care they might want in the future vary from one occasion to the next and are affected by the status of their present health.

In studies that examined the stability of advance directives, participants were asked to record their preferences for various life-sustaining treat-ments (e.g., CPR) in different medical scenarios (e.g., coma). After an interval ranging from 1 month to 2 years, these individuals recorded their preferences again. The average stability of preferences across all judgments was 71%, suggesting that over time peri-ods as short as 2 years, nearly one-third of individuals' stated treatment preferences changed (Ditto et al., 2003). Of course, a person could change his or her preferences for good reason—perhaps as a result of some relevant, intervening life experience such as a health crisis or a relative's use of life-sustaining treatment. But most people are unaware that their preferences change; they mistakenly believe that the preferences they express at the second interview are identical to those they provided at the first interview (Gready et al., 2000).

Preferences are also dependent on the context in which they are made. For example, when patients recently discharged from hospitals are asked about their desire for life-sustaining treatment, they show a characteristic "hospital dip"; they report less desire for interventions than they did prior to hospi-talization—and less than they report several months after their discharge (Ditto, Jacobson, Smucker, Danks, & Fagerlin., 2005). Apparently people have difficulty expressing stable preferences for medical care in the future.

The question of competence to consent to treatment usually arises when a patient refuses treatment that seems to be medically and psycho-logically justified. Under these circumstances, the first step might be to break down the explanation of the treatment decisions facing the patient into smaller bits of information (results from the MacArthur Treatment Competence Study have shown that patients are capable of significantly better understanding when treatment information is presented to them one element at a time). Using this kind of presentation might facilitate a patient's appreciation of whether a recommended treat-ment would be in his or her best interest. Should an impasse between the patient and treating professionals still exist after such a presentation, it would be important to have a clinical assess-ment instrument that could be administered in a brief period of time to determine whether a given patient lacks the necessary ability to reach a competent decision. The development of such an instrument—the MacArthur Competence Assessment Tool for Treatment Decisions (MacCAT-T)—has now been completed (Grisso & Appelbaum, 1998a) and is commercially available (Grisso & Appelbaum, 1998b).

Assessing Competence to Make Treatment Decisions

The research for the MacCAT-T, conducted as part of a larger MacArthur Research Network on Mental Health and Law study on competencies, coercion, and risk assessment, focused on the capacities of individuals with severe mental disorders to make decisions and give informed consent about their own psychiatric treatment. Can persons with seri-ous mental disorders make competent treatment decisions for themselves? Do their decision-making abilities differ from those of persons who do not suf-fer mental disorders? Researchers in the MacArthur Treatment Competence Study developed a series of structured interview measures to assess the four basic abilities—understanding information, applying information, thinking rationally, and expressing a choice—involved in legal competence (Grisso, Appelbaum, Mulvey, & Fletcher, 1995). For example, here is an item that taps a person's ability to apply information to the question of whether he or she has a condition that could be effectively treated:

> "Most people who have symptoms of a men-tal or emotional disorder like your doctor believes you have can be helped by treatment. The most common treatment is medication. Other treatments sometimes used for such disorders are having someone to talk to about problems, and participating in group therapy with other people with similar symptoms." ". . . [D]o

you believe that you have the kind of condition for which some types of treatment might be helpful?" "All right, you believe that . . . (paraphrase of the patient's expressed opinion). Can you explain that to me? What makes you believe that . . . (again paraphrase as above)?" For a patient who believes that treatment will not work because he or she is "just too sick," the interviewer would ask: "Imagine that a doctor tells you that there is a treatment that has been shown in research to help 90% of people *with problems just as serious as yours*. Do you think this treatment might be of more benefit to you than getting no treatment at all?" (Grisso et al., 1995, p. 133)

Standardized interviews, using items of this type, were conducted with three groups of patients—those with schizophrenia, those with major depression, and those with heart disease—and with groups of people from the community who were *not* ill but were demographically matched to the patient groups (Grisso & Appelbaum, 1995). Only a minority of the persons in all the groups showed significant impairments in competent decision making about various treatment options. However, the patients with schizophrenia and major depression tended to have a poorer understanding of treatment information and used less adequate reasoning in thinking about the consequences of treatment than did the heart patients or the members of the community sample. These impairments were more pronounced and consistent across different competence abilities for patients with schizophrenia than for patients with depression, and the more serious the symptoms of mental disorder (especially those involving disturbed thinking), the poorer the understanding.

These results obviously have implications for social policies involving persons with mental disorders. First, contrary to popular impressions, the majority of patients suffering from severe disorders such as schizophrenia and major depression appear to be capable of competent decision making about their treatment. On the other hand, a significant number of patients—particularly those with schizophrenia—show impairments in their decision-making abilities.

Assessing Competence to Execute a Will

Clinicians may also be asked to evaluate whether a person (called a "testator") was competent to execute a will; such competence is a requirement for the provisions of the will to be valid. Typically, challenges to this capacity are raised when there is suspicion that the testator lacked the requisite mental capacity to execute a valid will (Frolik, 1999). Ronald Eisaman challenged his aunt's will in a Pennsylvania probate court, arguing that his aunt, Harriet Schott, lacked **testamentary capacity**. Schott executed a will in 1993, leaving the bulk of her estate to Eisaman. But she executed a second will in 1997, reducing his share to 50 percent and passing the remaining 50 percent to the corporation that owned the assisted-living facility where she resided prior to her death. The expert witnesses who testified about Schott's mental capacity were equivocal. Thus, the judge determined that Eisaman had not established that his aunt lacked testamentary capacity to change her will. The 1997 version was admitted to probate.

According to one study, situations that may raise concern about capacity to execute a will include the following: there is a radical change from a previous will (72%), undue influence is alleged (56%), the testator has no biological children (52%), the testator executed the will less than a year prior to death (48%), and the testator suffered from co-morbid conditions such as dementia (40%), alcohol abuse (28%), and other neurological/psychiatric conditions (28%) (Shulman, Cohen, & Hull, 2004).

The legal standard for testators' competence to execute a will is derived from *Banks v. Goodfellow* (1870), in which the court held as follows:

1. Testators must know at the time of making their wills that they are making their wills.
2. They must know the nature and extent of their property.
3. They must know the "natural objects of [their] bounty."
4. They must know the manner in which the wills they are making distribute their property.

This type of competence has a lower threshold than other competencies because it requires only that persons making a will have a general understanding of the nature and extent of their property and of the effect of their will on members of their family or others who may naturally claim to benefit from the property cited in the will (Melton et al., 1997). A person cannot be deemed incompetent to execute a will simply on the basis of the presence of a mental illness, unless there is clear evidence that the mental illness specifically interfered with the individual's ability to meet the set standard at the time the will was written.

Assessment of this competence focuses on the individual's functional abilities at the time his or her will was written. Melton and colleagues. (1997) outline some strategies used by mental health professionals in assessing competence to execute a will. First, they recommend structuring the evaluation to conform to the associated legal elements. They suggest using the sources available (e.g., the testator, family, friends, records) to first determine the purpose of the will and why it was written at that time. Second, they recommend gathering information about the testator's property holdings, which may include asking questions about occupation and salary, tangible property, and intangibles (e.g., bank accounts, investments). Third, the clinician should determine the testator's "values and preferences" (p. 361) to gain insight into the family dynamics (e.g., with whom the testator has a good relationship, with whom he or she does not get along). This information can shed light on the testator's rationale for bequeathing his or her belongings to specific individuals. Finally, Melton and colleagues recommend that clinicians assess the general consequences of the dispositions outlined in the will.

One of the obvious difficulties that arises in these types of evaluations is that the testator, the subject of the evaluation, is often deceased at the time the question of competence to execute the will arises. Thus, the sources of information will be different; if the testator is alive, he or she will be a primary informational source—but if he or she is deceased, the evaluator must gather information from family, friends, acquaintances, medical records, and other available sources without the testator's specific input.

Psychological Autopsies

Like most clinical assessments, the typical forensic assessment involves a clinician interviewing, observing, and testing a client to arrive at an understanding of the case. However, in a few unusual circumstances, clinicians may be called on to give an opinion about a deceased person's state of mind as it existed at a specific time before death. Obviously, in these cases, the clinician must conduct an evaluation without any participation by the individual whose prior condition is in question. These evaluations are termed **psychological autopsies** or **equivocal death analyses** (Ogloff & Otto, 1993).

Psychological autopsies originated in the 1950s when a group of social scientists in the Los Angeles area began assisting the coroner's office in determining whether suicide, murder, or accident was the most likely mode of death in some equivocal cases. Their use has spread over the years, and now they are encountered most often in cases such as determining the cause of death in situations where an insurance company could deny death benefits if the policy holder committed suicide; assessing claims in workers' compensation cases that stressful working conditions or work trauma contributed to a worker's death or suicide; evaluating a deceased individual's mental capacity to execute or modify a will; and assessing the validity of an argument occasionally made by criminal defendants that a victim's mode of death was suicide rather than homicide.

Although there is no standard format for psychological autopsies, most of them rely on information from two sources: past records and interviews with third parties who knew the decedent. General guidelines for what should be included in psychological autopsies have been published (Ebert, 1987). Some investigators concentrate on more

IIII THE CASE OF

BOX 9.3 the *U.S.S. Iowa*

On April 19, 1989, 47 U.S. Navy sailors were killed when an explosion ripped through turret 2 of the *U.S.S. Iowa*. The Navy's investigation of this tragedy initially concluded that the explosion was caused by the suicidal acts of Gunner's Mate Clayton Hartwig, who was himself killed in the explosion. The major foundation for this conclusion was a psychological autopsy conducted by FBI agents working at the National Center for the Analysis of Violent Crime. The Navy's conclusions were later evaluated by a congressional committee, which commissioned its own panel of 14 psychological and psychiatric experts to review the FBI's analysis. Partly on the basis of this panel's input, the congressional committee rejected the FBI analysis as invalid. Ultimately, the U.S. Navy also concluded that the cause of the explosion could not be determined. Randy Otto and his colleagues

The U.S.S. Iowa, *damaged in an explosion*

asked 24 psychologists and psychiatrists to rate the reports prepared by the 14 experts commissioned by the U.S. House of Representatives to review the FBI analysis of the *U.S.S. Iowa* explosion (Otto, Poythress, Starr, & Darkes, 1993). Three raters judged each of the 14 reports, and although they failed to show precise agreement

in how they thought the reports should be interpreted, they did achieve a moderate amount of broad agreement in their ratings of the 14 reports. Note, however, that this agreement pertains only to how the raters interpreted the 14 panelists' reports, not to the contents or opinions in the reports themselves.

recent data, generated close in time to the person's death. What was the person's mood? How was the person doing at work? Were there any pronounced changes in the person's behavior? Others—especially those who take a psychodynamic perspective on behavior—look for clues early in the person's life. As a child, how did the person interact with his or her parents? What was the individual's approach to school? To competition with peers?

As with any assessment technique, the first question to be considered is the reliability of the psychological autopsy. There are several reasons to suspect that the reliability of psychological

autopsies is low. The person in question is not available to be interviewed or tested. The persons who are interviewed might not remember the past accurately, or they might have reasons to distort their answers.

We are aware of only one study that has addressed the question of reliability, and it did so in a very indirect fashion, using data from the investigation of the *U.S.S. Iowa* explosion (see Box 9.3).

No empirical information exists concerning the validity of psychological autopsies—that is, whether they accurately portray a person's state of mind at the time of death. Obviously, a major problem is that the decedent's "true" state of mind is unknown; in fact, were this not the case, the autopsy would be unnecessary. However, it might still be possible to examine the validity of psychological autopsies by giving reputed experts background information in cases that appear ambiguous (but in which the cause of death *is* actually known) and studying the opinions offered and the reasons for them.

How has testimony about psychological autopsies fared in court? In cases involving workers' compensation claims and questions of whether insurance benefits should be paid, the courts have usually admitted psychological autopsy testimony; in criminal cases or in cases involving the question of whether a person had the mental capacity to execute a will, the courts have been more reluctant to permit the testimony (Ogloff & Otto, 1993). Judges are more hesitant to allow expert testimony in criminal cases than in civil ones, perhaps because the risks of prejudicial testimony are greater when one's liberties can be taken away. One reason for the courts' hesitancy in permitting psychological autopsy testimony in cases involving the validity of wills might be that, in such cases, the state of mind of the deceased is the critical question for the jury. Allowing expert testimony on this matter might therefore be viewed as invading the province of the jury, a perception that judges usually want to avoid.

Child Custody and Parental Fitness

One of the most rapidly growing areas of forensic psychology is the evaluation of families for the purpose of recommending the particular custodial arrangement that is in the best interests of a child whose parents are divorcing or separating. The increase in these cases is attributable to two facts. First, half of all marriages in the United States now end in divorce. As a result, over one-third of children in the United States will spend some time living in a stepfamily, and more than half will spend some time in a single-parent household (Bray,

1991). Therefore, the issue of custody is a practical concern for millions of families. Second, from the end of the 19th century to about the middle of the 20th century, the prevailing assumption was that awarding custody of young children (sometimes called children of "tender years") to their mothers was usually in their best interests. This preference for maternal custody has diminished as we enter the 21st century; now many courts want to know about the parenting abilities of each parent before making a decision about custody (Liss & McKinley-Pace, 1999).

Currently, the prevailing standard for custody decisions is the **future best interests of the child**, but an alternative standard—the **primary caretaker standard**—has been applied in a few states. Under the latter standard, custody is awarded to the parent who has been primarily responsible for caring for and supervising the child. Although the child's "best interests" must be assessed on a case-by-case basis, the Uniform Marriage and Divorce Act indicates that courts should consider the following criteria: (1) the wishes of the child; (2) the wishes of the child's parents; (3) the relationships between the child and the parents, siblings, and significant others who interact with the child; (4) the child's adjustment at home and school and in the community; and (5) the physical and mental health of the parties involved.

Child custody evaluations usually arise in situations in which divorcing parents disagree about which of them can best meet the needs of their children and should therefore have custody. Most states permit two kinds of custodial arrangements, each with two aspects (physical and legal). "Physical custody" refers to the living arrangement, whereas "legal custody" concerns the responsibility for decision making. In **sole custody**, it has been decided that the child will live only with one parent (although the other parent may be granted visitation rights), and/or all legal decision-making authority for that child will rest with one parent. In **joint custody**, both parents retain parental rights concerning decisions about the child's general welfare, education, health care, and other matters (for joint legal custody), or the child alternates living in the home of the mother and in the home of the father according to the schedule provided in the custody decision (joint physical custody). Joint custody does not necessarily mean that the child spends equal time with each parent, however. Usually, one parent is designated the residential parent, and the child spends more time living at the home of that parent. In general, families that are functioning better at the time that custody is awarded are more likely to ask for joint custody than families that are experiencing ongoing difficulties (Gunnoe & Braver, 2001).

Psychologists have examined the effects of sole custody and of joint custody on children and parents. Although the findings are not clear-cut, there appear to be several advantages to joint-custody arrangements. In a meta-analysis of 21 studies, Bauserman (1997) concluded that children in joint custody fared better than children in sole custody on a number of measures related to adjustment and interpersonal relations. Fathers benefitted from joint custody because they had more frequent contact with their children. Joint custody was advantageous for mothers because it afforded them greater opportunity for courtship; as a result, these mothers repartnered more rapidly than mothers with sole responsibility for their children, a situation that may be beneficial for the children (Gunnoe & Braver, 2001).

The three main differences between sole custody and joint custody are as follows:

1. Joint custody distributes the frequency of interaction more evenly between the children and each parent.
2. Joint custody requires more interactions between the divorced parents and generates more demands for cooperation concerning the children.
3. Joint custody results in more alterations in caregiving arrangements, along with more separations and reunions between children and parents (Clingempeel & Reppucci, 1982).

Many mental health professionals regard child custody cases to be the most ethically and clinically difficult forensic evaluations they perform. First, the emotional stakes are extremely high, and both parents are often willing to spare no expense or tactic in the battle over which of them will win custody. The children involved are usually forced to live—for months, if not years—in an emotional limbo in which they do not know in whose home they will be residing, where they will be going to school, or how often they will see each parent.

Second, a thorough custody evaluation requires that the clinician evaluate the children, both parents, and—when possible—others who have interacted with the child, such as relatives, teachers, and family health care providers. Often, not all the parties agree to be evaluated or do so only under coercion, resulting in a lengthy and sometimes tense process.

Third, to render a valuable expert opinion, a clinician must be quite knowledgeable—about the children and parents under evaluation, but also about child development, bonding and attachment, family systems, the effects of divorce on children, adult and childhood mental disorders, and several different kinds of testing. Added to these factors are variations in what we have traditionally defined as a family. With increasing acceptance of different lifestyles and family structures, clinicians must often confront questions about whether parents' sexual orientation or ethnicity should have any bearing on custody decisions, something we consider in more detail in Chapter 14.

Finally, child custody evaluations are often highly adversarial, with each parent trying to expose all the faults of the other and each side vigorously challenging any procedures or opinion by an expert with which it disagrees. Clinicians who conduct custody evaluations must be prepared for challenges to their clinical methods, scholarly competence, and professional ethics.

In disputed custody cases, clinicians can conduct a custody evaluation under any of three scenarios: (1) A judge can appoint one clinician to conduct a custody evaluation that is available to all the parties, (2) each side can retain its own expert to conduct independent evaluations, or (3) the sides can agree to share the expenses of hiring an expert to conduct one evaluation (Weissman, 1991). Most clinicians prefer either the first or the third option because they do not want to be subjected to the pressures that are brought to bear when separate experts are hired by each side (Keilin & Bloom, 1986). Attorneys tend to agree with this preference, believing that option 2 leads to greater bias (LaFortune & Carpenter, 1998).

Specific guidelines for conducting custody evaluations have been developed by the American Psychological Association and the Association of Family and Conciliation Courts. Although the methods used in custody evaluations vary depending on the specific issues in each case, most evaluations include the following components: (1) clinical, social history, and mental status interviews of the parents and the children; (2) standardized testing of the parents and the children; (3) observation of interactions between each parent and the children, especially when the children are minors; (4) assessments or interviews with other people who have had opportunities to observe the family (adult children of the parents, grandparents, neighbors, the family physician, school teachers, etc.); and (5) documents or records that might be relevant to the case (medical records of children and parents, report cards, arrest records).

In a national survey of mental health professionals who conducted child custody evaluations, Ackerman and Ackerman (1997) found that experts spent an average of about 30 hours on each custody evaluation. Much of this time was devoted to interviewing and observing the parties in various combinations. In fact, more than two-thirds of the respondents indicated that they conducted individual interviews with each parent and each child, observed each parent interacting (separately) with each child, and conducted formal psychological testing of the parents and the children. The MMPI was the test most often used with parents; intelligence tests and projective personality tests were the instruments most commonly used with the children.

Experts also reported how often they recommended different kinds of custodial arrangements (Keilin & Bloom, 1986). Limited joint custody

(parents share the decision making, but one parent maintains primary physical custody) was the most common recommendation (42.8%), and single-parent custody without visitation was the least often recommended alternative (4.6%). Single-parent custody with visitation (30.4%) and joint custody (21.7%) were among the other preferred recommendations.

One question addressed by several research studies is whether children raised in joint-custody arrangements function better than children in sole custody. One could predict that to the extent that joint custody allows the child to maintain close ties to both parents, better child adjustment would be promoted by joint-custody arrangements. Alternatively, one might argue that because sole custody simplifies custodial arrangements, minimizes the child's confusion over where his or her home is, and keeps still-angry parents away from each other, better adjustment will occur with sole custody.

Based on several criteria, most studies report either no major differences between children in the two types of custody or somewhat better adjustment by joint-custody children (Bender, 1994). For example, in her study of 78 stepfamilies with adolescent children, Margaret Crosbie-Burnett (1991) found that joint custody was associated with greater family cohesion, improved adjustment by the adolescents, and better relationships with their stepparents. However, the gender of the child moderated the impact of the custodial arrangement on adjustment. Girls felt more upset in sole-custody families; boys expressed more anxiety in joint-custody families. Consistent with earlier research (Emery, 1982; Hetherington & Arasteh, 1988), continuing hostility and conflicts between the parents—regardless of the type of custody arrangement—were associated with poorer adjustment on the part of the children. At this point, most research suggests that the quality of the relationship between divorced parents is more important to the adjustment of their children than whether the children are raised in sole custody or joint custody.

THE CASE OF

BOX 9.4 ### Ciesluk v. Ciesluk: Can a custodial parent move away?

When Michelle and Christopher Ciesluk were divorced in 2002, they arranged to share joint legal custody of their son, Connor, who lived primarily with his mother. But when Michelle Ciesluk lost her job with Sprint in early 2003 and the company offered to rehire her provided that she was willing to move from Colorado to Arizona, Christopher Ciesluk objected. He opposed the move, fearing he would lose any relationship with his son and would miss his son's school and athletic activities. Unfortunately for Ms. Ciesluk, neither the Colorado legislature nor the courts have made it easy for her. In 2001, the legislature abolished a legal presumption that a custodial parent has the right to move away, and an appellate court has ruled that a parent who wishes to move must demonstrate a *direct* beneficial effect on the child. (The more commonly used test requires the parent to show that the move would have an *indirect* effect on the child, typically by enhancing the custodial parent's job opportunities.) Michelle Ciesluk has not been able to meet that test, so she remains in Colorado with her son, working for $10 an hour as an administrative assistant and feeling that her "whole life is on hold" (Eaton, 2004).

In recent years, divorced couples have sometimes returned to court to ask judges to resolve both ongoing and novel disputes. For example, Pamela Peck, a divorced mother, went to family court in Dallas to seek an injunction that would ban her ex-husband's girlfriend from spending the night at his house when his son was there. A Texas judge ruled in her favor, enjoining both parties from having overnight guests of the opposite sex when "in possession of" their 9-year-old son. One of the thorniest custody issues is whether a custodial parent can relocate. An example of a "move-away case" is described in Box 9.4.

Because divorce is a potent stressor for children and because protracted custody battles tend to leave a trail of emotionally battered family members in their wake, increasing attention is being given to helping parents and children cope with these transitions or to finding alternatives to custody fights (Grych & Fincham, 1992; Kelly, 1996). Many judges require divorcing couples to attempt to settle issues of custody, visitation, and support through **mediation**, a form of alternative dispute resolution that minimizes the adversarial quality of the typical custody dispute. (Mediation is discussed further in Chapter 2.) If mediation fails, the couple can return to court and have the judge decide the issues. The benefits of custody mediation are that resolutions are reached more quickly, and with better compliance among the participants, than with adversarial procedures.

It is *not* clear, however, that mediation always leads to better adjustment by divorcing parents or by their children. To assess the impact of mediated versus adversarial child custody procedures, Robert Emery and his colleagues randomly assigned divorcing couples to settle their custody disputes either through mediation or through litigation. They found that mediation reduced the number of hearings and the total amount of time necessary to reach a resolution. Parents who mediated did not differ in their psychological adjustment from those who litigated, but a consistent gender difference in satisfaction with the two methods did emerge. Fathers who went through mediation were much more likely to report feeling satisfied with the process than fathers who litigated. Mothers who went through mediation, on the other hand, were less likely to express satisfaction with its effects, and in some ways they actually preferred litigation to mediation (Emery, Matthews, & Kitzmann, 1994; Emery, Matthews, & Wyer, 1991). Mediation is most likely to be harmful when "domestic violence, child abuse, or substance abuse [has] resulted in drastic inequalities between partners [so that] a truly consensual mutual decision may be impossible" (Liss & McKinley-Pace, 1999, p. 362).

Evaluations of parental fitness involve different questions from the typical custody dispute (Azar & Benjet, 1994). In every state, the Department of Child Welfare will intervene if it receives a credible report that a child is being abused or neglected. After an investigation, the department might file a petition asking a court to remove the child from the home and arrange placement with a relative or in foster care. In such cases, the issue before the court is whether the child should be left with the parents or removed from the home because of parental unfitness. The issue for the evaluator is different from the issue in a custody case. In a custody case, the matter to be determined is what arrangement with the parents is in the best interests of the child. In abuse/neglect cases, the issue is what arrangement protects the child's well-being, while properly respecting the rights of the parents. Although parental rights are important, the state must protect children from parents who cannot or will not provide adequate food, shelter, and supervision. The state must also protect children from parents who abuse them, physically or psychologically. A clinician might recommend that the child be placed temporarily in foster care and that the parents receive training in parenting skills as a condition of having the child returned to them. In extreme cases—those in which parents abandon a child or are clearly incapable of caring for a child—the state might seek to terminate parental rights. This is done most often when relatives or others wish to adopt the child.

In an interesting twist on the usual circumstances of termination cases, 12-year-old Gregory Kingsley asked a Florida judge in 1992 to terminate his parents' right to function as parents on his behalf. Gregory had been removed from his home and placed in foster care, but when the state attempted to return him to his birth parents, Gregory objected and tried to sever his parents' ties to him. Courts had never before confronted the question of whether a 12-year-old can bring a termination petition, but both the trial judge and an appellate court ruled in Gregory's favor (Haugaard & Avery, 2002).

Civil Commitment and Risk Assessment

All 50 states and the District of Columbia have **civil commitment** laws that authorize the custody and restraint of persons who, as a result of mental illness, are a danger to themselves or others or who are so gravely disabled that they cannot care for themselves. This restraint is usually accomplished by compulsory commitment to a mental hospital. The courts also provide safeguards and rules for how these involuntary commitments are to be accomplished.

Many of these procedures were instituted in the 1970s in response to a concern that in the 1950s and 1960s, it was too easy to commit people to state psychiatric facilities. At that time, people who were mentally ill could be involuntarily committed whenever the state believed they needed treatment. Beginning around 1970, commitment proceedings began to be reformed, resulting in more legal rights for the mentally ill to resist compulsory commitment. A key case in this reform movement was *O'Connor v. Donaldson* (1975), in which the Supreme Court held that mental illness and a need for treatment were insufficient justifications for involuntarily committing mentally ill persons who were not dangerous.

Similar limits on involuntary hospitalizations have been upheld by the Supreme Court more recently (e.g., *Foucha v. Louisiana*, 1992). The standard for commitment changed from mere mental illness to mental illness that was associated with dangerousness or a grave lack of ability to care for oneself. Ironically, today many people believe "it's too hard to get people in and much too easy to get them out" of mental hospitals (Riechmann,

1985, p. 6). Mental health activists and patients' families feel that patients are often "dumped," without concern for their fate on the outside. Some of these deinstitutionalized people end up in the courts and jails after being on the streets (Teplin, 1984). Although the legislative changes of the 1970s were intended to protect the rights of the mentally ill, an exclusive concern with rights can sometimes leave patients without adequate care, housing, or the effective psychiatric treatment that can be provided in some hospitals (Turkheimer & Parry, 1992; Wexler, 1992).

Four Types of Commitment Procedures

The laws permit four types of civil commitment: (1) emergency detention, (2) voluntary inpatient commitment, (3) involuntary inpatient commitment, and (4) outpatient commitment. Emergency detention (which in some states does not require a court order) is the means by which most mental patients are initially admitted to hospitals; that is, detention is permitted under emergency or temporary commitment statutes. A police officer, a mental health professional, or sometimes a private citizen can initiate involuntary detention of another person. Usually, the cause is actual or anticipated harmful behavior by the patient either against self (e.g., attempted suicide) or against others. The examination is performed by a physician or a qualified mental health professional. Patients committed on an emergency basis are told that they can be detained for only a specified length of time before a review takes place, usually a matter of two or three days. Then a preliminary hearing must be held before the patient can be confined any longer.

A person may volunteer to enter a mental institution, although he or she still must meet the criteria for hospitalization (typically some version of "mentally ill and in need of treatment"). Schwitzgebel and Schwitzgebel (1980) note, "In actual practice, 'voluntary' admission is seldom as benign as the formalities make it appear. Usually there is considerable pressure from relatives, civil

authorities, and mental health personnel who are becoming worried or angry about a person's deviant behavior" (p. 8). But while voluntarily hospitalized, the patient may find that the hospital has instigated commitment proceedings to challenge or delay release. The following research investigation illustrates the tendency for patients, once committed to the hospital, to be seen as deserving to be there, whether they really are or not.

In 1973, David Rosenhan tested the ability of staff members at psychiatric hospitals to distinguish "normal" from "insane" behaviors. He and seven other normal persons gained admission to hospitals (in five states on the East and West Coasts) by complaining of hearing voices that repeated the word *one* and also said, "empty," "hollow," and "thud." The pseudopatients were a psychology graduate student, three psychologists, a pediatrician, a psychiatrist, a painter, and a homemaker—three women and five men. Seven were diagnosed as schizophrenic and one as manic depressive.

Immediately after being admitted, the pseudopatients stopped saying they heard voices. They gave false names and employment data, but otherwise they responded honestly to questions about their lives and tried to interact normally with the staff. It became apparent to them that a psychiatric label, once attached, distorted the staff's interpretations of patients' behavior. For example, the pseudopatients had been told to keep detailed notes about life in the wards. Members of the staff, in observing this behavior, concluded that they were obsessive-compulsive.

None of the pseudopatients was detected as such by the staff of any of the hospitals. In fact, the only ones who sometimes recognized the pseudopatients as normal were other patients. But the pseudopatients were eventually released. The hospital stays averaged 19 days, with a range of 7 to 52 days. Each of the pseudopatients who had been diagnosed as schizophrenic was eventually discharged with the label of "schizophrenia in remission." Thus, the diagnostic label stuck, despite changes in behavior.

The third type of commitment—involuntary inpatient commitment—requires a court order.

The criteria for obtaining an involuntary civil commitment vary from state to state; in general, however, the person must be mentally ill and must fulfill both of the following conditions: (1) be dangerous to self and others or so gravely disabled as to be unable to provide for his or her own basic needs, and (2) need treatment that is available in a setting no less restrictive than a hospital. Although the criterion of "dangerousness" is the most often discussed standard and therefore is deemed the most important for involuntary hospitalization, grave disability is the standard that determines most commitments (Turkheimer & Parry, 1992).

For an involuntary commitment to be obtained, the concerned persons must petition the court for a professional examination of the individual in question. A formal court hearing usually follows the examination. In most states, the hearing is mandatory, and persons whose commitment is sought can call witnesses and have their lawyer cross-examine witnesses who testify against them.

A fourth type of commitment procedure, known as outpatient commitment, is available in nearly all states and allows a patient to be mandated to receive treatment in an outpatient setting, such as a community mental health center, rather than in a hospital (Hiday & Goodman, 1982). Outpatient commitment often involves conditional release from a hospital; that is, formerly hospitalized patients are ordered to continue treatment in the community. Several legal and clinical complications arise with this approach. For example, what should be done with patients who refuse medication? Are therapists who treat these patients liable for any dangerous acts the patients might commit? And, most important, is effective community-based treatment available?

Dangerousness and Risk Assessment

Dangerousness is one of the central constructs of mental health law. Whether a person is now or could in the future be dangerous is an issue that underlies many decisions in our system of justice, including questions of civil commitment. Although the law often uses the terms *dangerous* and *dangerousness*, these terms are difficult to define. They actually merge three distinct constructs: (1) risk factors (variables associated with the probability that violence or aggression will occur), (2) harm (the nature and severity of the aggression predicted, and its results), and (3) risk level (the probability that harm will occur) (National Research Council, 1989). In some combination, these factors provide a major justification for involuntarily committing the mentally ill to hospitals.

As we saw in Chapter 1 when we discussed the *Tarasoff* case, dangerousness is the basis for requiring therapists to protect third parties from possible acts of violence against them by the patients of these therapists. Chapter 7 identified dangerousness as a reason for denying bail to certain defendants. In Chapter 8, we learned that dangerousness is the justification for hospitalizing defendants after they have been found not guilty by reason of insanity. And as you will learn in Chapter 15, some states use future dangerousness as one factor a jury can consider when deciding whether to sentence a convicted murderer to life in prison or death by execution. In Chapter 15, we also discuss the related question of predicting whether certain sex offenders will reoffend.

Difficulties in Assessing Dangerousness

For reasons described in the last section, it is clearer to use the term *violence risk* than *dangerous*. We will do so throughout the remainder of this chapter. Can mental health experts accurately assess a person's present violence risk and then predict whether that person will be violent in the future? Is mental illness a sign that a person is likely to be violent? Do certain types of mental illness make a person more prone to violent behavior? These questions have been examined extensively by researchers for more than three decades, and they are at the heart of many real-life cases. For example, should the mental health professionals who treated John Hinckley in the past have predicted that he posed a danger to

President Reagan? What about Jeffrey Dahmer? Was his brutal behavior predictable, given his early psychological problems?

Clinicians who attempt to answer these questions perform what are called **risk assessments**; using the best available data and research, they try to predict which persons are and which are not likely to behave violently in certain circumstances, give some estimate of the risk for violence, and offer suggestions on how to reduce the risks (Monahan & Steadman, 1994; Webster, 1998).

The original consensus of researchers was that mental illness was not linked to a risk of violence. Leading scholars such as John Monahan (1984) of the University of Virginia had once concluded that clinicians could not assess risks for future violent behavior with any acceptable degree of accuracy. The following summary of this research is typical: "In one study after another, the same conclusion emerges: for every correct prediction of violence, there are numerous incorrect predictions" (Pfohl, 1984). Another early summary of the research on clinicians' ability to predict violence was that their predictions were wrong in two of every three cases in which a "yes" prediction of future violence was made.

More recent research has modified the early pessimism about clinicians' ability to predict violence. Researchers have learned that these predictions can sometimes reach moderate to good levels of accuracy when certain conditions are present (Borum, 1996). Specifically, clinicians who consider a set of factors that years of research have shown to be related to future violence can predict the risk for violence considerably better than was the case 20 years ago (Douglas & Webster, 1999). Specifically, when clinicians are given information about a range of historical, personal, and environmental variables related to violence, when they limit their predictions to specific kinds of violent behavior, and when they concentrate on predicting risks in certain settings rather than in all situations, they can predict violence with a fair degree of accuracy. Although they still make a large number of errors, they do significantly better than chance.

Many factors can lower the accuracy of predictions of violence. For example, the base rate of violence in some groups is low, so clinicians are being asked to predict a phenomenon that rarely occurs. The clinical assessments of persons assessed for violence risk are usually conducted in hospitals or prisons, whereas the environment where violence is relevant for those being considered for release is the community. The predictions have often been for long-term risk, which is harder to predict than violence risk over a shorter time frame such as two weeks.

However, if we examine clinicians' ability to predict violent behavior on a short-term basis, particularly when they are familiar with whether a person has a history of prior violence or has stated an intention to behave violently, we find the predictions to be much more accurate (Klassen & O'Connor, 1988). Thus, reasonable accuracy in predictions can be expected under the following conditions: (1) the predictions are over the short term, (2) they are made for environments in which the clinician has information about the person's past behavior, (3) they consider the person's history of violent behavior, and (4) they are made for individuals belonging to groups with relatively high base rates of violence (Litwack & Schlesinger, 1987; Mossman, 1994).

As accustomed as psychologists once were to claiming that mental illness and violence were not associated, recent evidence suggests that this opinion may be wrong. Monahan himself has revised his stance on this issue; whereas he once concluded that there was no link between mental illness and violence, he now believes that a small but reliable connection exists. After reviewing recent studies that surveyed the prevalence of violent behavior among mentally ill people in the community and that measured levels of mental illness among violent citizens, Monahan (1992) concluded, "there appears to be a relationship between mental disorder and violent behavior. Mental disorder may be a robust and significant risk factor for the occurrence of violence" (p. 519).

On the basis of a review of risk assessment research, Kevin Douglas and Christopher Webster (1999) identified 20 predictor variables that are related to the risk of violence. Ten of these variables are *static predictors*, meaning that they are features about an individual or an individual's past that do not change. Five variables are termed *dynamic predictors* because they involve features about the individual (such as psychological condition, emotional state, and involvement in treatment) that can and do change over time. The final five variables, known as *risk management predictors*, are concerned with the nature of the environments in which a subject will live in the future.

STATIC PREDICTORS

In general, these variables tend to be the strongest predictors of future violence:

1. A *history of prior violence*
2. *The younger a person's age*, particularly if the person's first incidence of violence was committed at a young age
3. A *history of relationship instability or hostility*
4. A *history of employment instability* involving frequent unemployment or job terminations
5. A *pattern of drug or alcohol abuse*
6. A *major mental disorder* such as schizophrenia or severe mood disturbances
7. A diagnosis of *psychopathy or antisocial personality disorder*
8. A *history of early maladjustment at home or school*
9. A *diagnosis of any personality disorder*, but especially antisocial personality disorder and borderline personality disorder
10. A history of *attempted or actual escapes from custody or confinement*

DYNAMIC PREDICTORS

The following clinical variables have been shown to often correlate with increased risks for dangerous behavior:

11. A *lack of insight* into one's own personality and capacity for violent behavior, as well as a tendency to misunderstand the intentions of others
12. A tendency to be *angry and hostile* in multiple situations
13. Experiencing *psychotic symptoms such as delusions and hallucinations that threaten a person's self-control*
14. Tendencies toward *impulsivity and unstable negative emotions*
15. *Resistance or unresponsiveness to psychiatric treatment*

RISK MANAGEMENT PREDICTORS

These factors involve characteristics of social and physical environments that can elevate risks for violence:

16. *A lack of adequate supervision and monitoring for persons released from institutions*
17. *Easy access to victims, weapons, alcohol, and drugs*
18. *Lack of social support and tangible resources for effective living*
19. *Noncompliance with medication and other mental health treatments*
20. *Excessive stress in the areas of family, employment, and peers*

On the basis of this list, several risk assessment instruments have been developed to help clinicians utilize the most important variables for assessing risk and predicting violence. For example, the HCR-20 (meaning 20 historical, clinical, and risk management variables; Webster, Douglas, Eaves, & Hart, 1997) predicts violent behavior by released psychiatric patients. The Violence Risk Appraisal Guide (VRAG; Harris, Rice, & Quinsey, 1993) has been used to predict violent recidivism among offenders. Some tools have been designed to predict violence in specific subgroups, such as sex offenders (Hanson & Thornton, 2000), spouse abusers (Kropp & Hart, 2000), and those who are civilly committed (Monahan et al., 2005). Each of these instruments relies heavily on the presence and combination of the static variables that have proved to be the strongest predictors of violence.

SUMMARY

1. *What problems are associated with expert testimony, and what reforms have been proposed?* The main objections to expert testimony are that it invades the province of the jury, is too adversarial and thus insufficiently impartial, takes too much court time, introduces irrelevant information, and is often founded on an insufficient scientific base. Proposed reforms have focused on limiting the scope of expert testimony, reducing the partisanship involved in adversaries retaining their own experts, requiring judges to examine more strictly the scientific foundation of expert testimony, and referring to it as opinion testimony rather than as expert testimony. The limitation in scope and having judges consider the scientific foundation more carefully are proposals that have been implemented.

2. *Under what conditions can a plaintiff be compensated for psychological damages?* Plaintiffs can seek damages in civil trials if they are a victim of a tort, which is a wrongful act that can be proved to have caused them harm. Although the law has historically been skeptical of claims for psychological harm and emotional distress unless they are accompanied by physical injuries, the recent trend has been to allow plaintiffs to be compensated for emotional damages (without any physical injuries) resulting from intentionally outrageous or negligent conduct.

3. *What is workers' compensation, and how do mental health professionals participate in such cases?* Workers' compensation is a no-fault system now used by all states and in the federal system to provide a streamlined alternative for determining the compensation of workers who are injured in the course of their jobs. Although formal trials are not held or juries used in workers' compensation cases, it is not clear that these cases are handled as expeditiously as intended. Psychologists often testify in workers' compensation hearings about the extent, cause, and likely prognosis for psychological problems that have developed following a physical injury and/or work-related stress.

4. *What capacities are involved in civil competence?* Questions of civil competence focus on whether an individual has the mental capacity to understand information that is relevant to decision making in a given situation and then make an informed choice about what to do. The issue of civil competence is raised when it is not clear that an individual is capable of managing his or her financial affairs, giving informed consent to current or future medical treatments, or executing a will.

5. *What criteria are used for decisions about disputes involving child custody or parental fitness?* The future best interest of the child is the main criterion applied to disputes about which parent should have custody of a child following divorce. Evaluations of parental fitness address a different question: Should a parent's custody of a child be terminated because of indications of parental unfitness? Many mental health professionals regard custody and parental fitness assessments as the most difficult evaluations they perform. For this reason, and in an attempt to reduce the stress of custody battles, custody mediation has been developed as a less adversarial means of resolving these disputes.

6. *How well can clinicians assess the risk of dangerousness, or violent behavior, a key criterion for civil commitment?* Persons who are considered gravely disabled or dangerous to themselves or others may be committed to a state mental hospital against their will, but they have the right to a hearing shortly thereafter to determine whether they should be retained. After being hospitalized, some patients may continue on outpatient commitment. Long-term predictions of violence risk cannot be made with any acceptable degree of accuracy, but there is a reliable association among several static, dynamic, and environmental factors and dangerous behavior that provides a basis for reasonably accurate short-term assessments of risk.

KEY TERMS

advance medical
  directives
breached duty
civil commitment
civil competence
compensatory damages
dangerousness

duty
equivocal death analysis
future best interests of
  the child
harm
intentional behavior
joint custody

malingering
mediation
negligence
primary caretaker
  standard
proximate cause
psychological autopsy

punitive damages
risk assessment
sole custody
testamentary capacity
tort
validity scales

The Trial Process

ORIENTING QUESTIONS

1. *What is the purpose of a trial?*
2. *What are the steps the legal system follows in bringing a case to trial?*
3. *What is the order of procedures in the trial itself?*
4. *Do juries' verdicts differ from those of judges?*
5. *What is jury nullification?*
6. *How has race been involved in the debate over jury nullification?*

THE CASE OF

BOX 10.1   Bruno Richard Hauptmann: Arguments and evidence

Even though the trial occurred nearly 70 years ago, people still talk about it, books are still being published about it, and critics still speculate about whether the verdict was just (Behn, 1995; Berg, 1998). The offense has been termed one of the "crimes of the century" (Geis & Bienen, 1998). The violent treatment of the victim sickened our society, which then sought retribution.

Sometime during the night of March 1, 1932, the young son of Colonel Charles A. Lindbergh was kidnapped from a crib in the nursery of his parents' estate in Hopewell, New Jersey. Lindbergh, who ironically had been called "Lucky Lindy," was the quintessential American hero. In 1927, piloting the *Spirit of St. Louis*, he had become the first person to complete a solo flight from the United States to Europe.

A month after the baby's kidnapping, Col. Lindbergh, through a go-between, paid $50,000 to a shadowy figure he had arranged to meet in a Bronx, New York, cemetery; Lindbergh had been assured that the child would then be returned unharmed. But he was not. On May 12, 1932, two months after the kidnapping, the baby's body was found in a shallow grave about five

miles from Lindbergh's home. His skull had been bashed in, probably on the night he was kidnapped.

For more than two years, the police and the FBI sought the criminal. They had found several physical clues, including ransom notes, footprints under a first-floor window, and a makeshift ladder apparently used to climb to the second-floor nursery, but it was not until September 19, 1934, that the police arrested Bruno Hauptmann and charged him with the crime.

Bruno Richard Hauptmann, 34 at the time of his arrest, was German-born and was in the United States illegally. Through dogged persistence, he had entered the United States without money, passport, or source of income and had successfully adapted to a new country and a new language.

The trial began in Flemington, New Jersey, the day after New Year's in 1935. Public interest was intense; hundreds of reporters crowded into the small courthouse to cover the trial. Some media representatives went beyond calm, objective reporting: "no harmless rumor was too wild to print, no conjecture too fantastic to publish" (Whipple, 1937, pp. 46–47). Radio

CHARLES AND ANNE LINDBERGH

stations retained well-known attorneys daily to broadcast their opinions about the progress of the case and the likelihood of Hauptmann's conviction.

The public hoped that those chances were good; the whole country seemed to harbor a deep-felt desire that the defendant be convicted and executed. And he was. After a trial that lasted 40 days, the jury returned its unanimous verdict that Bruno Richard Hauptmann was guilty of murder and made no recommendation of mercy. After several unsuccessful appeals, he was electrocuted on April 3, 1936.

What Is the Purpose of a Trial?

Every trial, civil or criminal, presents two contrasting versions of the truth, just as the Hauptmann trial did. Both sides try to present the

"facts" of the matter in question in such a way as to convince the fact finder (the judge or the jury) that their claims are the truth. The fact finder must render judgments on the probable truth or falsity of each side's statements and evidence.

Was Bruno Hauptmann guilty? Here are the arguments and evidence used by each side in his trial. What do you think?

In the Lindbergh kidnapping trial, the prosecution presented the following evidence and arguments:

1. One of the ransom bills was found in a bank deposit from a gasoline station. In examining the bill, the FBI discovered written on it an automobile license plate number—that of a car registered to Hauptmann.
2. A thorough search of Hauptmann's garage revealed $14,600 of the Lindbergh ransom money secreted in an extraordinary hiding place.
3. Written on a strip of wood in a closet in Hauptmarm's house was the telephone number of the man who served as an intermediary in the transport of the ransom money.
4. When the police dictated to Hauptmann the contents of the ransom notes and asked him to transcribe them, he misspelled certain words, just as the author of the notes had. (The wording of the notes—

such as "The child is in gut care"—implied that they had been composed by a German-speaking person.)

5. Hauptmann stopped work on the very day the ransom was paid and never thereafter resumed steady employment. He bragged to friends that he could live without working because he knew how to beat the stock market, although in actuality he was losing money (Whipple, 1937).
6. Wood from the makeshift ladder could have come from a portion of the floorboards of Hauptmann's attic that had been removed.

The defense presented the following responses:

1. Several witnesses testified that they saw Hauptmann in the Bronx, New York, on the night of the kidnapping, implying that he could not have kidnapped the baby.
2. Expert witnesses claimed that the wood on the makeshift ladder did not match that from the attic.
3. The ransom money in his garage, he said, had belonged

to his friend Isidor Fisch. Fisch had returned to Germany and then died, so Hauptmann had kept the money safely hidden.

4. Hauptmann claimed that when the police dictated the ransom notes to him, they insisted that he spell the words as they were spelled in the notes. He knew, for example, that *boat* was not spelled "boad," as it was on the notes.

Hauptmann proclaimed his innocence to the day he died. So did his wife, who for 60 years sought to reverse the decision. As recently as 1985, the U.S. Third Circuit Court of Appeals rejected her request to reinstate a lawsuit against the state of New Jersey for wrongfully trying and convicting her husband. In that same year, a book by Ludovic Kennedy (1985) concluded that the prosecution withheld unfavorable evidence, perjured its witnesses, and capitalized on the public mood in order to frame Hauptmann. A more recent review of the case (Behn, 1995) reconsiders early speculation that Mrs. Lindbergh's sister was the real murderer.

If we were asked what the purpose of a trial is, our first response might be "to determine the truth, of course." Conflicts over the purposes of the legal system, however, raise the question of whether this really is the prime function of a trial. In fact, trials also serve other purposes in our society: They provide a sense of stability and a way to resolve conflicts so that the disputants can receive satisfaction. Miller and Boster (1977) have identified three images of the trial that reflect these contrasting conceptions. We will briefly consider each.

Courtroom scene with judge, witness, and jury

The Trial as a Search for the Truth

Many people see a trial as a rule-governed event involving the parties' collective search for the truth (Miller & Boster, 1977). This view assumes that what really happened can be clearly ascertained— that witnesses are capable of knowing, remembering, and describing events completely and accurately. Although this image of the trial recognizes that the opposing attorneys present only those facts that buttress their positions, it assumes that the truth will emerge from the confrontation of conflicting facts. It also assumes that judges or jurors, in weighing these facts, can "lay aside their prejudices and preconceived views regarding the case and replace such biases with a dispassionate analysis of the arguments and evidence" (Miller & Boster, 1977, p. 25).

The Trial as a Test of Credibility

The image of the trial as a rational, rule-governed event has been challenged on several grounds. Chapter 5 questioned the assumption that eyewitnesses are thorough and accurate reporters, as the legal system would like to believe. We saw in Chapter 6 that interrogations can sometimes result in false confessions and that jurors are not particularly good at distinguishing false confessions from true confessions. Sections of Chapters 11 and 12 review the limitations of jurors and judges as they seek to put aside their own experiences and prejudices. Although this image remains as an inspiring ideal, other images need to be considered as well.

A second conception—that the trial is a test of credibility—acknowledges that facts and evidence are always incomplete and biased. Hence the decision makers, whether judge or jury, must not only weigh the information and evidence but also evaluate the truthfulness of the opposing sources of evidence (Miller & Boster, 1977). Fact finders must focus on the way evidence is presented, the qualifications of witnesses, the omissions from a body of testimony, and the inconsistencies between witnesses. Competence and trustworthiness of witnesses take on added importance in this image.

These two images share the belief that the primary function of a trial is to produce the most nearly valid judgment about the guilt of a criminal defendant or the responsibility of a civil defendant.

The difference between the two images is one of degree, not of kind; Miller and Boster (1977) observe that "where the two images diverge is in the relative emphasis they place on weighing information and evidence per se as opposed to evaluating the believability of the sources of such information" (p. 29).

This image of the trial also has problems. Fact finders often make unwarranted inferences about witnesses and attorneys on the basis of race, gender, mannerisms, or style of speech. Judges' and jurors' judgments of credibility may be based more on stereotypes, folklore, or "commonsense intuition" than on the facts.

The Trial as a Conflict-Resolving Ritual

The third image shifts the function of the trial from determining the truth to providing a mechanism to resolve controversies. Miller and Boster (1977) express it this way: "At the risk of oversimplification we suggest that it removes primary attention from the concept of doing justice and transfers it to the psychological realm of *creating a sense that justice is being done*" (p. 34).

This third image gives priority to maintaining the perception that "our legal system provides an efficient means of resolving conflict peacefully" (p. 34). Truth remains a goal, but participants in the trial process also need both the opportunity to have their "day in court" and the reassurance that, whatever the outcome, "justice was done."

In 1935, the nation wanted to know the identity of the Lindbergh baby's kidnapper. Did Bruno Hauptmann really do it? But people also needed to know that the killer had been captured, tried, and convicted. The nation could not indefinitely tolerate any uncertainty in this matter. Thus, trials serve to stabilize society, provide answers, and give closure so that people can resume their normal business. They are useful rituals in our process of ensuring that evil acts are punished in a just manner.

A trial conducted in Oklahoma in 2004 exemplified this desire for closure. Several years before, Oklahoma City bombing suspect Terry Nichols was convicted on federal charges and sentenced to life in prison, rather than to death (his co-defendant, Timothy McVeigh, was executed in 2001). An Oklahoma prosecutor, responding to some victims' families who were eager to see Nichols also put to death, charged him in state court with 161 counts of first-degree murder (for the 160 people and one fetus who were killed in the blast) and requested the death penalty. But Nichols was again spared execution when this second jury, despite convicting him, deadlocked over his sentence. By law, Nichols was sentenced (again) to life in prison—161 consecutive life sentences, to be exact—and those families hoping for closure were disappointed (again).

The stabilizing function of a trial is worthless, of course, if the public doubts that justice was done in the process. Sometimes a sense of closure is not the result; the widespread dissatisfaction in some segments of our society with the outcome of O. J. Simpson's criminal trial (Brigham & Wasserman, 1999) ensured continued media interest and public fascination with his actions and statements. The belief that "he got away with murder" even led to proposals to reform and restrict the jury system, which we review in Chapter 12. However, other segments of society were equally dissatisfied with the verdict in Simpson's civil trial, in which he was found liable for the deaths of his ex-wife and her friend Ronald Goldman. Perhaps together, the verdicts in the two trials converged on a reasonable outcome—Simpson probably was the killer, but this couldn't be proven beyond a reasonable doubt, the level of certainty required for a criminal conviction.

These three contrasting images are guideposts for interpreting the findings presented in this and the next two chapters. Truth is elusive, and in the legal system, all truth seekers are subject to human error, even though the system seems to assume that they approach infallibility. The failure to achieve perfection in our decision making will become evident as the steps in the trial process are reviewed.

Steps in the Trial Process

The usual steps in a trial are sketched out here as a framework for issues to be evaluated in this and the next two chapters.

Preliminary Actions

In Chapter 7, we discussed **discovery**, the pretrial process by which each side tries to gain vital information about the case that will be presented by the other side. This information includes statements by witnesses, police records, documents, material possessions, experts' opinions, and anything else relevant to the case.

Statements from parties involved in a case may be taken in written form, called **written interrogatories**. These do not permit cross-examination. In carrying out discovery, particularly in civil cases, attorneys may also collect **depositions** from witnesses expected to testify at trial. A deposition is usually an oral statement by a potential witness, given under oath in the presence of a court reporter and attorneys from both sides. (A judge is seldom present.) It is taken in question-and-answer form, like testimony in court, with the opportunity for the opposing lawyer (or "adversary") to cross-examine the witness. In his now-famous deposition in the Paula Jones sexual harassment case, President Clinton stated that he had not had sexual relations with Monica Lewinsky. In her equally famous deposition given in the Senate impeachment trial of President Clinton, Lewinsky swore under oath that she had not been asked to lie about their relationship.

Before any trial, the decision must be made whether a judge or a jury will hear the evidence and render the verdict. The U.S. Constitution provides criminal defendants with the right to have the charges against them judged by a jury of their peers. In addition, the defendant is entitled to be acquitted unless the jury finds his or her guilt beyond a reasonable doubt.

Although most defendants opt for a jury trial, some choose to waive a jury trial and, if the prosecutor agrees, have a judge decide the case. Does it make any difference? We answer this important question in a later section of this chapter.

Civil lawsuits may also be decided by either a jury or a judge, depending on the preferences of the opposing parties. Many states have revised the size and **decision rule** from the traditional 12-person jury requiring a unanimous verdict. In some states, for some kinds of cases, juries as small as six persons or decision rules requiring only a three-fourths majority are in effect.

Jury Selection

If the trial is before a jury, the identification of jurors involves a two-step process. The first step is to draw a panel of prospective jurors, called a *venire*, from a large list (usually based on voter registration lists and lists of licensed drivers).

Once the *venire* for a particular trial has been selected—this may be anywhere from 30 to 200 people, depending on the customary practices of that jurisdiction and the nature of the trial—a process known as *voir dire* is employed to question and select the eventual jurors. (*Voir dire* is French for "to tell the truth.") Prospective jurors who reveal biases and are unable to be open-minded about the case are dismissed from service, so the task of jury selection is really one of elimination. Prospective jurors who appear free of these limitations are thus "selected." *Voir dire* can have important effects on the outcome of the trial; the process is described in detail in Chapter 11.

The Trial

Before we detail the procedures involved in trials, we briefly consider the advantages accorded to the prosecution and to the defense in criminal trials. You will notice that opposing sides have roughly offsetting advantages. For example, the prosecution gets the first and last chance to address the judge or jury, but it also has the burden of proving its case to the fact finder. The defense, on the other hand, is not given the opportunity to speak first or to speak last. But it has the advantage of not needing to prove anything to the judge or jury. If the prosecution is unable to meet its obligation to convince the fact finder of the defendant's guilt, then the defendant prevails. What other advantages accrue to each side in a criminal case?

ADVANTAGES TO THE PROSECUTION

The state, in its efforts to convict wrongdoers and bring justice to bear, has several advantages:

1. It has the full resources of the government at its disposal to carry out a prosecution. Detectives can locate witnesses and subpoena them. The state can marshal testimony from chemists, fingerprint examiners, medical examiners, psychiatrists, photographers, or whoever is an appropriate expert.
2. The prosecution can produce its evidence in a virtually unfettered way if a grand jury system is used to bring down indictments. (Chapter 7 describes the grand jury.)
3. In the trial itself, the prosecution presents its evidence before the defense, getting "first crack" at the jury. In presenting opening statements, which are not evidence but do provide a structure for the entire trial, the prosecution always goes first. And at the end of the trial, when both sides are permitted closing arguments (again, not part of the evidence), the prosecution usually gets to go first and then is permitted to offer a final rebuttal to the defense attorney's closing argument. Therefore, the prosecution has the advantages of both *primacy* and *recency* in its attempts at jury persuasion.

ADVANTAGES TO THE DEFENSE

The courts also provide defendants certain safeguards, including the following:

1. The defense is entitled to "discovery"; the prosecution must turn over exculpatory evidence, but the defense does not have to turn over incriminating evidence.
2. If a trial is before a jury, the defense may exercise more peremptory challenges—that is, opportunities to remove potential jurors without giving a reason (see Chapter 11)—than the prosecution.
3. Defendants do not have to take the stand as witnesses on their own behalf. In fact, they do not have to put on any defense at all; the burden is on the prosecution to prove beyond a reasonable doubt that the defendant is guilty of the crime.
4. Defendants who are found not guilty can never be tried again for that specific crime. For example, National Basketball Association star Jayson Williams was acquitted on the charge of aggravated manslaughter in the death of a chauffer at his mansion. (In a confusing verdict, the jury did convict Williams of trying to cover up the man's death as a suicide, hindering apprehension, and fabricating evidence.) But even if incontrovertible evidence of Williams's guilt on the manslaughter charge comes to light at some time in the future, he can never be retried for that offense.

The advantages that are accorded to the prosecution and defense pertain only to criminal trials. But all trials—whether related to criminal law or to civil law—include similar procedural steps. At the beginning of the trial itself, lawyers for each side are permitted to make **opening statements**. These are not part of the evidence (if the trial is before a jury, the jurors are instructed that these opening statements are not to be considered evidence), but they serve as overviews of the evidence to be presented. The prosecution or plaintiff usually goes first, because this side is the one that brought charges and bears the burden of proof. Attorneys for the defendant, in either a criminal or civil trial, can choose to present their opening statement immediately after the other side's or to wait until it is their turn to present evidence.

After opening statements, the prosecution or plaintiff calls its witnesses. Each witness testifies under oath, with the threat of a charge of **perjury** if the witness fails to be truthful. That witness is then cross-examined by the adverse counsel, after which the original attorney has a chance for **redirect questioning**. Redirect questioning is likely if the original attorney feels the opposition has "impeached" his or her witness; **impeach** in this context refers to a cross-examination that has effectively called into question the credibility (or reliability) of the witness.

The purpose of redirect examination is to "rehabilitate" the witness, or to salvage his or her original testimony. The defense, however, has one more chance to question the witness, a process called **recross** (short for "re-cross-examination").

After the prosecution's or plaintiff's attorneys have presented all their witnesses, it is the defense's turn. The same procedure of direct examination, cross-examination, redirect, and recross is used.

After both sides have presented their witnesses, one or both may decide to introduce additional evidence and witnesses and so petitions the judge for permission to present **rebuttal evidence**, which attempts to counteract or disprove evidence given by an earlier adverse witness.

Once all the evidence has been presented, each side is permitted to make a **closing argument**, also called a summation. Although jurisdictions vary, typically the prosecution or plaintiff gets the first summation, followed by the defense, after which the prosecution or plaintiff has an opportunity to rebut.

The final step in the jury trial is for the judge to give instructions to the jury. (In some states, instructions precede the closing arguments.) The judge informs the jury of the relevant law. For example, a definition of the crime is given, as well as a statement of what elements must be present for it to have occurred—that is, whether the defendant had the motive and the opportunity to commit the crime. The judge also instructs jurors about the standard they should use to weigh the evidence. We discuss jury instructions in more detail in Chapter 12.

With criminal charges, the jurors must be convinced **beyond a reasonable doubt** that the defendant is guilty before they vote to convict. Although the concept of "reasonable doubt" is difficult to interpret, generally it means that jurors should be strongly convinced (but not necessarily convinced beyond *all* doubt). Each of us interprets such an instruction differently, and as Chapter 12 illustrates, this instruction is often a source of confusion and frustration among jurors.

In a civil trial, in which one party brings a claim against another, a different standard is used. The **preponderance of the evidence** is all that is necessary for a finding in favor of one side. Usually, judges and attorneys translate this to mean, "Even if you find the evidence favoring one side to be only slightly more convincing than the other side's, rule in favor of that side." Preponderance is sometimes interpreted as meaning at least 51% of the evidence, but this number is misleading. Its meaning derives from the attempt to quantify a concept that is expressed verbally, and it implies that it is possible for juries or judges to evaluate evidence in a much more finely grained fashion (e.g., 49% versus 51%) than they can, or need to.

The jury is sometimes given instructions on how to deliberate, but these are usually sparse. Jurors are excused to the deliberation room, and no one—not even the bailiff or the judge—can be present during or eavesdrop on their deliberations. When the jury has reached its verdict, its foreperson informs the bailiff, who informs the judge, who reconvenes the attorneys and defendants (and plaintiffs in a civil trial) for announcement of the verdict.

Sentencing

If the defendant in a criminal trial is judged guilty, at some later point a punishment must be decided. In most jurisdictions, the trial judge makes this decision. In the past, judges have had wide discretion to impose sentences by taking into account all they knew about the defendant and his actions, regardless of whether those actions constituted a crime or were proven to a jury. But in a landmark 2004 decision, the U.S. Supreme Court ruled that judges may not increase defendants' sentences on the basis of what they perceive as aggravating factors. In *Blakely v. Washington* (2004), the Court reserved those determinations for juries.

The ruling came from a case in which the defendant, Ralph Blakely, pled guilty to kidnapping his estranged wife, a crime that carried a penalty of 53 months. But the judge, after deciding that Blakely acted with "deliberate cruelty"—a circumstance that

Blakely had not admitted and that no jury had decided—increased his sentence to 90 months. In overturning this sentence (and thereby striking down dozens of state sentencing laws and potentially affecting thousands of cases), the Court said the imposition of additional time violated Mr. Blakely's right to a jury trial. The U.S. Supreme Court relied on this case to hold that *federal* judges also may not increase sentences by deciding that aggravating factors were present in a case (*U.S. v. Booker*, 2005).

In a few states, sentencing is determined by a jury. After the verdict is rendered, the jury is reconvened, evidence relevant to the sentencing decision is presented by both sides, and the jury deliberates until it agrees on a recommended punishment. In cases involving the death penalty (described in Chapter 15), jurors, rather than judges, decide the critical sentencing issues (*Ring v. Arizona*, 2002).

The Appellate Process

Treatment of guilty defendants within the legal system does not end when they are sentenced to a prison term or to probation. To protect the rights of those who may have been convicted unjustly, society grants any defendant the opportunity to appeal a verdict to a higher level of courts. Appeals are also possible in virtually every civil suit.

As in earlier steps in the legal process, a conflict of values occurs as appeals are pursued. One goal is equality before the law—that is, to administer justice consistently and fairly. But appellate courts also try to be sensitive to individual differences in what at first appear to be similar cases. Appellate courts recognize that judges and juries can make errors. The appellate procedure is used to correct mistakes that substantially impair the fairness of trials; it also helps promote a level of consistency in trial procedures.

When a decision is appealed to a higher court, the appellate judges read the record (the transcript of the trial proceedings), the pleadings (motions and accompanying documents filed by the attorneys), and the briefs (written arguments, which are rarely brief, from both sides about the issues on appeal) and then decide whether to overturn the original trial decision or to let it stand. Appellate judges rarely reverse a verdict on the basis of the facts of the case or the apparent legitimacy of that verdict. When they do reverse, it is usually because they believe that the trial judge made a procedural error, such as allowing controversial evidence to be presented or failing to allow the jury to consider some evidence that should have been included.

If a verdict in a criminal trial is overturned or reversed, the appeals court will either order a retrial or order the charges thrown out. In reviewing the decision in a civil case, an appellate court can let the decision stand, reverse it (rule in favor of the side that lost rather than the side that won), or make some other changes in the decision and remand (return) the case to a lower court for reconsideration. One possible conclusion in either civil or criminal appeals is that certain evidence should not have been admitted or that certain instructions should not have been given; hence, a new trial may be ordered.

Judges' Decisions versus Juries' Decisions

As noted earlier, defendants in criminal trials ordinarily opt for a jury to decide their guilt or innocence, but if the prosecutor consents, they can choose to have a judge decide (such a proceeding is called a **bench trial**). This was the choice made by abortion opponent James Kopp in his 2003 trial stemming from charges that he intentionally murdered a Buffalo-area doctor who performed abortions. The doctor was killed by a single bullet fired through a window of his home after he returned with his family from a memorial service for his father. Following a one-day trial, Kopp was convicted by the judge and sentenced to between 25 years and life in prison.

Why do some defendants (and, in civil cases, some plaintiffs) choose to have their case decided by a jury or by a judge? And does it make any difference? A survey (MacCoun & Tyler, 1988) found that citizens believe a jury decision offers more procedural

TABLE 10.1 ◆ Agreement of Judges' and Juries' Verdicts Based on 3576 Trials (in percentage of all trials)

	JURY			
JUDGE	ACQUITS	CONVICTS	HANGS	TOTAL, JUDGE
Acquits	**13.4**	2.2	1.1	16.7
Convicts	16.9	**62.0**	4.4	83.3
Total, Jury	30.3	64.2	5.5	100.0

SOURCE: Adapted from Kalven and Zeisel (1966, p. 56). Figures in bold show cases in which judge and jury were in agreement on the verdict.

fairness (greater thoroughness, better representation of the community, fewer personal biases affecting decisions) than a decision by a judge.

We know that juries and judges sometimes disagree, but we don't know how frequently. When they do disagree, can we say which made the better decision? After all, jury verdicts are not systematically compared against some "correct," back-of-the-book answer—even if there were such a thing (which there is not, although see our discussion of "ground truth" in Chapter 6).

Jury verdicts are almost never "second-guessed" and reversed by the judge. One prominent exception is the case of Louise Woodward that riveted both sides of the Atlantic Ocean in the fall of 1997. Woodward, a young English au pair, was convicted by a Massachusetts jury of second-degree murder and sentenced to life imprisonment for the death of 8 ½-month-old Matthew Eappen. Declaring that the penalty was too harsh, the judge reduced her conviction to that of manslaughter and the life sentence to time already served, 279 days. The judge stated that he was seeking a "compassionate conclusion" to the case. On review of this case, the Massachusetts Supreme Court chastised the judge for not making the manslaughter verdict available as one option for the jury.

Such reversals are unusual, jury verdicts are rarely overturned on appeal because they were wrong, and not-guilty verdicts are final regardless of their validity. Therefore, we must rely on the social sciences and survey data to estimate how frequently judges and jurors agree.

Harry Kalven and Hans Zeisel (1966), professors at the University of Chicago, carried out an extensive survey of the outcomes of jury trials. In a classic application of the methods of social science to understand juries' decisions, Kalven and Zeisel asked each district court judge and federal judge in the United States to provide information about recent jury trials over which he or she had presided. Of approximately 3500 judges, only about 500 responded to a detailed questionnaire. But some judges provided information about a large number of trials—some, amazingly, about more than 50 trials—so the database for this analysis consisted of approximately 3500 trials.

Two questions are relevant to our present discussion: (1) What was the jury's verdict? and (2) Did the judge agree? By considering the frequency of this agreement, we can get hints about the extent of juries' deviations from application of the law.

In criminal trials, the judges reported that their verdict would have been the same as the jury's actual verdict in 75% of the cases (see Table 10.1 for detailed results). Thus, in three-fourths of the trials, two independent fact-finding agents would have brought forth the same result. Similar consistency was found for civil trials, as illustrated in Table 10.2. Although each of us may have our own opinion about the desirability of this degree of agreement, it does suggest that jurors are not deviating to a great extent from their narrow mandate to follow the judge's instructions about the law and use only that information plus the actual evidence to reach their verdict.

TABLE 10.2 ◆ Agreement of Judges' and Juries' Decisions in Civil Cases (in percentage of all trials)

	JURY FINDS FOR:		
JUDGE FINDS FOR	PLAINTIFF	DEFENDANT	TOTAL, JUDGE
Plaintiff	**47**	10	57
Defendant	12	**31**	43
Total, jury	59	41	100

SOURCE: Adapted from Kalven and Zeisel (1966, p. 63). Figures in bold show cases in which judge and jury were in agreement on the verdict.

In fact, we might speculate on what is an optimal degree of agreement between judge and jury. What if they agreed 100% of the time? That undesirable outcome would indicate that the jury was a rubber stamp of the judge. But if judge and jury agreed only 50% of the time, given only two possible outcomes of guilty and not guilty (putting aside "hung" juries momentarily), it would reflect a level of agreement no better than that which would occur by chance. (Two independent agents, choosing yes or no at random, would agree 50% of the time by chance alone.) Appropriately enough, the 75% level of agreement is halfway between chance and perfect agreement. And what is most important, all this speculation after the fact should not obscure the basic conclusion that in *the vast majority of cases, juries base their verdicts on the evidence and the law* (Visher, 1987).

Among the 25% of the criminal cases in which there was disagreement, 5.5% resulted in hung juries; that is, the jury members could not agree on a verdict. Thus, it is more appropriate to say that in only 19.5% of the criminal cases did the jury return a guilty verdict where the judge would have ruled not guilty, or vice versa.

In most of these discrepant decisions, the jury was more lenient than the judge. The judge would have convicted the defendant in 83.3% of these cases, whereas the jury convicted in only 64.2% of them. For every trial in which the jury convicted and the judge would have acquitted, there were almost eight trials in which the reverse was true. In only 2% of the cases would the judge have ruled not

guilty when the jury found the defendant guilty; in 17% of cases the opposite was true.

Determinants of Discrepancies

What accounts for the discrepancies between judge and jury? For their sample of cases, Kalven and Zeisel unfortunately have only one source to answer this: the judge's opinion. Yet on this basis, they offer a classification of cases. Through an analysis of these cases, we may be able to shed more light on the subject.

A few of these discrepancies apparently resulted from facts that one party knew but the other did not. For example, in several cases, the judge was aware of the defendant's prior arrest record (a matter not introduced into evidence) and would have found him guilty, but the jury acquitted him. Or, especially in a small community, a member of the jury might share with fellow jurors some information about a witness or the defendant that was not part of evidence and was not known to the judge at the time.

A second, smaller source of judge/jury discrepancies was the relative effectiveness of the two attorneys. In some trials, the jury was swayed by the apparent superiority of one lawyer over the other and produced a verdict that was, at least in the judge's opinion, contrary to the weight of the evidence. If this is a generalizable finding, it is a matter of some concern. At the same time, it is not surprising that some portion of jury verdicts would have such determinants, in light of findings on the impact of nonevidentiary information (to be described in the next two chapters).

Judge/jury discrepancies may also arise when the two disagree about the evidence. It is inevitable that, in cases in which the evidence is balanced and the decision rests on the evidence (i.e., issues of law are straightforward), the judge will occasionally disagree with the jury. In such disagreements, it is often unclear whether the judge or the jury has reached the "correct" verdict (MacCoun, 1999).

Consider a case of theft in which there is a solitary eyewitness and the accused person claims mistaken identity. In a "bare-bones" case like this, the issue boils down to whom one really believes. The judge may trust the eyewitness more; the jurors, though initially in disagreement, may eventually come to give the defendant the benefit of their collective doubt. In such cases, judge and jury may differ in their estimates of the probability that the defendant committed the crime or in their standards of reasonable doubt or in both. On such matters, there can be honest disagreement. (In fact, two judges could disagree over these issues.) Although any inconsistency between judge and jury may, to some, imply unreliability in the fact-finding process, this type of disagreement seems to rest on differences in standards for the acceptability of evidence.

Jury Sentiments

Perhaps the most important explanation of judge/jury differences involves what Kalven and Zeisel called **jury sentiments** (they account for roughly half of the disagreements). Kalven and Zeisel, after reviewing the multitude of discrepancies, used this term to cover all trials in which, *in the judge's view*, the jury's verdict was detrimentally determined by factors beyond the evidence and the law. (There is an implicit assumption here that the judge's decision was free of sentiments—a dubious claim, given that some judges admitted favoring conviction for defendants who the judge, but not the jurors, knew had a prior arrest!)

Sometimes, the judge concluded, the jurors felt that the "crime" was just too trivial for any punishment or at least for the expected punishment,

and hence they found the defendant not guilty, thus making sure that he or she would not be punished. In one case, a man was brought to trial for stealing two frankfurters. Because this was his second crime, if he had been convicted it would have been considered a felony conviction, and he would have been sentenced to prison. Whereas the judge would have found him guilty, the jury voted 10–2 for acquittal.

In other cases, the jury seemed to believe that a law was unfair and therefore voted to acquit. In trials for the sale of beer and liquor to minors who were in the military, juries have concluded that there was minimal social harm. Apparently they felt that if a young man can be forced to die for his country, "he can buy and consume a bottle of beer" (Kalven & Zeisel, 1966, p. 273).

In actuality, jury sentiments surfaced in many types of cases involving "unpopular" crimes—for example, in small misdemeanors such as gambling and in so-called victimless crimes such as prostitution. Often the jurors' brusque announcement of a not-guilty verdict, when technically the defendant most certainly had committed a crime, was their way of expressing frustration. "Why waste our time over such minor affairs?" they might have been thinking.

Relevant to the question of whether jury sentiments are sources of jury error or expressions of a different definition of justice are cases in which the jury, after due deliberation, concluded that the defendant had already been sufficiently sanctioned and that punishment by the legal system was therefore unnecessary. Here is an example in which the pivotal circumstances were unrelated to the crime: In a case of income tax evasion, the following series of misfortunes plagued the defendant between the crime and the trial: "His home burned, he was seriously injured, and his son was killed. Later he lost his leg, his wife became seriously ill, and several major operations were necessary . . . . his wife gave birth to a child who was both blind and spastic" (Kalven & Zeisel, 1966, p. 305). The jury found the defendant not guilty of income tax evasion, apparently concluding that he had already suffered divine retribution. The judge would have found him guilty.

As noted in Table 10.2, the level of agreement between the jury and the judge is also high in civil trials. Judges report that their verdict would have favored the side favored by the jury in 78% of the civil suits analyzed by Kalven and Zeisel. Also of importance is the lack of meaningful difference in the likelihood of finding for the plaintiff; the jury ruled for the plaintiff in 59% of the cases, whereas the judge did so in 57%.

These figures are a healthy empirical response to the critics (Huber, 1990; Olson, 1991) who conclude that in civil suits, especially those involving personal injury claims, juries are overly sympathetic to victims. In fact, in certain kinds of cases, plaintiffs who go to trial before juries win infrequently, a matter that we address further in Chapter 12.

Juries do occasionally make high awards to injured plaintiffs, and these are the decisions that are publicized in our newspapers and on talk shows (Bailis & MacCoun, 1996). But in controlled studies, juries make decisions—verdicts and awards—quite akin to those made by judges and experienced lawyers, and there is little evidence that juries are especially pro-plaintiff, as several critics have claimed. In fact, some would argue that because the jury can apply its sense of community standards to a case, their award of damages in a civil case might actually be more fitting than a judge's award: "The appreciation of pain and suffering, and the likely impact on an individual's life and his or her ability to earn a living, are not matters which judges are any more qualified to assess than is a member of the public applying his or her life experience" (Watson, 1996, p. 457). Any disagreement between judge and jury that *does* exist might be better attributed to the jury's interest in equity, to its consideration of a range of sensible factors that might be broader than those considered by an individual judge, or to its emotional closeness to the parties in the case than to its competence (Shuman & Champagne, 1997).

A Critique of the Kalven and Zeisel Study

The study by Kalven and Zeisel described in *The American Jury* (1966) was a massive undertaking supported by a $1.4 million grant from the Ford Foundation (Hans & Vidmar, 1991). But the actual data were collected between 1954 and 1961, and in the intervening decades, the methodological limitations of the study have become increasingly apparent:

1. Judges were permitted to choose which trial or trials they reported. Did they tend to pick those cases in which they disagreed with the jury, thus causing the sample's result to misrepresent the true extent of judge/jury disagreement? We do not know.

2. Only 555 judges out of 3500 provided responses to the survey; half of the cases in the study were provided by only 15% of the judges—an unrepresentative sampling of possible responses, leading us to question how well these results can be generalized to the entire population of judges and juries.

3. The focus is on disagreements in criminal trials; little information is provided on civil cases.

4. Juries have changed in many ways. In some jurisdictions, jury decisions no longer need be unanimous, and many states have shifted to smaller juries. The absence of a requirement for unanimous verdicts would probably decrease the percentage of "hung" juries.

5. Furthermore, the membership of juries has changed; "juries are today more representative and heterogeneous than in the 1950's when Kalven and Zeisel conducted their research" (Hans & Vidmar, 1986, p. 142). The increased heterogeneity in contemporary juries might increase their rate *of disagreement* with the judge's position because their broader experiences and cultural diversity might give them insights or perspectives on the trial evidence to which judges do not have access (Hans & Vidmar, 1986). For example, is a jury of African Americans as likely as a white judge to believe a white police officer's testimony that a drug dealer "dropped" a bag of cocaine?

6. As for *causes* of discrepancies between verdicts by the judge and jury, we have only the judge's attribution of what the jurors' feelings and sentiments were (Hans & Vidmar, 1991).

A New Look at Judge/Jury Differences

As Hans and Vidmar (1991, p. 347) observed, replication of this classic study has been long overdue. Fortunately, nearly 50 years after the trials reported by Kalven and Zeisel, an excellent replication now exists. To examine the applicability of these early findings to 21st-century juries, researchers at the National Center for State Courts collected data from jurors, judges, and attorneys in more than 350 trials in four jurisdictions: Los Angeles, Phoenix, the Bronx (in New York City), and the District of Columbia (Eisenberg et al., 2005). They asked some of the same questions that Kalven and Zeisel had asked, including how often judges and juries agreed on verdicts in criminal trials.

In a careful replication of earlier procedures, participants in noncapital felony trials completed questionnaires that asked about preferred verdicts and their evaluation of the evidence. There was a very high response rate (questionnaires were returned in 89% of cases, and 91% of judges responded—a very impressive number indeed, considering that many researchers are content with a 50% response rate!), so we can be fairly certain that the data are representative of most trials. As before, judges stated, prior to hearing the juries' verdicts, whether they would opt to acquit or convict and what they thought about the evidence. One obvious advantage of this study over its predecessor is that all groups (judges, attorneys, and jurors alike) gave their views of the evidence, thus reducing an important concern about Kalven and Zeisel's work, namely that all the information about a trial came from the judge.

Perhaps the most striking finding was how closely the new results mirrored those of the earlier study. The rate of jury/judge agreement was 70% (compared to Kalven and Zeisel's 75%), and when there was disagreement, it also mirrored the earlier asymmetry: Juries were more lenient. They were more likely to acquit when judges opted to convict than they were to convict when judges would acquit (see Table 10.3).

Kalven and Zeisel wondered whether one reason for jury/judge disagreement in criminal cases was that judges and juries interpreted "beyond a reasonable doubt" differently. Data from the more recent study included how different observers viewed the strength of the evidence favoring the prosecution in each case. On the basis of those assessments, the researchers showed that when the evidence was viewed as "moderately strong" or "strong," judges tended to convict more than juries, implying that juries applied a higher evidentiary threshold to convict than the judge. Stated otherwise, jurors required more proof to be convinced of a defendant's guilt beyond a reasonable doubt.

Eisenberg and his colleagues explored something that Kalven and Zeisel had not: regional differences in jury/judge agreement rates. They found that jury/judge agreement ranged from a low of 64% in Washington, D.C., to a high of 89% in Phoenix (agreement in the Bronx was 66% and in Los Angeles was 88%). Although these findings are hard to explain (the authors suggest that interpreting these results is as much an art as a science), one possibility is that different kinds of cases come to trial in these different jurisdictions.

Although there are limitations to this more recent study—it did not assess jury/judge agreement in civil cases, and its sample was smaller—it supports with additional rigor the important finding that judges and juries agree most of the time and that when they do not, it is because judges tend to convict when jurors would acquit. It is satisfying to know that Kalven and Zeisel's landmark study has withstood the test of time, even as the makeup of juries has changed in the intervening years.

We have more recent findings on how judges compare to juries in civil cases, as well. Neil Vidmar and his colleagues compared judges' and jurors' decisions in medical malpractice cases by asking the two groups to respond to the same trial evidence. A comparison of the damage awards of mock jurors with those of experienced legal professionals (not judges) showed no important differences. The legal professionals in this study (done by Vidmar in association with Jeffrey Rice and David Landau) were 21 lawyers who served as arbitrators for personal injury, contract, or labor disputes; five had previously been judges. In a case involving an accidentally scarred knee that occurred during bunion removal,

TABLE 10.3 ◆ **Agreement of Judges' and Juries' Verdicts Based on 350 Trials (National Center for State Court data, in percentage of all trials)**

| | JURY | | | |
JUDGE	ACQUITS	CONVICTS	HANGS	TOTAL, JUDGE
Acquits	**11.6**	5.0	1.9	18.5
Convicts	16.0	**58.5**	6.9	81.4
Total, jury	27.6	63.5	8.8	100.0

SOURCE: Adapted from Eisenberg et al. (2005). Figures in bold show cases in which judge and jury were in agreement on the verdict.

the lawyers gave the plaintiff a median award of $57,000, whereas mock jurors gave her a median award of $47,850. However, the awards by individual jurors were more variable than those of the lawyers; jurors awarded the plaintiff anywhere between $11,000 and $197,000, whereas the lawyers' awards ranged only from $22,000 to $82,000.

There is much controversy about whether jurors are able to make competent decisions about punitive damages. These damage awards, which are described further in Chapter 12, are intended to punish or to deter errant defendants and are levied most often against corporations that have engaged in egregious wrongdoing. Indeed, some punitive damage awards have been very high; since 1989, the Supreme Court has ruled on five occasions about whether a punitive damage award was excessively so. Thus, a reasonable question is whether jury awards for punitive damages are different from awards assessed by judges, and whether the two groups differ on the basis of those awards.

The most comprehensive study of jury/judge agreement on punitive damages, conducted by Theodore Eisenberg and his colleagues (Eisenberg, LaFountain, Ostrom, Rottman, & Wells, 2002), analyzed data from nearly 9000 trials that ended in 1996 from 45 of the nation's largest trial courts. The primary finding was that judges and juries did not differ substantially in these cases; they awarded punitive damages of about the same size, although the range of the jury awards was somewhat greater than that of the judicial awards. These results call

into question the notion that juries are unable to set reasonable limits on punitive damages.

But do jurors do as well as judges in attending to the relevant evidence in these cases, setting aside any sympathy for the plaintiff and focusing only on the factors that *should* matter to the determination of punitive damages (i.e., the actions of the defendant)? The answer is a qualified yes. Jennifer Robbennolt (2002) asked judges and jury-eligible citizens to read a vignette about a patient who experienced harmful side effects of a medication prescribed for depression. The trial evidence included a memo demonstrating that employees of the defendant, an HMO, knew about the potential side effects of the drug—effects that were not communicated to the plaintiff. Research participants were told that the defendant's liability had already been determined and that they were to make awards for pain and suffering and, if appropriate, punitive damages.

As we've seen before, the decision making of judges and that of laypeople with regard to punitive damages were quite similar; their awards were of roughly the same magnitude and variability. Just as important, both groups used the evidence in appropriate ways, relying on the severity of the plaintiff's injury to assess money for pain and suffering and on the nature of the defendant's conduct to determine punitive damages.

Returning to the question we posed earlier— whether jurors perform as well as judges when deciding damage awards—we find little evidence to suggest that jurors' reasoning processes are inherently

THE CASE OF

BOX 10.2   Laura Kriho: Jury nullifier

A 32-year-old University of Colorado researcher, Laura Kriho was a juror in the 1997 felony drug possession trial of a young woman charged with possession of methamphetamines. During deliberations, a fellow juror sent an anonymous note to the judge that Kriho had stated, "the criminal court system is no place to decide drug charges." The judge, Kenneth Barnhill, had no alternative but to declare a mistrial. He told the lawyers who assembled in his courtroom that May afternoon that he was "more than a little bit ticked."

Judge Barnhill also launched an investigation of Kriho that uncovered an arrest 12 years earlier for possession of LSD and membership in a hemp legalization organization. Because Kriho had not disclosed this information during jury selection, nor had she

discussed her views of drug laws, she was charged with criminal contempt.

At her trial in a small Gilpin County, Colorado, courtroom packed with her supporters, seven fellow jurors revealed her comments during their private deliberations; comments that were not denied by Kriho: "I can't send this girl to prison. . . . I'm against the drug laws and won't vote for guilt . . . . Drug cases should be handled by family and community . . . . Jurors can vote their conscience . . . . Jurors have the right to nullify laws they don't like." They also acknowledged that following the mistrial, Kriho had shared a pamphlet on jury nullification that she had acquired from the Libertarian party.

Although the prosecutor argued that Kriho was on trial not for her

beliefs but for her disobedience of a court order and her failure to tell the truth when questioned during jury selection, Kriho's testimony had a ring of truth: "If I had voted guilty, I would not be sitting here now," she stated. Her attorney declared, "If Laura Kriho can be prosecuted for contempt, no juror who thinks for himself can safely speak in the jury room. The court is trying to intimidate anybody with an independent mind. The government cannot tell its citizens not to think critically of the law or the government. The government cannot order a juror to violate her own conscience. And the court cannot banish all jurors who have consciences." Notwithstanding these pleas, Kriho was convicted and fined $1200, although her conviction was later overturned by a Colorado appellate court, and the case was eventually dismissed.

different from those of judges. Although some studies suggest that jurors render erratic and unpredictable awards, in part because their decision-making processes are influenced by various cognitive biases (see, for example, Sunstein, Hastie, Payne, Schkade, & Viscusi, 2002), judges are also human and apparently can fall prey to the same cognitive illusions as juries (Guthrie, Rachlinski, & Wistrich, 2001).

Jury Nullification

Do jurors have the right to disregard the judge's instructions and disobey the law when they render their verdicts? Laura Kriho apparently thought so (see Box 10.2).

Laura Kriho is not alone in her desire to ignore the law. A 1998 survey conducted by the *National Law Journal* showed that the vast majority of potential jurors would disregard the judge and the law and do what they thought was right. For example, a Kentucky jury acquitted actor Woody Harrelson on a misdemeanor charge of marijuana possession after deliberating only 25 minutes. Four years before, Harrelson had planted four hemp seeds, knowing that he would be arrested, in order to challenge a Kentucky law that outlawed possession of any part of the cannabis plant. Harrelson argued that the statute was unconstitutional because it didn't distinguish marijuana from hemp. According to Harrelson, the jury sent a very strong message that it's not right for someone to go to jail for growing industrial hemp.

Juries do, in fact, have the implicit power to acquit defendants despite evidence and judicial instructions to the contrary. This power, termed **jury nullification**, has permitted juries to acquit defendants who were legally guilty but morally upright (Horowitz & Willging, 1991). The jury's power to deliver a verdict that is counter to the law "resides in the fact that a general verdict of guilty or not guilty requires no other revelation as to the decision by the jurors" (Horowitz, 1988, pp. 439–440).

The concept of jury nullification reflects society's awareness that we have juries for a variety of reasons. Not only do we entrust them to resolve the facts and apply the law in a given case, but we also value juries because they represent the breadth of community values. This latter function reflects their historical role of serving as the conscience of the community (Abramson, 1994) and of bringing their commonsense to bear on matters between the government and private individuals. Even though juries in the United States are instructed that their task is only to evaluate the facts and then apply the law as described by the judge, the opportunity to apply a community perspective has existed for centuries, even if it ignores or "violates" the law. In fact, juries have sometimes been praised for their willingness to ignore the law rather than enforce it, particularly when the law is perceived as unjust.

For example, in a precedent-setting trial during colonial times, the printer John Peter Zenger was charged in 1735 with printing material that had not been authorized by the government; hence, he had committed sedition. The British law stated that the truth of the unauthorized material was irrelevant (Alexander, 1963). But Zenger's attorney, Andrew Hamilton, the foremost attorney in colonial times, told the jurors that they "had the right beyond all dispute to determine both the law and the facts." They did; they went against the judge's instructions and acquitted Zenger. The philosophy of "the jury as the judge," at least in criminal cases, was very prominent in post-Revolutionary America, partly in keeping with the resentment felt toward Crown-appointed judges (Rembar, 1980, p. 362). It even extended to the mid-1800s, when juries found defendants not guilty of aiding slaves to escape from the South, even though, by doing so, these abolitionists had violated the fugitive slave law.

Up until that time, federal and state judges often instructed juries that they had the right to disregard the court's view of the law. But after northern juries began acquitting abolitionists, judges started questioning jurors to find out whether they were prejudiced against the government, dismissing those who were. In 1895, the Supreme Court ruled in a bitter split decision (*Sparf and Hansen v. United States*) that criminal juries were obligated to apply the law as set out by the judge; they had no right to deviate from that law (Scheflin, 1972). But as Horowitz and Willging (1991) note, the controversy resurfaced in the turbulent Vietnam War period when the government began to prosecute antiwar activists, usually on charges of conspiracy. Defense attorneys sought ways that jurors could, within the law, take into account the morality of such actions. Several cases reached the federal appellate level, although none progressed as far as the Supreme Court for review. However, in a 1968 decision (*Duncan v. Louisiana*), the Supreme Court recognized the jury's power to decide cases *as a matter of conscience* as a characteristic so "fundamental to the American scheme of government that a state violates due process of law in eliminating a jury trial" (Kadish & Kadish, 1971, p. 204).

The U.S. Court of Appeals for the D.C. Circuit decided another important nullification case in 1972 (*U.S. v. Dougherty*). Several members of the Catholic clergy had been found guilty of ransacking Dow Chemical Company offices to protest the company's manufacture of napalm. The trial judge had refused their attorney's request that he instruct the jurors that they could acquit the defendants whether or not there had been a violation of criminal law. The appellate court, by a 2–1 vote, upheld this decision by the trial judge. In the majority opinion, Judge Harold Leventhal suggested that the jurors "knew quite well through informal channels that they could nullify without fear of reprisal. To make this power explicit would loosen any restraints jurors may feel" (Horowitz &

Willging, 1991, p. 171). Thus, the court acknowledged a curious irony: Jurors can thumb their noses at the law, but ordinarily they aren't told that they can.

In another sort of irony, jurors have the option to nullify the law but judges can apparently dismiss jurors who exercise that option. During the first day of deliberations in a sexual assault case, the foreperson of a Santa Clara, California, jury told the judge that one of the jurors refused to follow the court's instruction to uphold the law. When the juror in question told the judge that he thought the law was wrong and that he would be governed by the defense attorney's reference to jury nullification, the judge excused him and replaced him with an alternate juror. After the defendant was convicted, he appealed, claiming that the judge abused his discretion by discharging the juror. But the California Supreme Court did not agree; it ruled that although a juror has the ability to disregard a court's instructions, the judge is still authorized to discharge a juror who is unable or unwilling to follow those instructions (*People v. Williams*, 2001).

The real issue in the debate over jury nullification is whether jurors should be informed of this power. State and federal judges do not tell jurors that they have the power to disregard the law. What might happen if they did? Would we have anarchy and "runaway" juries, as opponents of nullification suggest? How would juries behave if they were informed that they have the option to disregard the law? Would they be less likely to convict? Possibly so; in two trials of Vietnam War protesters who broke into offices and destroyed records, the judge in one trial of the Camden 28 allowed a jury nullification defense and the jury acquitted all the defendants, whereas the judge in the other trial did not, and all nine defendants were convicted (Abramson, 1994).

Empirical evidence concerning jury nullification

Another way to assess the effects of nullification instructions is to look to the empirical evidence on this topic. What effect does explicit instruction about the jury's right to nullify have on verdicts in criminal cases? That question was addressed by Irwin Horowitz (1988) in an elegant study of the impact of judicial instructions concerning jury nullification on mock jurors. Each juror was exposed to one of three criminal cases and to either nullification or non-nullification instructions from the judge. Jurors participated in groups of six and delivered a group verdict on the defendant's guilt.

In all three cases, the weight of the evidence indicated that the defendant was guilty. In the drunk driving case, the defendant, while driving home from a party during which he was seen consuming numerous alcoholic drinks, killed one pedestrian and injured another. In the euthanasia case, a male nurse who had cared for a terminal cancer patient over a long period was tried for mercy killing. The defendant was portrayed sympathetically, reflecting his compassion for the patient and the family. In the illegal weapon possession case, a mentally disabled convicted felon stood trial for illegally obtaining a revolver that he thought was necessary for a mail-order detective course he wished to take.

The judge's instructions took one of two forms: either the standard, non-nullification instruction or a nullification instruction in which jurors were told that although they must give respectful attention to the laws, they have the final authority to decide whether or not to apply a given law to the acts of the defendant on trial. They were also instructed that nothing would bar them from acquitting the defendant if they felt that the law, as applied to the fact situation before them, would produce an inequitable or unjust verdict.

What effects did these experimental manipulations have on jury verdicts? First, there were clear differences in the frequency with which jurors convicted the defendant as a function of the case they heard. Juries who heard the drunk driving case were much harsher in their verdicts than were juries in either of the other two cases. The judge's nullification instructions also mattered and in a dramatic way: Pro-nullification information increased the likelihood of conviction in the drunk driving case and decreased the likelihood of conviction in the euthanasia and illegal possession cases. Apparently, when informed of the nullification option, jurors are more likely to acquit a sympathetic defendant and less likely to acquit a culpable, dangerous defendant.

What seems to drive the verdicts of juries with nullification instructions? Nullification instructions seem to change the way the evidence is weighed (Horowitz & Willging, 1991). The presence of these instructions shifts the focus of discussion away from the evidence per se, and in the direction of extra-evidentiary factors such as concerns about what is just rather than what is lawful (Hill & Pfeifer, 1992; Niedermeier, Horowitz, & Kerr, 1999). Nullification instructions seem to encourage jurors to think about what is moral and to fashion internal stories that help them interpret the evidence in light of this morality. However, according to other studies, the shift of focus has its limits; nullification does not cause jurors to completely ignore evidence or give full sway to their biases (Niedermeier, Horowitz, & Kerr, 1999), and the deliberation process apparently serves to diminish the importance of an individual's sentiments about justice (Meissner, Brigham, & Pfeifer, 2003).

We can think of instances where jurors' reliance on their sentiments may have influenced their verdicts. For example, prosecutions of police officers for using excessive force in the course of their duties are often unpopular and may lead to nullification. In fact, this may have been what kept Inglewood, California, police officer Jeremy Morse from being convicted on charges of excessive use of force related to the 2002 videotaped assault of a 16-year-old black youth. Morse was shown slamming the handcuffed teenager into the hood of a car and punching him in the face. At trial, the defense called experts who testified that what Morse did at the scene was reasonable, and the jury deadlocked—not once but twice—over the charges. At least some of the jurors may have been reluctant to convict a police officer for actions that they see as "just part of the job" of fighting crime.

As another example, some observers have labeled the verdict in the criminal trial of O. J.

Simpson an instance of jury nullification in that the jury—composed predominantly of African American and other minority jurors—chose to respond primarily to the claims that white police officers tampered with the evidence. But a claim that this verdict was an act of nullification per se fails to recognize the weaknesses in the prosecution's case and its failure to marshal enough evidence to meet the burden of proving guilt beyond a reasonable doubt.

In fact, decisions that turn on the question of reasonable doubt should probably not be classified as nullifications (Finkel, 2000). Nor should any misunderstanding of the law or misinterpretation of evidence that leads to a verdict at odds with the legal rule be classified as nullification. Jury nullification needs to be reserved for cases in which the jury, as the conscience of the community, believes a *law* is wrong and intentionally opts to nullify (Marder, 1999b). As Rosen (1996) observes about the O. J. Simpson case, "Nobody on the defense team ever suggested there is anything unjust about the laws prohibiting intentional homicide. Instead [Johnny] Cochran (Simpson's defense attorney) called on the jurors to refuse to apply a just law in order to punish the police and to express solidarity with the defendant" (p. 42).

Jury nullification and racial considerations

Although the Simpson verdict probably had more to do with the prosecution's failure to convince a predominantly African American jury than with jury nullification, the issue of race is a subtext to the nullification debate as well. There are notorious cases of nullification where white southern juries refused to convict members of the Ku Klux Klan and others who terrorized blacks during the early years of the civil rights movement. One such case concerns Byron de la Beckwith and the murder of civil rights leader Medgar Evers (Box 10.3).

Was jury nullification a factor in these trials? Did some of the jurors in the early trials of Beckwith and other Ku Klux Klan members set aside the law and refuse to convict these defendants because

THE CASE OF

BOX 10.3   Byron de la Beckwith: Jury nullification and race

Eager to see his children after a long day at work, civil rights leader Medgar Evers stepped out of his car in Jackson, Mississippi, on a hot June night in 1963 and, in the blink of an eye, was gunned down from behind by an assassin. The shooting ignited a firestorm of protest that ended in several more deaths and galvanized the civil rights movement.

The case against Byron de la Beckwith was strong but circumstantial. His rifle with his fingerprint was found at the scene, and a car similar to his was seen in the vicinity of Evers's home. But no one saw Beckwith pull the trigger, and his claim that he was 90 miles away at the time of the shooting was substantiated by two former police officers.

Beckwith was tried twice in 1964; both times the all-white, all-male jury deadlocked and failed to reach a verdict. This was an era of volatile race relations in which blacks were excluded from jury service and in which attorneys for Ku Klux Klan members charged with killing civil rights leaders openly appealed to white jurors for racial solidarity. The defense attorney for one alleged murderer of Emmett Till (a 14-year-old black boy whose abduction and killing in Mississippi in 1955 for supposedly whistling at a white woman helped spark the civil rights movement) appealed to an all-white jury by saying that he was sure that "every last Anglo-Saxon one of you has the

BYRON DE LA BECKWITH

MEDGAR EVERS

courage to free [the defendants]" http://www.intellectualcapital .com/issues/97/0109/icopinions1 .html). (Justice Department officials have recently reopened the investigation into the murder of Emmett Till, despite the fact that the two people originally charged in the crime are now dead. The investigation will focus on whether other people were involved, as Till's family has suspected for years.)

Beckwith's segregationist views were a common bond between himself and the juries that failed to convict him in 1964. But things were different in 1994. Despite the obstacles presented by stale evidence, dead witnesses, and constitutional questions, prosecutors tried Beckwith for the third time. They presented several witnesses who testified that Beckwith suggested—and in some cases bragged—that he had murdered Evers. Witnesses also described Beckwith's racist

views, including his description of blacks as "beasts of the field" and his belief that NAACP leaders should be exterminated.

This time, Beckwith's racist ideology was a liability. Despite pleas from defense attorneys that jurors not focus on Beckwith's sensational beliefs, a jury of eight blacks and four whites convicted Beckwith of murder in February of 1994. He was immediately sentenced to life in prison. Darrell Evers, the slain civil rights leader's son, who was 9 at the time of the shooting, said he attended the trial to confront Beckwith: "He never saw my father's face. All he saw was his back. I wanted him to see the face, to see the ghost of my father come back to haunt him" (http://newslibrary.krmediastream .com/cgi- . . . document/). National leaders of the NAACP called for other civil rights cases to be reopened and charges against aging Klansmen have been revived in at least one other case.

they supported the defendants' racist dogma? Because we can't talk to the jurors, we will never know for sure. And yet, it is telling that a racially mixed jury convicted Beckwith for the murder of Medgar Evers 30 years after two all-white juries were unable to agree on a verdict.

In an ironic twist, much of the nullification debate today revolves around the recommendation, championed primarily by law professor and former prosecutor Paul Butler, that African American jurors should nullify the law in certain kinds of cases where black men are the defendants. The rationale for this idea is not that the law is unjust but that black jurors have a moral right to practice jury nullification because, historically, they have not had the benefits of the rule of law (Butler, 2004). As a result, prosecutors in cities with large African American populations have come to expect to lose certain cases against black defendants (e.g., low-level drug cases) even when they persuade the jury beyond a reasonable doubt. Why? Because some black jurors may refuse to convict black defendants whom they know are guilty. Finally, to bring the story full circle from the days when segregationists refused to apply the law, members of extremist groups that support militia and white-supremacist movements are now calling for jurors to fight the government by essentially ignoring the law in cases they adjudicate.

But given the secrecy of jury deliberations, it is actually rather difficult to know why juries decide cases the way they do. Even in trials that result in a hung jury, there are explanations other than out-right nullification that can explain the verdict, including the nature of the evidence and the interpersonal dynamics of the deliberation (Hannaford-Agor & Hans, 2003). What do psychologists know about the role of nullification-related sentiments in hung juries?

To examine the frequency and causes (including nullification) of hung juries, the National Center for State Courts conducted an in-depth study of 382 felony trials in four large urban courts, focusing special attention on the 46 cases from the sample in which the jury hung on one or more charges (Hans, Hannaford-Agor, Mott, & Munsterman, 2003). By surveying jurors, attorneys, and judges about characteristics of the cases

and the interpersonal dynamics of the deliberations, the researchers were able to assess the role of these factors in cases in which the jury reached consensus and in cases where they deadlocked. They were also able to examine the influence of jurors' demographics and attitudes in order to ask, for example, whether the race and ethnicity of the jurors were related to the incidence of hung juries.

They found that jurors' concern about the fairness of a particular law was an important factor in hung juries, and although we cannot say for sure that jurors who "hung the jury" intentionally disregarded the law, it is easy to imagine that concerns about fairness might lead to nullification. Perhaps the most striking finding from this study, at least in regard to nullification, is that jurors' general views about the legitimacy of the police and the courts are better predictors of their notions of fairness than is their race.

Some final thoughts on jury nullification

Jury nullification has attracted significant attention in recent years. In January 1990, members of the antiabortion group Operation Rescue went on trial for attempting to shut down several family planning clinics in San Diego; they were charged with trespassing and resisting arrest. As one of the trials was about to start, a newspaper urged potential jurors to use their right of nullification to find the defendants not guilty. The ad's headline read, "You can legally acquit anti-abortion 'trespassers' even if they're guilty" (Abramson, 1994, p. 57). Arguing that the defendants had performed acts of civil disobedience, the advertisement reminded jurors that they had the right to act as the conscience of the community.

The city attorney and judges presiding over the trials were outraged; one judge admonished the jurors to "pay no attention to the ad, to ignore it" (Abramson, 1994, p. 58). Apparently they did; the defendants were convicted and sentenced to brief periods in the county jail. But the episode boosted awareness of the possibility of jury nullification and focused attention on an organization devoted to lobbying for laws to protect and extend the right of nullification. Founded in 1989, the Fully Informed Jury Association (FIJA) advocates that judges be required to inform jurors of their inherent right to bring in a verdict according to their conscience and suggests that defendants' motives be admissible evidence in all trials.

An instruction that would explicitly permit jurors to disregard the law puts a heavy burden of responsibility on them. And if jurors have a license to acquit regardless of the facts and the law, do they equivalently have the license to convict when the facts and the law fail to support that decision?

If the nullification procedure is ever implemented nationally, it must be available only in cases in which a jury wants to acquit in the face of law and evidence to the contrary. It should not be available to a jury that vindictively wants to convict even though the evidence would lead to acquittal.

As noted, it is most applicable in cases of civil disobedience, in which community sentiment points to a moral responsibility to disobey unjust laws.

In the end, what should we think about jury nullification? Should it be condemned as an inappropriate usurpation of legislative authority by rogue juries that have run wild? Or should it be interpreted as an example of the "democratic and populist role of the jury in shaping the application of legal rules to the living norms of the community" (Casper, 1993, p. 418)? Without a doubt, one person's jury nullification is another person's "tempering of justice with equity" (Casper, 1993, p. 418). Jury nullification clearly exemplifies the tension between treating all people equally before the law and providing individualized justice that reflects the conscience of the community.

SUMMARY

1. *What is the purpose of a trial?* Every trial presents two contrasting views of the truth. Although at first glance, the purpose of a trial seems to be determining truth, conflict resolution may be an equally valid purpose. This debate is exemplified by three contrasting images of a trial: (1) as a search for the truth, (2) as a test of credibility, and (3) as a conflict-resolving ritual.

2. *What are the steps the legal system follows in bringing a case to trial?* When a case is brought to trial, the legal system employs a series of steps. Pretrial procedures include discovery, or the process of obtaining the information about the case held by the other side. Interviews of potential witnesses, called depositions, are a part of the discovery procedure. Before the trial, attorneys may make motions to exclude certain witnesses or testimony from the trial. The decision whether a judge or jury will render the verdict is also made at this point.

3. *What is the order of procedures in the trial itself?* After the jury, if any, is selected (a process called *voir dire*), the following sequence of steps unfolds in the trial itself:

a. Opening statements by attorneys for the two sides (prosecution or plaintiff goes first)

b. Direct examination, cross-examination, and redirect and recross of witnesses, with prosecution witnesses first, then defense witnesses

c. Presentation of rebuttal witnesses and evidence

d. Closing statements, or summations, by the two sides, usually in the order of prosecution, then defense, then prosecution again

e. Judge's instructions to the jury (in some jurisdictions, these come before the closing statements)

f. Jury deliberations and announcement of a verdict

g. If the verdict is guilty, determination of the punishment

4. *Do juries' verdicts differ from those of judges?* The question of whether juries' and judges' verdicts differ significantly was answered in a massive empirical study by Harry Kalven and Hans Zeisel. In actual trials, 75% of the time the jury came to the same verdict that the judge would have reached. With respect to the discrepancies, in 5.5% of the cases, the jury was hung. In the remaining 19.5%, the judge and jury disagreed. In the vast majority of these disagreements, especially those involving minor offenses, the jury was more lenient than the judge would have been.

Among the sources of the discrepancies were facts that the judge possessed and the jury did not (accounting for a small percentage of disagreements), the relative effectiveness of the two attorneys (again, a small percentage), disagreements over the weight of the evidence, and what Kalven and Zeisel call "jury sentiments," or factors beyond the evidence and the law.

A recent replication of this classic study showed remarkably similar results: In criminal cases, the judge and jury agreed on a verdict in 70% of trials, and when there was disagreement, jurors were more likely than judges to acquit.

5. *What is jury nullification?* The doctrine of jury nullification provides a way for a jury to acquit a defendant in, for example, a mercy-killing case, even when the evidence would lead to a conviction. Jury nullification instructions give the jurors the explicit right to disregard the weight of the evidence and the law if, in their judgment, community standards argue for compassion.

6. *How has race been involved in the debate over jury nullification?* Abolitionists who helped slaves during the Civil War were found not guilty of violating the fugitive slave laws, even though their actions indicated that they were breaking the law. During the turbulent civil rights movement of the 1960s, jurors refused to convict white defendants who had murdered black civil rights leaders, perhaps because they supported the defendants' racist beliefs. Today, some African American jurors may refuse to apply the law in cases in which black men are defendants, although systematic data from the National Center for State Courts suggests that jurors' perceptions of fairness, rather than preconceived personal notions of justice, factor heavily in verdicts.

KEY TERMS

bench trial	depositions	opening statements	recross
beyond a reasonable doubt	discovery	perjury	redirect questioning
	impeach	preponderance of the evidence	*venire*
closing argument	jury nullification		*voir dire*
decision rule	jury sentiments	rebuttal evidence	written interrogatories

Jury Trials I: Jury Representativeness and Selection

ORIENTING QUESTIONS

1. *What does the legal system seek in trial juries?*
2. *What stands in the way of jury representativeness?*
3. *What procedures are used in voir dire?*
4. *What personality characteristics of jurors, if any, are related to their verdicts?*
5. *Are lawyers and psychologists effective in jury selection?*

The O. J. Simpson Criminal Trial as an Illustration of Jury Selection

The murder trial of O. J. Simpson could stake several claims on being the most influential trial of the 20th century. The defendant was a former Heisman Trophy winner, a beloved and glamorous sports hero to millions. His assemblage of high-priced lawyers, dubbed the "dream team," included several of America's most successful trial attorneys. The trial, televised daily for over a year, became the nation's favorite soap opera and made overnight celebrities out of expert witnesses, prosecutors, and several bit players in the Simpson saga. Highly technical, scientific evidence was often on center stage, and the courtroom oratory and legal arguments were frequently spellbinding. But perhaps the most distinctive element of the Simpson trial was the jury—how it was selected, the way it performed, and, ultimately, the verdict of not guilty that it returned.

Although the trial of O. J. Simpson was by no means typical with respect to the jury's selection and its deliberations, it still merits a detailed review as an illustration of how juries are composed and how they function in our justice system.

Drawing a Panel, or Venire

Jury selection begins with the drawing of a panel, or *venire*, of prospective jurors. In the Simpson case, an unusually large number, 304, were included on this "jury list." But Judge Lance Ito excluded a significant percentage of these prospects for "hardship" reasons, including poor health, job demands, and the presence of small children in the home. Hence, even if the original panel had been drawn in a manner that would have made it representative of the community, the exemption of hardship jurors threatened the representativeness of the remainder of the panel.

When it came time to "select" the jury in the criminal trial of O. J. Simpson, each side initially considered the input of a trial consultant. One of these consultants (Donald Vinson, a founder of two jury consulting firms, Litigation Sciences and DecisionQuest) volunteered his services to the prosecution. But his advice about "ideal jurors" clashed with the preconceptions of prosecutor Marcia Clark, who believed that if black women were on the jury, they would be sympathetic to the prosecution's contention that the murder of Nicole Brown Simpson was related to the history of domestic violence between her and O. J. Simpson.

Vinson's interviews with simulated jurors led to an opposite conclusion: Blacks in the jury simulation overwhelmingly voted for acquittal; in fact, African American women were Simpson's strongest supporters. When asked to assume that Simpson had beaten, threatened, and stalked his ex-wife, the uniform reaction of the African American women was that the use of physical force was not always inappropriate in a marriage. They said, "In every relationship, there's always a little trouble"; "People get slapped around. That just happens"; "It doesn't mean he killed her" (quoted by Toobin, 1996b, p. 62).

Marcia Clark's gut reactions prevailed, Dr. Vinson's recommendations were dismissed, and the prosecution welcomed the presence of black women on the jury. The prosecution did not even exercise all of its 20 peremptory challenges. According to Jeffrey Toobin (1996b, p. 66), Clark allowed Vinson to attend only a day and a half of the jury selection and then told him that his advice was no longer needed.

In contrast, the defense eagerly sought the assistance of a trial consultant. Late in the summer of 1994, Robert Shapiro, then still the lead attorney for the defense, hired Jo-Ellan Dimitrius of Forensic Technologies, Incorporated. Her previous successes had included assisting the defendants charged with child abuse in the McMartin Preschool case and the Los Angeles police officers charged with beating Rodney King. Dimitrius not only conducted surveys and focus groups, as Vinson did, but she was also in the courtroom every day to observe the extended process of jury selection.

Did the Jury Selection "Work"?

The eventual jury included one African American man, one Hispanic American man, two white women, and eight African American women. According to Vinson's analysis of their questionnaires, they possessed the following characteristics:

◆ All twelve were Democrats.

◆ Only two were college graduates.

◆ Not one juror read a newspaper regularly. (One juror said she read nothing at all "except the horse sheet.") Two had supervisory or management responsibilities at work; ten did not.

◆ Eight watched evening television tabloid news, such as "Hard Copy." (Vinson's polling data found a predilection for the tabloids to be a reliable predictor of belief in Simpson's innocence.)

◆ Five said that they or a family member had personally had a negative experience with law enforcement.

◆ Five thought that using physical force on a family member was sometimes justified.

◆ Nine—three-quarters of the jury—thought that O. J. Simpson was unlikely to have committed murder because he excelled at football (quoted by Toobin, 1996b, pp. 66–67).

Analysis of the juror questionnaires led the defense team's jury consultant to the same conclusion as Vinson's: This group of jurors leaned heavily toward the defense from the very beginning (Miller, 1995). Furthermore, the black women on the jury did not like Marcia Clark. They saw her as a "castrating bitch" who "was attempting to demean this symbol of black masculinity" (Toobin, 1996b, p. 67).

After listening to nine months of evidence, this jury deliberated for less than four hours before unanimously finding the defendant not guilty of each murder. A number of explanations have been offered for this outcome, but it was clearly a triumph for the jury selection decisions made by the defense team.

General Problems in Forming a Jury Panel

Was the selection procedure in this trial fair? Was the outcome just? This trial highlights some of the challenges to the legal system's goal of forming juries that are both representative *and* fair. When implementing this first step of forming a venire, each state—as well as the federal government—has its own procedures about how the sample of prospective jurors will be drawn.

But each method must neither systematically eliminate nor underrepresent any subgroups of the population. To encourage representativeness, U.S. Supreme Court cases going back to 1880 (*Strauder v. West Virginia*, 1880) have forbidden systematic or intentional exclusion of religious, racial, and other **cognizable groups** (who, because of certain shared characteristics, might also hold unique perspectives on selected issues) from jury panels. Despite these rulings, until about 40 years ago, the composition of most *venires* was homogeneous, with middle-aged, well-educated white men generally overrepresented (Beiser, 1973; Kairys, 1972. In some cities and counties, juries were composed exclusively of white men. Furthermore, 40 years ago there was no consistent standard for composing jury pools. In 1961, according to the Department of Justice, 92 federal courts employed 92 different methods of establishing the *venire* (Hyman & Tarrant, 1975). In some local jurisdictions, representativeness was totally ignored. It was customary in some towns to use as jurors retired or unemployed men who hung around the courthouse all day.

Judicial and Legislative Reforms

In a series of decisions, the Supreme Court and the U.S. Congress established the requirement that the pool from which the jury is selected must be a representative cross section of the community. One of the most noteworthy of these decisions, the Jury Selection and Service Act of 1968, led federal courts to seek uniform criteria for determining what groups are to be excused from jury service.

These decisions were propelled by two policy concerns, each of which entails psychological assumptions (Hans & Vidmar, 1982). First, the government believed that if the pools from which juries were drawn represented a broad cross section of the community, the resulting juries would be more heterogeneous; that is, they would be composed of people who were more diverse with respect to age, gender, ethnic background, occupation, and education. The courts assumed that this diversity would produce two benefits: (1) Heterogeneous juries would be better fact finders and problem solvers, and (2) juries composed of a diverse collection of people would be more likely to include minority group members, who might discourage majority group members from expressing prejudice.

This second assumption seems logically valid; casting a wider net will yield members of smaller religious and ethnic groups. But the first expectation—that more heterogeneous juries are better problem solvers—is an empirical question. Extensive research on the dynamics of groups studied in the psychological laboratory shows that, other things being equal, groups composed of people with differing abilities, personalities, and experiences are better problem solvers than groups made up of people who share the same background and perspective (Hoffman, 1965). Heterogeneous groups are more likely to evaluate facts from different points of view and to have richer discussions. Does this also happen in juries?

The answer is apparently yes. Samuel Sommers (2002) used actual jury pool members to examine the effects of racial heterogeneity on jury deliberations in a rape trial. He asked the jurors to take part in simulated (mock) trials in which he varied the racial mix of jurors and recorded their deliberations. Sommers found that mixed-race groups had several advantages over juries composed of only white jurors: The mixed-race groups had longer, more thorough deliberations and were more likely to discuss racially charged topics such as racial profiling. Furthermore, white jurors on racially mixed juries mentioned more factual information and were more aware of racial concerns than were their counterparts on all-white juries. On the basis of this study, we can conclude that one justification for requiring representative *venires*—that they will result in better, more thorough fact-finding—seems justified, both logically and empirically.

The second policy reason for the Court's and Congress's decisions on representativeness is related to the *appearance* of legitimacy, rather than to the jury's actual fact-finding and problem-solving skills (Hans & Vidmar, 1982). Juries should reflect the standards of the community. When certain components of the community are systematically excluded from jury service, the community is likely to reject both the criminal justice process and its outcomes as invalid.

We now know that the racial composition of a jury *can* affect public perceptions of the fairness and legitimacy of a trial and of the resulting verdict. To examine this issue, Leslie Ellis and Shari Diamond (2003) approached 320 adults in airports, bus and train stations, and parks, and asked them to participate in a short survey. These participants read a description of a shoplifting trial in which the racial makeup of the jury and the verdict were varied. Half of the respondents read that there were 12 whites on the jury (racially homogeneous), and half read that there were 8 whites and 4 African Americans (racially heterogeneous). For half the jury's verdict was a conviction, and for the other half it was an acquittal. The researchers measured observers' perceptions of the fairness and legitimacy of the trial procedures. When the verdict was an acquittal, fairness ratings were not influenced by the racial composition of the jury. But when the verdict was guilty, a different picture emerged. Here, the racial composition of the jury *was* important: Observers considered a trial with a homogeneous jury less fair than a trial with a heterogeneous jury (Ellis & Diamond, 2003, p. 1047).

It has been said that "justice must not only be done; it must be seen to be believed," and the different elements of the community must see that they are well represented among those entrusted with doing justice—that they have a voice in the process of resolving disputes (Hans, 1992).

The violent aftermath of the 1992 trial of four white Los Angeles police officers who were acquitted of assault for their role in beating black motorist Rodney King illustrates this problem as dramatically as any event in our nation's history. The panel eventually selected for the trial of these officers contained no black jurors (Box 11.1). After the jury found the police officers not guilty, the black community rejected the verdict as invalid and angrily challenged the legitimacy of the entire criminal justice system for black people. Shaken by the surprising verdicts and shocked by the ensuing riots, many Americans, regardless of their race, questioned the fairness of the jury's decision, in part because of the absence of black citizens from its membership.

So, too, might defendants reject the fairness of decisions made by juries whose members share few, if any, social or cultural experiences with them. Consider, for example, the probable reaction of a college sophomore, on trial for possession of marijuana, who is found guilty by a jury composed entirely of people in their fifties and sixties.

Representative juries not only preserve the legitimacy of the legal process but also solidify participants' positive feelings toward the process. If members of underrepresented groups—the poor, the elderly, blacks, youth—do not serve on juries, they are more likely to become angry and impatient with the legal process. For some participants, at least, the net result of serving on a jury is an increased appreciation for the jury as a worthwhile institution.

Devices Used for Drawing a Pool

Representativeness of jury pools is an eminently worthwhile goal. Given the guidelines from the federal courts and the legislature, how should local courts go about forming the *venire* in order to reach this goal? (It is important to note that these laws do not require any one pool to be representative; they require that a series of jury pools drawn over a period of several years be representative of the community's

composition; Farmer, 1976.) The 1968 law required that voter registration lists be used as "the primary source" for jury pool selection. But such lists underrepresent certain segments of the community. Compared with the general population, people who have recently reached voting age are less likely to have registered to vote. Smaller percentages of the poor, Latinos, and other minorities register to vote. Thus, the pool of prospective jurors may be unrepresentative of the community on a variety of relevant dimensions.

To increase the extent to which juries represent their communities, some courts have tried their hand at "rigging" the *venire*. For example, in Detroit, where African Americans are consistently underrepresented on jury *venires*, a federal court removed non–African Americans from the jury pool in order to increase the likelihood that African Americans would be represented in the panel. To do so, the jury commissioners removed one out of every five non–African Americans from the potential pool in order to make the *venires* more accurately reflect a cross section of the greater Detroit area. However, when two Hispanic defendants appealed their convictions on the grounds that increasing the percentage of African Americans disadvantaged other groups, specifically Hispanics, the appeals court agreed. The court ruled that although the desire to increase African Americans on Detroit juries was commendable, the district court's actual plan was fatally flawed because it eliminated persons from jury service solely on the basis of race (*United States v. Ovalle*, 1998).

Various changes in selection procedures can increase representativeness. These include supplementing voters' lists with other sources, such as lists of licensed drivers, persons receiving public assistance, and unemployment lists (Kairys, Kadane, & Lehoczky, 1977), and updating address lists to reduce the impact of greater mobility among lower-income citizens (Fukurai & Butler, 1994). Another option is to stratify the selection procedures so that historically underrepresented groups in a jurisdiction receive a larger number of jury summons, thereby increasing the ultimate

THE CASE OF

BOX 11.1   ### Rodney King: Does it matter who sits on the jury?

When the four white police officers were acquitted of beating Rodney King, most people were surprised and appalled. Indeed, a *Los Angeles Times* poll reported that 92% of people who had seen the videotaped confrontation thought that excessive force was used against King. The jury was severely criticized, and observers sought to understand the outcome. Critics sometimes raise broader concerns (fairness and justice, for instance) but fail to consider the problem from the perspective of the jury, which must make a decision based only the evidence presented. Often a major cause of a surprising verdict by a jury (especially an acquittal) is that the prosecution was not effective

in arguing its case or presenting its evidence. Or it may be that what the public hears or reads through the mass media is different from what the jury is exposed to. Even conceding the importance of the evidence (or the reporting of evidence) to trial outcomes, the composition of the jury needs to be examined as a determinant of verdicts, too.

The trial of the police officers in the King case was moved from urban Los Angeles to neighboring Ventura County as a result of pretrial publicity. The demographics of Ventura County favored the defense—suburban, white, a bedroom community with more than 2000 police families, a place to which people move to escape urban

problems. It could be expected that jurors would empathize with the defendants—the "thin blue line" regarded by many as protecting the citizenry from drugs and gang violence—rather than with Rodney King, a large, black, drunk driver.

The six-man, six-woman jury, whose verdict of acquittal sparked one of the worst riots in this nation's history, consisted of ten whites, one Hispanic, and one Asian American but included no African Americans. The median age of the jurors was 50 years. Three were members of the National Rifle Association, and two others had law enforcement backgrounds. Most of the jurors were married and owned or were purchasing their own homes.

yield of prospects from these groups (Ellis & Diamond, 2003).

Unfortunately, the Jury Selection and Service Act of 1968 did not make these recommendations into requirements. Even though states have added more sources (usually lists of people with drivers' licenses and state-issued identification cards), many were slow to broaden the source for potential jurors. For example, a study conducted almost a decade after the new law was passed documented the continued use of outdated voter registration lists, failure to contact those who had not returned their questionnaires, and very liberal granting of exemptions (Alker, Hosticka, & Mitchell, 1976).

Furthermore, some local courts have ruled that underrepresentation of such groups—in a 1973 Louisiana test case, it was those who were

poor—does not violate the purpose of the Jury Selection and Service Act (Handman, 1977). The courts have still not agreed about what "representativeness" means in practice.

Exclusions, Nonresponses, and Exemptions: Threats to Representativeness?

Once a pool of potential jurors has been drawn, each individual is sent a questionnaire to assess his or her qualifications and ability to serve. Some people may be excluded by law because their responses reveal personal limitations (e.g., blindness, mental incompetence), although these restrictions are changing.

The rationale for prohibiting the service of certain groups (the visually impaired, persons who are not mentally competent, those who do not speak

English, people who have felony convictions, those who are not U.S. citizens) may be justified, but other issues that arise during this phase of jury selection further erode the representativeness of the eventual jury. A national survey of state court administrators showed that an average of 12% of juror questionnaires are returned by the post office as undeliverable, and many people who receive questionnaires simply do not respond (as many as 20% of Dallas residents!) (Boatright, 1999).

Without a doubt, every jury commissioner (those courthouse employees responsible for securing jurors' participation) in the country could tell stories about the creative ways that people have tried to escape jury service. Vincent Homenick, the chief jury clerk of the courthouse in Manhattan, once received a summons that someone had returned with the word "deceased" scribbled on it, along with a plastic bag supposedly containing the ashes of the prospective juror (Green, 2004)!

Among those persons who are eligible for jury service and who return the questionnaire, members of the jury panel are randomly selected and summoned to appear for jury service on a designated date. But as many as half of qualified jurors ignore the jury duty summons, even though doing so constitutes a violation of law (Ellis & Diamond, 2003). Often, as long as enough prospective jurors appear to fill the needed juries, those no-shows are never contacted or punished. Better follow-up of nonresponders might reduce this problem, but most courts do not have the resources to do so.

Until recently, all members of certain occupations were automatically exempted from jury service. For example, the state of New York gave automatic exemptions to physicians, firefighters, veterinarians, podiatrists, phone operators, and embalmers. Why? The rationale extends back a hundred years, to a time when each of these occupations played a vital role in small-town life, and the person (usually there was only one physician or one telephone operator) had to remain available to the community. In many jurisdictions, elected officials, lawyers, and judges were also exempted from jury duty. But those exemptions are less common nowadays. When Arizona Senator John McCain showed up for jury duty in a

Phoenix courtroom in January of 2005, he reminded some surprised fellow potential jurors that he too was a citizen. Most states, including New York, have now eliminated all exemptions from jury duty (Kaye, 2001).

As recently as 1979, Missouri offered *all* women an automatic exemption, which allowed them to opt out of jury service simply by signing their name on the jury questionnaire. Before this policy was changed, women constituted only about 15% of the jurors in the Kansas City, Missouri, area. A ruling by the Supreme Court in 1979, stating that this exemption undermined the principle that the jury should be a "fair cross-section of the community," led to a fourfold increase in the percentage of Missouri jurors who are women (Mills, 1983).

Prospective jurors sometimes avoid jury service by claiming personal hardship. Some judges are sympathetic to claims of ill health, business necessity, vacation plans, and the like. But many other judges are unwilling to dismiss individual jurors because of perceived "hardships." During the jury selection for the O. J. Simpson civil trial, Judge Hiroshi Fujisaki responded to one prospective juror who had requested dismissal because she suffered from claustrophobia, "How big is your living room? Is it as big as this courtroom?" She remained in the pool. Another prospective juror complained of the likelihood of getting stiff from sitting too long. "That's why we take breaks," replied the unsympathetic judge.

Because only those prospective jurors who make the request are excused, the result can be a winnowing out of many who don't want to serve. Does this change the representativeness of the pool? Intuitively, it would seem that those who remain are more likely to regard jury service as a civic responsibility important enough for them to endure personal inconvenience.

Thus, even before the formal jury selection in the trial gets under way—that is, before jurors are chosen from among the people who are physically present in the courtroom—a selection process has already removed some people from the panel of prospective jurors from which the final jury will be drawn. These removals can distort the representativeness of panels whenever certain groups of people are overrepresented among those removed. As Hans and Vidmar (1982) stated after reviewing the evidence, "The ideal of a jury panel as a representative cross-section of the community is seldom realized" (p. 46).

Voir Dire: A Reasonable Process with Unreasonable Outcomes?

As if the steps in forming a *venire* had not already compromised the representativeness of the jury, the forum in which prospective jurors are questioned by the judge and/or the attorneys (called **voir dire**, a French term meaning *to speak the truth*) may further accentuate the resulting jury's bias, as we saw in the chapter-opening example. Paradoxically, the purpose of *voir dire* questioning is to eliminate biased jurors. As part of the constitutional right to be tried by a "fair and impartial" jury, a defendant is afforded the opportunity to screen prospective jurors to determine whether any of them are prejudiced (*Dennis v. United States*, 1966).

The ways in which *voir dire* is conducted are almost as numerous as the judges who hold trials (Hans & Jehle, 2003). Who asks the questions, what questions are asked and how they are phrased, how long the questioning goes on, and whether the questions are posed to individual jurors or to a group are all matters left to judges' discretion.

The most limited form of *voir dire* involves a small number of questions asked in yes-or-no format only by the judge and features group rather than individual questioning of prospective jurors. An example: "Do any of you have an opinion at this time as to the defendant's guilt or innocence?" Yes-or-no questions are effective in controlling the answers of witnesses, but they offer little insight into jurors' beliefs and attitudes. Also note that this form of questioning requires jurors to self-identify any biases and report them to the judge. But jurors may be unaware of their predispositions and/or hesitant to state them in public; thus, both of these obligations may be difficult for jurors to fulfill.

Several studies show that limited *voir dire* has several drawbacks as a means of identifying biased jurors (Johnson & Haney, 1994; Seltzer, Venuti, & Lopes, 1991). One of the most compelling demonstrations came from a project initiated by District of Columbia Superior Court Judge Gregory Mize (1999). Prior to this study, Judge Mize, like many judges, had conducted limited *voir dire* during which he asked questions in open court to a group of approximately 60 prospective jurors. He and the attorneys would then pose follow-up questions to those who responded affirmatively to the initial question. Judge Mize revised his procedures for the study; he interviewed all prospective jurors, regardless of whether they had responded affirmatively to the first question. In doing so, he determined that a number of jurors who were silent in response to a preliminary question actually had a great deal to say when prompted individually. Among the responses:

- "I was frightened to raise my hand. I have taken high blood pressure medications for twenty years. I am afraid I'll do what others tell me to do in the jury room."
- "I do not understand your questions or remember the past very well."
- "My grandson was killed with a gun so the topic of guns makes my blood pressure go up."
- And remarkably, this one: "I'm the defendant's fiancée."

Judges must find ways to induce jurors to talk, because a new trial may be required if it is later determined that one or more of the jurors should have been excused (Post, 2005).

Why is limited *voir dire* so ineffective at uncovering juror bias? Obviously, some jurors will fail to disclose important information because of privacy concerns, embarrassment, or a failure to recognize their own biases. But an important psychological dynamic, termed **social desirability effect**, is also a factor at this stage. Most people want to present themselves in a positive, socially desirable way. This desire to appear favorably, especially in the presence of a high-status person such as a judge, shapes how people answer questions and influences what they disclose about themselves. As Hans and Jehle (2003) point out, the leading questions that are of limited *voir dire* often elicit the socially desirable response (for example, a claim that one can set aside predispositions and biases when evaluating trial evidence, even if one would actually find that difficult or impossible to do).

At the other extreme is extended *voir dire*, in which both the judge and the attorneys ask questions, the questions are both closed-ended (yes-or-no questions) and open-ended (questions that require elaboration), they cover a wide range of topics, and jurors are questioned individually. Extended *voir dire* has several advantages in uncovering biases. Open-ended questions (for example, "What experiences have you had in your life that caused you to believe that a person was being discriminated against because of the color of his skin?") encourage jurors to talk more about their feelings and experiences. Individual questioning can result in disclosures that jurors might not otherwise offer, an advantage that prompted Judge Mize to conclude that individual *voir dire* is "an indispensable way of ferreting out otherwise unknown jurors qualities" (Mize, 1999, pg. 12). But because extended *voir dire* can take a long time, most courts tend not to favor it.

The typical *voir dire* procedures now involve a compromise between the limited and extended versions; both the attorneys and the judge pose questions to a group of prospective jurors, and then they ask brief follow-up questions of selected individuals. Judges usually impose severe time restrictions on questioning by attorneys (Rottman et al., 1998). The average length of *voir dire* in a felony case is 5.13 hours (Hans & Jehle, 2003). Remarkably, in the Enron fraud case—perhaps the most visible corporate prosecution ever—the judge delivered on his promise to select a jury in just one day (although jurors had answered a lengthy questionnaire before coming to the Houston courthouse in January of 2006).

Examination of jurors is typically conducted in open court, but if very sensitive topics are raised, the questioning may be done at the judge's bench or in the judge's chambers. This is likely to occur if, in the judge's opinion, issues that are ordinarily private, such as one's credit rating, health problems, religious beliefs, or history of victimization, may affect a juror's ability to be fair and impartial. Apparently, jurors consider many questions asked during jury selection to be either irrelevant or intrusive. Mary Rose interviewed 209 North Carolina jurors after they had served on juries; 43% believed they had been asked irrelevant questions, 27% said the questions made them feel uncomfortable, and approximately the same number said the questions were overly personal (Rose, 2003). Aware that jurors are more likely to disclose personal and sensitive information in writing than orally, some judges use written questionnaires in place of, or in addition to, questions asked in open court. The "mother of all juror questionnaires" was the 294-item questionnaire used in the O. J. Simpson case.

Can a potential juror refuse to answer questions that, in that juror's opinion, are invasive or irrelevant? Dianna Brandborg tried, as Box 11.2 explains.

Challenges for Cause and Peremptory Challenges

Technically, opposing attorneys do not select a jury; rather, the judge gives them the opportunity to exclude a number of potential jurors from the eventual jury. (For this reason, the procedure should perhaps be termed jury rejection rather than jury selection, although *rejection* is probably too strong a word!) There are two mechanism—challenges for cause and peremptory challenges—by which panelists are excluded from serving on a jury; both are explained in detail below. Here, we simply point out that after all the challenges have been made and ruled on, and some prospective jurors have been dismissed, the people who remain are sworn into service as the jury.

In any trial, each side can claim that particular jurors should be excluded because they are inflexibly biased or prejudiced or because they have a relationship to the parties or the issues that creates the appearance of bias. These exclusions are known

THE CASE OF

BOX 11.2 | **Dianna Brandborg: The juror who refused to talk**

When questioned as a potential juror in a Denton, Texas, murder trial, Dianna Brandborg refused to answer queries about her income, religion, political affiliation, and preferences in TV shows and books. Judge Sam Houston told her that her responses were insufficient and gave her a chance to reconsider. When she refused, he cited her for contempt and sentenced her to jail for three days. His rationale was that a prospective juror's right to privacy must defer to the urgency of a fair trial, particularly in an important case such as a murder trial. A federal magistrate thought otherwise, however, and set aside Ms. Brandborg's contempt citation, reasoning that she had a constitutional right to refuse to answer questions that unnecessarily pried into her personal life (*Brandborg v. Lucas, 1995*).

---

as **challenges for cause**. (For example, a relative or business associate of a defendant would be challenged, or excused, for cause.) Additionally, the judge may excuse a panelist for cause without either attorney requesting it if the prospective juror is unfit to serve. In theory, each side has an unlimited number of challenges for cause, but in reality, few prospective jurors are excused for reasons of prejudice. In a survey of New Mexico courts over a three-year period, only about 1 of every 20 jurors was dismissed for cause (Hans & Vidmar, 1986).

Potential jurors who are prejudiced against either party in a trial should be stricken from service, and that is the purpose of judges granting challenges for cause. But additionally, each side may exclude a designated number of prospective jurors "without a reason stated, without inquiry, and without being subject to the court's control" (*Swain v. Alabama*, 1965). This procedure is known as a **peremptory challenge**. Peremptory challenges are used by attorneys to challenge potential jurors who they believe will not be sympathetic, for whatever reason, to their client.

The number of peremptory challenges allocated to each side varies from one jurisdiction to another and also on the basis of the type of case (civil or criminal) and the seriousness of the charge. In criminal trials, the defense will have either the same number of peremptory challenges as the prosecution or a greater number. In civil litigation, the defense and the plaintiff are granted the same number of peremptory challenges, which are usually fewer than those granted in criminal trials in the same jurisdiction.

The peremptory challenge is more than a simple mechanism for removing jurors thought to be unsympathetic. The peremptory challenge also has a symbolic function: When the parties in a lawsuit play a role in selecting the people who decide the outcome, they may be more satisfied with that outcome (Saks, 1997).

The third function of peremptory challenges is to allow the attorney to indoctrinate prospective jurors and influence those who ultimately will make up the jury. For example, Holdaway (cited in Blunk & Sales, 1977, p. 44) gives the following example of how counsel can ask a question that will acquaint the juror with rules of law expected to arise in the case but pose it in such a way that it allies the juror with the attorney's position. The question is "Do you agree with the rule of law that requires acquittal in the event there is reasonable doubt?" The real purpose of this question is, of course, to alert the prospective juror right from the start that reasonable doubt could exist in the case and to make the juror aware of the rule in the hope that he or she will thus look for reasonable doubt and then vote to acquit.

The legal system also has three broad goals for *voir dire*, and one can ask whether an attorney's objectives in challenging prospective jurors match the legal system's goals for *voir dire*. Basically, the latter goals are (1) to determine whether a prospective juror meets the statutory requirements for jury service, (2) to discover any grounds for a challenge for cause, and (3) to discover information that can lead to the intelligent exercise of peremptory challenges (*United States v. Dellinger*, 1972). These goals underscore the overall aim of *voir dire*: ensuring that an impartial jury is empaneled. However, lawyers are well aware that jury selection, as practiced in an adversarial system, enables them to achieve other goals.

As we shall see in the next section, the Supreme Court has imposed more and more limits on the exercise of peremptory challenges. As a result, the overall status of this jury selection tool is in doubt. Although opinions about the importance of the peremptory challenge remain divided—some experts favor its elimination altogether, and others argue that it is crucial for fair trials—surprisingly little data have been published on the use of peremptory challenges in real trials. For example, are they used to remove minority jurors or other specific groups, a major concern that is addressed in the next section? Do the prosecution and defense repeatedly strike different types of jurors?

Some preliminary answers to these questions come from a study conducted by Mary Rose (1999), who examined 13 North Carolina felony trials that involved the questioning of 348 juror prospects (32% African American, 53% female). A total of 147 peremptory challenges were exercised, and the defense used the majority (66%) of them. The following pattern of dismissals was uncovered:

◆ African American jurors were no more likely to be peremptorily challenged than white jurors. However, 71% of the African Americans who were dismissed were challenged by the prosecution, whereas 81% of the white jurors who were dismissed were challenged by the defense.

◆ Men were more likely to be dismissed than women, but there was no association between gender and the probability of being removed by one side or the other.

◆ On most juries, the percentage of African American and female jurors mirrored their level of representation in the community.

These results provide both good news and bad news: It appears that peremptory challenges do not have a disparate impact on members of minority groups; however, these selection mechanisms result in differential treatment of people on the basis of their race, by prosecutors and defense attorneys alike.

The Batson *Decision: No Exclusion on Account of Race*

As a result of a series of Supreme Court decisions, it is forbidden to exercise peremptory challenges solely on the basis of a juror's race or gender. Consequently, these challenges are "less peremptory" than they used to be. The decision regarding race was triggered by an appeal by James Batson, a black man convicted of second-degree burglary by an all-white jury. During the *voir dire*, the prosecuting attorney had used four of his six peremptory challenges to dismiss all the black persons from the *venire*. In *Batson v. Kentucky*, decided in 1986, the Court held that a black defendant was denied his Fourteenth Amendment right to equal protection by the prosecution's strikes against black members of the panel (Pizzi, 1987). In *Holland v. Illinois* (1990), the Court held that a white defendant could also complain about the exclusion of blacks because the principle of representativeness was violated by the arbitrary exclusion of any racial group. Finally, and most significantly, the Court in 1991 held that striking jurors solely on the basis of race violates the equal protection rights of the jurors (*Powers v. Ohio; Edmonson v. Leesville Concrete Co.*). The *Edmonson* decision makes it clear that race-based peremptory strikes are forbidden in *civil* cases, and in the 1992 case of *Georgia v. McCollum*, the Supreme Court prohibited race-based strikes *by the defense* in criminal cases (previous cases had focused on the prosecution's peremptory challenges) (Bonora, 1995).

In a case in which a peremptory challenge might be motivated by racial factors, the judge will ask the attorney for an explanation. The attorney must then advance a race-neutral explanation for the strike—for example, that the juror has a brother in prison or has filed a lawsuit against the police. The judge then determines whether the explanation is genuine, taking into account the other jurors who were not struck by the attorney. For example, if an attorney were to explain that she struck a black juror because he had been robbed, the judge would want to know why she had not struck a white juror who also had been robbed.

In *Branch v. State* (1986), decided soon after the *Batson* case, the court accepted as genuine the prosecutor's "race-neutral" explanations for striking several black jurors. The various explanations included the following:

◆ Potential juror Montgomery: Being a scientist, Montgomery's presence on the jury would have put too great a burden on the prosecution, considering the background of the case and "knowing the problems with one hundred percent mathematical aspects of a case like this"; the prosecutors did not want "a scientific application in the decision."

◆ Potential juror Parmer: Parmer's general appearance was unkempt. Moreover, he worked in "credit management," and because the prosecutors were not able to question him about his specific job, they considered it too risky to leave Parmer on the jury. Parmer appeared to be a gruff individual, and the prosecution did not want a juror who would be at odds with other jurors.

Not only did the trial judge accept these as "race-neutral," but the appeals court concluded that the judge had applied *Batson* "with caution and sensitivity."

Do these results indicate that a judge will always accept a lawyer's race-neutral explanation for striking a juror? If so, *Batson* is a paper tiger. In fact, a minority of the Supreme Court justices used a similar label in reacting to the majority's opinion in *Purkett v. Elem* (1995), a case based on a *Batson*-like appeal. In a Missouri trial, a prosecutor had dismissed two prospective black jurors. Because the defendant, Jimmy Elem, who was charged with robbery, was black, the prosecutor was instructed to give a race-neutral reason for his strikes; he told the judge that the jurors' long hair, beards, and mustaches "look suspicious to me." An appeals court decided that such explanations had to be not only race-neutral but also "plausible," but the Supreme Court later decided that this requirement was too stringent; the trial judge need decide only whether the reason violates jurors' right to equal protection. In the dissenting opinion by Justices Stevens and Breyer, giving trial judges such broad latitude turned the inquiry into a "meaningless charade" in which "silly, fantastic, and implausible" explanations had to be tolerated.

It might appear that creative prosecutors can always find "race-neutral" reasons for excluding minorities from the jury. Indeed, the case of Thomas Miller-El, detailed in Box 11.3, exemplifies the difficulty of proving racial bias in jury selection.

Peremptory Challenges and Other Juror Characteristics

The Supreme Court has also extended the logic of *Batson* to peremptory challenges based on another cognizable characteristic—gender. The case of *J. E. B. v. Alabama ex rel. T. B.* (1994) is described in Box 11.4.

How many different cognizable groups are there and could limitations on peremptory challenges eventually be extended to cover all of them? Dominic Massaro, a judge in the state of New York, decided that Italian Americans were entitled to *Batson*-type protection (Alden, 1996), and a California law bans attorneys from removing jurors simply because they are homosexual. But in other trials, attempts to apply the rule to obese jurors (*United States v. Santiago-Martinez*, 1995) and bilingual jurors (*Hernandez v. New York*, 1991; Restrepo, 1995) were denied. Peremptory strikes based on religious affiliation should not be permitted, and some courts have held that such strikes

THE CASE OF

BOX 11.3   **Thomas Miller-El and the difficulty of proving racial bias in jury selection**

Texas death row inmate Thomas Miller-El must feel like a yo-yo, given the number of times his case has bounced back and forth between the 5th Circuit Court of Appeals and the Supreme Court. The issue is whether prosecutors engaged in purposeful discrimination during Miller-El's 1986 trial on charges that he robbed and murdered an Irving, Texas, hotel clerk. Probably no *voir dire* has ever been scrutinized as thoroughly as the one that occurred in this case.

Prosecutors in that trial used peremptory strikes to exclude 10 of the 11 blacks who were eligible to serve on the jury, and Miller-El was convicted and sentenced to death. For years he contended that prosecutors used peremptory challenges in a biased way to keep African American jurors off his jury panel, but courts rejected this claim four times. Finally, when the 5th Circuit refused to hear Miller-El's appeal, he appealed to the Supreme Court.

This time, with the support of some unusual allies (including numerous federal prosecutors and

judges who, along with the former director of the F.B.I., filed a brief supporting Miller-El's position), he found a receptive audience. In an 8–1 ruling (and a rare victory for Miller-El), the Supreme Court found that the lower courts had failed to fully consider the evidence he offered to show racial bias, and it ordered the 5th Circuit to reconsider Miller-El's claim (*Miller-El v. Cockrell*, 2003). (That evidence included a history of discrimination by Dallas prosecutors and a training manual from the Dallas District Attorney's Office that instructed prosecutors to exercise their peremptory strikes against minorities.) But when the 5th Circuit judges undertook such reconsideration and examined all the reasons prosecutors gave for striking *venire* members, they concluded that black and white jurors had been treated the same by prosecutors (*Miller-El v. Dretke*, 2004).

Miller-El again appealed to the Supreme Court, and again the high court ruled in his favor, overturning his conviction because of racial bias

Texas death row inmate, Thomas Miller-El, being told that he was granted a stay of execution in 2002. Miller-El challenged the prosecutor's use of peremptory challenges during his 1986 trial.

in jury selection. According to Justice Stephen Breyer, "[t]he right to a jury free of discriminatory taint is constitutionally protected. The right to use peremptory challenges is not." Justice David Souter was even more direct, writing that Miller-El's evidence of bias "is too powerful to conclude anything but discrimination" (*Miller-El v. Dretke*, 2005).

violate the constitutions of their states (e.g., *State v. Fuller*, 2004), but the Supreme Court has yet to hold that it is unconstitutional to base peremptory challenges on religious affiliation or on any other classification, for that matter. So critics' fears that the *J. E. B.* decision would effectively kill off the venerable peremptory challenge have not yet been realized. Attorneys' discretion in jury selection

remains relatively unfettered, except that jurors cannot be challenged because of their race or their gender.

Sometimes, trial attorneys attempt to extend the principle of "a jury of your peers" to an extreme degree. In Houston, Texas, the attorney for accused murderer Jeffrey Leibengood asked to include only people less than five feet tall in the

THE CASE OF

BOX 11.4   *J. E. B. v. Alabama ex rel. T. B.*: **Whose child is this and who gets to decide?**

The facts of the case are these: Teresia Bible gave birth to a child in May 1989; she named the child Phillip Rhett Bowman Bible, claimed that James E. Bowman, Sr. was the father, and filed a paternity suit against him to obtain child support. Even though a blood test showed that there was a 99.92% probability that he was the father, Mr. Bowman refused to settle, so a trial was held.

The jury pool was composed of 24 women and 12 men; after three prospective jurors were dismissed for cause, the plaintiff used nine of its ten peremptory challenges to remove males; the defendant used ten of his eleven to remove women

(he also removed one man). Thus the resulting jury was composed of 12 women. (Note that in this case, it was men who were systematically excluded from the jury.) The jury concluded that Mr. Bowman was the child's father and ordered him to pay child support of $415.71 per month.

Because the judge had dismissed his challenge to the procedure of striking male jurors, Bowman appealed to the higher courts. The U.S. Supreme Court ruled that peremptory challenges that were used to eliminate one gender were, like those used to exclude a race, unacceptable, and other grounds had to be justified.

The Court's decision acknowledged that peremptory strikes against women hark back to stereotypes about their competence and predispositions, traced from a long history of sex discrimination in the United States (Babcock, 1993).

In the aftermath of this case, critics contended that the limitations imposed by the justices would prove unworkable and would unleash a flood of collateral litigation. But the data show otherwise: In the five years immediately after *J. E. B. v. Alabama ex rel. T. B.* was decided, only 23 published cases in the entire U.S. federal and state court systems were reversed because of *J. E. B.* violations (Hightower, 2000).

jury pool because his client's height was four feet six inches. The attorney told the judge, "We say a short person is subject to discrimination, and we hope to have two or three short people end up on the jury. *Batson* should be extended to include the little people" (quoted by Taylor, 1992, p. 43). The judge disagreed.

There is an irony to court-ordered limitations on the use of peremptory challenges. Cognizable groups are defined in part by the fact that their members share certain attributes and points of view. But if this is the case, and if these views tend to be adverse to one side or the other (for example, compared to white jurors, African Americans tend to be more skeptical of the police), why shouldn't individual litigants be allowed to remove certain types of prospects who might be biased against them? In fact, despite the *Batson* and *J. E. B.* cases, many lawyers continue to consider race and gender in the

exercise of peremptory challenges. In 2005, John Quatman, former Alameda County (California) prosecutor, claimed that prosecutors routinely exclude Jews and blacks in capital cases because they assume that these groups would not vote for a death sentence.

If members of cognizable groups are systematically underrepresented on juries (although Rose's study would question that assumption), the community at large might doubt that the jury system is fair and sufficiently inclusive. But it seems inconsistent to argue that particular demographic segments of a community need to be included on jury panels to promote minority points of view, while at the same time denying attorneys the opportunity to base their peremptory challenges on those very demographic characteristics. Are these two arguments logically incompatible? In the end, both sides of this debate may have only weak empirical support. As discussed in the next sections, demographic variables tend not to be very powerful predictors of jury verdicts.

Lawyers' Theories: Stereotypes in Search of Success

Do the trial strategies of attorneys conflict with the goal of having unprejudiced fact finders? Do they perpetuate or extend the bias that might occur in the empaneling and questioning of prospective jurors? Before we answer these questions, we need to answer a more basic one: How do lawyers go about selecting or excluding jurors, and do their strategies work?

In everyday life, our impressions about others are governed largely by what psychologists have termed implicit personality theories. An **implicit personality theory** is a person's organized network of preconceptions about how certain attributes are related to one another and to behavior. Trial lawyers often apply their implicit personality theories to jury selection. For example, William J. Bryan (1971) advised prosecutors to "never accept a juror whose occupation begins with a P. This includes pimps, prostitutes, preachers, plumbers, procurers, psychologists, physicians, psychiatrists, printers, painters, philosophers, professors, phonies, parachutists, pipe-smokers, or part-time anythings" (p. 28). Another attorney vowed always to use a peremptory strike against any prospect who wore a hat indoors. Implicit personality theories lead to stereotypes, when a person believes that all members of a distinguishable group (e.g., a religious, racial, sexual, age, or occupational group) have the same attributes. They also produce assumptions that two qualities are associated—for example, when a lawyer assumes that slow-talking jurors are also unintelligent.

We tend to link qualities together and form our own implicit personality theories. Sometimes these judgments are rationally based; we may have had enough consistent experiences to draw a valid conclusion about the relationship. Other theories, however, such as the examples just presented, are only intuitive or are based on limited experiences and purely coincidental relationships. Stereotypes often formed on this basis.

The emergence of implicit personality theories is almost inevitable when we form impressions of others and make interpersonal decisions. After all, human behavior is very complex. We must simplify it in some way. Richard "Racehorse" Haynes, a highly successful lawyer, once defended two white Houston police officers charged with beating a black prisoner to death. Like all lawyers, Haynes had his ideas about the kind of juror who would be sympathetic to his police officer clients, but his candor was a surprise. After the trial was over, Haynes was quoted as saying, "I knew we had the case won when we seated the last bigot on the jury" (Phillips, 1979, p. 77).

The use of implicit personality theories and stereotypes was reflected by the jury selection decisions made by each side in the trial of *J. E. B. v. T. B.* Ms. Bible's attorney struck male jurors, assuming they would be sympathetic to the man alleged to be the baby's father, whereas the defense struck female jurors because of similar beliefs that women would be biased in favor of another woman. But the courts are beginning to prohibit the use of such stereotypes; in his majority opinion in the *J. E. B.* case, Justice Harry Blackmun wrote, "Virtually no support [exists] for the conclusion that gender alone is an accurate predictor of [jurors'] attitudes," and if gender does not predict a juror's predisposition, then there is no legitimacy in dismissing jurors on the basis of it only (quoted by Greenhouse, 1994, p. A10).

Despite such admonitions, books of advice for trial lawyers continue to perpetuate gender stereotypes as a basis for evaluating jurors. A jury selection primer, published in 1985 with endorsements by prestigious trial lawyers F. Lee Bailey and Melvin Belli, stated, "Women are born skeptics, generally as curious as the cat. . . . And they are skeptical in direct proportion to the physical beauty of a female witness" (quoted in Ruben, 1995, p. 188).

Lawyers must choose which prospective jurors to strike with their quota of peremptory challenges. Hence, their own implicit personality theories come into play. Typically, their decisions are based on little information beyond the juror's race, sex, street address, appearance, and occupation. Even if they are allowed to question jurors individually, lawyers cannot know for certain whether they are being told the truth. By necessity, they fall back on their own impressions. What attributes do lawyers find important? Textbooks and journal articles on trial advocacy provide a wealth of folklore about jurors' characteristics. Not surprisingly, characteristics that are visible or easily determined—age, gender, race, religion, occupation, country of origin—receive special attention.

In addition to applying their own theories of personality to juror selection, some attorneys use their understanding of group structure. For example, they play hunches about which jurors will be the most dominant during the deliberations. Who will be selected as foreperson (if, as in most jurisdictions, that choice is left up to the jury)? What cliques will form? Although an understanding of group dynamics is more sophisticated than simple stereotypes of individual jurors, lawyers who use such conceptions are still relying on their own assumptions about human behavior. Some lawyers maintain a simple "one-juror verdict" theory—that is, they believe that the final group decision is usually determined by the opinions of one strong-willed, verbal, and influential juror. Lawyers who adhere to this maxim look for one juror who is likely to be both sympathetic and influential and then, during the trial, concentrate their influence attempts on that individual. In pursuing this search for a "key juror," the typical attorney follows one basic rule of thumb: "In general, an individual's status and power within the jury group will mirror his status and power in the external world" (Christie, 1976, p. 270). If jurors themselves are asked who among them was most influential during their deliberations, three characteristics tend to emerge: male gender, an extroverted personality style, and height greater than that of their fellow jurors (Marcus, Lyons, & Guyton, 2000).

Another common attorney strategy is based on the assumption that jurors who are demographically or socially similar to a litigant will be predisposed to favor that litigant, a belief known as the **similarity–leniency hypothesis** (Kerr, Hymes, Anderson, & Weathers, 1995). Does this rule of thumb hold true? Are jurors more likely to favor litigants with whom they share certain characteristics?

I try to get a jury with little education but with much human emotion. The Irish are always best for the defense. I don't want a Scotchman, for he has too little human feelings; I don't want a Scandinavian, for he has too strong a respect for law as law. In general, I don't want a religious person, for he believes in sin and punishment. The defense should avoid rich men who have a high regard for the law, as they make and use it. The smug and ultra-respectable think they are the guardians of society, and they believe the law is for them. (Quoted in Sutherland & Cressey, 1974, p. 417.)

One could make the opposite prediction in some cases—sharing similar qualities with another might make a juror more skeptical of that person's excuses or justifications for behavior that the juror dislikes. Here, the so-called **black sheep effect** may apply: Although people generally favor individuals who are part of their in-group, they may sometimes strongly sanction those fellow members who reflect negatively on and could embarrass the in-group (Marques, Abrams, Paez, & Martinez-Taboada, 1998). Recent studies have produced conflicting evidence about this issue. Religious similarity between a defendant and mock jurors has been found to increase leniency, but when the evidence against the defendant was very strong, a black sheep effect was discovered whereby the defendant similar in religious affiliation was treated more harshly than an out-group defendant (Kerr et al., 1995).

Finally, some attorneys follow the "first 12 called" rule. Frustrated by past attempts to predict how jurors will behave, they simply accept the first prospects called to the jury box, sometimes deliberately drawing jurors' attention to their willingness to believe that everyone is fair and can be trusted to decide the case "correctly."

Demographic Characteristics of Jurors

Trial attorneys must make informed guesses about which prospective jurors will be more favorable to their side. On what basis should these choices be made? Are juror demographics the answer?

The prospect of relying on demographic features of jurors is appealing to attorneys because

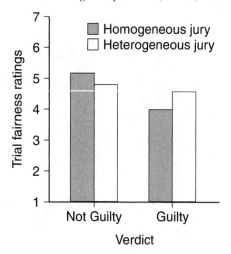

Including all respondents (N=320)

FIGURE 11.1 *Combined effect of verdict and racial composition of jury on fairness ratings for both sets of analyses*

many of these characteristics (e.g., age, race, gender, socioeconomic status) are easily observable (Kovera, Dickinson, & Cutler, 2002). Indeed, attorneys do actively select (or, rather, deselect) jurors on the basis of demographic information. When Olczak, Kaplan, & Penrod (1991) gave attorneys mock juror profiles that varied along demographic lines (jurors' gender, age, marital status, and nationality) and asked them to rate the extent to which each profiled juror would be biased toward the defense or prosecution, they found that attorneys could do this task easily and that they focused on one or two characteristics to the exclusion of others. Results of a separate study, however, showed that none of the juror characteristics actually predicted juror voting.

Demographic characteristics of jurors *are* related to their verdicts some of the time, but the relationships are weak and inconsistent from one type of trial to another (Baldus, Woodworth, Zuckerman, Weiner, & Broffit, 2001; Wissler, Hart, & Saks, 1999). The relationships that emerge are usually small; they permit researchers to claim "there's something there" but offer no guarantee of success to the attorney who deals with only a few individuals and one trial at a time.

The relationship between demographic characteristics and verdicts may depend on the type of case. For example, in trials that involve issues such as sexual assault, domestic violence, and sexual harassment, jurors' gender may matter: In general, women are more likely than men to convict the perpetrators of these crimes (Brekke & Borgida, 1988; Kovera, Gresham, Borgida, Gray, & Regan, 1997), and in civil trials, women are more inclined than men to perceive that sexual harassment has occurred in the workplace (Weiner, Hurt, Russell, Mannen, & Gasper, 1997). Even here, however, the gender effect is not particularly large (Blumenthal, 1998), and gender is not a reliable predictor of verdicts in other types of cases (Kovera, Dickinson, & Cutler, 2002).

The most consistent gender difference involves social influence rather than content; men play a more active role in the jury room than women. A man is more frequently selected as foreperson (Dillehay & Nietzel, 1985; Strodtbeck, James, & Hawkins, 1957), men speak more often during deliberations (James, 1959), and men are generally perceived by other jurors as more influential than women (Marcus et al., 2000). Men seem to be chosen more often to head the jury for two reasons: (1) They are more likely to make a personal statement about their status by choosing the end seat at the deliberation table, and (2) they are seen by other jurors as more experienced in such decisions (Strodtbeck & Lipinski, 1985).

Jurors' socioeconomic status and occupational level are related to their verdicts in only a very general way. In a survey of how jurors voted in 100 criminal trials, Adler (1973) found that jurors who voted to convict the defendant were of higher socioeconomic status (indicated by variables such as income, occupational level, and education) than those who voted for acquittal. This tendency for "well-off" jurors to be harsh on criminal defendants has been confirmed in controlled laboratory studies (Simon, 1967). And like men, jurors of higher socioeconomic status are more likely to be elected foreperson (Strodtbeck et al., 1957).

Attempts to relate jurors' ethnic origin to their verdicts have led some to a few tentative conclusions—for example, that jurors of German and British descent favor the prosecution, whereas those of Slavic and Italian descent favor the defense (Broeder, 1959)—but these generalizations must be viewed with great caution. For example, other factors, such as socioeconomic differences among ethnic groups, may provide a better explanation for their different reactions. When other demographic characteristics are studied (e.g., race, level of education, or place of residence), they are often found to interact so much with ethnicity, with one another, and with characteristics of the case that it is impossible to make even the most tentative conclusions about the influence of any one variable.

Using jurors' race to predict their verdicts is complicated (Kovera et al., 2002). Some psychologists (e.g., Bothwell, 1999) have concluded that black jurors are more lenient than whites in the typical criminal case. Indeed, even in the atypical case involving O. J. Simpson, blacks were less likely than whites to believe that Simpson murdered his ex-wife (Brigham & Wasserman, 1999). But other psychologists (e.g., Nietzel & Dillehay, 1986) have suggested that upwardly mobile black middle-class jurors may, in fact, be harsher toward black defendants in violent crimes such as murder and rape than are white jurors. In general, there is little evidence that jurors' demographic characteristics can predict reliably what verdicts will ensue.

Personality Characteristics of Jurors

If demographic qualities have an uncertain relationship to jury verdicts, what about the personality characteristics of the individual juror? Do attorneys' implicit personality theories and stereotypes work here? A number of studies have concluded that enduring aspects of personality may influence a person's courtroom decisions, but usually only to a modest degree. Many commentators suggest that personality factors typically do not predict more than 10% of the variance in jury verdicts, but other researchers claim that in certain cases, these variables can account for as much as 30% of the variance (Moran, Cutler, & Loftus, 1990).

Psychological research using simulated juries in laboratory settings has indicated that certain personality attributes of mock jurors, such as authoritarianism, internal or external locus of control, and belief in a just world, may at times be related to verdicts in a jury simulation. It is possible that lawyers improve their outcomes to a slight degree when they select jurors on the basis of those dispositions.

But we need to remember that the trials used in these studies were "close calls"; that is, the evidence for each side was manipulated to be about equally persuasive, and it is in such cases that individual juror characteristics may have their greatest influence (Hepburn, 1980; Nietzel & Dillehay, 1986; Penrod, 1990). In the real world, the evidence is often so conclusive for one side that the jurors' personality dispositions have no appreciable impact. And equally important—yet often overlooked—is the interaction between the jurors' personality characteristics and aspects of the specific trial.

Authoritarianism is one personality characteristic of jurors that is correlated with their verdicts (Dillehay, 1999). People with an authoritarian personality adhere rigidly to traditional values, identify with and submit to powerful figures, and are punitive toward those who violate established norms. In terms of the legal system, authoritarian subjects are more likely to vote for conviction in mock jury experiments (Narby, Cutler, & Moran, 1993) and impose more severe sentences than less authoritarian jurors (Bray & Noble, 1978). However, when highly authoritarian jurors encounter a defendant who symbolizes authority, their usual tendency to punish the defendant is reversed (Nietzel & Dillehay, 1986). In fact, about the only time that authoritarian mock jurors are not more conviction-prone is in trials in which the defendant is a police officer. In such cases, the more authoritarian jurors tend to identify with the powerful and punitive image of the officer. (This may be changing as jurors, mindful of recent cases of police corruption, have become less trusting of police testimony [Rovella, 2000a]).

Beliefs about what determines our outcomes in life form another personality variable that sometimes affects jurors' verdicts. Clinical psychologist

Julian Rotter (1966) proposed that people differ in their beliefs about whether their lives are controlled by internal factors, such as skill and effort, or by external factors, such as luck, fate, or the actions of others. Research has shown that this **internal/external locus of control** (or I-E, as it is abbreviated) is a potent influence on behavior in a variety of settings (Phares, 1976). In their verdicts, jurors seem to project their own orientations onto the behavior of the litigants. Criminal defendants may prefer jurors who have an external focus and who are likely to attribute criminal acts to forces beyond the defendant's control (Phares & Wilson, 1972). In civil cases, on the other hand, defendants may prefer jurors with an internal locus of control (those who believe in personal responsibility), whereas civil plaintiffs would probably opt for jurors who have an external locus of control (those who don't feel able to control their fate and who may feel victimized by events that happen to them).

Studies by the National Jury Project (1990) find that people differ a great deal in whether they hold individuals or outside forces responsible for negative happenings. Some prospective jurors hold a "personal responsibility" viewpoint, believing that individuals are completely responsible for the adversities that beset them, whereas others lean toward "social responsibilities," arguing that social and environmental factors are the key determinants of behavior. Such a variable is relevant to a number of personal injury and medical malpractice cases—an older woman slipping on the ice in front of a grocery store, a hunter who accidentally shoots himself and then sues his emergency physician for improper treatment. Jurors who hold a personal responsibility perspective take special notice whenever the plaintiff has assumed a risk and has contributed in even a minor way to the harm he or she suffered (Hans, 1992).

A third relevant personality characteristic of jurors is called **belief in a just world** (Lerner, 1970). Individuals differ in the extent to which they believe that people get what they deserve (and deserve what they get) in life. A person who believes in a just world has a need for explanation and justification; such a person is threatened by

the possibility that events happen by chance. Imagine that someone is killed in what appears to be a completely coincidental accident; he is walking along a sidewalk when a truck careens out of control and runs him down. Those who believe in a just world are so threatened by the idea that the victim died merely by chance that they will conclude that he must have deserved such a fate by having done something wrong to cause his misfortune. Relatives and friends of rape victims, instead of providing sympathy, may derogate them on the assumption that if they were raped, they must somehow have provoked, invited, or caused it. Consistent with this view, researchers have found that persons who believe in a just world will berate the victim of a crime or be tougher on the defendant in order to maintain their belief system (Gerbasi, Zuckerman, & Reis, 1977; Moran & Comfort, 1982).

One final juror characteristic that has been linked to jury outcomes is not a personality variable at all; it is the amount of prior experience jurors have had deciding other cases. Although the results of studies about the effects of prior juror experience on jury verdicts are somewhat inconsistent (Dillehay & Nietzel, 1999; Rovella, 2002), most criminal defense attorneys prefer jurors who have never served on a jury before—a preference that has some empirical support.

In an effort to learn whether prior jury service influences later verdicts, Dillehay and Nietzel (1985) studied 175 consecutive criminal trials across one calendar year in Lexington, Kentucky. Because jurors in this jurisdiction are "on call" for service for 30-day terms, they have the opportunity to serve on several trials in one month. Two indices of juror experience were found to be correlated with a greater likelihood of conviction: (1) the number of jurors per jury who had served on at least one prior jury and (2) the total number of juror experiences represented on each jury. Guilty verdicts increased when a majority of jurors on a given case had prior jury experience. A later study (Himelein, Nietzel, & Dillehay, 1991) found that juries with more experienced members handed down more severe sentences than inexperienced juries (Kentucky is one of the states where jurors sentence convicted defendants.) The results of other studies have been mixed, but when a relationship *is* discovered, it has been in the direction of juries with more experience being more conviction-prone (Dillehay & Nietzel, 1999).

Although many psychologists doubt that personality and demographic characteristics can predict individual jurors' verdicts well enough to be useful, other legal experts believe that specific attitudes and beliefs can be important influences in certain trials (Gayoso, Cutler, & Moran, 1994). With a few exceptions, practicing attorneys and authors of trial advocacy textbooks state that a case can be won or lost during *voir dire*. Attorneys take pride in their skill in selecting a proper jury. For example, a president of the Association of Trial Lawyers in America wrote, "Trial attorneys are acutely attuned to the nuances of human behavior, which enables them to detect the minutest traces of bias or inability to reach an appropriate decision" (Begam, 1977, p. 3). Yet Kalven and Zeisel (1966), two experts on jury decision making, suggest that lawyers often overestimate their own abilities to turn a jury verdict in a favorable direction.

Others are even more skeptical about how much lawyers can accomplish in *voir dire*. One social scientist observed the jury selection process in 23 consecutive trials in a federal court in the Midwest and concluded that "the *voir dire* was grossly ineffective not only in weeding out 'unfavorable' jurors but even in eliciting the data which would have shown particular jurors as very likely to prove 'unfavorable'" (Broeder, 1965, pp. 505–506).

In a test of this issue (Olczak, Kaplan, & Penrod, 1991), experienced trial attorneys were observed to use juror selection strategies that were not different from or better than those of inexperienced college and law students who were asked to evaluate mock jurors. As with other comparisons of experts and novices, trial attorneys do not appear to think any more accurately when making personality judgments than do nonprofessionals. Even when asked to perform a more realistic task—rating jurors from the videotapes of a previous *voir dire*—attorneys did not do better than chance in detecting jurors who were biased against them (Kerr, Kramer, Carroll, & Alfini, 1991).

In another study evaluating the effectiveness of *voir dire*, Cathy Johnson and Craig Haney (1994) observed the full *voir dires* used in four felony trials in Santa Cruz, California. As part of this study, they collected information on the criminal justice attitudes held by the jurors by administering Boehm's (1968) Legal Attitudes Questionnaire to prospective jurors. By comparing the attitudes of persons who were retained as jurors with those of persons who were challenged by the prosecutor or defense attorneys, they were able to gauge the effectiveness of each side's peremptory challenge strategy. Jurors who were peremptorily excused by prosecutors held stronger pro-defense attitudes than jurors excused by the defense, and jurors excused by the defense were more pro-prosecution than jurors excused by the prosecution. However, the overall score of the retained jurors was not significantly different from the average score of the first 12 jurors questioned or of a group of prospective jurors sampled at random. Apparently, although each side succeeded in getting rid of jurors most biased against it, the end result was a jury that would not have differed appreciably from a jury obtained by just accepting the first 12 people called or empaneling 12 jurors at random.

A few other findings are a bit more favorable to attorneys. In one experiment involving a simulated personal injury case, a social scientist (Strodtbeck, reported in Zeisel & Diamond, 1978) asked experienced civil attorneys to rank jurors according to the size of the damage award that each might advocate in the jury deliberations. He then compared their rankings with the actual awards proposed by these jurors. Both plaintiff and defense attorneys were good at predicting the variations in awards.

In a more sophisticated study, two social scientists (Zeisel & Diamond, 1978) assessed lawyers' selection skills by looking at how prospective jurors who were challenged and excused would have voted. For 12 criminal trials conducted at the U.S. District Court of Northern Illinois, the researchers had those *venire* members who had been excused remain as "shadow jurors," watch the trial from the spectator section of the courtroom, and then render their own verdicts. In this way, the researchers could compare the decisions of actual juries composed of those who had survived the *voir dire* with the verdicts of hypothetical juries composed simply of the first 12 *venire* members. (The latter, reconstituted juries were thus made up of both real jurors and those who had been excused.) Zeisel and Diamond estimated that, in 3 of the 12 cases, the actual verdicts were affected by the defense attorney's effective use of peremptory challenges. They concluded that trial attorneys apparently do win some of their cases because of their decisions during the *voir dire*. Interestingly, defense attorneys seem to exercise more peremptory challenges than prosecutors, even when the same number is granted to each side (a finding replicated in other studies; Rose, 1999). This "zealous" representation of clients may be one reason for their relative effectiveness in the preceding survey (Van Dyke, 1977).

"Scientific Jury Selection": Does It Work Any Better?

As we have noted in this chapter, for years trial lawyers have been "picking" jurors on the basis of their own theories about how people behave. To the extent that these hunches, superstitions, and stereotypes have validity—and sometimes they do—attorneys can increase their chances of winning cases that they might have lost if those cases had been decided by a jury with a different composition.

Many attorneys, convinced of the importance of jury selection but skeptical of their ability to do it well or limited in the time they can devote to it, have hired social scientists as jury selection consultants. These consultants try to use empirically based procedures, including focus groups and shadow juries, systematic ratings of prospective jurors, and surveys of the community, to detect bias (Strier, 1999). This collection of techniques is known by the label of "scientific" or "systematic" jury selection. Although these techniques were first used to aid defendants in several highly publicized "political" trials (McConahay, Mullin, & Frederick, 1977; Schulman, Shaver, Colman, Emrich, & Christie, 1973), they are now frequently practiced in the full range of criminal and civil trials, ranging from the high-profile cases of O. J. Simpson, Martha Stewart, Scott Peterson, and the "Whitewater scandal," to routine civil cases.

Earlier, in considering whether lawyers' strategies "work," we concluded that when attorneys in criminal trials have relied on empirically grounded scientific jury selection, they have often been successful. Although the procedure seems to work, the success rate may be inflated by any of the following factors: (1) Many of the more widely discussed cases involved weak or controversial evidence against defendants, (2) the trials have often been lengthy and complex, increasing the opportunity for juror characteristics to color perceptions of the evidence, and (3) attorneys who make the extra effort to enlist jury consultation resources may also be more diligent and thorough in other areas of their case preparation.

How does scientific jury selection compare to traditional selection methods when the two approaches are used to select jurors for the same trials? Horowitz (1980) carried out one empirical comparison using four criminal cases. Conventional jury selection methods used by attorneys, including their past experience, interactions with similar jurors in prior trials, and conventional wisdom, were pitted against social science methods. Neither approach was superior for all four trials. Scientific jury selection was more effective in cases in which there were clear-cut relationships between personality or demographic variables and jurors' votes, but when these relationships were weak, scientific selection lacked accuracy and precision. Reviewing a collection of studies that contrasted scientific jury selection with attorney methods, Fulero and Penrod (1990, p. 252) concluded, "If a defendant has his or her life . . . at stake, the jury selection advantages conferred by scientific jury selection techniques may well be worth the investment."

Observers disagree about the usefulness of consultants in jury selection. Not surprisingly, consultants themselves (as well as some attorneys) contend that they provide an essential service: "We've collected a lot of research and we can spot things a lawyer wouldn't normally be paying attention to. . . . Most attorneys do just one or two trials a year, if they're lucky. But a good consultant has studied hundreds of juries and knows which behaviors and characteristics to look out for" (quote by consultant Dan Wolfe, cited by McCann, 2004). But other attorneys are content to do their own jury-picking: "I've done this for a long time, and I know what I want and don't want in a juror. . . . I don't need someone distracting me from my own job" (quote by attorney Joseph Power, cited by McCann, 2004).

How effective *are* trial consultants at selecting juries? The answer to this question, like the answer to many questions involving human behavior in the legal system, is "It depends" (Greene, 2002). It depends on how many peremptory challenges are allowed, whether it is the judge or the attorneys who question prospective jurors, the extent to which questions delve into matters beyond superficial demographic details of prospective panel members, and whether attorneys act on the guidance of the consultant. The more freedom and flexibility inherent in the jury selection procedures, the more room for consultants to ply their trade and the greater the chances they can be effective.

Unfortunately, few empirical studies have investigated the effectiveness of scientific jury selection. Further, the research that has been published often involves simulated—mock jury—experiments, which may limit the extent to which the results apply to actual juries (Bornstein, 1999).

One study of scientific jury selection as it was practiced in a series of actual capital murder trials provides some data on the effectiveness of jury consultants. To evaluate the effectiveness of the defense's use of consultants in a series of death penalty cases, Nietzel and Dillehay (1986) examined the 35 outcomes of 31 capital trials (a couple of trials had two defendants). Juries recommended the death sentence in 61% of the trials in which consultants were not employed by the defense and in 33% of the trials with defense jury consultants. Of course, these cases differed on many variables beyond the use of consultants, so it is not possible to conclude that any differences were due to their presence alone. But the results are consistent with claims that jury consultants might be effective in cases in which jurors' attitudes are particularly important, as they are when a jury is asked to choose between life and death.

Recognizing that jurors' demographic and personality characteristics do not correlate strongly with verdicts in general, many jury consultants have shifted their focus from advising lawyers about jury selection to providing services in realms other than jury selection (Kressel & Kressel, 2002; Lisnek, 2003). This new strategy emphasizes the following methods:

1. Conducting public opinion surveys, small-group discussions (or focus groups), and jury simulation studies in which subjects hear abbreviated versions of the evidence, discuss it, and make individual and group decisions as the consultant watches and listens to their deliberations. In addition to determining whether any individual characteristics of subjects are systematically related to their reactions to the evidence, consultants can use respondent feedback to help attorneys craft their presentation of the evidence so that it has the greatest possible appeal to jurors. In the realm of civil trials, this pretrial analysis can help determine the value that a jury would place on a plaintiff's injuries, thereby facilitating settlement negotiations. These procedures were used effectively by the prosecutor in a recent civil rights trial about an old crime (Box 11.5).

2. Analyzing how different jurors form a narrative or private story that summarizes the evidence into a coherent, compelling account (Pennington & Hastie, 1986, 1988). This analysis is followed by an attempt on the consultant's part to derive central themes that can serve to organize and explain the evidence. These themes are then reinforced by voir dire questions, evidence presentation, opening statements, and closing arguments so that the most salient psychological factors of the case are repeatedly presented to the jurors in a manner that best supports the attorney's desired interpretation of the facts (Kressel & Kressel, 2002; Lisnek, 2003).

THE CASE OF

BOX 11.5   **Thomas Blanton: A church bombing and a jury consultant**

The 1963 bombing of the 16th Street Baptist Church in Birmingham, Alabama, is regarded by many as the most galvanizing moment of the civil rights era. Four African American girls were killed that Sunday morning as the bomb ripped through their church. Although the F.B.I. investigated the murders and quickly identified four suspects, the case was never prosecuted, presumably because the suspects—all white— would not have been convicted by a Birmingham jury, also presumably all white. But 40 years later, one of those suspects, Thomas Blanton, a former member of the Ku Klux Klan, stood trial for the murders.

The prosecution was aided by a jury consultant, Andrew Sheldon, who conducted two focus groups and polled nearly 500 residents of the Birmingham area to ascertain their attitudes about racial issues in general and about the church bombing in particular. According to Sheldon, this pretrial research convinced him that the prosecution should not focus on the Ku Klux Klan because the group had little relevance to most prospective jurors. Rather, Sheldon urged the prosecutor to query jurors and exercise challenges on the basis of whether they had children and were churchgoers. Other relevant attitudes concerned school desegregation and racial conflict. After a three-week

Aftermath of bombing of 16th Street Baptist Church in Birmingham, Alabama in 1963.

trial, the jury deliberated for barely two hours before convicting Blanton on four counts of murder. He was sentenced to life in prison.

Lawyers, Psychologists, and Ethics: Problems with Jury Selection

The legal system promulgates an idealized assumption that all members of the community have an equal chance of serving on juries, but widespread practices prevent that. All segments of the community are not fairly represented in the jury pools of many jurisdictions across the nation. Furthermore, attorneys do not seek neutral jurors; they seek those favorable to their own side. Proponents of the current system acknowledge this tendency but assume that if both parties are successful in rejecting those who are unfavorable to them, their respective challenges will balance out. In theory, both extremes will be eliminated, leaving those who are less biased and more open-minded.

This assumption is required by the logic of our adversarial system, which holds that fair process and just outcomes are achieved when two opponents work zealously to win outcomes favorable to themselves. But unfortunately, actual trials don't usually work out that way. Because some lawyers don't really care about jury selection ("Give me any 12 people and I'll convince 'em!") and others are inept in their selection of favorable jurors, this theoretical balance is seldom if ever achieved. As the O. J. Simpson criminal trial reflects, the effective use of jury consultants by only one side adds to the imbalance. In effect, when one of the attorneys is more motivated or more skilled at jury selection, the outcome is equivalent to giving that side a larger number of peremptory challenges.

Of course, this imbalance is not restricted to adversarial systems; resources are not equally distributed in education, medicine, government, or any of our other social institutions. But the

adversarial system may magnify the impact of unequally qualified participants; when opponents are not evenly matched, the superior one will win more often.

As the practice of scientific jury selection has expanded, so have legal and ethical objections to it. Critics often condemn these techniques as "jury rigging" that undermines public confidence in the jury system and gives rich litigants an unfair edge over poor or average-income citizens (Kressel & Kressel, 2002). Some critics (e.g., Lecci, Snowden, & Morris, 2004) raise concerns about shortcomings in the methodologies typically employed by trial consultants. Fueled by these criticisms, public concern has led to several suggested reforms. These include (1) prohibiting the use of jury consultants, (2) imposing greater restrictions on *voir dire* questioning, (3) curtailing or eliminating altogether the use of peremptory challenges, (4) requiring jury consultants to share with the other side any information on prospective jurors that they gather, and (5) regulating jury consultants through professional licensure and practice standards (Strier, 2001).

Few, if any, of these reforms have been implemented in the United States (although the American Society of Trial Consultants is considering licensure for people in that profession). Nor would they necessarily yield fairer outcomes. The American system of justice remains fundamentally adversarial. As long as litigants are expected to present their version of the case as zealously as possible, they should be expected to use every legal means available to woo the jury and counter the opposition in order to win the dispute. To single out jury consultation for special restrictions is a slippery slope premised on the faulty notion that the two sides in a trial can be required to be equal.

As we have previously noted, it is paradoxical that the legal system insists that jurors first be chosen in such a way as to be typical of their communities and then often allows this representativeness to be undone at the stage of *voir dire*. The jury selection process does sometimes conflict with the goals of representativeness. For this reason, even though the legal system seeks with equal fervor to achieve representativeness and fairness, these ideals may be incompatible.

Symposium: The Jury at a Crossroad: The American Experience

SYMPOSIUM EDITOR
Nancy S. Marder

Foreword
John Paul Stevens

Introduction to The Jury at a Crossroad: The American Experience
Nancy S. Marder

I. LESSONS FROM THE PAST

The Origins of Felony Jury Sentencing in the United States
Nancy J. King

II. THE JURY AND RACE

How Much Do We Really Know About Race and Juries? A Review of Social Science Theory and Research
Samuel R. Sommers and Phoebe C. Ellsworth

Race, Diversity and Jury Composition: Battering and Bolstering Legitimacy
Leslie Ellis and Shari Seidman Diamond

III. THE JURY IN PRACTICE

A *Voir Dire* of *Voir Dire*: Listening to Jurors' Views Regarding the Peremptory Challenge
Mary R. Rose

The Current Debate on Juror Questions: "To Ask or Not To Ask, That Is the Question"
Nicole L. Mott

Jurors and the Future of "Tort Reform"
Judge B. Michael Dann (ret.)

When All of Us Are Victims: Juror Prejudice and "Terrorist" Trials
Neil Vidmar

Avoid Bald Men and People with Green Socks? Other Ways To Improve the *Voir Dire* Process in Jury Selection
Valerie P. Hans and Alayna Jehle

Death of an Accountant: The Jury Convicts Arthur Andersen of Obstruction of Justice
Stephan Landsman

Nullification at Work? A Glimpse from the National Center for State Courts Study of Hung Juries
Paula L. Hannaford-Agor and Valerie P. Hans

IV. REINVIGORATING THE JURY

Jurors as Statutory Interpreters
Lawrence M. Solan

A Conservative Perspective on the Future of the American Jury Trial
Robert P. Burns

Proof Beyond All Possible Doubt: Is There a Need for a Higher Burden of Proof When the Sentence May Be Death?
Judge Leonard B. Sand and Danielle L. Rose

Chicago-Kent
College of Law

Illinois Institute of Technology

Source: *Chicago-Kent Law Review*, Volume 78, Number 3, 2003.

SUMMARY

1. *What does the legal system seek in trial juries?* Among its goals for juries, the legal system seeks that they be representative and unbiased. Each of these goals is hard to achieve. The jury selection process can, in some instances, create an unrepresentative jury.

2. *What stands in the way of jury representativeness?* Reforms have not been very successful in creating juries that are representative of local populations. Too many people are excused from service. Furthermore, the traditional source of names (voter registration lists) excludes too many people. To make jury pools representative, jurisdictions need to (1) broaden the sources, by using lists of licensed drivers, and (2) reduce automatic exemptions to persons in a limited number of occupations.

3. *What procedures are used in voir dire?* The process of selecting a jury from the panel of prospective jurors is called *voir dire*. Its goal is a jury that is unbiased. Each side may discharge a certain number of prospective jurors without giving any reasons; these are called *peremptory challenges*. Prospective jurors who have biases or conflicts of interest can be challenged for cause and discharged. Questioning of the prospective jurors is done at the discretion of the judge. In most trials, there is some combination of questions from the judge and the attorneys. When questioning jurors, most attorneys also try to sway jurors to their viewpoint through various ingratiation and indoctrination techniques.

4. *What personality characteristics of jurors, if any, are related to their verdicts?* In choosing jurors, lawyers often base their decisions on their implicit personality theories and stereotypes of what is a "good" juror. A few personality characteristics—authoritarianism, locus of control, and belief in a just world—are weakly to moderately related to juror verdicts.

5. *Are lawyers and psychologists effective in jury selection?* Whether lawyers' choices of jurors actually improve their chances of winning is controversial. Clearly, the relative weight of the evidence is the most important determinant of the jury's verdict. Initially, practitioners of "scientific jury selection" used community surveys to determine which demographic characteristics of jurors were related to their being sympathetic to one side or the other in trials. More recently, trial consultants have broadened their work to include pretrial assessments of reactions to the evidence and the development of themes that organize the evidence for specific jurors likely to be swayed by this approach. There is some evidence that science-oriented consultation may be useful in cases in which the evidence is equivocal or jurors' attitudes about the evidence are especially important.

KEY TERMS

authoritarianism	cognizable groups	peremptory challenges	*venire*
belief in a just world	implicit personality theories	similarity–leniency hypothesis	*voir dire*
black sheep effect	internal/external locus of control	social desirability effect	
challenges for cause			

Jury Trials II: Concerns and Reforms

ORIENTING QUESTIONS

1. *Describe the concern related to the competence of jurors and juries.*
2. *What is the impact of extralegal information on jurors?*
3. *Can jurors disregard inadmissible evidence?*
4. *How can jurors be helped to understand their instructions?*
5. *What is meant by the statement "Bias is inevitable in jurors"?*
6. *What reforms of the jury system do psychologists suggest?*

The right to trial by jury is protected by state constitutions and by the Sixth (for criminal cases) and Seventh (for civil cases) Amendments to the U.S. Constitution. The U.S. Supreme Court underscored the importance of the jury by stating that "[t]he guarantees of jury trial in the state and federal constitutions reflect a profound judgment about the way in which the law should be enforced and justice administered" (*Duncan v. Louisiana*, 1968, p. 149). More recently, the Supreme Court acknowledged the preeminent role of juries in our legal system when it announced that *any* contested fact that increases the penalty for a crime (with the exception of a prior conviction) must be determined by a jury (*Blakely v. Washington*, 2004).

Trial by jury is an institution that routinely, on every working day, draws ordinary citizens into the apparatus of the justice system. Although most legal disputes are resolved without a jury trial and the number of cases that are decided by juries has dropped recently (Galanter, 2004), there are still more than 150,000 jury trials conducted each year in the United States, and tens of thousands occur in other countries throughout the world. In fact, jury trials have recently been reintroduced in Russia and Spain, are being considered in Japan, and form an integral part of the legal system in countries in Africa (e.g., Ghana, Malawi), Asia (e.g., Sri Lanka, Hong Kong), South America (e.g., Brazil), and Europe (England, Ireland, Denmark) (Vidmar, 2000). Jurors decide many criminal cases in Canada.

More than one-fourth of all American adults report that they've served on a jury (Gallup Organization, 1989), and approximately three million U.S. citizens are called for jury duty every year. For many jurors, their participation demands major sacrifices of income, time, and energy. In a massive class action lawsuit against the Ford Motor Corporation, one juror continued to attend the trial even after suffering injuries in a hit-and-run accident and in spite of requiring constant pain medication; another juror whose family moved out of the county opted to live in a hotel near the courthouse in order to continue hearing the case. On the other hand, serving on a jury can be a very educational

and inspiring enterprise and, on occasion, can bring great personal satisfaction, as it did for Erika Ozer and Jeremy Sperling, who met in a New York City jury box in 2001 and were married in 2005.

The jury system casts its shadow well beyond the steps of the courthouse, however, because predictions about how juries would decide cases influence decisions to settle civil lawsuits and to accept plea bargains in criminal cases. Thus the jury trial is an important and influential tradition; no other institution of government places power so directly in the hands of the people and allows average citizens the opportunity to judge the actions of their peers (Abramson, 1994).

Antecedents of the contemporary jury system may be seen in English law established 700 years ago and earlier. Even the ancient Greeks had a form of citizen jury. Throughout its history, however, the jury system has been under attack. One critic described the jury as, at best, 12 people of average ignorance. The esteemed Judge Jerome Frank, who served on the federal appeals court, complained that juries apply law they don't understand to facts they can't get straight. Even Mark Twain took a swing at the jury system. In *Roughing It*, he called the jury "the most ingenious and infallible agency for defeating justice that wisdom could contrive." One anonymous commentator asked rhetorically, "How would you like to have your fate decided by twelve people who weren't smart enough to get out of jury duty?" (cited by Shuman & Champagne, 1997). Others have noted that when a judge makes an unpopular decision, that particular judge is criticized, but when a jury reaches an unpopular verdict, the entire jury system is indicted (Ellsworth & Mauro, 1998).

Many people cite the 1995 acquittal of O. J. Simpson on charges of murder as the prime example of flaws in the jury system. A public opinion poll taken exactly a year after the verdict found that only 25% of 3400 adults felt that it was the right decision (Price & Lovitt, 1996). However, 62% of the blacks questioned felt that Simpson was not guilty, compared to 20% of the whites. One of the many consequences of that trial has been a renewed call for jury reforms, including greater limits on peremptory challenges, bans against the use of jury consultants, and the end of jury sequestration (Nietzel, McCarthy, & Kern, 1999; Strier, 1999). We discuss jury reforms later in this chapter.

The civil jury, in particular, has been resoundingly vilified. In fact, one prominent scholar of the civil jury points out that "so many writings, both scholarly and journalistic, have been devoted to criticizing the institution of the civil jury that it becomes boring to recite the claims" (Vidmar, 1998, p. 849). According to Vidmar, civil juries have been criticized as incompetent, capricious, unreliable, biased, sympathy-prone, confused, gullible, hostile to corporate defendants, and excessively generous to plaintiffs. We examine some of these claims later in this chapter.

Much of the public outcry focuses on the seemingly excessive nature of jury damage awards. For example, Marc Bluestone of Sherman Oaks, California, received a jury award of $39,000 after his mixed-breed Labrador retriever, valued at $10, died a few days after returning home from a two-month stay at a pet clinic. Explains Steven Wise, a lawyer and animal rights activist: "The courts are beginning to realize that the bond between humans and animals is very powerful" (Hamilton, 2004).

Another large damage award came in the case against Exxon for its role in the 1989 *Exxon Valdez* oil spill (Box 12.1).

The jury system has been described as an expensive and time-consuming anachronism. Some critics want to restrict the use of juries; others would prefer to abandon them altogether. Advocates of radical revision of the jury have even included former Chief Justice Warren Burger of the U.S. Supreme Court, who publicly questioned the abilities of jurors to understand and sort out the complexities of protracted civil cases.

Not all the criticism comes from the outside. From the perspective of jurors themselves, the satisfaction of doing their civic duty often does not offset their apprehensions or discomfort about jury service. After their verdict in the first Rodney King police brutality trial was announced, the jurors were warned not to open their mailboxes because officials feared that bombs might have been placed inside them. Some trials challenge human endurance; the Los Angeles trial concerning the sexual abuse of children in the McMartin preschool took more than three years to complete. Other trials result in serious financial hardship for jurors. David Olson, a single father of two and a juror in a complex lawsuit between the state of Minnesota and major U.S. cigarette manufacturers, lost all his credit cards and nearly lost his home after serving on the jury for four months. The small contracting company he worked for was unable to pay him while he was away, and the state paid only $30 per day. (To jurors' dismay, the case settled just prior to closing arguments, but the judge granted the jury's unusual request to hear the plaintiffs' closing argument anyway.)

To be sure, the jury system also has its defenders. Many authors point out that claims about juries are often based on anecdotes that are unrepresentative or fabricated and on studies that lack scientific validity (see, for example, Greene & Bornstein, 2003; Hans, 2000). Indeed, most of us never hear about the hundreds of thousands of juries that each year toil out of the spotlight and, after careful deliberation, reach reasonable verdicts.

Proponents further argue that the notion of trial by jury epitomizes what is special about the justice system in that it ensures public participation in the process. Verdicts reached by representative juries can and often do increase the legitimacy of the process in the eyes of the public, particularly in controversial trials. Juries can serve as a check on the arbitrary or idiosyncratic nature of a judge. Because juries do not give a reason for their verdicts as judges are required to do, they retain a flexibility that is denied judges: They can nullify the law to achieve justice in particular cases. Finally, participating on a jury can both educate jurors and enhance regard for the justice system. Alexis de Tocqueville (1900), a 19th-century French statesman, wrote, "I do not know whether the jury is useful to those who are in litigation, but I am certain it is highly beneficial to those who decide the litigation; and I look upon it as one of the most efficacious means for the education of the people which society can employ" (p. 290).

THE CASE OF

BOX 12.1 the *Exxon Valdez* and the "excessive" damage award

On the night of March 24, 1989, with the third mate at the helm, a 900-foot oil tanker was ripped open when it ran aground in Prince William Sound, Alaska. Eleven million gallons of oil spilled into the open sea and washed up onto shorelines. Aboard the tanker was an inebriated Captain Joseph Hazelwood, who, moments before the accident, had left the bridge to do paperwork in his cabin.

In the years following the wreck, Exxon spent approximately $2.1 billion to remove oil from the water and surrounding shorelines, was fined $125 million for environmental crimes, was ordered to pay $900 million for restoration of the natural environment, and shelled out an additional $300 million to those parties who were financially affected by the oil spill.

Left out of the mix were commercial fishermen, who were not compensated for the losses they sustained when fishing habitats were destroyed. They sued in federal court in Alaska; a jury determined that Hazelwood's actions were reckless because he commanded the vessel while "so drunk that a non-alcoholic would have passed out" and that Exxon was to blame for giving command of an oil tanker to a known alcoholic. The jury awarded approximately $20 million to the commercial fisherman as compensation and assessed damages against Exxon at $5 billion, one of the largest damage awards in American history.

In most cases that result in large damages, awards are likely to

The Exxon Valdez after running aground in Prince William Sound, Alaska on March 24, 1989, causing the largest oil spill in U.S. history.

be reduced by the judge, renegotiated during post-trial settlement conferences, or (as in this case) overturned on appeal. In 2001, the 9th Circuit Court of Appeals deemed the $5 billion award against Exxon to be "unconstitutionally excessive."

Who's right? Are juries capable of making fair and intelligent decisions, or is the jury system so flawed that its use should be restricted or possibly even eliminated? Are criticisms of the jury justified? If so, can the legal system do anything to improve the functioning of juries?

Over the past several decades, researchers have subjected the jury to careful scientific scrutiny by applying theories and principles of social psychology (e.g., social influence, conformity, and small-group behavior) and cognitive psychology (e.g., persuasion and decision making). In fact, studies of juror and jury decision making have become so plentiful that they occupy a center seat in psychology and law research. Knowledge of how juries operate comes from simulation studies, archival research, court

documents, appellate opinions, and actual jurors who have granted interviews or written books about their experiences. (A particularly valuable review of studies on jury decision making was conducted by Dennis Devine and his colleagues [Devine, Clayton, Dunford, Seying, & Pryce, 2001]). From these sources, we have been able to obtain a better—though still somewhat incomplete—picture of how the jury system works.

What have we learned from these many studies? In this chapter, we focus on two broad categories of concern: first, that juries may not be competent to execute their duties properly, and, second, that juries may be biased and prejudiced. Within each of these broad categories we examine several related issues and rely on research studies to address the criticisms. Finally, we consider various proposals to reform the institution of the jury.

The Concern That Juries May Not Be Competent

In reaching their verdicts, jurors are expected to rely only on the evidence and to disregard that which is not evidence (e.g., preexisting beliefs; irrelevant information about the defendant, victim, plaintiff, or witnesses; and any information that the judge asks them to disregard). They are expected to listen attentively to expert testimony but not to give it undue weight. The legal system assumes that jurors will understand and correctly apply the judge's instructions on the law and that they have the necessary reasoning skills to understand protracted and complex cases.

The concern related to these issues is that jurors are lacking in all areas and that they are generally not competent to carry out their defined duties. Indeed, some psychologists have suggested that juries in criminal cases make more mistakes than the public should tolerate, in part because they are faced with tough cases—cases in which the evidence is neither flimsy enough to warrant dismissal nor compelling enough to induce a guilty plea (Arkes & Mellers, 2002).

Concern about the Effects of Extralegal Information

Perhaps the most fundamental criticism about the jury is that its decisions will be determined *not* by the evidence presented in court but instead by irrelevant information about the defendant's background or appearance, by what jurors read in the newspaper, or by other sources of irrelevant information, all of which constitute **extralegal information**.

Is this critique warranted? How capable are jurors of basing their verdicts only on the evidence that is brought out in court? These questions are hard to answer, because it is not obvious when juries incorporate extralegal information into their decision-making process. If they do so, no one necessarily knows the difference. Therefore, some jury decisions may be based on irrelevant considerations rather than on the evidence. But checking the reasons for a verdict following a trial is done only very infrequently, and the real reasons for a verdict or for trends in jury verdicts are often impossible to assess (Vidmar, 1994), even for the jurors themselves.

In general, though, we have learned that jurors in both criminal and civil cases pay considerable attention to the strength of the evidence. In fact, evidentiary strength is probably the most important determinant of jurors' verdicts (Devine, Clayton, Dunford, Seying, & Pryce, 2001; Greene & Bornstein, 2003, Taylor & Hosch, 2004). Differences in strength of the evidence can have profound effects on jury verdicts: Some studies have shown a 70% increase in conviction rates as the evidence against the accused becomes stronger (Devine et al., 2001).

Professor Stephen Garvey and his colleagues analyzed the verdicts of 3000 jurors in felony trials in four metropolitan areas to find out what explained jurors' first votes (Garvey et al., 2004). They measured (and controlled for) the strength of the evidence by asking the judge who presided in the case to estimate this evidentiary strength. They then determined that the judge's assessment of the strength of the evidence was powerfully associated with the jurors' first votes: The stronger the evidence against the defendant, the more likely the juror was to convict. (These data support the notion that the judge and jury tend to agree on the strength of the evidence.)

In the realm of civil litigation, jurors also place considerable weight on the evidence and, in particular, on the severity of the plaintiff's injury. More seriously injured plaintiffs receive greater compensation than less seriously injured plaintiffs across the tort system as a whole (Bovbjerg, Sloan, Dor, & Hsieh, 1991), in medical malpractice cases (Vidmar, Gross, & Rose, 1998), and in personal injury cases (Bovbjerg, Sloan, & Blumstein, 1989).

Some of what we know about jurors' attention to the evidence and disregard for the irrelevant comes from questioning jurors; other data come from archival analyses of past verdicts and from jury simulation studies. In simulation studies, some extralegal information is introduced by the researcher, who then measures the extent to which that information, as well as the actual evidence, influence jurors' reasoning and their verdicts. Although simulation studies sometimes cast extralegal information in a more prominent light than would be likely in real trials (e.g., a defendant's physical appearance might seem salient in an abbreviated and simulated trial but would lose its impact in a lengthy proceeding), they are nonetheless useful techniques for exploring how jurors reason and make decisions. On the basis of such studies, we have learned much about the impact of extralegal information in both criminal and civil cases.

Impact of Extralegal Information in Criminal Cases

THE INFLUENCE OF PRIOR-RECORD EVIDENCE

In 1993, Maria Ohler was convicted of possessing a small amount of methamphetamine and was sentenced to three years of probation. Four years later, customs inspectors found 84 pounds of marijuana behind a loose panel in the van that Ohler was driving into the United States from Mexico. When she was tried on the marijuana charge, evidence of her prior conviction was admitted at the trial in order to attack her credibility as a witness.

Once jurors have heard evidence about a defendant's prior criminal record, they may no longer be able to suspend judgment about that defendant and decide his or her fate solely on the basis of the evidence introduced at trial. Therefore, the prosecution is often not permitted to introduce evidence of a defendant's criminal record for fear that jurors would be prejudiced by it and judge the current offense in light of those past misdeeds. However, if defendants take the witness stand, then prosecutors may be able to question them about certain types of past convictions in order to impeach their credibility as witnesses. In that circumstance, the judge may issue a **limiting instruction** to the effect that evidence of a defendant's prior record can be used

for limited purposes only: to gauge the defendant's credibility but not to prove the defendant's propensity to commit the charged offense. Defense attorneys are decidedly suspicious of jurors' ability to follow this rule, as well they should be; limiting instructions are rarely effective (Shaw & Skolnick, 1995). Thus, attorneys often recommend to their clients with prior records that they not take the witness stand to testify on their own behalf.

An early study showed that attorneys' hunches were well founded. Mock jurors informed of a defendant's prior conviction were more likely than jurors who had no information about a prior record to convict the defendant on subsequent charges (Doob & Kirshenbaum, 1972). More recent research found that the similarity of the charges is an important variable: Conviction rates were higher when the prior conviction was for an offense similar to the one being decided (Wissler & Saks, 1985). One study found that deliberating juries spend considerable time talking about a defendant's prior record, not for what it suggests about credibility, but rather to decide whether the defendant has a criminal disposition (Shaffer, 1985).

Why does evidence of a prior conviction increase the likelihood of conviction on a subsequent charge? For some jurors, the prior record, in combination with allegations related to the subsequent charge, may show a pattern of criminality; together they point to an individual who is prone to act in an illegal or felonious manner. Other jurors, upon hearing evidence of a prior conviction, may need less evidence to be convinced of the defendant's guilt beyond a reasonable doubt on the subsequent charge. Prior-record evidence may lead a juror to think that because the defendant already has a criminal record, an erroneous conviction would not be serious. This juror might therefore be satisfied with a slightly less compelling demonstration of guilt.

THE INFLUENCE OF PRIOR-ACQUITTAL EVIDENCE

On some occasions, a jury will hear evidence not of a prior *conviction* but of a prior *acquittal* (i.e., the defendant was previously tried and found not guilty of charges unrelated to the present case). The U.S.

Supreme Court has held that the admission of prior-acquittal evidence does *not* unfairly prejudice the jury against the defendant (*Dowling v. U.S.*, 1990). In the *Dowling* case, Reuben Dowling was tried for armed robbery of a bank in the Virgin Islands. During his trial, the prosecutor introduced evidence from an unrelated home break-in—a charge on which Dowling had previously been acquitted. The judge admitted the evidence to prove that Dowling was present in the community in which the bank was located. Theoretically, jurors should disregard evidence of a prior acquittal when deciding whether a defendant is guilty in a subsequent case. But do they?

To test whether jurors conform to this expectation, Greene and Dodge (1995) presented a summary of the facts in the *Dowling* case to three groups of mock jurors who were deciding whether the defendant should be found guilty of armed robbery. One-third of the jurors learned that the defendant had been previously tried and convicted of charges stemming from the home break-in. Another third was informed that the defendant had been acquitted of the home break-in charges, and the final group had no information about the defendant's prior record. The results supported the Supreme Court's reasoning: Jurors who heard evidence of a prior acquittal were no more likely to convict the defendant than jurors who had no information about a prior record, and both groups were less likely to convict than jurors who had evidence of a prior conviction. These findings suggest that jurors may exercise some restraint in their use of prior-acquittal evidence and may indeed not be prejudiced by it.

THE IMPACT OF EVIDENCE ON MULTIPLE CHARGES

Can jurors show the same restraint when multiple charges are tried together in the same trial? Consider the case of Bryon Quinn, charged with 21 counts (including several for aggravated robbery) stemming from multiple robberies of office supply and pet stores in Colorado in 2003. Would jurors be able to keep the evidence straight on all of these charges?

Most courts permit a criminal defendant to be tried for two or more charges at the same time as long as the offenses are similar or are connected to the same act. This procedure, called **joinder**, exists primarily for purposes of efficiency: It is more efficient to try similar cases together than to stage separate trials. But does trying someone for two or more charges at the same time increase the likelihood that the jury will convict the defendant of at least one of these crimes? Was Quinn more likely to be convicted of any of those robberies because they were tried in conjunction with other robberies? A meta-analysis of simulation studies that have examined the effects of joinder (Nietzel, McCarthy, & Kern, 1999) concluded that such a procedure was clearly to the defendant's disadvantage. Criminal defendants are more likely to be convicted of any single charge when it is tried in combination with other charges than when it is tried alone. Some evidence indicates that jurors who hear multiple cases misremember and confuse evidence against the defendant across charges and conclude that the defendant has a criminal disposition because of the multiplicity of charges (Nietzel et al., 1999).

THE IMPACT OF CHARACTER AND PROPENSITY EVIDENCE

Historically, evidence about a defendant's character could not be used in court to prove that the defendant committed a crime. Likewise, evidence of other crimes or wrongdoing (so-called **propensity evidence**) is typically not admissible to suggest that because a defendant had the propensity to act in a criminal manner, he is guilty of the charge now at issue. Sex crimes, however, are treated differently in federal court and in some states. In 1994, Congress passed a law making evidence of other sex offenses admissible to show a defendant's propensity to commit the charged sex offense. (The promulgation of this law reflects a belief that sexual behavior is not solely situational and that some people have a propensity toward aggressive and sexual impulses.) The California legislature enacted a similar law in 1995, and the California Supreme Court upheld the law in the case described in Box 12.2.

THE CASE OF

BOX 12.2   **Charles Falsetta and his propensity to commit sex crimes**

When Charles Falsetta was tried for rape and kidnapping in Alameda County Court, the prosecutor introduced evidence of two prior uncharged sexual assaults allegedly committed by Falsetta. In the first, the defendant was alleged to have begun jogging beside a woman, asked her where she was going, and then tackled and raped her. In the second incident, the defendant allegedly blocked the path of a woman as she walked to work and later jumped out from behind some bushes, grabbed her, threw her into the bushes, and sexually assaulted

her. These incidents bore a striking resemblance to the Alameda County case in which the defendant was alleged to have stopped a 16-year-old girl as she was walking to her house from a convenience store. After initially refusing a ride, the girl eventually accepted and was driven to a darkened parking lot and raped. The defendant was convicted and appealed his conviction, contending that the admission of evidence of other uncharged rapes violated his rights.

On appeal to the California Supreme Court, Richard Rochman,

the deputy attorney general who argued the case on behalf of the state of California, stated that because victims of sex offenses often hesitate to speak out and because the alleged crimes occur in private, prosecutors are often faced with a "he said, she said" credibility problem. Allowing prosecutors to present propensity evidence in these cases would give jurors the full picture of the defendant's past sexual misconduct, reasoned Rochman. The California Supreme Court agreed (*People v. Falsetta*, 1999).

What effect might propensity evidence have on jurors? In its argument in the *Falsetta* case, the state of California assumed that jurors could properly use propensity evidence to gauge the defendant's disposition to commit sex crimes. Yet psychologists can point to a fundamental error in this assumption—the belief that this characteristic or trait is stable over time and that situational factors are irrelevant (Eads, Shuman, & DeLipsey, 2000). In short, making this assumption constitutes the fundamental attribution error.

At least one study raises questions about jurors' abilities to use propensity evidence properly. In their study of jury decision making in sexual assault cases, Bette Bottoms and Gail Goodman exposed some mock jurors to information about a defendant's past criminal acts and to other negative evidence bearing on the defendant's character. These jurors perceived the victim as more credible and the defendant as more likely to be guilty than did jurors not exposed to this character evidence (Bottoms & Goodman, 1994).

Impact of Extralegal Information in Civil Cases

When individuals have a dispute with their landlord, their insurance company, or the manufacturer of a product that they allege to have caused them harm, they can attempt to resolve that dispute through the workings of the civil justice system. Although the vast majority of civil cases are resolved outside the courtroom, typically in settlement discussions between the opposing lawyers, thousands of civil cases are tried before juries each year. Juries in these cases typically make two fundamental decisions: whether the defendant (or, in some instances, the plaintiff) is **liable** or responsible for the alleged harm and whether the injured party (typically the plaintiff) should receive any money to compensate for his or her losses, and if so, in what amount. These monies are called **damages**.

Although the vast majority of scholarly research on juror and jury decision making has focused on criminal cases, in recent years psychologists have devoted considerable attention to the workings of civil juries. As a result, they are increasingly able to address the concern that juries may be incompetent to decide civil cases fairly and rationally. Do jurors determine liability and assess damages in a rational way, or are they swayed by emotion and prejudice?

DETERMINING LIABILITY

An important decision that jurors must make in civil cases concerns the parties' respective responsibility for the harm that was suffered. When psychologists study juries' liability judgments, they are really asking how people assign responsibility for an injury. When a baby is stillborn, do jurors perceive the doctor to be at fault for not performing a cesarean section? Would the child have died anyway? When a smoker dies from lung cancer, do jurors blame the cigarette manufacturer for elevating the nicotine level in its product or the smoker who knowingly exposed herself to a dangerous product over the course of many years? Or do they blame both?

The severity of an injury or accident, sometimes referred to as **outcome severity**, is legally relevant to decisions about the damage award in a civil case, but it should be irrelevant to a judgment concerning liability or legal responsibility. The defendant should not be saddled with a liability judgment against him simply because the plaintiff was seriously injured. Rather, jurors should decide liability on the basis of the defendant's conduct. Were his actions reckless? Were they negligent? Were they malicious and evil? These are the questions that jurors should ask themselves in the course of deliberating on the defendant's liability. Are jurors able to use the evidence concerning outcome severity for the limited purposes for which it is intended—namely, to assess damages? Or do they factor it into their decision about responsibility as well?

In an important early study, Elaine Walster sparked interest in examining how the consequences of an accident affect judgments of responsibility for that accident (Walster, 1966). She presented participants with the facts of an accident and asked them to rate the responsibility of the actor who was potentially at fault. Some participants learned that the actor's conduct resulted in a dented fender (a low-severity outcome), and others learned that his actions resulted in major property damage or personal injury (a high-severity outcome). Walster found that participants assigned more responsibility to the actor in the high-severity condition than in the low-severity condition.

Why would we assign more responsibility to an individual as the consequences of his or her conduct become more serious? One explanation is **defensive attribution** (Fiske & Taylor, 1991): As the consequences of one's actions become more severe, they also become more unpleasant, and the notion that they might be accidental becomes less tolerable. Thus, we are likely to blame a person for their occurrence because doing so makes the incident somehow more controllable and avoidable.

Walster's study was conducted with college students who read a brief description of an accident and assigned responsibility judgments. One wonders whether the same or similar results occur in the real world of a jury deliberation room. When information concerning injury severity is presented in combination with other testimony, and when this complex set of evidence is discussed during deliberations, will jurors continue to focus inappropriately on the outcome of the incident? Will their liability judgments be improperly influenced?

This question was addressed by Greene and her colleagues (Greene, Johns, & Bowman, 1999; Greene, Johns, & Smith, 2001) in a reenactment of an automobile negligence case in which the defendant, a truck driver hauling 22 tons of asphalt, crashed into a highway median. Remarkably, one of the truck's axles took flight and landed on the cab of a small pickup truck being driven in the opposite direction by the plaintiff. These researchers manipulated the defendant's conduct that led to the accident by varying information about the driver's speed and the number of lane changes he undertook prior to the accident, as well as his braking technique and his use (or nonuse) of an available engine retarder. They also varied the severity of the injuries to the plaintiff by describing either a catastrophic head injury coupled with paraplegia (high-severity outcome) or a concussion with accompanying soft-tissue injury (low-severity outcome). In theory, jurors' judgments of liability should be affected by evidence of the defendant's conduct but not by evidence related to the severity of the outcome.

As is legally appropriate, the defendant's conduct had a strong impact on citizen–jurors' judgments of the defendant's liability, but evidence about the severity of the plaintiff's injuries mattered, too: The defendant was perceived to be more negligent when the plaintiff suffered more serious injuries. Perhaps most troubling, these effects were not erased during deliberation. (One might hope that jurors would correct each other's misuse of the evidence as they discussed it during deliberation.) Rather, individual jurors were more likely to rely on irrelevant information regarding the plaintiff's injuries *after* deliberating than they had been *before* deliberations.

When asked various questions about factors that influenced their verdicts, jurors who heard that the plaintiff had been severely injured were more likely than those with evidence of mild injuries to say that their negligence judgments were fueled by a desire to compensate the plaintiff for economic losses and his pain and suffering. In situations in which a plaintiff has suffered emotionally and financially (and in which the defendant has acted carelessly), jurors may decide to find the defendant liable so that the plaintiff can be compensated for his losses. These results are consistent with a meta-analysis (Robbennolt, 2000) showing that people attribute greater responsibility for the outcome of a negative incident when that outcome is severe than when it is minor.

ASSESSING DAMAGES

Pity the poor man. Michael Brennan, a St. Paul bank president, was simply responding to nature's call when he was sprayed with more than 200 gallons of raw sewage as he sat on the toilet in the bank's executive washroom. The geyser of water came "blasting up out of the toilet with such force that it stood him right up," leaving Brennan "immersed in human excrement." He sued a construction company working in the bank at the time, but the jury awarded Brennan nothing. Why, then, did a jury award $300,000 to a workman who slipped from a ladder and fell into a pile of manure (a story aired on CBS's "60 Minutes")?

One of the most perplexing issues related to juries is how they assess damages (Greene & Bornstein, 2003; Sunstein, Hastie, Payne, Schkade, & Viscusi, 2002). This complex decision seems especially subjective and unpredictable because people value money and injuries differently and because jurors are given scant guidance on how to award damages (Greene & Bornstein, 2000). The awards for punitive damages—intended to punish the defendant and deter future malicious conduct—are of special concern because the jury receives little instruction about how those awards should be determined. Consider the staggering $145 billion punitive damage award against the tobacco industry in 2000. Even the judge in the case was amazed. "A lot of zeros," he observed dryly, after reading the verdict.

Recently, psychologists have begun to study this issue. What have they learned? First, few people get rich by suing for damages. In 2001, the median award in tort cases—involving injury to persons or property—was $27,000; the median award in automobile accident cases was a mere $16,000 (Cohen, 2004). Although the media are eager to tell us about multimillion-dollar damage awards, these colossal awards are far from the norm. Second, in general, the more a plaintiff asks for, the more that plaintiff receives. Jurors tend to adjust their awards toward "anchor points," the most obvious of which is the plaintiff's requested damages (Chapman & Bornstein, 1996).

What factors do jurors consider in their decisions about damages? Data from interviews with actual jurors, experimental studies, and videotapes of actual jury deliberations (part of a project sanctioned by the Arizona Supreme Court) show that juries often consider attorneys' fees, the possible taxation of a damage award, and whether any loss is covered by insurance—issues that are all theoretically irrelevant to decisions about the amount of damages to award. According to psychologists Shari Diamond and Neil Vidmar (2001), discussions about insurance coverage are quite common in jury rooms. They examined the deliberations of 50 juries in Tucson, Arizona, as part of the landmark Arizona Jury Project (the research project evaluated a number of reforms in jury trials that we describe later in this chapter). They determined that conversations about insurance occurred in 85% of these cases; often, jurors expressed concern about overcompensating plaintiffs whose medical bills had already been covered by their own insurance. Consistent with this picture, Greene and Dunaway (2004) examined the frequency of discussion about insurance in mock jury deliberations and the relationship between those discussions and the compensatory damage award. They found that the more frequently juries discussed the plaintiff's insurance, the lower their award.

Another common (but theoretically forbidden) topic of discussion is attorneys' fees. Attorneys who represent plaintiffs in personal injury cases (a kind of civil case that is sometimes tried before a jury) typically work on a contingent fee basis. Plaintiffs do not pay their attorneys up front to represent them. Rather, if successful in securing a settlement or damage award for the client, the attorney takes some percentage (typically 25% to 35%) of it as a fee. If unsuccessful, the attorney (and the plaintiff as well) receive nothing. In their analysis of the Arizona jury deliberations, Diamond and Vidmar found that the topic of attorneys' fees came up in 83% of jury discussions. Rarely, however, did jurors make an explicit connection between attorneys' fees and their verdict preferences, a result supported by Greene and Dunaway's analyses.

Another question of considerable interest to psychologists is whether jurors tend to reduce their awards to errant plaintiffs. Oftentimes, both plaintiff and defendant share responsibility for the alleged wrongdoing. Consider a situation in which a home furnace malfunctions, setting fire to a house and injuring the homeowner. One might suspect that the furnace manufacturer was partially at fault for any injuries suffered. However, if the homeowner had rushed back into the burning house to retrieve some cherished possessions, many of us would also believe that he was partially at fault. In cases like this, which are called **comparative**

negligence cases because the jury compares and apportions the blame between the two parties, jurors are instructed to compensate the plaintiff fully for his losses and are informed that the judge will reduce the award in proportion to the plaintiff's fault. (For example, if the jury determines that 60% of responsibility rests with the defendant and 40% with the plaintiff, the judge will reduce the damages awarded to the plaintiff by 40%.) If jurors are supposed to compensate the plaintiff fully, they should not discount their awards to reflect their sentiments about the plaintiff's liability, a practice termed **double discounting**. (Double discounting means that after determining an amount that will compensate the plaintiff, jurors deduct from that award to reflect the plaintiff's wrongdoing, and then the judge *further* discounts the award for the same reason.)

Some research (e.g., Feigenson, Park, & Salovey, 1997; Wissler, Kuehn, & Saks, 2000) suggests that jurors tend to double-discount damage awards. In these studies, the experimenters manipulated the comparative fault of the plaintiff and found evidence of double discounting: When the plaintiff was partially at fault, mock jurors intuitively and inappropriately lowered the damages they awarded. Even when jurors were instructed to disregard the plaintiff's level of fault and were informed that the *judge* would reduce the award, their awards were apparently influenced by the degree of the plaintiff's responsibility (Wissler et al., 2000; Zickafoose & Bornstein, 1999).

Instructions to Disregard Inadmissible Evidence: How Effective?

Research on **inadmissible evidence** is also relevant to the assumption that jurors can separate evidence from nonevidence. Anyone who has ever watched television shows depicting courtroom drama is familiar with the attorney's "I object!" If the judge sustains an objection, then the opposing attorney's objectionable question or the witness's objectionable response will not be recorded, and the judge will instruct, or admonish, the jury to disregard the material. But are jurors able to do so?

Most of the empirical evidence indicates that they are not (e.g., Kassin & Sukel, 1997) and, furthermore, that a judge's admonition to disregard inadmissible evidence may boomerang (Tanford, 1990). For example, Pickel (1995) presented mock jurors with information that a defendant in a theft trial had a prior conviction. That information was admitted as evidence, ruled inadmissible with a simple admonition for the jury to disregard it, or ruled inadmissible and accompanied by an explanation of this ruling by the judge. Results showed that when the judge gave a legal explanation why the jurors were to disregard information about the defendant's prior conviction, they were *more* likely to convict him.

Broeder (1959) found a similar effect in a civil case in which mock jurors learned either that the defendant had insurance or that he did not. Half the subjects who were told that he had insurance were admonished by the judge to disregard that information. Juries who believed that the defendant had no insurance awarded damages to the plaintiff in an average amount of $33,000. Juries who believed that he did have insurance awarded an average of $37,000. But those juries that were aware of the insurance but had been admonished to disregard it gave the highest average award, $46,000.

These findings imply that admonishments to disregard certain testimony may heighten jurors' reliance on the inadmissible evidence. Several theoretical explanations have been offered for this phenomenon. A theory that relies on motivation as an explanation, **reactance theory** (Brehm, 1966; Brehm & Brehm, 1981), would propose that instructions to disregard evidence may threaten jurors' freedom to consider all available evidence. When this happens, jurors may respond by acting in ways that will restore their sense of decision-making freedom.

Alternatively, jurors' overreliance on evidence they are admonished not to use may reflect a cognitive process described in Wegner's (1989, 1994) **thought suppression** studies. Wegner and his associates (Wegner & Erber, 1992; Wegner, Schneider, Carter, & White, 1987) found that asking people

"not to think of a white bear" increased the tendency to do just that. In fact, the harder people try to control a thought, the less likely they are to succeed (Wegner, 1994). Likewise, jurors may think more about inadmissible evidence as a direct consequence of their attempts to follow the judge's request to suppress thoughts of it (Clavet, 1996).

Not all the empirical evidence indicates such a boomerang effect (Kagehiro & Werner, 1977). But the overall pattern of findings makes us very suspicious of an assumption that jurors are able to disregard inadmissible evidence, especially when such evidence would lead to conviction of the defendant (Nietzel et al., 1999). After a very thorough review of the experimental evidence, Tanford (1990) concluded, "the empirical research clearly demonstrates that instructions to disregard are ineffective in reducing the harm caused by inadmissible evidence and improper arguments" (p. 95).

But what happens when individual jurors come together to deliberate? Will the process, or even the expectation of discussion with other jurors, motivate jurors to follow the judge's instructions (Kerwin & Shaffer, 1994)? Limited research on mock juries indicates that jury deliberations can indeed lessen the impact of inadmissible evidence (London & Nunez, 2000).

The jury's decision could also be influenced by many other irrelevant factors in the trial presentation, including the gender, race, age, physical appearance, and attractiveness of the litigants and other witnesses, the personal style and credibility of attorneys, and the order of presentation of evidence (Devine et al., 2001). Are jurors able to eliminate such irrelevant considerations from their decisions? An early review by Gerbasi, Zuckerman, and Reis (1977) offered a summary that is, unfortunately, still relevant today: "It appears that extraevidential factors, such as defendant, victim, and juror characteristics, trial procedures, and so forth, can influence the severity of verdicts rendered by individual jurors" (p. 343). More recently, after reviewing a variety of extralegal influences ranging from speculative questions during cross-examination (Kassin, Williams, & Saunders, 1990) to hearsay as communicated by an expert witness (Schuller, 1995), two researchers concluded that "indeed, mock jury research has shown that verdicts can be influenced by a wide range of nonevidentiary factors presented both inside and outside the courtroom" (Kassin & Studebaker, 1998, p. 3).

Psychologists emphasize that, in contrast to the stated view of the legal system, jurors are active information processors. Their goal is to make a decision based on what they believe is just, not necessarily one that reflects what the judge says. Thus, for example, when mock jurors were told to disregard certain evidence because of a legal technicality, they still allowed that evidence to influence their verdicts when they thought that it enhanced the accuracy of their decisions (Sommers & Kassin, 2001). Because jurors want to be correct in their judgments, they may rely on information that *they* perceive to be relevant, regardless of whether that information meets the law's technical standards of admissibility.

To deal with the effects of inadmissible evidence, judges might provide juries at the start of every trial with a general warning that some of the information they will receive will be inadmissible (Kassin & Studebaker, 1998). A study in a nonlegal setting by Schul (1993) concluded that such an early warning, along with a later reminder, permitted participants both to suspend the processing of evidence and to think more critically about information that was subsequently discredited. As we describe in detail later in this chapter, jury instructions that come before the evidence are more effective than instructions that come after the evidence. An added boost would be for the judge to secure a public commitment from jurors during *voir dire* that they will disregard any information ultimately judged inadmissible (Tanford, 1990).

Concern about the Effects of Expert Testimony

As society has become increasingly specialized and technical knowledge has accumulated at a feverish pace, the judicial system has had to rely more often on expert witnesses to inform jurors of this professional information. Experts typically testify about scientific, technical, or other specialized knowledge with which most jurors are not familiar. In criminal cases, they may describe procedures used to gather and test evidence such as blood, fingerprints, DNA, and ballistics; in tort cases, they may describe the nature and causes of various claimed injuries; and in commercial cases, they may detail complex financial transactions and contractual arrangements. An example is given in Box 12.3.

A concern that arises when experts testify is that because jurors lack rigorous analytical skills, they may resort to irrational decision-making strategies when faced with highly specialized or technical testimony. Some people suspect, for example, that jurors will rely on superficial aspects of the expert's demeanor, including his or her appearance, personality, or presentation style to determine how much weight to put on the expert's testimony. Others fear that expert testimony will mesmerize jurors, causing them to discount their own commonsense and rely too heavily on the opinions of the experts. The opposite result has been forecast as well: that because jurors "know it all along," they do not need to hear from a supposed "expert" whose testimony they view as meaningless and gratuitous. The "battle of the experts"—a situation that arises when both opposing sides present their own experts—is thought to compound problems for the jury: "An especially perplexing task for lay jurors is to assimilate and select in some rational manner from the competing testimonies of expert witnesses. This battle of the experts tends to confound factfinders, especially juries" (Strier, 1996, p. 112).

Do jurors place undue weight on testimony from experts? How are their verdicts affected by expert testimony? A number of studies show that expert testimony exerts a small but reliable effect on jurors' decisions (Greene et al., 2002). When prosecutors introduce expert testimony, convictions are more likely; when experts testify on behalf of the defense, the likelihood of conviction decreases. In addition, expert testimony may help jurors make better decisions (Cutler, Penrod, & Dexter, 1989; Kovera, Gresham, Borgida, Gray, & Regan, 1997).

When questioned about their reliance on expert testimony, jurors have stated that they evaluated

THE CASE OF

BOX 12.3 **Alexander Pring-Wilson, his expert witness, and the issue of a concussion**

Had their paths not crossed on the night of April 12, 2003, Harvard graduate student Alexander Pring-Wilson might have gone on to a successful career as an environmental lawyer, and 18-year-old Michael Colono might have married the mother of his 3-year-old child (O'Connell, 2004). Instead, Pring-Wilson and Colono got into a late-night fight outside a pizza parlor, apparently after Colono made a wisecrack about Pring-Wilson's drunken demeanor. The Ivy-leaguer claimed that he had acted in self-defense as the victim and victim's cousin repeatedly punched and kicked him in the head, but in the end, Colono died as a result of five stab wounds inflicted by Pring-Wilson's pocket knife.

At his trial, Pring-Wilson enlisted the testimony of expert witness Jeremy Schmahmann, a neurologist from Massachusetts General Hospital, who reviewed the defendant's medical history (including a concussion sustained during a rugby match) and suggested that Pring-Wilson's confusion and inconsistent answers to police in the hours after the stabbing incident could indicate that he sustained another concussion as he was being beaten by the victim. Pring-Wilson was eventually convicted of manslaughter (but not the more serious charge of first-degree

ALEXANDER PRING-WILSON *describing fatal fight during his trial testimony in 2004.*

murder) and was sentenced to six to eight years in the Massachusetts Department of Corrections (although he was granted a new trial on the basis of an unrelated issue).

the testimony on the basis of the experts' qualifications, the quality of the experts' reasoning, and the experts' impartiality (Shuman & Champagne, 1997). Although jurors may not be especially attuned to the complexity of the experts' reasoning, it is fair to say that they do not routinely defer to the experts' assessments. A meta-analysis (Nietzel et al., 1999) supports this notion: Examining the effects of psychological expert testimony in 22 studies, Nietzel and his colleagues found little support for the concern that expert testimony will dominate jurors' decision making. Nor is it an expensive waste of time. Jurors appear to give reasoned and balanced consideration to experts whom they perceive as fair and professional.

To this point, we have assumed that expert testimony is based on valid scientific methodologies. But judges, who ultimately decide what expert evidence is admitted into court (*Daubert v.*

Merrell Dow Pharmaceuticals, Inc., 1993), may not assess correctly the quality of the scientific enterprise on which the expert relies and may allow unreliable expert testimony to be admitted into evidence (Kovera & McAuliff, 2000). Are jurors able to distinguish between reliable scientific evidence and "junk science"?

This question was addressed in the context of a hostile work environment trial (Kovera, Russano, & McAuliff, 2002). Mock jurors read a 15-page trial description that included variations in the validity of the plaintiff's expert testimony: The expert's research either was valid, contained a confounding variable, was lacking a control group, or involved a confederate who was not blind to the experimental condition. In general, jurors were unable to distinguish the valid from the flawed research. Other research shows that jurors may have difficulty understanding and using complex probabilistic evidence (McAuliff, Nemeth, Bornstein, & Penrod, 2003). Taken together, these studies suggest that jurors could benefit from information that would assist them in understanding scientific expert testimony (Kovera et al., 2002).

Concern about Jurors' Abilities to Understand and Apply Their Instructions

Jury instructions, provided by the judge to the jury near the end of a trial, play a crucial role in every case. They explain the laws that are applicable to the case and direct jurors to reach a verdict in accordance with those laws. Ironically, jurors are often treated like children during the testimonial phase of the trial—they are expected to sit still, pay attention, and not ask questions—but like accomplished law students during the reading of the judge's instructions, when they are expected to understand the complicated legal terminology of the instructions. Unfortunately, the greatest weakness for many juries is their inability to understand these instructions (Ellsworth, 1999; Lieberman & Sales, 2000).

One source of confusion is the legal language itself. Often, the instructions simply repeat statutory language and therefore are full of legal terms that are unfamiliar to laypeople. (For example, in most civil cases, jurors are informed that the burden of proof is on the plaintiff to establish his case by a *preponderance* of the evidence; the word *preponderance* appears 0.26 times per million words in the English language (Zeno, Ivens, Millard, & Duvvuri, 1995)! In addition, consider this example of how jurors are instructed about the meaning of *proximate cause*, an important concept in civil trials: "a cause which, in a natural and continuous sequence, produced damage, and without which the damage would not have occurred." Do you think the average layperson would understand the meaning of that term? Despite the fact that juries work hard to understand their instructions, spending 20% or more of their deliberation time trying to decipher the meaning of the judge's instructions (Ellsworth,

1989), they sometimes get it wrong simply because they do not understand the legal jargon.

Another source of confusion lies in the way the instructions are conveyed to jurors. Typically, the jury listens passively as the judge reads the instructions aloud. Jurors may or may not be provided with a written copy of the instructions, and they are almost never given the opportunity to ask questions in the courtroom to clarify misunderstandings they may have about the law. When jurors ask for assistance with the instructions in the course of deliberating, the judge often is unwilling to help, reasoning that rewording or clarifying the instructions could be grounds for appeal. In one of the cases studied by a Special Committee of the American Bar Association (1991), during deliberations the jury asked the judge to define the word *tortious*. His response: "Take away the *-ious*." Not exceedingly helpful, we suspect! (Recall that a *tort* is an injury to persons or to property.)

Judges generally assume that the instructions will have their intended effects of guiding jurors through the thicket of unfamiliar legal concepts. That was the sentiment of the U.S. Supreme Court in *Weeks v. Angelone* (2000). Lonnie Weeks confessed to killing a Virginia state trooper in 1993 and was tried for capital murder. During the penalty phase deliberations, jurors sent the judge a note asking for clarification of their instructions. The judge simply repeated the instruction. Two hours later the jurors, some in tears, sentenced Weeks to death. Weeks appealed, citing the jury's apparent confusion about the instructions. But the appeal fell on deaf ears. Chief Justice William Rehnquist, author of the opinion, wrote that there was only a "slight possibility" that jurors had been confused by the trial judge's instructions. Ironically, a study conducted by Cornell law professor Stephen Garvey and his colleagues challenges that assumption. Simulating the Weeks case, Garvey and his colleagues concluded that the jury might not have sentenced Weeks to death had they received clarification of their instructions (Garvey, Johnson, & Marcus, 2000).

Can this situation be rectified? Could the instructions be rewritten, or could their presentation be revised so that jurors have a better chance of understanding and implementing them properly?

Probably so. Borrowing principles from the field of **psycholinguistics** (the study of how people understand and use language), psychologists have been able to simplify jury instructions by minimizing or eliminating the use of abstract terms, negatively modified sentences, and passive voice and by reorganizing the instructions in a more logical manner. These simplified instructions are easier for jurors to understand and use (English & Sales, 1997; Steele & Thornburg, 1988).

It is one thing for psychologists to document improvements in jurors' comprehension when instructions are revised, but it is quite another for judges to embrace those changes and provide simplified instructions in their courtrooms. Even though there has been a steady accumulation of research showing that jurors have difficulty understanding their instructions, courts, legislatures, and rule-making commissions have not been especially receptive to reforms suggested by social scientists (Tanford, 1991).

That sentiment may be changing, however, and states have recently begun to adopt reforms that focus on how the judge communicates the law to jurors. Several states have revised portions of their civil jury instructions, and California has become the first state to finalize "plain-English" instructions for both civil and criminal trials (Post, 2004b). Consider these changes to the California civil jury instruction on "burden of proof":

> Old: "Preponderance of the evidence means evidence that has more convincing force than that opposed to it. If the evidence is so evenly balanced that you are unable to say that the evidence on either side of an issue preponderates, your finding on that issue must be against the party who had the burden of proving it."
>
> New: "When I tell you that a party must prove something, I mean that the party must persuade you, by the evidence presented in court, that what he or she is trying to prove is more likely to be true than not true. This is sometimes referred to as 'the burden of proof.' "

Not surprisingly, simplified instructions enhance jurors' comprehension of the law and result in far fewer questions to the judge about what the jury instructions mean (Post, 2004b).

Another method for improving jurors' understanding of the instructions is to restructure how they are presented. Although instructions are typically read at the close of the trial, after the evidence has been presented and just before the jury retires to deliberate, some states now require judges to provide preliminary instructions before any of the evidence is presented, and many individual judges do so of their own accord (Dann & Hans, 2004).

Instructing the jury at the conclusion of the trial reflects a belief in the **recency effect**: that the judge's instructions will have a more powerful impact on a jury's decision when they are given late in the trial, after the presentation of evidence. The recency effect suggests that immediate past events are generally remembered better than more remote ones, especially when the earlier events have unfolded over a longer period of time. Presenting the instructions after the evidence should thus increase the salience of the instructions and make the judge's directives more available for recall during deliberations. Having just heard the judge's instructions, deliberating jurors would have them fresh in their minds and be more likely to make references to them.

Logical as it might seem, this idea has been questioned by a number of authorities. Two lines of reasoning guide such criticism. First, Roscoe Pound, former dean of the Harvard Law School, and others have proposed what is essentially a "schema" theory—that jurors should be instructed before the presentation of testimony because this gives them a mental framework to appreciate the relevance or irrelevance of testimony as it unfolds and thus to make selective use of the facts. This line of reasoning gains support from research findings in experimental psychology showing (1) that people learn more effectively when they know in advance what the specific task is and (2) that schematic frameworks facilitate comprehension and recall (Bartlett, 1932; Neisser, 1976). Second, a number of judges (e.g., Frank, 1949) have objected to the customary sequence on the ground that instructions at the end of the trial are given after the jurors have already made up their minds. Research has shown that despite cautionary instructions, jurors often form very definite opinions before the close of the trial (Carlson & Russo, 2001). Judge E. Barrett Prettyman's (1960) position reflects this concern:

> It makes no sense to have a juror listen to days of testimony only then to be told that he and his conferees are the sole judges of the facts, that the accused is presumed to be innocent, that the government must prove guilt beyond a reasonable doubt, etc. What manner of mind can go back over a stream of conflicting statements of alleged facts, recall the intonations, the demeanor, or even the existence of the witnesses, and retrospectively fit all these recollections into a pattern of evaluations and judgments given him for the first time after the events; the human mind cannot do so. (p. 1066)

The delivery of jury instructions at the beginning of the trial rests on the notion of a **primacy effect**—that instructions will have their most beneficial effect if they are presented first, because jurors can then compare the evidence they hear to the requirements of the law and apply the instructions to the evidence in order to reach a verdict. In this way, jurors know the rules of the trial and the requirements of the law before the trial commences.

At what point in the trial proceedings, then, *should* the judge instruct the jury? ForsterLee and Horowitz (2003) reported that mock jurors who received instructions at the beginning of the trial recalled and used more of the evidence than did jurors who were instructed after the evidence.

The timing of the instructions also affects jurors' assignment of damages (ForsterLee, Horowitz, & Bourgeois, 1993). Jurors who were preinstructed on the elements of compensation made clearer differentiations among several plaintiffs than did jurors who had not been preinstructed: When jurors had been preinstructed, the most severely injured plaintiff received the highest award and the least severely injured plaintiff received the lowest award. There were no differences in compensatory awards as a function of injury severity for jurors who had received posttrial instructions.

Preliminary instructions have other beneficial effects. In a study conducted in Los Angeles Superior Court, jurors who received pretrial instructions said that they were able to focus better during the trial (Judicial Council of California, 2004). Judges also believe that substantive preliminary instructions help jurors to follow the evidence (Dann & Hans, 2004).

What practical applications can we draw from these findings? We would argue that judicial preinstructions are vastly underutilized. There is no reason why general instructions about the law (e.g., burden of proof, assessment of the credibility of witnesses) should not be given at both the beginning and the end of trials. Interim instructions can be given as needed to explain issues that come up during the trial, and instructions that depend on the specific evidence in a trial can be given at the end (Ellsworth & Reifman, 2000).

Other procedural remedies have been proposed to enhance jurors' comprehension of the instructions. One is provision of a written copy of the instructions and taping of the instructions for later playback by the jurors. Traditionally, judges have instructed jurors orally. There is good reason to expect that written instructions would improve comprehension. Trial-related information is processed more efficiently and recalled better when it is presented in writing in addition to being read aloud (Elwork, Alfini, & Sales , 1982). Also, less confusion about the instructions arises when they are in writing, which in turn leads to a reduction in the number of questions about the instructions during deliberation (Dann & Hans, 2004).

A Cambridge, Massachusetts, judge came to that realization rather slowly. After three weeks of testimony in the 2004 homicide trial of Alexander Pring-Wilson (see Box 12.3), she read instructions to the jurors (including those related to the crucial elements of self-defense, the claim made by the defendant to explain his actions), but she opted not to give the jury a written copy of her instructions. Only after jurors asked for clarification of self-defense did she reconsider and provide the instructions in writing.

Concern about Jurors' Abilities to Decide Complex Cases

Judge John V. Singleton looked up as his law clerk leaned against his office door as though to brace it closed. "You won't believe this," she said breathlessly, "but there are 225 lawyers out there in the courtroom!" (Singleton & Kass, 1986, p. 11). Judge Singleton believed it. He was about to preside over the first pretrial conference in *In re Corrugated Container Antitrust Litigation*, at that time one of the largest and most complicated class action cases ever tried by a jury. (A **class action case** involves many plaintiffs who collectively form a "class" and claim that they suffered similar injuries as a result of the defendants' actions. The plaintiffs portrayed in the movie *Erin Brockovich* and, more recently, in *North Country* constituted a class.)

The case actually entailed three trials: a 15-week criminal trial that involved 4 major paper companies, 27 corporate officers, scores of witnesses, and hundreds of documents; a 4-month-long class action trial with 113 witnesses and 5000 exhibits; and a second class action trial involving plaintiffs who had opted out of the original class action lawsuit. Discovery and trials took five years. In the midst of this organizational nightmare, Judge Singleton wondered whether the framers of the Constitution had ever imagined a case of such magnitude when they drafted the Sixth and Seventh Amendments, guaranteeing the right to trial by jury in criminal and civil cases. He also worried about the "unsuspecting souls out there in the Southern District of Texas whose destiny was to weigh the facts under the complex antitrust law" (Singleton & Kass, 1986, p. 11).

Some of the loudest and most vehement criticisms of the jury center on its role in complex cases. In product liability and medical malpractice cases, for example, there are difficult questions related to causation (i.e., who or what actually caused the claimed injuries), and in business cases there are intricate financial transactions that must be dissected and evaluated. These cases often require the jury to render decisions on causation, liability, and damages for multiple plaintiffs, multiple defendants,

The real Erin Brockovich

or both (Vidmar, 1998). In criminal cases, the use of forensic evidence contributes to case complexity (Heise, 2004).

Many arguments have been made against the use of juries in complex cases: The evidence is too difficult for a layperson to understand; the general information load on juries is excessive because of the large number of witnesses, particularly expert witnesses who testify in these cases; and, because of *voir dire* procedures that result in the exclusion of jurors with some understanding of or interest in the case, less capable jurors are left to decide. Some judges have gone on record expressing concerns about jurors' abilities in these cases: "I remain convinced that the highly complicated issues presented by this litigation are such that an attempt to dispose of them in a jury trial would result in nothing short of judicial chaos" (dissent of Judge Kilkenny in *In re U.S. Securities Litigation*, 1979, p. 431).

The two primary methods for assessing the abilities of jurors to decide complex cases are to conduct mock jury studies and to interview jurors after they have served in these cases. A third technique—to select a group of jurors who function, for all intents and purposes, like the real jury (i.e., they sit in the jury box throughout the entire trial and mingle with the actual jurors during the breaks) until the end of the case when they become "research jurors" whose deliberations are videotaped—was used by a Special Committee of the American Bar Association in the late 1980s. Regrettably, this method has not been tried since.

Interview studies (e.g., ABA Special Committee, 1991; Sanders, 1993) consistently point to a substantial spread in individual jurors' abilities to understand and summarize the evidence. Some jurors are willing and able to attend to the complicated nature of the testimony and the sometimes-arcane questions of law that they raise; other jurors are overwhelmed from the outset. Whether some capable jurors can compensate for others' failings is unclear. Sanders (1993) interviewed jurors in a products liability case against Merrell Dow Pharmaceuticals and concluded that the jury's deliberation appeared to fall short of full understanding of the case. But the Special ABA Committee (1991) that studied four complex cases in different jurisdictions across the country (involving sexual harassment, criminal fraud, antitrust, and trademark infringement) concluded that the stronger, more capable jurors, even when not designated as forepersons, were able to direct the deliberations and that defensible verdicts resulted. Richard Lempert, professor of law at the University of Michigan, systematically examined the reports of 12 complex trials, including those reported by Sanders and the ABA Committee (Lempert, 1993). He concluded that in 2 of the 12 cases, the expert testimony was so complicated and esoteric that only professionals in the field could have understood it. On the other hand, Lempert found little evidence of jury befuddlement and concluded that on balance, the juries' verdicts were defensible.

Oregon State University professor Irwin Horowitz and his colleagues have conducted several sophisticated studies of mock juror decision making in complex cases. These studies are inherently difficult to do because the conditions of a complex case (e.g., its length, the large number of expert witnesses, and the complicated nature of the testimony) are not easily simulated. Horowitz and his team dealt with this problem by basing their simulation studies on an actual toxic tort case involving manufacture of a chemical known as DBX, or dibenzodioxin. (The facts of their case resembled those described in the popular book and movie *A Civil Action*.) Residents adjacent to a chemical plant sued the chemical manufacturer for injuries alleged to have been caused when the company allowed DBX to leach from the plant into the surrounding drainage ditches and waterways, thus entering the plaintiffs' drinking water, contaminating the fish and wildlife the plaintiffs consumed, and threatening their recreational facilities. The studies typically involved multiple plaintiffs, all of whom complained, in varying degrees, of health problems such as skin rashes, chloracne, and elevated blood pressure; psychological distress; a fear of contracting cancer and future illnesses; and economic loss. Attorneys for the defendant chemical manufacturer refuted the allegations.

Using these facts and manipulating the structure of the trial and nature of the testimony, Horowitz and his colleagues have been able to examine, among other things, the effects of the number and order of decisions required of jurors, the complexity of the language, the number of plaintiffs, and the role of preliminary instructions and group deliberations.

The picture that emerges from this vast set of data is of a jury whose abilities and verdicts are significantly affected by nuances in trial procedure. For example, preinstructed jurors made more appropriate distinctions among plaintiffs who suffered different kinds of injuries (ForsterLee et al., 1993), complex language lessened jurors' ability to compensate plaintiffs who suffered injuries of varying severity (Horowitz, ForsterLee, & Brolly, 1996), and multiple plaintiffs increased the unpredictability of punitive damage awards (Horowitz & Bordens, 2002).

None of these findings suggests that jurors are inherently unable to decide matters of complexity, however. As psychologist Phoebe Ellsworth has noted, there is little support for the popular idea that bad jury decisions are caused by bad jurors (Ellsworth, 1999). Rather, the findings point to the need for care and consideration in the manner in which a complex case is presented to the jury. A judge has wide discretion to set the tone and pacing of the trial, to implement procedures to assist the jury, and, ultimately, to ensure equal justice under law. Indeed, there *is* no justice unless jurors understand the facts and the law in each case they decide.

We would not expect a college student to pass a course without taking any notes, asking questions to seek clarification, or discussing an interesting concept with a professor or fellow student. Yet all too often, we handicap jurors by forcing trial procedures on them that discourage or even forbid these simple steps toward better understanding. We suspect that jurors would have an easier time of it—and that their verdicts would be more reasoned—if judges were willing to structure jurors' tasks to be more conducive to their learning (e.g., preinstruction and simplifying the language of the instructions). Fortunately, some courts have begun that process, and we will discuss these jury reforms later in the chapter.

The Concern That Juries May Be Biased

The Assumption of a Blank Slate

Jurors are assumed to enter a trial as "blank slates," free of overwhelming biases. Courts assume that jurors can put aside any preconceptions about the guilt of a criminal defendant or the merits of civil defendants and plaintiffs when forming their judgments. If jurors cannot set aside their biases, they should be excused for cause. (In criminal cases, the "blank slates" should be tinted at the outset by a presumption that the defendant is innocent of the charges.)

Olivia Brodsky, summoned for jury duty in Connecticut, might have had difficulty setting aside her preconceptions. When asked what she would do as a juror, Brodsky responded, "I would wait until the bad guy talks. Then I would put him in jail." Brodsky was 4 years old at the time. In Connecticut, potential jurors can be culled from state income tax records that lack birth dates; the tax return on Olivia's trust fund was probably the reason why she was summoned to appear.

As we noted in Chapter 11, the judge and the attorneys inquire about a prospective juror's biases during the jury selection process. A frequent question during *voir dire* takes the following form: "Do you believe that you, as a juror, can set aside any negative feelings you might have toward the defendant because he is black or a police officer or a used-car salesman [whatever the group membership that possibly elicits prejudice] and make a judgment based on the law and the facts of this case?" If prospective jurors say yes, the judge usually believes them, and they are allowed to serve as jurors.

Less frequently, prospective jurors may have positive feelings about the defendant that could influence their ability to be impartial. Consider the lawsuit filed against basketball great Michael Jordan (see Box 12.4).

Prospective jurors who admit to discernible and resolute prejudices or vested interests in the outcome of the case can be identified and dismissed. But what can be done about prospective jurors who, during the jury selection process, consciously or unconsciously misrepresent their views?

In John Grisham's novel *The Runaway Jury* (1996), a central character develops a scheme by which he is impaneled on a jury in a huge lawsuit against a tobacco company; he then gets the tobacco industry to pay him for influencing the jury to decide in its favor. Jurors who proclaim neutrality while they possess and conceal a bias are called stealth jurors (Bodaken & Speckart, 1996). Stealth jurors may have a variety of reasons to misrepresent themselves—not just the

THE CASE OF

BOX 12.4   Michael Jordan: The search for unbiased jurors

When 36 prospective jurors filed into a drab, windowless courtroom in Chicago, a big surprise awaited them: Seated at the defense table was former basketball star Michael Jordan, undoubtedly one of the biggest sports heroes in American history. Jordan was being sued for allegedly reneging on a deal to star in the basketball film *Heaven Is a Playground*. The movie flopped without him. Dean Dickie, attorney for the plaintiff production company, anticipated difficulties in finding jurors who were not partial toward Jordan. Indeed, after five long hours of jury selection, only three jurors had been selected. Nearly all of the other prospective jurors stated that their admiration and adoration of Jordan would interfere with their neutrality in the case. In the end, the jury returned a judgment in Jordan's favor. In fact, jurors determined that the corporation that made the film owed Jordan $50,000 for failing to live up to its financial obligation to him.

Basketball star Michael Jordan

possibility of financial gain, as in the case of people who seek to be chosen for jury service on highly publicized trials, but also for revenge against one of the parties.

The courts assume that individual jurors can divest themselves of any improper "leaning" toward one side or the other and that through detailed, sometimes time-consuming jury selection procedures, the ideal of open-minded jurors can be achieved. Because prospective jurors whose preconceptions would affect their verdicts are identified and dismissed, the trial can begin with the expectation that the jury will reach a fair verdict. But this outcome faces at least three types of challenges. First, attorneys are motivated to select jurors who are favorable to their own side, rather than those who are neutral and thus unpredictable. Second, as seen in the foregoing example, if people systematically misrepresent their views during jury selection, no sure way exists to detect it. Finally, as we discuss in detail later, it is impossible for anyone to be completely uninfluenced by past experiences and resulting prejudices.

Inevitability of Juror Bias

Bias is an inevitable human characteristic. But even though the word *bias*, in this case **juror bias**, conjures up many unfavorable associations, we should not focus exclusively on its negative qualities. Rather, bias is simply part of the human condition, and accordingly colors all our decisions, including jury verdicts.

Bias, as we use the term here, is a human predisposition to make interpretations based on past experience—to try to fit new stimuli and information into one's already-developed system for looking at the world. When we are exposed to a new event, we respond to it by relying on past experiences. For example, when we view a traffic accident, it is hard to separate our perceptions from our interpretations. We may make judgments that one car was going too fast or that another car was in the wrong lane. We may assume that a particular driver was at fault simply because we happen to have a negative stereotype about, for example, teenage drivers, elderly drivers, or drivers from a particular state.

Bias in our responses to the actions of others is inevitable because people account for so many outcomes in our lives, and we must make assumptions about the causes of their behavior. Why was Emily so abrupt when she spoke to me this morning? Why did Juan decide to buy a new car? Why did the defendant refuse to take a lie detector test? Every day, we make decisions on the basis of our assumptions about other people. Criminal defense lawyers make recommendations to their clients on how to plead on the basis of their expectations about the reactions of prosecuting attorneys, judges, and jurors. College administrators decide who will be admitted as students on the basis of applicants' credentials and academic promise. Choices are always necessary, and our expectations about the outcomes of our choices rest partly on our biases.

Why do we have expectations? We probably could not tolerate life if people were constantly surprising us. We need assumptions about people to help us predict what they will do. Our expectations often help simplify our explanations for people's behavior. Such processes apply to the behavior of jurors too. When former Dallas Cowboys wide receiver Michael Irvin appeared before the grand jury with regard to a charge of cocaine possession, he was wearing a mink coat, a lavender suit, and a bowler hat. Did the jurors form any impressions of him on the basis of his attire?

Virtually all the legal and psychological conceptions of how a juror makes decisions in a criminal case propose that verdicts reflect the implicit operation of two judgments on the part of jurors. One judgment is an estimate of the probability of commission—that is, how likely it is that the defendant actually committed the crime. Most jurors base their estimates of this probability mainly on the strength of the specific evidence, but their previous beliefs and experiences also have an impact on how they interpret the evidence (Finkel, 1995).

A second judgment by the criminal juror concerns reasonable doubt. Judges instruct jurors in criminal cases that they should bring back a verdict of not guilty if they have any reasonable doubt of the defendant's guilt. Yet the legal system has difficulty defining reasonable doubt; a common, but not very informative, definition is that it is a doubt for which a person can give a reason. Jurors apply their own standards for the threshold of certainty deemed necessary for conviction.

On the basis of these factors, many jurors can be classified as having a pro-prosecution bias or a pro-defense bias. Jurors with a pro-prosecution bias view the conflicting evidence through the filter of their own past experiences and beliefs, which make them more likely to think that the defendant committed the crime. Consider, for example, the statement "Any suspect who runs from the police probably committed the crime." Agreement with this statement reflects a bias in favor of the prosecution. But persons with pro-defense biases also filter the evidence as a result of *their* past experiences and reactions. For example, agreement with the statement "Too many innocent people are wrongfully imprisoned" reflects filters leading to biases sympathetic to the defense.

Even if we accept the proposition that bias is inevitable, we must still ask whether such biases color the judgments of jurors. That is the bottom line. To determine whether bias affects one's verdicts, Kassin and Wrightsman (1983) asked potential jurors to complete a 17-statement attitude inventory containing statements such as those given as examples. Later, these mock jurors watched videotapes of reenacted actual trials or read transcripts of simulated trials. Five types of criminal trials were used. After being exposed to the trial, each mock juror was asked to render an individual verdict about the defendant's guilt or innocence. Jurors voting guilty were then compared with those voting not guilty to see whether their preliminary biases differed. In four of the five cases, they did. The average rate of conviction was 81% for the prosecution-biased jurors and only 52% for defense-biased ones. Thus, even though everyone was exposed to the same evidence, mock jurors holding a pro-prosecution bias were more likely to find the defendant guilty. It appears that, at least in some cases, each juror's reaction to the evidence is filtered through personal predispositions. Pretrial beliefs and values may influence, and occasionally even overwhelm, the evidence presented in court.

Pretrial beliefs may also affect the very way the evidence is evaluated. Jane Goodman-Delahunty and her colleagues found that mock jurors' beliefs about the death penalty influenced more than the penalty they imposed in a capital murder case; they also influenced jurors' perceptions of the evidence (Goodman-Delahunty, Greene, & Hsiao, 1998). Mock jurors in this study watched the videotaped murder of a convenience store clerk that had been captured on film. When asked questions about the defendant's motive and intentions, jurors who favored the death penalty were more likely than those who opposed capital punishment to "read" criminal intent into the actions of the defendant. For example, pro-death-penalty jurors were more likely than those opposed to infer from the videotape that the defendant intended to murder the victim and that his specific actions indicated premeditation. These findings remind us of the common situation in which two people experience the same event—a movie or a play, for example—and interpret the actions in very different ways, partly because of the "mindset" with which they watched or experienced that event. These beliefs, or schemas, can apparently influence the way jurors make sense of the evidence in a trial.

We now know something about *how* those schemas manage to influence jurors' decision making. When jurors are exposed to a new piece of evidence, they evaluate the evidence in a way that is consistent with their current verdict preferences rather than in an objective fashion. Assume that two jurors hear the same evidence that slightly favors the prosecution's case. Also assume that Juror A favors the prosecution and Juror B favors the defense. According to the notion of **predecisional distortion** (Carlson & Russo, 2001), these jurors will distort their evaluation of the evidence in a direction that supports their verdict choice. Thus, Juror A might evaluate this evidence as favoring the prosecution, whereas Juror B might evaluate it as favoring neither party, actually distorting his or her interpretation of the evidence away from its objective value and in the direction of the side that is favored. In short, tentative judgments bias jurors' evaluations of subsequent evidence.

A powerful source of premature beliefs and judgments about a defendant is prejudicial pretrial publicity (described in detail in Chapter 7). Exposure to this kind of publicity can distort how jurors search for, use, and evaluate subsequent evidence at trial, usually in favor of the prosecution (Hope, Memon, & McGeorge, 2004).

Do jurors' biases predispose them to favor one side over another in a civil case? A common perception is that jurors are generally biased in favor of injured plaintiffs. Are they? Was the Miami jury's decision to award $37 million to the family of 12-year-old honor student Jill Goldberg, who was killed in a 1997 car accident, fueled by feelings of sympathy for her grieving family members? It seems natural for people to have feelings of compassion for injured persons and for these feelings to translate into favorable verdicts and lavish damage awards for plaintiffs. But do they?

Surprisingly, perhaps, a variety of studies using different methodologies suggest that the answer is no. From posttrial juror interviews, we have learned that although elements of sympathy play *some* role in deliberations (and feelings of anger toward a defendant matter, too), this happens relatively infrequently. In her study of cases involving claims by individuals against corporate defendants, Valerie Hans (1996) interviewed jurors who decided these cases, conducted surveys of jurors' attitudes, and ran experimental studies that manipulated variables related to this **sympathy hypothesis**. All these sources of data pointed to the same conclusion: that the general public is "quite suspicious of, and sometimes downright hostile to, civil plaintiffs" (p. 244). A survey conducted by the consulting firm DecisionQuest yielded similar results: Eighty-four percent of the 1012 people polled agreed with the statement "When people are injured, they often try to blame others for their carelessness." According to the same survey, potential jurors do not think highly of civil defendants, either. For example, more than 75% of respondents believe that corporate executives often try to cover up evidence of wrongdoing by their companies, and more respondents say that product warnings are intended to protect manufacturers than say they are intended to keep consumers safe.

These views beg the next question: Do juries give larger awards when a defendant is wealthy? Some data would seem to support this so-called deep-pockets effect. Jury damage awards *are* consistently higher in products liability and medical malpractice cases than in automobile negligence cases. (The former group typically involves wealthy defendants, whereas the latter does not.) But a number of studies (e.g., Hans & Ermann, 1989; MacCoun, 1996) suggest that the wealth of the defendant alone is not the important variable. Rather, the public believes that businesses and corporations should be held to a higher standard of responsibility than individual defendants. Any inflation of awards against corporate defendants is apparently related to their status as a corporation and not to their wealth.

The jury that awarded $37 million to the family of Jill Goldberg clearly focused on the duties and responsibilities of the defendant, Florida Power and Light (FPL) Company. The victim was killed when a car driven by her mother, Rosalie, sailed through an intersection and was struck by a Ford Expedition on a rainy September afternoon. The role of the defendant? Ten minutes before the accident occurred, an FPL lineman pulled a fuse from a transformer box about 100 feet away from the intersection, cutting power to the traffic light. At trial, FPL lawyers told the jury that the utility couldn't be obligated to ensure that every traffic light in the county worked when it terminated power. The lineman testified that he never looked to see whether the traffic light had been affected. Neither of these contentions sat well with jurors. Said jury foreman Juan Perez, "To them, power outages were a fact of life and they throw switches all the time. But to say that in front of a jury is almost suicidal to the defense." After a week-long trial, the jury deliberated for three hours and determined that FPL was entirely at fault. But for the power outage, they reasoned, the accident would never have happened. They awarded $17 million to Walter Goldberg, Jill's father, and $20 million to Rosalie Goldberg, Jill's mother—far more than the plaintiffs had requested.

Jurors' Inferences and the Stories They Tell

We have seen that jurors' pretrial beliefs can affect their decisions in both criminal and civil trials (although the evidence is still the primary determinant of verdicts). But how do jurors make sense of the evidence that they hear *during* the trial? In many ways, the juror's task is like that of the reader of a mystery story. The joy of reading a mystery comes from savoring each clue, bouncing it off prior clues, and then evaluating its significance in the overall puzzle of who committed the crime. That is how most jurors operate. They form a schema, a mental structure that aids in the processing and interpretation of information. As indicated earlier, such schemata can—precisely because they provide a cognitive framework—produce a skewed perception and recall of reality. Just like mystery readers who remember those clues that fit their hypothesis and forget others that do not, jurors construct their own private stories about the evidence so that it makes sense to them; in the process, they pay inordinate attention to certain pieces of evidence while ignoring others.

Good lawyers know this. In fact, really great lawyers know that an important task for them at trial is to convince the jury that their story, and not their opponent's story, is the right one. Famed criminal defense attorney "Racehouse" Haynes once said, "The lawyer with the best story wins."

Psychologists Reid Hastie and Nancy Pennington developed the **story model** to describe inferences that individual jurors make when reaching a decision in a case (see, generally, Pennington & Hastie, 1993). Hastie and Pennington dubbed their theory the story model because they suspect that the core cognitive process involved in juror decision making is construction of a story or narrative summary of the events in dispute. To illustrate the role of narrative evidence summaries in juror decision making, Hastie and Pennington interpreted the dramatic differences between white Americans' and African Americans' reactions to the verdict in the

O. J. Simpson case. They suspected that because of their life experiences and beliefs, African Americans can more easily construct a story about police misconduct and police brutality than can white Americans. Thus, African Americans were more likely than whites to accept the "defense story" that racist police detective Mark Fuhrman planted incriminating evidence on Simpson's property (Hastie & Pennington, 1996).

In one of their early empirical studies, Pennington and Hastie (1986) interviewed mock jurors who had seen a filmed reenactment of a murder trial and who were asked to talk out loud while making a verdict decision. The evidence summaries constructed by jurors had a definite narrative story structure, and, importantly, jurors who reached different verdicts had constructed different stories.

In a later study, Pennington and Hastie (1988) assessed whether these stories were constructed spontaneously in the course of jurors' decision making and how jurors represented the evidence in memory. To answer these questions, they asked mock jurors to read a written description of the murder case that included sentences from different verdict stories gleaned from the previous interview study (e.g., sentences from stories that resulted in guilty verdicts as well as sentences from stories that led to not-guilty verdicts). All participants then determined a verdict and were asked to say whether various sentences had been included in the trial evidence or had not been presented before. Mock jurors were more likely to "recognize" as having been presented those sentences that were associated with their chosen verdict than sentences from stories associated with other, rejected verdicts!

Does the order in which evidence is presented influence jurors' judgments? Apparently, yes. In that same study, Pennington and Hastie (1988) found that stories were easy to construct when the evidence was presented in a temporal order that matched the occurrence of the original events ("story order") but harder to construct when the evidence was presented in an order that did not match the sequence of the original events ("witness order").

Prosecutors and defense attorneys might be wise to familiarize themselves with these findings; the study has significant implications for the practice of actual trials. When Pennington and Hastie manipulated the order of evidence, they affected the likelihood of a guilty verdict. For example, mock jurors were *most* likely to convict a criminal defendant when the prosecution evidence was presented in story order and the defense evidence in witness order. They were *least* likely to convict when the prosecution evidence was presented in witness order and the defense evidence in story order.

Is the story model a complete and accurate description of how jurors organize themselves to decide the verdict in a trial? No. For starters, it focuses only on *jurors* and does not address the complex nuances that come into focus when jurors deliberate as a jury. But as a mechanism for understanding the cognitive strategies employed by individuals to process trial information prior to deliberations, it is highly useful. Indeed, several other studies (e.g., Hastie, Schkade, & Payne, 1998; Olsen-Fulero & Fulero, 1997; Huntley & Costanzo, 2003) have been inspired by its elegant theorizing.

Jury Reform

The traditional legal model treated jurors as passive recipients of information who, like tape recorders, recorded a one-way stream of communication. Jurors were expected to process all incoming information passively, without immediate interpretation, until finally instructed by the judge to decide. As we pointed out earlier, this conception of juror-as-blank-slate is largely wrong; jurors actively evaluate the evidence through the lens of their personal experiences and frames of reference, pose questions to themselves, and construct narratives or stories to help them understand the evidence and make a judgment about it.

Acknowledging that most jurors are active "thought processors," psychologists and other social scientists began suggesting reforms to the jury system in the 1970s. Until recently, though, few people listened. For example, in 1991, Alexander Tanford, a professor of law at Indiana University, reviewed the impact of research on pretrial and written instructions on state court judges, legislatures, and rule-making commissions and concluded that the research had very little impact: Lawmakers were not being persuaded about the need for reform on the basis of empirical research studies alone. (This finding raises some interesting and difficult questions about whether psychologists, armed with sophisticated theories and well-honed research techniques, can effectively influence the landscape of the law.)

Many observers of the jury (e.g., Ellsworth, 1999; Marder, 1999a) now suspect that intense media coverage of a series of dramatic trials and controversial verdicts has accomplished for jury reform what decades of social science research could not. As the names O. J. Simpson, Martha Stewart, Scott Peterson, and Kobe Bryant became household words, as sensational trials were being broadcast in living rooms across the country, and as the media splashed news of a $2.7-million award to an 81-year-old New Mexico grandmother who was burned by hot coffee at McDonald's (the award was reduced by the judge to $480,000, and the plaintiff eventually settled for even less—something that the media generally failed to report), the public grew increasingly dissatisfied and occasionally even outraged about the failure of the jury system. Calls for reform became more frequent and more urgent.

Convinced that the time was right for serious discussion of reform to the jury system, the University of Michigan sponsored a symposium that brought together judges, lawyers, legal academics, social scientists, and even a thoughtful and experienced juror to share their concerns and suggest solutions. Despite the diversity in intellectual backgrounds and practical experience, there was remarkable convergence of opinion among participants. For example, none of them subscribed to the "bad juror" theory—the idea that bad jury decisions are caused by bad jurors. Rather, all shared the view, long advocated by psychologists, that the system is primarily to blame. According to the "bad system" theory, deficiencies in the performance of jurors reflect deficiencies in the jury system, and any jury

reform should be directed at how the task is presented to jurors, rather than at how people are selected to serve. As Phoebe Ellsworth (1999), one of the participants at the Michigan forum, aptly noted, "Before deciding that jurors are governed by their hearts, we should consider the possibility that the system does very little to encourage the intelligent use of their minds."

This perspective was echoed by a diverse array of attendees at the first-ever National Jury Summit in 2001 and led to the establishment of a nationwide project to increase use of effective jury reform methods (Mize & Connelly, 2004). The project seeks to enhance the conditions of jury service (thereby improving responses to jury summonses), provide assistance to courts in implementing innovative jury practices, and gather data on what courts are now doing in terms of jury reform.

Against the backdrop of increasing support for reform, many jury scholars, some creative court personnel, and a few courageous judges have proposed and implemented reforms that take advantage of jurors' natural inclinations and that provide tools to encourage jurors' active involvement in the trial process. Some of the reforms have been relatively uncontroversial and benign: providing notebooks that list the witnesses and summarize their testimony in long or complex cases; giving preinstructions or interim instructions during the course of a lengthy trial; allowing jurors to take notes; designating alternate jurors only after the trial is completed; providing a written copy of the judge's instructions to each juror; and allowing jurors to examine the demonstrative evidence during their deliberations.

Two reforms have been more radical: allowing jurors to pose questions to witnesses (questions are screened by the judge, who decides whether they are appropriate) and to discuss the evidence in the midst of trial (traditionally, jurors were forbidden from talking about the case until they began deliberating.) Not only have these reforms been implemented in many jurisdictions, but research studies have now been conducted to chart their effectiveness. What have we learned about the effects of these new practices on jurors' sentiments and decision-making abilities?

Results of a mock jury study that tested the effects of question asking on jurors' understanding of contested DNA presentations suggest that many jurors think the process enables them to comprehend the evidence better (Dann, Hans, & Kaye, 2004). Pilot studies conducted in several states have reached the same conclusion (Dann & Hans, 2004). An analysis of the content of more than 2000 questions posed in 164 actual trials (both civil and criminal) characterized the nature of the questions. This study revealed that jurors questioned both lay and expert witnesses in order to clarify previous testimony and to ask about common practices in unfamiliar professions (Mott, 2003). Finally, although some judges have expressed concern that jurors would be offended by having a question disallowed or would speculate about the reasons why a submitted question could not be asked, jurors themselves tend to accept that decision and drop the issue (Diamond, Rose, & Murphy, 2004). Therefore, we see no serious drawbacks to allowing jurors to ask questions. Although the process can take a bit of time, it can clarify jurors' understanding of the evidence, enhance their involvement in the trial process, and create an environment more conducive to learning.

The most radical reform permits jurors to discuss the evidence during the trial, rather than having to wait until their formal deliberations began. The rules were simple: All jurors must be present in the deliberation room during these discussions, and jurors must keep an open mind and avoid debating verdict options. Psychologists have described a number of potential advantages of such mid-trial discussions based on fundamental principles of cognitive and social psychology. For example, juror discussions about the evidence can

- improve juror comprehension by permitting jurors to sift through and organize the evidence into a coherent framework over the course of the trial;
- improve juror recollection of the evidence and testimony by emphasizing and clarifying points made during trial; and

- promote greater cohesion among jurors, thereby reducing the time needed for deliberations (Hans, Hannaford, & Munsterman, 1999).

But there are also several potential drawbacks to jury discussions during trial, and these are also based on well-established psychological principles. They include the possibility that jury discussions may

- facilitate the formation or expression of premature judgments about the evidence,
- diminish the quality of the deliberations as jurors become more familiar with each other's views, and
- produce more interpersonal conflicts prior to formal deliberations (Hans et al., 1999).

The first empirical test of this reform was a field experiment in which researchers randomly assigned approximately 100 civil jury trials to an experimental "trial discussion" condition and an equal number to a control "no discussion" condition (Hannaford, Hans, & Munsterman, 2000; Hans et al., 1999). For both conditions, questionnaires were distributed to jurors, judges, attorneys, and litigants to assess their impressions.

Perhaps surprisingly, given their general tendency to adhere to traditional courtroom procedures, judges were the most enthusiastic group. Three-quarters of the judges indicated that they supported the reform, and only 15% opposed it (others were neutral). Another large percentage (75%) agreed that juror discussions helped jurors understand the evidence; only 30% expressed concern that jurors who engaged in these discussions were likely to prejudge the evidence. Attorneys and litigants were more negative, however. Only approximately half of each group thought that trial discussions improved juror understanding of the evidence, and approximately half agreed that trial discussions might encourage premature decision making.

How did the innovation affect jurors' experiences and views? Of the 686 jurors who were permitted to discuss the evidence, approximately 70% reported that their jury had at least one such discussion, suggesting that even when permitted to talk about the case, a sizeable minority of juries do not. Experience with the reform apparently increases support for it. Jurors who reported having these discussions were quite positive about them. They said that trial evidence was remembered very accurately during these discussions, that discussions helped them understand the evidence in the case, and that all jurors' points of view were considered during the course of the discussions. The perceived drawbacks were mostly logistical: Jurors said that there were difficulties in getting all jurors together at the same time. (After all, these short breaks represent the only time in the course of several hours that jurors may use the rest rooms or smoke a cigarette. Some people's desire for these comforts undoubtedly outweighed their interest in talking about the evidence!)

The most useful data on the issue of jury discussions come from the analysis of videotapes of 50 civil jury trials in Arizona (the state that has been at the forefront of jury reform) (Diamond, Vidmar, Rose, Ellis, & Murphy, 2003). This study examined all mid-trial jury discussions, as well as the deliberations. These tapes make it clear that jurors seek information from one another, discuss questions they intend to ask, and talk about the as-yet-unpresented evidence they would like to hear. Such discussions led to modest enhancements in jurors' understanding of the evidence and did not result in premature judgments. These data provide a fascinating and previously unseen picture of the jury at work as it discusses the evidence in the midst of the trial and reaches a final verdict at the trial's conclusion. Just as for question asking, we perceive few negative effects of mid-trial discussion, and we believe that allowing jurors the opportunity to talk about the case simply legitimizes what they are likely to do anyway.

The Jury: Should It Be Venerated or Vilified? Revered or Reviled?

The trial jury is a remarkable institution and, in important ways, almost a unique one. Kalven and Zeisel (1966) make the following comments about the jury system:

> It recruits a group of twelve lay people, chosen at random from the widest population; it convenes them for the purpose of a particular trial; it entrusts them with great official powers of decision; it permits them to carry out deliberations in secret and report out their final judgment without giving reasons for it; and, after their momentary service to the state has been completed, it orders them to disband and return to private life. (p. 3)

The use of average citizens to determine outcomes for rich or politically powerful figures such as O. J. Simpson or the Microsoft Corporation underscores our country's commitment to egalitarian values. It is no exaggeration to claim that the trial jury is sanctified as one of our fundamental democratic institutions. Political scientist Jeffrey Abramson (1994), author of *We, the Jury*, put it eloquently:

> [T]here are all the jurors we never read about, who toil out of the limelight every day, crossing all kinds of racial and ethnic lines to defend a shared sense of justice. These examples convince me that the jury, far from being obsolete, is more crucial than ever in a multiethnic society struggling to articulate a justice common to [all] citizens. Though the jury system is a grand phenomenon—putting justice in the hands of the people—we still have lessons to learn about how to design an institution that gathers persons from different walks of life to discuss and decide upon one justice for all. (p. 5)

Although there remains much to learn, we now know a good deal about how juries function. We know that juries don't always get it right; on occasion, jurors are overwhelmed by the sheer volume of evidence, they misunderstand their instructions, they use evidence in inappropriate ways, and their biases and prejudices can rise to the surface and color their judgments. But by and large, we find little support for the extreme claims that charge juries with poor and irresponsible performance. On the contrary, we believe the institution of the jury is worth defending and worth improving.

SUMMARY

1. *Describe the concern related to the competence of jurors and juries.* Some critics have expressed concern that jurors and juries are overly attentive to extralegal information that, in theory, is irrelevant to the guilt decision in criminal cases and to the liability judgment in civil cases. Others have voiced concerns that jurors will be mesmerized by the testimony of an expert or, conversely, that they will not understand such testimony and dismiss it outright. Whether jurors and juries are able to understand and apply their instructions is another concern. Finally, critics of the jury system claim that jurors are poorly equipped to decide the complicated issues that arise in so-called complex cases.

2. *What is the impact of extralegal information on jurors?* Research studies suggest that on occasion, jurors may be influenced by evidence of a defendant's prior record, multiple charges, or character and propensity to commit crimes. In civil cases, evidence related to an accident victim's injury may influence the judgment of a defendant's liability, and evidence related to the plaintiff's negligence may inappropriately deflate damage awards.

3. *Can jurors disregard inadmissible evidence?* When a question posed or an answer offered during a trial is ruled inadmissible by the judge, jurors are instructed to disregard it. Psychological evidence indicates that it is difficult for jurors to disregard this testimony; in fact, the stronger the judge's admonition, the less effective it may be.

4. *How can jurors be helped to understand their instructions?* Jurors can be instructed before the trial begins about the relevant elements of the law that they will apply to the facts they hear. Judges can provide written copies of the instructions for all jurors. Unfortunately, judges rarely answer jurors' questions about their instructions.

5. *What is meant by the statement "Bias is inevitable in jurors"?* *Bias*, as used here, refers to the human predisposition to make interpretations on the basis of past experience. Bias is inevitable because it is inescapable human nature to make assumptions about human behavior.

6. *What reforms of the jury system do psychologists suggest?* The information-processing demands placed on jurors should be simplified. More clearly worded instructions, in written as well as oral form, delivered at the beginning and at the conclusion of the trial would be helpful. In complex trials in which multiple verdicts must be decided, preinstruction, access to a trial transcript, and simplifying complex language may be especially helpful. During the trial, jurors should be able to pose questions that the judge would then ask of the witnesses. Finally, midtrial discussion of the evidence might have great value; such discussion might help jurors to organize the evidence in a thematic framework and thus improve their memory of the testimony.

KEY TERMS

class action case	extralegal information	limiting instruction	psycholinguistics
comparative negligence	inadmissible evidence	outcome severity	reactance theory
damages	joinder	predecisional distortion	recency effect
defensive attribution	juror bias	primacy effect	story model
double discounting	liable	propensity evidence	sympathy hypothesis
			thought suppression

ORIENTING QUESTIONS

1. *What is the frequency of crime victimization?*
2. *What types of research have psychologists conducted on victimization?*
3. *What factors predict the development of PTSD after being a crime victim?*
4. *What are the components of the battered woman syndrome?*
5. *How have the laws about rape changed?*
6. *How can rape be prevented?*
7. *What are two types of sexual harassment recognized by the courts?*

Perception of Victims

One element of almost every crime is the presence of at least one victim. Even so-called victimless crimes—crimes such as prostitution, ticket scalping, and gambling—have victims, even if they do not immediately recognize it or would not describe themselves that way. The social burdens and psychological costs of these offenses are often delayed—the squandering of a person's income as a consequence of the inevitable losses from habitual gambling or the physical abuse and underworld crimes that surround prostitution—but ultimately, society and individuals are victimized by these crimes.

Society has conflicting feelings toward victims. At the same time that most individuals feel sympathy toward them, we also tend to question why they became victims, and sometimes we even blame them for their plight. One reason for this inclination is the need to believe in a "just world." The thought of becoming victims ourselves is so threatening that we feel compelled to find an explanation why other people are victimized (Lerner, 1980). These justifications often take the form of singling victims out as the primary cause of their own plight.

Such judgments are predicted by the perspective known as **attribution theory**, which originated with the work of Fritz Heider (1958). Heider stated that people operate as "naive psychologists"; they reach conclusions about what caused a given behavior by considering both personal and environmental factors. Generally, when considering someone else's actions, we use *dispositional attributions* that rely on the person's ability level, personality, or even temporary states (such as fatigue or luck) as explanations for the conduct in question. To explain a person's misfortune on the basis of his or her physical disabilities, lack of effort, or loose morals reflects a kind of defensive attribution that puts the onus for bad outcomes on the person rather than on the environment. Such reactions help shape our responses to victims. The norms of our society demand that we help others if they deserve our help. But if people are responsible for their own suffering, we feel less obligated to help them (Mulford, Lee, & Sapp, 1996).

Since 1970, the term *blaming the victim* has been increasingly heard. The term was first popularized in a widely read book by William Ryan (1970), in which the author observed that people on welfare were often seen as lazy or shiftless and hence responsible for their fate. A literature search (cited by Downs, 1996) found no use of the term *blaming the victim* before 1970, but there was a steep increase in its use from the early 1980s up through 1993, and there were more than 1000 references that year. This remains the most recent published estimate, but a literature review for publications between 1997 and 2004 found nearly 200 references, suggesting that the concept of *blaming the victim* continues to be cited regularly.

An extreme example of blaming the victim is offered by trial attorney Robert Baker, who represented O. J. Simpson in his civil trial for the wrongful deaths of Nicole Brown and Ronald Goldman. His opening statement for the defense included a scorching attack on Nicole Brown, whom he portrayed as a heavy-drinking party girl whose dangerous lifestyle often included companions who were prostitutes and drug dealers. Sometimes by implication and sometimes by direct comment, he communicated that she had many boyfriends and had had at least one abortion. As a trial observer noted, "it was as close to calling her a slut [as one could come] without using the word" (quoted by Reibstein & Foote, 1996, p. 64). Baker demeaned the victim for a reason, of course; he wanted to imply that a sordid lifestyle had led to her becoming involved with someone other than O. J. Simpson and that this putative individual had killed her (Toobin, 1996a). Simpson himself has echoed this claim, stating that he feels angry at Nicole because he believes her careless lifestyle contributed to her being murdered.

Types of Victims

There is no shortage of victims in our society. Estimates of the numbers of children who are sexually abused, of adults who are battered by their partners, and of women and men who are assaulted, robbed, or raped run into the millions each year.

The primary source of information on crime victims in the United States is the Bureau of Justice Statistics' National Crime Victimization Survey, which can be found at www.ojp.usdoj .gov/bjs/. Each year, data are collected from a national sample of 50,000 households on the frequency and consequences of criminal victimization in the form of rape and other sexual assaults, robbery, theft, assault, household burglary, and car theft. From these figures, the rate of victimization nationwide can be calculated. For example, it is estimated that in 2003, approximately 24.2 million criminal victimizations occurred; more than 18.6 million involved property crimes (a rate of 163 incidents per 1000 households), and over 5.4 million were crimes of violence (23 incidents per 1000 persons). Additional statistics on the frequency, consequences, and prevention of criminal victimization can be found at the National Center for Victims of Crime website (www.ncvc.org/).

For other offenses, it is difficult to assess the frequency of victimization, but what we do know is that they happen all too often. Included here, for example, are acts of racial or religious discrimination in which the recipient is denied rights that are accorded to others. Homophobic attitudes are frequently expressed (Herek, 1987; Larsen, Reed, & Hoffman, 1980); 90% of gay men report having been threatened or subjected to verbal abuse, and more than 33% were victims of violence (Segell, 1997). Compared with gay adults, homosexual youth are at higher risk for violent victimization, and the psychological consequences of the victimization may be more severe for them (D'Augelli, 1998). One study examined data from self-report measures of victimization and found that gay students were significantly more likely than others to be victims of violent and property crimes while at school (Faulkner & Cranston, 1998). Specifically, homosexual students were more than twice as likely to report having been threatened or injured with a weapon at school, and they were more than three times as likely to report not going to school because they felt unsafe. In addition, these students were significantly more likely than others to report having

their property damaged or stolen while they were at school. Gay students were also several times more likely to have been in ten or more physical fights in the previous year. In terms of the consequences of this increased victimization, homosexual students were significantly more likely to report substance abuse and suicidal ideation. Specifically, homosexual students were nine times more likely to report using alcohol on each of the 30 days preceding the survey, six times more likely to report recently using cocaine, and nearly 50% more likely to report seriously considering or attempting suicide in the 12 months prior to the study.

Persons diagnosed with AIDS are frequently stigmatized in our society (Crandall, Glor, & Britt, 1997); not only laypersons but even medical professionals rate people with AIDS more negatively than they rate people with cancer, diabetes, or heart disease (Katz et al., 1987). In fact, being threatened by the risk of illness can harden our attitudes toward

seriously ill people and cause us to stigmatize them (Jones et al., 1984). We often come to believe that someone's disease is not just a consequence of his or her behavior or physical predisposition but that the illness somehow reflects the afflicted person's intrinsic value (Sontag, 1978).

Technological advancements and cultural changes have brought new forms of victimization to the fore. "Cyberstalking" is a recently emerged technique favored by some sexual predators as a way to target victims. "Identity theft," in which information about an individual's personal and financial life is stolen by computer hackers and then used fraudulently, has become a major fear of people in the 21st century. Nationwide, 9% of all students in secondary schools report feeling afraid that they will be attacked at school and avoid certain places within their schools because they believe these places to be unsafe (Verlinden, Hersen, & Thomas, 2000); millions more are traumatized by bullying and other forms of peer victimization that cause them to dread going to school (Hanish & Guerra, 2000).

This chapter concentrates on three types of victims and the effects of victimization on them: targets of sexual harassment, battered women, and victims of violent crime—particularly rape, the violent crime that has been studied most often. For each of these, the field of psychology has generated theory and research relevant to the laws and court decisions instituted to protect such victims. The responses of the legal system reflect conflicting views in our society about the nature of victims, especially victims of sex-related offenses. For example, how extreme does a situation need to be before we conclude that sexual harassment exists, and how distressed does the response of the victim need to be? In the case of a battered woman who kills her batterer, will a claim of self-defense be accepted by a jury? And why do as many as two-thirds of rape victims never report the attack to the police?

Victims of Violent Crime

The dilemmas confronted throughout this book, especially the quest to preserve both the rights of suspects and the rights of victims, come into sharp focus when we consider the victims of crime, particularly victims of violent crimes such as rape. Until recently, society had not paid much attention to crime victims. Their trial testimony was necessary to obtain convictions, but most of the legal rights formally protected in the adversarial system are extended to defendants, not victims. As a result, the needs and rights of crime victims have often been ignored. This imbalance began to change in the late 1970s and early 1980s as victim advocacy groups, mental health professionals, police, and court officials all began to acknowledge the need to better recognize and serve crime victims. Several developments reflect the growing stature and influence of the victims' rights movement:

- The emergence of the interdisciplinary field of **victimology**, which concentrates on studying the process and consequences of victimization experiences and how victims (or survivors, which is the term preferred by many) recover
- The increasing availability of services to crime victims, including compensation and restitution programs, victim assistance programs in the courts, self-help programs, and formal mental health services
- The expanded opportunity for victims to participate in the trials of their victimizers through mechanisms such as victim impact statements
- The heightened focus on victims brought about by new journals (one example is *Victimology*; a second is *Violence and Victims*), organizations such as the National Organi-zation for Victim Assistance, and commissions such as the President's Commission on Victims of Crime (1982) and the American Psychological Association's Task Force on the Victims of Crime and Violence

For their part, psychologists have conducted research on and delivered clinical services to a diverse array of crime victims. Three areas have received special attention: the consequences of physical/sexual abuse on child victims; the role of violent victimization as a cause of psychological disorders, particularly posttraumatic stress disorder; and the psychology of rape. We review the latter two of these topics in this chapter, and the consequences of abuse on child victims will be discussed in more detail in Chapter 14.

Is Violence Inherited?

Cathy Spatz Widom (1989, 1992) used court records to identify a group of 908 children in a midwestern American city who had suffered abuse (i.e., sexual abuse or physical assault leading to injury) or severe neglect (i.e., inadequate food, clothing, shelter, or medical care) between 1967 and 1971. This "abuse/neglect" group was matched to a group of 667 children who had not been exposed to abuse or neglect but who were similar in gender, age, ethnicity, and family socioeconomic status. Matching the abused and nonabused groups on these variables was important, because it enabled Widom to assume that any differences between the groups in terms of violent behavior in adolescence or adulthood were not due to differences in demographic characteristics.

Widom's analysis of police and court records showed that, as earlier research had suggested, abused or neglected children were significantly more likely than the comparison group to have been arrested for violent crimes as juveniles or as adults. In addition, the abused or neglected individuals were, on average, a year younger than comparison subjects at the time of their first arrest and had committed twice as many total offenses over the 15- to 20-year period studied. These differences were seen in boys and girls and in European Americans and African Americans; however, the relationship between abuse and violence was particularly strong among African Americans.

As disturbing as these results are, they may actually *underestimate* the risks created by childhood abuse. For one thing, only offenses that resulted in arrest or trial were included in this study. Many undetected or unreported crimes may have been committed by the abused/neglected group. Furthermore, this aspect of the study did not assess group differences in mental disorders, substance abuse, educational and occupational difficulties, or other possible long-term consequences of childhood abuse.

Data on this sample were collected again 22 to 26 years after the abuse or neglect (Maxfield & Widom, 1996). The researchers found that by age 32, almost half of the abused/neglected group (49%) had been arrested for a nontraffic offense. This percentage was considerably greater than for the matched control sample (38%). Furthermore, victims of abuse and neglect were more likely than members of the control group to have been arrested for violent crimes, even after controlling for age, race, and gender.

More recently, Widom and her colleagues examined the impact of sexual abuse, physical abuse, and neglect in childhood on adult mental health outcomes (Horwitz, Widom, McLaughlin, & White, 2001). Findings suggested that both men and women with histories of childhood abuse and neglect displayed increased levels of dysthymia and antisocial personality characteristics when compared with matched controls. The abused and neglected women also reported more alcohol problems than both the men and the matched groups. Although this line of research has suggested a strong association between childhood experiences of abuse and neglect and elevated levels of mental health problems in adulthood, these differences dissipated after controlling for other stressful life events. These findings highlight the importance of including early child abuse and neglect as part of a broader constellation of life stressors rather than isolating them as independent predictors of adult outcomes.

Violent Victimization and Posttraumatic Stress Disorder

Individuals who suffer a severe trauma and, weeks or months later, continue to experience intense, fear-related reactions when reminded of the trauma, may be experiencing **posttraumatic stress disorder** (PTSD). Usually, the trauma must be severe enough to have threatened the victim, or someone close to the victim, with mortal danger or serious bodily harm. We saw an example of this trauma as we watched the victims of Hurricane Katrina try to reconstruct their homes and their lives. Most instances of violent crime qualify as trauma severe enough to trigger PTSD in at least some victims.

The symptoms of PTSD fall into three broad classes:

1. Frequent reexperiencing of the event through intrusive thoughts, flashbacks, and repeated nightmares and dreams
2. Persistent avoidance of stimuli associated with the trauma and a general numbing or deadening of emotions (feeling detached or estranged from others)
3. Increased physiological arousal resulting in exaggerated startle responses or difficulty sleeping

The case of Jim (Box 13.1) reveals how these diagnostic criteria apply to a real-life case. Shot and left to die, Jim suffered an extremely traumatic event; guns and related stimuli would trigger a reexperiencing of the trauma; he avoided stimuli associated with the trauma; and he was hyperaroused and reactive. These symptoms must last longer than one month to qualify as PTSD. Trauma-related symptoms beginning within one month after the trauma and lasting more than two days but less than one month are diagnosed as *acute stress disorder*. In some cases of PTSD, the symptoms may not emerge for months or even years following the actual event.

How common is PTSD? As part of the Epidemiological Catchment Area studies, door-to-door diagnostic interviews of thousands of residents of the United States found PTSD in about 0.5% of males, most of whom were veterans of the Vietnam War. About 1.3% of females carried this diagnosis; most had suffered sexual or physical assault or had witnessed others being assaulted

THE CASE OF

BOX 13.1 **Jim: Posttraumatic stress disorder**

When Jim appeared for treatment at age 40, he had been suffering from anxiety and depressive symptoms for eight years. He dated his problems to the autumn day when he foiled a burglary attempt across the street from his workplace. A distance runner, Jim decided to pursue the fleeing burglar and to attract help along the way. After a chase, Jim slowed and looked around for help. Turning again to the burglar, he found himself staring down the barrel of a handgun. Then the burglar shot him. Jim was hit in the legs with three bullets and immobilized. He begged the young man to spare his life. Instead, the assailant continued firing until the gun was empty. He then fled, leaving Jim to die.

Fortunately, Jim was found and rushed to surgery. After eight days in the hospital, he knew he would recover. He felt elated just to be alive. Soon, however, the elation wore off, and Jim began thinking of what might have occurred had he not been found in time. With increasing frequency, everyday sights and sounds in Jim's life began to evoke the memory of the shooting and the panic he had experienced. The sight of guns or depictions of violence on TV triggered waves of strong emotion. Sirens and the sight of ambulances would startle him, and then panic and despair would set in. By the following year, even the cool fall weather could reactivate the event in his mind. He had frequent

nightmares involving looking into a gun barrel.

As time went on, Jim felt more on edge. He became wary of people, and he kept to himself. He no longer experienced life's joy and excitement. Because of injury-related leg pain, he had to stop running, giving up one of his major pleasures and outlets for stress. Leg pain also evoked images of the shooting that, in turn, brought fear, hyperventilation, and a racing heart. Episodes in which Jim felt deeply depressed and suicidal would sometimes follow exposure to various stimuli. After eight years of nightmares and daily reminders of the trauma, Jim sought treatment and was able to make substantial improvements in his condition.

(Helzer et al., 1987). However, estimates of PTSD prevalence from other studies are much higher. For example, Heidi Resnick and her colleagues (1993) conducted a diagnostic survey of 4008 females and found that 12% of the sample had symptoms of PTSD at some time in their lives and that 4.6% were currently suffering PTSD symptoms. These percentages suggest that in the United States alone, 11,800,000 women have had PTSD at some time in their lives and that 4,400,000 currently suffer from it (Resnick et al., 1993). Resnick et al. (1993) found that 26% of women whose trauma was related to crime developed PTSD, whereas only 9% of women who had sustained a noncriminal trauma developed PTSD symptoms. The extent of injury during trauma also predicts whether PTSD symptoms will develop. Women who were injured by a trauma are more likely to develop

PTSD symptoms than those who were not. Victims' perceptions of trauma are also important in determining the likelihood of PTSD. The belief that the victim's life is in danger and that he or she has no control over the trauma increases risk for PTSD (Foa & Kozak, 1986; Green et al., 1990; Kushner et al., 1992). One study suggests that cognitive processing during the trauma (such as persistent dissociation) and beliefs after the trauma (such as negative interpretations of trauma memories) predict PTSD symptoms to a greater degree than objective and subjective measures of the severity of the trauma (Halligan, Michael, Clark, & Ehlers, 2003).

Although traumas are unfortunate facts of life, there is reason to believe that PTSD—in some trauma victims, at least—can be prevented. For one thing, although many persons who experience severe trauma may develop acute stress disorder, most do not go on to develop PTSD. One reason may be that those experiencing trauma, but not PTSD, tend to receive high levels of social support from family, friends, or counselors immediately following the event (e.g., Sutker et al., 1995). Thus, providing immediate social support for trauma victims may prevent their experiences from progressing into posttraumatic stress disorder.

Two other characteristics distinguish people who develop PTSD from those who do not. Individuals who suffer PTSD often perceive the world as a dangerous place from which they must retreat, and they come to view themselves as helpless to deal with stressors. If these two misconceptions could be eliminated, full-blown cases of PTSD might be prevented in many victims. Edna Foa has developed a four-session prevention course designed to attack these two misconceptions in women who have been raped or assaulted. Foa includes the following elements in her PTSD prevention course:

1. Education about the common psychological reactions to assault in order to help victims realize that their responses are normal
2. Training in skills such as relaxation so that the women are better prepared to cope with stress
3. Emotionally reliving the trauma through imaginal exposure methods to allow victims to defuse their lingering fears of the trauma
4. Cognitive restructuring to help the women replace negative beliefs about their competence and adequacy with more realistic appraisals

Ten women who had recently been raped or assaulted completed the four-week course. Their PTSD symptoms were then compared with those of ten other women who had also been assaulted or raped but who did not take part in the course. At the times of two follow-up assessments (2 months and 5.5 months, respectively, after the assaults) victims who had completed the prevention course had fewer PTSD symptoms than control subjects who had not received treatment. Two months after their trauma, 70% of the untreated women, but only 10% of the treated women, met the criteria for PTSD (Foa, Hearst-Ikeda, & Perry, 1995). These results suggest that a brief program that facilitates emotionally reexperiencing trauma *and* correcting beliefs about personal inadequacy can reduce the incidence of PTSD.

Battered Spouses

PREVALENCE RATE

The extent of physical abuse directed toward spouses and romantic partners in American society is difficult to estimate, but many observe that it is extensive. It has been estimated that some form of physical aggression occurs in one-fourth to one-third of all couples (Straus & Gelles, 1988). More recent estimates suggest that 33% of men and 25% of women have been involved in a physically aggressive altercation, with the most severe episodes occurring in or near a bar for the men and in the home for the women (Leonard, Quigley, & Collins, 2002). Although relationship aggression by women against men is as frequent as male-to-female aggression (Magdol et al., 1997), male aggression is significantly more likely to result in serious injuries; 39% of female physical assault victims and 24.8% of male assault victims reported having been injured during the most recent assault upon them (Tjaden & Thoennes, 2000). About 30% of all the women murdered in the United States each year are killed by their male partners; in fact, women are 3.7 times more likely to be killed by their partner than by a stranger (Kellerman & Mercy, 1992). For this reason, most of the research on relationship aggression has concentrated on male aggression against female partners (Rosenbaum & Gearan, 1999); we echo that emphasis in this chapter.

Despite these disturbing statistics and the continuing research on relationship aggression, myths about battered women still abound. The mass media often pay little attention to this kind of violence (except in highly publicized cases, such as those of Nicole Simpson and Whitney Houston). Some professionals, such as physicians and police, fail to ask appropriate questions when a battered woman reports an attack by her intimate partner. Arrest and prosecution of perpetrators of partner violence remain unpredictable, and protective restraining orders against batterers are often not consistently enforced.

MYTHS AND EXAGGERATED BELIEFS

Experts emphasize that many oversimplified beliefs, exaggerations, and myths about battered women exist. Follingstad (1994) identified the following misconceptions:

1. Battered women are masochists.
2. They provoke the assaults inflicted on them.
3. They get the treatment they deserve.
4. They are free to leave these violent relationships any time they want to.
5. Violence among intimate partners is not common.
6. Men who are nonviolent in their dealings with outsiders behave the same way in their dealings with their intimates.
7. Middle-class and upper-class men don't batter, and middle-class and upper-class women don't get beaten.
8. Battering is a lower-class, ethnic-minority phenomenon, and such women don't mind because this is a part of their culture.
9. "Good" battered women are passive and never try to defend themselves (1994, p. 15).

Although these misconceptions do not reflect the reality of domestic violence, a recent survey regarding attitudes and beliefs shows that most respondents think of domestic violence as stemming from individual problems, relationships, and families, but not from the nature of our society. Not many think that women cause their own abuse, but about 25% believe that some women want to be abused, and most believe that women can end abusive relationships (Worden & Carlson, 2005).

Research examining U.S. perceptions of domestic violence is nearly two decades old, so it may not reflect current attitudes in this area. More recent studies on the topic, conducted in other countries, have yielded mixed results. For instance, a national study conducted in Singapore found that the overwhelming majority of the 510 participants disapproved of battery, and only about 6% agreed that under some circumstances it is acceptable for a husband to use physical force against his partner (Choi & Edleson, 1996). However, another study conducted with Israeli husbands found that although the majority of participants (58%) agreed that "there is no excuse for a man to beat his wife" (p. 199), nearly one-third believed that wife-beating is justified on certain occasions (e.g., unfaithful sexual behavior, disrespect of relatives) (Haj-Yahia, 2003). The attitudes of this latter group are consistent with the belief that women provoke domestic assaults and are treated in the way they deserve.

The misconceptions listed above also obscure several truths about the plight of battered women: Battered woman face many real obstacles that make it difficult for them to leave their abusers, and when they do attempt to leave abusive relationships—as many women do—they often suffer further threats, recriminations, and attacks.

THE CAUSES OF BATTERING

What are the main risk factors for battering? Researchers who have studied the causes of battering have focused on ecological factors, the characteristics of the battering victim, the nature of violent intimate relationships, and the psychological makeup of batterers. A recent review of this literature points to several risk factors as important (Rosenbaum & Gearan, 1999). Although batterers come from all socioeconomic and ethnic backgrounds, they are more likely than nonbatterers to be unemployed, less well educated, members of minority groups, and of lower socioeconomic status. Batterers tend to have been raised in families in which they either suffered physical abuse as children or observed an abusive relationship between their parents. Adolescents who later become batterers have experienced a higher rate of conduct problems and are more likely to have engaged in early substance abuse; early experiences with coercive or aggressive behavior may set the stage for similar strategies in adult relationships (Magdol, Moffitt, Caspi, & Silva, 1998). In addition, batterers usually have poor self-concepts, are not very good problem solvers, and often have limited verbal skills. They are prone to extreme jealousy and fear being abandoned by their partners. As a result, they monitor their partners' activities closely and exert excessive control over their partners' whereabouts and activities. They overreact to signs of rejection and alternate between rage and desperation.

Although research suggests that batterers have many characteristics in common, not all batterers share a common profile. For instance, one comprehensive study revealed three distinct types of batterers: generally violent, psychopathological, and family-only (Waltz, Babcock, Jacobson, & Gottman, 2000). These groups were distinguished by the degree of violence within the relationship and the degree of general violence reported, as well as by personality characteristics. For instance, generally violent batterers displayed the highest levels of aggressive-sadistic behavior, psychopathological batterers exhibited more passive-aggressive/dependant characteristics, and family-only batterers displayed violent behaviors but generally did not hold violence-supportive beliefs and attitudes. Findings from this study further indicated that differences in life experiences accounted for some of the variations in each of the group's behavior. For instance, when the generally violent batterers and the family-only batterers were compared, both groups were found to have experienced physical abuse as children, but significant differences existed in the frequency and severity of interparental violence witnessed; the generally violent batterers had witnessed more frequent and severe parental violence. These findings suggest that understanding the risk factors associated with batterers may be more complex than once was believed.

THE CYCLE OF VIOLENCE

Batterers are sometimes described as displaying a **cycle of violence** involving a Jekyll-and-Hyde pattern of emotional and behavioral instability that makes their victims all the more fearful of the battering they believe is inevitable. A man may be loving and attentive to a woman's needs early in their relationship as he cultivates her affection and relies on her to satisfy his dependency needs. However, when disappointments or disagreements occur in the relationship, as they invariably do, a *tension-building phase* begins, characterized by increased criticism of the partner and perhaps even minor physical assaults.

This phase leads to a second stage in the cycle, an *acute battering incident*. By the time this more serious form of aggression occurs, the woman has become too dependent on the man to break off the relationship easily. He has succeeded in controlling her behavior and curtailing her contact with friends who might have possibly helped extract her from her plight. The woman also tends to believe that if only she can find the right way to mollify the man's anger and reassure him of her faithfulness and obedience, he will change his behavior.

Following a battering incident, a third stage (called the *contrite phase*) occurs, in which the batterer apologizes for his attack, promises never to do it again, and persuades the woman that he is a changed man. Often this is an empty pledge. Indeed, sometimes the humiliation that the man feels over having apologized so profusely to his partner simply fuels more intense anger and violence, and the cycle repeats itself.

How pervasive is the cycle of violence? Even though Walker (1979) portrays it as a significant dynamic faced by battered women, she did not identify it in about a third of the 400 women she studied. What the *cycle of violence* may actually be describing is an underlying personality disorder that typifies a certain category of batterer. According to Donald Dutton (1995, 2000), a psychologist at the University of British Columbia and one of the experts who testified for the prosecution in O. J. Simpson's murder trial, as many as 40% of batterers have the features of **borderline personality disorder**, a severe disturbance that is characterized by unstable moods and behavior. People with borderline personality disorder are drawn into intense relationships in which they are particularly unable to tolerate certain emotions. They are demandingly dependent, which causes them to feel easily slighted, which leads to jealousy, rage, aggression, and subsequently guilt. These emotional cycles repeat themselves, providing the underlying motivation for the cycle of violence. In addition to emotional instability, batterers also are prone to believing the worst about others; for example, they are quick to attribute hostile intentions to their partners (Eckhardt, Barbour, & Davison, 1998). Dutton traces the origin of this personality disorder to insecure attachments that batterers experienced with their parents, which later cause them to feel intense anger toward partners whenever things go awry in a relationship.

RESPONSES TO VICTIMS OF BATTERING

The prevalence of many myths about battered women reflects the negative feelings toward crime victims described earlier in this chapter. A deep uneasiness, even hostility, exists toward some victims of battering (Jones, 1994). They are often seen as pathological "doormats" or delusional alarmists "crying wolf" over minor disagreements. When victims retaliate against their abusers—when battered women kill their batterers—they may receive a greater punishment than men who commit acts with similar outcomes. Do women receive harsher sentences than men for domestic homicide? The question is difficult to answer because the circumstances may be quite different. Jenkins and Davidson (1990) analyzed the court records of ten battered women charged with the murder of their abusive partners in Louisiana between 1975 and 1988; all pleaded guilty or were convicted at trial. Their sentences ranged from five years' probation to life in prison; with half received the latter sentence.

Ewing (1987) surveyed a larger number of women who had killed their batterers. All 100 were charged with murder, manslaughter, or some form of criminal homicide. The outcomes were as follows: 3 were found not guilty by reason of insanity, 3 had their charges dropped, 9 pleaded guilty, and 85 went to trial. Of these 85, a total of 63 were convicted. For those convicted, 12 were given life in prison, 1 was sentenced to 50 years without parole, and the others received anywhere from 4 years' probation to 25 years in prison, with 17 receiving prison sentences longer than 10 years.

BATTERED WOMAN SYNDROME AS A DEFENSE

Only a very small minority of battered women kill their attackers, but these victims receive a great deal of public scrutiny, usually in connection with their trial for murder. When they go to trial, most battered women have used either insanity or self-defense as a defense; in either type of defense, **battered woman syndrome** is likely to be part of the defense. Battered woman syndrome is defined as a collection of symptoms and reactions by a woman to a pattern of continued physical and psychological abuse inflicted on her by her mate. Lenore Walker (1984), the psychologist who is recognized for naming this syndrome, emphasizes the following elements:

1. As a result of chronic exposure to repeated incidents of battering, the woman develops a sense of *learned helplessness,* in which she comes to believe that there is nothing she can do to escape from the batterer or improve her life; finally, she gives up trying to make a change.
2. As a result of her social isolation and often her economic dependence on the batterer, the woman falls more and more under his domination. She believes that she has diminished alternatives for solving her problem.
3. As she restricts her outside activities and has less contact with friends or relatives, the woman grows increasingly fearful of the threats and attacks of the batterer. Most of the women Walker interviewed stated that they believed that their batterer would eventually kill them.
4. Trapped in this existence, the woman experiences several emotional and psychological reactions. Her self-esteem is diminished, she feels guilty and ashamed about what she sees as her multiple failures and shortcomings, and she also feels increasing rage and resentment toward her partner, whose control over her seems to grow over time.

5. After years of victimization, the woman grows *hypervigilant*; she notices subtle things—reactions by the batterer that others wouldn't recognize as a signal of upcoming violence (for example, her partner's words come faster, he assumes a specific posture, or his eyes get darker). This heightened sensitivity to danger cues often motivates the woman to kill her assailant and accounts for her belief that she acted in self-defense.

Conflicts between the values of discretion and equality often surface in cases in which a woman is charged with murdering a partner who has been abusive to her throughout their relationship. For example, the last three pardons granted in New Hampshire—a state in which pardons are rarely given—were to women who had been victims of domestic abuse and had killed their husbands. The most recent such pardon was to June Briand, 33, who had served nearly ten years in prison for killing her physically and emotionally abusive husband.

JUNE BRIAND

EVALUATING BATTERED WOMAN SYNDROME

How have claims of battered woman syndrome fared in court? Does battered woman syndrome really exist? Does it advance the cause of victims who feel they are forced to retaliate? A battered woman's claim of self-defense often faces both legal hurdles and the skepticism of jurors (Dodge & Greene, 1991; Schuller, McKimmie, & Janz, 2004). These obstacles might account for the fact that the majority of battered women charged with murdering their abusive partner are convicted.

Historically, a claim of **self-defense** has applied to homicides in which, at the time of the killing, the individual reasonably believed that he or she was in imminent danger of death or great bodily harm from an attacker. The defense was usually invoked in cases in which a specific attack or fight put defendants in fear for their lives. However, the typical case in which a battered woman relies on a theory of self-defense to exculpate her from charges of murdering her partner is much different. The violence does not involve a specific episode; rather, it is ongoing. The woman's response may seem disproportionate to

what a "reasonable" person believes was necessary; often she kills her abuser while he is unarmed or even is sleeping. To help jurors understand how battered woman syndrome leads to a woman's perception that she is acting in self-defense, defendants often try to introduce expert testimony about the characteristics and consequences of the syndrome. Some mock jury research has explored the effect of expert testimony in a criminal homicide case in which the defendant was a battered woman (Schuller et al., 2004). Participants were more inclined to accept the woman's claim of self-defense when they heard from an expert testifying for the defense. In addition, compared to the no-expert control condition, those exposed to expert testimony on battered woman syndrome believed that the defendant's options were far more limited.

It is important to remember that no single set of reactions or characteristics can describe all victims of battering. One study (Button, Perrin, Chrestman,

& Halle, 1990) that investigated the characteristics of battered women seeking help at a counseling program identified five distinct personality types, with different patterns of psychological functioning among them, including profiles that were "normal."

Although battered women share the experience of being victimized by a violent partner, their reaction to this aggression and how they cope with it takes many different forms. This variation has implications for developing the most effective types of intervention for these women. Rather than assuming that they need traditional services such as psychotherapy or couples counseling, it would be more effective to provide battered women with special advocates who would support these survivors and help them find the resources they need to improve their lives. Just such an intervention has proved very effective in helping bring about changes that allowed battered women to become violence-free (Sullivan & Bybee, 1999). After providing battered women with a personal advocate who helped them gain access to the resources that each needed to reduce her risk of partner abuse, Sullivan and Bybee found that the women who received advocacy services were twice as likely, during the two-year outcome period, to be free of any battering than were women without such a service.

The Psychology of Rape

Until recently, rape victims were singled out for misunderstanding, harassment, and neglect. For example, if a rape victim did not resist her attacker, people might incorrectly assume that she wanted to be raped; in contrast, people never raise the question of whether a robbery victim wanted to be robbed, even when he or she didn't resist (Scroggs, 1976). Furthermore, society struggles over how to deal with convicted rapists. Is rape a sexual crime or an act of violence? Is it the act of a disordered mind or of a normal one?

Among serious crimes, rape is perhaps the most appropriate for psychological analysis (Allison &

Wrightsman, 1993). Myths abound about the nature of rapists and their relationship to their victims. Rape is a crime in which the interaction between the criminal and his prey is central to attributions of responsibility and blame (Stormo, Lang, & Stritzke, 1997). Since the 1970s, there has been an explosion of psychological research directed toward understanding sexual assaults (Ellis, 1991; Hall & Hirschman, 1991; Marshall, Fernandez, & Cortoni, 1999; Beech, Fisher, & Thornton, 2003; Jones, Wynn, Kroeze, Dunnuck, & Rossman, 2004). For these reasons, we devote special attention to the crime of rape and its victims. We focus on female rape victims, but the fact that men are also raped should not be overlooked, even though the law has only recently recognized them as victims.

MYTHS ABOUT RAPE

Myths and misleading stereotypes about rape, rapists, and rape victims take three general forms: (1) Women cannot be raped against their will, (2) women secretly wish to be raped, and (3) most accusations of rape are faked. For example, we are told, "Only bad girls get raped." But we are also told, "All women want to be raped" and "Women ask for it." We also learn that "any healthy woman can resist a rapist if she really wants to." These falsehoods create a climate hostile to rape victims, often portraying them as willing participants in or even instigators of sexual encounters. In fact, these attitudes often function as self-serving rationalizations and excuses for blaming the victim.

RAPE ATTITUDE SURVEYS

Rape means different things to different people, and these differing attitudes and perceptions affect behaviors toward both offenders and their victims (Feild, 1978). Some respondents feel more empathy toward rape victims than others do; some feel empathy toward defendants charged with the crime of rape (Deitz, Blackwell, Daley, & Bentley, 1982; Deitz, Littman, & Bentley, 1984; Deitz, Russell, & Hammes, 1989; Weir & Wrightsman, 1990). Thus, the measurement of attitudes about rape can clarify what different people believe about this crime, its victims, and its perpetrators.

In his groundbreaking studies 'of attitudes toward rape, Herbert S. Feild (1978, 1979; Barnett & Feild, 1977; Feild & Barnett, 1978; Feild & Bienen, 1980) hypothesized that a person's view of rape cannot be summarized by one score on a single scale. After constructing a 75-item Attitudes toward Rape questionnaire and analyzing responses to it, Feild concluded that seven different attitude clusters contribute to our overall perspective. Among these factors were the degree to which:

1. women were seen as responsible for preventing their own rape,
2. a desire for sex is seen as the main motive for rape,
3. severe punishment is advocated for rapists, and
4. a woman is seen as instigating rape through flirtatious behavior or provocative dress.

WHAT ACCOUNTS FOR STEREOTYPES AND MYTHS ABOUT RAPE?

Individuals who, on the basis of answers to Feild's questionnaire, are unsympathetic to victims and tolerant of rapists also tend to believe in many of the myths about rape described earlier. Such persons have developed a broad ideology that encourages the acceptance of myths about rape (Burt, 1980). This ideology embraces the following beliefs:

1. *Sexual conservatism.* This attitude emphasizes restrictions on the appropriateness of sexual partners, sexual acts, and circumstances under which sexual activity should occur. Burt (1980) observes, "Since many instances of rape violate one or more aspects of this conservative position, a sexually conservative individual might feel so strongly threatened by, and rejecting of, the specific circumstances of rape that he or she would overlook the coercion and force involved, and condemn the victim for participating" (p. 218).

2. *Adversarial sexual beliefs.* This component refers to the belief that sexual relationships are fundamentally exploitive—that participants in them are manipulative, unfaithful, and not to be trusted. To a person holding this ideology, "rape might seem the extreme on a continuum of exploitation, but

not an unexpected or horrifying occurrence, or one justifying sympathy or support" (Burt, 1980, p. 218).

3. *Acceptance of interpersonal violence.* Another part of the ideology is the belief that force and coercion are legitimate behaviors in sexual relationships. This ideology approves of men dominating women and overpowering passive partners with violence and control.

4. *Sex-role stereotyping.* The last component of Burt's ideology casts each gender into the traditional mold of behaviors associated with that gender.

Burt constructed a set of attitude statements and administered them to a sample of 598 Minnesota adults to determine whether each of these components contributed to acceptance of myths about rape. When subjects' responses on the ideology clusters were compared to their answers on a scale measuring beliefs in myths about rape, Burt found that three of the four clusters had an impact (sexual conservatism did not). The strongest predictor of believing the myths was the acceptance of interpersonal violence. The subjects, both men and women, who felt that force and coercion were acceptable in sexual relationships were the ones who agreed with items such as "Women who get raped while hitchhiking get what they deserve" and "Any healthy woman can successfully resist a rapist if she really wants to."

A review of more than 70 studies that employed a variety of measures of attitudes about rape supports Burt's conclusions (Anderson, Cooper, & Okamura, 1997). Those subjects who are more tolerant of rape are more likely to have traditional beliefs about gender roles, more adversarial sexual beliefs, greater needs for power and dominance, and heightened expressions of aggressiveness and anger.

FACTS ABOUT RAPE

As we have seen, mistaken beliefs about rape are related to general attitudes toward law and crime. But what are the facts about rape? The United States has one of the highest rates of forcible rape among the world's industrialized countries (Marshall et al., 1999). Between 75 and 85 forcible rapes are reported annually to the police for every 100,000 females (Butterfield, 1997). Findings from the National Violence against Women Study, conducted in 2000, revealed that 14.8% of women reported being victims of rape, and an additional 2.8% of women reported being victims of attempted rape, at some time in their lives (Tjaden & Thoennes, 2000). This rate is three times that of England and twice that of countries such as France, Norway, and Spain (Kutchinski, 1988; Quinsey, 1984; Russell, 1984).

However, experts estimate that reported rapes are only a minority of all those that occur, representing perhaps only a fifth or a tenth of actual rapes (Koss, 1992; Russell, 1984). Estimates are that between 20% and 30% of women in the United States suffer at least one rape or rape attempt in their lifetime (Ellis, 1989; Koss & Oros, 1982; Muehlenhard & Linton, 1987), up to twice as many rapes or attempts as are reported (Tjaden & Thoennes, 2000). Several factors account for the low report rates (Feldman-Summers, & Ashworth, 1981): The woman may be convinced that reporting won't do any good, that she will suffer further embarrassment as a result of reporting, and/or that law enforcement officers will not believe her. Many victims are afraid that the attacker will retaliate if charges are made, and these expectations are sometimes fulfilled. According to FBI figures, only about half of reported rapes result in an arrest. And if a suspect is charged and the victim is a witness at his trial, his defense attorney may ridicule her testimony and impugn her character.

Women of all ages, social classes, and ethnic groups are vulnerable to rape. According to a study by the U.S. Bureau of Justice Statistics, the high-risk age groups are children and adolescents; victims younger than age 12 account for 15% of those raped and victims aged 12 to 17 account for an additional 29% (Butterfield, 1997). Other surveys report that between 1% and 12% of victims are over 50 years of age.

RAPE STATISTICS: THE NATIONAL WOMEN'S STUDY

A major study of rape, published in 2000, provided valuable data on the frequency of rape and on women's reactions to this crime. The National Women's Study was organized and funded by several governmental agencies and crime victim organizations. A nationwide, stratified sample of 8000 adult women and 8005 adult men were interviewed over the telephone about their experiences as victims of sexual aggression.

Because children and adolescents were excluded from the sample, the figures underestimate the total number of rapes, but they do give us an idea of the magnitude of the problem with adults. Among the study's findings are the following:

1. In the sample surveyed, 17.6% of all women said they had been the victim of rape or attempted rape sometime in their lifetime, and 21.6% of these women reported that they were younger than 12 years old at the time of their first rape.
2. Among rape victims, 31.5% reported being physically injured during their most recent rape.
3. An estimated 9.1 million women in the United States have been raped at least once in their lifetime.

MOTIVATIONS AND CHARACTERISTICS OF RAPISTS

Not all rapists have the same motives. Rape involves diverse combinations of aggressive and sexual motivation and deviant lifestyles for different offenders (Barbaree & Marshall, 1991). Experts have developed typologies of rapists, some proposing as many as nine types (Prentky & Knight, 1991), others as few as two or three (Groth, 1979). Most typologies have emphasized four factors that distinguish different types of rapists: (1) the amount and type of aggression the rapist used; (2) when the level of aggression was high, whether it heightened sexual arousal in a sadistic manner; (3) whether the offender showed evidence of psychopathy or antisocial personality disorder; and (4) whether the offender relied on deviant sexual fantasies to produce sexual arousal.

Theories of sexual aggression combine several causal factors into an integrated scheme that accounts for the different types of rapists

(Sorenson & White, 1992). For example, Hall and Hirschman (1991) rely on four factors, similar to those just identified, to describe most rapists: (1) high levels of sexual arousal that are not inhibited by aggression, (2) attitudes toward women that justify aggressiveness toward females, (3) loss of control over emotions such as anger and hostility that are acted out in sexual aggression, and (4) long-standing antisocial personality disorder.

Ellis (1989) identified three theories of rape: the *feminist theory*, emphasizing rape as a pseudosexual act of male domination and exploitation of women (Donat & D'Emilio, 1992; White & Sorenson, 1992); the *social-learning approach*, suggesting that sexual aggression is learned through observation and imitation; and the *evolutionary theory*, holding that natural selection favors men who use forced sexual behavior (Buss & Malamuth, 1996). Ellis (1991) also suggests that high levels of testosterone increase the proclivity to rape by increasing the man's sexual urges and decreasing his sensitivity to aversive outcomes such as a victim's suffering.

These different approaches illustrate that rape cannot be easily explained by any one theory. However, every one of these classification systems fails to capture the full spectrum of behaviors and motivations that typify rapists. Some of these systems are also limited by the fact that they are based on studies of convicted rapists who have been sentenced to prison. The majority of rapists are never imprisoned for their offenses; fewer than 10% of rapes result in convictions or prison sentences (Frazier & Haney, 1996).

ACQUAINTANCE RAPE AND "DATE RAPE"

Over three-fourths of rapes are committed by acquaintances (Koss, 1992; Warshaw, 1988), and these are the assaults that women are least likely to report. Sometimes these actions are not even interpreted as rape. Kanin (1957, 1971) found that, over a 20-year period, between one-fourth and one-fifth of college women he had surveyed reported forceful attempts at sexual intercourse by their dates, during which the women resorted to such reactions as screaming, fighting, crying, and pleading. But usually they did not label the event as attempted rape.

More recent surveys draw similar conclusions; 22% of college females in Yegidis's (1986) survey reported being a victim at least once of an attempted or a completed rape; 25.3% of a sample of undergraduates in New Zealand reported being raped or having a rape attempted against them (Gavey, 1991). Muehlenhard and Linton (1987) reported that 78% of females had experienced some kind of unwelcome sexual initiative during a date. Even among college males, 6% in one study reported having been sexually assaulted at least once (Lott, Reilly, & Howard, 1982).

The 2000 National Women's Study reported that only 14.6% of rapes were committed by a stranger to the victim; 16.4% were committed by a nonrelative acquaintance; 6.4% by a relative; and 64% by an intimate partner. In general, date rapes differ from sexual assaults by a stranger in several ways. They tend to occur on weekends, between 10:00 P.M. and 1:00 A.M., and they usually take place at the assailant's home or apartment. Date rapes tend to involve situations in which both the attacker and the victim have been using alcohol or drugs. But they are less likely to involve the use of weapons; instead, the date rapist employs verbal threats and physical prowess to overpower his victim.

Responding to Rape Victims

Rape victims suffer physical injuries, emotional pain and humiliation, and sometimes severe psychological aftereffects. Recovery from the trauma of rape can be very slow, and victims often describe a sense that they will never be the same again. Providing psychological assistance to rape victims is of utmost importance.

The plight of rape victims has received increased attention through a number of highly publicized cases in which women have come forward to report their experiences. As these cases have unfolded in the public eye, sexual aggression has become a topic of increased discussion among men and women. The gang rape of the Central Park jogger during a "wilding" spree, Patricia Bowman's claim that she was raped by William

Kobe Bryant enters the courthouse

Kennedy Smith after meeting him in a bar, Desiree Washington's rape charges that resulted in the conviction of former heavyweight boxing champion Mike Tyson, the arrest of more than a dozen men for a string of daylight sexual assaults on scores of women in Central Park during Puerto Rican National Day celebrations, and, most recently, the Vail, Colorado, resort employee who accused Kobe Bryant of rape have focused this nation's attention on matters of sexual conduct and on the plight of the victims of sexual aggression.

One part of this discussion has been a debate about whether the names of victims of sexual assault should be made public. The tradition in this country has been to protect the identity of rape victims by not using their names in media coverage. However, in the trial of William Kennedy Smith, both NBC News and the *New York Times* broke with this tradition and published the name of Smith's accuser, Patricia Bowman. Defenders of this decision argued that not naming rape victims perpetuates the stigma of having been raped, making it more difficult in the long run for victims to come forward and confront their attackers. Critics of the practice claimed that publishing the victim's name invaded her privacy and perhaps ruined her future because she would forever be branded as a rape victim. According to the National Women's Study, most rape victims prefer not to have their names published; over three-quarters of the respondents said they would be less likely to report a rape if they knew their names would be made public.

HOW DO WOMEN REACT TO BEING RAPED?

Burgess and Holmstrom (1974, 1979) describe a collection of symptoms experienced by many rape victims. This pattern—**rape trauma syndrome**—comprises three kinds of reactions: emotional responses, disturbances in functioning, and changes in lifestyle. The primary emotional response is fear, including fear of being left alone and fear of situations similar to the one in which the rape occurred (Calhoun, Atkeson, & Resick, 1982). Even the most general of associations with the rape or rapist may trigger an emotional response.

Judith Rowland (1985), a deputy district attorney, describes a reaction of a white rape victim, Terri Richardson, as the trial of her alleged attacker began. Her attacker was a black man.

> Now, in the summer of 1979 the San Diego Municipal Court had one black judge among its numbers. As it happened . . . his chambers were next door. As Terri and I stood . . . while the bailiff scurried out to reassemble the jury, this lone black judge was also preparing to take the bench. I was aware of him standing in his doorway, wearing his ankle-length black robes. It was only when his bailiff held the courtroom door open for him and he was striding toward it that Terri saw him. In less than the time it took him to get through the door, Terri had bolted from the corridor, through the courtroom, and into the main hallway. By the time I got to the outside corridor, I found only a group of startled jurors. I located Terri in a nearby ladies' room, locked in a stall, crying. With a bit more comforting, she was able to regain her composure and get through both my direct and the defense's cross-examination with only minor bouts of tears, particularly while describing the attack itself. (pp. 166–167)

Guilt and shame are also frequent emotional responses. Victims may blame themselves: "Why was I at a bus stop in a strange part of town?" "Did I check that the back door was locked that night?" They may worry that they didn't resist the attacker vigorously enough. The victim often feels a loss of autonomy and of control over her body. She may no longer trust others, a loss that may never be fully repaired throughout her lifetime. One victim describes the feeling this way: "I never feel safe. I couldn't stand the apartment where I lived, but I'm so afraid to be alone anywhere. I never was like that before. I carry things with me, like kitchen knives and sticks, when I go out" (quoted in Rowland, 1985, p. 146).

The second type of reaction, a disturbance in functioning, also frequently appears among rape victims. Specific disturbances include changes in sleep patterns (insomnia, nightmares, and early awakening), social withdrawal, changes in appetite, and problems in sexual functioning. Feldman-Summers, Gordon, and Meagher (1979) studied the impact of rape on victims' sexual satisfaction. Although the sample consisted of only 15 victims, the study did include a comparison group of women who had not been sexually assaulted. Compared with this group, the rape victims reported no difference in frequency of sexual behavior or degree of satisfaction with sexual activities since the rape. However, the victims reported less satisfaction with most areas of sexual *functioning* one week after the rape than in the period before the rape. The level of dissatisfaction diminished somewhat over the next two months, but women who had been raped did not, during this period, approach the level of sexual satisfaction they had experienced before the attack.

Changes occur not only in emotions and general functioning but also in lifestyle. Some victims report obsessively checking doors to make sure they are double-locked; one of the victims whose attacker was prosecuted by Rowland (1985) took 45-minute showers two or three times daily, trying to remove the rapist's odor from her body. Other women make major changes in lifestyle, breaking up with their boyfriends, changing jobs, and moving to new residences. The overall socioeconomic impact of rape can be profound; victims of sexual assault are at greater risk of subsequently losing income, becoming unemployed, and going through a divorce (Byrne, Resnick, Kilpatrick, Best, & Saunders, 1999). Women who have been sexually assaulted in the past or who were sexually abused as children are two to three times more likely to suffer a subsequent sexual attack than women without prior sexual victimizations (Nishith, Mechanic, & Resick, 2000).

Although the reasons for the heightened risk are not clear, one possibility is that some women who have been victimized before are slower to recognize when they are at risk and therefore are more likely to remain in situations where they are vulnerable (Wilson, Calhoun, & Bernat, 1999). Women with more than one sexual victimization across their childhood and adult years are more likely to report unplanned and aborted pregnancies (Wyatt, Guthrie, & Notgrass, 1992).

The impact of rape trauma tends to change over time as well. In fact, observers (Burgess & Holmstrom, 1974; Ellison & Buckhout, 1981) have described the typical rape victim's response as a crisis reaction that unfolds in a series of discrete phases.

The *acute phase* begins with the attack and lasts a few hours or a day. During this acute phase, the primary needs of the victim are to understand what is happening, regain control over her life, predict what will happen next, and ventilate her feelings to someone who will listen without passing judgment (Ellison & Buckhout, 1981). At this point, police officers investigating the crime can either help or hinder the victim. For example, a pelvic examination and the collection of any semen samples are necessary at this point; it is unlikely that the suspect can be prosecuted in the absence of such evidence. But the examination may cause a resurgence of the initial feelings of disruption, helplessness, hostility, and violation—a reaction known as *secondary victimization*. In fact, negative experiences with legal and medical authorities have been shown to increase rape victims' symptoms of posttraumatic stress disorder (Campbell et al., 1999).

Within a few hours or days of the attack, many victims slip into a period of false recovery. Denial occurs: "I'm OK; everything is the same as before." Then a secondary crisis occurs—a sort of flashback—in which some of the symptoms of the acute crisis phase, particularly phobias and disturbances in eating and sleeping, return (Ellison & Buckhout, 1981, p. 59). This phase may last for hours or days before another "quiet period" emerges in which the victim feels a range of negative emotions such as loneliness, anger, and guilt.

Because of increased public awareness of the needs of rape victims, rape crisis centers have been established in many cities. These centers provide crisis counseling to victims. Most follow up with at least one further interview (usually by phone), and a third of their clients have from two to six follow-up interviews. The crisis center also checks for pregnancy and sexually transmitted disease.

Long-term counseling for rape victims is more difficult to provide because of the lack of staff at some rape crisis centers and, in some cases, because of a feeling that counseling is no longer needed. Burgess and Holmstrom (1979), in a follow-up of their earlier sample, found that 74% of rape victims felt that they had recovered and were "back to normal" four to six years after the rape. But 26% did not. A longitudinal study of 20 rape victims (Kilpatrick et al., 1981) measured the personality and mood of these victims and of a matched control group at three time intervals: one month, six months, and one year after the rape. Even at a one-year follow-up, many victims continued to suffer emotionally from the sexual assault. Among the major problems were fear and anxiety, often severe enough to constitute a diagnosis of posttraumatic stress disorder. Several factors contributed to the severity of the victim's reaction. Another study involved interviewing 35 rape victims between 2 and 46 years after their rape and compared their responses to 110 matched, nonabused participants to determine the long-term psychological effects of rape (Santiago, McCall-Perez, Gorcey, & Beigel, 1985). Findings were consistent with those of Kilpatrick and colleagues: fear and anxiety were significantly higher in the rape victim population, compared to the nonabused sample, regardless of the length of time since their rape. Findings also indicated that the rape victims were significantly more depressed than those who had not been raped and that fear, anxiety, and depression were highest in women who had been raped more than once

Providing social support is one of the most helpful interventions. The therapeutic power of social support may derive in part from the fact that women, in particular, tend to react to stress by seeking opportunities for attachment and caregiving—or what psychologist Shelley Taylor has termed the "tend-and-befriend" response (Taylor et al., 2000). (Men, on the other hand, are more likely to respond to stress with the well known "fight-or-flight" strategy.) Therefore, it might be especially useful to female crime victims to have ample opportunities for social support so that their preference to be with others in times of need can be fully addressed.

RAPE TRAUMA SYNDROME IN COURT

Psychologists, along with psychiatrists and other physicians, often testify as expert witnesses in rape trials, especially about the nature and consequences of rape trauma syndrome (Fischer, 1989; Frazier & Borgida, 1985, 1988). This syndrome is usually thought of as an example of a posttraumatic stress disorder, similar to that experienced by veterans of combat, survivors of natural disasters, and victims of other violent crimes. The expert can be of special use to the prosecution in those trials in which the defendant admits that sexual intercourse took place but claims that the woman was a willing participant; evidence of rape trauma syndrome can be used to corroborate the complainant's version of the facts (Frazier & Borgida, 1985). In addition, jurors are often not familiar with the reactions that rape victims frequently experience (Borgida & Brekke, 1985), so psychological experts can educate the jury. Courts around the country are divided, however, on the admissibility of such testimony, and the resulting controversy has generated considerable debate.

The main argument against admitting expert testimony on rape trauma syndrome is as follows: The psychological responses of rape victims are not unique to rape and are not uniform, so it is impossible to say with certainty that a woman exhibiting any given set of responses has been raped. Therefore, a psychologist should not be allowed to testify that a woman is suffering from rape trauma syndrome because to do so is tantamount to telling the jury that she has been raped, which should remain a matter for the jury to decide. Many courts also reject expert testimony on rape trauma syndrome on the ground that the reliability of the syndrome has not been established.

Legislation and Court Decisions

Throughout history, rape has had a rather uncertain status within whatever legal system was in effect. Laws about rape in the United States, rooted in English common law, changed little for three centuries (Harper, 1984). The first American law about rape, created in Massachusetts, imposed the death penalty on the rapist except when the victim was unmarried, reflecting a view that women belonged to their husbands (Estrich, 1987). But beginning in the 1970s, legislation about rape began to undergo dramatic review and revision. Since Michigan initiated its reform in 1974, most of the other states have modified their rape statutes or passed new ones. These changes are correlated with our increased knowledge about rape, generated by social science research and feminist groups. The revisions have usually involved replacing the term *rape* with the term *sexual assault*, reflecting the view that this crime primarily involves the sexual expression of violence (Harper, 1984). This term also eliminates any lingering requirements that the state provide corroborating evidence for the victim's testimony, and it devotes more attention to the extent of physical and psychological injury inflicted on the victim.

The basic definition of sexual assault is nonconsenting sexual contact (such as intercourse) that is obtained by using force or coercion against the victim. But how do we distinguish between rape and a consensual sexual act? No single standard defines what is meant by *nonconsent*, which is why, despite legal reforms, the nature of the victim's conduct in a sexual assault often remains an issue.

SHIFTS IN RAPE LAWS

How much does the victim's behavior contribute to the determination of nonconsent? Is resistance relevant or necessary? Until the 1980s, about four-fifths of the states still imposed a resistance standard—it had to be shown that the victim attempted to resist a sexual assault—in their definition of rape (Largen, 1988). But the sexual assault statutes in most states now concentrate more on the behavior of the assailant and have expanded their definition of force to include coercion or intimidation by the alleged assailant. The standard of resistance has been weakened or eliminated almost entirely.

A second shift in sexual assault laws has been to define several different crime levels. Previously, some states found that with only one degree of offense, which carried possibly severe penalties, juries saw the sentence (which could be life in prison) as too extreme for some cases; hence, they opted for not-guilty verdicts. Many of the newer laws divide sexual assault into degrees according to the extent of force or threat that was used. For example, a *first-degree* sexual assault (rape) would involve sexual intercourse by forcible compulsion under aggravated circumstances (e.g., using a deadly weapon or kidnapping the victim). A *second-degree* rape would require sexual intercourse by forcible compulsion. A *third-degree* rape would be defined as sexual intercourse without consent or with threat of substantial harm to property rights.

One other legislative change is that up until approximately 1980, most states did not consider the sexual assault of a spouse to be rape. Now, all the states have eliminated this exception and recognize **spousal rape** as a crime. In Florida in 1984, a 41-year-old man was found guilty of kidnapping and raping his wife. He was the first man to be convicted of a sexual assault that occurred while the couple was married and living together.

Even though spousal rape is now considered a crime in every state, it is not always treated the same as a sexual assault involving unmarried persons. For example, some states impose a shorter "reporting period" on victims of spousal rape than on victims of other violent crimes. If a victim does not report the assault within this period, the spouse cannot be prosecuted. Another difference between spousal rape and nonspousal rape is the requirement that force or threat of force by the spouse must be proved, rather than just the lack of consent by the victim, which is the requirement in many nonspousal sexual assault statues.

THE RAPE VICTIM AS A TRIAL WITNESS

One frequently used defense strategy in rape prosecutions is to portray the sexual contact as consensual. Shifts in the rape laws have also addressed a persistent problem in the trials of alleged rapists. Before such laws were changed, another defense strategy involved attacking the victim's truthfulness and her general morality. Jurors can be influenced by testimony about the woman's character, reputation, and lifestyle (Lee, 1985), and this has led all states to adopt **rape shield laws** to provide victims with more protection as trial witnesses. In addition, the Privacy

Protection for Rape Victims Act of 1978 amended the federal rules of evidence with regard to the admissibility of testimony on the victim's sexual history with parties other than the defendant. As a result, it is more difficult for defense attorneys to introduce evidence regarding a victim's sexual history, and today defense attorneys probably rely much more often on the argument that the sexual contact was consensual.

Rape shield laws are designed to protect victims' rights to privacy during trial and to exclude evidence about past sexual behavior that might influence the jury's decision in the case. Findings from a recent study of jurors' use of sexual history evidence underscore the importance of this protection. Schuller and Hastings (2002) varied the evidence of prior sexual history of the complainant and defendant in a mock sexual assault trial. In the condition in which the complainant and defendant had a history of involvement including sexual intercourse, compared with the no-sexual-history control condition, the complainant was perceived as less credible, more likely to have consented, and more blameworthy. Prior sexual history also affected jurors' verdicts: The more intimate the prior contact between complainant and defendant, the less guilty the defendant was believed to be. Jurors apparently gauge the credibility of the complainant and the culpability of the defendant through the lens of the parties' prior sexual encounters.

Despite the frequent application of rape shield laws, there is some debate about whether they serve their intended purpose. Many jurisdictions have exceptions that allow the introduction of sexual history evidence at trial when the judge deems it relevant and helpful to the jury (Schuller & Klippenstine, 2004). For example, in the Kobe Bryant rape case, the judge decided, prior to trial, that evidence of the complainant's sexual forays in the three days prior to her encounter with Bryant could be admitted at trial. The rape shield law in Colorado allows evidence of prior sexual conduct when such evidence is relevant to determining the source of vaginal injuries or semen. (Bryant contended that the woman suffered injury during her earlier sexual encounters.) The case against Bryant was dismissed after his accuser opted not to testify.

Although these laws differ from jurisdiction to jurisdiction (Borgida, 1981), they usually prohibit inquiries about the victim's previous sexual conduct unless it can be shown that the questions are relevant to specific issues of the case (as they were in Bryant's case). In Connecticut, for example, testimony about prior sexual activity is admissible only if it does one of the following:

1. Raises the issue of consent by showing prior sexual conduct between the victim and the defendant
2. Shows that the defendant was not the source of semen, pregnancy, or sexually transmitted disease
3. Attacks the victim's credibility, provided that she has testified on direct examination about her past sexual conduct
4. Is otherwise so relevant to a critical issue in the case that excluding it would violate the defendant's constitutional rights

An example of evidence that is so relevant that excluding it would violate the defendant's constitutional rights is found in *Commonwealth v. Wall* (1992). A child victim had been placed in an aunt's home following a sexual assault by her mother's boyfriend. The child was unhappy in the aunt's home and allegedly fabricated a sexual assault claim against her uncle in an attempt to be removed. The Pennsylvania court held that it was relevant to the defense to introduce evidence of the earlier sexual assault.

Wide latitude is still allowed in questioning rape victims, and in some jurisdictions, rape shield laws may not shield the victim from very much. Borgida (1980, 1981) classified these laws into three categories, based on the extent to which evidence is excluded, and then assessed how mock jurors reacted to different versions of a rape trial reenactment reflecting each of these categories. Consider, for example, the following:

> The complainant testifies that she met the defendant at a singles bar, danced and drank with him, and accepted his offer to drive her home. She testifies that at the front door he refused to leave, forced his way into her apartment, and raped her.

> The defendant wants to prove that the complainant had previously consented to intercourse with casual acquaintances she had met at singles bars. Is the evidence relevant? (Borgida, 1981, p. 234)

In a few states, a judge would probably rule that the evidence of the victim's past liaisons is relevant to the fact at issue and admit the evidence. But under the more restrictive statutes of most states (Borgida, 1981, p. 213), such evidence probably would be excluded. These states have concluded that such evidence would be prejudicial (against the victim). As it turns out, Borgida's (1981) study supported this expectation. The "jurors" were reluctant to convict the defendant when testimony was introduced regarding the victim's past sexual relationships with other men. Although no state permits defense attorneys to offer evidence of the victim's sexual history in all situations, some states recognize defense arguments that the victim's sexual history can bear directly on the crime charged in certain situations. For example, North Carolina allows evidence of "a pattern of sexual behavior so distinctive and so closely resembling the defendant's version of the alleged encounter with the complainant as to tend to prove that such complainant consented to the acts charged, or behaved in such a manner as to lead the defendant to reasonably believe that the complainant consented" (*North Carolina Evidence Rule 412*, 1983).

Even if stringent rape shield laws are in force, some jurors will continue to doubt the testimony of rape victims or will use the testimony to make attributions about the witnesses' honesty. For example, mock jurors who are relatively lacking in empathy for rape victims are less likely to see an attacker as responsible for a rape (Dietz, Littman, & Bentley, 1984).

One experience that increases empathy for rape victims is to be personally acquainted with a woman who has been raped. In a laboratory study in which subjects read summaries of witness testimony and then rated the responsibility of a man charged with rape, men and women who themselves knew a rape victim were twice as likely to find the accused guilty of rape as were men and women who did not personally know a rape victim (Wiener, Wiener, & Grisso, 1989).

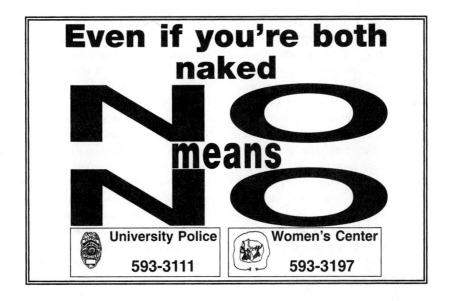

Even if you're both naked

NO means NO

University Police	Women's Center
593-3111	593-3197

The recent changes in rape laws cover several aspects of the crime. Although these changes are impressive, their impact on the courts is unclear. One thorough review of the effects of rape law reforms (Goldberg-Ambrose, 1992) concluded that some have been quite successful but others have had little impact. Myths and false assumptions held by judges, juries, and trial attorneys remain an obstacle; it is easier to change laws than to change attitudes (Largen, 1988).

Preventing Rape

As more is learned about the frequency and consequences of rape, a primary goal of concerned citizens, law enforcement officials, and social scientists has been to develop effective interventions for preventing rape. Two basic strategies have been emphasized: (1) training potential victims how best to protect themselves against rape and (2) designing effective treatment for rapists so that they do not repeat their crimes.

TRAINING POTENTIAL VICTIMS TO REDUCE THE RISK OF RAPE

If a woman finds herself in a situation in which a man begins to sexually assault her, what should she do? Should she scream? Should she fight back, or should she try to reason with him? Should she submit to the attack, especially if the assailant has a weapon, all the while trying to notice as many identifying features of the attacker as possible? There is no uniformly correct response, just as there is no one type of rapist. However, on the issue of passive compliance, a Justice Department survey of over a million attacks (quoted in Meddis & Kelley, 1985) found that women who did not resist a rape attack were twice as likely to suffer a completed rape as women who tried to protect themselves.

As we have already seen, national surveys suggest that between one-fifth and one-quarter of college women have suffered a sexual assault and that the majority of victims were acquainted with their assailants before the assault. Research has also uncovered several risk factors associated with sexual assault. For example, individuals who were sexually victimized are at an increased risk for subsequent victimization (Smith, White, & Holland, 2003; Tjaden & Thoennes, 2000). Acquaintance rape is more frequent (1) when both the victim and the assailant have been drinking or using drugs, (2) on dates in which the man pays all the expenses, and (3) when the date is at an isolated location. Several colleges and universities have incorporated this information about risk factors into rape prevention programs aimed at changing attitudes about sexuality, challenging rape myths and sex-role stereotypes, and improving women's coping responses in potentially dangerous situations.

In the typical rape prevention program, participants discuss several facts and myths about rape, learn how to avoid situations involving heavy use of alcohol, practice resisting pressure for unwanted sexual activity, and role-play other strategies for protecting themselves. The programs try to help women change behaviors and to dispel the notion that victims cause sexual assault. They also strive to minimize the blaming of women that results after sexual victimization. Evaluation of the success of these programs in preventing assaults is just beginning.

In one large experimental study (Hanson & Gidycz, 1993), 181 college women participated in a nine-week acquaintance rape prevention program, while 165 others were assigned to a no-program control group. The prevention program was designed to debunk common myths about rape, educate women about how to protect themselves against rape, alter risky dating practices, improve communication between men and women about sexual behavior, and prevent sexual assaults. Participants discussed rape myths and protective behaviors, watched videotapes that depicted risky situations and the protective behaviors that women can use in these situations, and shared general information about how to prevent acquaintance rape.

The effects of the program were assessed nine weeks later. The prevention program appeared effective for women who had never been victimized before the study; 14% of the women in the control group reported that they had suffered a sexual victimization during the period studied, compared with only 6% of the women in the prevention program. However, among women who had histories of sexual victimization, there was no difference in the victimization rates of the program and control groups. (It should be added that despite the demonstrable risk reduction value of this program, the figures of either 6% or 14% of university women

reporting sexual victimization over a nine-week period are staggeringly high and should serve as a wake-up call to every university that has not yet taken this problem very seriously and implemented policies to prevent such victimization.)

These results confirm that previous sexual assaults are a potent risk factor for future assaults. What they do not explain is why prior sexual assault is such a strong risk factor for repeated victimization. Perhaps victimization lowers self-esteem so that a woman thinks she has already been so damaged that subsequent victimizations don't matter. Alternatively, victimization may convince a woman that she will not be wanted for any reason other than sex, so she continues to place herself in sexually risky situations. Whatever the explanation, these results send a clear message for other prevention programs: The earlier the attempt at prevention, the better. If women participate in assault prevention services before they are ever victimized, it appears that the success of such services will be substantially greater.

DESIGNING EFFECTIVE TREATMENTS FOR RAPISTS

Society is rightfully concerned about the likelihood of sex offenders repeating their crimes (Quinsey, Lalumiere, Rice, & Harris, 1995). In some states, men convicted of sex crimes are required to complete a sex-offender program before being considered for parole (see Chapter 15). In such programs, the offender must acknowledge responsibility for his actions and participate in special treatment programs (Glamser, 1997).

The treatment of rapists can involve psychological, physical, and medical procedures; in many treatment programs, different interventions are often combined. On the international scene, psychosurgery and surgical castration (described in Chapter 15) have been used, but their effectiveness is unclear. Because of the ethical controversies that surround these procedures, few experts advocate their use in the United States (Marshall, Jones, Ward, Johnston, & Barbaree, 1991).

In the United States it is not uncommon for antiandrogen drugs to be prescribed to sex offenders in order to reduce their sex drive, a procedure sometimes referred to as *chemical castration*. The most common treatment involves giving offenders a synthetic female hormone, MPA, which has the trade name of Depo-Provera. MPA decreases the level of testosterone in the body, thereby decreasing sexual arousal in most men. Its use with sexually aggressive offenders has met with mixed success (Bund, 1997). But the drug has also been associated with a number of negative side effects, including weight gain, hair loss, feminization of the body, and gall bladder problems.

In some cases, men were told they would not have to serve any time in prison if they agreed to submit to drug treatments. In 1983, Joseph Frank Smith, 30, of San Antonio, Texas, became the first convicted rapist actually to receive drug treatments as a condition of his ten-year probation. Feminists, on the one side, and defense attorneys, on the other, have raised a number of concerns and criticisms regarding this procedure. For instance, its effectiveness has yet to be fully assessed, even though its advocates claim a very high success rate.

Antiandrogen treatments have problems other than negative side effects. The rate of men dropping out of such treatment prematurely is very high, and failure to complete treatment is one of the strongest predictors of recidivism for sex offenders (Hanson & Bussiere, 1998). Of greater concern is the fact that the treatment does not always reduce sexual arousal and sexual offenses. In some men, arousal is not dependent on their level of testosterone, so the drugs have little effect on their sexual behavior. This point is related to the fact that rape is often an act of violence, not of inappropriate sexual arousal; consequently, drugs aimed at reducing sexual desire may be pointing at the wrong target. Even if the drugs inhibit sexual appetites, they may not control violent outbursts. Hence, they would not meaningfully control these offenders.

Another major approach to treating aggressive sexual offenders involves combining several behavior therapy techniques into an integrated treatment package designed to increase offenders' self-control, improve their social skills, modify their sexual preferences, and teach them how to prevent relapses of their offenses. These programs are usually situated in institutions because of the prison sentences imposed on offenders, but they have also been implemented in the community. Some programs are run in a group format; others rely on individual treatment (Hall, 1996).

These integrated programs employ a wide range of treatment techniques. Sex education and training in social skills are common ingredients because of the widespread belief that sex offenders are often socially incompetent. Biofeedback and aversive conditioning are often used to decrease inappropriate sexual arousal and replace it with arousal to nonaggressive sexual cues. Existing programs appear able to produce short-term decreases in recidivism, but longer-term improvements have been difficult to achieve. As a result, relapse prevention techniques (which have proved useful in the treatment of drug addictions and cigarette smoking) have been added to some programs.

California's Sex Offender Treatment and Evaluation Project (SOTEP), a two-year intensive treatment program focusing on cognitive, behavioral, and skill training, incorporated relapse prevention techniques into the treatment protocol (Marques, Wiederanders, Day, Nelson, & van Ommeren, 2005). The primary goals of the treatment program were focused on relapse prevention by (1) creating a sense of responsibility within the participants, (2) decreasing justifications for sexual deviance, and (3) improving skills for avoiding and coping with high-risk situations. Once released on parole, the participants were mandated, as part of their parole requirements, to participate in a one-year Sex Offender Aftercare Program. Data were collected for an additional five years to establish rates of reoffending. Participants' outcomes were compared to two other groups of sexual offending inmates, one group that volunteered to participate in treatment but were randomly selected to be in the control group, and a second group that declined treatment. Results indicated that individuals who met the program's treatment goals had lower reoffense rates that those who did not, although these differences were very small (the sexual reoffense rate was 21.6% for the treatment group, 23.8% for the volunteer control group, and 23% for the second control group that declined treatment). This suggests that further research will be quite important in designing treatment programs for sexual offenders.

Detecting the Rapist

What methods exist to determine whether a given suspect committed a rape? The late 1980s saw the introduction of a device that initially was acclaimed as the greatest advance in the science of crime detection in a century (Lohr, 1987). The technique, sometimes informally called "genetic fingerprinting," relies on genetic X-ray analyses of DNA (deoxyribonucleic acid) samples, which produce patterns for each of us as distinctive as our fingerprints. As we pointed out in Chapter 5, DNA samples can be taken from any kind of biological material, including hair or skin, as well as from substances such as blood, saliva, and semen. Geneticists have claimed that the identifying patterns are absolutely specific for each individual.

An early use of the procedure in a highly publicized case in Great Britain was described in a nonfiction book by Joseph Wambaugh, *The Blooding* (1989). On separate occasions, three years apart but in the same location, two 15-year-old girls were sexually assaulted and strangled to death. For several years, despite intensive efforts by the police, no killer was found. But with the development of DNA technology, the Leicestershire police decided to obtain blood samples from every possible perpetrator of the crimes and compare these with analyses of the semen taken from the bodies of the victims. All men living in the vicinity who had been born between 1953 and 1970—which turned out to be thousands of men—were asked to present themselves for a "blooding"; if they did not appear, the police sought them out. Despite the trampling of civil liberties involved in forcing thousands of innocent people to submit to the test, and even though the killer tried to cheat, the police found their man (Walker, 1989). When confronted, the murderer ultimately confessed.

Genetic fingerprinting is a rapidly growing industry in the United States. The FBI uses the procedure, as do most state crime labs. The results of DNA testing proved to be one of the most controversial elements of the O. J. Simpson criminal trial, and it is increasingly being used, as we discussed in Chapter 8, to evaluate prisoners' claims that they are innocent of crimes for which they were convicted and in some cases sentenced to capital punishment. An increasing number of states require genetic profiling of people convicted of sex offenses before they are released.

There are, however, concerns about genetic fingerprinting, even beyond the violations of civil rights that compulsory testing might involve. For example, the crime laboratory at the Orange County, California, Sheriff's Department sent about 50 blood and semen samples drawn from about 20 people to each of three labs. The labs were asked to identify which specimens came from the same people. One lab was wrong on 1 of the 44 matches it found; a second was wrong on 1 out of 50. The third, more cautious lab offered no conclusions on about 14 of the samples but got all 37 of its reported matches correct (M. Thompson, 1989). Across the board, the accuracy rate was 98%, but not absolutely perfect. It may be that technology available at the time was unable to make matches perfectly, or it may be that certain assumptions about the characteristics of DNA identification are false (Thompson & Ford, 1989). However, with increasingly sophisticated technology, DNA testing is becoming more precise. For instance, one estimate of the accuracy of DNA typing as a method of determining the guilt of a suspected rapist indicated that it was 3.3 billion times more likely that the defendant's DNA had been at the crime scene than that of any other individual in the population of a South American city in which the rape occurred (da Silva, Goes, de Carvalho, & de Carvalho, 2004).

Sexual Harassment

Even though sexual harassment is a significant problem in educational and work environments, the term itself was not used until 1974. At that time, a group of

Andrea Mackris, who accused Bill O'Reilly of sexual harassment

Talk show host Bill O'Reilly

women at Cornell University, after becoming aware that several of their female colleagues had been forced to quit because of unwanted advances from their supervisors, began to speak out against such harassment (Brownmiller & Alexander, 1992). Also in the early 1970s, the United States Equal Employment Opportunity Commission (EEOC) emerged as a major tool for redressing sexual harassment by employers.

Prevalence Rates

Within the past decade, several cases involving sensational charges of sexual harassment have received widespread attention and focused awareness on the problem of sexual harassment. A well-known case involved the four-year legal battle in which Paula

Jones, a former secretary in Arkansas state government, charged that then-governor Bill Clinton had pressured her to perform oral sex in a Little Rock hotel room. Although he admitted no wrongdoing and refused to apologize to Jones, President Clinton finally paid her $850,000 to drop the lawsuit. The consequences of the case went well beyond this, however, in that Clinton's apparently less than truthful testimony in a deposition in this case was a primary impetus for his eventual impeachment.

More recently, Bill O'Reilly, the host of a top-rated television and radio talk show and the author of several best-selling books, was accused of subjecting the producer of his television show, Andrea Mackris, to "unwanted sexual conduct" and "a hostile work environment" by detailing his sexual fantasies during multiple phone calls (Spilbor, 2004). O'Reilly filed a countersuit claiming extortion. About two weeks after the suit was filed, O'Reilly agreed to drop the extortion charges, and, although he acknowledged no culpability, agreed to pay Ms. Mackris approximately $2 million to settle the case (Kurtz, 2004).

How frequent is sexual harassment? A survey of 20,000 federal employees found that 42% of the female workers reported having experienced sexual harassment on the job in the previous two years (Brownmiller & Alexander, 1992). Similarly, 43% of the women lawyers in large law firms reported that they had been recipients of deliberate touching, pinching, or cornering in the office (Slade, 1994). One survey of female graduate students reported that 60% had experienced some form of harassment by male faculty members, and 22% had been asked out on dates by such faculty (Schneider, 1987). A nationwide survey of female psychologists revealed that over half of them had experienced sexual harassment from a psychotherapy client at some point in their careers (deMayo, 1997). In a study examining sexual harassment in academic medicine, data were collected from over 3000 full-time faculty members at 24 medical schools across the United States (Carr et al., 2000). Findings indicated that about half of female faculty experienced some form of sexual harassment, compared to very few male faculty, and these experiences were similarly prevalent across different institutions in the sample and across all regions of the United States. Estimates of sexual harassment were found to be lower for medical students; one study suggested that about a quarter of female medical students (27.5%) experienced at least one incident of sexual harassment or gender discrimination while enrolled in medical school (Stratton et al., 2005).

Sexual harassment is typically assumed to involve a male perpetrator and a female victim, but men also experience sexual harassment. One survey of 480 nursing students and faculty found that although more women than men experienced mild or moderate forms of sexual harassment (e.g., teasing, attempts to initiate romantic relationships), men were more likely to experience severe types of sexual harassment (e.g., intimate touch, forcing the respondent to touch someone else in an intimate

way) (Bronner, Peretz, & Ehrenfeld, 2003). The Supreme Court has ruled in the case of *Oncale v. Sundowner Offshore Industries* (1998) that male-on-male and female-on-female harassment is also prohibited. Although popular depictions of sexual harassment of males, such as Michael Crichton's novel *Disclosure* and the movie based on it, feature an aggressive female boss demanding sex from a male subordinate, men more often report that other men sexually harass them. One survey of nearly 1000 male workers found that just under 50% of the men had experienced at least one incident involving potential sexual harassment at work, and other men were the perpetrators in over half of these incidents (Waldo, Berdahl, & Fitzgerald, 1998). Similarly, a more recent survey of over 2000 male workers found that 37% had experienced sexual harassment in the workplace, with 53% of these experiences perpetrated by other men (Stockdale, Visio, & Batra, 1999). Although lewd sexual comments, negative comments about men, and unwanted sexual attention were the most common types of harassment, the form of harassment that these men found most upsetting involved statements or actions that belittled them for acting too "feminine" or that pressured them to adopt stereotypical "masculine" behavior.

Defining Sexual Harassment

Title VII of the Civil Rights Act of 1964 prohibits discrimination in the workplace because of a person's gender. It therefore provides the legal basis for banning sexual harassment. Even as more cases come forward, there is continued confusion about the nature of sexual harassment. "Can I tell my assistant that she looks especially nice today?" "What kinds of jokes are okay at the office party?" Questions like this reflect the uncertainty that men in particular seem to have about the possibility that a comment will be viewed by a woman as sexually harassing if it attempts to reflect a compliment or to be humorous (Gutek, 1985; Terpstra & Baker, 1987). U.S. federal law defines harassment as follows:

> Unwelcome sexual advances, requests for sexual favors, and other verbal or physical conduct of a sexual nature constitute sexual harassment when (1) submission to such conduct is made

either explicitly or implicitly a term or condition of an individual's employment, (2) submission to or rejection of such conduct by an individual is used as the basis for employment decisions affecting such individual, or (3) such conduct has the purpose or effect of unreasonably interfering with an individual's work performance or creating an intimidating, hostile, or offensive working environment (16 Code of Federal Regulations Section 1604.11: http://ecfr.gpoaccess.gov/cgi/t/text/text-idx?c= ecfr&sid=9601b0de3a77676a1445d27ae9585 e38&rgn=div8&view=text&node=29:4.1.4.1.5 .0.21.11&idno=29).

One problem with this definition is that it leaves key terms such as *unwelcome* and *unreasonably interfering* open to varying interpretations. When men and women differ in their evaluations of potentially harassing interactions, women are more likely to classify a specific act as harassing than are men (Frazier, Cochran, & Olson, 1995). However, this gender difference is small (Blumenthal, 1998). Who, then, determines when an act is harassing— the alleged victim, the alleged perpetrator, or an outside, "neutral" observer?

What can psychology and other social sciences contribute to understanding sexual harassment? As Frazier and colleagues. (1995) noted, one contribution of psychological research is to provide information about just what behaviors people consider sexually harassing. The following research indicates a gender difference in assessment of what legal standard should be used in evaluating claims of sexual harassment.

When psychologists study the way individuals define sexual harassment, they usually do this by presenting participants with a set of facts and asking them whether they believe those facts show that sexual harassment occurred. In some studies, the subjects read a summary of the facts; in others they watch or listen to a taped description of the events. Some fact patterns are taken from cases that have previously been tried in court; others are hypothetical scenarios created for the purpose of the study. These methodological variations can affect the results. For example, most studies use college students as subjects, which is a potential problem because under-

graduates tend to define sexual harassment more leniently than older adults (Blumenthal, 1998). Along similar lines, studies using genuine case materials from litigation tend to find smaller "gender effects" than studies employing other kinds of stimuli (Blumenthal, 1998).

Some studies consider the impact of subject characteristics other than, or in addition to, gender. For example, Richard Wiener and his colleagues conducted a complex experiment that simultaneously assessed the impact of subject gender, sexist attitudes, and the legal standard used to define harassment (Wiener, Hurt, Russell, Mannen, & Gasper, 1997). In addition to replicating the finding that females were more likely than men to find that sexual harassment had occurred in two workplace situations, Wiener and colleagues (1997) examined the impact of a psychological variable—sexist attitudes—on perceptions of sexual harassment. Subjects were classified as being either high or low in *hostile sexism* and *benevolent sexism*. Hostile sexism involves antipathy toward women, reflecting a belief that males are superior to women and should be dominant over them. Benevolent sexism is an attitude of protection toward women; it reflects a belief that as the "weaker sex," women need to be shielded from the world's harshness. Wiener and his colleagues hypothesized that subjects who scored high on a measure of benevolent sexism would be more likely to find that sexual harassment had occurred, especially when they were directed to judge the behavior from the perspective of the woman. Conversely, they predicted that subjects high in hostile sexism would be less inclined to conclude that sexual harassment had occurred. The results supported most of their predictions. Subjects high in hostile sexism were less likely than subjects who scored low on this dimension to find that the defendant's behavior constituted sexual harassment. However, this difference was not seen when subjects were high on both hostile and benevolent sexism—these individuals did not differ, in their judgments regarding harassment, from subjects who were low in sexism.

As it turns out, the influence of the harasser's status relative to the victim is much more influential than gender on perceptions of sexual harassment. In his meta-analysis of 111 empirical studies examining how sexual harassment is evaluated by different observers, Blumenthal (1998) found that both men and women were more likely to perceive behavior directed by someone of higher status at someone of equal or lesser rank in the workplace as harassment than if such behavior occurred between peers. This is a reassuring result, given that the law also tends to assume greater liability on behalf of a defendant in cases where harassment by a supervisor or manager, as opposed to a peer or co-worker, is alleged (Goodman-Delahunty, 1998).

Structured measures of sexual harassment, such as the Sexual Experiences Questionnaire (Fitzgerald, Gelfand, & Drasgow, 1995), identify three forms of sexual harassment: (1) *gender harassment*, which involves lewd and negative comments directed at a person's gender; (2) *unwanted sexual attention*, which involves overtures for sexual contact ranging from flirting to uninvited touching; and (3) *sexual coercion*, which involves the offer of bribes or the threat of retaliation in exchange for sexual contact. As you would expect, reactions to these behaviors vary widely. Fewer than 10% of respondents consider staring, flirting, or nonsexual touching to be harassment, but almost 100% believe that pressure for sexual favors or sexual bribery constitutes harassment (Frazier et al., 1995). Findings from another study, however, suggest that individuals who are the victims of sexual harassing behaviors experience negative outcomes regardless of whether they label these experiences as sexually harassing (Munson, Miner, & Hulin, 2001). The severity of the sexual harassment, rather than whether the recipient labels the experience as "sexual harassment," is more predictive of the level of negative consequences. Consider a woman who was threatened with termination from her job if she did not engage in sexual acts with her boss. This experience is significantly more severe than listening to her boss tell jokes with sexual content. After having experienced the former scenario, such an employee might not label the latter scenario as sexual harassment; however, research suggests that she may still suffer negative outcomes as a result of the latter experience.

The courts, following the EEOC guidelines, have recognized two types of sexual harassment. The *quid pro quo* type involves sexual demands that are made in exchange for employment benefits; it is comparable to sexual coercion on the Sexual Experiences Questionnaire. **Quid pro quo** harassment is seen in an implicit or explicit bargain in which the harasser promises a reward or threatens punishment, depending on the victim's response (Hotelling, 1991). When a teacher says to a student, "Sleep with me or you fail this course," it qualifies as *quid pro quo* sexual harassment (McCandless & Sullivan, 1991).

The second type of harassment, usually referred to as **hostile workplace harassment**, involves the other two dimensions of the Sexual Experiences Questionnaire—gender harassment and unwanted sexual attention. Under Title VII, it is illegal for employers to create or tolerate "an intimidating, hostile, or offensive working environment" made so by harassment. In Paula Jones's lawsuit against President Clinton, the plaintiff claimed that Clinton's behavior constituted hostile workplace harassment. How is this defined? How disabling must the environment be for the victim? The courts have answered these questions in several relevant cases.

In the 1986 case of *Meritor Savings Bank v. Vinson*, the U.S. Supreme Court recognized for the first time that sexual harassment creating a hostile work environment also violates Title VII of the 1964 Civil Rights Act. However, the legal standards differ between the two types of harassment. For instance, one incident alone can constitute *quid pro quo* harassment. In the 1998 case *Burlington Industries, Inc. v. Ellerth*, the Supreme Court held that to prove *quid pro quo* harassment, one need only show that the harassment occurred; it is not necessary, in order for the perpetrator to be guilty of *quid pro quo* harassment, for the stated or implied threats to have been carried out or to have led to material harm.

In contrast, isolated incidents of sexual misconduct may not necessarily constitute *hostile workplace* harassment; evidence of repeated offensive behavior or behavior of a severe nature is usually required. However, as the Supreme Court stated in *Harris v. Forklift Systems, Inc*, (1993; see Box 13.2), the effects of such harassment need not "seriously

THE CASE OF

BOX 13.2 **Teresa Harris: Sexual harassment on the job**

Teresa Harris was the rentals manager at Forklift Systems in Nashville. Her boss (the company president) made a number of suggestive and demeaning comments to her. At first she tried to ignore him, and then she confronted him. He promised to stop, but a month later, in public, he asked whether she had slept with a client to get his account. This was the last straw; after working there two years, Harris quit. She sought relief from the EEOC and the courts, claiming that the boss's behavior had created a hostile workplace. She asked for back wages as part of the litigation.

When she did not receive satisfaction from the lower courts, she brought her appeal to the U.S. Supreme Court, which agreed to hear the case because different circuit courts had been inconsistent in their decisions in such cases. Some courts had adopted a subjective approach, focusing on the impact of the alleged harassment on the plaintiff. Others, taking a more objective approach, had asked whether a reasonable person would have found the environment abusive. Also unclear was the question of degree of impact. Was it sufficient that the environment interfered with the complainant's work performance, or was it necessary for

"psychological injury" to have occurred? Even though there is ample evidence that sexual harassment produces psychological damage (Fitzgerald, Buchanan, Collinsworth, Magley, & Ramos, 1999), should plaintiffs be forced to prove that they were psychologically harmed in order to persuade a jury that the sexual harassment has occurred? It has been suggested that plaintiffs not be required to prove that they suffered specific psychological symptoms, but only to establish nonspecific pain and suffering. If plaintiffs claim nonspecific pain and suffering, they are not required to offer expert testimony about that suffering. In contrast, however, if plaintiffs claim that specific psychological disorders resulted from the sexual harassment (such as posttraumatic stress disorder or major depression), they are required to proffer expert testimony to support these claims. In response, defense counsel may wish to hire their own expert to evaluate the accuracy of these claims (Kovera & Cass, 2002). These evaluations contribute to the already traumatic situation that the plaintiff faces.

The unanimous decision of the Court, announced by Justice O'Connor, ruled in favor of Harris

and held that it was not always necessary for plaintiffs to prove that they had suffered psychological injuries. The case was returned to the lower court, which was instructed to examine the ruling and decide how much back pay, if any, Harris deserved. (Several months later, Forklift Systems settled with Harris out of court, for an unpublicized amount.) The Supreme Court decision listed several criteria by which to decide whether an action constitutes sexual harassment, including the frequency and severity of the behavior, whether the behavior was physically threatening or humiliating, and whether it would unreasonably interfere with an employee's work performance.

Noteworthy in the Court's decision was the use of the "reasonable person" standard. For example, Justice O'Connor wrote, if conduct was not sufficiently severe and pervasive as to create an "objectively hostile" work environment as defined by a reasonable person, then it was not sexual harassment. Her decision reflected an intermediate position. Harassment was no longer defined by responses of the "reasonable man," but Justice O'Connor did not go so far as to permit the victim to define what is hostile.

affect [an employee's] psychological well being" or lead the plaintiff to "suffe[r] injury" (pp. 3–6) to constitute *hostile workplace* harassment. The standard for evaluating a hostile environment is from the perspective of a "reasonable person."

Experts remain divided about whether sexual harassment should be viewed from the perspective of the "reasonable woman" or the "reasonable person" (Wiener & Gutek, 1999). One position is that the latter standard ignores the perspective of women, who are more likely to be victims than are men and who therefore can provide the more appropriate perspective. The other viewpoint holds that use of a "reasonable woman" standard would perpetuate a stereotype that women are less able than men to cope with ordinary job pressures.

Although women are more likely than men to describe an act as sexual harassment, the gender difference is usually small. Extreme behaviors, such as coercive threats to have sex or lose one's job, are rated as sexual harassment by 99% of each gender—it is the more ambiguous behaviors for which gender differences emerge. For this reason, Gutek and O'Connor (1995) argue that a "reasonable woman" standard is not advisable in sexual harassment cases. That standard can focus attention on the recipient's behavior and away from the perpetrator's, as well as perpetuating the very sexist attitudes it seeks to eliminate.

On the other hand, using a "reasonable woman" standard could make employees more aware of the perspective of potential victims perhaps thereby prevent some acts of sexual harassment (Wiener & Hunt, 1999). As a compromise, some commentators have recommended a "reasonable *victim*" standard that would encourage jurors to examine several factors—including gender of the victim—in evaluating claims of sexual harassment (Goodman-Delahunty, 1999).

Applying Psychological Knowledge to Detecting Harassment

Psychological approaches contribute to our understanding of sexual harassment in two other ways. First, some psychologists have attempted to predict when sexual harassment will occur. Other psychologists have tried to determine the likelihood of a favorable outcome in litigation when a person who alleges sexual harassment files a complaint. We consider these issues next.

When does sexual harassment occur? Pryor, Giedd, and Williams (1995) proposed that certain individuals are inclined toward behavior that would be sexual harassment and that the norms in specific organizations function to encourage the expression of harassment. For example, a factory that permits its workers to display *Playboy* centerfolds or nude

calendars in their work areas may encourage harassment on the part of a worker who, in another environment, would not exhibit such behavior. Similarly, a company that provides sexually oriented entertainment at office parties or has work-related parties that exclude one gender is expressing a norm that gives tacit approval to at least some forms of harassment.

But men also differ in their likelihood to harass. Pryor (1987) asked men to imagine themselves in a series of scenarios in which they had power over an attractive woman. In one scenario, for example, the man is a college professor meeting with a female student who is seeking to raise her grade in the class. The subjects were asked to rate how likely they were to engage in an act of *quid pro quo* sexual harassment in each scenario, given that they could do so without being punished. Men who scored relatively high on the Likelihood to Sexually Harass (LSH) scale were more accepting of myths about rape, indulged in more coercive sexual fantasies, and endorsed more stereotypical beliefs about male sex roles (Pryor et al., 1995). They had strong needs to dominate women and to seek sex for the sake of their own gratification. In a series of laboratory experiments, Pryor and his colleagues found that men high in likelihood to sexually harass engaged in harassment in social situations in which harassing behavior was convenient and not conspicuous, and under conditions in which local norms encouraged such behavior.

A more recent study yielded findings consistent with these results using a similar assessment protocol (Begany & Milburn, 2003). This study also indicated that authoritarian personality characteristics (such as a belief in obeying authority above all else) predicted men's self-reported likelihood of engaging in sexual harassment; men who reported higher levels of authoritarian characteristics are more likely to engage in sexual harassment. Other personality characteristics have also been associated with higher scores on the LSH scale, including a less feminine personality, more traditional beliefs about women's roles, more negative attitudes toward women, and less concern with social desirability (Driscoll, Kelly, & Henderson, 1998).

Which types of harassment claims succeed, and which ones fail? Terpstra and Baker (1988) examined

81 sexual harassment charges filed with the Illinois State Equal Employment Opportunity Commission over a two-year period to determine what factors influenced their outcomes. About 31% of these cases were settled in favor of the complainant. The researchers identified three characteristics that were significantly related to EEOC decisions. Sexual harassment charges were more likely to be resolved in favor of the complainant when:

1. the harassing behaviors were serious,
2. the complainant had witnesses to support the charges, and
3. the complainant had given notice to management prior to filing formal charges.

This analysis was repeated for another sample of 133 court decisions between 1974 and 1989 (Terpstra & Baker, 1992). A total of 38% of these cases were decided in favor of the complainants—higher than the 31% of the EEOC cases—even though the complainants' cases were generally not as strong as those heard by the EEOC. In these cases, complainants were more likely to win their cases if:

1. the harassment was severe,
2. witnesses supported their claims,
3. documents supported their claims,
4. they had given notice to management prior to filing charges, and
5. their organization had taken no action.

If a complainant had none of these factors in his or her favor, the odds of winning the case were less than 1%; if he or she had all five, the odds of winning were almost 100% (Terpstra & Baker, 1992).

Offenders as Victims

When offenders are at the same time victims, or claim to be victims, society's reaction becomes even more complex, and decisions made by the legal system become even more controversial. Consider the trials of Lorena Bobbitt, Lyle and Erik Menendez, and Michael Jackson. What do these trials have in common? In each case, the defendant or defendants, charged with serious crimes, claimed the role of victim and argued that they were retaliating against an unwanted act or trying to prevent a feared attack. Lorena Bobbitt was outraged over an act earlier that evening that she considered to be spousal rape by her husband John, so while he was sleeping, she cut off his penis. At their trials, the Menendez brothers described episodes of physical and sexual abuse from their father, with their mother as a passive accomplice; fearing the worst, they said, they decided to kill their parents first. Michael Jackson was charged with sexually molesting a young boy and holding his family captive at his "Neverland" ranch. Jackson claimed that the boy and his family had fabricated these accounts in an attempt to obtain money from him.

How did the juries react to these defenses? Lorena Bobbitt was found not guilty by reason of insanity. Jurors' reactions in the Menendez brothers' trials were more complicated. In the first trials, the jurors could not agree, producing a hung jury. The jurors agreed that each brother was guilty of a crime, but they could not agree on whether each should be convicted of murder or manslaughter (Thornton, 1995). With each jury deadlocked over the appropriate charge for conviction, the result was a mistrial. At the second trial, both brothers were found guilty of murder and sentenced to life in prison. Michael Jackson was acquitted on all charges after arguing that family members of his alleged victim were essentially con artists trying to take advantage of his celebrity.

In cases like those of Bobbitt and the Menendez brothers, in which a defendant claims to be a victim, critics are concerned that jurors will be tempted to accept what has been called the **abuse excuse**—"the legal tactic by which criminal defendants claim a history of abuse as an excuse for violent retaliation" (Dershowitz, 1994, p. 3). Although Dershowitz concluded that an increasing number of defense lawyers are using the abuse excuse and that juries increasingly are accepting it, evidence in support of the latter claim is sparse at best. In fact, such defenses seem to be met with increasing skepticism and with a willingness to blame the offender, exactly as the "just world" theory predicts they would be.

SUMMARY

1. What is the frequency of crime victimization? According to the National Crime Victimization Survey, crime victimization occurs at a rate of 217 incidents per 1000 persons. But this figure underestimates the true extent of victimization that befalls an unknown number of individuals in homes, schools, and the workplace.

2. What types of research have psychologists conducted on victimization? Three areas of victimization have received special attention from psychologists: violent victimization and posttraumatic stress disorder, including the psychology of rape; domestic violence (particularly battered spouses), and sexual harassment.

3. What factors predict the development of PTSD after being a crime victim? The extent of injury suffered in the crime and the belief that the victim has no control over his or her life heightens the risk of developing PTSD. Treatments that help restore a sense of control and that help victims reexperience the trauma so that its emotional power is drained are the most effective interventions for preventing and reducing PTSD after a crime victimization.

4. What are the components of battered woman syndrome? Battered woman syndrome consists of a collection of responses, many of which are displayed by individuals who are repeatedly physically abused by their intimate partners. These include learned helplessness, lowered self-esteem, impaired functioning, fear or terror, loss of the assumption of invulnerability, and anger or rage.

5. How have the laws about rape changed? Beginning in the 1970s, state legislatures and the courts began to modify longstanding laws about rape. One general type of shift was to de-emphasize resistance as a requirement in showing that a rape took place. A second shift was to divide rape into several degrees of offense, enabling juries to render guilty verdicts more frequently. Virtually all states now permit a husband to be charged with rape against his wife. Most states now have rape shield laws that restrict the defense attorney's questioning of the victim about her sexual history.

6. How can rape be prevented? Prevention of rape has taken two routes. One is to determine what responses by potential victims are most effective in warding off a sexual assault. The other is to use effective treatments for convicted rapists. Antiandrogen drugs, which reduce sex drive, and a combination of various behavior therapy techniques have shown some effectiveness as treatment for convicted rapists.

7. What are two types of sexual harassment recognized by the courts? The first type of harassment, *quid pro quo* harassment, consists of sexual demands made in conjunction with offers of benefits in exchange for complying or threats of punishment if the respondent does not comply. The second type is harassment that creates a hostile work environment; it often involves demeaning comments, acts of touching or attempted intimacy, or the display of provocative photographs or artwork.

KEY TERMS

abuse excuse	borderline personality	posttraumatic stress	rape trauma
attribution	disorder	disorder	syndrome
theory	cycle of violence	*quid pro quo*	self-defense
battered woman	hostile workplace	harassment	spousal rape
syndrome	harassment	rape shield laws	victimology

Children, Adolescents, and the Law

ORIENTING QUESTIONS

1. *What are the characteristics of juvenile courts and how has juvenile justice changed in recent years?*

2. *What are the short-term and long-term effects of child maltreatment?*

3. *Can children accurately report on their experiences of victimization? What factors affect the accuracy of their reports?*

4. *Contrast nurturance rights and self-determination rights. What do the data suggest about adolescents' capacities to make their own treatment decisions?*

5. *How has the traditional family structure changed and how do children fare when raised in households headed by gays and lesbians?*

Juvenile Offenders

The Juvenile Justice System

As the criminal law developed in England and the American colonies, children under 7 were treated in the same way as were insane persons—that is, as not being criminally responsible for their actions. If the child was between 7 and 14, the state was required to prove that the child understood what he or she was doing and knew the difference between right and wrong. Children 14 or older were treated as adults (Lou, 1927).

Juvenile courts were first established in the late 19th century. Social reformers believed that misbehaving children should be corrected but not subjected to adult punishment (Schwartz, Weiner, & Enosh, 1998). In 1899, the Illinois legislature created for the city of Chicago the first juvenile court in the United States. The premise of the court was that it should treat law-breaking children in the same way as a kind but stern parent would treat a child—with corrective measures rather than punishment.

Consider a 1909 description:

> Why is it not just and proper to treat these juvenile offenders as we deal with the neglected children, as a wise and merciful father handles his own child whose errors are not discovered by the authorities? Why is it not the duty of the state, instead of asking merely whether a boy or girl has committed a specific offense, to find out what he is, physically, mentally, morally, and then if it learns that he is treading the path that leads to criminality, to take him in charge, not so much to punish as to reform, not to degrade but to uplift, not to crush but to develop, not to make him a criminal but a worthy citizen. (Mack, 1909, p. 107)

The Chicago experience started a trend. During the first three decades of the 20th century, all but three states established juvenile courts, in which criminal offenses were termed "acts of juvenile delinquency," punishment became "rehabilitation," and "reform school" (for the most incorrigible) replaced the prisons and jails to which children had previously been sent. The movement was based on the belief that wayward youths could be reclaimed and go on to lead orderly and productive lives (Ryerson, 1978). Another premise of the juvenile court movement was that juvenile misbehavior resulted as much from the environment as from the child; therefore, the child should not be treated as a criminal (Lou, 1927). The distinction between neglected and delinquent children became blurred; probation, rather than institutionalization, became the preferred disposition for juvenile offenders; courtroom procedures were informal and lacked the adversarial nature of adult courts. The public selected juvenile court judges who, it was hoped, were imbued with humanistic and sympathetic skills that would inspire trust from youthful offenders (Olson-Raymer, 1984). It was assumed that these offenders wanted to be good and had the potential and desire to be productive citizens (Ryerson, 1978).

These days, juvenile courts maintain many of the same external trappings. In a relatively informal setting, a juvenile court judge hears evidence about the alleged offense and determines whether a youthful offender should be adjudicated as delinquent, in which case the youth is sanctioned at a disposition hearing. After reviewing a report typically prepared by the probation department, the judge determines the most appropriate punishment, choosing from a range of options that include commitment to an institution; placement in a group home, foster care, or another residential facility; probation; day treatment or mental health treatment; the imposition of a fine; community service; and restitution.

But not all juveniles are handled with velvet gloves. In recent years, instead of receiving the relatively benevolent adjudication of juvenile courts, some youthful offenders have faced more serious penalties imposed in adult criminal courts. Indeed, in the early years of the 21st century, the public's attitude toward juvenile offenders is far different than it was at the beginning of the 20th century. Now the public, believing that juvenile courts are "kiddie courts," clamors for "adult time for adult crimes." As a result, all states now have provisions that allow juveniles charged with serious crimes to be prosecuted and punished as adults. These **transfer laws** have generally increased the range of offenses for which juveniles can be transferred to adult court and have lowered the minimum age for that transfer (Grisso & Schwartz, 2000).

The public's get-tough attitude stems in part from a significant increase in juvenile crimes of violence between 1980 and 1993. Arrests of juveniles for aggravated assault and homicide doubled in that period before starting to decline in 1994. Gun-related homicides, often highly publicized, showed the largest increase—up almost 300% by 1993 (Zimring, 1998). Though relatively small in numbers (2800 homicides out of a total caseload of 1.7 million cases in 1995), murders committed by juveniles captured headlines and sparked demands to be tough on crime (Office of Juvenile Justice and Delinquency Prevention, 1999).

Transfer laws generally focus on three criteria related to a juvenile's functioning: potential dangerousness (which is typically considered to mean risk of reoffending), sophistication/maturity, and amenability to treatment (Salekin, 2002); juvenile offenders who are deemed dangerous, who appear more "adult-like" in their sophistication and maturity, and who are believed to lack amenability to treatment are destined for transfer to adult court. The juvenile justice system relies on psychological and psychiatric assessment of these factors. In fact, court-ordered evaluations are accorded significant weight by the judges who ultimately determine whether a youthful offender will be tried as a juvenile or an adult.

Does it make sense to treat a 14-year-old, or even a 17-year-old, like an adult? In some respects this is a moral question revolving around notions of personal responsibility and maturity. But empirical research studies can lend a scientific perspective as well.

Research by developmental and child-clinical psychologists suggests that juveniles differ in important ways from adults and therefore should not be held to the same legal standards. Whereas adults have developed stable and enduring personality styles, adolescents typically experience fluctuations in their personality and behavior as they develop and mature. Thus, assessing the risk that they will offend again may be more complex with adolescents than with adults (Salekin, 2002). In addition, many adolescents who engage in antisocial behaviors eventually desist in their early to mid-20s and lead law-abiding lives as adults (Moffit, 1993). Determining which youthful offenders will persist in antisocial behaviors and which will desist is a difficult task. Because adolescents are in the process of developing their personal identities, their criminal behavior may be less indicative of a bad character than is the criminality of adults (Steinberg & Scott, 2003). In terms of maturity and sophistication, adolescents' judgment and decision-making abilities often lag behind those of adults. Adolescent offenders have more difficulty weighing and comparing the consequences of decisions and contemplating the long-term effects of their decisions (Woolard, 2002). Perhaps the most intriguing explanation for impulsive adolescent behavior is the fact that the human brain, once thought to be fully formed by age 12, is now known to continue developing until well into the third decade of life. Neuroscience research has shown that the last part of the brain to mature is the prefrontal cortex, which is responsible for impulse control, regulating emotions, and evaluating risks and rewards (Spear, 2000). Finally, although psychologists have suggested that youth are more malleable than adults and therefore more amenable to treatment (Salekin, 2002), it is difficult to predict which adolescents will be helped by treatment. In general, adolescents differ from adults in predictable ways, and determining which *particular* adolescents deserve adult treatment is problematic.

Nonetheless, in 1999, 100 years after the first juvenile offender statute, Illinois made sweeping changes in its juvenile laws in order to emphasize punishment and accountability over rehabilitation. Other states did the same. These new statutes often include "purpose provisions"—that is, statements of what the legislation is intended to accomplish. The purpose provision of the pre-1999 juvenile statute in Illinois spoke to the "safety and moral, emotional, mental and physical welfare of the minor," but the purpose provision of the 1999 statute speaks to the need to "protect the community, impose accountability for violations of law, and equip juvenile offenders with the competencies to live responsibly and productively." The law was changed to reflect this shift in purpose. For example, in deciding whether to transfer a child to adult court, Illinois judges are now to be guided primarily by the seriousness of the offense rather than by the best interests of the child (Geraghty & Rhee, 1998). Recently passed transfer statutes in other states focus on the circumstances of the offense rather than on the child's amenability to treatment, a focus that is consistent with a goal of punishment ("just desserts") rather than rehabilitation (Feld, 1997, p. 80).

Most states set a minimum age for transfer to adult court. Consider, for example, a Jonesboro, Arkansas, case in which Mitchell Johnson, age 13, and Andrew Golden, age 12, lay in ambush and opened fire on their schoolmates with stolen rifles, killing four students and a teacher. They were tried in juvenile court because they were too young to be transferred to adult court (Johnson turned 14, the age for transfer, after the shootings). Judge Ralph Wilson sentenced the pair to confinement until they turn 21, at which time the juvenile court will lose jurisdiction and the boys will go free. In sentencing Johnson and Golden, Judge Wilson expressed frustration because he could not impose a more severe sentence (Moehringer, 1998). Some states set the minimum age for transfer as young as 10, and a few states have no minimum age (Sickmund, 1996). In one of those states, Johnson and Golden could have been tried as adults and subjected to adult penalties.

Although states have made it easier to transfer juveniles to adult courts, the vast majority of juveniles stay in juvenile court. In 1998, only 7135 juvenile defendants were transferred to adult criminal courts in 40 of the largest urban counties in the United States (Rainville & Smith, 2003). Of these, nearly two-thirds were charged with violent offenses, 18% with property crimes, and 15% with drug offenses. (The corresponding figures for adults were 24% charged with violent crimes, 28% with property crimes, and 39% with drug offenses.) Notably, 43% of the convicted adolescent defendants were sentenced to prison, compared to only 25% of convicted adults.

Juveniles' Due Process Rights

The idealized juvenile court of the early 20th century made a virtue of informality. Consider this 1909 description:

> The child who must be brought into court should, of course, be made to know that he is face to face with the power of the state, but he should at the same time, and more emphatically, be made to feel that he is the object of its care and solicitude. The ordinary trappings of the court-room are out of place in such hearings. The judge on a bench, looking down upon the boy standing at the bar, can never evoke a proper sympathetic spirit. Seated at a desk, with the child at his side, where he can on occasion put his arm around his shoulder and draw the lad to him, the judge, while losing none of his judicial dignity, will gain immensely in the effectiveness of his work. (Mack, 1909, pp. 119–120)

Unlike adult courts, juvenile courts of the early 20th century were not adversarial. Children were not represented by counsel, hearings were informal, and evidence rules were nonexistent. "By separating children from adults and providing a rehabilitative alternative to punishment, juvenile courts rejected both the criminal law's jurisprudence and its procedural safeguards such as juries and lawyers" (Feld, 1997, p. 71). But juvenile courts' focus on protecting children's interests tended to overlook the child's perspective, and eventually, unfettered discretion led to unequal and unfair treatment (Woolard, 2002). The case of Gerald Gault (see Box 14.1) changed that; it recognized that even children have constitutionally protected interests, and it extended due process rights to them.

After the *Gault* case, it appeared that the Supreme Court would rule that juveniles were entitled to the same constitutional protections as adults. One year after *Gault*, however, the Court held that the Due Process Clause did not require states to provide jury trials for juveniles. The Court had held that an adult facing a serious charge is entitled to trial by jury (*Duncan v. Louisiana*, 1968), but in *McKeiver v. Pennsylvania* (1971), the

THE CASE OF

BOX 14.1   Gerald Gault: The rights of juveniles

Fifteen-year-old Gerald Francis Gault and another boy were arrested on June 8, 1964, and charged with making an obscene telephone call to a neighbor. The hearing was informal, and Gerald did not have a lawyer. Gerald testified that he had only dialed the number and the other boy had made the call. The neighbor did not testify. The judge found Gerald to be a delinquent and committed him to the State Industrial School until he turned 21. If it had been committed by an adult, the maximum penalty for that obscene call would have been two months in custody.

Gerald objected to the procedures that led to his conviction and confinement. The case eventually went to the United States Supreme Court, which described the Gila County, Arizona, juvenile

court as a "kangaroo court." The Supreme Court held that the Due Process Clause of the Fourteenth Amendment applies to juvenile court proceedings and that Gerald had been denied due process. The Court held that Gerald had the following rights, which had been denied him by the Arizona court:

- ◆ Notice of the charges
- ◆ The right to an attorney
- ◆ The right to confront and cross-examine the witnesses against him
- ◆ The privilege against self-incrimination (*In re Gault*, 1967).

The *Gault* case changed the way juvenile courts operated. Prior to *Gault*, it was unusual for an attorney to represent the child; after *Gault*,

lawyers (most appointed) began to appear on behalf of the child, turning juvenile hearings into adversarial affairs (though without juries). *In re Winship*, decided in 1970, held that the Due Process Clause requires the state to prove every element of the case against the child beyond a reasonable doubt. Professor Feld asserts that *Gault* and *Winship* "unintentionally, but inevitably, transformed the juvenile court system from its original Progressive conception as a social welfare agency into a wholly-owned subsidiary of the criminal justice system" (Feld, 1997, p. 73). Juvenile courts have moved away from the rehabilitative model of old and are now more concerned about protecting the community than about protecting the child (Woolard, 2002).

Court held that it was not unconstitutional for a state to deny jury trials to juveniles.

Sanctioning Juvenile Offenders: The Death Penalty for Teens?

The *Gault* case provided youthful defendants with many of the constitutional protections guaranteed to adult offenders. But it also raised the question of whether juveniles should be subjected to the same penalties as adults. For example, should they be executed for committing violent crimes prior to age 18?

Since the age of responsibility at common law was 7, it is not surprising to find accounts of young children sentenced to death in 18th- and 19th-century America. However, death sentences were

rarely carried out on children who were under 14 at the time of the crime. Only 16 children under the age of 14 at the time of the offense were executed in the period 1642–1899, and only two children under 14 were executed after 1900. However, there was little reluctance to execute those who were 16 or 17 when the crime was committed. Of 287 juveniles executed in the United States from 1642 to 1982, 196 were 17 at the time of the offense, and 52 were 16 at the time of the offense (Streib, 1983).

In 1988, the Supreme Court drew the line at age 16, reasoning that contemporary standards of decency bar the execution of a person who was under the age of 16 at the time of the offense (*Thompson v. Oklahoma*, 1988). Although this ruling forbade executions of 15-year-old offenders, it allowed executions of people who were 16 and 17 when they committed their crimes. But even this standard was relatively short-lived, as the Court determined, in 2005, that it was cruel and unusual to execute a person who was under 18 when the crime was committed (*Roper v. Simmons*, 2005). In his majority opinion in the *Roper* case, Justice Anthony Kennedy looked to the "evolving standards of decency that mark the progress of a maturing society." By that yardstick, the practice of executing juveniles had become outdated and even rare. (In 2005, only 19 states allowed executions of convicted murder who were under 18 at the time of the crime, and the United States was one of only a handful of countries in the world that condoned this practice.) The practical effect of sparing this age group from execution will be life sentences without parole—lengthy periods of imprisonment for relatively young offenders.

Other than the lack of a death penalty for those under 18, juveniles transferred to adult court face the same penalties as adults convicted of the same crimes. Thus, they might face very lengthy terms of imprisonment. In states with "blended sentence" options, such incarceration might begin in a juvenile facility and then involve transferring the individual to an adult prison at the age of 18. In states without such an option, adolescent offenders convicted as adults are incarcerated in the adult system—although some states have developed specialized facilities for these young offenders, or specific wings of an adult facility with no contact permitted between adolescents and adults.

Lionel Tate, 12 years old when he killed a playmate in a wrestling match, is believed to be the youngest person in the United States to have been sentenced to life in prison without parole. At his trial, Tate claimed that he was not guilty and that he had been imitating wrestling moves he had seen on TV when he killed his young friend. Because she was certain of his innocence, Tate's mother, a Florida state trooper, had rejected offers by the prosecutor to have her son plead guilty to second-degree murder and accept a sentence of three years in a juvenile detention center and 10 years of

AP/Wide World Photos

Fourteen-year old Lionel Tate after being sentenced to life imprisonment

probation. In fact, Lionel Tate was released from prison in 2004 after serving just three years. An appellate court set aside his conviction because he had not been given a hearing to determine whether he was competent to stand trial. (Life on the outside has not been easy for Tate, however; in the months following his release, he was arrested for violating the terms of his probation, jailed for robbing a pizza deliveryman at gunpoint, and charged with criminal mischief stemming from damage to his jail cell.)

Life sentences for juveniles overlook the obvious: A 12-year-old is an adolescent, with the mood swings and lack of judgment that come with adolescence. As a matter of policy, youth should operate as a mitigating factor; that is, a 13-year-old should not be sentenced as severely as a 16-year-old, and a 16-year-old should not be sentenced as severely as a 21-year-old (Feld, 1997). Scott and Grisso (1997) use the following example to illustrate three factors that influence adolescents' decisions: (1) conformity and compliance in relation to peers, (2) the youth's attitude toward and perception of risk, and (3) a short-sighted perspective.

> A youth hangs out with his buddies on the street. Someone suggests holding up a nearby convenience store. The boy's decision to go along with the plan may proceed in the following way. He has mixed feelings about the proposal but doesn't think of ways to extricate himself—although perhaps a more mature person might develop a strategy; the possibility that one of his friends has a gun and the consequences of that [don't] occur to him. He goes along, mostly because he fears rejection by his friends, a consequence that he attaches to a decision not to participate—and that carries substantial negative weight. Also the excitement of the hold-up and the possibility of getting some money are attractive. These weigh more heavily in his decision than the cost of possible apprehension by the police, or the long-term costs to his future life of conviction of a serious crime. (p. 166)

Is there is a constitutionally required minimum age for criminal responsibility? For example, would it be constitutional to try a 7-year-old in adult court and subject the child to adult penalties? At common law, it was conclusively presumed that a child younger than 7 was not criminally responsible—that is, did not know the difference between right and wrong or the nature and quality of his or her acts. In the get-tough atmosphere of the 21st century, perhaps the Supreme Court will fall back on the common law and hold that 7 is the minimum age at which a person may be subjected to criminal penalties.

The Miranda *Capacities of Juvenile Defendants*

When juveniles are arrested, they are often subjected to police interrogations, just as adults are. Also like adults, juveniles are encouraged to confess to crimes in which they are suspects. (Recall the false confessions given by the juvenile defendants in the Central Park jogger case, described in Chapter 6.) This practice raises two basic questions: Are juveniles able to understand their *Miranda* rights, and are they competent to waive them and offer valid confessions to the police?

Prior to the decision *In re Gault*, the courts had treated juvenile defendants differently from adults under the theory that the state should assume a parental interest in rehabilitating youthful offenders rather than punishing them. In exchange for this presumably less adversarial attitude (known as **parens patriae**), juveniles relinquished some of the constitutional rights of adult defendants because these protections were deemed unnecessary. The *Gault* decision replaced the former parental stance toward juveniles with a more adversarial posture in which juveniles were to be accorded many of the same constitutional protections as adults. As more states changed their laws to make it easier to transfer juveniles to adult courts and to increase the punishment of juveniles, questions about juveniles' competence have become more pressing (Grisso, 1997). Constitutional rights need to be understood if they are to fully protect accused persons. Thus, a major question is whether juveniles possess adequate capacities to waive their *Miranda* rights knowingly, intelligently, and voluntarily and to make a confession during interrogations by the police.

Thomas Grisso (1981), the leading expert on juveniles' capacities to waive *Miranda* rights, describes two approaches to evaluating these capacities. First, the totality of the circumstances surrounding the **waiver** can be considered. Included in such an evaluation would be the juvenile's age, intelligence, and prior experience in criminal proceedings, as well as the methods used by the police in obtaining the waiver and in questioning the youth. A second strategy, known as the *per se* approach, assumes that juveniles are limited in their understanding of these matters; it requires that they be given special assistance from an interested adult to help them grasp the meaning of their rights and the implications of waiving them. Without such assistance, regardless of the court's assessment of the totality of the circumstances, the waiver would probably not be deemed valid.

The totality approach prevails in most U.S. courts, although some states follow the *per se* approach. The leading case on this topic is *Fare v. Michael C.* (1979), in which the Supreme Court adopted the totality approach as the constitutional standard. The defendant was a 16-year-old boy taken into custody by police and questioned about the murder of a man in Van Nuys, California. The boy had a long record of legal trouble and had been on probation in juvenile court since he was 12. Before questioning him, the police read Michael C. his *Miranda* rights but then refused his request to see his probation officer. Michael C. finally agreed to talk to them without an attorney present, and he went on to make statements and draw pictures that incriminated him in the murder. The Supreme Court held that "the totality of circumstances surrounding the interrogation" made it clear that Michael had knowingly and voluntarily waived his rights and that the statements he made could be admitted into evidence against him. The Court based its decision partly on the fact that Michael had an extensive prior police record and therefore, the Court assumed, possessed sufficient knowledge about police methods.

To evaluate adults' and juveniles' comprehension of *Miranda* warnings, Grisso (1981) conducted a series of studies that measured subjects' understanding of (1) the vocabulary and phrases used in the warnings and (2) the purposes of the rights involved. He also examined the relationships between these measures and several background characteristics of juveniles. Grisso developed three different measures of vocabulary and phrase comprehension. In addition, subjects' perceptions of the function and significance of the warnings were assessed through a structured interview in which they described their understanding of four drawings depicting scenes such as police questioning a suspect and a suspect consulting with an attorney. These measures have recently been published in a manual, so clinicians now have a standardized format for assessing juveniles' understanding and appreciation of the *Miranda* warnings (Grisso, 1998). Among the most important findings were the following:

1. At least one of the four crucial elements of the *Miranda* warning was inadequately paraphrased by 55% of the juveniles and 23% of the adults.

2. At least one of six crucial vocabulary words was completely misunderstood by 63% of the juveniles and 37% of the adults.

3. The majority of juveniles younger than 15 years had significantly poorer comprehension of the significance or function of the warnings than did the adults.

4. Prior court experience was not related to understanding of the vocabulary and phrases in the warnings, but juveniles with more court experience had a greater appreciation of the significance of *Miranda* rights.

On the basis of these results, Grisso (1981) concluded that juveniles younger than 15—and especially those 13 or younger—do not understand all of their *Miranda* rights and that they would require assistance to waive these rights knowingly. He recommended a *per se* approach that would rely on one of four special protections: (1) using a simplified *Miranda* warning appropriate for juveniles, (2) requiring a pre-interrogation screening of juveniles to assess whether they comprehend the warnings adequately, (3) requiring the presence of an interested adult to advise the juvenile during the interrogation, or (4) requiring that an attorney for the juvenile be present during the interrogation. Grisso prefers the last alternative. Data from more recent studies are consistent with Grisso's results (Goldstein, Condie, Kalbeitzer, Osman, & Geier, 2003), and these recommendations remain applicable to the youth of today.

Although juveniles 15 or older comprehended better than younger juveniles, they still showed gaps in their *Miranda* understanding (as did a substantial percentage of adults). Therefore, a *per se* approach may be justified even for older juveniles, especially if we heed the admonition in *Gault* that other courts give the "greatest care" to evaluating juveniles' waivers of rights. On the other hand, if priority is given to efficient, vigorous police investigation of crime, courts' general satisfaction with the totality standard will continue. Currently, unless a juvenile is so severely intellectually disabled or mentally disordered that he or she couldn't understand what a waiver meant, or unless it can be

© Billy E. Barnes/PhotoEdit

A juvenile offender with his attorney in court

shown that the police took improper advantage of a suspect's psychological disorder in their interrogation methods, a waiver of *Miranda* rights will probably be judged an act made with sufficient relevant capacities.

Whether one prefers a *per se* or a totality standard will also reflect the personal emphasis one places on the competing values introduced in Chapter 1. Should we provide extra protections to people who have special needs even if these protections handicap society in certain ways, or should individual rights sometimes give way to society's interest in identifying criminals and protecting itself from them?

In addition to documenting juveniles' lack of understanding about their rights, psychologists have asked how comprehension can be improved. Experience in the juvenile justice system—thought by some to provide an opportunity to learn about and assert rights—apparently falls short (Peterson-Badali & Koegl, 1998), as does assistance from parents (probably because parents' understanding of the consequence of waiving rights is no better than that of their children). After interviewing

young Canadian offenders and determining that many of them waived their right to silence and agreed to talk to police without a lawyer present, Peterson-Badali and colleagues advocated better legal education in schools, a neutral, noncoercive atmosphere during questioning, and practical advice about how to contact a lawyer (Peterson-Badali, Abramovitch, Koegl, & Ruck, 1999).

The Adjudicative Competence of Juveniles

In some respects, the adjudicative competence (also known as competence to stand trial) of juveniles is very similar to that of adults. Much of the discussion of trial competence in Chapter 8 of this book applies to both adults and juveniles, including the legal standard set forth in *Dusky v. United States* (1960): "(the defendant must have a) sufficient present ability to consult with [his] attorney with a reasonable degree of rational understanding, and . . . a rational, as well as factual understanding of the proceedings against him." As we noted in the previous section on *Miranda* waiver capacities, the important *Winship and Gault* decisions resulted in juveniles being accorded more rights when being prosecuted for criminal behavior—rights that make them more similar to adults in the course of such prosecution. In this respect, adjudicative competence for juveniles is important in the same way that *Miranda* waiver is important; if the individual being prosecuted cannot adequately carry out the necessary legal tasks, then it is not fair to proceed with such prosecution.

It is only in recent years that competence to stand trial has been considered in juvenile court. Prior to the 1990s, the issue was rarely raised (Grisso, Miller, & Sales, 1987), but a recent survey (Grisso & Quinlan, 2005) indicates that competence to stand trial is addressed in a substantial number of cases in juvenile court in 87 of the largest U.S. jurisdictions. There are probably three reasons for this increased number of referrals. First, courts and attorneys have been increasingly attentive to the legal rights of juveniles since the *Winship and Gault* decisions. Second, researchers have spent much time in the last decade considering the judgment and decision making of adolescents, and their work has yielded important information about the psychosocial maturity of adolescents as it is related to the juvenile court process (Grisso & Schwartz, 2000). Third, as we have shown, there has been an increasing trend during the last 15 years in the United States to try juveniles charged with serious crimes in adult court, which means that competence to stand trial (firmly established as a concept in adult criminal court for many years) is likely to become a consideration for younger adolescents (those under 16) both for reasons of mental/emotional disorder and for reasons of immaturity.

Do courts recognize developmental immaturity as a basis for incompetence to stand trial in juvenile court? This is not a settled question in the law, although some states have changed their statutes such that an adolescent whose adjudicative competence is impaired by immaturity, but not by mental or emotional disorder, can still be considered as possibly incompetent to stand trial (Grisso & Quinlan, 2005). The question of whether developmental

immaturity may be considered when the juvenile has been transferred to adult court is also very important, considering that current transfer laws in many states allow 14-, 13-, and 12-year-olds to be tried as adults. (In some states, even younger children can be tried as adults, because there is no lower age limit specified.) A recent study using the MacCAT-CA (see Chapter 8) with adolescents raised serious concerns about the capacities of many 13- and 14-year-old adolescents to "understand and assist" in adult court—and strongly suggested that most 12-year-olds had neither the cognitive nor the psychosocial maturity to function as reasonably effective adult criminal defendants (Grisso et al., 2003).

Considering that the legal concept of competence to stand trial is comparable between adult and juvenile court, but that the individuals being evaluated are different—both developmentally (in terms of their thinking, judgment, and maturity) and clinically—it would be helpful for the field to have a specialized measure for evaluating the competence of adolescents to stand trial. We have not yet reached the point where there is a well-validated measure (such as Grisso's *Miranda* waiver capacities tool discussed in the last section). However, Dr. Grisso (the leading researcher in the forensic evaluation of juveniles) has developed a structured approach to considering the adjudicative competence capacities of adolescents that incorporates recent developmental research in addition to other important considerations (Grisso, 2005). This approach will undoubtedly receive further research attention in the coming decade, and it presently offers important guidance for psychologists and psychiatrists who evaluate adolescents' competence to stand trial.

Children as Victims

Child Maltreatment, the Cycle of Abuse, and Abuse Prevention

Over the past 30 years, psychologists as well as the general public have become increasingly aware of the problem of child abuse and neglect. Today, the term **child maltreatment** is used to encompass various forms of child abuse and neglect, including physical abuse, sexual abuse, emotional or psychological abuse (such as habitual verbal harassment by way of disparagement, criticism, or ridicule), and neglect (the failure to provide for a child's fundamental needs).

It is difficult to know how widespread these abuses are because of the many problems involved in documenting their occurrence. But some experts point to frequencies of epidemic proportions. In 2003, Child Protective Services received 2.9 million referrals for alleged child maltreatment in the United States and, after investigation, determined that 906,000 children were victims of maltreatment. More than 60% of the victims had been neglected, approximately 20% were physically abused, and 10% had been sexually abused. Children under the age of 3 had the highest risk of victimization, and girls were slightly more likely to be victimized than boys (National Association of Counsel for Children, 2005). About 1500 children die from abuse annually in the United States, and 80% of these deaths are caused by actions of their parents (U.S. Department of Health and Human Services, 2004).

Data on the prevalence of child sexual abuse come primarily from **retrospective accounts** by adults. Some question these figures because self-reports of long-held memories can be unreliable; sometimes people claim that their memories of abuse were repressed for years. Given these caveats, between 12% and 35% of women and between 4% and 9% of men report unwanted sexual experience prior to age 18 (Putnam, 2003). Where they exist, studies of rates of child sexual abuse in other countries are comparable with those in the United States. Add to these figures the problem of victimization by peers in which boys and girls are bullied, attacked, or singled out for other forms of prolonged abuse while at school (19% of elementary students in the United States, 11% in Finland, and 50% in Ireland report such experiences [Dake, Price, & Telljohan, 2003]), and it is obvious that the majority of youth have had one or more potentially serious victimization experiences by the time they reach adulthood.

What are the effects of the physical and sexual abuse of children? The direct effects include short-term consequences such as increased mood and anxiety disorders, as well as inappropriate sexual behavior and impaired school performance (Prentky, 1999). Victims of physical abuse on average are more aggressive than nonvictims, and children who experience repeated abuse tend to be more aggressive than those who experience lower levels of maltreatment (Goodman, Emery, & Haugaard, 1998). But more concern has been raised by the possibility of long-term effects from physical and sexual child abuse—effects that include a much greater risk for developing mental disorders, suffering subsequent **revictimization** experiences, abusing drugs and alcohol, and engaging in criminal conduct. Many victims have great difficulty talking about their experiences of abuse, even as adults. Laveranues Coles, a top receiver in the National Football League, came forward with his story of devastating sexual abuse by his stepfather between the ages of 10 and 13 only after receiving unconditional support from his team, the New York Jets. Said Coles, "Some kids do look up to us. Even if it's one kid who I can touch, who my story gives him the strength to come out and say something, I feel like it's worth it."

Long-term effects of child sexual abuse are highly variable; some children show no detectable negative effects, and others show extremely harmful reactions, including symptoms of psychopathology (Saywitz, Mannarino, Berliner, & Cohen, 2000). This variability makes sense, given the highly variable nature of sexual victimization of children. In fact, as with any traumatic event, one's reaction will depend not only on characteristics of the incident but on other situational factors, such as social support and financial resources, as well as dispositional factors such as temperament, resilience, and emotional maturity. But the experience of being sexually abused as a child stays with many people throughout their lives, affecting their psychological well-being and causing significant distress later in life. Many victims experience sexual behavior problems as adolescents and adults (Loeb et al., 2002), and estimates suggest that more than half of all sexually abused children meet the criteria for posttraumatic stress disorder.

Does being abused as a child lead to criminal behavior in later years? This issue is controversial because studies that report a higher prevalence of abuse in the childhoods of aggressive adults have usually relied on retrospective methods, often using self-reported memories of abuse. It would be better, of course, to base any conclusions about the relationship between childhood abuse and adult violence on long-term *prospective* studies in which abused children are identified and then repeatedly assessed into adulthood. However, such as study could not be done without also providing assistance to the children identified as being abused (of whom there are many, tragically) and prosecuting their abusers. Of course this is as it should be, morally and legally, but it does keep researchers from fully understanding the impact of abuse on children.

Are maltreated children likely to grow up to be abusers themselves? The data show a relationship between early victimization and later abusive, sexualized, or aggressive behavior both in general and toward children—in other words, a **cycle of violence** (Goodman et al., 1998). But the relationship is not straightforward, and many abuse victims become caring, nonabusive caregivers of their offspring. Psychologists have asked why some abuse victims become abusers themselves and have attempted to discern risk factors for perpetrating child abuse and prolonging the cycle of abuse (Nietzel, Speltz, McCauley, & Bernstein, 1998). They have found that compared to nonabusers, abusive parents tend to:

- possess less knowledge about normal child development;
- hold unrealistic expectations for their children, such as the age by which they should be toilet trained;
- become easily annoyed when under stress;
- choose aggressive means of resolving conflicts;
- have limited access to social support and help with child care; and
- disagree with each other about child rearing and discipline.

One wonders whether these risks can be reduced or overcome. Several studies have shown that when parents learn more effective child management skills, abusive interactions with children are reduced. Home visitation programs have reduced (but not eliminated) child maltreatment, other violence, conduct disorders, and prenatal health risks (McFarlane, Doueck, & Levine, 2002). Abusive parents can be taught to change their behavior and learn the skills necessary to manage their children. However, child maltreatment is not caused solely by the problems of individual parents. Social factors also play a role. A comprehensive plan to reduce child abuse should combine parent training with larger-scale interventions aimed at helping families. Community day care centers to relieve mothers of child care demands and crisis intervention to help parents cope with personal stress are two examples of needed social services.

Children as Witnesses

Sometimes a child is the only witness to a crime— or its only victim. Even in some civil cases, the only dispassionate observers of accidents may be children. A number of questions arise in cases in which children are witnesses. Is it appropriate to ask children about the precise details of these incidents? Is it appropriate for them to testify in a courtroom? Can children distinguish between fact and fantasy? Is it therapeutic for children to testify against people who may have hurt them? Can suggestive interviewing techniques distort a child's report?

In keeping with the initial dilemma posed at the beginning of this book, society's desire for criminals to be prosecuted and punished demands that all relevant witnesses be allowed to testify, but defendants also have the right not to be convicted on the basis of inaccurate testimony. Can we guarantee that right when the witnesses to crimes are children?

Two separate concerns emerge here: One deals with the accuracy of children as witnesses, and the other concerns threats to their well-being that may be caused by subjecting them to the stress of testifying in court. Later in this chapter, we discuss the potentially traumatic impact of testifying. Here we turn to the issue of whether child witnesses are reliable—both as eyewitnesses to crimes and as victims of child sexual abuse.

The Reliability of Children's Eyewitness Memories

Although children interact with the legal system mostly as victims of abuse who know their perpetrators (a situation we explore in detail later in this chapter), they are sometimes called upon to identify strangers or to describe what they witnessed regarding crimes. In some instances—a kidnapping or an assault—the child may be the only witness to a crime committed by a stranger. To test children's eyewitness capabilities, researchers create situations that closely match real-life events. In these studies, children typically interact with an unknown adult (the "target") for some period of time in a school classroom or a doctor's office. They are later questioned about what they experienced and what the target person looked like, and they may attempt to make an identification from a lineup.

Two general findings emerge from these studies. First, children's narrative accounts are more accurate when they participate in an incident rather than merely observing it (Tobey & Goodman, 1992). Second, children over the age of 6 can make reasonably reliable identifications from lineups, provided that the perpetrator is actually in the lineup and that the child had extended contact with the perpetrator (Gross & Hayne, 1996). Yet many of the factors that influence adult eyewitnesses—stress, weapon focus, leading questions—affect child witnesses as well. In fact, children are generally less accurate than adults when making an identification from a lineup in which the suspect is absent. In these situations, children are more likely than adults to select someone—usually a foil—from the lineup, thereby making a "false-positive" error (Lindsay, Pozzulo, Craig, Lee, & Corber,

1997). Such mistakes are troubling to the criminal justice system because they discourage police and prosecutors from using the identification evidence of a child witness in subsequent investigations.

Psychologists have attempted to devise identification procedures for children that will maintain identification accuracy when the suspect is present in the lineup but reduce false-positive choices when the suspect is absent. Unfortunately, training tasks and instructions about the risk of false identifications and the importance of choosing no one rather than making a false identification have not been effective in reducing false-positive selections (Pozzulo & Lindsay, 1997). Children tend to make false identifications even when viewing a sequential lineup (Lindsay et al., 1997). One procedure that has shown some success is the elimination lineup, in which witnesses are asked to eliminate all but one lineup member before being asked whether that person is the perpetrator. Elimination lineups decreased false-positive responding in a group of 10- to 14-year-old children without significantly affecting correct identification rates (Pozzulo & Lindsay, 1999).

Children as Witnesses in Child Sexual Abuse Cases

The concern about a child's witnessing ability is perhaps most vexing in cases of child sexual abuse. Here the issue is not who committed the crime but, rather, what exactly happened to the child. Most child sexual abuse cases rest solely on the words of the victim, because these cases typically lack any physical evidence. (The most frequent forms of sexual abuse perpetrated on children are fondling, exhibitionism, and oral copulation.) Yet anyone who has spent time with young children knows that their descriptions of situations can sometimes be fanciful mixes of fact and fantasy. Can preschoolers and even older children be trusted to provide accurate details about what happened to them? Are they aided or hindered by the questions asked by adults? Will they readily disclose experiences of abuse? Will they accurately remember those experiences? These questions have prompted a great deal of empirical research by developmental psychologists in recent years, typically relying on staged events and interviews of the children who watched those events, or interviews with actual abuse victims. With the aid of these studies, some questions about children's witnessing abilities have now been answered.

One feature of child sexual abuse cases has emerged as crucial to the accuracy of child witnesses: the investigative interview. Good interviewers ask a child to describe the event in his or her own words before posing specific questions. ("You said there was a man. Tell me about him.") Analysis of responses to these so-called open-ended questions suggests that many preschool children recall little, even when they just witnessed the event (Fivush & Shukat, 1995), either because they are shy or because they fail to understand the questions. Older children can provide more details, of course, and although their reports are also incomplete, their free-recall accuracy tends to be fairly high (Gee & Pipe, 1995).

Some interviewers have now been trained to use a structured questioning protocol that encourages suspected sexual abuse victims to first provide details in their own words (in response to questions such as "Tell me what happened") and discourages the use of **suggestive questions** (questions that assume information not disclosed by the child or that suggest the expected answer, such as "He touched you, didn't he?"). Police officers trained in this protocol interviewed 4- to 8-year-old children who claimed that they had been abused. Most children (83%) freely disclosed their experiences in response to open-ended questions (Lamb et al., 2003). These findings suggest that central details (the "gist") of abusive experiences can be remembered well if they are elicited through the use of open-ended questions.

After a child has recounted an experience in his or her own words and in response to open-ended questions, investigators may ask specific questions about the event. For example, if a child said that she was touched, a follow-up question might be "Where were you touched?" Although children tend to provide more detail in response to

specific questions than to open-ended questions, the use of specific questions comes at a cost: Children are much less accurate in answering specific questions. This difficulty is not restricted to very young children. For example, 6-year-olds were inaccurate about one-third of the time when questioned about two videos they had just seen (Roebers & Schneider, 2002). Why are children less accurate in answering specific questions than more general queries? Specific questions demand precise memories of details that the child may never have encoded or may have forgotten (Dickinson, Poole, & Laimon, 2005). Additionally, the child may answer a question that she or he does not fully understand in order to appear to be cooperative (Waterman, Blades, & Spencer, 2001). Obviously, lack of question understanding can result in inaccurate responses. Finally, the more specific the question, the more likely it is that the interviewer will accidentally include information that the child has not stated.

A substantial number of children experience multiple incidents of sexual abuse, and although the central features of the experiences may be constant, peripheral details may change. But before prosecutors can file multiple charges, they may have to provide evidence that reflects the critical details of each separate incident. In other words, the child will be asked to "particularize" his or her report by providing precise details about each specific allegation (Dickinson et al., 2005). Can a child do this? Studies that examine children's recall of repeated events typically expose them to a series of similar incidents with certain constant features and some details that vary across episodes. Although source-monitoring (identifying the source of a memory) improves with age (Quas & Schaaf, 2002), children often recall information from one event as having occurred in another (Roberts, 2002). In fact, exposure to recurring events is a double-edged sword: Repetition enhances memory for aspects of the incident that are held constant but impairs the ability to recall details that vary with each recurrence and to match particular details to the event in which they occurred (Dickinson et al., 2005).

The Effects of Suggestive Questioning

Up to this point, we have considered only the ways in which children respond to questions that are free from contaminating influences—questions that do not suggest an answer. In some cases, children may be reluctant to disclose abusive experiences and may even deny them when asked. How, then, should these children be questioned? Some people believe that leading questions are needed to elicit reports or details from sexually abused children who feel embarrassed, ashamed, or guilty about the abuse and hesitate to talk about it. But questioning in a suggestive manner sometimes elicits false reports. In fact, many people have speculated that suggestive questioning led to the notorious allegations of bizarre and ritualistic abuse in day care centers across the country in the 1980s, including the McMartin Preschool in California, Little Rascals Day Care Center in North Carolina, Wee Care Day Nursery in New Jersey, Old Cutler Presbyterian Day Care in Florida, and the Fells Acres Daycare Center in Massachusetts (see Box 14.2). Estimates of false-positive cases (cases in which the interview of a child leads to the false allegation of sexual abuse) range from 5% to 35% (Poole & Lindsay, 1998), suggesting that up to one-third of all claims of child sexual abuse may be invalid.

How do suggestive interviewing techniques lead to the false claim of child sexual abuse? In its decision in the *Michaels* case, the New Jersey Supreme Court reasoned that the interrogations of the children revealed a lack of impartiality on the part of the interviewers and many instances in which children were asked leading questions that furnished information the children themselves had never mentioned. Consider the following exchange between an investigator and R.F., a 3-year-old girl:

>   *Detective*: Do you think Kelly can hurt you?
>   R.F.: No.
>
>   *Detective*: Did Kelly say she can hurt you? Did Kelly ever tell you she can turn into a monster?
>   R.F.: Yes.

>   *Detective*: What did she tell you?
>   R.F.: She was gonna turn into a monster.

Or this conversation between an investigator and B.M., a 6-year-old boy:

>   *Investigator*: I want to ask you something.
>   B.M.: No.
>
>   *Investigator*: Don't be a baby. You're acting like a nursery school kid. Come here. Come here . . . we're not finished yet. Sit down.
>   B.M.: No.
>
>   *Investigator*: Come here. Seriously, we are going to need your help on this.
>   B.M.: No I'm not.
>
>   *Investigator*: How do you think she hurt boys and girls, with a fork? A fork in the face? Sticking on the legs? The arms or on the neck? Does that hurt?

Note the suggestive nature of these last questions. The technique of suggestive questioning involves introducing into the interview new information that the child has not already provided. Psychologists have known for many years that suggestive questions reduce children's accuracy, and we now know that children become somewhat less susceptible to suggestion as they grow older (Poole & Lindsay, 2001). Even adults are somewhat susceptible to suggestion, however, as we noted in Chapter 5.

In the wake of the highly publicized cases of child sexual abuse in the 1980s and 1990s, researchers have focused considerable attention on how children's reports can be influenced by suggestive questioning. In particular, they have attempted to cast an empirical eye on the interview process itself in order to discover how various interviewing techniques can mold a child's responses. Although suggestive questioning is probably not the norm, it can have profound effects on a child's memory when it is used.

One factor that characterizes suggestive interviewing is **interviewer bias**. When interviewers have some preconceived notions about the occurrence or nonoccurrence of a certain event, they can

THE CASE OF

BOX 14.2 **Margaret Kelly Michaels: Real or surreal memories?**

When 26-year-old Margaret Kelly Michaels resigned from her job at the Wee Care Nursery School in Maplewood, New Jersey, in April 1985, she probably thought that her connection to Wee Care was over. Little could she have imagined the story that was about to unfold. Four days later, while having his temperature taken rectally at a doctor's office, a 4-year-old former student of Michaels told the nurse, "That's what my teacher does to me at school." That afternoon, the boy's mother notified child protective services. Two days after that the boy was questioned by a prosecutor. During the course of the interview, he inserted his finger into the rectum of an anatomical doll (a tool used by professionals to help reluctant children enact sexual acts that were allegedly perpetrated on them) and stated that two other boys had also had their temperatures taken this way. Although neither boy confirmed this claim, one of them stated that Michaels had touched his penis.

The Wee Care Nursery distributed a letter to all parents, alerting

them to the investigation of a former employee regarding "serious allegations made by a child," and encouraged them to examine their children for genital soreness and to notice any incidents of bed wetting, masturbation, nightmares, or other changes in behavior.

Various therapists and investigators interviewed the children and their families over the next two months to determine the extent of the abuse. Many of the children were interviewed several times and, after persistent questioning, began to disclose some bizarre and horrifying details: that Michaels had licked peanut butter off their genitals, played the piano while nude, made children drink her urine and eat her feces, and raped children with knives, forks, spoons, and Lego blocks. These acts were alleged to have occurred during regular school hours over the course of seven months. (Surprisingly, the acts had not been reported by the children to their parents or noticed by other staff at the time they were alleged to have occurred; neither did any

parents report unusual behavior in their children at the time.)

In 1988, Margaret Kelly Michaels was convicted of 115 counts of sexual abuse against twenty 3- to 5-year-old children and was sentenced to 47 years in prison. She served 5 years of her sentence before her conviction was reversed on grounds that the interrogations of the children were coercive and highly suggestive (*State v. Michaels*, 1994) and the prosecution dropped all charges against Michaels in 1994. Ironically, though, when Michaels tried several years later to sue the Essex County prosecutors who had so badly botched the investigatory stages of the case, a judge ruled that Michaels could not hold prosecutors liable for abiding by the law as they reasonably believed it to be. The judge noted that although the prosecutor's office had no internal instructions for interviewing child witnesses and few other guidelines for prosecutors to follow, they had acted reasonably in light of the information they possessed at the time.

frame their questions in such a way as to elicit responses from the child that are consistent with their prior beliefs. Biased interviewers would probably not ask children open-ended questions such as "What happened?" Rather, they would use specific questions that presuppose the answer. The question asked of a child in the Michaels case is a good example: "How do you think she hurt boys and girls, with a fork?" If the child does not immediately

provide the expected answer, he or she may be repeatedly questioned until that answer is given (Bruck, Ceci, & Hembrooke, 2002).

Social influence can also play a role in these interviews. Regardless of the precise nature of the questions, the manner in which those questions are asked can vary greatly. Some interviewers may be warm and supportive; others may be hostile and intimidating. Although children interviewed by a highly supportive interviewer may be more resistant to leading questions than those interviewed in an environment that lacks support (Davis & Bottoms, 2002), highly supportive interviewers can lose their impartiality if they selectively reinforce statements that are consistent with their beliefs and ignore statements that are inconsistent with those beliefs. This can happen when the interviewer gives praise, rewards, approval, or agreement to a child who says something desirable or expresses disappointment when a child says something that is undesirable.

Yet another technique used occasionally by professional interviewers involves **guided imagery** or memory work. An interviewer may first ask a child to try to remember whether a certain event occurred and then to pretend that the event *did* occur and to create a mental picture that provides details about the event. The concern here is that interviewers may ask children to imagine events that had not been reported by the children but that are suspected by the interviewer. And the very act of imagining may make the event seem real (Garry & Polaschek, 2000).

There is much support for the premise that suggestive techniques influence responses; children questioned in a suggestive manner have been led to remember events they did *not* experience—for example, getting their finger caught in a mousetrap (Ceci, Huffman, Smith, & Loftus, 1994) and seeing a thief steal food from a day care center (Bruck, Ceci, & Hembrooke, 2002)—and nonexistent details within events that they *did* experience—for example, having a man put something "yucky" in their mouths (Poole & Lindsay, 2001).

At this point you may wonder whether investigative interviews of children really encompass these practices. Do interviewers really reward children who provide the desired answer and chastise those who don't? Do they really ask child witnesses to imagine events that the children themselves have never reported? The answer is yes. Maggie Bruck and her colleagues (1998) analyzed interview transcripts provided to them by attorneys, judges, parents, and medical and mental health professionals who had concerns about the suggestive nature of

a particular interview and its potential impact on a child's report. Although Bruck and colleagues acknowledge that their sample may not be representative of the vast number of interviews conducted with children, still their description is troubling. Other evidence suggests that interviewers sometimes do use specific and leading questions and introduce into the interview information that the child had not volunteered (Lamb et al., 1996; Warren, Woodall, Hunt, & Perry, 1996). Interviews conducted in the Kelly Michaels day care case and the McMartin Preschool case included several suggestive procedures.

Some psychologists have assessed the possibility that allegations of ritualistic abuse that arose in these cases were induced by suggestive interviewing techniques (Wood et al., 1998). They performed a **content analysis** (a careful, sometimes painstaking analysis of the content of a discussion or conversation) of 14 interview transcripts from the McMartin Preschool case, 20 interviews from the Margaret Kelly Michaels case, and 20 interviews of alleged sexual abuse victims conducted by a child protective service.

To measure the type of interviewing techniques that were used in these three situations, the researchers coded each exchange (they defined an exchange as one interviewer "turn" in the interview transcript, followed by one child "turn"). They then scored each exchange for the presence or absence of several interviewing techniques, including:

- ◆ Positive consequences (giving, promising, or implying praise, approval, or other reward to a child)
- ◆ Negative consequences (criticizing or disagreeing with a child's statement)
- ◆ Inviting speculation (asking the child to offer opinions or speculations about past events or to use imagination or solve a mystery)
- ◆ Suggestiveness (introducing into the interview information that goes substantially beyond what the child has already said)

Using this framework, the researchers found that the interviews conducted in the McMartin case were characterized by positive consequences (19% of all exchanges), inviting speculation (8%), and suggestiveness (18%). Interviews in the Michaels case tended to involve positive consequences (10% of all exchanges), negative consequences (17%), and suggestiveness (18%). Contrast these numbers with interviews conducted by the child protective service: 7% of exchanges contained positive consequences, 4% implied negative consequences, 2% were suggestive, and less than 1% invited speculation.

What effect do those questioning styles have on the children's reports? Do children's reports differ when they are questioned in different ways? To find out, Sena Garven and her colleagues questioned 120 children 5 to 7 years old about a classroom visitor, using techniques employed in the McMartin interviews (Garven, Wood, & Malpass, 2000). In particular, they explored more fully the impact of positive consequences or reinforcement from interviewers (i.e., praising a child who answered "Yes" to any question). What they found was remarkable: More than one-third (35%) of children who received reinforcement from an interviewer made false allegations against a classroom visitor, whereas only 12% of control subjects (children who did not receive reinforcement) falsely implicated the visitor. Even more impressive, more than half of the children who were questioned about "fantastic" events (e.g., being flown from the school in the helicopter, being taken on a horseback ride) made false allegations, as did only 5% of controls. The false allegations persisted in a second interview, even though the reinforcement was discontinued. Moreover, even when challenged, the children insisted that the false allegations were based on their own memories. These findings suggest that reinforcement from an interviewer can make a powerful, lasting impression on a child that can lead to the inducement of false allegations.

If interviewer tactics can influence a child's responses, can the reverse also be true? In other words, can the child's behavior affect the interviewer's questioning style? More important, can individual differences in children influence the "social climate" of the interview to such an extent that the child's memory becomes distorted? These questions were posed by psychologists Livia Gilstrap and Paul Papierno, who analyzed the interviews of 38 preschool and elementary school students questioned about a magic show staged at their school (Gilstrap & Papierno, 2004). These researchers distinguished characteristics of the child that were visible, or marked (e.g., shyness, sociability, emotionality, withdrawal) from those that were invisible, or unmarked (IQ, source monitoring, suggestibility). They found that visible behaviors on the part of a child were more predictive of interviewer behavior than invisible behaviors in the child and that on occasion, the child's behavior influenced the adult's responses, which, in turn, affected subsequent responding from the child. Apparently, children can be influenced either directly by the nature of the questions posed during an interview, or indirectly by the impression they make on interviewers who then respond differently to different kinds of children.

Is Suggestive Questioning Necessary?

In light of compelling evidence that children are influenced by suggestive questioning, one might wonder whether such heavy-handed tactics are necessary. Arguably, these kinds of intrusive probes may be useful in inducing a child to disclose details about sexual abuse that he or she might not be willing to volunteer. But analyzing data from 17 studies of children with substantiated diagnoses of abuse who had not been subjected to suggestive interviewing, Kamala London and her colleagues observed that most children *did* disclose their abuse when directly asked (London, Bruck, Ceci, & Shuman, 2005). Suggestive questioning techniques were not needed to prompt the disclosures.

Suggestive questioning might be useful in cases where a child is so traumatized by the experience that he or she, in an effort to cope, represses a memory of the whole ordeal. Suggestive questions in these cases might prompt a child to recall details from an otherwise impoverished memory. But do children really repress abuse experiences? Some psychologists think so (Terr, 1991; van der Kolk, 1997). Many others believe that children remember significant details of abuse experiences and, if directly asked, can describe them. Some recent data support that position.

To study the accuracy of memory in victims of documented child sexual abuse, several developmental psychologists contacted approximately 200 adolescents and young adults who, during the 1980s, had been involved in a study of the effects of criminal prosecutions on child victims of sexual abuse. Participants had been 3 to 17 years old at the time of the original data collection (Alexander et al., 2005). All of them had been sexually abused. Upon renewing contact years later, psychologists asked questions about participants' mental health, victimization experiences, legal involvement, and maternal support, and they also provided a list of traumatic events (including child sexual abuse) and asked respondents to indicate which events happened to them and, among those events, which was the most traumatic. Respondents who designated child sexual abuse as their most traumatic experience were remarkably accurate in reporting details of their experiences. These data suggest that memory for emotional, even traumatic, victimization experiences can be quite well retained even decades after the incidents occurred.

Fortunately, not all interviews contain elements of suggestive questioning, and many interviewers are careful to avoid the controversial techniques we have described. Furthermore, professionals who interview, assess, and treat children have begun to receive training in interviewing techniques, child development, or both. But still more needs to be done. Although interviewers have been aided by the use of professionally designed **protocols** for interviewing children (Lamb et al., 2003; Orbach et al., 2000), some of the training programs have apparently fallen short (Doris, Mazur, & Thomas, 1995), and many interrogators lack up-to-date information about the latest scientific findings related to interviewing. Unfortunately, until professionals begin to incorporate research findings into their practices, we will continue to wonder about the reliability of the children's testimony.

The Child Witness in the Courtroom

Although only a small percentage of sexual abuse cases actually result in a trial (many more end in admissions of guilt or plea bargains), tens of thousands of children have to testify in sexual abuse trials each year. A disproportionate number of them may be preschool children. In one study of child witnesses in sexual abuse cases, although only 18% of these cases involved children 5 years old or younger, 41% of all the cases that went to trial involved children of this age (Gray, 1993).

The traditional legal view of children, supported by early research that focused on children's *incapacities*, was that young children were not reliable witnesses because they had limited memory capabilities and could not distinguish truth from falsehood or fact from fantasy. Thus, for many years, American courts were reluctant to accept the uncorroborated statements of child witnesses. As a result, children under a certain age were not permitted to testify in court (Perry & Wrightsman, 1991). More recently, developmental psychologists have suggested that early studies may have underestimated children's abilities because of the unnecessarily complicated assessment tasks those studies used (Saywitz & Lyon, 1998). In fact, it appears that children as young as 3 years of age may be able to show that they understand the meaning of truth and lying if they can demonstrate that understanding in an age-appropriate way. Thus, whether a child is allowed to testify is now determined more by the child's linguistic repertoire, ability to distinguish a truth from a lie, and willingness to speak than by age. In fact, most jurisdictions allow children to testify regardless of the nature of the crime or the child's age and expect that juries will accord the child's testimony its appropriate weight.

How *do* jurors perceive child witnesses? Do they tend to doubt the truthfulness of children's testimony, reasoning that children often make things up and leave things out? Or do they tend to "believe the children," as a popular bumper sticker would like us to do?

In mock jury studies, child bystander witnesses are generally viewed as less credible than

A child witness, 12-year-old Quinlan Junta, testifying during his father's trial on charges stemming from a fight between Thomas Junta and fellow hockey father, Michael Costin, that resulted in Costin's death.

adult bystander witnesses, although the age of the witness apparently does not influence judgments of the defendant's guilt (Goodman, Golding, Helgeson, Haith, & Michelli, 1987). But something quite different happens in child sexual abuse cases. Here, younger victims are viewed as *more* credible than adolescents or adults, probably because jurors suspect that younger children lack the sexual knowledge to fabricate an allegation (Bottoms & Goodman, 1994). Jurors may also be cognizant of the effects of suggestive questioning; mock jurors who read a transcript of the child's forensic interview and heard other evidence in the case tended to discount the child's testimony when it had been elicited through a highly suggestive interview (Castelli, Goodman, & Ghetti, 2005).

Procedural Modifications When Children Are Witnesses

We have already noted many issues related to the reliability of children's testimony. An equally troubling concern is the effect *on the child* of having to

discuss these difficult issues in court. Talking about atrocities in a public setting may increase the trauma for many children. Some children can, in private session, describe in graphic detail how they were abused. But when these children find themselves in a courtroom full of strangers, a judge in a long black robe, a jury, and the person accused of harming them, they can become speechless, evasive, or immobilized by fear (Goodman et al., 1992). They may feel that they are being victimized all over again. Especially when children know their abuser, they may experience tremendous conflict. They may be frightened by an attacker who has threatened them with further abuse. Defense lawyers may try to intimidate the child. In fact, one study found that 8- to 10-year-olds interviewed in a courtroom had poorer memory performance and gave higher stress ratings than children questioned at their school (Saywitz & Nathanson, 1993).

These concerns have been addressed in various ways. One innovation to protect children from the potential stress of testifying is the placement of a one-way screen in front of the defendant so that he or she can't be seen by the child witness while the latter testifies. This type of screen was used in the trial of John Avery Coy, who was convicted of sexually assaulting two 13-year-old girls while they were sleeping outdoors in a tent. At the trial, a screen was placed in front of Coy when the two girls testified. (He was able to see the girls, but they could not see him.) Coy appealed his conviction on two grounds: (1) that the presence of the screen caused the jury to presume that he was guilty and (2) that the screen deprived him of the opportunity to confront the girls face-to-face. In a 1988 decision, the Supreme Court agreed with Coy about the second claim; by a 6–2 vote, it overturned his conviction, saying that the defendant's Sixth Amendment constitutional right to confront his accusers face-to-face was not outweighed "by the necessity of protecting the victims of sexual abuse" (*Coy v. Iowa*, 1988).

Justices Blackmun and Rehnquist dissented; they stated that the right to cross-examination (which Coy still had) was central to the Sixth Amendment's confrontation clause, whereas the right to a face-to-face confrontation was only peripheral (Hans, 1988). Their minority opinion reflected the fact that child victims could be psychologically injured even more by having to testify as they faced their alleged abusers. The dissent also noted that such concerns "may so overwhelm the child as to prevent the possibility of effective testimony, thereby undermining the truth finding function of the trial itself." In the *Coy* decision, the Court left the door open for a state to use one-way closed-circuit television (CCTV) to present the testimony of a child unable to testify in open court. In the case of *Maryland v. Craig* (1990), the Court upheld a Maryland law permitting such a procedure when the trial court has found that the child is likely to suffer significant emotional distress not just by testifying in court but specifically by being in the presence of the defendant. *Craig* thus modifies the rule of the *Coy* case.

Proponents of CCTV claim that aside from reducing the trauma experienced by the child, this technology will also provide more complete and accurate reports. Opponents claim that the use of CCTV erodes the presumption of innocence (the child witness does not need to be protected from the accused unless the accused is actually guilty) and violates the defendant's right to face-to-face confrontation of witnesses. (The Sixth Amendment right to confrontation is based in part on the assumption that the witness will find it more difficult to lie about the defendant in the presence of that defendant.)

Gail Goodman and her colleagues conducted an elaborate study to test these ideas (Goodman et al., 1998). Each child in this study individually played with an unfamiliar male confederate. In the "defendant guilty" condition, the confederate helped the children place stickers on bare skin (e.g., the children's arm, toes, bellybutton). In the "defendant not guilty" condition, the confederate helped the children place stickers on their clothes. Each child then testified in a separate mock trial held in a courtroom. The child's testimony was presented either live in open court or via CCTV. Mock jurors viewed the trials, rated the child witness and the defendant, and deliberated to a verdict.

The use of CCTV had varying effects: It generally promoted more accurate testimony in children (young children who testified in open court made more errors in response to leading questions) and reduced the children's pretrial experience of stress, yet it had no effect on the likelihood of conviction or perceptions of fairness to the defendant. On the basis of these findings alone, one might argue for its use in every case in which a child feels anxious about testifying. But things aren't quite so simple. Children who testified via CCTV were viewed as less believable than children who testified in open court, despite the fact that they were more accurate. It appears that jurors want to see children in person in order to assess the truthfulness of their reports. Clearly, the impact of CCTV on jurors' decisions in child sexual abuse cases is complex; perhaps it should be reserved for cases in which the prospect of testifying in open court is so terrifying to children that they would become inept witnesses. In most cases, however, testimony taken in an adjoining room and shown to jurors via CCTV is preferable to no testimony at all.

Courts have made several other accommodations in cases in which children must testify. These include providing the child with an advocate who can familiarize the child with the courtroom setting, permitting a support person to sit with the child during testimony, making structural changes to the courtroom, and, on rare occasions, closing the courtroom to the public and the press (Myers, 1996).

Finally, we should note that although testifying has the potential to inflict further trauma on the child, it can also be a beneficial, therapeutic experience for some children. It can engender a sense of control over events and provide some satisfaction to the child if the defendant is found guilty. As an example, one 15-year-old girl said, "If I, as a young person, were a victim of a sexual abuse or rape case, I would *want* to testify before a full court. I might be scared at first or a little embarrassed, but I'd want to be present to make my assailant look like a complete fool. I'd want to see him convicted—with my own eyes. It would make me stronger" (quoted in Gunter, 1985, p. 12A).

Juveniles' Right to Self-determination

For most of recorded history, children were considered the property of their parents, valued for the economic benefits they could provide to families. They toiled in fields and factories for long hours to enhance the family's assets. Only since the mid-1800s have children been recognized as needing protection and nurturance, and only recently have we begun to regard minors as fully developed young people who possess certain rights of self-determination (Schmidt & Reppucci, 2002). Whereas **nurturance rights** focus on a child's entitlement to protection, sustenance, and other benefits (including the benevolent orientation of juvenile courts), **self-determination rights** allow juveniles to exercise control over their environments and make independent choices about their well-being.

Some commentators point to the case *Tinker v. Des Moines* (1969) as the first instance in which the U.S. Supreme Court recognized a child's right to self-determination. The issue here was whether children—expelled from school for wearing black armbands to protest the Vietnam War—possessed the fundamental right to freedom of speech. (Interestingly, some of the children were only 8 years old at the time, leading others to question whether the children were simply reflecting the sentiments of their parents.) In his majority opinion, Justice Abe Fortas recognized that "students in school as well as out of school are 'persons' under our Constitution" (p. 511), implying that they should be accorded the same rights as adults.

Whereas people have generally favored extending nurturance rights to children, there is ambivalence about whether juveniles should have self-determination rights. Should they be allowed to make their own decisions about accepting medical treatments, or should parents retain the right to make decisions on their behalf? In recent years, states have gradually begun to recognize the self-determination rights of juveniles, and many have passed laws that allow minors to give consent and make their own decisions about accepting certain forms of treatment (e.g., for substance abuse, pregnancy prevention, and sexually transmitted diseases).

Particularly contentious is the debate about an adolescent's right to self-determination in the decision to have an abortion. Many states require some sort of parental involvement in this decision, either in the form of **parental notification** (one or both parents must be notified prior to the adolescent having an abortion) or **parental consent** (one or both parents must explicitly permit the adolescent to have an abortion). In fact, most adolescents seek the advice and counsel of their parents even without these mandates, but certain situations—those involving incest or abusive or absent parents, for example—may make it impossible to secure their consent. Some adolescents fear negative consequences related to informing their parents of their pregnancy and desire to abort.

One of the first Supreme Court cases to consider the issue of parental involvement in an adolescent's decision about abortion was *Planned*

Parenthood of Central Missouri v. Danforth (1976). Here, the Supreme Court deemed unconstitutional a Missouri law that required a minor to have parental consent for an abortion during the first trimester of pregnancy. Since then, states have fashioned statutes that provide alternative means for seeking an abortion in situations where parental consent is unavailable. One procedure, known as judicial bypass, gives an adolescent the opportunity to go before a judge to demonstrate either that she is mature enough to make the decision on her own or that it is in her best interest to obtain an abortion. This is a cumbersome procedure and may require fortitude on the part of the adolescent, but in practice, judges rarely deny such requests (Crosby & English, 1991). The Supreme Court has generally upheld statutes that require parental notification as long as they provide for some kind of judicial bypass (*Hodgson v. Minnesota*, 1990). In general, state laws regulating adolescent abortion have become more restrictive in recent years.

The stated rationale of most parental involvement laws is twofold: to protect adolescents from making rash or adverse decisions about their pregnancies and to promote family functioning by involving parents in their daughters' decision and care. Implicit in this rational are a number of assumptions about adolescents and abortion, including the notion that abortions might be particularly harmful to adolescents, that teens are not capable of making independent, informed choices, and that family communication is enhanced by involving parents in the abortion decision (Adler, Ozer, & Tschann, 2003). Fortunately, research psychologists have examined each of these issues, and their data can cast light on these assumptions.

Do adolescents suffer serious psychological harm from an abortion? Alhough there are only minimal psychological risks associated with abortion generally (Alder & Dolcini, 1986), one might imagine that a teenager, with a less well-developed sense of self and fewer emotional and financial resources, might be adversely affected. One group of researchers followed 360 adolescents for two years after they were interviewed at a pregnancy clinic; some of these young women terminated their

pregnancies, others carried to term. The adolescents who underwent abortions actually fared better than those who gave birth: They experienced less anxiety over the course of the study and had a stronger internal locus of control. They were more likely to be in school or to graduate from high school, were less likely to get pregnant again, and fared better economically (Zabin, Hirsch, & Emerson, 1989). Other studies suggest that minors do not differ appreciably from adults in their reactions to abortion (e.g., Quinton, Major, & Richards, 2001).

A second rationale for involving parents in an adolescent's abortion decision stems from the belief that teens are not competent to make informed decisions—that they lack the ability to understand the complex issues involved or forecast the long-term consequences of their choices. Indeed, we have already seen that juvenile defendants may lack adjudicative competence (Grisso & Schwartz, 2000). But some commentators have argued that competence is domain specific; that performance in one area does not necessarily generalize to performance in other areas, and that the competencies needed to assist in one's defense at trial are different from those needed to decide about pregnancy (Adler, Ozer, & Tschann, 2003). They also suggest that adolescents seeking abortion may have more psychological and social resources at their disposal than youthful offenders, who have higher than average rates of mental disorder (Kazdin, 2000).

What have psychologists learned about the competence of adolescents to make decisions regarding abortion? Do young people differ from adults in their decision-making processes? The available data do not suggest that there are meaningful differences between adolescents and adults in the quality of their decisions about abortion. For example, one study compared the decision processes of three groups of young women who sought a pregnancy test: 14–15-year-olds, 16–17-year-olds, and 18–21-year-olds (legal adults). Some were considering abortion, and others planned to give birth. Their interviews with a pregnancy counselor were evaluated on several dimensions, including quality of reasoning, awareness of the consequences of various decisions, and factors considered in reaching a decision. Among those considering abortion, neither of the adolescent groups differed from the legal adults on any of these measures (Ambuel & Rappaport, 1992).

Finally, we consider the assumption that parental involvement will enhance family communication and promote family functioning. Some health care providers worry about physical or emotional harm that could come to some adolescents who are forced to involve parents in the abortion decision (Council and Ethical and Judicial Affairs, 1993). When adolescents have been asked why they do not want to tell their parents, they cite fears about disappointing and angering them, as well as concerns about punishment and physical violence (Henshaw & Kost, 1992). Adolescents whose parents found out about their pregnancy indirectly reported more adverse consequences than adolescents who volunteered this information to their parents (Henshaw & Kost, 1992).

In general, then, when psychologists have cast an empirical eye on the assumptions underlying parental involvement requirements, they have seen little support in their data. Without a doubt, parental support is desirable and of great comfort to many young, pregnant women, but there is little evidence that adolescents *need* parental involvement. Even so, given the contentious political climate and the moral issues surrounding abortion, it is not surprising that the findings from empirical research studies have been largely overlooked.

Children in Nontraditional Families

In her essay entitled "Definitions of Family: Who's In, Who's Out, and Who Decides," Harvard Law School professor Martha Minow pondered what constellation of people, connected through what kinds of relationships, constitutes a family (Minow, 1993). These "Leave it to Beaver"-like families are now a relic of the past. Whereas legal rules might define a family as a married couple

with children either born to them or adopted by them, this definition fails to account for the myriad groupings of people who function as families today.

The majority of American households in the 1950s fit the stereotype of a breadwinner father, stay-at-home mother, and their offspring. As we pointed out in Chapter 9, that situation is now a relic of the past. These days, half of all children will live in a single-parent household at some point during their childhood, and a third of all Americans will live in some sort of stepfamily arrangement during their lifetime. Nearly 7 million Americans come from mixed-race families, and approximately 10 million children in the United States now live with gay, lesbian, or bisexual parents. Conventional images of family are giving way to nontraditional groupings of adults and children who provide family-like support (and family-like dissension) for one another. Of particular interest, given current controversies over same-sex marriage, is an increase in the number of families headed by gays and lesbians.

Shortly after Massachusetts became the first state in the United States to recognize **same-sex marriage** (often referred to as gay marriage) in 2003, Provincetown town clerk Doug Johnstone was inundated with phone calls and e-mail messages, asking how, when, and where marriage licenses could be obtained. One of the first licenses issued by Johnstone's office was his own, as he and his partner of 25 years made it official in the eyes of the Commonwealth.

Same-sex marriages and **civil unions** (a legal arrangement that grants same-sex couples access to most of the benefits enjoyed by married opposite-sex couples) have emerged as two of the most contentious social issues of recent times. Gay marriage is legal in four countries: Canada, Belgium, The Netherlands, and Spain. In the United States, gays and lesbians have pushed for the legal protections accorded to married couples in such areas as health insurance, hospital visitation privileges, social security survivor benefits, and child custody. But only Massachusetts recognizes same-sex marriage (in 2005, a bill to allow gay marriage was passed by the

California legislature but vetoed by Governor Schwarzenegger), although two states (Vermont and Connecticut) allow civil unions, and in three other states (Hawaii, Maine, and New Jersey) same-sex couples enjoy some of the benefits accorded to opposite-sex couples. The advent of gay marriage has also ushered in a countermovement to endorse the traditional marriage of a union between a man and a woman: Several states have constitutional amendments that bar same-sex marriage, and more than one-quarter of the states have laws that define marriage as the union of two people of opposite sexes.

Apart from the legal issues that swirl around same-sex marriage, gay and lesbian couples have lived together in committed, monogamous relationships for years and have raised families. Many gays and lesbians function as single parents to their children. Psychologists have asked whether and how children raised in these families differ from those raised by heterosexual parents.

Parenting arrangements in families headed by gays and lesbians arise in one of two ways: Lesbian and gay parents either had children in a previous heterosexual relationship or opted to have children in the context of an already established gay or lesbian identity. Children are born to lesbian mothers through artificial insemination at a clinic or through self-insemination with donated sperm. Some gay men have co-parenting arrangements with lesbian mothers (with or without any biological connection to the child); others become fathers through surrogacy agreements.

The legal landscape for families of gays and lesbians is in considerable flux. A handful of states have reenacted laws in recent years that prohibit lesbian and gay couples from adopting minor children, and a parent's sexual orientation is sometimes considered in custody and visitation arrangements. One such case, *Bottoms v. Bottoms* (1995), is described in Box 14.3.

Courts that have denied or restricted custody or visitation on the basis of a parent's sexual orientation have generally cited three main concerns about children reared by gay and lesbian parents: the children's sexual identity, their personal development, and, as in the *Bottoms* case, their relationships with

other children (Patterson, Fulcher, & Wainwright, 2002). Research psychologists and other social scientists have data on each of these issues. Most of their studies compared children reared by divorced heterosexual mothers with children raised by divorced lesbian mothers, although a few have examined children raised by gay fathers or born to gay or lesbian parents. Data from these studies can address concerns about the sexual identity, personal development, and peer relations of children raised in gay and lesbian households.

There are actually three facets to **sexual identity**: gender identity (self-identification as a male or female), sexual orientation (choice of sexual partners), and gender-role behavior (how much one conforms to cultural norms of masculinity and femininity). Research has examined the possibility that children raised by gay and lesbian parents experience disruptions in each of these three areas. In general, though, studies have failed to uncover any significant impact of parents' sexual orientation on children's sexual identity or gender-role behavior (e.g., Tasker, 2005). For example, children of gays and lesbians tend to prefer the same sorts of toys, games, activities, and friends as children of heterosexual parents.

Are children of lesbians and gay men more likely than children reared by heterosexuals to choose same-sex partners? From interviews conducted with a group of teenagers, half of whom were raised by lesbians and half by heterosexual women, Huggins (1989) concluded that the great majority of children reared by a gay or lesbian parent self-identify as heterosexual. Studies of children raised by gay men point to the same conclusion. For example, more than 90% of gay fathers who were asked whether their sons older than 17 were heterosexual, gay, or bisexual reported that they were heterosexual. Sons of half of these fathers were questioned as well and confirmed the data supplied by their fathers (Bailey, Bobrow, Wolfe, & Mikach, 1995). None of the environmental factors that *might* be related to sons' sexual orientation (the number of years they had lived with their gay fathers, their acceptance of their fathers' gay identity, or the quality of the father–son relationship)

THE CASE OF

BOX 14.3   *Bottoms v. Bottoms*: **Children of gays and lesbians**

This case pitted a lesbian daughter against her mother over the questions of whether the daughter's sexual orientation (among other things) rendered her unfit to be a parent and whether her lesbianism had adverse effects on her child. Sharon Bottoms gave birth to a son, Tyler, in 1991. Two years later, Bottoms's mother, Pamela, who had a significant caregiver role in Tyler's life, petitioned a Virginia court to remove Tyler from Sharon's custody and award temporary custody to her, claiming that "the infant is currently living in an environment which is harmful to his mental and physical well-being." At the hearing, evidence was presented that the mother, "although devoted to her son, refuses to subordinate her own

desires and priorities to the child's welfare. For example, the mother disappears for days without informing the child's custodian of her whereabouts. She moves her residence from place to place, relying on others for support, and uses welfare funds to "do" her fingernails before buying food for the child. . . . The mother has difficulty controlling her temper [and] neglects to change and cleanse the child" (*Bottoms v. Bottoms*, p. 108).

Citing this evidence as well as "immoral conduct" related to lesbianism, the trial court awarded custody to the grandmother and restricted the mother to visitation rights, a decision that was affirmed by the Virginia Supreme Court. They ruled that the evidence was sufficient to support the trial

court's finding that the mother was an unfit parent and that the child's best interests would be promoted by awarding custody to his grandmother.

Although this decision did not include a *per se* ruling that a lesbian mother is an unfit parent, it did note that courts should consider the fact that "conduct inherent in lesbianism" is punishable as a felony in Virginia. The opinion also stated that "living daily under conditions stemming from active lesbianism practiced in the home may impose a burden upon a child by reason of the "social condemnation" attached to such an arrangement, which will inevitably afflict the child's relationships with its peers and the community at large" (p. 102).

predicted the sons' sexual orientation. Bailey and colleagues conclude that there may be a small effect of genetic transmission on sexual orientation.

Certain aspects of a child's personal development—self-esteem, psychological well-being, moral judgment, and intelligence—have been thought to be affected by a parent's sexual orientation. Some people worry that children of homosexuals will be exposed to prejudice because of their family structure and that this will make them vulnerable to emotional distress. But these claims lack empirical support (Tasker, 2005). In many respects, psychosocial development in children raised by gay and lesbian parents is comparable to that of children raised by heterosexual parents. For example, when teachers were asked to report on the psychological adjustment of young children, those children raised in lesbian-headed homes were viewed no differently from children

reared in heterosexual homes. Studies that tracked these children into early adulthood also showed no differences between the groups in psychological well-being (Tasker & Golombok, 1997), although adolescents who perceived high levels of stigma associated with their mothers' sexual identity experienced reduced self-esteem (Gershon, Tschann, & Jemerin, 1999). Children born to lesbian mothers and children born to heterosexual mothers did not differ in psychological adjustment as reported by both teachers and parents (Flaks, Ficher, Masterpasqua, & Joseph, 1995).

In the *Bottoms* case (Box 14.3), the Virginia Supreme Court raised concerns that children of lesbian parents experience difficulty in social relations and face social condemnation from their peers. Other courts have made similar assumptions. How children deal with the social stigma of homosexuality depends on how much the parent self-identifies as gay or lesbian, how much the child identifies with the parent, the child's age, where the child lives, and whether the child lives with the gay or lesbian parent. Some anecdotal data do reflect children's worries about being stigmatized by their friends as a result of their parents' sexual orientation (Pollack & Vaughn, 1987).

Although data on this topic are sparse, there is little evidence that children raised by lesbian mothers experience difficulty in their peer rela-tions or excessive harassment from those peers. When asked whether they had experienced teasing or bullying during their high school years, young adults from lesbian-led families were no more likely than those from heterosexual single-parent families to report feeling stigmatized by their peers during adolescence. However, the daughters, and particularly the sons, of lesbian mothers were more likely than those in the comparison group to recollect peer group teasing about their *own* sexuality (Tasker & Golombok, 1997).

SUMMARY

1. *What are the characteristics of juvenile courts and how has juvenile justice changed in recent years?* Children under 18 who commit crimes are usually prosecuted in juvenile courts, where they are treated less harshly than adults who have committed the same crime. Historically, the objective was rehabilitation rather than punishment; presently, most jurisdictions stress public safety, accountability for the offending, and building competencies to reduce reoffense risk. Adolescents who commit serious crimes may be transferred to adult courts and treated the same as adults. In some states, there is no minimum age for such transfer.

2. *What are the short-term and long-term effects of child maltreatment?* Short-term effects include an increased propensity for mood and anxiety disorders, inappropriate sexual behavior, and (for victims of physical abuse) increased aggressiveness. Although highly variable, long-term consequences can include psychological disorders, repeat victimization experiences, and criminality later in life.

3. *Can children accurately report on their experiences of victimization? What factors affect the accuracy of their reports?* Psychologists are concerned by the possibility that suggestive interviewing techniques can influence the accuracy of a child's report of abuse. When children are questioned in a nonsuggestive manner, are asked open-ended questions, and are given little or no reinforcement for their answers, the resulting report will be more accurate than when suggestive interrogation procedures are used.

4. *Contrast nurturance rights and self-determination rights. What do the data suggest about adolescents' capacities to make their own treatment decisions?* Historically, children were thought to be property of their parents with few rights of their own. Gradually, their rights to be nurtured and protected by adults, their so-called nurturance rights, were recognized. Recently, juveniles have been allowed to exercise control over their environments and make independent choices about their well-being, reflecting a concern about rights to self-determination. Psychological research data show that adolescents are generally capable of making reasoned decisions about their own treatment.

5. *How has the traditional family structure changed and how do children fare when raised in households headed by gays and lesbians?* Many fewer families mirror the stereotypic nuclear family of the past. These days, children are more likely to live in single-parent households and be part of stepfamily arrangements. Children raised in families headed by gays and lesbians appear comparable to children reared by heterosexual parents: They tend to self-identify as heterosexual, their psychosocial development is like that of other children, and there is little evidence that they experience difficulty in peer relations.

KEY TERMS

child maltreatment

civil union

content analysis

cycle of violence

guided imagery

interviewer bias

juvenile courts

nurturance rights

parens patriae

parental consent

parental notification

protocols

retrospective
accounts

revictimization

same-sex marriage

self-determination
rights

sexual identity

social influence

suggestive questions

transfer laws

waiver

ORIENTING QUESTIONS

1. *What are the purposes of punishment?*
2. *How are the values of discretion and fairness reflected in sentencing decisions?*
3. *What factors influence sentencing decisions?*
4. *What special factors are considered in the sentencing of repeat sex offenders?*
5. *How is the death penalty decided by juries?*
6. *What legal rights do prisoners have?*

Although crime rates have declined in recent years, no other industrialized country except Russia incarcerates its citizens at the rate of the United States. According to United States Department of Justice statistics, on December 31, 2003, there were over 2 million people in prisons and jails and an additional 4.8 million people on probation or parole. The comparable figures for 1995 are 1.5 million in prisons and jails and 3.7 million on probation or parole. At the end of 2003, about 3.2% of the population—1 in 32 adults—were incarcerated or on probation or parole (Bureau of Justice Statistics, 2003b). African Americans are much more likely to be in the correctional system than whites; a 2005 press release of the Bureau of Justice estimates that they are five times more likely (Bureau of Justice Statistics, 2005b), and a 2002 report by Human Rights Watch (www.hrw.org/press/2002) indicated that they were seven times more likely to be incarcerated. Drug offenders account for much of the increase in incarceration rates; in just 17 years, from 1980 to 1997, the rate of incarceration of drug offenders increased tenfold (Blumstein & Beck, 1999). Expanded use of mandatory prison sentences and the gradual disappearance of parole have also increased the rates of incarceration.

What can be done about crime? How should we respond to individual criminals? With an inmate population over 2 million, does it make sense to continue locking up more offenders every year? Incarceration comes at a price; every dollar spent on corrections means one less dollar for public schools, health care, parks, and higher education (assuming a fixed budget—but Congress often seems more inclined to maintain and increase spending for crime control and national security than for education and health care). As an example, adjusting for inflation, state spending for prisons increased 30% from 1987 to 1995, while state spending on higher education declined 18% in the same period (Caplow & Simon, 1999).

Crime Control and the Purposes of Punishment

We described two models of the criminal justice system in Chapter 1: the due process model and the crime control model. The latter, which has heavily influenced police, prosecutors, and many judges over the past 25 years, interprets the primary aim of law enforcement as the apprehension and punishment of criminals. Its major purpose is to punish offenders so that they will not repeat their offenses and others will be deterred from similar acts.

Punishment of criminals, whether by community service, fines, or imprisonment, can have several purposes. At least seven different goals have been identified (see, for example, Greenberg & Ruback, 1984):

1. *General deterrence.* The punishment of an offender—and the subsequent publicity that comes with it—are assumed to discourage other potential lawbreakers. Some advocates of the death penalty, for example, believe that fear of death may be our strongest motivation; hence, they believe the death penalty serves as a general deterrent to murder.

2. *Individual deterrence.* Punishment of the offender is presumed to keep that person from committing other crimes in the future. Some theories assume that many criminals lack adequate internal inhibitors; hence, punitive sanctions must be used to teach them that their behavior will be controlled—if not by them, then by society.

3. *Incapacitation.* If a convicted offender is sent to prison, society can feel safe from that felon while he or she is confined. One influential position (Wilson, 1975) sees a major function of incapacitation as simply to age the criminal—an understandable goal, given that many more crimes are committed by the young than by the old and that the rate of offending declines with age.

4. *Retribution.* Society believes that offenders should not benefit from their crimes; rather,

they should receive their "just desserts." The moral cornerstone of punishment is that it should be administered to people who deserve it as a consequence of their misdeeds.

5. *Moral outrage.* Punishment can give society a means of catharsis and relief from the feelings of frustration, hurt, loss, and anger that result from being victims of crime; it promotes a sense of satisfaction that offenders have paid for what they have done to others.

6. *Rehabilitation.* One hope in sentencing has always been that offenders will recognize the error of their ways and develop new skills, values, and lifestyles so that they can return to normal life and become law-abiding. Rehabilitation as a goal received a boost from an influential book by the psychiatrist Karl Menninger (1966). In *The Crime of Punishment*, Menninger proposed that criminals are capable of change if they are placed in humane prisons. However, the data generally indicate that correctional rehabilitation has not been as effective as Menninger theorized.

7. *Restitution.* Wrongdoers should compensate victims for their damages and losses. Typical statutes require judges, in imposing a criminal sentence, to make defendants pay for victims' out-of-pocket expenses, property damage, and other monetary losses. Restitution is often a condition of probation.

Most of these goals are **utilitarian**: They are intended to accomplish a useful outcome, such as compensating the victim, deterring crime, or incapacitating or rehabilitating the defendant. Two of the goals, however, involve looking back at the offense and determining what the criminal "deserves" as a consequence of committing it. These goals are retribution (or "just desserts") and moral outrage, a close cousin of retribution (Kaplan, 1996).

The stark contrast between utilitarian and **retributive** approaches begs the question of why we punish people. What are our motives for punishing others? How might one begin to research this question? One possibility is simply to ask people which

philosophy they prefer and to assume that they can report their true beliefs. But in studies that measured people's agreement with various sentencing policies, people tended to agree with all of them (Anderson & MacCoun, 1999)! Furthermore, people are sometimes unaware of the factors that influence their preferences (Wilson, 2002). An alternative research design involves considering the length of sentences that judges actually order and working backward from these sentences to discern the underlying motives (i.e., just desserts, deterrence, incapacitation). But this method can be fallible, too.

The punishment motives of ordinary people were assessed by Carlsmith, Darley, and Robinson (2002) using an innovative research technique called **policy capturing**. The specific motives for punishment that they contrasted were just desserts (focusing on atonement for the harm committed) and deterrence (focusing on preventing future harms). Using scenarios that described a variety of harmful actions, the researchers attempted to understand (or "capture") the policies underlying the punishments that people assigned. They varied different elements of the crimes described, elements that should or should not matter to respondents depending on which motive they preferred. (For example, the seriousness of the offense should matter to people who are motivated by just desserts, and the difficulty of detecting the crime should matter to those who are concerned with future deterrence.) Carlsmith and his colleagues then measured the degree to which each respondent's sentence was influenced by these variables. The data showed a high sensitivity to factors associated with just desserts and relative insensitivity to factors associated with deterrence. Apparently, people's preferences focus on their retrospective sense of what punishment is appropriate for a given harm—that is, what an offender deserves. It would be interesting to know whether judges' underlying motives in sentencing are comparable.

Although the original purpose of prisons was to rehabilitate (the root of the word *penitentiary* is *penitent*, and many prisons are still called *correctional* institutions), it is now assumed that prisons are not very effective at rehabilitating offenders. This opinion, which in its extreme form was dubbed the "nothing works" position, first appeared in a review article about rehabilitation by Robert Martinson (1974). After reviewing a large number of outcome studies, Martinson concluded that most attempts at offender rehabilitation fail. Although it is now recognized that this conclusion was too pessimistic—Martinson (1979) himself revised his opinion and acknowledged that there is more evidence supporting rehabilitation than he originally believed—the "nothing works" view has prevailed among many politicians, policymakers, and the public at large (Haney, 1997b).

When rehabilitation was the dominant goal, criminal sentences were expected to accomplish something other than incarceration and punishment. In the 21st century, however, rehabilitation as a goal of sentencing has lost much of its popular appeal. As the goal of rehabilitation has fallen into disrepute, criminal sentences have become longer, and prison conditions have grown harsher. It now appears that the public wants to punish convicts, and politicians are happy to respond. Sheriff Joe Arpaio of Maricopa County, Arizona (Phoenix), is a "get tough" icon. His philosophy, which has gained him national publicity and notoriety, is to make jail so unpleasant that no one would want to come back—while simultaneously saving money. When he took office, he put prisoners in "leaky, dilapidated military-surplus tents set on gravel fields surrounded by barbed wire" and fed them "bologna streaked with green and blue packaging dye" (Morrison, 1995). He put prisoners on chain gangs in black and white striped uniforms (as in the movie "Oh Brother, Where Art Thou?") and claimed credit on his website for the first woman's chain gang—an "equal opportunity" chain gang ("Joe Arpaio," 2004). Sheriff Arpaio said that he did not consider the chain gangs to be punishment but, rather, a "form of rehabilitation," a way "to help inmates contribute to the community and do something productive." He claimed that "rather than being a source of public humiliation that critics claim, chain gangs are a hit with the inmates." The chain gangs do public service work, including burying indigents in the county cemetery ("Joe Arpaio," 2004).

First introduced in the House of Representatives in 1995, and kept alive in subsequent Congresses, the "No Frills Prisons Act" would require states receiving federal money to eliminate "luxurious" prison conditions, which include unmonitored telephone calls, in-cell television viewing, personally owned computers, in-cell coffee pots, weight-lifting equipment, and practice on any musical instrument for more than an hour a day. For violent offenders, the bill would require states to deny all television and more than an hour a day spent in sports or exercise. Because they must run the institutions in which these punitive measures would be implemented, correctional officials are appalled at the prospect of prisons full of idle men denied opportunities for recreation, education, and entertainment. "Take away television, they say, and you take away a legitimate means of occupying an inmate's time and mind. Without that diversion . . . prisons will have to hire more guards, which means more money from taxpayers" (Curriden, 1995, p. 74).

Jails and prisons are generally designed to punish, not to rehabilitate. Authority is centralized, communication is formalized, and rules are strictly maintained. The original purpose of prisons included the goal of creating a controlled environment that would separate the offender from the corrupting influences of the outside world. Today, however, overcrowded prisons seem to offer inmates more opportunities to learn new criminal behaviors and attitudes from one another. Given this state of affairs, it is worthwhile to examine the system of assigning criminal punishments.

Sentencing: Difficult Choices

The sentencing of a convicted criminal lies at the very center of society's efforts to ensure public order. Hoffman and Stone-Meierhoefer (1979) go so far as to state, "Next to the determination of guilt or innocence, a determination waived by a substantial proportion of defendants who plead guilty (around 90%), the sentencing decision is probably the most important decision made about the criminal defendant in the entire process" (p. 241).

Sentencing is a judicial function, but sentencing decisions are largely controlled by the legislative branch—Congress and state legislatures. The legislative branch dictates the extent of judges' discretion, and many legislators argue that judges should have little or no discretion. They emphasize retribution and argue that the punishment should fit the crime. Mandatory sentences, sentencing guidelines, and the abolition of parole are the primary ingredients in these "get tough" schemes. On the other hand, a few legislators still maintain that the sentence should fit the offender—that judges should have discretion to make the sentence fit not only the crime but the criminal as well.

In the federal system and in some states, the legislative branch has imposed a **determinate sentencing** system on the judiciary. In these systems, sentences are determined (fixed) by statutes and sentencing guidelines. Judges have little control over the sentences, and there is no parole. In such systems, the primary goals are retribution and moral outrage. There is little concern for the offender's personal characteristics, apart from his criminal record.

In other states, judges have wide discretion, and parole is available. All seven of the sentencing goals listed earlier are taken into account. The focus tends to be more on the offender than on the offense. Judges (and parole boards) consider the reasons why the offender committed the crime and the likelihood of rehabilitation if the offender is placed on probation or paroled.

Many sentencing systems are mixed; that is, judges and parole boards have discretion in some cases but not in others. Mandatory minimum sentences are often used in a system in which judges otherwise have wide discretion. These sentencing statutes must be applied even when their results seem unjust. For example, in *United States v. Angelos*

(2004), Federal District Judge Paul Cassell was forced to sentence a first-time offender who had sold marijuana on three occasions to $61\frac{1}{2}$ years in custody with no parole. The reason: He carried a gun during the marijuana sales. The statute imposed a 5-year minimum term for the first gun count and a minimum of 25 years for each subsequent count, which added up to 55 years to be served consecutively in addition to $6\frac{1}{2}$ years for the sale of the marijuana. Offended by the injustice imposed by the mandatory minimum requirement of the gun statute, Judge Cassell (a conservative judge who as a law professor had argued in the United States Supreme Court that *Miranda v. Arizona* should be overruled) wrote a 36-page opinion, pointing out that the 738-month sentence for Angelos was longer than the sentences prescribed under the federal sentencing guidelines for a three-time aircraft hijacker and a kingpin of three major drug-trafficking rings in which three deaths occurred. He noted that on the same day he sentenced Angelos, he sentenced a murderer under the sentencing guidelines to 262 months, about a third of Angelos's sentence. Judge Cassell asked the president to commute Angelos's sentence and asked Congress to reconsider mandatory minimum sentencing (*United States v. Angelos*, 2004).

The American Psychological Association has spoken out against mandatory minimum sentences: "[T]hey have done nothing to reduce crime or put big-time drug dealers out of business. What they have done . . . is to fill prisons with young, nonviolent, low-level drug offenders serving long sentences at enormous and growing cost to taxpayers" (Hansen, 1999, p. 14).

Discretion Justified as a Value

Discretion allows judges to capitalize on their perceptions of the crime, the criminal, and the circumstances so that their decisions can "serve, within limits set by law, that elusive concept of justice which the law in its wisdom refuses to define" (Gaylin, 1974, p. 67). Those who advocate individually tailored sentences note that each offender is different and deserves to be treated as an individual.

But Tonry (1996) observes that "theories [that] place primary emphasis on linking deserved punishments to the severity of crimes, in the interest of treating cases alike . . . lead to disregard of other ethically relevant differences between offenders—like their personal backgrounds and the effects of punishments on them and their families—and thereby treat unlike cases alike" (p. 15).

To save money and relieve prison overcrowding, many states (but not the federal government) have embraced the concept of **intermediate sanctions** for nonviolent offenders (Carlson, Hess, & Orthmann, 1999). Intermediate sanctions serve utilitarian goals—rehabilitation, deterrence, restitution—and are tailored to fit the offender. An example of an intermediate sanction is intensively supervised probation. A probationer serving such a sentence might be required to report daily to the probation officer, submit to random drug tests, stay away from certain people, and work or go to school.

In Vermont, although violent offenders still go to prison, community boards fix the sanctions for people convicted of nonviolent misdemeanors and low-level felonies. A woman who wrote bad checks was ordered to write letters of apology and an essay on what she had learned. A reckless driver was ordered to issue a public apology and spend time with brain-damaged children. This approach, called **restorative justice**, is designed to repair the damage caused by the offender, to promote reconciliation, and to restore relationships between victims and offenders (Hansen, 1997). It now forms the core of many dispute resolution schemes around the world. Restorative justice emphasizes three basic principles:

◆ Crimes injure victims, communities, and offenders; therefore, the criminal justice system should repair those injuries.

◆ Victims, offenders, and communities—not just the government—should be actively involved in the criminal justice process.

◆ In promoting justice, the government should keep order and the community should keep the peace (Carlson et al., 1999, p. 31).

A focus on reconciliation and restoration of relationships is a radical departure from the retributive view that offenders deserve punishment proportionate to the seriousness of the offense. Given the newness of this paradigm, it is reasonable to ask what people think of it. Do they generally embrace the principles of reconciliation between offenders and victims or do they prefer more traditional notions of retribution and incapacitation? Do they think that criminals get off too easily when they are sentenced in a restorative justice setting?

These questions were addressed in a review of research published in England between 1982 and 2002 (Roberts & Stalans, 2004). This study revealed widespread support for restorative sentencing options such as restitution, community service, and compensation, but only for less serious offenses and younger offenders. For adult offenders, particularly those who have committed serious crimes, the public tends to favor a sentence that reflects retributive principles (a sentence that is proportionate to the severity of the crime).

A contrasting viewpoint is that of Professor Dan Kahan, a leading advocate of alternatives to imprisonment, who argues that to be acceptable to the public, a sentence must *express* society's outrage. He maintains that the expressive dimension of punishment is not satisfied by "straight" probation, "mere" fines, or direct community service. Probation appears to be no punishment, a fine appears to be a means to "buy one's way out," and community service is something everyone ought to do. Kahan argues that attaching a **shaming penalty** to an intermediate sanction will make it more acceptable to the public and more meaningful to offenders.

Shaming is a traditional means by which communities punished offenders. In colonial days, those who committed minor offenses were put in stocks in a public place for several hours for all to see and ridicule. Serious offenders were branded or otherwise marked so they would be "shamed" for life. In Williamsburg, Virginia, thieves were nailed to the stocks by the ear; after a period of time the sheriff would rip the offender from the stocks, thus "ear-marking" the offender for life (Book, 1999).

THE CASE OF

BOX 15.1 **Curtis Lee Robin and his 30 nights in the doghouse**

After Curtis Lee Robin pled guilty to charges that he had whipped his 11-year-old stepson with a car antenna, forced him to chop wood, and made him sleep in a doghouse, Orange County, Texas, Judge Buddie Hahn offered Robin a choice: 30 days in jail or 30 nights in a doghouse. Robin chose the doghouse in order to continue to work as the foreman for a demoli-tion company. Judge Hahn then asked the state to provide a 2-by-3-foot doghouse, about the same size as the one that the boy claimed he slept in. Robin's attorneys argued that their client needed a bigger doghouse, a sleeping bag, and some mosquito netting. But Judge Hahn wouldn't budge, claiming that what Robin did was horrible: "He had beaten this kid and left him out at night. The kid climbed in the doghouse to sleep, so yeah, it was pretty appropriate and proba-bly got more attention than giving him 30 days in jail" (Baldas, 2004). (Judge Hahn did allow the defen-dant to sleep with either his head or his feet outside of the doghouse, however.) The deal also required Robin to serve eight years of proba-tion and pay a $1000 fine.

Increasingly employed in state courts, the modern counterpart to shaming (without mutila-tion) is to allow offenders to avoid all or part of a jail sentence by publicly renouncing their crimes in a humiliating way. Federal judge Vaughn Walker sentenced a young mail thief to two months in jail and three years supervised release, on condition that he apologize to those whose mail he had stolen and stand in front of the post office for eight hours wearing a two-sided sandwich board stating, "I stole mail; this is my punishment" (*United States v. Gementra*, 2004). Innovative sentences like this one are being used with increasing fre-quency as judges grapple with problems of repeat offenders and the ever-mounting costs of incar-ceration. One innovative sentence is described in Box 15.1.

Innovative sentences are becoming increas-ingly common as judges look for creative ways to punish criminals. The impetus for these alter-native sentences is twofold. First, judges have become frustrated with revolving-door justice: Approximately one-third of offenders who are released from prison eventually return, suggest-ing that their punishments had little long-term effectiveness. Second, judges are aware of the longstanding problem of prison overcrowding and the high costs of incarceration. (The average cost for incarceration of a federal inmate is more than $22,000 per year.) The American Bar Association has urged judges to provide alterna-tives to incarceration for offenders who might benefit from them.

Some judges have been happy to oblige, and many of the sentences they have imposed are truly ingenious. Consider the following:

1. A construction manager who was an avid golfer was convicted of diverting $300,000 in material and labor from a California building project in order to build a house near the famous Pebble Beach golf course. The judge ruled that for nine months he had to go to a busy public golf course and schedule tee times for other golfers. He was not allowed to play himself and was incarcerated except during working hours (Neff, 1987).

2. The punishment that dentist Michael Koplik received for sexually abusing a heavily sedated female patient was to provide free treatment for six AIDS patients who had been rejected by other dentists (Sachs, 1989).

3. Houston judge Ted Poe ordered a piano teacher who had molested two students not to play the

piano for 20 years and to give his piano to a school (Reske, 1996).

4. Judge Poe also ordered a teenager who had stolen and damaged a woman's car to turn his car over to the woman while her car was being fixed (Reske, 1996).

5. Judge Michael Foellger regularly gives "Deadbeat Dads,"—fathers owing more than $10,000 in child support to more than three women—a choice: jail or a vasectomy (McAree, 2004).

As you might expect, alternative sentences like these are highly controversial. Some lawyers, defense attorneys and prosecutors alike, applaud them, acknowledging that judges have discretion in sentencing and that incarceration is costly and does not always work. But others worry that the shaming inherent in these sentences is sometimes extreme.

Shaming has intuitive appeal as a penal sanction because everyone has experienced shaming in childhood. Parents teach their children to "be good" by making them ashamed of their bad behavior. A child forced to confess to the store owner that he stole a piece of candy should associate theft with embarrassment from that time on (Book, 1999). However, the 21st century lacks the social cohesiveness of earlier societies, such as 18th-century American colonial communities and pre–World War II Japan, in which shaming was effective in controlling behavior. For this reason, some perceive modern shaming as ineffective and unnecessarily cruel. Although shaming sanctions may satisfy society's need to condemn the offender, Professor Sharon Lamb argues that externally produced shame causes the offender to feel not remorse but resentment—and therefore may be counterproductive (Lamb, 2003). An extreme example of counterproductive shaming: A 19-year-old was ordered to publish his name, photo, and offense in the local paper after his third DUI conviction. His mother saw the paper and left it on the breakfast table with a note saying she was ashamed of him. He wrote her a letter of apology and shot himself in the head (Braudway, 2004).

Sentencing Disparity and the Quest for Equal Treatment

In Chapter 1, we described the competing objectives of equality (treating all people in an equivalent way regardless of circumstances) and discretion (tailoring an intervention to the specific needs of the situation). One by-product of discretion (and of individualized sentences) is **sentencing disparity**, the practice of sentencing similar defendants in a dissimilar fashion. The current federal sentencing system was developed to remedy problems of sentencing disparity. By the 1970s, the ideal of rehabilitation was in collapse, and many commentators blamed sentencing disparity for much of the unrest and discontent in U.S. prisons (Stith & Cabranes, 1998). Therefore, the Sentencing Reform Act of 1984 abolished parole and established a Sentencing Commission charged with the responsibility of developing mandatory sentencing guidelines. The act acknowledged the goals of deterrence, incapacitation, just punishment, and rehabilitation, but Congress did not want the Sentencing Commission to allow the goal of rehabilitation to undermine the overriding goal of sentencing uniformity.

The commission's guidelines are very complicated. Each offense is graded—from 1 (least severe) to 43 (most severe); the higher the level, the longer the term of imprisonment. The offense level can be adjusted up or down in the grid, depending on the characteristics of the offense and the offender's criminal history. The judge must then sentence within a narrow range prescribed by the grid. For example, if the adjusted offense level is 20 and the defendant has no criminal history, the judge has discretion to impose a sentence between 33 months and 41 months in length.

The Sentencing Guidelines take into account not only the charged crime but also the circumstances of the crime. For example, the Guidelines provide that "if the defendant knew or should have known that a victim of the offense was unusually vulnerable, due to age, physical or mental condition, or that a victim was otherwise particularly vulnerable to the criminal conduct, increase by 2 levels" (Federal Sentencing Guidelines, 1995). In other words, all other things being equal, a longer sentence will be given for robbery of an elderly and infirm person than for robbery of a young and healthy person.

Although applications of mandatory guidelines result in injustices at times, proponents of guideline sentencing point to our society's tradition of equal treatment under the law. Writing in 1997, Charles Sifton, chief judge of a New York federal court, praised the guidelines for having brought rationality to sentencing—making the sentencing decision less dependent on personalities and "gut instincts" and more dependent on the facts of the case (Sifton, 1997).

But the guidelines have been controversial. In fact, in 2005, the United States Supreme Court held the mandatory nature of the guidelines to be unconstitutional (as interfering with defendants' right to jury trial) but also opined that judges should look to the guidelines in determining the parameters of a reasonable sentence (*United States v. Booker*, 2005). Since the *Booker* case, federal judges have continued to sentence within the guidelines except in extraordinary circumstances (MacLean, 2005).

Determinants of Sentencing: Relevant and Irrelevant

To be morally acceptable, punishment should be consistent with the seriousness of the crime. Punishment does correlate strongly with the severity of the crime; even in systems in which judges retain wide sentencing discretion, graver crimes earn greater punishments.

But factors other than the seriousness of the crime also influence sentencing. Should they? Which factors *should* be considered in determining punishment and which factors are irrelevant? Should an offender's past be taken into account? Should it matter that a convicted offender was deprived as a child, hungry, abused, and denied opportunities to go to school or look for work? The Federal Sentencing Guidelines do not consider such factors, but many states still do. An offender's

record is relevant in every jurisdiction. In fact, most states require those with prior offenses to serve longer terms. California's famous "three strikes and you're out" law, mentioned in Chapter 1, is an example. A third-time offender with two prior convictions for violent felonies can be sentenced to life imprisonment without parole, even if the third offense is minor (*Ewing v. California*, 2003).

What other factors might affect the sentence? Many people would agree that it shouldn't matter whether the defendant in any particular case is a man or woman; what should matter is the individual's criminal history and the seriousness of the offense. Indeed, determinate sentencing has evolved to ensure that variations in sentencing are *not* attributable to extralegal factors such as the offender's race, social class, or gender. But gender does have an impact (as does the offender's race, as we describe later). An examination of the sentences meted out to 77,236 federal offenders showed that after controlling for criminal history and socioeconomic variables, males received significantly longer sentences than females (Mustard, 2001).

Female defendants are treated more leniently than males because of assumptions about the physical and emotional characteristics of women and stereotypes about the social roles that women are thought to fulfill. Notions of chivalry still exist in courtroom settings, and judges (predominantly men) who ascribe passivity, weakness, or dependence to women may believe that they are in need of protection rather than punishment from the criminal justice system. There is some evidence that gender disparities in sentencing arise because judges do not have complete information on either the offenders or their crimes. To manage the uncertainty inherent in these decisions, judges rely on well-honed stereotypes to fill in gaps in their information (Albonetti, 1991). They may attribute certain qualities to offenders on the basis of their gender, believing, for example, that female offenders are less dangerous and less blameworthy than their male counterparts because they have more family responsibilities, greater ties to their communities, and greater potential for reform (Steffensmeier, Ulmer, & Kramer, 1998).

Although most of the research on the influence of gender on sentencing has focused on the gender of the *offender*, crime victims' gender also has an impact on sentencing decisions. Relying on data on Texas offenders who had been convicted of three violent crimes in 1991, Curry, Lee, and Rodriguez (2004) found that offenders who victimized females received substantially longer sentences than those who victimized males. Because this analysis controlled for the type and severity of crime, we cannot assume simply that the offenses perpetrated against women were more serious and hence more deserving of a longer sentence. Rather, this finding may reflect some subtle form of sexism, paternalism, or an implicit belief that a female crime victim would suffer more than a male victim.

Another important demographic characteristic that influences sentencing decisions is the race of the offender. Determinate sentencing and sentencing guidelines have been only minimally successful in reducing racial disparity. A representative study using data from Maryland showed that on average, African Americans receive 20% longer sentences than whites (Bushway & Piehl, 2001). Other studies (e.g., Everett & Wojtkiewicz, 2002) have found that Hispanics and Native Americans also receive harsher sentences than white offenders.

These differences cannot be fully explained by characteristics of the offenses committed by people of varying races, so observers have looked for alternative explanations. Again, attribution theory and stereotypic beliefs of judges may explain this apparent bias in sentencing decisions. According to attribution theory, people make assumptions about whether the cause of crime was a bad person or a bad environment and then convert their assumptions into sentencing decisions (Bridges & Steen, 1998). Judges may attribute the deviant behavior of minority offenders to negative attitude and personality traits (rather than to environmental factors) and assume that these offenders are more likely to repeat their crimes, thus believing that a longer sentence is more appropriate. Judges may view minorities as more evil and threatening than whites who commit similar crimes (Hagan & Peterson, 1995).

Another factor that influences judicial sentencing patterns is the way a conviction came about: whether by guilty plea, bench trial, or jury trial. In Chapter 7, we explained that defendants who plead guilty are often given a reduced sentence, partly to encourage them to do so, thereby reducing costs for court time and personnel. But overlaying the guilty plea is the requirement that judges adhere to sentencing guidelines that have been established in most states. Few guidelines recognize "plea agreement" as an acceptable reason for judges to depart from rigid application of the guidelines. But analysis of differences in sentences imposed for the same offense in five states with sentencing guidelines showed significant discounts for guilty pleas (King, Soule, Steen, & Weidner, 2005). Defendants who were convicted by a jury received the longest sentences. Judges (and prosecutors who advocate for a particular sentence) apparently factor the cost savings of a guilty plea into their sentencing decisions.

Some judges give more severe sentences in order to punish the offender for lying on the stand as well as for committing the initial crime. Paul A. Bilzerian, a Florida investor who was one of the most successful corporate raiders of the 1980s, was sentenced to four years in prison and fined $1.5 million for conspiracy to violate securities laws. Federal Judge Robert Ward stated that the sentence was stiff in part because he believed that Bilzerian had perjured himself when he testified in his own defense: "I do believe that if Mr. Bilzerian had not testified at all at the trial, his sentence would not be what it was" (quoted in Eichenwald, 1989, p. 29). In another case, *Grayson v. United States* (1978), the trial judge said, "[I]t is my view that your defense was a complete fabrication without the slightest merit whatsoever. I feel it is proper for me to consider that fact in the sentencing and I will do so" (p. 44). In upholding the conviction, the Supreme Court rejected the defendant's contention that allowing a judge to penalize someone for perceived perjury chilled the right to testify in one's own behalf. Not so, said the Court, for the right to testify is the right to testify *truthfully*.

Judges are human. When latitude exists in the punishments they can give, their backgrounds and personal characteristics may influence their decisions (Hogarth, 1971). They may be prejudiced for or against certain groups—racial minorities, antiwar protestors, homosexuals. A Dallas judge told a reporter that he was giving a lighter sentence to a murderer because the victims were "queers." A judge in Jackson County, Missouri, said in court that he would like to shoot people who vandalize automobiles "in the head so they can't testify" (Blakeman, 1988, p. A1). Both judges later apologized, and the Dallas judge was censured by the Texas State Commission on Judicial Conduct.

The Sentencing Process

The procedure used in most courts for sentencing has several components. The judge receives a file on the offender, prepared by the probation officer. It contains the probation officer's written report on the case, the offender's personal history, the offender's prior convictions (if any), and a number of documents describing various procedures (e.g., the date of the arraignment, the formal indictment). The judge reviews the file before the sentencing hearing.

The Sentencing Hearing

At the hearing, recommendations for a sentence are presented to the judge by the prosecutor and by the attorney representing the offender. The judge has the probation officer's report and recommendation as well. The judge may ask the offender questions and will usually permit the offender to make a statement. Two social psychologists, Ebbe Ebbesen and Vladimir Konecni (1981), observed more than 400 sentencing hearings in San Diego in 1976 and 1977 in order to determine which factors seemed to influence judges' decisions. They discovered that very few of the sentencing hearings in San Diego lasted more than *five minutes*. On average, judges took 42% of this time, and defense attorneys took the next biggest chunk of time—38%. Participation by offenders averaged

only 3% of these hearings' total time. Usually anything said by the offender came at the end of the hearing, in response to the judge asking whether the offender wanted to make a statement.

What Predicts the Sentence?

In Ebbesen and Konecni's (1981) sample, four factors accounted for nearly all the systematic variations among sentences: (1) type of crime, (2) extent of the offender's past record, (3) status of the offender between arrest and conviction—that is, whether the offender was released on his or her own recognizance, was freed on bail, was held in jail, or was originally held in jail and then released on bail, and (4) the probation officer's sentence recommendation. The judge's sentence agreed with the probation officer's recommendation in more than 84% of the cases. When they disagreed, the judge was more lenient 10% of the time and more severe 6% of the time. Across the eight judges who supplied most of the data for this study, the range of agreement with probation officers was from 93% to 75%, with a median of 87% agreement with the recommendation. A more recent study in New Zealand found similar levels of agreement; judges agreed with the probation officer's recommendation 77% of the time (Rush & Robertson, 1987).

Ebbesen and Konecni concluded that sentencing works this way: The probation officer's recommendation is determined by the prior record, the seriousness of the current crime, and the offender's present status. An extensive criminal record strongly increases the likelihood that a severe sentence will be recommended. The probation officer incorporates all these factors into his or her recommendation, which is one reason why the judge's agreement with it is so high.

The Sentencing of Sex Offenders

Many people believe that sex offenders are especially likely to reoffend sexually and therefore require different kinds of punishment than other offenders. In the most comprehensive study to date of the behavior of sex offenders who were released from prison, the Department of Justice tracked subsequent arrest rates of 9691 convicted male sex offenders released from state prison in 1994 (Langan, Schmitt, & Durose, 2003). (The study also documented levels of recidivism among 272,000 men and women released from state prison in 1994.) Sex offenders were actually *less* likely than those convicted of other crimes to be later arrested for any offense (43% of sex offenders and 68% of other offenders were rearrested for any crime within three years). However, sex offenders were four times more likely than other offenders to be arrested for another sex crime in the three years after their release from prison (5.3% of sex offenders and 1.3% of other offenders were arrested for a sex crime).

A 25-year follow-up study of sex offenders in Canada provides a more nuanced picture of sexual reoffending and shows that child sexual abusers and exhibitionists were more likely to reoffend than offenders who committed incest (Langevin et al., 2004). This study also found that the typical sex offender's criminal career spanned two decades, which suggests that recidivism can remain a problem over much of a sex offender's adult life. Indeed, the public fears sexual predators, and legislatures have adopted special measures to protect the public from sex offenders.

There are three ways in which sex offenders are treated differently than other offenders, largely on the basis of the belief that they are particularly likely to reoffend: (1) Sex offenders in many jurisdictions are required to register with state officials, and these officials then publicly notify the community about the location of the offender's residence when that individual is released from prison. (2) Sex offenders can be involuntarily committed to a mental health facility following the completion of their criminal incarceration. (3) Sex offenders can be subjected to extraordinary sanctions, including enhanced sentences, mandatory treatments, and surgical or chemical castration.

Sentencing for sex crimes, particularly those against children, has been singled out for special attention by the states. Probation for serious sex offenses is no longer an option in most states; in fact, sentences for sex offenses against children can be as severe as sentences for murder. For example, rape of a child is a capital offense in Louisiana.

Registration and Notification

Most convicted sex offenders are required to register with local law enforcement after they are released from prison and to notify the authorities of subsequent changes of address. The period of required registration depends on the classification of the offender, which is a product of a formal risk assessment. In Kentucky, for example, high-risk offenders are required to register for life, whereas moderate- or low-risk offenders are required to register for ten years after their formal sentence is completed. Mandatory registration is based on the premise that sex offenders are more likely to reoffend than those convicted of other crimes.

Notification is more controversial than registration. In some states (New Jersey, for example) police go door-to-door to notify neighbors that a high-risk sex offender has moved into the neighborhood (Witt & Barone, 2004). Most states and the federal government rely on the Internet as a means of notification. (The federal government website is a compilation of data on an estimated 500,000 sex offenders listed on separate websites maintained by the states.) Typically, offenders' names are placed on the World Wide Web for the period of their required registration, and law enforcement officials take no further steps to notify the community. Website notification appears to be plagued by the worst of two extremes. On the one hand, it is over-inclusive; the entire world can learn about the offender, even though only one or a few communities really need to. At the same time, Web notification is underinclusive; persons who cannot or do not regularly access the sex offender website will not be made aware of a sex offender living in the neighborhood. Not surprisingly, most website hits appear to involve idle browsers rather than citizens who are concerned that an offender might be living in their neighborhood.

Website posting also raises serious concerns about invasion of privacy. No matter how minor the offense, most states and the federal government post offenders' personal information (including their photos) on the Web for all to see during the period of required registration. Other information is also available. On the federal sex offender registry (www.nsopr.gov), for example, one can search by offender's name, city, county, or ZIP code; a ZIP code inquiry yields all offenders currently living in that ZIP code. Clicking on a name pulls up a photo, home address, description of physical characteristics including scars and tattoos, and identification of the crime for which the offender was convicted. Offenders must inform law enforcement of changes in address so that postings can be updated. An offender posted on the Web will live under the shadow of his conviction in a way that no other type of offender must endure. A murderer could move to a new community, safe in the knowledge that his past, although it is a matter of public record, is not readily accessible to friends and neighbors. On the other hand, a sex offender will know that his past is available to anyone in the world at the click of a mouse.

When someone learns that an offender is living nearby, the result may be public hysteria. In Danville, Kentucky, a recently released parolee classified as a "high-risk offender" was taken in by a middle-class couple who wanted to put their newfound Christian faith to work. The couple wasn't prepared for their neighbors' reaction when they were notified that there was a high-risk sex offender in their suburban neighborhood. Fliers appeared in mailboxes and on light poles, anonymous letters were written, children were kept in their homes and off the streets, and the couple was shunned by the neighbors. When a crew from the television program *Extra* showed up, the ex-offender packed his bags and left without a word (Breed, 1999). After the community was notified about a released offender in Waterloo, Iowa, children started carrying bats and sticks as they walked to school; the recently released offender was threatened and was ultimately hounded out of the community (VanDuyn, 1999).

Involuntary Commitment

A second form of sanction on repeat sex offenders is involuntary commitment to a mental health facility after the prison term has been completed. The leading case on this topic is *Kansas v. Hendricks* (1997). Leroy Hendricks was "every parent's nightmare" (Kolebuck, 1998, p. 537). He was in his sixties at the time he was scheduled to be released from a Kansas state prison where he had served ten years for child molestation. But Kansas had recently passed a Sexually Violent Predator (SVP) Act, allowing for the involuntary commitment of offenders suffering from a "mental abnormality" that would make them likely to commit predatory acts of sexual violence. A Kansas court found Hendricks to be a sexually violent predator and committed him to a mental hospital. His case is described more fully in Box 15.2.

Predictably, other states passed statutes similar to the Kansas statute that was upheld in *Kansas v. Hendricks*. As of 2003, 16 states had enacted some form of civil proceedings for the involuntary commitment of sex offenders. Once such an individual is committed, release is rare. By 2003, almost 2500 persons had been committed as sexually violent predators, but only 82 had been subsequently released (Janus & Prentky, 2003).

The Supreme Court's rulings on the Sexually Violent Predator Act make clear that selected individuals must have a "mental abnormality" or personality disorder that predisposes them to sexual violence. In making assessments of "mental abnormality," evaluators typically use the diagnostic criteria for pedophilia, paraphilia, or antisocial personality disorder set out in the *Diagnostic and Statistical Manual-IV* (Becker, Stinson, Tromp, & Messer, 2003).

The U.S. Supreme Court has also said that individuals subjected to Sexually Violent Predator laws must be likely to commit future sexually violent crimes. How does one assess the likelihood of some possible event in the future? The risk of reoffending is typically determined via actuarial risk assessment instruments. These tests compare a given individual to individuals who have similar characteristics and for whom the rates of recidivism are known. Obviously, these instruments cannot predict with certainty that a given individual will behave in any particular way, but they can be quite useful in gauging the likelihood of future behavior (Levenson, 2004).

THE CASE OF

BOX 15.2   Leroy Hendricks: Lock 'em up and throw away the key?

LEROY HENDRICKS

Leroy Hendricks had done his time—or so he thought. By August 1994, he had served ten years for taking indecent liberties with two 13-year-old boys. Unfortunately for Hendricks, his reputation preceded him. In fact, he had a long history of sexually abusing children, beginning in 1955 and including five convictions for sex crimes involving children. Hendricks readily admitted to having difficulty controlling his urges. In fact, he told a Kansas state court judge that only his death would guarantee that he would never commit another sexual offense on a child. In 1994, shortly before Hendricks was to be released, the state invoked the Sexually Violent Predator Act and sought his involuntary commitment.

Hendricks challenged the constitutionality of the act, claiming, among other things, that it violated the double-jeopardy and *ex post facto* clauses of the Constitution. (The double-jeopardy clause prevents the government from punishing people twice for the same crime, and the *ex post facto* clause forbids the enactment of new laws that extend punishment for past crimes.) Resolution of the issue turned on whether Hendricks's continued confinement was considered "punishment."

Writing for the 5–4 majority of the Supreme Court, Justice Clarence Thomas concluded that it was not (*Kansas v. Hendricks*, 1997). Thomas reasoned that Hendricks's confinement could not be considered "punishment" because, in constitutional terms, punishment derives from criminal proceedings, not civil ones. He also pointed to the indefinite duration of the confinement (theoretically, individuals can be released when their "abnormality" is no longer threatening) as proof of its nonpunitive nature. In a bit of irony, Thomas dismissed the fact that the state failed to provide treatment for Hendricks. By analogy to cases upholding quarantine of persons with communicable diseases, Thomas held that the state

could lock up those for whom no treatment was available but who posed a danger to others.

Professor Stephen Morse has raised concerns about the role of the *Hendricks* case in striking a balance between the due process and crime control models of criminal justice (Morse, 1998). He asserted that in its quest for public safety, society is now willing to punish people who are merely *at risk for* reoffending, in essence punishing them more severely than they deserve.

Civil commitment evaluations are conducted around the time the offender is scheduled to be released from prison and typically rely on such actuarial instruments as the Sex Offender Risk Appraisal Guide (SORAG; Quinsey, Harris, Rice, & Cormier, 1998), the Violence Risk Appraisal Guide (VRAG; Harris, Rice, & Quinsey, 1993), the Rapid Risk Assessment for Sex Offense Recidivism (RRASOR; Hanson, 1997), and the Static-99 (Hanson & Thornton, 2000). A study of the predictive accuracy of these instruments (the ability of the tests to predict violent and sexual recidivism, or the absence of such recidivism) in a sample of approximately 400 sex offenders showed accuracy rates of 0.90 when the VRAG and SORAG were used (Harris et al., 2003; Harris & Rice, 2003). (Perfect prediction using this approach, called Receiver Operating Characteristics, or ROC analysis, would yield an accuracy value of 1.0, and chance prediction would yield an accuracy value of 0.50.)

Actuarial assessments are, in general, more reliable than subjective clinical assessments. In evaluations made for the purposes of involuntary commitments, examining clinicians may offer their opinion about whether the defendant is suffering from a mental abnormality (or illness) that will render him a substantial risk to reoffend. Compared to actuarial prediction schemes, such clinically based predictions of reoffense risk are notoriously inaccurate (Falk, 1999) and should not be used as the sole basis for risk-based decisions concerning involuntary commitment. Janus and Prentky (2003) argue that psychologists should use one of the standard instruments as part of any evaluation of propensity to reoffend.

Sex Offender Treatments

Unlike other offenders, sex offenders are often required to undergo treatment designed to "cure" them of their antisocial tendencies. Offenders sentenced to prison are required to participate in offender treatment programs or give up hope of parole; offenders offered probation are required to participate in counseling sessions. In these counseling sessions, offenders must acknowledge their wrongdoing and are taught to recognize situations that might lead them to reoffend. These sessions often include an assortment of behavior modification techniques, including aversive conditioning and, in some cases, medications designed to diminish the sex drive (Becker & Murphy, 1998).

The most controversial forms of treatment are **surgical castration** and **chemical castration**— the former involving removal of the testes (termed orchiectomy) and the latter involving the administration of hormones to reduce testosterone levels and lower most men's sex drives. Surgical castration is effective in reducing sexual recidivism; sexual desires are diminished in men who have been castrated, even though these men are still able to develop an erection in response to sexual stimuli (Weinberger, Sreenivasan, Garrick, & Osran, 2005). The effectiveness of chemical castration as a treatment for repeat sex offenders (**paraphiles**) is still in question. Some studies report dramatic decreases in recidivism by male sex offenders following hormone treatment (Beckman, 1998). Other studies, however, report that the drug is effective only for sex offenders who want to control their behavior but feel unable to do so; that it does not inevitably suppress erections or prevent sexual arousal; and that it is less effective than a combination of interventions involving counseling, medication, and behavior modification (Bund, 1997). In the past, some courts have given convicted sex offenders a choice: prison or hormone treatment. It is not surprising that some men have opted for the drug, even though the possible side effects include lethargy, hot flashes, nightmares, hypertension, and shortness of breath (Keene, 1997).

California was the first state to pass a law requiring repeat child molesters (**pedophiles)** to be treated with hormones as a condition of parole. Recognizing that not all pedophiles are repeat sex offenders, the California statute requires that a clinician conclude that the offender will benefit from the treatment. This issue is similar to the question that a clinician must answer in civil commitment proceedings for sexually violent predators: Does the offender suffer from a condition (e.g., paraphilia) that creates a substantial risk of reoffending? If so, the California legislature reasoned, it makes sense to deny parole unless the offender agrees to the treatment. At the time the California Chemical Castration Bill was being considered, Assemblyman Bill Hoge, one of the sponsors, reasoned as follows:

> What we're up against is the kind of criminal who, just as soon as he gets out of jail, will immediately commit this crime again at least 90% of the time. So why not give these people a shot to calm them down and bring them under control, or alternatively, give them the option of going under the knife? (Ayres, 1996, p. A1)

Although Assemblyman Hoge clearly overstated the probability of reoffending, there may be a certain logic in requiring sex offenders to take a drug that diminishes their sex drive.

Since 1996, nine states have followed California's lead and passed laws authorizing the use of either chemical or surgical castration. In those states, repeat offenders are eligible for probation or parole only if they accept mandated chemical castration (Scott & Holmberg, 2003).

The Death Penalty: The Ultimate Punishment

The ultimate punishment, of course, is death, and the United States is one of just a few countries in the world that sanction this form of punishment. Citizens of the United States can be executed by the federal government and by the governments of 38 states. But capital punishment has had a controversial and volatile history in this country. Although a majority of Americans apparently support capital punishment, and politicians and appellate judges have tended to make decisions that reflect that support (Ogloff & Chopra, 2004), in 1997 the American Bar Association called for a nationwide moratorium on capital punishment, citing concerns about the way the death penalty was administered. In 2003, during his last few days as governor of Illinois, George Ryan effectively closed down Illinois's death row, commuting (or canceling) the death sentences of 156 condemned prisoners. Most of them are now serving life sentences.

The modern era in the history of capital punishment in the United States began in 1972 when the U.S. Supreme Court effectively abolished the death penalty on the grounds that it constituted "cruel and unusual punishment" (*Furman v. Georgia*, 1972). After the *Furman* case, state legislatures revised their death penalty laws to address the Court's concern that capital punishment was being applied in an arbitrary and discriminatory fashion as a consequence of the "unbridled discretion" in sentencing given to juries.

To remedy this problem, states passed statutes that guided the capital sentencing discretion of juries. First, they made only certain crimes eligible for the death penalty. Second, they changed the structure of capital trials. Now, if a defendant is charged with one of these crimes, the trial is conducted in two phases. The jury decides the guilt or

innocence of the defendant in the first phase (the "guilt phase"). If the defendant is found guilty, then the second phase, or "sentencing phase," of the trial is held. During this phase, the jury hears evidence of **aggravating factors** (facts that argue for a death sentence, such as killing a police officer, killing in an especially heinous manner, killing for hire) and **mitigating factors** (facts that argue for a sentence less than death, such as a defendant's mental illness or voluntary intoxication at the time of the offense). Specific aggravating and mitigating factors are listed in the statutes, but a jury is not required to consider only those factors in its deliberations. Before reaching a sentencing decision, jurors hear instructions from the judge on how to weigh the aggravating and mitigating factors. Generally, a jury cannot vote for a sentence of death unless it finds at least one aggravating factor. However, even if it finds one or more aggravating circumstances to be present, it may still, after considering the mitigating factors, return a sentence of less than death.

In 1976, in the case of *Gregg v. Georgia*, and in response to these newly enacted laws and procedures, the Supreme Court reinstituted the possibility of the death penalty. Since that time, the Court has issued many death penalty opinions, focusing often on the behavior of capital juries (Haney & Wiener, 2004).

Following the *Gregg* decision, state after state began to execute those convicts who had been sentenced to death. The first to be executed, on January 17, 1977, was Gary Gilmore, in Utah, who gave up his right to challenge his conviction and resisted the efforts of his relatives to save him from the firing squad. (Gilmore is the only person to have been executed in the United States by firing squad since the death penalty was re-instituted.) Gilmore, whose story is told in Norman Mailer's (1979) book *The Executioner's Song*, was the first of many to die at the hand of the executioner (although he did so as a "volunteer"—a person who wanted to die rather than spend the rest of his life in confinement). Since the death penalty was reinstated in 1976, more than 975 persons have been put to death. The greatest number (98) were executed in 1999, and the number has declined

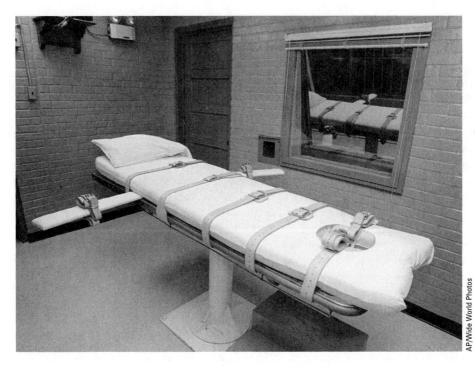

Gurney on which the prisoner is executed by lethal injection

since that time (Bureau of Justice, 2005a). More than 80% of these executions have occurred in southern states, and Texas alone accounts for approximately one-third of them.

The Question of Innocence

We do not know exactly how many innocent individuals have been executed, but we do know that some have been. David Protess, a Northwestern University journalism professor, drew attention to the possibility of "executing the innocent" when students under his supervision tracked down and obtained confessions from true killers, thereby exonerating two men on death row. Professor Protess's student investigators uncovered other instances of conviction of the innocent, and 13 inmates were ultimately exonerated from death row in Illinois. This led outgoing Governor George Ryan to commute the death sentences of all remaining death row inmates in Illinois (Marshall, 2002). In a speech he delivered at Northwestern University at the time, Ryan was quoted as saying, "Our capital system is haunted by the demon of error: error in determining guilt and error in determining who among the guilty deserves to die" (www.cnn.com, 2003).

According to the Death Penalty Information Center, since executions resumed after the *Gregg* case, 123 people have been freed from death rows upon proof of their innocence (Death Penalty Information Center, 2005). Some of these condemned convicts were cleared when new evidence came to light or when witnesses changed their stories. Another frequently used source of exoneration has been sophisticated DNA testing. DNA evidence has been credited with proving the innocence of scores of death row inmates in the United States and Canada (Shapiro, 1998). Many of these cases involved defendants who had originally been convicted on the basis of faulty eyewitness identifications or false confessions.

The moratorium on executions gained further momentum from a large-scale Columbia University Law School study, "A Broken System: Error Rates in Capital Cases" (Liebman, 2000). This study analyzed every capital conviction in the United States between 1973 and 1995 and revealed that serious mistakes had been made in two-thirds of the cases, a startling indictment of the criminal justice system. The most common problems included incompetent defense attorneys (37%), faulty jury instructions (20%), and misconduct on the part of prosecutors (19%). Of those defendants whose capital sentence was overturned because of an error, 82% received a sentence less than death at their retrials, including 7% who were found not guilty of the capital crime with which they had originally been charged.

As a result of these widely publicized errors, a number of states have passed laws that give death row inmates the right to postconviction DNA testing. (On the other hand, laws that allowed prisoners to petition courts for postconviction DNA testing have expired in Florida and Ohio.) In 2004, Congress established a grant program to help states defray the costs of such testing. The grant program bears the name of Kirk Bloodsworth, the first death row inmate exonerated by DNA testing. We tell his story in Box 15.3.

Not all cases end as satisfactorily as Bloodworth's did. In 1992, Roger Dale Coleman was executed by the state of Virginia for the brutal rape and slaying of his sister-in-law. Coleman maintained his innocence to the end, but appellate courts refused to consider evidence, discovered after the trial, that pointed to Coleman's innocence because his attorneys failed to file a motion on time. What is unusual about the case is that in the week before his death, Coleman became a media celebrity—appearing on the cover of *TIME* magazine (under the headline "This Man May Be Innocent") and participating in extraordinary live interviews on CNN's "Larry King Live" and NBC's "Today" show.

A similar fate may have befallen Gary Graham, executed in Texas in 2000. He was convicted for the murder of a man during a stickup in a grocery store parking lot. Protesting his innocence to the end, Graham was forcibly hauled to the execution chamber and strapped to the gurney with extra restraints. The only evidence against Graham was an eyewitness who said she saw the killer through her car windshield. Two eyewitnesses who would have testified that Graham was not the killer did not testify, and three jurors, after watching the videotaped statements of the two potential witnesses, signed affidavits that they would have acquitted if the witnesses had been called. The Texas Board of Pardons wasn't convinced that an injustice had been done and voted not to recommend clemency. Without a recommendation of clemency, Governor (and then presidential candidate) George W. Bush did not stop the execution (Duggan, 2000).

Is the death penalty still justified if we know that innocent people have been executed? Some proponents insist that it is, invoking the analogy that administering a vaccine is justified even though a child might have an adverse—even lethal—reaction to it.

Justifications for the Death Penalty

Many reasons have been advanced for endorsing the irrevocable penalty of death. While he was the mayor of New York City, Ed Koch contended that the death penalty "affirms life." By failing to execute murderers, he said, we "signal a lessened regard for the value of the victim's life" (quoted in Bruck, 1985, p. 20). Nineteenth-century philosopher Immanuel Kant put it this way:

> Even if a civil society resolved to dissolve itself with the consent of all its members, the last murderer lying in the prison ought to be executed before the resolution was carried out. This ought to be done in order that every one may realize the desert of his deeds, and that blood-guiltiness may not remain upon the people; for otherwise they might all be regarded as participators in the murder as a public violation of justice. (Dressler, 2003, p. 41)

Most justifications for the death penalty reflect value choices and thus extend beyond the capacity

THE CASE OF

BOX 15.3   **Kirk Bloodsworth: The worth of his blood and his exoneration on death row**

Kirk Bloodsworth was the first death row inmate to be exonerated by DNA testing. A Marine veteran, Bloodsworth had never been in trouble with the law until 1985, when he was convicted of the rape and murder of 9-year-old girl who had been strangled, raped, and beaten with a rock. Bloodsworth was sentenced to die in Maryland's gas chamber. Bloodsworth's arrest was based in part on an identification by an eyewitness from a police sketch that was compiled from the recollections of five other eyewitnesses. At trial, all five eyewitnesses testified that they had

seen Bloodsworth with the victim. All were wrong.

In 1992, prosecutors in the case agreed to DNA testing in which blood found on the victim's clothing was compared to her own blood and to Bloodsworth's; testing excluded Bloodsworth as the perpetrator, and he was released from prison in 1993. DNA evidence ultimately led police to the true killer, Kimberly Ruffner, who was arrested in 2003. In an ironic twist to the story, Bloodsworth had known Ruffner in prison. When Ruffner was arrested, Bloodsworth was

Kirk Bloodsworth (at left), the first death row inmate exonerated by DNA testing, being introduced at a rally

quoted as saying, "My God, I know him. He lifted weights for us. I spotted weights for him." (Levine, 2003, A01)

---

of empirical research to prove or disprove them. But a central argument for capital punishment is the belief that it acts as a deterrent to criminal activity. Proponents of this position suggest that (1) the death penalty accomplishes general, as well as specific, deterrence, (2) highly publicized executions have at least a short-term deterrent effect, and (3) murderers are such dangerous people that allowing them to live increases the risk of injury or death to other inmates and prison guards.

A variety of empirical approaches have been used to evaluate the deterrent effects of the death penalty, and these studies consistently lead to a conclusion that the death penalty does not affect the rate of crimes of violence (e.g., Peterson & Bailey, 2003). Evidence also contradicts the view that murderers are especially dangerous inmates. Some data indicate that capital murderers tend to commit fewer violent offenses and prison infractions than the general population of prison inmates

(Cunningham & Reidy, 1998; Cunningham & Vigen, 2002; Reidy, Cunningham, & Sorensen, 2001).

Not only is there little support for the deterrent effects of capital punishment, but some researchers contend that capital punishment actually *enhances* crime, an effect known as **brutalization**. Brutalization theorists argue that executions increase violent crime by sending the message that it is acceptable to kill those who have wronged us. However, the evidence in support of brutalization effects is no stronger than the data in favor of deterrence (Radelet & Akers, 1996).

Equality versus Discretion in Application of the Death Penalty

Does the death penalty further the goal of equal treatment before the law? About a fourth of the states, plus the District of Columbia, do not permit it, and vastly different rates of execution occur in those states that do. For example, even though the state of New Hampshire has the death penalty, no one has been executed or even sent to death row in that state since the penalty was reestablished. As we have noted, about a third of all executions in the United States since 1977 have taken place in one state—Texas. If discretion is the operating principle, it is discretion run amok. The death penalty is administered in only a minority of eligible cases, and its determinants often seem inconsistent and unpredictable.

Furthermore, there is the question of race. The victims of intentional homicide are equally divided between blacks and whites, and yet the chances of a death sentence are much greater for criminals who kill whites than those who kill blacks (U.S. General Accounting Office, 1990). In fact, data from governmental and capital case defense organizations show that between the late 1970s and the early 2000s, there was tremendous racial disparity in when capital punishment was sought by prosecutors and imposed by juries; in particular, death sentence rates in black-defendant/white-victim cases far exceeded those in cases where offender and victim were of the same race (Blume, Eisenberg, & Wells, 2004). This means that black defendants who kill black victims and white defendants who kill white victims are actually underrepresented on death row.

The leading Supreme Court case on the issue of race and application of the death penalty, *McCleskey v. Kemp* (1987), considered this issue. The question before the Court was whether the death penalty discriminated against blacks—or, more specifically, whether it discriminated against persons who murdered whites. We describe McClesky's case in Box 15.4.

Capital Jury Decision Making

The *Furman* and *Gregg* cases, two pivotal challenges to the constitutionality of the death penalty, focused attention on the role of the jury in capital cases. For this reason, it is not surprising that there has been intense public and scientific scrutiny of two important aspects of capital jury decision making: the process of selecting jurors in capital cases, and the ability of those jurors to understand and apply the sentencing instructions they receive from the judge.

THE SELECTION OF JURORS IN CAPITAL CASES: "DEATH QUALIFICATION"

In most cases, sentencing decisions are made by the trial judge. But capital cases are different because juries usually decide the sentence, essentially choosing either life or death for the defendant. When jurors are empaneled to serve on cases in which the death penalty is being sought, they are required to answer *voir dire* questions about their attitudes toward capital punishment in a procedure called **death qualification**. If, in response to those questions, jurors indicate extreme beliefs about the death penalty, they may be excused "for cause"—that is, dismissed from that case. More precisely, prospective jurors are excluded if their views of capital punishment would "prevent or substantially impair the performance of [their] duties as juror[s] in accordance with [their] instructions and [their] oath" (*Witherspoon v. Illinois*, 1968, pp. 516–517). Prospective jurors dismissed for this reason are termed "excludables," and those who remain are termed "death qualified." (Another group of prospective jurors—those who would automatically impose the death penalty at every opportunity—so-called "automatic death penalty" jurors—are also dismissed for cause, although they are fewer in number than "excludables.") Colloquially, death-qualified jurors are qualified to impose the death penalty because they do not hold strong scruples or reservations about its use.

Death qualification raises some important constitutional questions. Recall that capital cases involve two phases but only one jury to decide both guilt and punishment. Although excludable jurors might be unwilling to impose the death penalty, they are not necessarily unable to determine fairly the guilt or innocence of the defendant. Yet death qualification procedures both deny them the opportunity to make a decision and raise concerns about the leanings of jurors who *do* assess guilt.

THE CASE OF

BOX 15.4 Warren McClesky: Does race matter?

Warren McCleskey was a black man who was convicted in 1978 of armed robbery and the murder of a white police officer who had responded to an alarm while the robbery was in progress. McCleskey was sentenced to die in Georgia's electric chair. With the assistance of the NAACP Legal Defense and Educational Fund, he challenged the constitutionality of the death penalty on the ground that it was administered in a racially discriminatory manner in Georgia. In the words of one of his attorneys, "When you kill the organist at the Methodist Church, who is white, you're going to get the death penalty, but if you kill the black Baptist organist, the likelihood is that it will be plea bargained down to a life sentence" (quoted in Noble, 1987, p. 7).

The foundation for Warren McCleskey's appeal was a comprehensive study of race and capital sentencing in the state of Georgia.

David Baldus, a law professor at the University of Iowa, and his colleagues analyzed the race of the offender and the race of the victim for about 2000 murder and manslaughter convictions from 1973 to 1979 and concluded that those who killed whites were 11 times more likely to receive the death penalty than those who killed blacks (Baldus, Pulaski, & Woodworth, 1983). In line with the Supreme Court guidelines we discussed earlier, Georgia juries must weigh aggravating and mitigating circumstances before deciding to sentence a convicted murderer to death rather than life in prison. Anticipating the argument that some murders were more heinous than others, Baldus and colleagues identified 230 different aggravating or mitigating factors. Then they eliminated cases in which extreme violence or other aggravating circumstances virtually ensured the death

penalty. They also eliminated those in which overwhelming mitigating circumstances almost guaranteed a life sentence. For the remaining cases—which permitted the greatest jury discretion—they found that defendants were about four times more likely to be sentenced to death if their victims were white. Similar patterns have been reported for capital sentencing in Arkansas, North Carolina, Illinois, Ohio, Texas, Mississippi, and several other states (Nietzel, Hasemann, & McCarthy, 1998).

Despite the mass of statistical evidence, the Supreme Court upheld McCleskey's death sentence. Because there was no evidence that individual jurors in his trial were biased, the Court was unwilling to assume that McCleskey's jury represented an instance of what Baldus's study strongly suggested: that Georgia juries at that time valued white lives more than black lives.

Intuitively, one might expect that "death-qualified" juries (those made up of people who are not opposed to the death penalty) would be somewhat more "conviction-prone" than the general population. This was the argument made in the case of *Witherspoon v. Illinois*, which was decided by the U.S. Supreme Court in 1968. In his argument to the Supreme Court, Witherspoon presented evidence from three social science research studies that death-qualified juries were more conviction-prone than excludable jurors. The Court decided that the data were too tentative and fragmentary to support his contention but left the door open for

future consideration. In a rare statement of encouragement to social scientists (Ogloff & Chopra, 2004), the Court stated that "a defendant convicted by such a jury in some future case might still attempt to establish that the jury was less than neutral with respect to guilt" (p. 520).

The question that the *Witherspoon* court left open was whether a death-qualified jury is more disposed toward conviction than a jury that also includes excludable jurors. Responding to this implicit "invitation" to undertake further studies, psychologists and other social scientists were only too happy to oblige. In particular, Professor Phoebe

Ellsworth (then at Stanford University) and her colleagues conducted an integrated set of empirical studies that demonstrated the conviction-proneness of death-qualified juries.

In their first study, Fitzgerald and Ellsworth (1984) surveyed a random sample of 811 eligible jurors in Alameda County, California. A total of 64% favored the death penalty (37% did so "strongly"). Another 17% said they could never vote to impose the death penalty and thus were excludable under the *Witherspoon* criterion. In response to questions about the criminal justice system, death-qualified jurors were more inclined to favor the prosecutor's viewpoint, more likely to mistrust criminal defendants and their counsel, more in sympathy with a punitive approach toward offenders, and more concerned with crime control than with due process (a dilemma we discussed in Chapter 1).

A follow-up study by Cowan, Thompson, and Ellsworth (1984) involved showing a two-hour videotape of a murder trial reenactment to 288 mock jurors who were either death qualified or excludable, using the *Witherspoon* criterion. (Thirty of the 288 were excludable.) These adults were divided into juries. About half of the juries were composed entirely of death-qualified jurors; the others contained from two to four excludables, although the majority of jurors were death qualified. Three-fourths of the death-qualified jurors found the defendant guilty; only 53% of the juries that included the excludables did. The "mixed" juries took a more serious approach to their deliberation task; they were more critical of witnesses and better able to remember the evidence.

In a final study, Thompson, Cowan, Ellsworth, and Harrington (1984) examined why death-qualified jurors voted guilty more often than excludable jurors. The researchers found that the death-qualified jurors tend "to interpret evidence in a way more favorable to the prosecution and less favorable to the defense" (p. 104). The two groups expressed different kinds of regret over making a mistaken decision; death-qualified jurors were more upset about acquitting a guilty defendant, whereas excludables were more disturbed about convicting an innocent one.

Overall, the death qualification studies consistently indicated that death-qualified juries are more disposed toward conviction than juries that include jurors with scruples against the death penalty (Bersoff, 1987). Ardia McCree apparently thought so, anyway. At his trial in Arkansas, McCree asked for two juries—one to decide guilt or innocence, and a second, death-qualified jury to decide the penalty if the first jury convicted. The judge denied his request and excluded eight prospective jurors who said that they could not under any circumstances impose a death sentence (Taylor, 1986). McCree was convicted and sentenced to death. He appealed his conviction to the U.S. Supreme Court, and the American Psychological Association submitted an *amicus curiae* ("friend of the court") brief in support of his position. It summarized three decades of social science research showing that the process of death qualification produced juries that were likely to be conviction-prone and that were unrepresentative of the larger community (Bersoff, 1987).

In spite of this concerted effort and the substantial body of empirical support for McCree's position, the Supreme Court, in a 6–3 vote, held that the jury in McCree's trial was not an improper one (*Lockhart v. McCree*, 1986). Former Chief Justice Rehnquist wrote the majority opinion. On the issue of representativeness of death-qualified juries, he noted that the only requirement was to have representative *venires*, not necessarily to have representative juries. Exclusion of groups who were "defined solely in terms of shared attitudes" was not improper.

The majority opinion also rejected the claim that death-qualified juries were less than neutral in determining guilt and innocence. An impartial jury, Justice Rehnquist wrote, "consists of nothing more than jurors who will conscientiously apply the law and find the facts." He noted that McCree conceded that each of the jurors who convicted him met that test. Accordingly, the Supreme Court upheld the state's use of a death-qualified jury for the decision at the guilt-or-innocence phase.

In effect, the majority opinion dismissed 30 years of psychological research as irrelevant to their ultimate decision (W. C. Thompson, 1989). The conflict between social science and the law was never more sharply delineated than in the majority opinion's final view:

> We will assume for purposes of this opinion that the studies are both methodologically valid and adequate to establish that "death-qualification" in fact produces juries somewhat more "conviction-prone" than "non-death-qualified juries." We hold, nonetheless, that the Constitution does not prohibit the states from "death-qualifying" juries in capital cases. (p. 1764)

Whereas the *Witherspoon* opinion invited further psychological research, the *Lockhart* opinion essentially closed the door on any future discussion of this topic, holding, in essence, that whether death-qualified juries were more conviction-prone was irrelevant (Ogloff & Chopra, 2004).

COMPREHENSION OF JURY INSTRUCTIONS IN CAPITAL CASES

Jurors in capital cases receive a set of complex instructions that outline their duties and explain how to evaluate and weigh aggravating and mitigating circumstances to reach a sentencing decision. Several studies indicate that jurors do not adequately comprehend the instructions they receive about mitigating factors because, much like other types of judicial instructions, mitigation instructions are often couched in legal jargon and are unusually lengthy and grammatically complex (Haney & Lynch, 1994, 1997; Lynch & Haney, 2000). If jurors do not understand a judge's instructions about mitigation, they are more likely to rely on other, more familiar factors to guide their verdicts, such as the heinousness of the crime or extralegal considerations such as racial stereotypes, sympathy for victims, or the expertise of the lawyers. The race of the defendant and that of the victim also appear to affect sentences to a significantly greater extent when comprehension of instructions is low than when it is high. In a study by Lynch and Haney (2000), jury-eligible subjects who scored low on their comprehension of instructions recommended death 68% of the time for black-defendant/white-victim cases versus 36% of the time for white-defendant/black-victim cases. Among subjects who comprehended the sentencing instructions well, neither the race of the defendant nor that of the victim affected sentences.

Would jurors fare better if these all-important instructions were presented in a different format? This question was posed by Richard Wiener and his colleagues, who tested various methods of improving jurors' **declarative knowledge** (their understanding of legal concepts) and **procedural knowledge** (their ability to know what to do in order to reach a sentencing decision) in a highly realistic trial simulation (Wiener et al., 2004). Their study involved both the guilt and sentencing phases of a capital murder trial based on an actual case, used death-qualified community members as jurors, and included jury deliberations. The modifications to the instructions involved (1) simplifying the language of the instructions, (2) presenting the instructions in a flowchart format so that jurors could understand the progression of decisions they were expected to make, (3) giving jurors the chance to review and practice using the instructions in a mock case so that they would gain some experience prior to the real trial, and (4) offering corrections to common misconceptions that jurors have about aggravating and mitigating circumstances. For example:

> [Some] people believe that an aggravating circumstance is a factor that aggravated or provoked the defendant to kill the victim. This definition is based on the common use of the word *aggravation*. However, this in an incorrect definition of aggravating circumstance and should not be used in imposing a sentence upon the defendant.

Each of these modifications was helpful in enhancing some aspect of jurors' declarative and procedural knowledge in capital cases.

Mental Retardation

Another highly controversial aspect of the death penalty concerns its use in cases where the defendant, for reasons of mental illness, youth, or limited mental abilities, may not be fully culpable. Noting that many states prohibit the execution of the mentally retarded, the Supreme Court acknowledged that applying the death penalty to the mentally retarded does not further the legitimate goals of deterrence and retribution. The Court therefore declared that it was cruel and unusual punishment, in violation of the Eighth Amendment, to execute mentally retarded individuals but left it to the states to determine whether inmates are retarded (*Atkins v. Virginia*, 2002).

This decision stemmed from the case of Daryl Atkins, who was convicted of abducting and killing an airman from the Langley Air Force Base in Virginia and was sentenced to death. His successful appeal to the Supreme Court led to the ruling that it is unconstitutional to execute the mentally retarded, but the Court returned the case to the Virginia courts to decide whether Atkins fit Virginia's definition of mental retardation: "a disability originating before the age of 18 characterized concurrently by . . . significantly sub-average intellectual functioning" and "significant limitations in . . . conceptual, social and practical adaptive skills."

Atkins became one of the first death row inmates to have a jury trial on the question of whether he was mentally retarded. If a jury were to deem him retarded, he would be spared the death penalty and sentenced to life imprisonment. But in a 2005 trial in which the defense portrayed Atkins's capabilities as so limited that he was cut from the football team because he could not understand the plays and the prosecution blamed his poor performance on alcohol and drugs the jury decided that Atkins was not mentally retarded. In an ironic twist, the defendant whose case resulted in a moratorium on executing the mentally retarded was deemed fully culpable and was scheduled to be executed.

In the *Atkins* case, the Supreme Court referred to definitions of *mental retardation* of the American Association of Mental Retardation and the American Psychiatric Association (DSM IV): These definitions require manifestation prior to age 18 and are characterized by below-average functioning in at least two adaptive skill areas, such as communication, use of community resources, work, etc. The Court also referred to typical IQs of the mildly mentally retarded, between approximately 50–55 and 70–75 (Atkins's IQ was measured at different times as 59, 67, 74, and 76).

Commenting on *Atkins*, a student note in the *Harvard Law Review* points out that the test should *really* be functional impairment in life activities, not an IQ below a certain number; that a person with an IQ above 70–75 might be seriously functionally impaired and should be classified as retarded; and that some people with IQs below 70–75 function well ("Implementing Atkins," 2003). Defining mental retardation—and hence exemption from the death penalty—solely by IQ score is insufficient and hence unfair.

Another problem associated with reliance on IQ scores is that they are known to fluctuate over time (Ceci, Scullin, & Kanaya, 2003), just as Atkins's scores did. In fact, Evan Nelson, a clinical psychologist who tested Atkins in 1998 and 2004, surmised that his scores rose "as the result of a forced march towards increased mental stimulation provided by the case itself" (Liptak, 2005). According to Dr. Nelson, "Oddly enough, because of his constant contact with the many lawyers that worked on his case, Mr. Atkins received more intellectual stimulation in prison than he did during his late adolescence and early adulthood." (Indeed, Atkins dropped out of school after failing in his third attempt to pass tenth grade.) Ironically, by helping to end execution of the mentally retarded, Atkins may have made his own execution more likely.

Voluntary Executions

Some defendants "volunteer" to be executed. Gary Gilmore, the first person executed after the *Furman* case, resisted all efforts to appeal his case after a certain point and willingly faced a Utah firing squad (Mailer, 1979). The state of Indiana upheld a plea bargain in which the defendant agreed to plead guilty if he would receive the death penalty. The trial court accepted the plea bargain, the state proved an aggravating circumstance, the defendant produced no mitigating evidence, and the judge imposed the death penalty, which was upheld on automatic appeal to the state supreme court (*Smith v. State*, 1997). Jason Blume has listed 106 people who "volunteered" for the death penalty by foregoing mitigating evidence or dropping their appeals (Blume, 2005).

A competent defendant might rationally decide that death is preferable to lengthy imprisonment, raising the question of whether society should force defendants to attempt to prevent their own executions. Free will is a premise of our criminal justice system, and the right to make basic decisions is a corollary of that premise. However, no one has the right to state-assisted suicide. Professor Blume would require courts to look at the motivation of offenders who want to be executed. He would have courts ask whether the offender's motivation is primarily suicidal or, rather, indicates acceptance of the justness of the penalty. In his view, acceptance of the justness of the penalty is a legitimate reason to forgo appeal, but a court should not—must not—allow the defendant to use the state to commit suicide (Blume, 2005).

In terms of current understanding of free will, whatever his motivation, a competent offender may plead guilty, forgo mitigating evidence, and forgo appeals. In 2005, Michael Ross was the first person executed in New England in decades. After 18 years on Connecticut's death row, he found a lawyer to argue that he had a right to drop his appeals and be executed (Thornburgh, 2005). Of course, there must be a competency hearing to determine whether the defendant is voluntarily and knowingly "choosing death" (Chandler, 1998). For example, after his murder conviction was affirmed on appeal, Alan Willett elected to waive his postconviction remedies and be executed. A psychiatrist examined Willett and found that he was competent to decide whether to continue his appeals. The trial court accepted Willett's waiver of further proceedings, and the Supreme Court of Arkansas affirmed the decision (*Willett v. State*, 1999).

Society has an interest in preventing the imposition of a death penalty that is not warranted by the facts. In addition to ensuring nonsuicidal motivation, Professor Blume would require that the death penalty be objectively fair. Suppose a man, drunk and distraught over the loss of his job, kills his wife and children and attempts to kill himself. Failing in his attempt at suicide, he is arrested and charged with capital murder. He then asks for the death penalty and refuses to allow his lawyer to present mitigating evidence or to argue that the death penalty would not be the correct sentence. In such cases, we believe that the judge should appoint an *amicus curiae* (friend of the court) to investigate the case and present relevant mitigating evidence. The jury should not be denied evidence that might indicate that the death penalty is inappropriate.

Psychologists' Roles in Capital Cases

Psychologists have played a variety of roles in capital cases. Some have served as jury consultants. Others have been called on to render opinions about defendants' competence to plead guilty, to forgo mitigating evidence, and even to be executed. Psychologists have been involved in assessing defendants' mental retardation. In some states, they have been asked to predict dangerousness. In all states, mental health professionals, including psychologists, have a role in presenting mitigating evidence at the penalty phase.

Defendants have a Sixth Amendment right to competent counsel in the penalty phase of a capital case. This means that defense counsel must investigate the defendant's background and offer evidence discovered in the investigation that might cause the jury to reject the death penalty (*Wiggins v. Smith*, 2003). The American Bar Association guidelines for the defense of capital cases recommend that the defense team always include a mitigation specialist:

> Mitigation specialists possess clinical and information-gathering skills and training that most lawyers simply do not have. They have the time and the ability to elicit sensitive, embarrassing and often humiliating evidence (e.g., family sexual abuse) that the defendant may never have disclosed. They have the clinical skills to recognize

such things as congenital, mental or neurological conditions, to understand how these conditions may have affected the defendant's development and behavior, and to identify the most appropriate experts to examine the defendant or testify on his behalf. . . . The mitigation specialist compiles a comprehensive and well-documented psycho-social history of the client based on an exhaustive investigation [and] analyses the significance of the information in terms of impact on development, including effect on personality and behavior (ABA *Guidelines*, 2003, p. 959).

Clinical psychologists and social workers may be well suited for the role of mitigation specialist in capital cases because they are trained to look for behavioral clues in a person's history. Mitigation evidence is nearly always psycho-social—an explanation of the events and relationships that shaped the offender's development and contributed to the offender's criminal conduct (Fabian, 2003).

Consider the case of Ronald Rompilla, beginning with his horrible childhood. His parents were alcoholics; his father yelled at him, beat him, and locked him and his brother in a dog pen. Rompilla became an alcoholic at an early age and exhibited signs of schizophrenia and poor adjustment in school and later in prison. However, the jury that sentenced Rompilla to death heard none of this potentially mitigating evidence because his public defenders accepted the statements of Rompilla and his family that he had a normal childhood, and they did not look for the documents (school and prison records) that showed otherwise. By a 5–4 vote the Supreme Court set aside Rompilla's death sentence (*Rompilla v. Beard*, 2005). The Court held that his lawyers were obligated to seek out the records that might have explained his conduct. Significantly, the Court relied on the ABA *Guidelines*, which call for a mitigation specialist in all death penalty cases, to be paid for by the state if necessary. The message from the *Rompilla* case is clear: In death penalty cases, states must provide funds for public defenders to investigate the defendant's background, and such an investigation is best done by a mitigation specialist with mental health training.

The Rights of Prisoners

Although the first jail in America was established in the Massachusetts Bay Colony in 1632, it wasn't until the 19th century that imprisonment became the preferred penalty for convicted criminals. In colonial times, jails were used only to hold people awaiting trial. After conviction, depending on the severity of the crimes, they were fined, whipped, put in stocks, branded, or hanged (Carlson et al., 1999). The Quakers were appalled by these barbaric penalties and pressured the Pennsylvania legislature to provide more humane punishments. In 1794, the legislature funded a separate wing of the Philadelphia Walnut Street Jail to hold convicted felons, thus establishing the first prison in the United States.

Prisoners in the Walnut Street Jail and other early U.S. prisons were kept in solitary confinement with only the Bible for companionship. The hope was that the felons would read the Bible and repent of their sins (hence the word *penitentiary*) so that they would emerge from prison as changed men. The reality, of course, was very different.

From the beginning, prisons were places of strict confinement in which prisoners were punished, often brutally, for violations of prison rules. Prison administrators had free rein to abuse the inmates as they wished. There were no "prisoner's rights." In 1871 a Virginia judge stated that a prisoner has "forfeited not only his liberty, but all his personal rights except that which the law in its humanity accords to him. He is for the time being the slave of the State" (*Ruffin v. Virginia*, 1871, p. 794). The courts deferred to the supposed expertise and "tender mercies" of prison officials and largely maintained a "hands-off" policy toward prisoners' complaints (Bronstein, 1980).

But word began to spread about abuses—including, as Bronstein (1980) noted, "abuses of the cruelest sort: physical brutality, gross medical neglect, the silence rules, racial discrimination, kangaroo courts for disciplinary matters, incredible tortures . . . chain gangs, bread and water diets and worse, economic exploitation by the convict lease system ... along with meaningless and brutally hard work" (p. 20). Slowly, the courts' "hands-off" policy was replaced by a willingness to intervene to stop the worst of the abuses. Although prison administrators are still accorded much discretion (*Bell v. Wolfish*, 1979), prisoners do have rights that will be protected by the courts. For example, a decision involving the notorious Pelican Bay State Prison in California (*Madrid v. Gomez*, 1995) illustrates the willingness of some courts to intercede in matters of prison management.

The Pelican Bay State Prison was opened in 1989. It is a maximum-security prison with a special unit, the Security Housing Unit (SHU), built to house the "worst of the worst": inmates with serious disciplinary infractions in other institutions, habitual criminals, and prison gang members. A class action was filed in federal court over the conditions within Pelican Bay and the SHU. The case was assigned to Judge Thelton Henderson, who presided over the lengthy and complex lawsuit. After hearing from 57 witnesses who provided more than three months of testimony, looking at more than 6000 exhibits, and spending two days touring Pelican Bay, Judge Henderson issued a 120-page opinion examining every aspect of Pelican Bay and the SHU. He agreed with many of the plaintiffs' complaints and ordered the state to revise its procedures for the use of physical force, to improve physical and mental health care, and conduct fair hearings before assigning alleged gang members to the SHU.

Due Process Rights

Do prisoners lose their due process rights during confinement? Yes and no. In *Wolff v. McDonnell* (1974), the Supreme Court held that prisoners charged with a serious disciplinary offense have a right to call witnesses and present evidence at their disciplinary hearings. However, the Court held that "procedural due process" does not require that prison officials allow the prisoner to confront or cross-examine the witnesses against him. Thus a prisoner might never know what information was considered by the hearing committee. For example, in the Pelican Bay case, Judge Henderson ruled that it was constitutionally permissible for prison officials to assign alleged gang members to the SHU on the basis of hearsay statements and statements by confidential informants.

Washington v. Harper (1990) is an important case involving due process rights and forced medication. A competent person has the right to refuse unwanted medication, and the Court held in *Harper* that prisoners also are entitled to due process protection against forcible administration of psychoactive medication. Only after it has been determined that the drug is medically appropriate and essential to the safety of the prisoner or of others can it be administered against the will of the prisoner.

Cruel and Unusual Punishment

The Eighth Amendment to the United States Constitution protects us from "cruel and unusual" punishments, but in general, the Supreme Court has not been very sympathetic to Eighth Amendment protests regarding U.S prison conditions (Haney & Zimbardo, 1998). In fact, the Court has focused less on prison conditions themselves and more on the expressed motivations or justification of the officials in charge of these conditions. As a result, prison officials' explanations for any of a number of extreme measures are usually accepted by judges. In *Bass v. Perrin* (1999), for example, the federal court accepted a Florida prison administrator's explanation for keeping two prisoners in solitary confinement for two years. The official claimed that both men were serious security risks: One had killed a guard, and the other had attempted to escape five times. It is only at the extreme—where the use of force or the conditions of confinement "shock the conscience"— that a judge will interfere with the administration of a prison.

The effect of solitary confinement on prisoners' mental health should be cause for concern. After extensive testimony, including testimony that a SHU prisoner was found sitting on the floor in a catatonic state, staring "bug-eyed" at the walls and ceiling, Judge Henderson ordered the state to

The maximum-security prison at Pelican Bay

increase its mental health staffing, keep adequate records, and provide adequate mental health care to the Pelican Bay inmates. Rebman (1999) described studies of solitary confinement conducted by Dr. Stuart Grassian and others in the early 1980s. Grassian studied prisoners incarcerated in the maximum-security unit at Massachusetts's Walpole prison. He found that they suffered strikingly consistent symptoms, including sensory disturbances, primitive aggressive fantasies, and disturbances of memory and attention.

Because most prisoners ultimately will be released, prison authorities should prepare even those held in solitary confinement for life on the outside. But some Texas inmates are released from solitary confinement directly to the streets with little preparation for what awaits them. (To prevent gang violence, Texas places potentially troublesome gang members in solitary confinement.) The results are predictable. After years of isolation, they emerge from prison dysfunctional and likely to fail, which

they often do. Out of nine inmates released this way in 2002, all but two were back behind bars by the summer of 2005 (Johnson, 2005).

In 2004, the Justice Kennedy Commission (which bears the name of Justice Anthony Kennedy) made the following recommendations to the American Bar Association on appropriate prison conditions and procedures for prisoner reentry:

- Safe, secure environments with effective supervision by trained staff
- Substance abuse treatment, educational and job training, and mental health counseling
- For those reentering society, transitional housing, job placement assistance, and counseling in staying away from drugs and alcohol abuse

The Commission added the following commentary to these recommendations:

[W]here prison conditions and reentry are concerned, three steps need to be taken: 1) prison conditions must be safe and humane, for prisoners and staff alike; 2) prison programming must be developed and implemented to help prisoners prepare for their return to the free community; and 3) the legal system must be scrutinized to ensure that it does not itself aggravate the problem of reentry by presenting criminal offenders with insuperable obstacles to reintegration into the community. If the legal system is preventing prisoners from obtaining a true second chance, the alternative for them may be a return to criminality (American Bar Association Justice Kennedy Commission, 2004, p. 8).

For the sake of both the offender and the society to which the offender will return, states should attempt to ensure that the offender's prison time renders him less likely, not more likely, to reoffend.

Any discussion of modern prison conditions must include the United States government's confinement of prisoners at Guantanamo Bay, Cuba, and the myriad issues that surround it. In the aftermath of the 2001 victory over the Taliban government of Afghanistan, the United States shipped some of the battlefield prisoners to the naval base at Guantanamo Bay, Cuba, to be held as "unlawful combatants." The U.S. government contended that the prisoners were not entitled to the protections provided to prisoners of war by the Geneva Convention because they had not fought as conventional troops are supposed to fight—uniformed, in regular units, and with a command structure. Those sent to Guantanamo were suspected of having some involvement in terrorist activities, though not necessarily in the 9/11 attack on the World Trade Center and the Pentagon. In subsequent years, Guantanamo has served as a holding station for persons suspected of involvement in terrorism. Those incarcerated were questioned, sometimes returned to their home countries, but rarely charged with a crime. As some prisoners were sent home, others were brought in from Iraq, Afghanistan, or elsewhere, keeping the population between 500 and 600. In June 2003, 20 children were among the prisoners from 42 countries held in conditions more restrictive than those of a "supermax" prison (Conover, 2003).

Guantanamo Bay detainees

As years passed, the world press zeroed in on the strange world at the tip of Cuba, a sliver of land occupied by the United States under an ancient treaty but not part of the United States. In fact, the U.S. government had sent the prisoners to Guantanamo rather than bringing them to the states because the naval station that served as the prison is not on U.S. soil. (The United States leased the land from Cuba in 1903 for a yearly rental of $4085, with Cuba maintaining sovereignty.) The government believed that federal courts could not consider detainees' complaints because they were not being held in the United States. However, detainees filed suits in federal courts, claiming they were being held illegally. They claimed they were not "unlawful combatants" and were entitled to release, or at least to the protections afforded prisoners of war. (It is important to note that the Geneva Convention requires a hearing by a "competent tribunal" if there is any doubt about a whether a prisoner is an "unlawful combatant" or a "prisoner of war.") Some of the detainees claimed that they were innocent civilians and were entitled to release, and others claimed that they should be treated as "lawful combatants" and hence entitled to the full protection of the Geneva Convention.

In June of 2004, the Supreme Court held that Guantanamo was effectively part of the United States and that the federal courts therefore could hear the detainees' claims. The Court opined that the detainees were entitled to hearings and that they could not be held indefinitely without charge, but it did not decide what kinds of hearings were necessary (*Rasul v. Bush*, 2004).

In June 2005, *TIME* magazine's cover story exposed the Guantanamo interrogation log of "Detainee 063," Mohammed al-Qahtani, who may have been the 20th hijacker—the person who was supposed to be a member of the team that hijacked United Airlines Flight 93 that crashed in Pennsylvania on September 11. Some of the recorded interrogation methods used on al-Qahtani border on torture. He was forced to urinate in his clothes, go without sleep, and bark like a dog. The revelations of the al-Qahtani log prompted Anthony Lewis to write, "We Americans have a sense of ourselves as a moral people. We have led the way in the fight for human rights in the world. Mistreating prisoners makes the world see our moral claims as hypocrisy" (Lewis, 2005, p. A23). In the article, Lewis referred to FBI reports of abuse similar to that reported in the al-Qahtani log, including prisoners chained in the fetal position for lengthy periods, deprived of food and water, and forced to defecate and urinate in their clothes.

The conditions at Guantanamo Bay raise many issues, including the definition of torture as a legal and moral matter, whether combatant hearings may be held by military tribunals, what due process rights detainees are accorded, whether those detained as "unlawful combatants" may be held for the duration of the "war against terror" (and how the end of such a war is declared), and whether those charged with a crime against the United States may be tried by a military commission as opposed to a civilian court.

Rights to Free Communication

Inmates have the right to communicate with others, but this right may be limited in the name of "legitimate penological interests." In *Turner v. Safley* (1987), the Supreme Court set out three factors to be considered in right-to-communicate claims by prisoners: (1) whether there is a clear connection between regulations on inmates' communication and the prison's legitimate interest in ensuring the security of the institution, (2) whether there are alternative means by which the inmate can exercise the right of communication (e.g., by mail rather than by phone), and (3) whether the regulation represents an "exaggerated response" to the prison's concerns about matters such as security.

Applying this standard, prisons (and the courts) often distinguish between incoming and outgoing mail: Incoming mail is much more subject to being opened and inspected because it might contain contraband; outgoing mail normally will be opened only if the officials suspect that criminal activity is being planned. Mail between an inmate and his or her attorney is generally treated differently. Incoming mail is opened in the presence of the inmate to check for contraband but is not read; outgoing attorney mail is not opened (Palmer & Palmer, 1999).

Most prisoners are allowed to have visitors, but the courts have not recognized a constitutional right to visitation for persons other than attorneys. Contact visitation is generally restricted to prisoners who do not pose a security risk or a serious risk of introducing contraband.

Religious Rights

In 2000 Congress passed the Religious Land Use and Institutionalized Persons Act, which requires states to show a compelling need for a regulation that interferes with prisoners' exercise of religion. In 2005 the Supreme Court held that this act does not violate the Establishment Clause of the First Amendment (*Cutter v. Wilkinson*, 2005). Prisons must make reasonable accommodations for genuine religious exercises, but this does not mean they must allow exercises that are dangerous or otherwise threaten security. In *Hamilton v. Schirro* (1996), for example, a federal court refused to require a prison to provide a "sweat lodge" to Native Americans who believed that their prayers must be preceded by sweating impurities out in a sauna-type structure. The court accepted the prison's argument that allowing prison inmates to congregate around a tent fire was impractical and potentially dangerous.

SUMMARY

1. *What are the purposes of punishment?* Punishment is associated with seven purposes: general deterrence, individual deterrence, incapacitation, retribution, expression of moral outrage, rehabilitation, and restitution. Although rehabilitation formerly played a greater role as a justification, deterrence, incapacitation, and retribution are now advocated as the major justifications for punishment.

2. *How are the values of discretion and fairness reflected in sentencing decisions?* The allocation of punishments is second only to the determination of guilt or innocence in importance to the criminal defendant. The sentencing process reflects many of the conflicts that permeate a psychological approach to the legal system. Historically, judges were given broad discretion in sentencing. Some judges are much more severe than the norm; others are more lenient. In recent years, concern over sentencing disparity led to greater use of determinate sentencing and tighter controls over judicial discretion in sentencing. Now, sentencing guidelines are sometimes merely advisory.

3. *What factors influence sentencing decisions?* Determinants of sentencing can be divided into relevant and irrelevant factors. For example, seriousness of the crime is a relevant factor, and there is a general relationship between it and the severity of the punishment. But a number of other, less relevant factors also are related to severity of sentence, such as race and gender of the offender and race and gender of the victim.

The sentencing hearing is usually a brief, routine procedure. Factors that predict the sentence include (1) type of crime, (2) extent of the offender's criminal record, (3) status of the offender between arrest and conviction, and (4) the recommendation made by the probation officer.

4. *What special factors are considered in the sentencing of repeat sex offenders?* Because they are believed to be at high risk for reoffending, sex offenders have been singled out for three types of special punishment: (1) mandatory registration and community notification, (2) involuntary commitment, and (3) extreme sanctions such as enhanced sentences and treatments such as castration.

5. *How is the death penalty decided by juries?* Jurors who oppose the death penalty regardless of the nature of the crime or the circumstances of the case are excluded from both the guilt phase and the sentencing phase of capital trials. Social science research has shown that the remaining so-called death-qualified jurors are conviction-prone. But the Supreme Court has not been responsive to these findings.

6. *What legal rights do prisoners have?* Convicted prisoners have fewer rights than other institutionalized persons because the courts have generally assumed that prison officials should be granted considerable latitude in the way they administer their institutions. Prisoners do retain the right to avoid "cruel and unusual punishment," to express religious beliefs, and to have certain due process protections.

KEY TERMS

aggravating factors

brutalization

chemical castration

death qualification

declarative knowledge

determinate
   sentencing

intermediate sanctions

mitigating factors

paraphile

pedophile

policy capturing

procedural knowledge

restorative justice

retributive

sentencing
   disparity

shaming penalty

surgical castration

utilitarian

Glossary

absolute judgment An eyewitness's process of deciding, when looking at a sequential lineup, whether anyone included in the lineup is the perpetrator.

abuse excuse A legal tactic by which a person charged with a crime claims that past victimization justified his or her retaliation.

adjudicative competence The set of abilities necessary for a criminal defendant to understand the proceedings in which he or she is participating and to make rational decisions about the alternative courses of action that are available.

advance medical directives Legal documents in which patients indicate what kinds of future medical treatments they will agree to should they later become incapacitated and therefore be incompetent to make treatment decisions for themselves.

adversarial system A system of resolving disputes in which the parties, usually represented by counsel, argue and present evidence to a neutral fact finder, who makes a decision based on the evidence and arguments presented by the parties; as distinguished from an *inquisitorial system*, in which the fact finder takes an active part in determining what occurred.

advocate A professional person whose goal is to represent the interests of another party.

affidavit A signed, written statement by a potential witness, bearing on issues relevant to a dispute or trial.

affirmative defense In a trial, a position by the defendant that places the burden on the defendant to prove his or her claim. Insanity and self-defense are examples of affirmative defenses.

aggravating factors Conditions that make a criminal act more serious—for example, to knowingly create a risk of death or serious injury to other persons as well as to the victim.

alternative dispute resolution Any legal mechanism used to settle a conflict without going to trial.

amicus curiae brief "Friend of the court" brief; a legal document written by someone not a party to the action (i.e., not a defendant or a plaintiff) that argues a particular point relevant to the case.

analog studies Studies that simulate real-life situations.

anomie A sense of alienation or meaninglessness.

antisocial personality disorder A personality disorder characterized by a pattern of disregard for the rights of others, as reflected by behavior such as criminal behavior, deceitfulness, impulsivity, irritability, reckless disregard for the safety of self or others, consistent irresponsibility, and lack of remorse. Antisocial personality disorder cannot be diagnosed until the individual is 18 years old, but there must be evidence of this kind of pattern between the ages of 15 and 18.

applied scientists Scientists who apply their knowledge to solving real-world problems.

arbitration A form of dispute resolution in which a neutral third party makes a decision that is binding on the disputants.

attribution theory A theory in social psychology that deals with the explanations people make for the causes of their behavior and the behavior of others.

authoritarianism A set of beliefs and characteristics that include submissiveness to authorities, demands for obedience from subordinates, intolerance of minorities and other outgroups, and endorsement of the use of power and punishment to ensure conformity to conventional norms.

451

autobiographical memory   Memory for one's own life experiences.

base rate   The frequency with which some event occurs.

basic scientists   Scientists who study phenomena in order to understand them, without concern for whether their work will be used in solving real-world problems.

battered woman syndrome   A collection of symptoms many of which are manifest in women who have suffered prolonged and extensive abuse from their spouses.

behavioral confirmation   A situation in which people's expectations cause them to act in ways that confirm those expectations.

belief in a just world   The belief that justice exists in the world and that people get what they deserve.

bench trial   A trial in which the judge, rather than the jury, makes the decision.

best interests of the child   The broad legal standard used by courts to decide the custodial arrangements for the child when parents or other custodians are involved in a divorce.

beyond a reasonable doubt   The standard of proof required in a criminal trial; generally means that jurors (or the judge) should be strongly convinced (but not necessarily convinced beyond all doubt) that the defendant is guilty before they convict.

binding arbitration   A form of dispute resolution in which a neutral third party makes a decision that is binding on the disputants.

biological theory of crime   An explanation for the causes of criminal behavior that invokes heredity and constitutional characteristics of the lawbreaker.

bioterrorism   A form of terrorism in which biological "weapons," such as viruses and bacteria, are used to harm or threaten to harm others.

black letter law   Basic principles of law generally accepted by courts and embodied in statutes.

black sheep effect   The tendency to be more punitive toward those members of one's own group who violate the norms of that group.

borderline personality disorder   A personality disorder characterized by impulsivity and instability in moods, behavior, self-image, and interpersonal relationships.

brain fingerprinting   A procedure that involves the measurement of brainwaves in response to a stimulus to assess whether the brain recognizes that stimulus.

Brawner rule   The principle that a defendant is not responsible for criminal conduct when, as a result of a mental disease or defect, he or she lacks substantial capacity either to appreciate the criminality (wrongfulness) of the conduct or to conform his or her conduct to the requirements of the law. (Also known as the *ALI rule*.)

breached duty   The violation, through either negligence or intentional wrongdoing, of a duty that one party legally owes to another party.

brutalization   The proposition that the use of capital punishment actually increases the crime rate by sending a message that it is acceptable to kill those who have wronged us.

burnout   A syndrome that occurs in people who work with other people; symptoms include emotional exhaustion, depersonalization, and reduced personal accomplishment.

case law   A law made by rulings of judges in individual cases.

challenge for cause   Employed when individuals are interviewed during jury selection. If the judge agrees that there is a justification for the attorney's claim of bias, a juror may be excused for cause. Also, a judge may excuse a prospective juror for cause without a request to do so from either attorney.

change blindness   The phenomenon in which individuals do not notice changes in their environment.

change of venue   A decision by a trial judge to move a trial to another locality, usually because extensive pretrial publicity has prevented (or would prevent) the empaneling of an open-minded jury.

charge bargaining   A form of plea bargaining in which a prosecutor reduces the number or the severity of charges against a criminal defendant in exchange for a guilty plea.

chemical castration The use of injections of a female hormone into male rapists as a method of lowering their sex drive.

child maltreatment Any form of abuse or neglect of a child, including physical, sexual, emotional, or psychological maltreatment.

civil commitment The legal proceeding by which a person who is mentally ill and imminently dangerous is involuntarily committed to a psychiatric hospital.

civil competence The ability of an individual to act appropriately in such noncriminal decisions as executing a will or determining medical treatment.

civil union A civil status similar to marriage, typically created for the purposes of allowing homosexual couples access to the rights and benefits enjoyed by married heterosexual couples.

class action case A case that involves many plaintiffs who collectively form a "class" and who claim that they suffered similar injuries as a result of a defendant's actions.

classical conditioning A procedure in which one learns to associate a new response with a stimulus.

classical school of criminology The point of view that evolved in the 1700s and 1800s, emphasizing the role of free will and cost/benefit analysis in determining criminal behavior.

closing argument A summation of evidence, made by an attorney at the end of a trial.

coerced-compliant false confession A false confession that a suspect knows to be false but is pressured to make.

coerced-internalized false confession A false confession that a suspect believes to be true.

cognitive interview A procedure used to help victims recall aspects of a crime or other traumatic event.

cognitive psychophysiology The measurement of mental activity during physiological responses.

cognizable group A group of persons, usually defined in terms of demographic characteristics such as race or gender.

commonsense justice Ordinary citizens' basic notions of what is just and fair, in contrast to the dictates of formal, statutory law.

community-based policing A policy that increases direct contact between the police and citizens within a neighborhood.

comparative negligence A doctrine in civil law under which the negligence of the plaintiff and defendant are measured in terms of percentages.

compensatory damages The payment or restitution owed to a plaintiff for the damages and harm that have been determined to have been caused by a civil defendant.

competence The ability to understand the implications of making legal decisions.

competence to plead guilty The ability of a defendant to understand the possible consequences of pleading guilty to criminal charges instead of going to trial, and to make a rational choice between these alternatives.

competence to stand trial Sufficient ability to understand the legal proceedings in which one is involved and to consult with one's attorney.

concordance rate The extent of similarity in a behavior or characteristic between two twins.

conditioned stimulus An act that, through association, comes to elicit a learned response.

confabulation One effect of hypnosis, in which the hypnotized subject adds false information to accurate recollections.

confirmation bias A tendency to search for information that confirms one's preconceptions.

containment theory The proposition that societal pressure controls the rate of crime.

content analysis Scientific analysis of the content of a conversation or discussion.

context reinstatement An interviewing technique that involves questioning about particular details of a situation.

contingency fee system An agreement between a plaintiff in a civil suit and the plaintiff's attorney by which the attorney receives a portion of any award to the plaintiff but otherwise is not paid by the plaintiff.

Control Question Test A polygraph technique in which the subject is asked a question that elicits an emotional response.

control theory The proposition that people will act in an antisocial way unless they are prevented from doing so.

crime control model A point of view that emphasizes procedures that detect suspects and prosecute defendants.

criminal profiling The use of psychological principles as a crime investigation technique to guide police toward suspects who have certain personal characteristics as revealed by the way a crime was committed.

criminology The study of crime and criminal behavior.

cycle of violence A pattern of periodic violence in a domestic context, often exhibited by batterers, that makes their victims all the more fearful of the battering they believe is inevitable.

damages Money awarded to a person injured by the unlawful act or negligence of another.

dangerousness Behavior that involves acts of physical violence or aggression by one person against another.

death qualification Requiring prospective jurors to answer *voir dire* questions about their attitudes toward the death penalty in order to exclude persons whose views on capital punishment would prevent them from performing their sworn duty as jurors.

decision rule The rule that governs whether a jury must reach a unanimous verdict or a majority vote will suffice for a verdict.

declarative knowledge In the context of jury behavior, jurors' understanding of legal concepts.

defensive attribution An explanation for behavior that enables people to deal with perceived inequities in others' lives and to avoid feelings of vulnerability.

deferred prosecution A procedure whereby offenders (usually first-time offenders) who admit their guilt are placed on probation and the charges against them are dismissed if they successfully complete probation.

delayed-reporting statutes Those laws that suspend the statute of limitations to permit alleged victims of child sex abuse to report this abuse after their memory for it has been reinstated.

deposition A witness's pretrial statement given under oath.

determinate sentencing The provision of strict limits for the sentences that judges can give for particular crimes.

differential association reinforcement theory A learning-theory approach that asserts that criminal behavior is the result of socialization into a system of values that is conducive to violations of the law.

diminished capacity A variation of the insanity defense that is applicable if the defendant (in the words of the law) lacks the ability to "meaningfully premeditate the crime."

discounting principle The notion that jurors should put less weight on information provided under threat than on information given in the absence of threats.

discovery A procedure in which the attorney for one side seeks to become aware of the materials being used by the other side to form its case.

discretion The application of judgment to temper a response after weighing of the circumstances.

dissociation The act of a person "escaping" from a traumatic event by detaching himself or herself from it.

distributive justice Concerns about what is right or just with respect to the allocation of goods within a society.

dizygotic twins Fraternal twins—that is, those who share about half of the same genes.

double-blind testing procedures Experimental procedures in which both the participant and the experimenter are unaware of the particular conditions being tested.

double discounting A situation that occurs when jurors reduce the damage award to an injured plaintiff to account for that plaintiff's contributions to his or her injuries, and then a judge further reduces the award for the same reason.

drug courts Courts that deal with offenders' addiction through counseling, treatment, and supervision.

due process model The view that the goal of the criminal justice system is to protect innocent suspects from prosecution and conviction.

duty The obligation that one party legally owes to another party.

ecological theorists A group of criminologists who believed that crime was caused primarily by a combination of social, environmental, and cultural factors.

encoding The process of entering a perception into memory.

entrapment A defense invoked by criminal defendants; the government's use of procedures that encourage criminal activity in otherwise law-abiding persons.

equality The goal of treating people in the legal system the same, regardless of their eminence, income, or power.

equivocal death analysis The application of psychological procedures to determine whether the mode of death was accident, suicide, homicide, or due to natural causes.

estimator variable In eyewitness identifications, a variable whose impact on an identification can only be estimated, not controlled.

evaluation apprehension Concern about the ways others evaluate us.

event-related brain potentials Components of brain waves that are affected by stimuli.

euthanasia The act of killing an individual for reasons that are considered merciful.

exclusionary rule The principle that rules as off-limits any material that was obtained illegally.

exculpatory Evidence that clears a defendant of fault or guilt.

executive function The cognitive ability to plan and regulate behavior carefully.

experimenter bias An experimenter's influence on the results of a research study.

expert witness A person with special training or experience in a field who is permitted to state his or her opinion concerning those technical matters in court.

extralegal information Information about a particular case that is not presented in a legal context.

extroversion The personality cluster characterized by outgoing orientation, enthusiasm, and optimism.

family courts Courts dealing with divorce, custody, and neglect of children.

field studies Studies conducted in real-life situations.

fitness-for-duty evaluation The psychological assessment of an employee to determine whether that individual is too mentally, emotionally, or behaviorally impaired to continue his or her workplace duties. It is often used with those in dangerous occupations, such as police work, firefighting, and the military.

focal concerns theory A theory that relates the criminal activities of lower-class gangs to their need to achieve, through the simplest possible means, those ends that are most culturally valued.

forensic psychology The application of the methods, theories, and concepts of psychology to the legal system. Forensic psychologists may serve as expert witnesses, carry out competence evaluations, and otherwise assist litigators and fact finders.

fundamental attribution error The belief that behavior is caused by stable factors internal to a person rather than by situational factors external to a person.

future best interests of the child The legal standard by which most child custody decisions are made in the United States.

gag order A trial judge's order to the press not to print or broadcast certain information; gag orders of this type are usually found to violate the First Amendment. More common are court orders to attorneys and witnesses not to talk to the press about an upcoming trial; gag orders are entered to prevent pretrial publicity from affecting prospective jurors.

general pretrial publicity Media coverage of issues that are not specifically related to a particular case but are thematically relevant to the issues at hand; jurors exposed to pretrial publicity about other crimes are more likely to judge a defendant guilty than jurors who have not been exposed to such publicity.

grand jury　A group of citizens who receive evidence in closed proceedings and decide whether to issue an indictment.

ground truth　A clear-cut criterion of accuracy.

guided imagery　The technique of helping a person to form a mental picture of an experience.

Guilty Knowledge Test　A polygraph technique in which the subject is asked a series of questions the answers to which would be known only by the perpetrator.

harm　The losses or adversities suffered by a person who is the victim of wrongdoing.

hearsay　Testimony by one person about what another person said.

homeless courts　Courts that deal with minor offenses of the homeless.

hostile workplace harassment　A form of workplace harassment that does not involve a specific response (see "*quid pro quo* harassment") but instead involves gender harassment and unwanted sexual attention, resulting in an intimidating, hostile, or offensive working environment.

hyperamnesia　One effect of hypnosis, in which the subject remembers more material than when he or she was not hypnotized.

impeach　To cross-examine a witness with the purpose of calling into question his or her credibility or reliability.

implicit personality theory　A person's preconceptions about how certain attributes are related to one another and to behavior.

inadmissible evidence　That testimony that the judge rules is not proper and, hence, instructs the jury to disregard.

indictment　An accusation issued by a grand jury charging the defendant with criminal conduct.

in-group/out-group differences　An in-group shares a common identity and sense of belonging; an out-group lacks these things. Eyewitness identifications are easier among in-group members.

inquisitorial approach　The procedure used in Europe, in which questioning is the responsibility solely of the judge.

insanity　A legal term for a mental disease or defect that, if proved to be present at the time a person committed a criminal act and combined with functional criteria (such as inability to understand the wrongfulness of one's behavior and the inability to conform one's conduct to the requirements of the law) can result in the person being found not guilty by reason of insanity of criminal charges.

intention　The purpose for an act.

intentional behavior　Conduct in which an actor means for the outcomes of his or her behavior to occur.

intermediate sanctions　A probationary sanction, tailored to the offender, with rehabilitation, deterrence, and restitution as its goals.

internal/external locus of control　The tendency for people to believe that their lives are controlled by internal factors such as skill and effort or by external factors such as luck or the actions of others.

interviewer bias　Bias sometimes exhibited by an interviewer who has some knowledge or preconceived ideas about the topic in question.

jail diversion programs　Programs that attempt to keep certain populations of citizens, such as the mentally ill, out of jail by providing special forms of supervision and treatment in lieu of incarceration.

joinder　The joining together of multiple defendants or multiple charges in one trial.

joint custody　A legal outcome in which divorcing parents share or divide various decision-making and control responsibilities for their children.

juror bias　The tendency of any juror to evaluate the facts of the case in such a way that the juror favors one side or the other.

jury nullification　An option for the jury that allows it to disregard both the law and the evidence and acquit the defendant if the jury believes that an acquittal is justified.

jury sentiments　Factors beyond the evidence and the law that jurors may rely on to decide a case.

juvenile court　A court to decide criminal charges brought against children under 18;

these courts often handle cases of abused or neglected children.

learned helplessness A condition in which people come to believe that they have no personal influence over what happens to them and, as a result, passively endure aversive treatment rather than trying to control or avoid it.

learning theory A form of criminological theory that emphasizes how specific criminal behaviors are learned directly from reinforcement and modeling influences.

legal precedent A judgment or decision that serves as a model for the disposition of a similar case arising afterwards. Courts attempt to decide cases on the basis of principles established in prior cases.

liable Responsible or answerable for some action.

limiting instruction A jury instruction that allows a prior criminal record to be used only to gauge the defendant's credibility.

M'Naghten rule A rule applied in the history of the insanity defense. Under this rule, a defendant may be deemed insane by the court if, as a result of a "disease of the mind," he or she (1) did not know what he or she was doing, or (2) did not know that what he or she was doing was wrong.

malingering The intentional fabrication or exaggeration of physical or psychological symptoms in order to gain an incentive or advantage.

mass murderer A person who kills four or more victims in one location during a period of time that lasts anywhere from a few minutes to several hours.

mediation A form of alternative dispute resolution in which a neutral third party helps the disputing parties agree on a resolution to their conflict; a mediator's recommendation is not binding on the parties.

memory hardening A process sometimes associated with hypnotically aided recall whereby a subject transforms a belief or experience into a "memory" that he or she is convinced is accurate.

mens rea A guilty mind; the mental state accompanying a forbidden act.

mental health court A type of criminal court designed to reduce the criminalization of persons with severe mental illness who have been charged with misdemeanor crimes.

mitigating factors Factors (such as age, mental capacity, motivations, and/or duress) that lessen the degree of guilt in a criminal offense and thus affect the nature of the punishment.

monozygotic twins Commonly called identical twins.

motion *in limine* A legal request for a judge to make a pretrial ruling on some matter of law expected to arise at the trial.

negligence Behavior that fails to meet the legal standard for acting in a way that would protect others from unreasonable risks.

negotiation The process of conferring with another to attempt to settle a legal matter.

neuroticism A major dimension of personality involving the tendency to experience negative emotions such as anxiety, anger, and depression, often accompanied by distressed thinking and behavior.

nolo contendere A plea of no contest.

nonbinding arbitration A form of dispute resolution in which a neutral third party makes a decision that is not binding; a disputant dissatisfied with the third party's decision may ask a judge (or jury) to decide the matter.

notification law A law that citizens must be notified when a sex offender has been released in their area.

nurturance rights The right to protection, sustenance, and nurturing.

opening statements Not part of the evidence, these orations made by the lawyers on each side give an overview of the evidence that will be presented.

operant learning A form of learning in which the consequences of a behavior influence the likelihood of its being performed in the future.

other-race effect The tendency for people to less accurately recognize faces of individiuals of other races.

outcome severity The severity of an accident or injury.

paraphile A person for whom sexual arousal and gratification are dependent on fantasizing about and engaging in sexual behavior that is atypical and extreme; it is thought that sexual offenders who are paraphiles are likely to reoffend.

parens patriae The parent-like role of guardian assumed by the state to protect the interests of persons with disabilities.

parental consent In the context of abortion, permission from one or both parents of a minor for her to seek an abortion.

parental notification In the context of abortion, informing one or both parents of a minor about her decision to seek an abortion.

pedophile A person who derives sexual gratification from sexual contact with children.

peremptory challenge The opportunity to exclude a certain number of potential jurors from the jury without having to give any reasons; the number of peremptory challenges is determined by the judge and varies from one jurisdiction to another.

perjury Lying while under oath.

physiognomic variability Perceived differences based on physical features.

plea bargaining In exchange for the defendant's promise to forgo a trial, the government may promise to charge the defendant with a lesser crime or ask the judge for a reduced sentence. When the "bargain" is reached, the defendant pleads guilty and no trial is held.

policy capturing Research to determine (capture) policy preferences and inclinations (e.g., the objectives that ordinary people believe punishment should achieve).

policy evaluator A psychologist in the role of evaluation researcher, who determines the effectiveness of some governmental or other intervention.

polygraph "Lie detector"; an instrument for recording variations in several physiological functions that may indicate whether a person is telling the truth or lying.

positive coercion bias The tendency for jurors to conclude that a suspect is guilty when he or she has been promised leniency for confessing to the crime.

positivist school of criminology A school of thought characterized by the view that criminal behavior by a person was determined, rather than a product of free will.

postevent information Details about an event to which an eyewitness is exposed after the event has occurred.

posttraumatic stress disorder An anxiety disorder in which the victim experiences a pattern of intense fear reactions after being exposed to a highly stressful event.

predecisional distortion A phenomenon by which jurors' initial inclinations affect the way they interpret evidence presented during a trial.

predictive validity One form of psychometric validity, involving the accuracy with which a measure can predict something that it should theoretically be able to predict.

preponderance of the evidence The standard for a verdict in a civil suit; evidence that is more convincing than the evidence that is offered against it.

primacy effect The influence of information that is presented first in a series.

primary caretaker standard An alternative to the best-interests-of-the-child standard, it states that custody of a child should be awarded to the parent who has been primarily responsible for caring for and supervising that child.

primary deviance Behavior that violates a law or norm for socially acceptable conduct.

principle of proportionality The legal principle that the severity of punishment should be consistent with the seriousness of the offense.

procedural justice A sense that the methods for resolving a dispute have been fair.

procedural knowledge In the context of jury behavior, jurors' ability to know what to do to reach a decision.

propensity evidence Evidence of a defendant's past wrongdoings that suggest that the defendant had the propensity, or inclination, to commit a crime.

protocols Structured formats for conducting research studies that are used with all participants in the studies.

proximate cause A cause that constitutes an obvious or substantial reason why a given harm occurred.

psycholinguistics The psychological study of how people use and understand language.

psychological autopsy An attempt to determine the mode of death (whether by an accident, suicide, homicide, or natural causes) via an examination of what was known about the deceased.

psychological stress evaluator A device that analyzes vocal characteristics to determine whether the speaker is lying.

psychological theory of crime The approach to explaining criminal behavior that relies on factors within the person, such as motivation, ability level, and aspirations.

psychopathy A long-term pattern of unsocialized or criminal behavior by a person who feels no guilt about such conduct.

psychoticism A major element in Eysenck's theory of personality, characterized by insensitivity, trouble-making, and lack of empathy.

punitive damages Financial compensation provided to a plaintiff in a civil lawsuit and assessed against a defendant to punish that defendant and to deter future misconduct by the defendant and others.

quid pro quo **harassment** An implicit or explicit bargain in which the harasser either promises a reward or threatens punishment in exchange for a specific response (often sexual in nature) from a workplace supervisee.

racial bias Prejudice based on racial factors.

racial profiling The police practice of using race as a factor in determining actions such as traffic stops, arrests, and questioning of suspects.

rape shield laws Laws that prevent or restrict the questioning of an alleged rape victim during that person's time on the witness stand; specifically, questioning about the alleged victim's past sexual activities is prohibited or limited.

rape trauma syndrome A collection of behaviors or symptoms that are frequent aftereffects of having been raped.

rational choice theory The theory that, if the reasons for committing a crime outweigh the reasons for not committing it, the likelihood of the crime being committed increases.

rational crime theory The theory that some illegal behavior "makes sense" because of the reward expected and the unlikelihood of detection.

reactance theory The theory that when something is denied or withheld from a person, the person's desire for it increases.

reality principle In psychoanalysis, the ego's task of reaching rational compromises between the instincts of the id and the moral demands of the superego.

rebuttal evidence Evidence presented to counter or disprove facts previously introduced into evidence by the opposing party.

recency effect The influence of information that is presented last in a series.

recross To cross-examine a witness a second time, after redirect examination.

redirect questioning Questioning by the original attorney that follows the opposing counsel's cross-examination.

relative judgment An eyewitness's process of deciding, when looking at a simultaneous lineup, which of the people shown in the lineup looks most like the perpetrator.

released on recognizance (ROR) A court order releasing a defendant from custody on the defendant's written promise to appear in court when her or his case is scheduled for a hearing, trial, or other proceeding; a defendant who is released on recognizance is not required to deposit money or other property with the court in order to be released.

relevant/irrelevant procedure A polygraph technique in which the subject is asked a series of questions, some of which are relevant to the crime and some of which are not.

repression The removal of certain unpleasant thoughts or memories into the unconscious.

restorative justice   Programs to reconcile offenders with their victims; such programs are designed to cause the offender to realize how much pain the victim has gone through and to help the victim understand why the offender committed the crime.

retributive approach   The notion that punishment should be inflicted on a person who has taken something from another.

retrieval   The process by which a memory is returned to a conscious state.

retrospective accounts   Descriptions of events provided after events have occurred; accounts provided after a lengthy time period may lack accuracy.

revictimization   The process of being victimized again.

risk assessment   The assessment of the probability that a person will behave violently in certain circumstances, often accompanied by suggestions for how to reduce the likelihood of violent conduct.

risk averse   Unwilling to take a chance.

same-sex marriage   A marriage of two people of the same gender; legal in only a few jurisdictions.

secondary deviance   A deviant identity created or intensified in a person through the use of official labels or formal legal sanctions.

self-defense   A legal defense often relied on by criminal defendants charged with homicide; it asserts that the defendant's actions were justified by a reasonable belief that he or she was in imminent danger of death or bodily harm from an attacker.

self-determination rights   The right to make independent choices about one's own well-being.

sentence bargaining   A form of plea bargaining in which a prosecutor recommends a reduced sentence in exchange for a guilty plea.

sentencing disparity   The tendency of different judges to administer a variety of penalties for the same crime.

sequential presentation   A lineup presentation in which the choices are shown one at a time.

serial killer   A person who kills four or more victims on separate occasions, usually in different locations.

settlement negotiation   In civil cases, the pretrial process whereby plaintiffs and defendants agree to an outcome that ends their legal disagreement.

sexual identity   A constellation of behaviors influenced by one's identification as male or female, choice of sexual partners, and gender-relevant actions.

shaming penalty   A criminal sanction designed to embarrass an offender by publicizing the offense; shaming penalties are thought to express the community's moral outrage and to deter others from committing this type of crime.

similarity–leniency hypothesis   The idea that fact finders will treat those they perceive as like themselves differently from the way they treat those they perceive as different.

simultaneous presentation   A lineup presentation in which all choices are shown at the same time.

social desirability effect   People's wishes to present themselves in a socially appropriate and favorable way.

social influence   The influence of other people and of the social context on behavior.

social labeling theory   The theory that the stigma of being branded deviant by society can influence an individual's beliefs about himself or herself.

social learning theory   A theory that acknowledges the importance of differential reinforcement for developing new behaviors but gives more importance to cognitive factors and to observational or vicarious learning.

social-psychological theory of crime   The theory that proposes that criminal behavior is learned through social interaction.

sole custody   The awarding of custody of a child to one parent, while the other parent is granted rights of visitation and other types of contact with the child.

source confusion   Confusion about the origin of a memory.

source misattribution Mistaking memories that arise from one context with those that come from another.

spousal rape Sexual assault (rape) upon a spouse.

specific pretrial publicity Media coverage concerning the details of one specific case prior to trial.

spree killer A person who kills victims at two or more different locations with no "cooling-off" interval between the murders.

stare decisis To stand on the decisions of the past. This principle holds that courts and judges should follow prior decisions and judicial rulings in the interest of predictability, fairness, and certainty.

stimulation-seeking theory The theory that psychopathic behavior is due to individuals' attempts to raise their sensory and arousal experiences to an optimal level through repeated thrill-seeking and risk-taking.

stipulate To agree about a fact in a legal proceeding without further argument or examination.

Stockholm syndrome The feelings of dependency and emotional closeness that hostages sometimes develop toward their kidnappers—and their kidnappers toward them—in prolonged hostage situations.

storage The phase of the memory process that consists of the retention of information.

story model The notion that people construct a story or narrative summary of the events in a dispute.

structural explanations A sociological theory of crime that emphasizes that individuals may have similar interests and motivations but different opportunities.

structured interviews Interviews in which the wording, order, and content of the questions are standardized in order to improve the reliability of the information an interviewer obtains.

subcultural explanations A sociological theory of crime that emphasizes class differences in values, and their subsequent impact on the likelihood of criminal behavior.

suggestive questioning Questioning that suggests an answer.

suicide by cop A citizen precipitating his or her own death by behaving in such a fashion that a police officer is forced to use lethal force.

summary jury trial A brief presentation of both sides of the case, usually lasting only one day, in which a jury renders a verdict that is only advisory to a judge.

surgical castration Removal of the testes to reduce the male sex drive.

sympathy hypothesis The assumption that jurors' decisions will be influenced by feelings of sympathy.

system variable In eyewitness identifications, a variable whose impact on an identification can be controlled by officials of the criminal justice system. Examples include the way a lineup is presented and the way a witness is questioned.

team policing A policy of less-centralized decision making within police organizations.

terrorism The use of violence and threats of violence to achieve certain organizational goals.

testamentary capacity Having the mental capacity to execute a will when the will is signed and witnessed, including the capacity to resist the pressures or domination of any person who might try to exert undue influence on the distribution of the estate of the person writing the will.

therapeutic jurisprudence The view that one aspect of the study of the law should be consideration of the impact of the legal system on the mental health of its participants and clients.

thought suppression The attempt to avoid thinking about something.

"three-strikes" law A law that mandates severe penalties for those who are multiple offenders.

tort A civil suit that does not involve a contract; thus, examples of tort litigation include a suit by one automobile driver against another, most medical malpractice cases, and other personal injury suits.

transfer laws Laws that allow juveniles who are charged with committing serious crimes to be tried as adults.

trial consultants Individuals who provide assistance to trial lawyers about effective ways to try cases.

ultimate opinion testimony Testimony that offers a conclusion about the specific defendant or a specific witness, in contrast to testimony about a general phenomenon.

unconditioned stimulus An original stimulus, not associated with a new or conditioned response.

unconscious transference Generation of a memory that is based on the recall of several past occurrences, such that an innocent person may be confused with an offender.

utilitarian approach The notion that criminal sentences should be designed to accomplish a useful outcome, such as compensating the victim or rehabilitating the offender.

validity scales Those measures whose goal is to access whether the test taker is telling the truth.

venire A panel of prospective jurors drawn from a large list.

vicarious learning Learning by observing the actions of another person and their outcomes.

victimology The study of the process and consequences of victim's experiences, including recovery.

voir dire The process by which the judge and/or attorneys ask potential jurors questions and attempt to uncover any biases.

waiver The intentional or voluntary relinquishment of a right.

weapon focus effect The tendency of a victim, when confronted by an armed attacker, to focus on the weapon and fail to notice other stimuli.

with prejudice When a suit is dismissed, a judicial dismissal "with prejudice" means that it cannot be resubmitted.

women's courts Early 20th-century courts for women reflecting an outlook similar to that of the juvenile court movement: Wayward women are not criminal but merely misguided and should be treated like children. Women's courts disappeared prior to World War II.

writ of *certiorari* An order by an appellate court allowing an appeal from a lower court; used in cases when the appellate court may, but is not required to, allow the appeal.

written interrogatories Questions given to a witness, and the responses made in writing, prior to a trial.

zero tolerance An approach to law enforcement in which the police attempt to arrest all lawbreakers, even those who have committed what are traditionally viewed as petty or nuisance crimes.

References

Abbate v. United States, 359 U.S. 187 (1959).

Abram, K. M., & Teplin, L. A. (1991). Co-occurring disorders among mentally ill jail detainees: Implications for public policy. *American Psychologist, 46*, 1036–1045.

Abramson, J. (1994). *We, the jury*. New York: Basic Books.

Abshire, J., & Bornstein, B. (2003). Juror sensitivity to the cross-race effect. *Law and Human Behavior, 27*, 471–480.

Adams, R. E., Rohe, W. M., & Arcury, T. A. (2005). Awareness of community-oriented policing and neighborhood perceptions in five small to midsize cities. *Journal of Criminal Justice, 33*, 43–54.

Addicott, J. (2004). Into the star chamber: Does the United States engage in the use of torture or similar illegal practices in the war on terror? *Kentucky Law Journal, 92*, 849–912.

Adler, F. (1973). Socioeconomic factors influencing jury verdicts. *New York University Review of Law and Social Change, 3*, 110.

Adler, N., & Dolcini, P. (1986). Psychological issues in abortion in adolescents. In G. Melton (Ed.), *Adolescent abortion: Psychological and legal issues*. Lincoln: University of Nebraska Press.

Adler, N., Ozer, E., & Tschann, J. (2003). Abortion among adolescents. *American Psychologist, 58*, 211–217.

Administrative Office of the Courts, Annual report (2004), www.uscourts .gov (2005).

Adorno, T., Frenkel-Brunswik, E., Levinson, D., & Sanford, N. (1950). *The authoritarian personality*. New York: Harper & Row.

Ake v. Oklahoma, 105 S.Ct. 977 (1985).

Akers, R. L., Krohn, M. D., Lanz-Kaduce, L., & Radosevich, M. (1996). Social learning and deviant behavior: A specific test of a general theory. In D. G. Rojek & G. F. Jensen (Eds.), *Exploring delinquency: Causes and control* (pp. 109–119). Los Angeles: Roxbury.

Albonetti, C. (1991). An integration of theories to explain judicial discretion. *Social Problems, 38*, 247–266.

Alden, B. (1996, September 9). Italian-Americans win "Batson" shield. *National Law Journal*, p. A8.

Alexander, F., & Healy, W. (1935). *Roots of crime*. New York: Knopf.

Alexander, J. (Ed.). (1963). *A brief narration of the case and trial of John Peter Zenger*. Boston: Little, Brown.

Alexander, K., Quas, J., Goodman, G., Ghetti, S., Edelstein, R., Redlich, A., et al. (2005). Traumatic impact predicts long-term memory for documented child sexual abuse. *Psychological Science, 16*, 33–40.

Alison, L., Smith, M. D., & Morgan, K. (2003). Interpreting the accuracy of offender profiles. *Psychology, Crime and Law, 9, 2*, 185–195.

Alker, H. R., Jr., Hosticka, C., & Mitchell, M. (1976). Jury selection as a biased social process. *Law and Society Review, 11*, 9–41.

Alkus, S., & Padesky, C. (1983). Special problems of police officers: Stress-related issues and interventions. *Counseling Psychologist, 11*, 55–64.

Allison, J. A., & Wrightsman, L. S. (1993). *Rape: The misunderstood crime*. Thousand Oaks, CA: Sage.

Alpert, J. L., Brown, L. S., & Courtois, C. A. (1998). Symptomatic clients and memories of childhood abuse: What the trauma and child sexual abuse literature tells us. *Psychology, Public Policy, and Law, 4*, 941–995.

Alschuler, A. W. (1968). The prosecutor's role in plea bargaining. *University of Chicago Law Review, 36*, 50–112.

Ambuel, B., & Rappaport, J. (1992). Developmental trends in adolescents' psychological and legal competence to consent to abortion. *Law and Human Behavior, 16*, 129–154.

American Bar Association. (1989). *ABA criminal justice mental health standards*. Washington, D.C.: Author.

American Bar Association. (1992). *Narrowing the gap*. St. Paul, MN: West.

American Bar Association. (1993a). *Standards for criminal justice*. Chicago: Author.

American Bar Association. (1993b). *ABA formal opinion 93379*. Chicago: Author.

American Bar Association. (2003). Guidelines for the appointment of counsel in capital cases. *Hofstra Law Review, 31*, 913–1090.

American Bar Association Commission on Ethnic and Racial Diversity in the Profession. (2005). *Statistics about minorities in the profession from the census*. Retrieved September 1, 2005, from http://www.abanet.org/minorities/links/2000census.html

American Bar Association Justice Kennedy Commision. (2004). *Reports with recommendations to the ABA house of delegates*. Retrieved October 10, 2005, from http://www.abanet.org/crimjust/kennedy/JusticeKennedy-CommissionReportsFinal.pdf

American Bar Association Special Committee. (1991). *Jury comprehension in complex cases*. Washington, DC: American Bar Association.

American Psychological Association. (1992). Ethical principles of psychologists and code of conduct. *American Psychologist, 47*, 1597–1611.

American Psychiatric Association. (1982). APA statement on the insanity defense. *American Journal of Psychiatry, 140*, 681–688.

Anderson, D. (1988). *Crimes of justice*. New York: Times Books.

Anderson, K. B., Cooper, H., & Okamura, L. (1997). Individual differences and attitudes toward rape: A meta-analytic review. *Personality and Social Psychology Bulletin, 23*, 295–315.

Anderson, M., & MacCoun, R. (1999). Goal conflict in juror assessments of compensatory and punitive damages. *Law and Human Behavior, 23*, 313–330.

Anderson, P. (1994). *Janet Reno: Doing the right thing*. New York: Wiley.

Anderson, R. (1984). Did I do it or did I only imagine doing it? *Journal of*

Experimental Psychology: General, 113, 594–605.

The Andrea Yates' case: Chronology of the Yates' case. (2005, January 7). *Houston Chronicle*, p. A10.

Andrews, D. A., & Bonta, J. (1994). *The psychology of criminal conduct*. Cincinnati, OH: Anderson.

Andrews, J. A., Foster, S. L., Capaldi, D., & Hops, H. (2000). Adolescent and family predictors of physical aggression, communication, and satisfaction among young adult couples. *Journal of Consulting and Clinical Psychology, 68*, 195–208.

Appelbaum, P. S., & Grisso, T. (1995). The MacArthur Treatment Competence Study. I: Mental illness and competence to consent to treatment. *Law and Human Behavior, 19*, 105–126.

Archer, J. (1991). The influence of testosterone on human aggression. *British Journal of Psychology, 82*, 128.

Arens, R., Granfield, D. D., & Susman, J. (1965). Jurors, jury charges, and insanity. *Catholic University Law Review, 14*, 129.

Ares, C. E., Rankin, A., & Sturz, H. (1963). The Manhattan bail project: An interim report on the use of pre-trial parole. *New York University Law Review, 38*, 67–95.

Argersinger v. Hamlin, 407 U.S. 25 (1972).

Arizona v. Fulminante, 111 S.Ct. 1246 (1991).

Arkes, H., & Mellers, B. (2002). Do juries meet out expectations? *Law and Human Behavior, 26*, 625–639.

Arrigo B. A. & Claussen N. (2003) Police corruption and psychological testing: A strategy for preemployment screening. *International Journal of Offender Therapy & Comparative Criminology, 47*, 272–290.

Aspin, L., & Hall, W. (1994), Retention elections and judicial behavior, *Judicature, 77*, 306–315.

Associated Press. (1988, January 13). Former Kansas woman identifies man in attack. *Kansas City Times*, p. B5.

Associated Press. (2000, July 14). *Analysis of Philadelphia arrest: 59 blows in 28 seconds*. Retrieved online July 18, 2005, from http://archives.cnn. com/2000/ US/ 7/14/police.beating.02/index.html

Atkins v. Virginia, 536 U.S. 304 (2002).

Ayres, B. D., (1996, August 27). California child molesters face "chemical castration." *New York Times*, p. A1.

Babb, S. (2003). Fear and loathing in America: Application of treason law in times of national crisis and the case of John Walker Lindh. *Hastings Law Journal, 54*, 1721–1744.

Babcock, B. (1993). A place in the palladium: Women's rights and jury service. *University of Cincinnati Law Review, 61*, 1139–1180.

Backster, C. (1974). The anticlimax dampening concept. *Polygraph, 3*, 28–50.

Baer, R., Wetter, M., Nichols, J., Greene, R., & Berry, D. (1995). Sensitivity of MMPI-2 validity scales to underreporting of symptoms. *Psychological Assessment, 7*, 419–423.

Bagby, R. M., Nicholson, R. A., Rogers, R., & Nussbaum, D. (1992). Domains of competency to stand trial: A factor analytic study. *Law and Human Behavior, 16*, 491–508.

Bailey, D. (2003). Who is learning disabled? Psychologists and educators debate over how to identify students with learning disabilities. *APA Monitor, 34*, 58.

Bailey, J., Bobrow, D., Wolfe, M., & Mikach, S. (1995). Sexual orientation of adult sons of gay fathers. *Developmental Psychology, 31*, 124–129.

Bailis, D., & MacCoun, R. (1996). Estimating liability risks with the media as your guide: A content analysis of media coverage of tort litigation. *Law and Human Behavior, 20*, 419–429.

Bailis, D. S., Darley, J. M., Waxman, T. L., & Robinson, P. H. (1995). Community standards of criminal liability and the insanity defense. *Law and Human Behavior, 19*, 425–446.

Baker, L. (1983). *Miranda: Crime, law, and politics*. New York: Atheneum.

Baldas, T. (2004, November 15). Considering the alternatives. *National Law Journal*, p. 18.

Baldus, D., Pulaski, C., & Woodworth, G. (1983). Comparative review of death sentences: An empirical study of the Georgia experience. *Journal of Criminal Law and Criminology, 74*, 661–753.

Baldus, D., Woodworth, G., Zuckerman, D., Weiner, N. A., & Broffitt, B. (1998). Race discrimination and the death penalty in the post-*Furman* era: An empirical and legal overview with recent findings from Philadelphia. *Cornell Law Review, 83*, 1638–1770.

Baldus, D. C., Woodworth, G., Zuckerman, D., Weiner, N. A., & Broffit, B. (2001). The use of peremptory challenges in capital murder trials: A legal and empirical analysis. *University of Pennsylvania Journal of Constitutional Law, 3*, 3–10.

Bandura, A. (1973). *Aggression: A social learning analysis*. Englewood Cliffs, NJ: Prentice-Hall.

Bandura, A. (1976). Social learning analysis of aggression. In E. Ribes-Inesta & A. Bandura (Eds.), *Analysis of delinquency and aggression* (pp. 203–232). Hillsdale, NJ: Erlbaum.

Bandura, A. (1986). *Social foundations of thought and action: A social cognitive theory*. Englewood Cliffs, NJ: Prentice-Hall.

Banks v. Goodfellow, L.R. 5 Q.B. 549 (1870).

Barbaree, H. E., & Marshall, W. L. (1991). The role of male sexual arousal in rape: Six models. *Journal of Consulting and Clinical Psychology, 59*, 621–630.

Bard, J. S. (2005). Re-arranging deck chairs on the *Titanic*: Why the incarceration of individuals with serious mental illness violates public health, ethical, and constitutional principles and therefore cannot be made right by piecemeal changes to the insanity defense. *Houston Journal of Health Law and Policy, 5*. Retrieved online on August 22, 2005, from LexisNexis database.

Bard, M. (1969). Family intervention police teams as a community mental health resource. *Journal of Criminal Law, Criminology, and Police Science, 60*, 24.

Bard, M., & Berkowitz, B. (1967). Training police as specialists in family crisis intervention: A community psychology action program. *Community Mental Health Journal, 3*, 209–215.

Barker v. Wingo, 407 U.S. 514 (1972).

Barnard, G. W., Thompson, J. W., Freeman, W. C., Robbins, L, Gies, D., & Hankins, G. L. (1991). Competency to stand trial: Description and initial evaluation of a new computer-assisted assessment tool. *Bulletin of the American Academy of Psychiatry and Law, 19*, 367–381.

Barnett, N., & Feild, H. S. (1977). Sex differences in attitudes toward rape. *Journal of College Student Personnel, 18*, 93–96.

Barovick, H. (1998, June). DWB: Driving while black. *Time*, p. 35.

Barr, W. (1992, March). *Comments by the attorney general of the United States*. Speech delivered at the University of Kansas, Lawrence.

Barth, P. S. (1990). Workers' compensation for medical stress cases. *Behavioral Sciences and the Law, 8*, 349–360.

Bartlett, F.C. (1932). *Remembering: A study of experimental and social psychology.* New York: Cambridge University Press.

Bartol, C. (1983). *Psychology and American law.* Belmont, CA: Wadsworth.

Bartol, C. R. (1991). Predictive validation of the MMPI for small-town police officers who fail. *Professional Psychology: Research and Practice, 22*, 127–132.

Bartol, C. (1996). Police psychology: Then, now, and beyond. *Criminal Justice and Behavior, 23*, 70–89.

Bashore, T. R., & Rapp, P. E. (1993). Are there alternatives to traditional polygraph procedures? *Psychological Bulletin, 113*, 3–22.

Bass v. Perrin, 170 F.3d 1312 (11th Cir. 1999).

Bass, E., & Davis, L. (1988). *The courage to heal: A guide for women survivors of child sexual abuse.* New York: Harper & Row.

Bates v. State Bar of Arizona, 433 U.S. 350 (1977).

Batson v. Kentucky, 476 U.S. 79 (1986).

Bayles, F. (1984, May 7). Law professor has a taste for controversial cases. *Lawrence Journal-World*, p. 16.

Bazelon, D. (1974). Psychiatrists and the adversary process. *Scientific American, 230*, 18–23.

Bechara, A., Damasio, H., Tranel, D., & Damasio, A. R. (1997). Deciding advantageously before knowing the advantageous strategy. *Science, 275*, 1293–1294.

Beck, A. (1987, July 25). Recruits graduate to police duties. *Lawrence Journal-World*, p. 3A.

Becker, J. V., & Murphy, W. D. (1998). Sex offenders: Scientific, legal and policy perspective. The science of sex offenders: Risk assessment, treatment and prevention. What we know and do not know about assessing and treating sex offenders. *Psychology, Public Policy and Law, 4*, 116–137.

Becker, J. V., Stinson, J., Tromp, S., & Messer, G. (2003). Characteristics of individuals petitioned for civil commitment. *International Journal of Offender Therapy and Comparative Criminology, 47*, 185–195.

Beckman, L. (1998). Chemical castration: Constitutional issues of due process, equal protection, and cruel and unusual punishment. *West Virginia Law Review, 100*, 853–859.

Beech, A. R., Fisher, D. D., & Thornton, D. (2003). Risk assessment of sex offenders. *Professional Psychology—Research and Practice, 34*, 339–352.

Begam, R. (1977). Voir dire: The attorney's job. *Trial, 13*, 3.

Begany, J. J., & Milburn, M. A. (2002). Psychological predictors of sexual harassment: Authoritarianism, hostile sexism, and rape myths. *Psychology of Men and Masculinity, 3*, 119–126.

Behn, N. (1995). *Lindbergh: The crime.* New York: Onyx.

Beiser, E. N. (1973). Are juries representative? *Judicature, 57*, 194–199.

Bell v. Wolfish, 99 S.Ct. 1861 (1979).

Belluck, P. (2005). Accuser testifies at trial of ex-priest in abuse case. Retrieved from *New York Times*: http://www.nytimes.com/2005/01/27/national/27shanley.html

Benner, A. W. (1986). Psychological screening of police applicants. In J. T. Reese & H. A. Goldstein (Eds.), *Psychological services for law enforcement* (pp. 11–20). Washington, D.C.: U.S. Government Printing Office.

Ben-Shakhar, G., Bar-Hillel, M., & Lieblich, I. (1986). Trial by polygraph: Scientific and juridical issues in lie detection. *Behavioral Sciences and the Law, 4*, 459–479.

Berg, A. S. (1998). *Lindbergh.* New York: G. P. Putnam.

Berkemer v. McCarty, 468 U.S. 420 (1984).

Berman, L. M., & Osborne, Y. H. (1987). Attorneys' referrals for competency to stand trial evaluations: Comparisons of referred and nonreferred clients. *Behavioral Sciences and the Law, 5*, 373–380.

Berman, M. E. (1997) Biopsychosocial approaches to understanding human aggression: The first 30 years. *Clinical Psychology Review, 15*, 585–588.

Berman, M. E., Tracy, J. I., & Coccoaro, E. F. (1997). The serotonin hypothesis of aggression revisited. *Clinical Psychology Review, 17*, 651–665.

Bersoff, D. N. (1987). Social science data and the Supreme Court: Lockhart as a case in point. *American Psychologist, 42*, 52–58.

Betts v. Brady, 316 U.S. 455 (1942).

Beutler, L. E., Storm, A., Kirkish, P., Scogin, F., & Gaines, J. A. (1985). Parameters in the prediction of police officer performance. *Professional Psychology: Research and Practice, 16*, 324–335.

Binder, A. (1988). Juvenile delinquency. In M. R. Rosenzweig & L. W. Porter (Eds.), *Annual review of psychology* (pp. 253–282). Palo Alto, CA: Annual Reviews.

Bittner, E. (1967). Police discretion in emergency apprehension of mentally ill persons. *Social Problems, 14*, 278–292.

Blair, I., Judd, C., & Chapleau, K. (2004). The influence of Afrocentric facial features in criminal sentencing. *Psychological Science, 15*, 674–679.

Blakely v. Washington, 124 S. Ct. 2348 (2004).

Blakeman, K. (1988, January 16). Baker says he regrets remark about vandals. *Kansas City Times*, pp. A1, A16.

Blau, T. H. (1986). Deadly force: Psychosocial factors and objective evaluation: A preliminary effort. In J. T. Reese & H. A. Goldstein (Eds.), *Psychological services for law enforcement* (pp. 315–334). Washington, D.C.: U.S. Government Printing Office.

Blau, T. H. (1994). *Psychological services for law enforcement.* New York: Wiley.

Blau, T. H., Super, J. T., & Brady, L. (1993). The MMPI Good Cop/Bad Cop Profile in identifying dysfunctional law enforcement personnel. *Journal of Police and Criminal Psychology, 9*, 2–4.

Blume, E. S. (1990). *Secret survivors: Uncovering incest and its aftereffects in women.* New York: Ballantine.

Blume, J. (2005). Killing the willing: "Volunteers," suicide, and competency. *Michigan Law Review, 103*, 939–1009.

Blume, J., Eisenberg, T., & Wells, M. (2004). Explaining death row's population and racial composition. *Journal of Empirical Legal Studies, 1*, 165–207.

Blumenthal, J. A. (1998). The reasonable woman standard: A meta-analytic review of gender differences in perceptions of sexual harassment. *Law and Human Behavior, 22*, 33–58.

Blumstein, A., & Beck, A. J. (1999). Population growth in U.S. prisons, 1980–1996. *Crime and Justice: A Review of the Research, 26*, 17–61.

Blunk, R., & Sales, B. (1977). Persuasion during the voir dire. In B. Sales (Ed.), *Psychology in the legal process* (pp. 39–58). New York: Spectrum.

Boatright, R. (1999). Why citizens don't respond to jury summonses, and what courts can do about it. *Judicature, 82*, 156–157.

Boccaccini, M. T., & Brodsky, S. L. (1999). Diagnostic test usage by forensic psychologists in emotional injury cases. *Professional Psychology: Research and Practice, 30*, 253–259.

Bodaken, E. M., & Speckert, G. R. (1996). To down a stealth juror, strike first. *National Law Journal*, pp. B7, B9, B13.

Boehm, V. (1968). Mr. Prejudice, Miss Sympathy, and the authoritarian personality: An application of psychological measuring techniques to the problem of jury bias. *Wisconsin Law Review, 1968*, 734–750.

Boehnert, C. (1989). Characteristics of successful and unsuccessful insanity pleas. *Law and Human Behavior, 13*, 31–40.

Boersema, C., Hanson, R., & Keilitz, S. (1991), State court-annexed arbitration: What do attorneys think? *Judicature, 75*, 28–33.

Bonneau, C. (2001). The composition of state supreme courts 2000. *Judicature, 85*, 26–31.

Bonnie, R. J. (1993). The competence of criminal defendants: Beyond *Dusky* and *Drope. University of Miami Law Review, 47*, 539–601.

Bonnie, R. J., & Grisso, T. (1998). Adjudicative competence and youthful offenders. In T. Grisso & R. G. Schwartz (Eds.), *Youth on trial: A developmental perspective on juvenile justice* (pp.73–103). Chicago: University of Chicago Press.

Bonnie, R. J., & Slobogin, C. (1980). The role of mental health professionals in the criminal process: The case for informed speculation. *Virginia Law Review, 66*, 427–522.

Bonora, B. (1995, February 27). Bias in jury selection continues. *National Law Journal*, pp. B8–B9.

Book, A. S. (1999). Shame on you: An analysis of modern shame punishment as an alternative to incarceration. *William and Mary Law Review, 40*, 653–686.

Bordenkircher v. Hayes, 434 U.S. 357, 363 (1978).

Borgida, E. (1980). Evidentiary reform of rape laws: A psycholegal approach. In P. D. Lipsitt & B. D. Sales (Eds.), *New directions in psycholegal research* (pp. 171–197). New York: Litton.

Borgida, E. (1981). Legal reform of rape laws. In L. Bickman (Ed.), *Applied social psychology annual* (Vol. 2, pp. 211–241). Newbury Park, CA: Sage.

Borgida, E., & Brekke, N. (1985). Psycholegal research on rape trials. In A. Burgess (Ed.), *Research handbook on rape and sexual assault* (pp. 313–342). New York: Garland.

Borgida, E., & Park, R. (1988). The entrapment defense: Juror comprehension and decision making. *Law and Human Behavior, 12*, 19–40.

Bornstein, B. H. (1999). The ecological validity of jury simulations: Is the jury still out? *Law and Human Behavior, 23*, 75–92.

Bornstein, B., Rung, L., & Miller, M. (2002). The effects of defendant remorse on mock juror decisions in a malpractice case. *Behavioral Sciences and the Law, 20*, 393–409.

Bornstein, B., Whisenhunt, B., Nemeth, R., & Dunaway, D. (2002). Pretrial publicity and civil cases: A two-way street? *Law and Human Behavior, 26*, 3–17.

Borum, R. (1996). Improving the clinical practice of violence risk assessment: Technology, guidelines, and training. *American Psychologist, 51*, 945–956.

Borum, R., Deane, M. W., Steadman, H. J., & Morrissey, J. (1998). Police perspectives on responding to mentally ill people in crisis: Perceptions of program effectiveness. *Behavioral Sciences and the Law, 16*, 393–406.

Borum, R., & Fulero, S. M. (1999). Empirical research and the insanity defense and attempted reforms: Evidence toward informed policy. *Law and Human Behavior, 23*, 375–394.

Borum, R., & Stock, H. V. (1993). Detection of deception in law enforcement applicants: A preliminary investigation. *Law and Human Behavior, 17*, 157–166.

Bothwell, R. K. (1999). The ethnic factor in voir dire. In W. F. Abbott & J. Batt (Eds.), *A handbook of jury research.* (pp. 10.1–10.11). Philadelphia: ALI-ABA.

Bottoms v. Bottoms, 457 S.E. 2d 102 (1995).

Bottoms, B., & Goodman, G. (1994). Perceptions of children's credibility in sexual assault cases. *Journal of Applied Social Psychology, 24*, 702–732.

Bottoms, B. L., Shaver, P. R., & Goodman, G. S. (1996). An analysis of ritualistic and religion-related child abuse allegations. *Law and Human Behavior, 20*, 1–34.

Bovbjerg, R., Sloan, F., & Blumstein, J. (1989). Valuing life and limb in tort: Scheduling "pain and suffering."

Northwestern University Law Review, 83, 908–976.

Bovbjerg, R., Sloan, F., Dor, A., & Hsieh, C. (1991). Juries and justice: Are malpractice and other personal injuries created equal? *Law and Contemporary Problems, 54*, 5–42.

Bower, B. (1984). Not popular by reason of insanity. *Science News, 126*, 218–219.

Bowlby, J. (1949). In Why delinquency? Report of the conference on the scientific study of juvenile delinquency. London: National Association for Mental Health.

Bowlby, J. (1953). *Child care and the growth of love.* Baltimore: Penguin.

Bowlby, J., & Salter-Ainsworth, M. D. (1965). *Child care and the growth of love.* London: Penguin.

Boyer, P. J. (2000, January 17) DNA on trial. *The New Yorker*, 42–53.

Bradfield, A., & Wells, G. (2000). The perceived validity of eyewitness identification testimony: A test of the five *Biggers* criteria. *Law and Human Behavior, 24*, 581–594.

Bradfield, A., Wells, G., & Olson, E. (2002). The damaging effect of confirming feedback on the relation between eyewitness certainty and identification accuracy. *Journal of Applied Psychology 87*, 112–120.

Bradwell v. State, 83 U.S. 130 (1872).

Brady v. Maryland, 373 U.S. 83 (1963).

Brady v. United States, 397 U.S. 742 (1970).

Brame, R. (2000). Investigating treatment effects in a domestic violence experiment with partially missing outcome data. *Journal of Quantitative Criminology. 16, 3*, 283–314.

Branch v. State, 40 Cr.L. Rpts. (BNA) 2215 (Ala. 1986).

Brandborg v. Lucas, 891 F. Supp. 352 (E.D. Tx. 1995).

Braudway, B. (2004). Scarlet letter punishments. *Campbell Law Review, 27*, 63–90.

Braun, K., Ellis, R., & Loftus, E. (2002). Make my memory: How advertising can change our memories of the past. *Psychology and Marketing, 19*, 1–23.

Bray, R. M., & Noble, A. M. (1978). Authoritarianism and decisions of mock juries: Evidence of jury bias and group polarization. *Journal of Personality and Social Psychology, 36*, 1424–1430.

Breed, A. G. (1999, September 2). "Love thy neighbor" tested in Danville. Lexington (Ky.) *Herald-Leader, 1*, 13.

Brehm, J. W. (1966). *A theory of psychological reactance.* Orlando, FL: Academic Press.

Brehm, S. S., & Brehm, J. (1981). *Psychological reactance.* New York: Academic Press.

Brekke, N., & Borgida, E. (1988). Expert psychological testimony in rape trials: A social-cognitive analysis. *Journal of Personality and Social Psychology, 55,* 372–386.

Bremer, C. & Todd, S. (2004). Reducing judicial stress through mentoring. *Judicature, 87,* 244–251.

Brennan, A. (1998, August 17). Women having it all. *National Law Journal,* p.1.

Brennan, P. A., & Raine, A. (1997). Biosocial bases of antisocial behavior: Psychophysiological, neurological, and cognitive factors. *Clinical Psychology Review, 17,* 589–604.

Brewer, N., & Burke, A. (2002). Effects of testimonial inconsistencies and eyewitness confidence on mock-juror judgments. *Law and Human Behavior, 26,* 353–364.

Brewster, J., & Stoloff, M. (2003). Relationship between IQ and first-year overall performance as a police officer. *Applied H.R.M. Research, 8,* 49–50.

Bridges, G., & Steen, S. (1998). Racial disparities in official assessments of juvenile offenders: Attribution stereotypes as mediating mechanisms. *American Sociological Review, 63:* 554–570.

Brigham, J., & Wasserman, A. (1999). The impact of race, racial attitude, and gender on reactions to the criminal trial of O. J. Simpson. *Journal of Applied Social Psychology, 29,* 1333–1370.

Bright, S. (1994). Counsel for the poor: The death sentence not for the worst crime but for the worst lawyer. *Yale Law Review, 103,* 1895–1883.

Bright, S. (1997). Political attacks on the judiciary: Can justice be done amid efforts to intimidate and remove judges from office for unpopular decisions? *New York University Law Review,* 308–336.

Brimacombe, C., Jung, S., Garrioch, L., & Allison, M. (2003). Perceptions of older adult eyewitnesses: Will you believe me when I'm 64? *Law and Human Behavior, 27,* 507–522

Broder, J. (2004, June 27). Starting over, 24 years after a wrongful conviction. *New York Times.* Retrieved from http://www.nytimes/com/2004/06/21/national/

Broderick, R. (1991), Court-annexed compulsory arbitration is providing litigants with a speedier and less expensive alternative to the traditional courtroom trial, *Judicature, 75,* 41–44.

Broeder, D. W. (1959). The University of Chicago jury project. *Nebraska Law Review, 38,* 744–760.

Broeder, D. W. (1965). Voir dire examinations: An empirical study. *Southern California Law Review, 38,* 503–528.

Bronner, G., Peretz, C., & Ehrenfeld, M. (2003). Sexual harassment of nurses and nursing students. *Journal of Advanced Nursing. 42,* 637–644.

Bronstien, A. J. (1980). Prisoner's rights: A History. In G.P. Alpert (Ed.), *Legal rights of prisoners* (pp. 14–45). Newbury Park, CA: Sage.

Brown v. Board of Education, 347 U.S. 483 (1954).

Brown v. Mississippi, 297 U.S. 278 (1936).

Brown, J. M., & Campbell, E. A. (1990). Sources of occupational stress in the police. *Work and Stress, 4,* 305–318.

Brownmiller, S., & Alexander, D. (1992, January/February). From Carmita Wood to Anita Hill. *Ms.,* pp. 70–71.

Bruck, D. (1985, May 20). The death penalty: An exchange. *New Republic,* 20–21.

Bruck, M., Ceci, S., & Hembrooke, H. (1998). Reliability and credibility in young children's reports: From research to policy and practice. *American Psychologist, 53,* 136–151.

Bruck, M., Ceci, S., & Hembrooke, H. (2002). The nature of children's true and false narratives. *Developmental Review, 22,* 520–554.

Bryan, W. J. (1971). *The chosen ones.* New York: Vantage Press.

Buchan, L. (2005). Jail diversion for mentally ill top priority in Miami-Dade. *County News Online, 37,* 12. Retrieved July 5, 2005, from http://www.naco.org/CountyNewsTemplate.cfm?template=/ContentManagement/ContentDisplay. cfm & Content ID=8091

Bund, J. M. (1997). Did you say chemical castration? *University of Pittsburgh Law Review, 59,* 157.

Bureau of Justice Statistics. (1995). *Sourcebook of criminal justice statistics – 1994.* Washington D.C.: U.S. Department of Justice.

Bureau of Justice Statistics (1999). *National crime victimization survey.* Washington, D.C.: U.S. Department of Justice.

Bureau of Justice Statistics. (2003a). *Criminal victimization in the United States, 2002 statistical tables.* Retrieved June 20, 2005, from http://www.ojp.usdoj.gov/bjsi/pub/pdf/cvus02.pdf

Bureau of Justice Statistics. (2003b). *Sourcebook of criminal justice statistics.* Retrieved September 1, 2005, from http://www.albany.edu/sourcebook

Bureau of Justics Statistics. (2005a). *Capital punishment statistics.* Retrieved September 1, 2005, from http://www. ojp.usdoj.gov/

Bureau of Justice Statistics. (2005b). *Nation's prison and jail population grew by 932 inmates per week, number of female inmates reached more than 10,000.* Retrieved September 1, 2005, from http://www.ojp.usdoj.gov/

Bureau of Justice Statistics. (2005c). *State and local law enforcement statistics.* Retrieved July 18, 2005, from http://www.ojp.usdoj.gov/bjs/sandlle.htm#education

Burger, W. E. (1975). Dissenting opinion in *O'Connor v. Donaldson. U. S. Law Week, 42,* 4929–4936.

Burgess, A. W., & Holmstrom, L. L. (1974). *Rape: Victims of crisis.* Bowie, MA: Robert J. Brady.

Burgess, A. W., & Holmstrom, L. L. (1979). Rape: Sexual disruption and recovery. *American Journal of Orthopsychiatry, 49,* 648–657.

Burgess, R. L., & Akers, R. L. (1966). A differential-reinforcement theory of criminal behavior. *Social Problems, 14,* 128–147.

Burlington Industries, Inc. v. Ellerth, 524, U.S., 742 (1998).

Burnet v. Coronado Oil and Gas Co., 285 U.S. 393, 406, 52 S.Ct. 443, 447, 76 L.Ed. 815 (1932).

Burt, M. R. (1980). Cultural myths and supports for rape. *Journal of Personality and Social Psychology, 38,* 217–230.

Burt, R., & Morris, N. (1972). A proposal for the abolition of the incompetency plea. *University of Chicago Law Review, 40,* 66–95.

Bush v. Gore, 531 U.S. 98 (2000).

Bush v. Schiavo, 885 So.2d 321(Fla. 2004).

Bushway, S., & Piehl, A. (2001). Judging judicial discretion: Legal factors and racial discrimination in sentencing. *Law and Society Review, 35,* 733–764.

Buss, A. H. (1966). *Psychopathology.* New York: Wiley.

Buss, D. M., & Malamuth, N. M. (Eds.). (1996). *Sex, power, conflict: Evolutionary and feminist perspectives.* New York: Oxford University Press.

Butler, P. (2004). In defense of jury nullification. *Litigation, 31,* 46–49.

Butler, W. M., Leitenberg, H., & Fuselier, D. G. (1993). The use of mental health consultants to police hostage negotiation teams. *Behavioral Sciences and the Law, 11,* 213–221.

Butterfield, F. (1996, March 8). Tough law on sentences is criticized. *New York Times,* p. A8.

Butterfield, F. (1997, February 3). '95 data show sharp drop in reported rapes. *New York Times,* pp. A1, A14.

Byrne, C. A., Resnick, H. S., Kilpatrick, D. G., Best, C. L., & Saunders, B. E. (1999). The socioeconomic impact of interpersonal violence on women. *Journal of Consulting and Clinical Psychology, 67,* 362–366.

Cable News Network. (2004, June 25). *No charges against man beaten during arrest.* Retrieved June 20, 2005, from http://www.cnn.com/2004/US/West/06/25/lapd.video/index.html

Caetano, R., McGrath, C., Ramisetty-Mikler, S., & Field, C.A. (2005). Drinking, alcohol problems and the five-year recurrence and incidence of male to female and female to male partner violence. *Alcoholism: Clinical & Experimental Research. 29,* 1, 98–106.

Calhoun, K., Atkeson, B., & Resick, P. (1982). A longitudinal examination of fear reactions in victims of rape. *Journal of Counseling Psychology, 29,* 656–661.

Callahan, L. A., & Silver, E. (1998). Factors associated with the conditional release of persons aquitted by reason of insanity: A decision tree approach. *Law and Human Behavior, 22,* 2, 147–163.

Callahan, V. A., McGreevey, M. A., Cirincione, C., & Steadman, H. J. (1992). Measuring the effects of the guilty but mentally ill (GBMI) verdict: Georgia's 1982 GBMI reform. *Law and Human Behavior, 16,* 447–462.

Campbell, R., Sefl, T., Barnes, H. E., Ahrens, C. E., Wasco, S. M., & Zaragoza-Diesfeld, Y. (1999). Community services for rape survivors: Enhancing psychological well-being or increasing trauma? *Journal of Consulting and Clinical Psychology, 67,* 847–858.

Cantor, N. L. (1998). Making advance directives meaningful. *Psychology, Public Policy, and Law, 4,* 629–652.

Caplow, T., & Simon, J. (1999). Understanding prison policy and population trends. *Crime and justice: A review of research, 26,* 63–120.

Cardozo, M. (1993). Racial discrimination in legal education. *Journal of Legal Education, 43,* 79–84.

Carlsmith, K., Darley, J., & Robinson, P. (2002). Why do we punish: Deter-rence and just deserts as motives for punishment. *Journal of Personality and Social Psychology, 83,* 284–299.

Carlson, H., Thayer, R. E., & Germann, A. C. (1971). Social attitudes and personality differences among members of two kinds of police departments (innovative vs. traditional) and students. *Journal of Criminal Law, Criminology, and Police Science, 62,* 564–567.

Carlson, K., & Russo, J. (2001). Biased interpretation of evidence by mock jurors. *Journal of Experimental Psychology: Applied, 7,* 91–103.

Carlson, N. A., Hess, K. M., & Orthmann, C. M. (1999). *Corrections in the 21st century.* Belmont CA: West/Wadsworth Press.

Carp, R., Manning, K., & Sitdham, R. (2004). The decision-making behavior of George W. Bush's judicial appointees. *Judicature, 88,* 20–28.

Carr, P. L., Ash, A. S., Friedman, R. H., Szalacha, L., Barnett, R. C., Palepu, A., & Moskowitz, M. M. (2000). Faculty perceptions of gender discrimination and sexual harassment in academic medicine. *Annals of Internal Medicine, 132,* 889–896.

Carroll, J. S., Kerr, N. L., Alfini, J. J., Weaver, F. M., MacCoun, R. J., & Feldman, V. (1986). Free press and fair trial: The role of behavioral research. *Law and Human Behavior, 10,* 187–201.

Carter, T. (1998, November), Terms of embitterment. *American Bar Association Journal, 84,* 42.

Carter, T. (2003, May). Arbitration pendulum. *American Bar Association Journal, 89,* 14–16.

Carter, T. (2004, June). Red Hook experiment. *American Bar Association Journal, 90,* 37–42.

Carter, T. (2005, February). Mud and money. *American Bar Association Journal, 91,* 40–45.

Casey, T. (2004). When good intentions are not enough: Problem-solving courts and the impending crisis of legitimacy. *Southern Methodist University Law Review, 57,* 1459–1519.

Casper, J. (1993). Restructuring the traditional civil jury: The effects of changes in composition and procedures. In R. Litan (Ed.), *Verdict: Assessing the civil jury system.* (pp. 419–459). Washington, D.C.: The Brookings Institute.

Casper, J. D. (1972). *American criminal justice: The defendant's perspective.* Englewood Cliffs, NJ: Prentice-Hall.

Cassell, P. G. (1999). The guilty and the "innocent": An examination of alleged cases of wrongful convictions from false confessions. *Harvard Journal of Law and Public Policy, 22,* 523–603.

Castelli, P., Goodman, G., & Ghetti, S. (2005). Effects of interview style and witness age on perceptions of children's credibility in sexual abuse cases. *Journal of Applied Social Psychology, 35,* 297–319.

Ceci, S., Huffman, M., Smith, E., & Loftus, E. (1994). Repeatedly thinking about a non-event: Source misattribution among preschoolers. *Consciousness and Cognition, 3,* 388–407.

Ceci, S., Scullin, M., & Kanaya, T. (2003). The difficulty of basing death penalty eligibility on IQ cutoff scores for mental retardation. *Ethics & Behavior, 13,* 11–17.

Cernkovich, S. A., & Giordano, P. C. (1996). School bonding, race, and delinquency. In D. G. Rojek & G. F. Jensen (Eds.), *Exploring delinquency: Causes and control* (pp. 210–218). Los Angeles: Roxbury.

Chambliss, W. J., & Seidman, R. B. (1971). *Law, order, and power.* Reading, MA: Addison-Wesley.

Chandler, C. (1998). Voluntary executions. *Stanford Law Review, 50,* 1897–1927.

Chandler, M., & Moran, T. (1990). Psychopathy and moral development: A comparative study of delinquent and nondelinquent youth. *Development & Psychopathology, 2*(3), 227–246.

Chapman, G., & Bornstein, B. (1996). The more you ask for, the more you get: Anchoring in personal injury verdict. *Applied Cognitive Psychology, 10,* 519–540.

Charles, M. T. (1986). *Policing the streets.* Springfield, IL: Thomas.

Chermack, S. T., & Giancola, P. R. (1997). The relation between alcohol and aggression: An integrated biopsychosocial conceptualization. *Clinical Psychology Review,* 17, 621–649.

Chevigny, P. (1969). *Police power: Police abuse in New York City.* New York: Vintage Books.

Choi, A., & Edleson, J.L. (1996). Social disapproval of wife assaults: A national survey of Singapore. *Journal of Comparative Family Studies,* 27(1), 73–88.

Choo, K. (2001). The right equation. *American Bar Association Journal,* 87(8), 58–62.

Christiansen, K. O. (1977). A preliminary study of criminality among twins. In S. A. Mednick & K. O. Christiansen (Eds.), *Biosocial bases of criminal behavior.* New York: Wiley.

Christie, R. (1976). Probability v. precedence: The social psychology of jury selection. In G. Bermant, C. Nemeth, & N. Vidmar (Eds.), *Psychology and the law: Research frontiers* (pp. 265–281). Lexington, MA: Lexington Books.

Cirincione, C., & Jacobs, C. (1999). Identifying insanity acquittals: Is it any easier? *Law and Human Behavior,* 23, 487–497.

Clancy, P. (1987, July 22). Cops battle stress: "I'm hurting . . . ." *USA Today,* pp. 1A–2A.

Clavet, G. J. (1996, August). *Ironic effects of juror attempts to suppress inadmissible evidence.* Paper presented at the meeting of the American Psychological Association, Toronto, Canada.

Cloninger, C., Sigvardsson, S., Bohman, M., & vonKnorring, A. (1982). Predisposition to petty criminality in Swedish adoptees. II: Cross-fostering analysis of gene–environment interaction. *Archives of General Psychiatry,* 39, 1242–1249.

Cloud, J. (1998). Of arms and the boy. *Time,* 152.

Cloward, R. A., & Ohlin, L. E. (1960). *Delinquency and opportunity: A theory of delinquent gangs.* New York: Free Press.

Coccaro, E., Kavoussi, R., & Lesser, J. (1992). Self- and other-directed human aggression: The role of the central serotonergic system. *International Clinical Psychopharmacology,* 6, 70–83.

Cochran, P. A. (1971). A situational approach to the study of police– Negro relations. *Sociological Quarterly,* 12, 232–237.

Cohen, M. I., Spodak, M. K., Silver, S. B., & Williams, K. (1988). Predicting outcome of insanity acquittees released to the community. *Behavioral Sciences and the Law,* 6, 515–530.

Cohen, T. (2004). Tort trials and verdicts in large counties, 2001. *Bureau of Justice Statistics Bulletin,* NCJ 206240.

Colbach, E. (1981). Integrity checks on the witness stand. *Bulletin of the American Academy of Psychiatry and the Law,* 9, 285–288.

Colorado v. Connelly, 107 S.Ct. 515 (1986).

Colorado v. Spring, 479 U.S. 564 (1987).

Committee on Ethical Guidelines for Forensic Psychologists. (1991). Specialty guidelines for forensic psychologists. *Law and Human Behavior,* 15, 655–665.

Commonwealth v. Wall, 606 A.2d 449 (Pa. 1992).

Conger, R. (1980). Juvenile delinquency: Behavior restraint or behavior facilitation? In T. Hirschi & M. Gottfredson (Eds.), *Understanding crime: Current theory and research* (pp. 131–142). Newbury Park, CA: Sage.

Conover, T. (2003, June 29). In the land of Guantanamo. *New York Times Sunday Magazine,* p. 40.

Cook, B. (1993). Moral authority and gender difference, Georgia Bullock and the Los Angeles Women's Court. *Judicature,* 77, 144–153.

Cook, S. W. (1984, August). Participation by social scientists in litigation regarding school desegregation: Past contributions and future opportunities. Paper presented at the meeting of the American Psychological Association, Toronto.

Cooper v. Oklahoma, 116 S.Ct. 1373 (1996).

Cooper, J., & Neuhaus, I. M. (2000). The hired gun effect: Assessing the effect of pay, frequency of testifying, and credentials on the perception of expert testimony. *Law and Human Behavior,* 24, 149–172.

Copson, G., Badcock, R., Boon, J., and Britton, P. (1997). Articulating a systematic approach to clinical crime profiling. *Criminal Behaviour and Mental Health,* 7, 13–17.

Cornish, D. B., & Clarke, R. V. (1986). *The reasoning criminal: Rational choice perspectives on offending.* New York: Springer.

Council on Ethical and Judicial Affairs (1993). Mandatory parental consent

to abortion. *Journal of the American Medical Association,* 269, 82–86.

County of Riverside v. McLaughlin, 111 S.Ct. 1661 (1991).

Cowan, C. L., Thompson, W. C., & Ellsworth, P. C. (1984). The effects of death qualification on jurors' predispositions to convict and on the quality of deliberation. *Law and Human Behavior,* 8, 53–79.

Cowan, J., Crisham, T., Keating, M., Mahoney G., Pole, D., Pope, M., Schwarzer, W. & Wester, J., (2003). What attorneys think of jury trial innovations, *Judicature,* 86, 192–99.

Cox, D. (1999, June 28). Arbitration is no simple matter, *National Law Journal,* p. 1.

Coy v. Iowa, 487 U.S. 1012, (1988).

Coyle, M. (2004). Death row inmate back at high court: Is 5th Circuit defying a Supreme Court ruling? *National Law Journal,* 26(42), 6.

Crandall, C. S., Glor, J., & Britt, T. W. (1997). AIDS-related stigmatization: Instrumental and symbolic attitudes. *Journal of Applied Social Psychology,* 27, 95–123.

Crosby, M., & English, A. (1991). Mandatory parental involvement judicial bypass laws: Do they promote adolescents' health? *Society for Adolescent Medicine,* 12, 143–147.

Cruzan v. Director, Missouri Department of Health, 497 U.S. 261 (1990).

Cunningham, M. D., & Reidy, T. J. (1998). Integrating base rate data in violence risk assessment at capital sentencing. *Behavioral Sciences and the Law,* 16, 71–96.

Cunningham, M. D., & Vigen, M. P. (2002). Death row inmate characteristics, adjustment, and confinement: A critical review of the literature. *Behavioral Sciences and the Law,* 20, 191–210.

Cureton, S. R. (2000). Justifiable arrests or discretionary justice: Predictors of racial arrest differentials. *Journal of Black Studies,* 30(5), 703–719.

Curriden, M. (1995, July). Hard time. *American Bar Association Journal,* 81, 72–74.

Curriden, M. (2001, August). Power of 12. *American Bar Association Journal,* pp. 36–41.

Curry, T., Lee, G., & Rodriquez, S. (2004). Does victim gender increase sentence severity? Further explorations of gender dynamics and sentencing outcomes. *Crime and Delinquency,* 50, 319–343.

Cutler, B. L., & Penrod, S. D. (1988). Improving the reliability of eyewitness identification: Lineup construction and presentation. *Journal of Applied Psychology*, 73, 281–290.

Cutler, B. L., Penrod, S. D., & Dexter, H. R. (1989). The eyewitness, the expert psychologist, and the jury. *Law and Human Behavior*, 13, 311–332.

Cutler, B. L., Penrod, S. D., & Dexter, H. R. (1990). Juror sensitivity to eyewitness identification evidence. *Law and Human Behavior*, 14, 185–192.

Cutter v. Wilkerson, 03-9877 (2005).

D'Agostino, C. (1986). Police psychological services: Ethical issues. In J. T. Reese & H. A. Goldstein (Eds.), *Psychological services for law enforcement* (pp. 241–248). Washington, D.C.: U.S. Government Printing Office.

Dahir, V., Richardson, J., Ginsburg, G., Gatowski, S., Dobbin, S., & Merlino, M. (2005). Judicial application of Daubert to psychological syndrome and profile evidence. *Psychology, Public Policy, and Law*, 11, 62–82.

Dake, J., Price, J., & Telljohan, S. (2003). The nature and extent of bullying at school. *Journal of School Health*, 73, 173–180.

Dann, B., & Hans, V. (2004). Recent evaluative research on jury trial innovations. *Court Review*, 41, 12–19.

Dann, B., Hans, V., & Kaye, D. (2004). *Testing the effects of selected jury trial innovations on juror comprehension of contested DNA evidence*. Final technical report. Washington, D.C.: National Institute of Justice.

Darley, J., Fulero, S., Haney, C., & Tyler, T. (2002). Psychological jurisprudence. In J. Ogloff (Ed.), *Taking psychology and law into the twenty-first century* (pp. 37–39). New York: Kluwer Academic/Plenum Publishers.

Darley, J., Sanderson, C., & LaMantha, P. (1996). Community standards for defining attempt: Inconsistencies with the Model Penal Code. *American Behavioral Scientist*, 39, 405–420.

da Silva, D. A., Goes, A. C., de Carvalho J. J., & de Carvalho, E. F (2004). DNA typing from vaginal smear slides in suspected rape cases. *Sao Paulo Medical Journal*, 122, 70–72.

Daubert v. Merrell Dow Pharmaceuticals, Inc., 113 S.Ct. 2786 (1993).

D'Augelli, A. R. (1998). Developmental implications of victimization of lesbian, gay, and bisexual youths. In G. M. Herek (Ed.), *Stigma and sexual orientation: Understanding prejudice against lesbians, gay men and bisexuals (psychological perspectives on lesbian and gay issues)* (4th ed., pp. 187–210). Thousand Oaks, CA: Sage Publications.

Davis v. United States, 411 U. S. 233 (1994).

Davis, S., & Bottoms, B. (2002). Effects of social support on children's eyewitness reports: A test of the underlying mechanism. *Law and Human Behavior*, 26, 185–215.

Davis, S., Haire, S. & Songer, D. (1993). Voting behavior and gender on the U.S. courts of appeal, *Judicature*, 77, 129–133.

Dawes, R. M. (1994). *House of cards: Psychology and psychotherapy built on myth*. New York: Free Press.

Dawes, R. M., Faust, D., & Meehl, P. E. (1989). Clinical versus actuarial judgment. *Science*, 243, 1668–1674.

Death Penalty Information Center. (2005). *Innocence: Freed from death row*. Retrieved September 1, 2005, from http://www.deathpenaltyinfo. org/

Deffenbacher, K., Bornstein, B., Penrod, S., & McGorty, E. (2004). A meta-analytic review of the effects of high stress on eyewitness memory. *Law and Human Behavior*, 28, 687–706.

Deitz, S. R., Blackwell, K. T., Daley, P. C., & Bentley, B. J. (1982). Measurement of empathy toward rape victims and rapists. *Journal of Personality and Social Psychology*, 43, 372–384.

Deitz, S. R., Littman, M., & Bentley, B. J. (1984). Attribution of responsibility for rape: The influence of observer empathy, victim resistance, and victim attractiveness. *Sex Roles*, 10, 261–280.

Deitz, S. R., Russell, S. A., & Hammes, K. M. (1989, August). Who's on trial?: Information processing by jurors in rape cases. Paper presented at the meeting of the American Psychological Association, New Orleans.

deMayo, R. A. (1997). Patient sexual behavior and sexual harassment: A national survey of female psychologists. *Professional Psychology: Research and Practice*, 28, 58–62.

Demuth, S., & Steffensmeier, D. (2004). The impact of gender and race-ethnicity in the pretrial release process. *Social Problems*, 51, 222–242.

Dennis v. United States, 384 U.S. 855 (1966).

Denno, D. (2002). Crime and consciousness. *Minnesota Law Review*, 87, 269–399.

Department of Justice (1999). Post-conviction DNA testing: Recommendations for handling requests. Retrieved from http://www.ncjrs.org/pdffiles1/nij/177626.pdf

Dershowitz, A. M. (1994). *The abuse excuse*. Boston: Little, Brown.

De Tocqueville, A. (1900). *Democracy in America*, 1, (Henry Reeve, Trans.). New York: Colonial Press.

Detrick, P., & Chibnall, J. T. (2002). Prediction of police officer performance with the Iwald Personality Inventory. *Journal of Police & Criminal Psychology*, 17, 9–17.

Detrick, P., Chibnall, J. T., & Rosso, M. (2001). Minnesota Multiphasic Personality Inventory–2 in police officer selection: Normative data and relation to the Inwald Personality Inventory. *Professional Psychology*, 32, 484–490.

Devenport, J., Stinson, V., Cutler, B., & Kravitz, D. (2002). How effective are the cross-examination and expert testimony safeguards? Jurors' perceptions of the suggestiveness and fairness of biased lineup procedures. *Journal of Applied Psychology*, 87, 1042–1054.

Devine, D., Clayton, L., Dunford, B., Seying, R., & Pryce, J. (2001). Jury decision making: 45 years of empirical research on deliberating groups. *Psychology, Public Policy, and Law*, 7, 622–727.

Dewolf, C., Duron, B, & Loas, G. (2002). Electroencephalographics abnormalities in psychopaths: A controlled study. *Annales Médico-psychologiques, revue psychiatrique*, 160, 5–6, 451–455.

Dhami, M. (2003). Psychological models of professional decision making. *Psychological Science*, 14, 175–180.

Diamond, B. L. (1980). Inherent problems in the use of pretrial hypnosis on a prospective witness. *California Law Review*, 68, 313–349.

Diamond, S., Rose, M., & Murphy, B. (2004). Jurors' unanswered questions. *Court Review*, 41, 20–29.

Diamond, S., & Vidmar, N. (2001). Jury room ruminations on forbidden topics. *Virginia Law Review*, 87, 1857–1915.

Diamond, S., Vidmar, N., Rose, M., Ellis, L., & Murphy, B. (2003). Civil juror discussions during trial: A study of Arizona's rule 39(f) from videotaped discussions and deliberations. Retrieved October 5, 2005, from http://www.law.northwestern.edu/diamond/papers/arizona_civil_discussions.pdf

Dickerson v. United States, 2000 U.S. Lexis 5911 (2000)

Dickinson, J., Poole, D., & Laimon, R. (2005). Children's recall and testimony. In N. Brewer & K. Williams (Eds.), *Psychology and Law: An empirical perspective* (pp. 151–175). New York: Guilford Press.

Dietz, P. E., & Reese, J. T. (1986). The perils of police psychology: 10 strategies for minimizing role conflicts when providing mental health services and consultation to law enforcement agencies. *Behavioral Sciences and the Law, 4*, 385–400.

Deitz, S. R., Littman, M., & Bentley, B. J. (1984). Attribution of responsibility for rape: The influence of observer empathy, victim resistance, and victim attractiveness. *Sex Roles, 10*, 267–280.

DiLalla, L. F., & Gottesman, I. (1991). Biological and genetic contributors to violence: Widom's untold tale. *Psychological Bulletin, 109*, 125–129.

Dillehay, R. C. (1999). Authoritarianism and jurors. In W. F. Abbott & J. Batt (Eds.), *A handbook of jury research*. (Pp. 13.1–13.18). Philadelphia: ALI-ABA.

Dillehay, R. C., & Nietzel, M. T. (1985). Juror experience and jury verdicts. *Law and Human Behavior, 9*, 179–191.

Dillehay, R. C., & Nietzel, M. T. (1999). Prior jury service. In W. F. Abbott & J. Batt (Eds.), *A handbook of jury research*. (pp. 11.1–11.17). Philadelphia: ALI-ABA.

Ditto, P., Jacobson, J., Smucker, W., Danks, J., & Fagerlin, A. (2005). *Context changes choices: A prospective study of the effects of hospitalization on life-sustaining treatment preferences*. Unpublished manuscript, University of California–Irvine.

Ditto, P., Smucker, W., Danks, J., Jacobson, J., Houts, R., Fagerlin, A., et al. (2003). Stability of older adults' preferences for life-sustaining medical treatment. *Health Psychology, 22*, 605–615.

Ditton, P. M. (1999, July). *Mental health treatment of inmates and probationers*. Washington D.C.: U.S. Department of Justice. Retrieved September 20, 2005, from http://www.ojp.usdoj.gov/bjs/pub/pdf/mhtip.pdf

Dodge, M., & Greene, E. (1991). Jurors and expert conceptions of battered women. *Violence and Victims, 6*, 271–282.

Donat, P. L. N., & D'Emilio, J. (1992). A feminist redefinition of rape and sexual assault: Historical foundations and change. *Journal of Social Issues, 48*(1), 9–22.

Doob, A., & Kirschenbaum, H. (1972). Some empirical evidence on the effect of S. 12 of the Canada Evidence Act upon the accused, *Criminal Justice Quarterly, 15*, 88–96.

Doren, D. M. (1987). *Understanding and treating the psychopath*. New York: Wiley.

Doris, J., Mazur, R., & Thomas, M. (1995). Training in child protective services: A commentary on the amicus brief of Bruck and Ceci (1993/1995). *Psychology, Public Policy, and Law, 1*, 479–493.

Dougall, A. L., Hayward, M. C. & Baum, A. (2005). Media exposure to bioterrorism: Stress and the anthrax attacks. *Psychiatry, 68*, 1, 28–43.

Douglas, J. E., Ressler, R. K., Burgess, A. W., & Hartman, C. R. (1986). Criminal profiling from crime scene analysis. *Behavioral Sciences and the Law, 4*, 401–421.

Douglas, K. S., & Webster, C. D. (1999). Predicting violence in mentally and personality disordered individuals. In R. Roesch, S. D. Hart, & J. R.P. Ogloff (Eds.), *Psychology and Law: The state of the discipline* (pp. 175–239). New York: Kluwer/Plenum.

Dowling v. U.S., 110 S.Ct. 668 (1990).

Downs, D. A. (1996). *More than victims: Battered women, the syndrome society, and the law*. Chicago: University of Chicago Press.

Dressler, J. (2003). *Criminal law*. St. Paul, MN: West.

Driscoll, D. M., Kelly, J. R., & Henderson, W. L. (1998). Can perceivers identify likelihood to sexually harass? *Sex Roles, 38*, 557–588.

Drizin, S. (1999), The juvenile court at 100, *Judicature, 83*, 9–15.

Drizin, S., & Colgan, B. (2004). Tales from the juvenile confession front: A guide to how standard police interrogation tactics can produce coerced and false confessions from juvenile suspects. In G. D. Lassiter (Ed.), *Interrogations, confessions, and entrapment* (pp. 127–162). New York: Kluwer Academic/Plenum.

Drizin, S., & Leo, R. (2004). The problem of false confessions in the post-DNA world. *North Carolina Law Review, 82*, 891–1007.

Duggan, P. (2000, June 23). Texas executes Graham after appeals fail; Death penalty case dogs Bush in his bid for the presidency. *Washington Post*, p. A1.

Duncan v. Louisiana, 391 U.S. 145 (1968).

Duning, C., & Hanchette, J. (1985, March 28). Don't shoot, Court tells police. *USA Today*, p. 2A.

Dunning, D., & Perretta, S. (2002). Automaticity and eyewitness accuracy: A 10–12 second rule for distinguishing accurate from inaccurate positive identifications. *Journal of Applied Psychology, 87*, 951–962.

Durham v. United States, 214 F.2d 862 (1954).

Dusky v. United States, 362 U.S. 402 (1960).

Dutton, D. G. (1987). The criminal justice response to wife assault. *Law and Human Behavior, 11*, 189–206.

Dutton, D. G. (1995). Male abusiveness in intimate relationships. *Clinical Psychology Review, 15*, 567–582.

Dutton, D. G. (2000). *The domestic assault of women* (3rd ed.). Vancouver: University of British Columbia Press.

Dwyer, J., Neufeld, P., & Scheck, B. (2000). *Actual innocence: Five days from execution and other dispatches from the wrongly convicted*. New York: Doubleday.

Dywan, J., & Bowers, K. S. (1983). The use of hypnosis to enhance recall. *Science, 222*, 184–185.

Eads, L., Shuman, D., & DeLipsey, J. (2000). Getting it right: The trial of sexual assault and child molestation cases under Federal Rules of Evidence 413–415. *Behavioral Sciences and the Law, 18*, 169–216.

Eaton, L., & Kaufman, L. (2005, April 26). In problem-solving courts, judges turn therapist. *New York Times*, p. A1.

Ebbesen, E. B., & Konecni, V. J. (1981). The process of sentencing adult felons: A causal analysis of judicial decision. In B. D. Sales (Ed.), *The trial process* (pp. 413–458). New York: Plenum.

Ebert, B. W. (1987). Guide to conducting a psychological autopsy. *Professional Psychology: Research and Practice, 18*, 52–56.

Ebreo, A., Linn, N., & Vining, J. (1996). The impact of procedural justice on opinions of public policy: Solid waste management as an example. *Journal of Applied Social Psychology, 26*, 1259–1285.

Eckhardt, C. L, Barbour, K. A., & Davison, G. C. (1998). Articulated thoughts of maritally violent and nonviolent men during anger arousal. *Journal of Consulting and Clinical Psychology, 66*, 259–269.

Eckholm, E. (1985, July 4). Stockholm syndrome: Hostages' reactions. *Lawrence Journal-World*, p. 6.

Edmonson v. Leesville Concrete Co., 111 S.Ct. 2077 (1991).

Edkins V., and Wrightsman, L. (2004). The psychology of entrapment. In G. D. Lassiter (Ed.), *Interrogations, confessions and entrapment* (pp. 215–246). New York: Kluwer Academic/Plenum.

Egeth, H. (1995). Expert psychological testimony about eyewitnesses: An update. In F. Kessel et al. (Eds.), *Psychology, science, and human affairs: Essays in honor or William Bevan* (pp. 151–166). Boulder, CO: Westview Press.

Eichenwald, K. (1989, September 28). Bilzerian gets four years in jail, stiffest in stock crackdown. *New York Times*, pp. 29, 36.

Eisele, G. T. (1991), The case against mandatory court-annexed ADR programs, *Judicature, 75*, 34–40.

Eisenberg, T., Hannaford-Agor, P., Hans, V., Waters, N., Munsterman, T., Schwab, S., & Wells, M. (2005). Judge–jury agreement in criminal cases: A partial replication of Kalven and Zeisel's *The American Jury. Journal of Empirical Legal Studies, 2,* 171–207.

Eisenberg, T., LaFountain, N., Ostrom, B., Rottman, D., & Wells, M. (2002). Juries, judges, and punitive damages: An empirical study. *Cornell Law Review, 87,* 743–782.

Ekman, P. (1985). *Telling lies.* New York: Norton.

Ekman, P., O'Sullivan, M., & Frank, M. (1999). A few can catch a liar. *Psychological Science, 10,* 263–266.

Eley, T. C. (1997). General genes: A new theme in developmental psychopathology. *Current Directions in Psychological Science, 6,* 90–95.

Elliott, D. S., Huizinga, D., & Ageton, S. S. (1985). *Explaining delinquency and drug use.* Thousand Oaks, CA: Sage.

Elliott, R. (1993). Expert testimony about eyewitness identification: A critique. *Law and Human Behavior, 17,* 423–436.

Ellis, L. (1989). *Theories of rape: Inquiries into the causes of sexual aggression.* New York: Hemisphere.

Ellis, L. (1991). A synthesized (biosocial) theory of rape. *Journal of Consulting and Clinical Psychology, 59,* 631–642.

Ellis, L., & Diamond, S. (2003). Race, diversity, and jury composition: Battering and bolstering legitimacy.

Chicago-Kent Law Review, 78, 1033–1058.

Ellison, K., & Buckhout, R. (1981). *Psychology and criminal justice.* New York: Harper & Row.

Ellsworth, P. C. (1989). Are twelve heads better than one? *Law and Contemporary Problems, 52*(4), 205–224.

Ellsworth, P. C. (1999). Jury reform at the end of the century: Real agreement, real changes. *University of Michigan Journal of Law Reform, 32,* 213ff. Retrieved December 7, 1999, from Lexis-Nexis.

Ellsworth, P. C., & Mauro, R. (1998). Psychology and law. In D. Gilbert, S. Fiske, et al. (Eds.) *The handbook of social psychology,* Vol. 2, (pp. 684–732), Boston: McGraw-Hill.

Ellsworth, P. C., & Reifman, A. (2000). Juror comprehension and public policy: Perceived problems and proposed solutions. *Psychology, Public Policy, and Law, 6,* 788–821.

Elwork, A., Alfini, J. J., & Sales, B. D. (1982). Toward understandable jury instructions. *Judicature, 65,* 433–442.

Elwork, A., Sales, B. D., & Suggs, D. (1981). The trial: A research review. In B. D. Sales (Ed.), *The trial process* (pp. 1–68). New York: Plenum.

English, P. W., & Sales, B. D. (1997). A ceiling or consistency effect for the comprehension of jury instructions. *Psychology, Public Policy, and Law, 3,* 381–401.

Ennis, B. J., & Litwack, T. R. (1974). Psychiatry and the presumption of expertise: Flipping coins in the courtroom. *California Law Review, 62,* 693–752.

Eron, L. (1987). The development of aggressive behavior from the perspective of developing behaviorism. *American Psychologist, 42,* 435–442.

Eron, L. (1990). Understanding aggression. *Bulletin of the International Society for Research on Aggression, 12,* 59.

Estrich, S. (1987). *Real rape.* Cambridge, MA: Harvard University Press.

Everett, R., & Wojtkiewicz, R. (2002). Difference, disparity, and race/ethnic bias in federal sentencing. *Journal of Quantitative Criminology, 18,* 189–211.

Everington, C. T., & Luckasson, R. (1992). *Competence assessment for standing trial for defendants with mental retardation (CASTMR) test manual.* Columbus, Ohio: International Diagnostic Systems, Inc.

Ewing v. California, 538 U.S. 11 (2003).

Ewing v. Goldstein, 120 Cal. App. 4th 807 (2004).

Ewing, C. (1987). *Battered women who kill: Psychological self-defense as legal justification.* Lexington, MA: Lexington Books.

Ewing, C. (1991). Preventive detention and execution: The constitutionality of punishing future crimes. *Law and Human Behavior, 15,* 139–164.

Ewing, C. P., & Aubrey, M. (1987). Battered women and public opinion: Some realities about the myths. *Journal of Family Violence, 2,* 257–264.

Ewing, C. P., Aubrey, M., & Jamieson, L. (1986, August). The battered woman syndrome: Expert testimony and public attitudes. Paper presented at the meeting of the American Psychological Association, Washington, D.C.

Eysenck, H. J. (1964). *Crime and personality.* Boston: Houghton Mifflin.

Eysenck, H. J., & Gudjonsson, G. H. (1989). *The causes and cures of criminality.* New York: Plenum.

Fabian, J. (2003). Death penalty mitigation and the role of the forensic psychologist. *Law and Psychology Review, 27,* 73–120.

Falk, A. J. (1999). Sex offenders, mental illness and criminal responsibility: The constitutional boundaries of civil commitment after *Kansas v. Hendricks. American Journal of Law and Medicine, 25,* 117–147.

Fare v. Michael C., 21 Cal. 3d 471, 519, p.2d 7 (1979).

Faretta v. California, 422 U.S. 806 (1975).

Farmer, M. W. (1976). Jury composition challenges. *Law and Psychology Review, 2,* 45–74.

Farrington, D. P. (1995). The development of offending and antisocial behavior from childhood: Key findings from the Cambridge Study in Delinquent Development. *Journal of Child Psychology and Psychiatry, 360,* 929–964.

Faulkner, A. H. & Cranston, K. (1998). Correlates of same-sex sexual behavior in a random sample of Massachusetts high school students. *American Journal of Public Health, 88,* 262–266.

Faust, D., & Ziskin, J. (1988). The expert witness in psychology and psychiatry. *Science, 241,* 31–35.

FBI Academy. (2002). *Countering terrorism: Integration of practice and theory.* Retrieved online July 22, 2005, from http://www.apa.org/releases/countering_terrorism.pdf

Federal sentencing guidelines. (1995). St. Paul, MN: West.

Feeley, M. M. (1983). *Court reform on trial.* New York: Basic Books.

Feigenson, N., Park, J., & Salovey, P. (1997). Effect of blameworthiness and outcome severity on attributions of responsibility and damage awards in comparative negligence cases. *Law and Human Behavior, 21,* 597–617.

Feild, H. S. (1978). Attitudes toward rape: A comparative analysis of police, rapists, crisis counselors, and citizens. *Journal of Personality and Social Psychology, 36,* 156–179.

Feild, H. S. (1979). Rape trials and jurors' decisions: A psycholegal analysis of the effects of victim, defendant, and case characteristics. *Law and Human Behavior, 3,* 261–284.

Feild, H. S., & Barnett, N. J. (1978). Simulated jury trials: Students vs. "real" people as jurors. *Journal of Social Psychology, 104,* 287–293.

Feild, H. S., & Bienen, L. B. (1980). *Jurors and rape: A study in psychology and law.* Lexington, MA: Heath.

Fein, S., McCloskey, A. L., & Tomlinson, T. M. (1997). Can the jury disregard that information? The use of suspicion to reduce the prejudicial effects of pretrial publicity and inadmissible testimony. *Personality and Social Psychology Bulletin, 23,* 1215–1226.

Feinblatt, J., & Denckla, D. (2001). Prosecutors, defenders, and problem-solving courts. *Judicature, 84,* 207–214.

Feld, B. (1997). Abolish the juvenile court: Youthfulness, criminal responsibility and sentencing policy. *Journal of Criminal Law and Criminology, 88,* 68–136.

Feldman, M. P. (1977). *Criminal behavior: A psychological analysis.* New York: Wiley.

Feldmann, T. B. (2001). Characteristics of hostage and barricade incidents: Implications for negotiation strategies and training. *Journal of Police Crisis Negotiations 1*(1), 3–33.

Feldman-Summers, S., & Ashworth, C. D. (1981). Factors related to intentions to report rape. *Journal of Social Issues, 37,* 71–92.

Feldman-Summers, S., Gordon, P. E., & Meagher, J. R. (1979). The impact of rape on sexual satisfaction. *Journal of Abnormal Psychology, 88,* 101–105.

Fenster, G. A., & Locke, B. (1973). Neuroticism among policemen: An examination of police personality. *Journal of Applied Psychology, 57,* 358–359.

Fentiman, L. (1986). Whose right is it anyway? Rethinking competency to stand trial in light of the synthetically sane insanity defendant. *University of Miami Law Review, 40,* 1109–1169.

Ferri, E. (1917). *Criminal sociology* (Joseph I. Kelley & John Lisle, Trans.). Boston: Little, Brown.

Finkel, N. (1989). The Insanity Defense Reform Act of 1984: Much ado about nothing. *Behavioral Sciences and the Law, 7,* 403–419.

Finkel, N. (1991). The insanity defense: A comparison of verdict schemas. *Law and Human Behavior, 15,* 533–556.

Finkel, N. (1995). *Commonsense justice: Jurors' notions of the law.* Cambridge, MA: Harvard University Press.

Finkel, N. (2000). Commonsense justice and jury instructions: Instructive and reciprocating connections. *Psychology, Public Policy, and Law, 6,* 591–628.

Finkel, N., & Groscup, J. L. (1997). When mistakes happen: Commonsense rules of culpability. *Psychology, Public Policy, and Law, 3,* 65–125.

Finkel, N., & Slobogin, C. (1995). Insanity, justification, and culpability toward a unifying theme. *Law and Human Behavior, 19,* 447–464.

Finz, S., & Walsh, D. (2004, December 15). *The stuff of crime novels finally has an end.* Retrieved September 1, 2005, from www.sfgate.com

Fischer, K. (1989). Defining the boundaries of admissible expert psychological testimony on rape trauma syndrome. *University of Illinois Law Review,* 691–734.

Fischer, P. J., & Breakey, W. R. (1991). The epidemiology of alcohol, drug, and mental disorders among homeless persons. *American Psychologist, 46,* 1115–1128.

Fisher, R. P., & Geiselman, R. E. (1992). *Memory enhancing techniques for investigative interviewing: The cognitive interview.* Springfield, IL: Thomas.

Fiske, S., & Taylor, S. (1991). *Social cognition* (2nd ed.). New York: McGraw-Hill.

Fitzgerald, L. F., Buchanan, N. T., Collinsworth, L. L., Magley, V. J., and Romos, A. M. (1999). Junk logic: The abuse defense in sexual harassment litigation. *Psychology, Public Policy, and Law, 5,* 730–759.

Fitzgerald, L. F., Gelfand, M., & Drasgow, F. (1995). Measuring sexual harassment: Theoretical and psychometric advances. *Basic and Applied Social Psychology, 17,* 425–445.

Fitzgerald, R., & Ellsworth, P. C. (1984). Due process vs. crime control: Death qualification and jury attitudes. *Law and Human Behavior, 8,* 31–51.

Fivush, R., & Shukat, J. (1995). Content, consistency, and coherence of early autobiographical recall. In M. Zaragoza, J. Graham, G. Hall, R. Hirschman, & Y. Ben-Porath (Eds.), *Memory and testimony in the child witness* (pp. 5–23). Thousand Oaks, CA: Sage.

Flaks, D., Ficher, I., Materpasqua, F., & Joseph, G. (1995). Lesbians choosing motherhood: A comparative study of lesbian and heterosexual parents and children. *Developmental Psychology, 31,* 105–114.

Flammer, E., & Bongartz, W. (2003). On the efficacy of hypnosis: A meta-analytic study. *Contemporary Hypnosis, 2003,* 179–197.

Foa, E. B., Hearst-Ikeda, D., & Perry, K. J. (1995). Evaluation of a brief cognitive behavioral program for the prevention of chronic PTSD in recent assault victims. *Journal of Consulting and Clinical Psychology, 63,* 948–955.

Foa, E. B., & Kozak, M. J. (1986). Emotional processing of fear: Exposure to corrective information. *Psychological Bulletin, 99,* 20–35.

Folger, R., Cropanzano, R., Timmerman, T. A., Howes, J. C., & Mitchell, D. (1996). Elaborating procedural fairness: Justice becomes both simpler and more complex. *Personality and Social Psychology Bulletin, 22,* 435–441.

Folger, R., Sheppard, B. H., & Buttram, R. T. (1995). Equity, equality, and need: Three faces of social justice. In B. B. Bunker & J. Z. Rubin and Associates (Eds.), *Conflict, cooperation, and justice* (pp. 261–289). San Francisco: Jossey-Bass.

Follingstad, D. R. (1994, March 10). *The use of battered woman syndrome in court.* Workshop for the American Academy of Forensic Psychology, Santa Fe, NM.

Footlick, J. (1978, May 8). Insanity on trial. *Newsweek,* pp. 108–112.

Ford v. Wainwright, 477 U.S. 399 (1986).

Ford Motor Credit Co. v. Sheehan, 373 So.2d 956 (Fla. App. 1979).

Ford, W. (1998). *Managing police stress.* Walnut Creek, CA: The Management Advantage.

ForsterLee, L., & Horowitz, I. (2003). The effects of jury-aid innovations on juror performance in complex civil trials. *Judicature, 86,* 184–190.

ForsterLee, L., Horowitz, I. A., & Bourgeois, M. J. (1993). Juror competence in civil trials: Effects of preinstruction and evidence technicality. *Journal of Applied Psychology, 78,* 14–21.

Forth, A. (1995). *Psychopathy and young offenders: Prevalence, family background, and violence.* Canada: Ministry of the Solicitor General of Canada.

Forth, A. E., & Burke, H. C. (1998). Psychopathy in adolescence: Assessment, violence, and developmental precursors. In D. Cooke, A. E. Forth, and R. D. Hare (Eds.), *Psychopathy: Theory, research, and implications for society* (pp. 205–229). Dordrecht, The Netherlands: Kluwer.

Forth, A. E., Hart, S. D., & Hare, R. D. (1990). Assessment of psychopathy in male young offenders. *Psychological Assessment, 2,* 342–344.

Foucha v. Louisiana, 112 S.Ct. 1780 (1992).

Fox, D., Gerson, A., & Lees-Haley, P. (1995). Interrelationship of MMPI-2 validity scales in personal injury claims. *Journal of Clinical Psychology, 51,* 42–47.

Fox, J. A., & Levin, J. (1998). Multiple homicide: Patterns of serial and mass murder. *Crime and Justice, 23,* 407–455.

Fox, S. G., & Walters, H. A. (1986). The impact of general versus specific expert testimony and eyewitness confidence upon mock juror judgment. *Law and Human Behavior, 10,* 215–228.

Frank, J. (1949). *Courts on trial.* Princeton, NJ: Princeton University Press.

Frazier v. Cupp, 394 U.S. 731 (1969).

Frazier, P., & Borgida, E. (1985). Rape trauma syndrome evidence in court. *American Psychologist, 40,* 984–993.

Frazier, P., & Borgida, E. (1988). Juror common understanding and the admissibility of rape trauma syndrome evidence in court. *Law and Human Behavior, 12,* 101–122.

Frazier, P. A., Cochran, C. C., & Olson, A. M. (1995). Social science research on lay definitions of sexual harassment. *Journal of Social Issues, 51*(1), 21–37.

Frazier, P. A., & Haney, B. (1996). Sexual assault cases in the legal system:

Police, prosecutor, and victim perspectives. *Law and Human Behavior, 20,* 607–628.

Frederick, R. (1997). *Validity Indicator Profile manual.* Minnetonka, MN: NSC Assessments.

Frederick, R. (2000). Mixed group validation: A method to address the limitations of criterion group validation in research on malingering detection. *Behavioral Sciences and the Law, 18,* 693–718.

Frederick, R. I., & Crosby, R. D. (2000). Development and validation of the Validity Indicator Profile. *Law and Human Behavior, 24,* 59–82.

Fredrickson, R. (1992). *Repressed memories: A journey to recovery from sexual abuse.* New York: Simon & Schuster.

Freedman, J. L. (1984). Effect of television violence on aggressiveness. *Psychological Bulletin, 96,* 227–246.

Freedman, J. L. (1986). Television violence and aggression: A rejoinder. *Psychological Bulletin, 100,* 372–378.

Frendak v. United States, 408 A.2d 364 (D.C. 1979).

Freud, S. (1961). *The complete psychological works of Sigmund Freud* (Vol. 19). London: Hogarth.

Friedrich-Cofer, L., & Huston, A. C. (1986). Television violence and aggression: A rejoinder. *Psychological Bulletin, 100,* 364–371.

Frolik, L.A. (1999). Science, common sense, and the determination of mental capacity. *Psychology, Public Policy, and Law, 5*(1), 41–58.

Frye v. United States, 293 F. 1013, 34 A.L.R. 145 (D.C. Cir. 1923).

Fukurai, H., & Butler, E. (Fall 1994). Sources of racial disenfranchisement in the jury and jury selection system. *National Black Lawyers Journal, 13,* 238–275.

Fulero, S., & Everington, C. (2004). Mental retardation, competency to waive *Miranda* rights, and false confessions. In G. D. Lassiter (Ed.), *Interrogations, confessions, and entrapment* (pp. 163–180). New York: Kluwer Academic/Plenum.

Fulero, S. M., & Finkel, N. J. (1991). Barring ultimate issue testimony: An "insane" rule? *Law and Human Behavior, 15,* 495–508.

Fulero, S. M., & Penrod, S. D. (1990). Attorney jury selection folklore: What do they think and how can psychologists help? *Forensic Reports, 3,* 233–259.

Furman v. Georgia, 408 U.S. 238 (1972).

Fyfe, J. J. (1982). Blind justice: Police shootings in Memphis. *Journal of Criminal Law and Criminology, 73,* 707–722.

Fyfe, J. J. (1988). Police shooting: Environment and license. In J. E. Scott & T. Hirschi (Eds.), *Controversial issues in crime and justice* (pp. 79–94). Newbury Park, CA: Sage.

Gaines, L. K., & Falkenberg, S. (1998). An evaluation of the written selection test: Effectiveness and alternatives. *Journal of Criminal Justice, 26,* 175–183.

Galanter, M. (2004). The vanishing trial: An examination of trials and related matters in state and federal courts. *Journal of Empirical Legal Studies, 1,* 459–570.

Gale, A. (Ed.). (1988). *The polygraph test: Lies, truth and science.* London: Sage.

Gallagher, T., et al. (2003). Patients' and physicians' attitudes regarding the disclosure of medical errors. *Journal of the American Medical Association, 289,* 1001–1008.

Gallagher, W. (1996). *I.D.: How heredity and experience make you who you are.* New York: Random House.

Gallup Organization. (1989, June 23). A jury of one's peers. *Lawrence Journal-World,* p. 1B.

Ganis, G., Kosslyn, S. M., Stose, S., Thompson, W. L., & Yurgelun-Todd, D. A. (2003). Neural correlates of different types of deception: An fMRI investigation. *Cerebral Cortex, 13,* 8, 830–836.

Gannett Co. v. DePasquale, 443 U.S. 368 (1979).

Gardner, J., Scogin, F., Vipperman, R., & Varela, J.G. (1998). The predictive validity of peer assessment in law enforcement: A 6-year follow-up. *Behavioral Sciences and the Law, 16,* 473–478.

Garner, J., Fagan, J., & Maxwell, C. (1995). Published findings from the spouse assault replication program: A critical review. *Journal of Quantitative Criminology, 11,* 3–28.

Garofalo, R. (1914). *Criminology* (R. W. Millar, Trans.). Boston: Little, Brown.

Garrioch, L., & Brimacombe C. (2001). Lineup administrators' expectations: Their impact on eyewitness confidence. *Law and Human Behavior, 25,* 299–315.

Garry, M., & Polaschek, D. L. (2000). Imagination and memory. *Current Directions in Psychological Science, 9,* 6–10.

Garven, S., Wood, J. M., & Malpass, R. S. (2000). Allegations of wrongdoing: The effects of reinforcement on children's mundane and fantastic claims. *Journal of Applied Psychology, 85*, 38–49.

Garvey, S., Hannaford-Agor, P., Hans, V., Mott, N., Munsterman, G. T., & Wells, M. (2004). Juror first votes in criminal trials. *Journal of Empirical Legal Studies, 1*, 371–399.

Garvey, S. P., Johnson, S. L., & Marcus, P. (2000). Correcting deadly confusion: Responding to jury inquiries in capital cases. *Cornell Law Review, 85*, 627.

Gatland, L. (1997, December). Dangerous dedication. *American Bar Association Journal, 83*, 28.

Gatowski, S., Dobbin, S., Richardson, J., Ginsburg, G., Merlino, M., & Dahir, V. (2001). Asking the gatekeepers: A national survey of judges on judging expert evidence in a post-*Daubert* world. *Law and Human Behavior, 25*, 433–458.

Gavey, N. (1991). Sexual victimization prevalence among New Zealand University students. *Journal of Consulting and Clinical Psychology, 59*, 464–466.

Gaylin, W. (1974). *Partial justice: A study of bias in sentencing.* New York: Vintage Books.

Gaylin, W. (1982). *The killing of Bonnie Garland: A question of justice.* New York: Simon & Schuster.

Gayoso, A., Cutler, B. L., & Moran, G. (1994). Assessing the value of social scientists as trial consultants: A consumer research approach. *Forensic Reports.*

Gee, S., & Pipe, M. (1995). Helping children to remember: The influence of object cues on children's accounts of a real event. *Developmental Psychologoy, 31*, 746–758.

Geis, G., & Bienen, L. B. (1998). *Crimes of the century.* Boston: Northeastern University Press.

Geiselman, R. E., Fisher, R. P., MacKinnon, D. P., & Holland, H. L. (1985). Eyewitness memory enhancement in the police interview. *Journal of Applied Psychology, 70*, 401–412.

Gelles, R. J., & Cornell, C. P. (1985). *Intimate violence in families.* Newbury Park, CA: Sage.

Gellhorn, E. (1968). The law schools and the Negro. *Duke Law Journal, 1968*, 1069–1099.

Georgia v. McCollum, 112 S.Ct. 2348 (1992).

Geraghty, T., & Rhee, W. (1998). Learning from tragedy: Representing children in discretionary hearings. *Wake Forest Law Review, 33*, 595–650.

Gerbasi, K. C., Zuckerman, M., & Reis, H. T. (1977). Justice needs a new blindfold: A review of mock jury research. *Psychological Bulletin, 84*, 323–345.

Gerber, M. R., Ganz, M. L., Lichter, E., Williams, C. M., & McCloskey, L. A. (2005). Adverse health behaviors and the detection of partner violence by clinicians. *Archives of Internal Medicine, 165*(9) 1016–1021.

Gergen, K. J. (1994). Exploring the postmodern: Perils or potentials? *American Psychologist, 49*, 412–416.

Gerry, M., Garry, M., & Loftus, E. (2005). False memories. In N. Brewer & K. Williams (Eds.), *Psychology and law: An empirical perspective* (pp. 222–252). New York: Guilford Publications.

Gershon, T., Tschan, J., & Jemerin, J. (1999). Stigmatization, self-esteem, and coping among the adolescent children of lesbian mothers. *Journal of Adolescent Health, 24*, 437–445.

Gibson, C. (2005, January 7). Andrea Yates case interview with Andrea Yates' mother [ABC News Transcript, Good Morning America]. Retrieved online August 7, 2005, from NexisLexis database.

Gideon v. Wainwright, 372 U.S. 335 (1963).

Gilstrap, L., & Papierno, P. (2004). Is the cart pushing the horse? The effects of child characteristics on children's and adults' interview behaviours. *Applied Cognitive Psychology, 18*, 1059–1078.

Gist, R. M., & Perry, J. D. (1985). Perspectives on negotiation in local jurisdictions, Part 1: A different typology of situations. *FBI Law Enforcement Bulletin, 54*(11), 21.

Glaberson, W. (2004, June 20). New trend before grand juries: Meet the accused. *New York Times*, p. 1.

Glamser, D. (1997, January 27). Washington State testing therapy for sex felons. *USA Today*, p. 3A.

Gleick, J. (1978, August 21). Getting away with murder. *New Times*, pp. 21, 27.

Godinez v. Moran, 113 S.Ct. 2680 (1993).

Goldberg-Ambrose, C. (1992). Unfinished business in rape law reform. *Journal of Social Issues, 48*(1), 173–186.

Goldfarb, R. L. (1965). *Ransom.* New York: Harper & Row.

Golding, S. L., Roesch, R., & Schreiber, J. (1984). Assessment and conceptualization of competency to stand trial: Preliminary data on the Interdisciplinary Fitness Interview. *Law and Human Behavior, 8*, 321–334.

Goldkamp, J. S., & Gottfredson, M. R. (1988). *Guidelines for bail and pretrial release in three urban courts.* Unpublished final report.

Goldkamp, J. S., Gottfredson, M. R., Jones, P. R., & Weiland, D. (1995). *Personal liberty and community safety: Pretrial release in the criminal court.* New York: Plenum.

Goldman, S., & Saronson, M. (1994). Clinton's nontraditional judges: Creating a more representative bench. *Judicature, 78*, 68–73.

Goldstein, N. E. S., Condie, L. O., Kalbeitzer, R., Osman, D., & Geier, J.L. (2003). Juvenile offenders' *Miranda* rights comprehension and self-reported likelihood of offering false confessions. *Assessment, 10*(4), 359–369.

Goleman, D. (1987, April 7). The bully: New research depicts a paranoid, lifelong loser. *New York Times*, p. 23.

Gonsalves, B., Reber, P., Gitelman, D., Parrish, T., Mesulam, M., & Paller, K. (2004). Neural evidence that vivid imagining can lead to false remembering. *Psychological Science, 15*, 655–660.

Goodman, G., Emery, R., & Haugaard, J. (1998). Developmental psychology and law: Divorce, child maltreatment, forster care, and adoption. In I. Sigel & A. Renninger (Eds.), *Handbook of child psychology: Vol. 4, Child psychology in practice* (pp. 775–876). New York: Wiley.

Goodman, G. S., Golding, J., Helgeson, V., Haith, M., & Michelli, J. (1987). When a child takes the stand: Jurors' perceptions of children's eyewitness testimony. *Law and Human Behavior, 11*, 27–40.

Goodman, G. S., Pyle-Taub, E., Jones, D., England, P., Port, L., Rudy, l., & Prado, L. (1992). Testifying in criminal court: Emotional effects of criminal court testimony on child sexual assault victims. *Monographs of the Society for Research in Child Development: Vol. 57, No. 5.* (Serial No. 229), i+ii+v+1–159.

Goodman-Delahunty, J. (1997) Forensic psychological expertise in the wake of *Daubert. Law and Human Behavior, 21*, 121–140.

Goodman-Delahunty, J. (1998). Approaches to gender and the law: Research and applications. *Law and Human Behavior, 22*, 129–143.

Goodman-Delahunty, J. (1999). Pragmatic support for the reasonable standard in hostile workplace sexual harassment cases. *Psychology, Public Policy, and Law, 5*, 519–555.

Goodman-Delahunty, J., Greene, E., & Hsiao, W. (1998). Construing motive in videotaped killings: The role of jurors' attitudes toward the death penalty. *Law and Human Behavior, 22*, 257–271.

Gordon, E. (2002). What role does gender play in mediation of domestic relations cases? *Judicature, 86*, 135–143.

Gordon, N., & Fleisher, W. (2002). *Effective interviewing and interrogation techniques.* San Diego: Academic Press.

Gordon, R. A. (1986, August). *IQ commensurability of black–white differences in crime and delinquency.* Paper presented at the meeting of the American Psychological Association, Washington, D.C.

Gorer, G. (1955). Modification of national character: The role of police in England. *Journal of Social Issues, 11*(2), 24–32.

Gothard, S., Rogers, R., & Sewell, K. W. (1995). Feigning incompetency to stand trial: An investigation of the Georgia Court Competency Test. *Law and Human Behavior, 19*, 363–374.

Gothard, S., Viglione, D. J., Jr., Meloy, J. R., & Sherman, M. (1995). Detection of malingering in competency to stand trial evaluations. *Law and Human Behavior, 19*, 493–506.

Gottfredson, L. (1986, August). *IQ versus training: Job performance and black–white occupational inequality.* Paper presented at the meeting of the American Psychological Association, Washington, DC.

Gowan, M. A. & Gatewood, R. D. (1995). Personnel selection. In N. Brewer & C. Wilson (Eds.) *Psychology and policing* (pp. 177–204). Mahwah, NJ: Erlbaum.

Gray, E. (1993). *Unequal justice: The prosecution of child sexual abuse.* New York: Macmillan.

Grayson v. United States, 438 U.S. 41 (1978).

Gready, R., Ditto, P., Danks, J., Coppola, K., Lockhart, L., & Smucker, W. (2000). Actual and perceived stability of preferences for life-sustaining treatment. *Journal of Clinical Ethics, 11*, 334–346.

Green, A. (2004, August 30). The waiting room: August. *The New Yorker,* 37–38.

Green, B., Grace, M., Lindy, J., Gleser, G., & Leonard, A.C. (1990). Risk factors for PTSD and other diagnoses in a general sample of Vietnam veterans. *American Journal of Psychiatry, 147,* 729–733.

Green, S. (2005, January 31). When justice is delayed. *National Law Journal,* p. 22.

Greenberg, M. S., & Ruback, R. B. (1982). *Social psychology of the criminal justice system.* Pacific Grove, CA: Brooks/Cole.

Greenberg, M. S., & Ruback, R. B. (1984). Criminal victimization: Introduction and overview. *Journal of Social Issues 40*(1), 1–8.

Greene, E. (1988). Judge's instruction on eyewitness testimony: Evaluation and revision. *Journal of Applied Social Psychology, 18*, 252–276.

Greene, E. (2002). How effective? [Review of the book *Stack and sway: The new science of jury consulting*]. *Judicature, 85*, 1–3.

Greene, E., & Bornstein, B. (2000). Precious little guidance: Jury instructions on damage awards. *Psychology, Public Policy, and Law, 6*, 743–768.

Greene, E., & Bornstein, B. (2003). *Determining damages: The psychology of jury awards.* Washington, D.C.: American Psychological Association.

Greene, E., Chopra, S., Kovera, M., Penrod, S., Rose, V., Schuller, R., & Studebaker, C. (2002). Jurors and juries: A review of the field. In J. Ogloff (Ed.), *Taking psychology and law into the twenty-first century* (pp. 225–285). New York: Kluwer Academic/Plenum.

Greene, E., & Dodge, M. (1995). The influence of prior record evidence on juror decision making. *Law and Human Behavior, 19*, 67–78.

Greene, E., & Dunaway, K. (2004). *The impact of silent factors on jury damage awards.* Paper presented at the American Psychology-Law Society, Scottsdale.

Greene, E., Goodman, J., & Loftus, E. (1991). Jurors' attitudes about civil litigation and the size of damage awards. *American University Law Review, 40*, 805–820.

Greene, E., Johns, M., & Bowman, J. (1999). The effects of injury severity on jury negligence decisions. *Law and Human Behavior, 23*, 675–693.

Greene, E., Johns, M., & Smith, A. (2001). The effects of defendant conduct on jury damage awards. *Journal of Applied Psychology, 86*, 228–237.

Greene, E., & Loftus, E. (1985). When crimes are joined at trial. *Law and Human Behavior, 9*, 193–207.

Greene, E., & Wade, R. (1988). Of private talk and public print: General pretrial publicity and juror decision making. *Applied Cognitive Psychology, 2*, 123–135.

Greene, J. A. (1999). Zero tolerance: A case study of police policies and practices in New York City. *Crime and Delinquency, 45*, 171–187.

Greenhouse, L. (1994, April 20). High court bars sex as standard of picking jurors. *New York Times,* pp. A1, A10.

Gregg v. Georgia, 428 U.S. 153 (1976).

Gregory, W. L., Mowen, J. C., & Linder, D. E. (1978). Social psychology and plea bargaining: Applications, methodology, and theory. *Journal of Personality and Social Psychology, 36*, 1521–1530.

Gretton, H., Hare, R., & Catchpole, R. (2004). Psychopathy and offending from adolescence to adulthood: A 10-year follow-up. *Journal of Consulting and Clinical Psychology, 72*, 636–645.

Gretton, H. M., McBride, H. L., O'Shaughnessy, R., & Hare, R. D. (1997, June). *Sex offender or generalized offender? Psychopathy as a risk marker for violence in adolescent offenders.* Paper presented at the 5th International Conference on the Disorders of Personality, Vancouver, British Columbia.

Grimes, J. (1996). On the failure to detect changes in scenes across saccades. In K. Akins (Ed.), *Vancouver studies in cognitive science: Vol. 5, Perception* (pp. 89–110). New York: Oxford University Press.

Grisham, J. (1996). *The runaway jury.* New York: Doubleday.

Grisso, T. (1981). *Juveniles' waivers of rights: Legal and psychological competence.* New York: Plenum.

Grisso, T. (1986). *Evaluating competencies: Forensic assessments and instruments.* New York: Plenum.

Grisso, T. (1997). The competence of adolescents as trial defendants. *Psychology, Public Policy, and Law, 3*, 3–32.

Grisso, T. (1998). Instruments for assessing understanding and appreciation of *Miranda* rights. Sarasota, Forida: Professional Resource Press.

Grisso, T. (2003). *Evaluating competencies: Forensic assessments and instruments* (2nd ed.). New York: Kluwer/Plenum.

Grisso, T. (2005). *Evaluating juveniles' adjudicative competence: A guide for clinical practice.* Sarasota, FL: Professional Resource Press.

Grisso, T., & Appelbaum, P. S. (1995). The MacArthur Treatment Competence

Study. III: Abilities of patients to consent to psychiatric and medical treatments. *Law and Human Behavior, 19*, 149–174.

Grisso, T., & Appelbaum, P. (1998a). *Assessing competence to consent to treatment: A guide for physicians and other health professionals.* New York: Oxford University Press.

Grisso, T., & Appelbaum, P. (1998b). *MacArthur competence assessment tool for treatment (MacCAT-T).* Professional Resource Press: Sarasota, FL.

Grisso, T., Appelbaum, P. S., Mulvey, E. P., & Fletcher, K. (1995). The MacArthur Treatment Competence Study. II: Measures of abilities related to competence to consent to treatment. *Law and Human Behavior, 19*, 127–148.

Grisso, T., Cocozza, J. J., Steadman, H. J., Fisher, W. H., & Greer, A. (1994). The organization of pretrial forensic evaluation services: A national profile. *Law and Human Behavior, 18*, 377–394.

Grisso, T., Miller, M., & Sales, B. (1987). Competency to stand trial in juvenile court. *International Journal of Law and Psychiatry, 10*, 1–20.

Grisso, T., & Quinlan, J. (2005). *Juvenile court clinical services: A national description.* Worcester, MA: Law and Psychiatry Program, University of Massachusetts Medical School.

Grisso, T., & Saks, M. J. (1991). Psychology's influence on constitutional interpretation: A comment on how to succeed. *Law and Human Behavior, 15*, 205–211.

Grisso, T., & Schwartz, R. (2000). *Youth on trial: A developmental perspective on juvenile justice.* Chicago: University of Chicago Press.

Grisso, T., & Siegel, S. K. (1986). Assessment of competency to stand criminal trial. In W. J. Curran, A. L. McGarry, & S. A. Shah (Eds.), *Forensic psychiatry and psychology* (pp. 145–165). Philadelphia: F. A. Davis.

Grisso, T., Steinberg, L., Woolard, J., Cauffman, E., Scott, E., Graham, S., Lexcen, F., Reppucci, N., & Schwartz, R. (2003). Juveniles' competence to stand trial: A comparison of adolescents' and adults' capacities as trial defendants. *Law and Human Behavior, 27*, 333–363.

Groscup, J., Penrod, S., Studebaker, C., Huss, M., & O'Neil, K. (2002). The effects of *Daubert* on the admissibility of expert testimony in state and federal criminal cases. *Psychology, Public Policy and Law, 8*, 339–372.

Gross, J., & Hayne, H. (1996). Eyewitness identification by 5- to 6-year old children. *Law and Human Behavior, 20*, 359–373.

Groth, A. N., with Birnbaum, H. J. (1979). *Men who rape.* New York: Plenum.

Group for the Advancement of Psychiatry. (1974). *Misuse of psychiatry in the criminal courts: Competency to stand trial.* The Committee on Psychiatry and Law, Vol. VIII, Report 89, 896–897. New York: GAP Publications.

Grove, W. M., & Barden, R. C. (1999). Protecting the integrity of the legal system: The admissibility of testimony from mental health experts under Daubert/Kumho analyses. *Psychology, Public Policy, and Law, 5*, 224–242.

Grutter v. Bollinger, 137 F. Supp. 2d 821 (E.D.Mich. 2001).

Grutter v. Bollinger, 123 S. Ct. 2325 (2003).

Guastello, S. J., & Rieke, M. L. (1991). A review and critique of honesty test research. *Behavioral Sciences and the Law, 9*, 501–523.

Gudjonsson, G. H. (1988). How to defeat the polygraph tests. In A. Gale (Ed.), *The polygraph test: Lies, truth and science* (pp. 126–136). London: Sage.

Gudjonsson, G. H. (2003). *The psychology of interrogations and confessions.* Chichester, England: Wiley.

Gudjonsson, G. H. and Copson, G. (1997) The role of the expert in criminal investigation. In J. L. Jackson and D. A. Bekerian (Eds), *Offender Profiling: Theory, Research, and Practice* (pp. 61–76). Chichester, England: Wiley.

Gunnoe, M.L. & Braver, S.L. (2001). The effects of joint legal custody on mothers, fathers, and children, controlling for factors that predispose a sole maternal vs. joint legal award. *Law and Human Behavior, 25*, 25–43.

Gunter, G. (1985 January 25). Voices across the USA. *USA Today*, p. 12A.

Gutek, B. A., & O'Connor, M. (1995). The empirical basis for the reasonable woman standard. *Journal of Social Issues, 51*(1), 151–166.

Guthrie, C., Rachlinski, J., & Wistrich, A. (2001). Inside the judicial mind. *Cornell Law Review, 86*, 777–830.

Hagan, J., & Peterson, R. (1995). *Crime and inequality.* Stanford, CA: Stanford University Press.

Haj-Yahia, M.M. (2003). Beliefs about wife-beating among Arab men in Israel: The influence of their patriar-chal ideology. *Journal of Family Violence, 18*(4), 193–206.

Hall, D. F., Loftus, E. F., & Tousignant, J. P. (1984). Postevent information and changes in recollection for a natural event. In G. L. Wells & E. F. Loftus (Eds.), *Eyewitness testimony: Psychological perspectives* (pp. 124–141). New York: Cambridge University Press.

Hall, G. C. (1996). *Theory-based assessment, treatment, and prevention of sexual aggression.* New York: Oxford University Press.

Hall, G. C., & Hirschman, R. (1991). Toward a theory of sexual aggression: A quadripartite model. *Journal of Consulting and Clinical Psychology, 59*, 662–669.

Halligan, S. L., Michael, T., Clark, D. M., & Ehlers, A. (2003). Posttraumatic Stress Disorder following assault: The role of cognitive processing, trauma memory, and appraisals. *Journal of Consulting & Clinical Psychology, 71*, 419–431.

Hamilton v. Schirro, 74 F.3d 1545 (9th Cir. 1996).

Hamilton, A. (2004, December 13). Woof, woof, your honor. *Time*, 46.

Handman, L. R. (1977). Underrepresentation of economic groups on federal juries. *Boston University Law Review, 57*(1), 198–224.

Haney, C. (1984). Editor's introduction. *Law and Human Behavior, 8*, 16.

Haney, C. (1997a). Commonsense justice and capital punishment: Problematizing the "will of the people." *Psychology, Public Policy, and Law, 3*, 303–337.

Haney, C. (1997b). Psychology and the limits to prison pain: Confronting the coming crisis in Eighth Amendment law. *Psychology, Public Policy, and Law, 3*, 499–588.

Haney, C., & Lynch, M. (1994). Comprehending life and death matters: A preliminary study of California's capital penalty instructions. *Law and Human Behavior, 18*, 411–436.

Haney, C., & Lynch, M. (1997). Clarifying life and death matters: An analysis of instructional comprehension and penalty phase closing arguments. *Law and Human Behavior, 21*, 575–596.

Haney, C., & Wiener, R. (2004). Death is different: An editorial introduction to the theme issue. *Psychology, Public Policy, and Law, 10*, 373–378.

Haney, C., & Zimbardo, P. (1998). The past and future of U. S. prison policy:

Twenty-five years after the Stanford Prison Experiment. *American Psychologist, 53*, 709–727.

Hanish, L. D., & Guerra, N. G. (2000). The roles of ethnicity and school context in predicting children's victimization by peers. *American Journal of Community Psychology, 28*, 201–224.

Hannaford, P., Hans, V., & Munsterman, G.T. (2000). Permitting jury discussions during trial: Impact of the Arizona reform. *Law and Human Behavior, 24*, 359–382.

Hannaford-Agor, P., & Hans, V. (2003). Nullification at work? A glimpse from the National Center for State Courts study of hung juries. *Chicago-Kent Law Review, 78*, 1249–1277.

Hans, V. P. (1988, November). Confronting the accused. *APA Monitor*, p. 35.

Hans, V. P. (1992). Judgments of justice. *Psychological Science, 3*, 218–220.

Hans, V. P. (1996). The contested role of the civil jury in business litigation. *Judicature, 79*, 242–248.

Hans, V. P. (2000). *Business on trial: The civil jury and corporate responsibility*. New Haven, CT: Yale Univeristy Press.

Hans, V. P., & Ermann, M. D. (1989). Responses to corporate versus individual wrongdoing. *Law and Human Behavior, 13*, 151–166.

Hans, V. P., Hannaford, P., & Munsterman, G. T. (1999) The Arizona jury reform permitting civil jury trial discussions: The views of trial participants, judges, and jurors. *University of Michigan Journal of Law Reform, 32*, 349ff. Retrieved December 7, 1999, from Lexis-Nexis.

Hans, V. P., Hannaford-Agor, P. L., Mott, N. L., & Munsterman, G. T. (2003). The hung jury: *The American Jury's* insights and contemporary understanding. *Criminal Law Bulletin, 39*, 33–50.

Hans, V. P., & Jehle, A. (2003). Avoid bald men and people with green socks. Other ways to improve the voir dire process in jury selection. *Chicago-Kent Law Review, 78*, 1179–1201.

Hans, V. P., & Slater, D. (1983). John Hinckley, Jr., and the insanity defense: The public's verdict. *Public Opinion Quarterly, 47*, 202–212.

Hans, V. P., & Vidmar, N. (1982). Jury selection. In N. L. Kerr & R. M. Bray (Eds.), *The psychology of the courtroom* (pp. 39–82). Orlando, FL: Academic Press.

Hans, V. P., & Vidmar, N. (1986). *Judging the jury*. New York: Plenum.

Hans, V. P., & Vidmar, N. (1991). The American jury at twenty-five years. *Law and Social Inquiry, 16*, 323–351.

Hansen, M. (1997, September). Repairing the damage. *American Bar Association Journal, 83*, 20.

Hansen, M. (1999, April). Mandatories going, going, . . .going. *American Bar Association Journal, 85*, 14.

Hanson, K. A., & Gidycz, C. A. (1993). Evaluation of a sexual assault prevention program. *Journal of Consulting and Clinical Psychology, 61*, 1046–1052.

Hanson, R. K. (1997). *The development of a brief actuarial risk scale for sexual offense recidivism*. User Report 97-04. Ottawa: Department of the Solicitor General of Canada.

Hanson, R. K., & Bussiere, M. T. (1998). Predicting relapse: A meta-analysis of sexual offender recidivism studies. *Journal of Consulting and Clinical Psychology, 66*, 348–362.

Hanson, R. K., & Thornton, D. (2000). Improving risk assessments for sex offenders: A comparison of three actuarial scales. *Law and Human Behavior, 24*, 119–136.

Harding v. State (of Maryland), 5 Md.App. 230, 246, A,2d, 302 (1968), 252 Md. 731, Cert. denied, 395 U.S. 949, 89 S.Ct. 2030, 23 L.Ed.2d 468 (1969).

Hare, R. D., Hart, S. D., & Harpur, T. J. (1991). Psychopathy and the DSM-IV criteria for Antisocial Personality Disorder. *Journal of Abnormal Psychology, 100*, 391–398.

Hare, R. D., & McPherson, L. M. (1984). Violent and aggressive behavior by criminal psychopaths. *International Journal of Law and Psychiatry, 7*, 35–50.

Harper, T. (1984, April 29). State rape laws see decade of change. *Lawrence Journal-World*, p. 1B.

Harpold, J. A. & Feemster, S. L. (2002). Negative influences of police stress. *FBI Law Enforcement Bulletin, 71*(9), 1–7. Retrieved July 18, 2005, from http://www.fbi.gov/publications/leb/2002/sept2002/sept02leb.htm#page_2

Harris v. Forklift Systems, Inc., 114 S.Ct. 367 (1993).

Harris v. Forklift Systems, Inc., 510 U.S. 17 (1993).

Harris v. New York, 401 U.S. 222 (1971).

Harris, G., & Rice, M. (2003). Actuarial assessment of risk among sex offenders. *Annals of the New York Academy of Sciences, 989*, 198–210.

Harris, G. T., Rice, M. E., & Quinsey, V. L. (1993). Violent recidivism of mentally disordered offenders: The development of a statistical prediction instrument. *Criminal Justice and Behavior, 20*, 315–335.

Harris, G., Rice, M., Quinsey, V., Lalumiere, M., Boer, D., & Lang, C. (2003). A multisite comparison of actuarial risk instruments for sex offenders. *Psychological Assessment, 15*, 413–425.

Hart, P. M., Wearing, A. J., & Headey, B. (1993). Assessing police work experiences: Development of the Police Daily Hassles and Uplifts Scales. *Journal of Criminal Justice, 21*, 553–572.

Hart, P. M., Wearing, A., & Headey, B. (1995). Police stress and well-being: Integrating personality, coping, and daily work experiences. *Journal of Occupational and Organizational Psychology, 68*, 133–156.

Hasemann, D. (1997). Practices and findings of mental health professionals conducting workers' compensation evaluations. Unpublished doctoral dissertation. Lexington, KY: University of Kentucky.

Hashemi, L., & Webster, B. S. (1998). Non-fatal workplace violence workers' compensation claims (1993–1996). *Journal of Occupational & Environmental Medicine, 40*(6) 561–567.

Hastie, R., & Pennington, N. (1996). The O. J. Simpson stories: Behavioral scientists' reflections on *The People of the State of California v. Orenthal James Simpson. University of Colorado Law Review, 67*, 957ff. Retrieved December 7, 1999, from Lexis-Nexis.

Hastie, R., Schkade, D. A., & Payne, J. W. (1998). A study of juror and jury judgments in civil cases: Deciding liability for punitive damages. *Law and Human Behavior, 22*, 287–314.

Hatcher, C., Mohandie, K., Turner, J., & Gelles, M. G. (1998). The role of the psychologist in crisis/hostage negotiations. *Behavioral Sciences and the Law, 16*, 455–472.

Haugaard, J. J., & Avery, R. J. (2002). Termination of parental rights to free children for adoption: Conflicts between parents, children, and the state. In Bottoms, B., Kovera, M., & McAuliff, B. D.(Eds.), *Children, social policy, and U.S. law*. Boston: Cambridge University Press.

Haw, R., & Fisher, R. (2004). Effects of administrator-witness contact on eyewitness identification accuracy. *Journal of Applied Psychology, 89*, 1106–1112.

Hazelwood, R. R., & Douglas, J. E. (1980). The lust murderer. *FBI Law Enforcement Bulletin, 49*(4), 18–22.

Hazelwood, R. R., Ressler, R. K., Depue, R. L. & Douglas, J. C. (1995). Criminal investigative analysis: An overview. In A. W. Burgess and R. R. Hazelwood (Eds.), *Practical aspects of rape investigation: A multidisciplinary approach* (2nd ed.). Boca Raton, FL: CRC, pp. 115–126.

Heaps, C., & Nash, M. (2001). Comparing recollective experience in true and false autobiographical memories. *Journal of Experimental Psychology: Learning, Memory, and Cognition, 27*, 920–930.

Heide, K. M. (1997). Juvenile homicide in America: How can we stop the killing? *Behavioral Sciences and the Law, 15*, 203–220.

Heider, F. (1958). *The psychology of interpersonal relations.* New York: Wiley.

Heilbrun, K. S. (1987). The assessment of competency for execution: An overview. *Behavioral Sciences and the Law, 5*, 383–396.

Heilbrun, K. S. (2001). *Principles of forensic mental health assessment.* New York: Kluwer/Plenum.

Heilbrun, K., & Collins, S. (1995). Evaluation of trial competency and mental state at the time of offense: Report characteristics. *Professional Psychology: Research and Practice, 26*, 61–67.

Heilbrun, K. S., Heilbrun, P., & Griffin, N. (1988). Comparing females acquitted by reason of insanity, convicted, and civilly committed in Florida: 1977–1984. *Law and Human Behavior, 12*, 295–312.

Heilbrun, K., & McClaren, H. (1988). Assessment of competency for execution? A guide for mental health professionals. *Bulletin of the American Academy of Psychiatry and the Law, 16*, 206–216.

Heise, M. (2004). Criminal case complexity: An empirical perspective. *Journal of Empirical Legal Studies, 1*, 331–369.

Heller, E. (2004, November 8). "Chamber" scores big in judicial election. *National Law Journal*, p. 6.

Helzer, J. E., Robins, L. N., & McVay, L. (1987). Posttraumatic stress disorder in the general population. *New England Journal of Medicine, 317*, 1630–1634.

Henkel, L., & Coffman, K. (2004). Memory distortions in coerced false confessions: A source monitoring framework analysis. *Applied Cognitive Psychology, 18*, 567–588.

Henshaw, S., & Kost, K. (1992). Parental involvement in minors' abortion decisions. *Family Planning Perspectives, 24*, 196–213.

Hepburn, J. R. (1980). The objective reality of evidence and the utility of systematic jury selection. *Law and Human Behavior, 4*, 89–102.

Herek, G. M. (1987). Can functions be measured? A new perspective on the functional approach to attitudes. *Social Psychology Quarterly, 50*, 285–303.

Hernandez v. New York, 111 S.Ct. 1859 (1991).

Hersch, P. D., & Alexander, R. W. (1990). MMPI profile patterns of emotional disability claimants. *Journal of Clinical Psychology, 46*, 795–799.

Heuer, L., & Penrod, S. (1988). Increasing jurors' participation in trials: A field experiment with jury notetaking and question asking. *Law and Human Behavior, 12*, 231–262.

Heumann, M. (1978). *Plea bargaining.* Chicago: University of Chicago Press.

Heussanstamm, F. K. (1975). Bumper stickers and the cops. In D. J. Steffensmeier & R. M. Terry (Eds.), *Examining deviance experimentally: Selected readings* (pp. 251–255). Port Washington, NY: Alfred.

Hiatt, D., & Hargrave, G. E. (1988). Predicting job performance problems with psychological screening. *Journal of Police Science and Administration, 16*, 122–125.

Hiday, V. A., & Goodman, R. R. (1982). The least restrictive alternative to involuntary hospitalization, outpatient commitment: Its use and effectiveness. *Journal of Psychiatry and Law, 10*, 81–96.

Higgins, M. (1999, March). Tough luck for the innocent man. *ABA Journal, 85*, 46–52.

Hightower, S. (2000). Sex and the peremptory strike: An empirical analysis of J.E.B. *Stanford Law Review, 52*, 895–928.

Hill, E., & Pfeifer, J. (1992). Nullification instructions and juror guilt ratings: An examination of modern racism. *Contemporary Social Psychology, 16*, 6–10.

Himelein, M. J., Nietzel, M. T., & Dillehay, R. C. (1991). Effects of prior juror experience on jury sentencing. *Behavioral Sciences and the Law, 9*, 97–106.

Hirschi, T. (1969). *Causes of delinquency.* Berkeley: University of California Press.

Hirschi, T. (1978). Causes and prevention of juvenile delinquency. In H. M. Johnson (Ed.), *Social systems and legal process* (pp. 322–341). San Francisco: Jossey-Bass.

Hishon v. King & Spaulding, 467 U.S. 69 (1984).

Hodgson v. Minnesota, 497 U.S. 417 (1990).

Hoffman, L. R. (1965). Group problem solving. In L. Berkowitz (Ed.), *Advances in experimental social psychology* (Vol. 2, pp. 99–127). Orlando, FL: Academic Press.

Hoffman, P. B., & Stone-Meierhoefer, B. (1979). Application of guidelines to sentencing. In L. E. Abt & I. R. Stuart (Eds.), *Social psychology and discretionary law* (pp. 241–258). New York: Van Nostrand Reinhold.

Hogan, R. (1971). Personality characteristics of highly rated policemen. *Personnel Psychology, 24*, 679–686.

Hogarth, J. (1971). *Sentencing as a human process.* Toronto: University of Toronto Press.

Hoge, S. K., Bonnie, R. J., Poythress, N., Monahan, J., Eisenberg, M., & Feucht-Haviar, T. (1997). The MacArthur adjudicative competence study: Development and validation of a research instrument. *Law and Human Behavior, 21*, 141–179.

Hogg, A., & Wilson, C. (1995). *Is the psychological screening of police applicants a realistic goal? The successes and failures of psychological screening.* National Police Research Unit Report Series No. 124. Payneham, Australia: National Police Research Unit. Retrieved June 20, 2005, from http://www.acpr.gov.au/pdf/ACPR124.pdf

Holland v. Illinois, 493 U.S. 474 (1990).

Holmes, D. (1995). The evidence for repression: An examination of sixty years of research. In J. Singer (Ed.), *Repression and dissociation: Implications for personality theory, psychopathology, and health,* pp. 85–102. Chicago: University of Chicago Press.

Holmes, O. (1881). *The common law.* Boston: Little, Brown.

Holmes, R. M., & DeBurger, J. (1988). *Serial murder.* Newbury Park, CA: Sage.

Homant, R. J., & Kennedy, D. B. (1998). Psychological aspects of crime scene profiling. *Criminal Justice and Behavior, 25*, 319–343.

Honts, C. R., Raskin, D. C., Kircher, J. C., & Hodes, R. L. (1984). Effects of spontaneous countermeasures on the detection of deception. *Psychophysiology, 21*, 583.

Hooton, E. A. (1939). *Crime and the man.* Cambridge, MA: Harvard University Press.

Hope, L., Memon, A., & McGeorge, P. (2004). Understanding pretrial publicity: Predecisional distortion of evidence by mock jurors. *Journal of Experimental Psychology: Applied, 10*, 111–119.

Hopt v. Utah, 110 U.S. 574 (1884).

Horgan, D. D. (1988, August). *The ethics of unexpected advocacy.* Paper presented at the meeting of the American Psychological Association, Atlanta.

Horowitz, I. A. (1980). Juror selection: A comparison of two methods in several criminal cases. *Journal of Applied Social Psychology, 10*, 86–99.

Horowitz, I. A. (1988). The impact of judicial instructions, arguments, and challenges on jury decision making. *Law and Human Behavior, 12*, 439–453.

Horowitz, I., & Bordens, K. (2002). The effects of jury size, evidence complexity, and note taking on jury process and performance in a civil trial. *Journal of Applied Psychology, 87*, 121–130.

Horowitz, I. A., ForsterLee, L., & Brolly, I. (1996). Effects of trial complexity on decision making. *Journal of Applied Psychology, 81*, 757–768.

Horowitz, I. A., & Willging, T. E. (1984). *The psychology of law.* Boston: Little, Brown.

Horowitz, I., & Willging, T. (1991). Changing views of jury power: The nullification debate, 1787–1988. *Law and Human Behavior, 15*, 165–182.

Horwitz, A. V., Widom, C. S., McLaughlin, J., & White, H. R. (2001). The impact of childhood abuse and neglect on adult mental health: A prospective study. *Journal of Health and Social Behavior, 42*, 184–201.

Hosch, H. M., Beck, E. L., & McIntyre, P. (1980). Influence of expert testimony regarding eyewitness accuracy on jury decisions. *Law and Human Behavior, 4*, 287–296.

Hostetler, A. J. (1988, June). Indictment, Congress send message on fraud. *APA Monitor*, p. 5.

Hotelling, K. (1991). Sexual harassment: A problem shielded by silence. *Journal of Counseling and Development, 69*, 497–501.

Houlden, P. (1981). Impact of procedural modifications on evaluations of plea bargaining. *Law and Society Review, 15*, 267–292.

Houston, C. (1935). The need for Negro lawyers. *Journal of Negro Education, 4*, 49–52.

Hovey v. Superior Court of California, 28 Cal.3d 1 (1980).

Howard, R. C., & Clark, C. R. (1985). When courts and experts disagree: Discordance between insanity recommendations and adjudications. *Law and Human Behavior, 9*, 385–395.

Huber, P. (1990). *Liability: The legal revolution and its consequences.* New York: Basic Books.

Huesmann, L. R., Eron, L. D., Lefkowitz, M. M., & Walder, L. O. (1984). Stability of aggression over time and generations. *Developmental Psychology, 20*, 1120–1134.

Huesmann, L. R., Eron, L. D., & Yarmel, P. W. (1987). Intellectual functioning and aggression. *Journal of Personality and Social Psychology, 52*, 232–240.

Huesmann, L., Moise-Titus, J., Podolski, C., & Eron, L.D. (2003). Longitudinal relations between children's exposure to TV violence and their aggressive and violent behavior in young adulthood: 1977–1992. *Developmental Psychology, 39*, 201–221.

Huggins, S. (1989). A comparative study of self-esteem of adolescent children of divorced lesbian mothers and divorced heterosexual mothers. In F. Bozett (Ed.), *Homosexuality and the family* (pp. 123–135). New York: Harrington Park Press.

Human Rights Watch. (2002). *World Report 2002.* Retreieved September 1, 2005, from http://www.hrw.org

Huntley, J., & Costanzo, M. (2003). Sexual harassment stories: Testing a story-mediated model of juror decision-making in civil litigation. *Law and Human Behavior, 27*, 29–51.

Huston, A. C., Donnerstein, E., Fairchild, H., Fesbach, N. D., Katz, P. A., Murray, J. P., et al, (1992). *Big world, small screen: The role of television in American society.* Lincoln, NE: University of Nebraska Press.

Hvistendahl, J. (1979). The effect of placement of biasing information. *Journalism Quarterly, 56*, 863–865.

Hyman, H. M., & Tarrant, C. M. (1975). Aspects of American trial jury history. In R. J. Simon (Ed.), *The jury system in America: A critical overview* (pp. 21–44). Newbury Park, CA: Sage.

Hyman, I. E., Husband, T. H., & Billings, F. J. (1995). False memories of childhood experiences. *Applied Cognitive Psychology, 9*, 181–197.

Hyman, J., & Huemann, M. (1996). Minitrials and matchmakers, *Judicature, 80*, 123–129.

Implementing *Atkins.* (2003). *Harvard Law Review, 116*, 2565–2587.

Imwinkelreid, E. J. (1994). The next step after *Daubert*: Developing a similarly epistemological approach to ensuring the reliability of nonscientific expert testimony. *Cardozo Law Review, 15*, 2271–2294.

Inbau, F., Reid, J., Buckley, J., & Jayne, B. (2004). *Criminal interrogation and confessions* (4th ed.), Gaithersburg, MD: Aspen.

Innocence Project (2005). Retrieved September 1, 2005, from http://www.innocenceproject.org/ *In re Corrugated Container Antitrust Litigation*, 614 F2d 958 (5th Circuit, 1980).

In re Gault, 387 U.S. 1, 87 S.Ct. 1428 (1967).

In re Guardianship of Schiavo, 780 So.2d 176 (Fla. App. 2001).

In re U.S. Securities Litigation, 609 F2d 411, (9th Circuit, 1979).

In re Winship, 397 U.S. 358 (1970).

Inwald, R. E. (1986). Issues and guidelines for mental health professionals conducting pre-employment psychological screening programs in law enforcement agencies. In J. T. Reese & H. A. Goldstein (Eds.), *Psychological services for law enforcement* (pp. 47–50). Washington, D.C.: U.S. Government Printing Office.

Inwald, R. E. (1992). *Inwald Personality Inventory technical manual* (rev. ed.). Kew Gardens, NY: Hilson Research.

Inwald, R. E., Knatz, H., & Shusman, E. (1983). *Inwald Personality Inventory manual.* New York: Hilson Research.

Irvin v. Dowd, 366 U.S. 717 (1961).

Irwin, J. (1970). *The felon.* Englewood Cliffs, NJ: Prentice-Hall.

Ivkovic, S. K., & Hans, V. P. (2003). Juror's evaluation of expert testimony. *Law & Social Inquiry, 28*, 2, 441.

J. E. B. ex rel. T. B., 114 S.Ct. 1419 (1994).

Jackson v. Denno, 378 U.S. 368 (1964).

Jackson v. Indiana, 406 U.S. 715 (1972).

Jackson, S. E., & Maslach, C. (1982). After-effects of job-related stress: Families as victims. *Journal of Occupational Behavior, 3*, 63–77.

Jackson, S. E., & Schuler, R. S. (1983, March–April). Preventing employee burnout. *Personnel*, pp. 58–68.

Jackson, R. L., Rogers, R., & Sewell, K. W. (2005). Forensic applications of the Miller Forensic Assessment of

Symptoms Test (MFAST): Screening for feigned disorders in competency to stand trial evaluations. *Law and Human Behavior, 29*(2), 199–210.

Jacobson v. United States, 112 S.Ct. 1535 (1992).

James, D. J. (2004). *Bureau of Justice Statistics special report: Profile of jail inmates, 2002.* U.S. Department of Justice: Author.

James, R. (1959). Status and competence of juries. *American Journal of Sociology, 64,* 563–570.

Janus, E., & Prentky, R. (2003). Forensic use of actuarial risk assessment with sex offenders: Accuracy, admissibility and accountability. *American Criminal Law Review, 40,* 1443–1499.

Jeffers, H. P. (1991). *Who killed Precious?* New York: Pharos Books.

Jenkins, P., & Davidson, B. (1990). Battered women in the criminal justice system: An analysis of gender stereotypes. *Behavioral Sciences and the Law, 8,* 161–170.

Joe Arpario 2004. (2004). Retrieved September 1, 2005, from http://www.reelectjoe.com

Johnson v. Zerbst, 304 U.S. 458 (1938).

Johnson, C., & Haney, C. (1994). Felony voir dire: An explanatory study of its content and effect. *Law and Human Behavior, 18,* 487–506.

Johnson, C. C., Jr. with Hampikian, G. (2003). *Exit to freedom.* Athens, GA: University of Georgia Press.

Johnson, K. (2005, June 9). Ex-cons face long odds on release from isolation. *USA Today,* p. 1.

Jones v. United States, 463 US 354 (1983).

Jones, A. (1994). *Next time, she'll be dead: Battering and how to stop it.* Boston: Beacon Press.

Jones, E. E. (1990). *Interpersonal perception.* New York: Freeman.

Jones, E. E., Farina, A., Hastorf, A. H., Markus, H., Miller, D. T., & Scott, R. A. (1984). *Social stigma: The psychology of marked relationships.* New York: Freeman.

Jones, J. S., Wynn, B. N., Kroeze, B., Dunnuck C., & Rossman, L. (2004). Comparison of sexual assaults by strangers versus known assailants in a community-based population. *American Journal of Emergency Medicine, 22,* 454–459.

Judicial Council of California (2004). *Final report: Task force on jury system improvements,* p. 68.

Kadish, M. R., & Kadish, S. H. (1971). The institutionalization of conflict: Jury aquittals. *Journal of Social Issues, 27*(2), 199–218.

Kagehiro, D. K., & Werner, C. M. (1977, May). *Effects of authoritarianism and inadmissibility of evidence on jurors' verdicts.* Paper presented at the meeting of the Midwestern Psychological Association, Chicago.

Kairys, D. (1972). Juror selection: The law, a mathematical method of analysis, and a case study. *American Criminal Law Review, 10,* 771–806.

Kairys, D., Kadane, B., & Lehoczky, P. (1977). Jury representativeness: A mandate for multiple source lists. *California Law Review, 65,* 776–827.

Kalven, H., & Zeisel, H. (1966). *The American jury.* Boston: Little, Brown.

Kamisar, Y., LaFave, W. R., & Israel, J. (1999). *Basic criminal procedure: Cases, comments and questions.* St. Paul, MN: West.

Kane, J. (2004, Fall). Giving trials a second look. *Judges' Journal,* 28–31.

Kanin, E. (1957). Male aggression in dating-courtship situations. *American Journal of Sociology, 63,* 197–204.

Kanin, E. (1971). Sexually aggressive college males. *Journal of College Student Personnel, 12*(2), 107–110.

Kansas v. Hendricks, 117 S.Ct.2013 (1996).

Kaplan, J. (1996). *Criminal law.* Boston: Little, Brown.

Kassin, S., Goldstein, C., & Savitsky, K. (2003). Behavioral confirmation in the interrogation room: On the dangers of presuming guilt. *Law and Human Behavior, 27,* 187–203.

Kassin, S., & Gudjonsson, G. (2004). The psychology of confessions: A review of the literature and issues. *Psychological Science in the Public Interest, 5,* 33–67.

Kassin, S. M. (2005). On the psychology of confessions: Does innocence put innocents at risk? *American Psychologist, 60,* 3, 215–228.

Kassin, S. M., & Kiechel, K. L. (1996). The social psychology of false confessions: Compliance, internalization, and confabulation. *Psychological Science, 7,* 125–128.

Kassin, S. M., & McNall, K. (1991). Police interrogations and confessions: Communicating promises and threats by pragmatic implication. *Law and Human Behavior, 15,* 233–251.

Kassin, S. M., & Studebaker, C. A. (1998). Instructions to disregard and the jury: Curative and paradoxical effects. In

J. M. Golding & C. M. MacLeod (Eds.), *Intentional forgetting: Interdisciplinary approaches* (pp. 413–434). Hillsdale, NJ: Erlbaum.

Kassin, S. M., & Sukel, H. (1997). Coerced confessions and the jury: An experimental test of the "harmless error" rule. *Law and Human Behavior, 21,* 27–46.

Kassin, S. M., Williams, L. N., & Saunders, C. L. (1990). Dirty tricks of cross-examination: The influence of conjectural evidence on the jury. *Law and Human Behavior, 14,* 373–384.

Kassin, S. M., & Wrightsman, L. S. (1980). Proir confessions and mock juror verdicts. *Journal of Personality and Social Psychology, 37,* 1877–1887.

Kassin, S. M., & Wrightsman, L. S. (1981). Coerced confessions, judicial instruction, and mock juror verdicts. *Journal of Applied Social Psychology, 11,* 489–506.

Kassin, S. M., & Wrightsman, L. S. (1983). The construction and validation of a juror bias scale. *Journal of Research in Personality, 17,* 423–441.

Kassin, S. M., & Wrightsman, L. S. (1985). Confession evidence. In S. M. Kassin & L. S. Wrightsman (Eds.), *The psychology of evidence and trial procedure* (pp. 67–94). Newbury Park, CA: Sage.

Katz, I., Hass, R. G., Parisi, N., Astone, J., Wackenhut, G., & Gray, L. (1987). Lay people's and health care personnel's perceptions of cancer, AIDS, cardiac and diabetic patients. *Psychological Reports, 60,* 615–629.

Katz, J. (1988). *Seductions of crime.* New York: Basic Books.

Kaye, J. (2001). *State of the Judiciary Address.* Delivered by New York Chief Judge Judith Kaye.

Kazdin, A. (2000). Treatments for aggressive and antisocial children. *Child and Adolescent Psychiatric Clinics of North America, 9,* 841–858.

Kebbell, M., & Wagstaff, G. (1998). Hypnotic interviewing: The best way to interview eyewitnesses? *Behavioral Sciences and the Law, 16,* 115–129.

Keene, B., (1997). Chemical castration: An analysis of Florida's new "cutting-edge" policy towards sex criminals. *Florida Law Review, 49,* 803–820.

Kellerman, A. L., & Mercy, J. M. (1992). Men, women, and murder: Gender-specific differences in rates of fatal violence and victimization. *Journal of Trauma, 33,* 1–5.

Kelley, H. H. (1971). *Attribution in social interaction*. Morristown, NJ: General Learning Press.

Kellough, G., & Wortley, S. (2002). Remand for plea: Bail decisions and plea bargaining as commensurate decisions. *British Journal of Criminology, 42*, 186–210.

Kennedy, J. (1998). Personality type and judicial decision making. *The Judges' Journal, 3*, 4–10.

Kennedy, L. (1985). *The airman and the carpenter: The Lindbergh kidnapping and the framing of Richard Hauptmann*. New York: Viking Press.

Kent, D. A., & Eisenberg, T. (1972). The selection and promotion of police officers: A selected review of recent literature. *Police Chief, 39*, 20–29.

Kerr, N. L., Hymes, R. W., Anderson, A. B., & Weathers, J. E. (1995). Defendant–juror similarity and mock juror judgments. *Law and Human Behavior, 19*, 545–568.

Kerr, N., Kramer, G. P., Carroll, J. S., & Alfini, J. J. (1991). On the effectiveness of voir dire in criminal cases with prejudicial pretrial publicity: An empirical study. *American Law Review, 40*, 665–701.

Kerwin, J., & Shaffer, D. R. (1994). Mock jurors versus mock juries: The role of deliberations in reactions to inadmissible testimony. *Personality and Social Psychology Bulletin, 20*, 153–162.

Ketterman, T., & Kravitz, M. (1978). *Police crisis intervention: A selected biography*. Washington, D.C.: U.S. Government Printing Office.

Kiesler, C. A. (1982). Public and professional myths about mental hospitalization: An empirical reassessment of policy-related beliefs. *American Psychologist, 37*, 1323–1339.

Kilpatrick, D. G., Resick, P., & Veronen, L. (1981). Effects of a rape experience: A longitudinal study. *Journal of Social Issues, 37*(4), 105–112.

Kimonis, E., Frick, P., & Barry, C. (2004). Callous-unemotional traits and delinquent peer affiliation. *Journal of Consulting and Clinical Psychology, 72*, 956–966.

King, N., Soule, D., Steen, S., & Weidner, R. (2005). When process affects punishment: Differences in sentences after guilty plea, bench trial, and jury trial in five guidelines states. *Columbia Law Review, 105*, 959–1009.

King, R., & Mauer, M. (2001). Aging behind bars: "Three strikes" seven years later. Retrieved from http:// www. sentencingproject.org/pdfs/9087.pdf

Kipnis, K. (1979). Plea bargaining: A critic's rejoinder. *Law and Society Review, 13*, 555–564.

Kirchner, J. C., Horowitz, S. W., & Raskin, D. C. (1988). Meta-analysis of mock crime studies of the control question polygraph technique. *Law and Human Behavior, 12*, 79–90.

Kirschman, E. (1997). *I love a cop: What police families need to know*. New York: Guilford.

Klassen, D., & O'Connor, W. A. (1988). A prospective study of predictors of violence in adult male mental health admissions. *Law and Human Behavior, 12*, 143–158.

Klein, C. (1996, May 6). Women's progress slows at top firms. *National Law Journal*, p. 1.

Kleinberg, H. (1989, January 29). It's tough to have sympathy for Bundy. *Lawrence Journal-World*, p. 5A.

Kleinmuntz, B., & Szucko, J. J. (1984). Lie detection in ancient and modern times: A call for contemporary scientific study. *American Psychologist, 39*, 766–776.

Klockars, C. (1985). *The idea of police*. Thousand Oaks, CA: Sage.

Knight, R. A., Warren, J. I., Reboussin, R., & Soley, B. J. (1998). Predicting rapist type from crime-scene variables. *Criminal Justice and Behavior, 25*, 30–45.

Koch, K. (2000). Zero tolerance. *CQ Researcher, 10*(9), 185.

Kolebuck, M. D. (1998). *Kansas v. Henricks*: Is it time to lock the door and throw away the key for sexual predators? *Journal of Contemporary Health and Law Policy, 14*, 537–561.

Konecni, V. J., & Ebbesen, E. B. (1986). Courtroom testimony by psychologists on eyewitness identification issues: Critical notes and reflections. *Law and Human Behavior, 10*, 117–126.

Kornfeld, A.D. (2000). Harris-Lingoes MMPI-2 Pd subscales and the assessment of law enforcement candidates. *Psychological Reports, 86*(1), 339–343.

Koss, M. P. (1992). The underdetection of rape: Methodological choices influence incidence estimates. *Journal of Social Issues, 48*(1), 61–75.

Koss, M. P., & Oros, C. (1982). Sexual experiences survey: A research instrument investigating sexual aggression and victimization. *Journal of Consulting and Clinical Psychology, 50*, 455–457.

Kovera, M. (2002). The effects of general pretrial publicity on juror decisions: An examination of moderators and mediating mechanisms. *Law and Human Behavior, 26*, 43–72.

Kovera, M., & Cass, S. A. (2002). Compelled mental health examinations, liability decisions, and damage awards in sexual harassment cases: Issues for jury research. *Psychology, Public Policy, and Law, 8*, 96–114.

Kovera, M., Dickinson, J., & Cutler, B. (2002). Voir dire and jury selection. In A. Goldstein (Ed.), *Comprehensive handbook of psychology, Vol. 11: Forensic psychology*. New York: Wiley.

Kovera, M., Gresham, A., Borgida, E., Gray, E., & Regan, P. (1997). Does expert testimony inform or influence decision-making? A social cognitive analysis. *Journal of Applied Psychology, 82*, 178–191.

Kovera, M., & McAuliff, B. (2000). The effects of peer review and evidence quality on judge evaluations of psychological science: Are judges effective gatekeepers? *Journal of Applied Psychology, 85*, 574–586.

Kovera, M., Russano, M., & McAuliff, B. (2002). Assessment of the commonsense psychology underlying *Daubert*: Legal decision makers' abilities to evaluate expert evidence in hostile work environment cases. *Psychology, Public Policy, and Law, 8*, 180–200.

Kraemer, G. W., Lord, W. D., & Heilbrun, K. (2004). Comparing single and serial homicide offenses, *Behavioral Sciences and the Law, 22*(3), 325–343.

Kramer, G. P., Kerr, N. L., & Carroll, J. S. (1990). Pretrial publicity, judicial remedies, and jury bias. *Law and Human Behavior, 14*, 409–438.

Kranz, H. (1936). *Lebenschicksale krimineller Zwillinge*. Berlin: Springer-Verlag OHG.

Kranz, H. (1937). *Untersuchungen an Zwillingen* in Furosorgeer-jiehungsanstalten. *Zeitschrift für Induktive Abstammungs-Vererbungslehre, 73*, 508–512.

Kravitz, H. M. & Kelly, J. (1999). An outpatient psychiatry program for offenders with mental disorders found not guilty by reason of insanity. *Psychiatric Services, 50*, 1597–1605.

Kressel, N., & Kressel, D. (2002). *Stack and sway: The new science of jury consulting*. Boulder, CO: Westview Press.

Kropp, P. R., & Hart, S. D. (2000). The Spousal Assault Risk Assessment (SARA) Guide: Reliability and validity in adult male offenders. *Law and Human Behavior, 24*, 101–118.

Kumho Tire Co. v. Carmichael, 526 U. S. 137 (1999).

Kunen, J. (1983). *"How can you defend those people?" The making of a criminal lawyer.* New York: Random House.

Kurtz, H. (1988, December 511). Take a number, cop a plea. *Washington Post National Weekly Edition*, pp. 9–10.

Kurtz, H. (2004, October 29). Bill O'Reilly, producer settle harassment suit: Fox host agrees to drop extortion claim. *Washington Post.* Retrieved online September 1, 2005, from http://www.washingtonpost.com/wp-dyn/articles/A7578–2004Oct28.html

Kushner, M., Riggs, D., Foa, E., & Miller, S. (1992). Perceived controllability and the development of posttraumatic stress disorder (PTSD) in crime victims. *Behavior Research & Therapy, 31*, 105–110.

Kutchinski, B. (1988, June). *Pornography and sexual violence: The criminological evidence from aggregated data in several countries.* Paper presented at the Fourteenth International Congress on Law and Mental Health, Montreal.

Laboratory of Community Psychiatry, Harvard Medical School. (1973). *Competency to stand trial and mental illness.* DHEW Publication No. (ADM) 77–103. Rockville, MD: NIMH, Department of Health, Education, and Welfare.

LaFave, W. (1965). *Arrest: The decision to take a suspect into custody.* Boston: Little, Brown.

Lafortune, K. A., & Carpenter, B. N. (1998). Custody evaluations: A survey of mental health professionals. *Behavioral Sciences and the Law, 16*, 207–224.

Lake, D. A. (2002, Spring). Rational extremism: Understanding terrorism in the twenty-first century. *Dialog-IQ,* 15–29. Retrived June 23, 2005, from http://journals.cambridge.org/bin/bladerunner?30REQEVENT=&REQAUTH=0&500001REQSUB=&REQSTR1=S777777770200002X

Lamar, J. V. (1989, February 6). "I deserve punishment." *Time*, p. 34.

Lamb, H. R., Weinberger, L. E., & DeCuir, W. J. (2002) The police and mental health. *Psychiatric Services, 53*(10), 1266–1271.

Lamb, M. E., Hershkowitz, I., Sternberg, K. J., Esplin, P. W., Hovav, M., Manor, T., et al. (1996). Effects of investigative utterance types on Israeli children's responses. *International Journal of Behavioral Development, 19*, 627–637.

Lamb, M., Sternberg, K., Orbach, Y., Esplin, P., Stewart, H., & Mitchell, S. (2003). Age differences in children's responses to open-ended invitations in the course of forensic interviews. *Journal of Consulting and Clinical Psychology, 71*, 926–934.

Lamb, S. (2003). The psychology of condemnation: Underlying emotions and their symbolic expression in condemning and shaming. *Brooklyn Law Review, 68*, 929–958.

Lambros, T. (1993). The summary jury trial: An effective aid to settlement, *Judicature, 77*, 6–8.

Langan, P., Schmitt, E., & Durose, M. (2003). *Recidivism of sex offenders released from prison in 1994.* Washington, D.C.: Department of Justice (Bureau of Justice Statistics Report NCJ-198281).

Langbein, J. H. (1978). Torture and plea bargaining. *University of Chicago Law Review, 46*, 12–13.

Lange, J. (1929). *Verbrechen als Schiskal.* Leipzig: Georg Thieme.

Langevin, R., Curnoe, S., Federoff, P., Bennett, R., Langevin, M., Peever, C., et al. (2004).

Largen, M. A. (1988). Rape-law reform: An analysis. In A. W. Burgess (Ed.), *Rape and sexual assault* (Vol. 2, pp. 271–292). New York: Garland.

Larsen, K. S., Reed, M., & Hoffman, S. (1980). Attitudes of heterosexuals toward homosexuality: A Likert-type scale and construct validity. *Journal of Sex Research, 16*, 245–257.

Larson, J. (2004, April 10). *Behind the death of Timothy Thomas: Shooting of 19-year-old brings to light pattern of ticketing that raises questions of racial profiling.* Dateline NBC. Retrieved September 24, 2005, from http://www.msnbc.msn.com/id/4703574/

Larson, J. A. (1932). *Lying and its detection.* Chicago: University of Chicago Press.

Lassiter, G. D. (Ed.) (2004). *Interrogations, confessions, and entrapment.* New York: Kluwer/Plenum.

Lassiter, G. D., & Geers, A. (2004). Bias and accuracy in the evaluation of confession evidence. In G. D. Lassiter (Ed.), *Interrogations, confes-*

sions, and entrapment. New York: Kluwer/Plenum.

Lecci, L., Snowden, J., & Morris, D. (2004). Using social science rsearch to inform and evaluate the contributions of trial consultants in voir dire. *Journal of Forensic psychology Practice, 4*, 67–78.

Lee v. Martinez, 96 P. 3d 291 (N.M. 2004).

Lee, F. (1985, May 16). Women are put "on trial" in rape cases. *USA Today*, p. 1A.

Lees-Haley, P. (1991). A fake bad scale on the MMPI-2 for personal injury claimants. *Psychological Reports, 68*, 203–210.

Lees-Haley, P. (1992). Efficacy of MMPI-2 validity scales and MCMI-2 modifier scales for detecting spurious PTSD claims: F, F-K, Fake Bad Scale, Ego Strength, Subtle-Obvious subscales, DIS, and DEB. *Journal of Clinical Psychology, 48*, 681–689.

Lefkowitz, J. (1975). Psychological attributes of policemen: A review of research and opinion. *Journal of Social Issues, 31*(1), 3–26.

Lemert, E. M. (1951). *Social pathology.* New York: McGraw-Hill.

Lemert, E. M. (1972). *Human deviance, social problems, and social control* (2nd ed.). Englewood Cliffs, NJ: Prentice-Hall.

Lempert, R. (1993). Civil juries and complex cases: Taking stock after twelve years. In R. E. Litan (ed.), *Verdict: Assessing the civil jury system* (pp. 181–247). Washington, D.C.: The Brookings Institution.

Lentz, B., & Laband, D. (1995). *Sex discrimination in the legal profession.* Westport, CT: Quorum Books.

Leo, R. (2004) The third degree and the origins of psychological interrogation in the United States. In G. D. Lassiter (Ed.), *Interrogations, confessions, and entrapment* (pp. 37–84). New York: Kluwer/ Plenum.

Leo, R., & Ofshe, R. (1998). The consequences of false confessions: Deprivations of liberty and miscarriages of justice in the age of psychological interrogation. *Journal of Criminal Law and Criminology, 88*, 429–496.

Leonard, K. E., Quigley, B. M., & Collins, R. L. (2002). Physical aggression in the lives of young adults. *Journal of Interpersonal Violence, 17*, 533–550.

Lerner, M. J. (1970). The desire for justice and reactions to victims. In J. Macaulay & L. Berkowitz (Eds.), *Altruism and helping behavior* (pp. 205–229). Orlando, FL: Academic Press.

Lerner, M. J. (1980). *The belief in a just world*. New York: Plenum.

Lester, D., Babcock, S. D., Cassissi, J. P., & Brunetta, M. (1980). Hiring despite the psychologists' objections. *Criminal Justice and Behavior, 7*, 41–49.

Levenson, J. (2004). Reliability of sexually violent predator civil commitment criteria in Florida. *Law and Human Behavior, 28*, 357–368.

Levin, J., & Fox, J. A. (1985). *Mass murder*. New York: Plenum.

Levine, S. (2003, September 26). Death-row inmate hears hoped-for-words: We found killer. *Washington Post*, p. A01.

Levinger, G. (1966). Marital dissatisfaction among divorce applicants. *American Journal of Orthopsychiatry, 36*, 803–807.

Levy, R. J. (1967). Predicting police failures. *Journal of Criminal Law, Criminology, and Police Science, 58*, 265–276.

Lewin, T. (1994, October 21). Outrage over 18 months for a killing. *New York Times*, p. A18.

Lewis, A. (1964). *Gideon's trumpet*. New York: Knopf.

Lewis, A. (2005, June 21). Guantanamo's long shadow, *New York Times*, p. A23.

Lewis, C. (1996, April 3). Keep trying to improve relations between black and white police officers. *Kansas City Star*, p. C11.

Lieberman, J., & Sales, B. (2000). Jury instructions: Past, present, and future. *Psychology, Public Policy, and Law, 6*, 587–590.

Liebman, J. S. (2000). A broken system: Error rates in capital cases, 1973–1995. Retrieved October 1, 2005, from the Criminal Justice Reform Education Fund website: http:// ccjr.policy.net/ cjedfund/jpreport/

Lifetime sex offender recidivism: A 25-year-follow-up study. *Canadian Journal of Criminology and Criminal Justice, 46*, 531–552.

Lilly, J. R., Cullen, F. T., & Ball, R. A. (1989). *Criminological theory: Context and consequences*. Newbury Park, CA: Sage.

Lind, E. A. (1975). The exercise of information influence in legal advocacy. *Journal of Applied Social Psychology, 5*, 127–143.

Lind, E. A. (1982). The psychology of courtroom procedure. In N. L. Kerr & R. M. Bray (Eds.), *Psychology in the courtroom* (pp. 13–37). Orlando, FL: Academic Press.

Lind, E. A., Erickson, B. E., Friedland, N., & Dickenberger, M. (1978). Reactions to procedural models for adjudicative conflict resolution. *Journal of Conflict Resolution, 22*, 318–341.

Lind, E. A., Thibaut, J., & Walker, L. (1973). Discovery and presentation of evidence in adversary and non-adversary proceedings. *Michigan Law Review, 71*, 1129–1144.

Lind, E. A, & Tyler, T. R. (1988). *The social psychology of procedural justice*. New York: Plenum.

Lindsay, D., Hagen, L., Read, J., Wade, K., & Garry, M. (2004). True photographs and false memories. *Psychological Science, 15*, 149–154.

Lindsay, D. S., & Read, J. D. (1995). "Memory work" and recovered memories of childhood sexual abuse: Scientific evidence and public, professional, and personal issues. *Psychology, Public Policy, and Law, 1*, 846–908.

Lindsay, J. (2004, May 20). *Man convicted in 1974 murder is released from prison*. The Associated Press State & Local Wire. Retrieved July 18, 2005, from Lexis-Nexis database.

Lindsay, R. C., Pozzulo, J. D., Craig, W., Lee, K., & Corber, S. (1997). Simultaneous lineups, sequential lineups, and showups: Eyewitness identification decisions of adults and children. *Law and Human Behavior, 21*, 391–404.

Lindsay, R., & Wells, G. (1985). Improving eyewitness identification from lineups: Simultaneous versus sequential lineup presentations. *Journal of Applied Psychology, 70*, 556–564.

Lipsitt, P. D., Lelos, D., & McGarry, A. L. (1971). Competency for trial: A screening instrument. *American Journal of Psychiatry, 128*, 105–109.

Liptak, A. (2005). Inmate's rising I.Q. score could mean his death. Retrieved February 8, 2005, from http://www .nytimes.com/2005/02/06/national/06 atkins.html/

Lipton, J. P. (1977). On the psychology of eyewitness testimony. *Journal of Applied Psychology, 62*, 90–95.

Lisnek, P. (2003). *The hidden jury: And other secret tactics lawyers use to win*. Naperville, IL: Source Books.

Litwack, T. R., & Schlesinger, L. B. (1987). Assessing and predicting violence: Research, law and applications. In I. B. Weiner & A. K. Hess (Eds.), *Handbook of forensic psychology* (pp. 205–257). New York: Wiley.

Lockhart v. McCree, 106 S.Ct. 1758 (1986).

Loeb, T., Rivkin, I., Williams, J., Wyatt, G., Carmona, J., Chin, D., et al. (2002). Child sexual abuse: Association with the sexual functioning of adolescents and adults. *Annual Review of Sex Research, 8*, 307–345.

Loeber, R., & Stouthamer-Loeber, M. (1986). Family factors as correlates and predictors of juvenile conduct problems and delinquency. In M. Tonry & N. Morris (Eds.), *Crime and justice: An annual review of research* (Vol. 7, pp. 291–249). Chicago: University of Chicago Press.

Loftus, E. F. (1974). Reconstructing memory: The incredible witness. *Psychology Today, 8*, 116–119.

Loftus, E. F. (1975). Leading questions and the eyewitness report. *Cognitive Psychology, 7*, 560–572.

Loftus, E. F. (1979). *Eyewitness testimony*. Cambridge, MA: Harvard University Press.

Loftus, E. F. (1984). Expert testimony on the eyewitness. In G. L. Wells & E. F. Loftus (Eds.), *Eyewitness testimony: Psychological perspectives* (pp. 273–282). New York: Cambridge University Press.

Loftus, E. F. (1992). When a lie becomes memory's truth: Memory distortion after exposure to misinformation. *Psychological Science, 1*, 121–123.

Loftus, E. F. (1993). Psychologists in the eyewitness world. *American Psychologist, 48*, 550–552.

Loftus, E. F. (1997a). Creating childhood memories. *Applied Cognitive Psychology, 11*, S75–S86.

Loftus, E. F. (1997b). Creating false memories. *Scientific American, 277*, 70–75.

Loftus, E. F., & Greene, E. (1980). Warning: Even memory for faces may be contagious. *Law and Human Behavior, 4*, 323–334.

Loftus, E. F., & Pickrell, J. E. (1995). The formation of false memories. *Psychiatric Annals, 25*, 720–725.

Loftus, E. F., & Wagenaar, W. (1990). Ten cases of eyewitness identification: Logical and procedural problems. *Journal of Criminal Justice, 18*, 291–305.

Loh, W. D. (1984). *Social research in the judicial process*. Newbury Park, CA: Sage.

Lohr, S. (1987, November 30). For crime detection, "genetic fingerprinting." *New York Times*, p. 5.

Lombroso, C. (1876). *L'Uomo delinquente*. Milan: Hoepli.

London, K., Bruck, M., Ceci, S., & Shuman, D. (2005). Disclosure of child sexual abuse: What does the research tell us about the ways that children tell? *Psychology, Public Policy, and Law, 11*, 194–226.

London, K., & Nunez, N. (2000). The effect of jury deliberations on jurors' propensity to disregard inadmissible evidence. *Journal of Applied Psychology, 85*, 932–939.

Loomis, S. D. (1965). EEG abnormalities as a correlate of behavior in adolescent male delinquents. *American Journal of Psychiatry, 121*, 1003.

Lott, B., Reilly, M. E., & Howard, D. R. (1982). Sexual assault and harassment: A campus community case study. *Signs: Journal of Women in Culture and Society, 8*, 296–319.

Lou, H. (1927). *Juvenile courts in the United States*. Chapel Hill: University of North Carolina Press.

Loucks, A., & Zamble, E. (1994). Some comparisons of female and male serious offenders. *Forum on Corrections Research, 6*(1), 22–25.

Love, A., & Childers, J. (1963). *Listen to leaders in law*. New York: Holt, Rinehart & Winston.

Ludwig, E. (2002). The changing role of the trial judge, *Judicature, 85*, 216–217.

Lunde, D. T., & Morgan, J. (1980). *The die song: A journey into the mind of a mass murderer*. New York: Norton.

Lurigio, A. J., & Skogan, W. G. (1994). Winning the hearts and minds of police officers: An assessment of staff perceptions of community policing in Chicago. *Crime and Delinquency, 40*, 315–330.

Lurigio, A., Watson, A., Luchins, D., & Hanrahan, P. (2001). Therapeutic jurisprudence in Action. *Judicature, 84*, 184–189.

Luus, C. A. E., & Wells, G. L. (1994). The malleability of eyewitness confidence: Co-witness and perseverance effects. *Journal of Applied Psychology, 79*, 714–724.

Lykken, D. T. (1981). *A tremor in the blood: Uses and abuses of the lie detector*. New York: McGraw-Hill.

Lykken, D. T. (1985). The probity of the polygraph. In S. M. Kassin & L. S. Wrightsman (Eds.), *The psychology of evidence and trial procedure* (pp. 95–123). Newbury Park, CA: Sage.

Lynam, D. (1996). Early identification of chronic offenders: Who is the fledgling psychopath? *Psychological Bulletin, 120*, 209–234.

Lynam, D. R. (1998). Early identification of the fledgling psychopath: Locating the psychopathic child in the current nomenclature. *Journal of Abnormal Psychology, 107*, 566–575.

Lynam, D., Moffitt, T., & Stouthamer-Loeber, M. (1993). Explaining the relation between IQ and delinquency: Class, race, test motivation, school failure, and self-control. *Journal of Abnormal Psychology, 102*, 187–196.

Lynch, D., & Evans, T. (2002). Attributes of highly effective criminal defense negotiators. *Journal of Criminal Justice, 30*, 387–396.

Lynch, M., & Haney, C. (2000). Discrimination and instructional comprehension: Guided discretion, racial bias, and the death penalty. *Law and Human Behavior, 24*, 337–358.

MacCoun, R. J. (1996). Differential treatment of corporate defendants by juries: An examination of the "deep pockets" hypothesis. *Law and Society Review, 30*, 121–161.

MacCoun, R. J. (1999). Epistemological dilemmas in the assessment of legal decision making. *Law and Human Behavior, 23*, 723–730.

MacCoun, R. J., & Tyler, T. R. (1988). The basis of citizens' perceptions of the criminal jury: Procedural fairness, accuracy, and efficiency. *Law and Human Behavior, 12*, 333–352.

Mack, J. (1909). The juvenile court. *Harvard Law Review, 23*, 104–122.

MacLean, P. (2005, February 14). Circuits wrestle with fallout from *Booker*. *National Law Journal*, p. 1.

Madden-Derdich, D. A., Leonard, S. A., & Gunnell, G. A. (2002). Parents' and children's perceptions of family processes in inner-city families with delinquent youths: A qualitative investigation. *Journal of Marital and Family Therapy, 28*, 355–370.

Maddox, K., & Gray, S. (2002). Cognitive representations of Black Americans: Re-exploring the role of skin tone. *Personality and Social Psychology Bulletin, 28*, 250–259.

Madonna, J. M. & Kelly, R. E. (2002). *Treating police stress: The work and the words of peer counselors*. Springfield, IL: Thomas.

Madrid v. Gomez, 889 F.Supp. 1146 (N.D. Cal. 1995).

Magdol, L., Moffitt, T. E., Caspi, A., Newman, D. L., Fagan, J., & Silva, P. A. (1997). Gender differences in rates of partner violence in a birth cohort of 21-year-olds: Bridging the gap between clinical and epidemiological approaches. *Journal of Consulting and Clinical Psychology, 65*, 68–78.

Magdol, L., Moffitt, T. E., Caspi, A., & Silva, P. A. (1998). Developmental antecedents of partner abuse: A prospective-longitudinal study. *Journal of Abnormal Psychology, 107*, 373–389.

Maguin E. & Loeber R. (1996). Academic performance and delinquency. In M. Torry and N. Morris (Eds.), *Crime and justice* (pp.145–264). Chicago: Chicago University Press.

Maguire, K., & Flanagan, T. J. (Eds.) (1991). *Sourcebook of criminal justice*. Washington, D.C.: U. S. Department of Justice, Bureau of Justice Statistics.

Mailer, N. (1979). *The executioner's song*. Boston, MA: Little, Brown.

Malpass, R. S., & Devine, P. G. (1981). Eyewitness identification: Lineup instructions and the absence of the offender. *Journal of Applied Psychology, 66*, 482–489.

Malpass, R. S., & Devine, P. G. (1984). Research on suggestion in lineups and photospreads. In G. L. Wells & E. F. Loftus (Eds.), *Eyewitness testimony: Psychological perspectives* (pp. 64–91). New York: Cambridge University Press.

Mandel, S. (September, 2003). Firms and family. *American Bar Association Journal 89*, 45.

Mankoff, M. (1971). Societal reaction and career deviance: A critical analysis. *Sociological Quarterly, 12*, 204–218.

Manson v. Braithwaite, 432 U.S. 98 (1977).

Mapp v. Ohio, 367 U.S. 643 (1961).

Marcus, D.R., Lyons, P.M., & Guyton, M. R. (2000). Studying perceptions of juror influence *in vivo*: A social relations analysis. *Law and Human Behavior, 24*, 173–186.

Marder, N. (1999b). The myth of the nullifying jury. *Northwestern University Law Review, 93*, 877–886.

Marder, N. S. (1999a). The interplay of race and false claims of jury nullification. *University of Michigan Journal of Law Reform, 32*, 285ff. Retrieved December 7, 1999, from Lexis-Nexis.

Marques, J., Abrams, D., Paez, D., & Martinez-Taboada, J. (1998). The role of categorization and in-group norms on judgments of groups and their members. *Journal of Personality and Social Psychology, 75*, 976–988.

Marques, J. K., Wiederanders, M., Day, D. M., Nelson, C., & van Ommeren,

A. (2005). Effects of a relapse prevention program on sexual recidivism: Final results from California's sex offender treatment and evaluation project (SOTEP). *Sexual Abuse: Journal of Research & Treatment. 17*, 79–107.

Marshall, J. (1968). *Intention in law and society*. New York: Minerva.

Marshall, L. (2002). Do exonerations prove that the system works? *Judicature, 86*, 83–89.

Marshall, W. L., Fernandez, Y. M., & Cortoni, F. (1999). Rape. In V. Van Hasselt & M. Hersen (Eds.), *Handbook of psychological approaches with violent offenders*. (pp. 245–266) New York: Kluwer/Plenum.

Marshall, W. L., Jones, R., Ward, T., Johnston, P., & Barbaree, H. E. (1991). Treatment outcome with sex offenders. *Clinical Psychology Review, 11*, 465–485.

Martinson, R. (1974). What works? Questions and answers about prison reform. *Public Interest, 35*, 22.

Martinson, R. (1979). New findings, new views: A note of caution regarding sentencing reform. *Hofstra Law Review, 7*, 243.

Maryland v. Craig, 110 S.Ct. 3157 (1990).

Maslach, C., & Jackson, S. E. (1984). Burnout in organizational settings. In S. Oskamp (Ed.), *Applied social psychology annual* (pp. 133–154). Newbury Park, CA: Sage.

Matthews, A. R. (1970). Observations on police policy and procedures for emergency detention of the mentally ill. *Journal of Criminal Law, Criminology & Police Science, 61*(2), 283–295.

Maxfield, M. G., & Widom, C. S. (1996). The cycle of violence: Revisited 6 years later. *Archives of Pediatrics & Adolescent Medicine. 150*, 390–395.

Maxwell, C. D., Garner, J. H., & Fagan, J. A. (2002). The preventive effects of arrest on intimate partner violence: Research, policy and theory. *Criminology and Public Policy*. Retrieved June 23, 2005, from http://www.jcjs.org/Products/Domestic%20Violence/SARP/CCP.SARP%20article.pdf

Mazzoni, G. A., Loftus, E. F., Seitz, A., & Lynn, S.J. (1999). Changing beliefs and memories through dream interpretation. *Applied Cognitive Psychology, 13*, 125–144.

Mazzoni, G., & Memon, A. (2003). Imagination can create false autobiographical memories. *Psychological Science, 14*, 186–188.

McAree, D. (2004, May 31). Deadbeat dads face ban on procreation, *National Law Journal*, p. 4.

McAuliff, B., Nemeth, R., Bornstein, B., & Penrod, S. (2003). Juror decision-making in the twenty-first century: Confronting science and technology in court. In D. Carson & R. Bull (Eds.), *Handbook of psychology in legal contexts* (2nd Ed.) (pp. 303–327). New York: Wiley.

McCandless, S. R., & Sullivan, L. P. (1991, May 6). Two courts adopt new standard to determine sexual harassment. *National Law Journal*, pp. 18–20.

McCann, T. (2004, August 21). Jury consultants try to turn voir dire into a science. Retrieved October 1, 2005, from http://www.zmf.com/

McCleskey v. Kemp, 107 S.Ct. 1756 (1987).

McConahay, J. B., Mullin, C., & Frederick, J. (1977). The uses of social science in trials with political and racial overtones: The trial of Joan Little. *Law and Contemporary Problems, 41*, 205–229.

McDonough, M. (2004, October). Summary time blues. *American Bar Association Journal, 90*, 18.

McDonough, M. (2005, March). Demanding diversity. *American Bar Association Journal, 91*, 52

McFarlane, M., Doueck, H., & Levine, M. (2002). Preventing child abuse and neglect. In B. Bottoms, M. Kovera, & B. McAuliff (Eds.), *Children, social science, and the law*. Cambridge: Cambridge University Press.

McGee, H. (1971). Black lawyers and the struggle for racial justice in the American social order. *Buffalo Law Review, 20*, 423–433.

McGee, R., Feehan, M., Williams, S., & Anderson, J. (1992). DSM III disorders from age 11 to age 15 years. *Journal of the American Academy of Child and Adolescent Psychiatry, 31*, 50–59.

McKay v. Ashland Oil Inc., 120 F.R.D. 43, 49 (E.D.Ky. 1988).

McKeiver v. Pennsylvania, 403 U.S. 528 (1950).

McLaurin v. Oklahoma State Regents for Higher Education, 339 U.S. 637 (1950).

McManis, M. J. (1986). Post shooting trauma: Demographics of professional support. In J. T. Reese & H. A. Goldstein (Eds.), *Psychological services for law enforcement* (pp. 361–364). Washington, D.C.: U.S. Government Printing Office.

McNatt, D. (2000). Ancient Pygmalion joins contemporary management: A meta-analysis of the result. *Journal of Applied Psychology, 85*, 314–322.

McNiel, D., Borum, R., Douglas, K., Hart, S., Lyon, D., Sullivan, L., et al. (2002). Risk assessment. In J. Ogloff (Ed.). *Taking psychology and law into the twenty-first century* (pp. 148–171). New York: Kluwer Academic/Plenum.

McNiel, D. E. & Binder, R. L. (2005). Psychiatric emergency service use and homelessness, mental disorder, and violence. *Psychiatric Services, 56*, 699–704.

Meddis, S. S., & Kelley, J. (1985, April 8). Crime drops but fear on rise. *USA Today*, p. A1.

Medina v. California, 112 S.Ct. 2572 (1992).

Mednick, S. A., & Christiansen, K. O. (Eds.). (1977). *Biosocial bases of criminal behavior*. New York: Gardner Press.

Mednick, S. A., Gabrielli, W. F., Jr., & Hutchings, B. (1984). Genetic factors in the etiology of criminal behavior. In S. A. Mednick, T. E. Moffitt, & S. A. Stack (Eds.), *The causes of crime: New biological approaches* (pp. 74–91). Cambridge: Cambridge University Press.

Meissner, C., & Brigham, J. (2001). Thirty years of investigating the own-race bias in memory for faces: A meta-analytic review. *Psychology, Public Policy, and Law, 7*, 3–35.

Meissner, C., Brigham, J., & Pfeifer, J. (2003). Jury nullification: The influence of judicial instruction on the relationship between attitudes and juridic decision-making. *Basic and Applied Social Psychology, 25*, 243–254.

Meissner, C., & Kassin, S. (2004). "You're guilty, so just confess!" Cognitive and behavioral confirmation biases in the interrogation room. In G.D. Lassiter (Ed.), *Interrogations, confessions, and entrapment* (pp. 85–106). New York: Kluwer Academic/Plenum.

Meloy, J. R. & Felthous, A. R. (2004). Introduction to this issue: Serial and mass homicide. *Behavioral Sciences and the Law, 22*(3), 289–290.

Meloy, J. R., Hempel, A. G., Gray, B. T., Mohandie, K., Shiva, A., & Richards, T. C. (2004). A comparative analysis of North American adolescent and adult mass murderers. *Behavioral Sciences and the Law, 22*(3), 291–309.

Melton, G. B., Petrila, J., Poythress, N. G., & Slobogin, C. (1997). *Psy-*

chological evaluation for the courts: A handbook for mental health professionals and lawyers (2nd edition). New York: Guilford.

Memon, A., Bartlett, J., Rose, R., & Gray, C. (2003). The aging eyewitness: Effects of age on face, delay, and source-memory ability. Journal of Gerontology, 58B, 338–345.

Memon, A., Hope, L., Bartlett, J., & Bull, R. (2002). Eyewitness recognition errors: The effects of mugshot viewing and choosing in young and old adults. Memory and Cognition, 30, 1219–1227.

Menninger, K. (1966). The crime of punishment. New York: Viking Press.

Meritor Savings Bank v. Vinson, 106 S.Ct. 2399 (1986).

Merrick, R. A. (1985). The tort of outrage: Recovery for the intentional infliction of mental distress. Behavioral Sciences and the Law, 3, 165–175.

Merton, R. K. (1968). Social theory and social structure. New York: Free Press.

Meyer, P. (1982). The Yale murder. New York: Empire Books.

Milgram, S. (1963). Behavioral study of obedience. Journal of Abnormal and Social Psychology, 67, 371–378.

Miller, A. (1988, April 25). Stress on the job. Newsweek, pp. 40–45.

Miller, G. R., & Boster, F. J. (1977). Three images of a trial: Their implications for psychological research. In B. D. Sales (Ed.), Psychology in the legal process (pp. 19–38). New York: Spectrum.

Miller, H. A. (2001). M-FAST: Miller Forensic Assessment of Symptoms Test professional manual. Odessa, FL: Psychological Assessment Resources, Inc.

Miller, H. A. (2004). Examining the use of the M-FAST with criminal defendants incompetent to stand trial. International Journal of Offender Therapy and Comparative Criminology, 48(3), 268–280.

Miller, M. (1995, October 30). The road to Panama City. Newsweek, p. 84.

Miller, W. B. (1958). Lower-class culture as a generating milieu of gang delinquency. Journal of Social Issues, 14, 5–19.

Miller-El v. Cockrell, 537 U.S. 322 (2003).

Miller-El v. Dretke, 361 F. 3d 849 (5ᵗʰ Cir. 2004).

Miller-El v. Dretke, No. 03–9659 (2005).

Mills, K. (1983, September 19). Some lawyers alter tactics as more women take seats on juries. Kansas City Times, p. A1.

Mills, L. G. (1998). Mandatory arrest and prosecution policies for domestic violence: A critical literature review and the case for more research to test victim empowerment approaches. Criminal Justice and Behavior, 25, 306–318.

Mills, M. C., & Stratton, J. G. (1982). MMPI and the prediction of job performance. FBI Law Enforcement Bulletin, 51, 10–15.

Mills, R. B., McDevitt, R. J., & Tonkin, S. (1966). Situational tests in metropolitan police recruit selection. Journal of Criminal Law, Criminology, and Police Science, 57, 99–104.

Mills, S. (1998, April 29). "Killer" in jail when crime committed; Teen accuses cops of coercing him into admitting guilt. Chicago Tribune, p. 1.

Minow, M. (1993). Definitions of family: Who's in, who's out, and who decides. In M. Minow (Ed.). Family matters: Readings on family lives and the law. New York: The New Press.

Miranda v. Arizona, 384 U.S. 486 (1966).

Mitchell, P. (1976). Act of love: The killing of George Zygmanik. New York: Knopf.

Mize, G. (1999, Spring). On better jury selection: Spotting UFO jurors before they enter the jury room. Court Review, 10–15.

Mize, G., & Connelly, C. (2004). Jury trial innovations: Charting a rising tide. Court Review, 41, 4–10.

Moehringer, J. (1998, August 12). Boys sentenced for Arkansas school murders. Los Angeles Times, p. A1.

Moenssens, A. (2002). Brain fingerprinting: Can it be used to detect the innocence of persons charged with crime? University of Missouri, Kansas City Law Review, 70, 891–920.

Moffitt, T. (1993). Adolescence-limited and life-court–persistent antisocial behavior: A developmental taxonomy. Psychological Review, 100, 674–701.

Moffitt, T., & Lynam, D. (1994). The neuropsychology of conduct disorder and delinquency: Implications for understanding antisocial behavior. In D. Fowles, P. Sutker, & S. Goodman (Eds.), Psychopathy and antisocial behavior: A developmental perspective (pp. 233–262). New York: Springer-Verlag.

Moffitt, T. E., & Mednick S. A. (1988). Biological contributions to crime causation. New York: Martinus Nijhoff.

Moffitt, T. E., & Silva, P. A. (1988). IQ and delinquency: A direct test of the differential detection hypothesis. Journal of Abnormal Psychology, 97, 330–333.

Monahan, J. (1984). The prediction of violent behavior: Toward a second generation of theory and practice. American Journal of Psychiatry, 141, 10–15.

Monahan, J. (1992). Mental disorder and violent behavior: Perceptions and evidence. American Psychologist, 47, 511–521.

Monahan, J., & Steadman, H. (Eds.) (1994). Violence and mental disorder: Developments in risk assessment. Chicago: University of Chicago Press.

Monahan, J., Steadman, H. J., Robbins, P.C., Appelbaum, P., Banks, S., Grisso, T., Heilbrun, K., Mulvey, E. P., Roth, L., & Silver, E. (2005) An actuarial model of violence risk assessment for persons with mental disorders. Psychiatric Services, 56, 810–815.

Monahan, J., & Walker, L. (1990). Social sciences in law: Cases and materials (2nd ed.). Westbury, NY: Foundation Press.

Monson, C. M., Gunnin, D. D., Fogel, M. H. & Kyle, L. L. (2001). Stopping (or slowing) the revolving door: Factors related to NGRI acquittees' maintenance of a conditional release. Law and Human Behavior, 25(3), 257–267.

Montgomery, G., DuHamel, K., & Redd, W. (2000). A meta-analysis of hypnotically induced analgesia: How effective is hypnosis? International Journal of Clinical and Experimental Hypnosis, 48, 138–153.

Moran v. Burbine, 475 U.S. 412 (1986).

Moran, G., & Comfort, J. C. (1982). Scientific juror selection: Sex as a moderator of demographic and personality predictors of impaneled felony juror behavior. Journal of Personality and Social Psychology, 43, 1052–1063.

Moran, G., & Cutler, B. L. (1991). The prejudicial impact of pretrial publicity. Journal of Applied Social Psychology, 21, 345–367.

Moran, G., & Cutler, B. L. (1997). Bogus publicity items and the contingency between awareness and media-induced pretrial prejudice. Law and Human Behavior, 21, 339–349.

Moran, G., Cutler, B. L., & Loftus, E. F. (1990). Jury selection in major controlled substance trials: The need for extended voir dire. Forensic Reports, 3, 331–348.

Morgan, A. B., & Lilienfled, S. O. (2000). A meta-analytic review of the relation between antisocial behavior and neuropsychological measures of executive function. *Clinical Psychology Review, 20*, 113–136.

Morgan, C., Hazlett, G., Doran, A., Garrett, S., Hoty, G., Thomas, P., Baranoski, M., & Southwick, S. (2004). Accuracy of eyewitness memory for persons encountered during exposure to highly intense stress. *International Journal of Law and Psychiatry, 27*, 265–279.

Morier, D., Borgida, E., & Park, R. C. (1996). Improving juror comprehension of judicial instructions on the entrapment defense. *Journal of Applied Social Psychology, 26*, 1838–1866.

Morrison, P. (1995, August 21). The new chain gang. *National Law Journal*, pp. A1, A22.

Morse, S. J. (1978). Law and mental health professionals: The limits of expertise. *Professional Psychology, 9*, 389–399.

Morse, S. J. (1998). Fear of danger, flight from culpability. *Psychology, Public Policy, and Law, 4*, 250–267.

Mossman, D. (1987). Assessing and restoring competency to be executed: Should psychiatrists participate? *Behavioral Sciences and the Law, 5*, 397–410.

Mossman, K. (1994). Assessing predictors of violence: Being accurate about accuracy. *Journal of Consulting and Clinical Psychology, 62*, 783–792.

Mott, N. (2003). The current debate on juror questions: "To ask or not to ask, that is the question." *Chicago-Kent Law Review, 78*, 1099–1125.

Muehlenhard, C. L., & Linton, M. A. (1987). Date rape and sexual aggression in dating situations: Incidence and risk factors. *Journal of Counseling Psychology, 34*, 186–196.

Muir, W. K., Jr. (1977). *Police: Streetcorner politicians*. Chicago: University of Chicago Press.

Mulford, C. L., Lee, M. Y., & Sapp, S. C. (1996). Victim-blaming and society-blaming scales for social problems. *Journal of Applied Social Psychology, 26*, 1324–1336.

Mulvey, E., & Cauffman, E. (2001). The inherent limits of predicting school violence. *American Psychologist, 56*, 797–802.

Mu'Min v. Virginia, 111 S.Ct 1899 (1991).

Munson, L. J., Miner, A. G., & Hulin, C. (2001). Labeling sexual harassment in the military: An extension and replication. *Journal of Applied Psychology, 86*, 293–303.

Munsterman, G., & Hannaford-Agor, P. (2004). Building on bedrock: The continued evolution of jury reform. *The Judges' Journal, 43*, 10–16.

Murdoch, D., Pihl, R., & Ross, R. (1985). Alcohol and crimes of violence: Present issues. *International Journal of Addiction, 25*, 1065–1081.

Murdoch, D., Pihl, R. O., & Ross, D. (1990). Alcohol and crimes of violence: Present issues. *International Journal of the Addictions, 25*(9), 1065–1081.

Mustard, D. (2001). Racial, ethnic, and gender disparities in sentencing: Evidence from the U.S. Federal Courts. *Journal of Law and Economics, 44*, 285–314.

Myers, B., Rosol, A., & Boelter, E. (2003). Polygraph evidence and juror judgments: The effects of corroborating evidence. *Journal of Applied Social Psychology, 33*, 948–962.

Myers, J. (1996). A decade of international reform to accommodate child witnesses. *Criminal Justice and Behavior, 23*, 402–422.

Myers, M., Stewart, D., & Brown, S. (1998). Progression from conduct disorder to antisocial personality disorder following treatment for adolescent substance abuse. *American Journal of Psychiatry, 155*, 479–486.

Narby, D. J., Cutler, B. L., & Moran, G. (1993). A meta-analysis of the association between authoritarianism and jurors' perceptions of defendant culpability. *Journal of Applied Psychology, 78*, 34–42.

National Advisory Commission on Criminal Justice Standards and Goals. (1973). *Corrections*. Washington, D.C.: U.S. Government Printing Office.

National Association of Counsel for Children. (2005). *Child maltreatment*. Retrieved September 2, 2005, from http://www.naccchildlaw.org/

National Association of Law Placement. (2005). *Employment of new graduates just shy of 89%*. Retrieved September 1, 2005, from http://www.nalp.org/assets/45_ersini03.pdf

National Center for Education Statistics (2003). *Indicators of school crime and safety: 2003*. Retrieved September 1, 2005, from http://nces.ed.gov/

National Center for Education Statistics (2004). *Crime and safety in America's public schools: Selected findings from the School Survey on Crime and Safety*. Retrieved September 1, 2005, from http://nces.ed.gov/

National Jury Project. (1990). *Jurywork: Systematic techniques*. Release No. 9. New York: Clark Boardman Company.

National Research Council (1989). *Improving risk communication*. Washington, D.C.: National Academy Press.

National Research Council (2003). *The polygraph and lie detection*. Washington, D.C.: National Academy of Sciences.

National Women's Study. (2000). *National Institute on Druge Abuse*. Retrieved October 1, 2005, from http://data.library.ubc.ca/java/jsp/database/production/detail.jsp?id = 528

Neary, A. M. (1990). *DSM-II and psychopathology checklist assessment of antisocial personality disorder in black and white female felons*. Unpublished Master's thesis, Univeristy of Missouri, St. Louis.

Nebraska Press Association v. Stuart, 427 U.S. 539 (1976).

Neff, C. (1987, April 8). Scorecard. *Sports Illustrated*, p. 28.

Neil v. Biggers, 409 U.S. 188 (1972).

Neil, M. (2003, October). Let's get away from it all. *American Bar Association Journal, 89*, 70.

Neil, M. (2005, January). Litigation over arbitration, *American Bar Association Journal, 91*, 50–53.

Neisser, U. (1976). *Cognition and reality: Principles and implications of cognitive psychology*. San Francisco: Freeman.

Nestor, P. G., Daggett, D., Haycock, J., & Price, M. (1999). Competence to stand trial: A neuropsychological inquiry. *Law and Human Behavior, 23*, 397–412.

Nettler, G. (1974). *Explaining crime*. New York: McGraw-Hill.

Newman, A. (2001). The rise and fall of forensic hypnosis in criminal investigation. *Journal of the American Academy of Psychiatry and Law, 29*, 75–84.

New York v. Quarles, 467 U.S. 649 (1984).

Nicholson, R. A. (1999). Forensic assessment. In R. Roesch, S. D. Hart, & J. R. Ogloff (Eds.), *Psychology and law: The state of the discipline* (pp. 122–173). New York: Kluwer/Plenum.

Nicholson, R. A., Briggs, S. R., & Robertson, H. C. (1988). Instruments for assessing competency to stand trial: How do they work? *Professional Psychology: Research and Practice, 19*, 383–394.

Nicholson, R. A., & Kugler, K. E. (1991). Competent and incompetent criminal defendants: A quantitative review of comparative research. *Psychological Bulletin, 109,* 355–370.

Nicholson, R. A., Norwood, S. (2000). The quality of forensic psychological assessments, reports, and testimony: Acknowledging the gap between promise and practice. *Law and Human Behavior, 24,* 9–44.

Nicholson, R. A., Norwood, S., & Enyart, C. (1991). Characteristics and outcomes of insanity acquittees in Oklahoma. *Behavioral Sciences and the Law, 9,* 487–500.

Nicholson, R. A., Robertson, H., Johnson, W., & Jensen, G. (1988). A comparison of instruments for assessing competency to stand trial. *Law and Human Behavior, 12,* 313–321.

Niederhoffer, A. (1967). *Behind the shield: The police in urban society.* New York: Anchor Books.

Niedermeier, K. E., Horowitz, I. A., & Kerr, N. L. (1999). Informing jurors of their nullification power: A route to a just verdict or judicial chaos? *Law and Human Behavior, 23,* 331–352.

Nietzel, M. T. (1979). *Crime and its modification: A social learning perspective.* New York: Pergamon Press.

Nietzel, M. T., & Dillehay, R. C. (1982). The effects of variations in voir dire procedures in capital murder trials. *Law and Human Behavior, 6,* 1–13.

Nietzel, M. T., & Dillehay, R. C. (1986). *Psychological consultation in the courtroom.* New York: Pergamon Press.

Nietzel, M. T., Hasemann, D., & Lynam, D. (1998). Behavioral perspectives on violent behavior. In J. B. Van Hasselt & M. Hersen (Eds.), *Handbook of psychological approaches with violent criminal offenders: Contemporary strategies and issues* (pp. 56–89). New York: Plenum.

Nietzel, M. T., Hasemann, D., & McCarthy, D. (1998). Psychology and capital litigation: Research contributions to courtroom consultation. *Applied and Preventive Psychology,* 7(2), 121–134.

Nietzel, M. T., McCarthy, D., & Kern, M. (1999). Juries: The current state of the empirical literature. In R. Roesch, S. D. Hart, & J. R. P. Ogloff (Eds.), *Psychology and law: The state of the discipline* (pp. 25–52). New York: Kluwer/Plenum.

Nietzel, M. T., Speltz, M., McCauley, E., & Bernstein, D. (1998). *Abnormal psychology.* Boston: Allyn and Bacon.

Nishith, P., Mechanic, M. B., & Resick, P. A. (2000). Prior interpersonal trauma:

The contribution to current PTSD symptoms in female rape victims. *Journal of Abnormal Psychology, 109,* 20–25.

Nix, C. (1987, July 9). 1000 new officers graduate to New York City streets. *New York Times,* p. 15.

Nobile, P. (1989, July). The making of a monster. *Playboy,* pp. 41–45.

Noble, K. B. (1987, March 23). High court to decide whether death penalty discriminates against blacks. *New York Times,* p. 7.

Nordheimer, J. (1989, January 25). Bundy is put to death in Florida, closing murder cases across U.S. *New York Times,* pp. 1, 11.

Note (1953). Voluntary false confessions: A neglected area in criminal investigation. *Indiana Law Journal, 28,* 374–392.

Nunn, S. (2004). Thinking the inevitable: Suicide attacks in America and the design of effective public safety policies. *Journal of Homeland Security and Emergency Management,1,* 4, 401–423.

Obiakor, F., Merhing, T., & Schwenn, J. (1997). *Disruption, disaster, and death: Helping students deal with crises.* Reston, VA: Council for Exceptional Children.

O'Connell, C. (2004). *Murder trial renews division between Ivy Leaguers, blue-collar locals.* Retrieved from http:// www.courttv.com/trials/pring-wilson/cambridge_091704_ctv.html

O'Connor v. Donaldson, 422 U.S. 563 (1975).

O'Connor, M., Sales, B. D., & Shulman, D. (1996). Mental health professional expertise in the courtroom. In B. D. Sales & D. W. Shulman (Eds.), *Law, mental health, and mental disorder* (pp. 40–60). Pacific Grove, CA: Brooks/Cole.

Office of Juvenile Justice and Delinquency Prevention. (1999). Web site: http://ojjdp.ncjrs.org

Ofshe, R. (1992). Inadvertent hypnosis during interrogation: False confession due to dissociative state: Misidentified multiple personality and the satanic cult hypothesis. *International Journal of Clinical and Experimental Hypnosis,* 40(3), 125–156.

Ofshe, R. J. (1989). Coerced confessions: The logic of seemingly irrational action. *Cultic Studies Journal, 6,* 1–14.

Ofshe, R., & Watters, E. (1994). *Making monsters: False memories, psychotherapy,*

and sexual hysteria. New York: Scribners.

Ogloff, J. R. P. (1991). A comparison of insanity defense standards on juror decision making. *Law and Human Behavior, 15,* 509–532.

Ogloff, J., & Chopra, S. (2004). Stuck in the dark ages: Supreme Court decision making and legal developments. *Psychology, Public Policy, and Law, 10,* 379–416.

Ogloff, J. R., & Finkelman, D. (1999). Psychology and law: An overview. In R. Roesch, S. D. Hart, & J. R. P. Ogloff (Eds.), *Psychology and law: The state of the discipline* (pp. 1–20). New York: Kluwer.

Ogloff, J. R. P., & Otto, R. (1993). Psychological autopsy: Clinical and legal perspectives. *Saint Louis University Law Journal, 37,* 607–646.

Ogloff, J. R. P., & Vidmar, N. (1994). The impact of pretrial publicity on jurors: A study to compare the relative effects of television and print media in a child sex abuse case. *Law and Human Behavior, 18,* 507–525.

Olczak, P. V., Kaplan, M. F., & Penrod, S. (1991). Attorneys' lay psychology and its effectiveness in selecting jurors: Three empirical studies. *Journal of Social Behavior and Personality, 6,* 431–452.

Olsen-Fulero, L. & Fulero, S. (1997). Commonsense rape judgments: An empathy-complexity theory of rape juror story making. *Psychology, Public Policy, and Law, 3,* 402–427.

Olson, W. K. (1991). *The litigation explosion.* New York: Dutton.

Olson-Raymer, G. (1984). National juvenile justice policy: Myth or reality? In S. H. Decker (Ed.), *Juvenile justice policy: Analyzing trends and outcomes* (pp. 19–57). Newbury Park, CA: Sage.

Olweus, D. (1995). Bullying or peer abuse at school: Facts and interventions. *Current Directions in Psychological Science, 4,* 196–200.

Oncale v. Sundowner Offshore Services, Inc., 118 S. Ct. 998 (1998).

Orbach, Y., Hershkowitz, I., Lamb, M., Sternberg, K., Esplin, P., & Horowitz, D. (2000). Assessing the value of structured protocols for forensic interviews of alleged child abuse victims. *Child Abuse and Neglect, 24,* 733–752.

Ornstein, P. A., Ceci, S. J., & Loftus, E. F. (1998). Adult recollections of childhood abuse: Cognitive and developmental perspectives. *Psychology, Public Policy, and Law, 4,* 1025–1051.

Ostrov, E. (1986). Police/law enforcement and psychology. *Behavioral Sciences and the Law, 4*, 353–370.

Otto, R. K., Poythress, N. G., Nicholson, R. A., Edens, J. F., Monahan, J., Bonnie, R. J., et al. (1998). Psychometric properties of the MacArthur competence assessment tool—criminal adjudication. *Psychological Assessment, 10*, 435–443.

Otto, R., Poythress, N., Starr, K., & Darkes, J. (1993). An empirical study of the reports of APA's peer review panel in the congressional review of the *USS Iowa* incident. *Journal of Personality Assessment, 61*, 425–442.

Packer, H. L. (1964). Two models of the criminal process. *University of Pennsylvania Law Review, 113*, 1–68.

Padawer-Singer, A. M., & Barton, A. H. (1975). The impact of pretrial publicity on jurors' verdicts. In R. J. Simon (Ed.), *The jury system in America: A critical overview* (pp. 123–139). Newbury Park, CA: Sage.

Palermo, G. B. (2002). Criminal profiling: The uniqueness of the killer. *International Journal of Offender Therapy & Comparative Criminology, 46*(4), 383–385.

Palmer, J., & Palmer, S.E. (1999). *Constitutional rights of prisoners.* Cincinnati: Anderson.

Parker, R. (2004). Alcohol and violence: Connections, evidence and possibilities for prevention. *Journal of Psychoactive Drugs, suppl. 2*, 157–163.

Pasewark, R. A., Bieber, S., Bosten, K. J., Kiser, M., & Steadman, H. J. (1982). Criminal recidivism among insanity acquittees. *International Journal of Law and Psychiatry, 5*, 365–374.

Pasewark, R. A., & Pantle, M. L. (1981). Opinions about the insanity plea. *Journal of Forensic Psychiatry, 8*, 63.

Patterson, C., Fulcher, M., & Wainright, J. (2002). Children of lesbian and gay parents: Research, law, and policy. In B. Bottoms, M. Kovera, & B. McAuliff (Eds.), *Children, social science, and the law.* Cambridge: Cambridge University Press.

Patterson, G. R. (1982). *Coercive family process.* Eugene, OR: Castalia.

Patterson, G. R. (1986). Performance models for antisocial boys. *American Psychologist, 41*(4), 432–444.

Patton v. Yount, 467 U.S. 1025 (1984).

Peak, K., Bradshaw, R., & Glensor, R. (1992). Improving citizen perceptions of the police: "Back to the basics" with a community policing strategy. *Journal of Criminal Justice, 20*, 24–40.

Pearce, J. B., & Snortum, J. R. (1983). Police effectiveness in handling disturbance calls: An evaluation of crisis intervention training. *Criminal Justice and Behavior, 10*, 71–92.

Pearl, D., Bouthilet, L., & Lazar, J. (Eds.). (1982). *Television and behavior: Ten years of scientific progress and implications for the eighties.* (Vols. 1 & 2). Washington, D.C.: U.S. Government Printing Office.

Pennington, N., & Hastie, R. (1986). Evidence evaluation in complex decision-making. *Journal of Personality and Social Psychology, 51*, 242–258.

Pennington, N., & Hastie, R. (1988). Explanation-based decision making: Effects of memory structure on judgment. *Journal of Experimental Psychology: Learning, Memory, and Cognition, 14*, 521–533.

Pennington, N., & Hastie, R. (1993). The story model for juror decision making. In R. Hastie (Ed.), *Inside the juror: The psychology of juror decision making* (pp. 192–221). New York: Cambridge University Press.

Penrod, S. D. (1990). Predictors of jury decision making in criminal and civil cases: A field experiment. *Forensic Reports, 3*, 261–278.

Penrod, S. D. & Cutler, B. (1999). Preventing mistaken convictions in eyewitness identification trials: The case against traditional safeguards. In Roesch, R., Hart, S. D., & Ogloff, J. (Eds.), *Psychology and law: The state of the discipline.* New York: Kluwer/Plenum.

Penrod, S. D., Fulero, S. M., & Cutler, B. L. (1995). Expert psychological testimony on eyewitness reliability before and after *Daubert*: The state of the law and the science. *Behavioral Sciences and the Law, 13*, 229–260.

Penrod, S. D., Loftus, E. F., & Winkler, J. (1982). The reliability of eyewitness testimony: A psychological perspective. In N. L. Kerr & R. M. Bray (Eds.), *The psychology of the courtroom* (pp. 119–168). Orlando, FL: Academic Press.

People v. Falsetta, 986 P.2d 182 (1999).

People v. Williams, 21 P.3d 1209 (California, 2001).

Perlin, M. (1996). The insanity defense: Deconstructing the myths and reconstructing the jurisprudence. In B. D. Sales & D. W. Shulman (Eds.), *Law, mental health, and mental disorder* (pp. 341–359). Pacific Grove, CA: Brooks/Cole.

Perry, N. W., & Wrightsman, L. S. (1991). *The child witness.* Newbury Park, CA: Sage.

Peterson, R., & Bailey, W. (2003). Is capital punishment an effective deterrent for murder? An examination of social science research. In J. Acker, R. Bohm, & C. Lanier (Eds.), *America's experiment with capital punishment: Reflections on the past, present, and future of the ultimate penal sanction* (pp. 251–282). Durham NC: Carolina Academic Press.

Peterson-Badali, M., Abramovitch, R., Koegl, C., & Ruck, M. (1999). Young people's experience of the Canadian youth justice system: Interacting with police and legal counsel. *Behavioral Sciences and the Law, 17*, 455–465.

Peterson-Badali, M., & Koegl, C. (1998). Young people's knowledge of the Young Offenders Act and the youth justice system. *Canadian Journal of Criminology, 40*, 127–152.

Petrella, R. C., & Poythress, N. G. (1983). The quality of forensic evaluations: An interdisciplinary study. *Journal of Consulting and Clinical Psychology, 51*, 76–85.

Pfohl, S. J. (1984). Predicting dangerousness: A social deconstruction of psychiatric reality. In L. A. Teplin (Ed.), *Mental health and criminal justice* (pp. 201–225). Newbury Park, CA: Sage.

Pfohl, S. J. (1985). *Images of deviance and social control: A sociological history.* New York: McGraw-Hill.

Phares, E. J. (1976). *Locus of control in personality.* Morristown, NJ: General Learning Press.

Phares, E. J., & Wilson, K. G. (1972). Responsibility attribution: Role of outcome severity, situational ambiguity, and internal–external control. *Journal of Personality, 40*, 392–406.

Phillips, A. (2004, February 8). Training to be police officers: What does it take to join the force? These cadets are finding out. *The Austin American Statesman.* Retrieved July 15, 2005, from http://www.statesman.com/opinion/content/editorial/cadets/0208apdcadets.html

Phillips, D. A. (1979). *The great Texas murder trials: A compelling account of the sensational T. Cullen Davis case.* New York: Macmillan.

Phillips, M., McAuliff, B., Kovera, M., & Cutler, B. (1999). Double-blind photoarray administration as a safe-guard against investigator bias. *Journal of Applied Psychology, 84*, 940–951.

Pickel, K. L. (1995). Inducing jurors to disregard inadmissible evidence: A legal explanation does not help. *Law and Human Behavior, 19*, 407–424.

Pickel, K. L. (1998). The effects of motive information and crime unusualness on jurors' judgments in insanity cases. *Law and Human Behavior, 22*, 571–584.

Pickel, K. L. (1999). The influence on context on the "weapon focus" effect. *Law and Human Behavior, 23*, 299–311.

Pickel, K., French, T., & Betts, J. (2003). A cross-modal weapon focus effect: The influence of a weapon's presence on memory for auditory information. *Memory, 11*, 277–292.

Pinizzotto, A. J., & Finkel, N. J. (1990). Criminal personality profiling: An outcome and process study. *Law and Human Behavior, 14*, 215–234.

Pizzi, W. T. (1987). Batson v. Kentucky: Curing the disease but killing the patient. In P. K. Kurland, G. Casper, & D. Hutchinson (Eds.), *The Supreme Court review, 1987* (pp. 97–156). Chicago: University of Chicago Press.

Planned Parenthood of Central Missouri v. Danforth, 428 U.S. 52 (1976).

Platt, J. J., & Prout, M. F. (1987). Cognitive-behavioral theory and interventions for crime and delinquency. In E. K. Morris & C. J. Braukmann (Eds.), *Behavioral approaches to crime and delinquency: A handbook of application, research, and concepts* (pp. 477–497). New York: Plenum.

Plessy v. Ferguson, 163 U.S. 537 (1896).

Poland, J. M. (1978). Police selection methods and the prediction of police performance. *Journal of Police Science and Administration, 6*, 374–393.

Pollack, S., & Vaughn, J. (1987). *Politics of the heart: A lesbian parenting anthology.* Ithaca, NY: Firebrand Books.

Pollina, D., Dollins, A., Senter, S., Krapohl, D., & Ryan, A. (2004). Comparison of polygraph data obtained from individuals involved in mock crimes and actual criminal investigations. *Journal of Applied Psychology, 89*, 1099–1105.

Polvi, N., Jack, L., Lyon, D., Laird, P., & Ogloff, J. (1996). *Mock jurors' verdicts in a child sexual abuse case: The effects of pretrial publicity.* Paper presented at the Biennial Convention of the American Psychology-Law Society. Hilton Head, SC.

Poole, D. A., & Lindsay, D. S. (1998). Assessing the accuracy of young children's reports: Lessons from the investigation of child sexual abuse. *Journal of Applied and Preventive Psychology, 7*, 1–26.

Poole, D., & Lindsay, D. (2001). Children's eyewitness reports after exposure to misinformation from parents. *Journal of Experimental Psychology: Applied, 7*, 27–50.

Porter, B. (1983). Mind hunters. *Psychology Today, 17*, 44–52.

Porter, S., & Yuille, J. C. (1996). The language of deceit: An investigation of the verbal clues to deception in the interrogation context. *Law and Human Behavior, 20*, 443–458.

Porter, S., Yuille, J., & Lehman, D. (1999). The nature of real, implanted, and fabricated memories for emotional childhood events: Implications for the recovered memory debate. *Law and Human Behavior, 23*, 517–538.

Posey, A., & Dahl, L. (2002). Beyond pretrial publicity: Legal and ethical issues associated with change of venue surveys. *Law and Human Behavior, 26*, 107–126.

Post, C. G. (1963). *An introduction to the law.* Englewood Cliffs, NJ: Prentice-Hall.

Post, L. (2004a, June 7). Courts mix justice with social work. *National Law Journal,* p. 1.

Post, L. (2004b, November 8). Spelling it out in plain English. Retrieved November 11, 2004, from the *National Law Journal* Web site: www.law.com/jsp/nlj

Post, L. (2004c, June 21). Report: Civil trials fall by half. *National Law Journal,* p. 6.

Post, L. (2005, January 3). DA seeks jail time for lying jurors. *National Law Journal,* p. 5.

Powers v. Ohio, 111 S.Ct. 1364 (1991).

Poythress, N. (1982). Concerning reform in expert testimony. *Law and Human Behavior, 6*, 39–43.

Poythress, N. G., Bonnie, R. J., Hoge, S. K., Monahan, J., & Oberlander, L. B. (1994). Client abilities to assist counsel and make decisions in criminal cases: Findings from three studies. *Law and Human Behavior, 18*, 437–452.

Poythress, N. G., Nicholson, R., Otto, R. K., Edens, J. F., Bonnie, R. J., Monahan, J., et al. (1999). *The MacArthur Competence Assessment Tool–Criminal Adjudication: Professional Manual,* Odessa, FL: Psychological Assessment Resources.

Pozzulo, J. D., & Lindsay, R. C. (1997). Increasing correct identifications by children. *Expert Evidence, 5*, 126–132.

Pozzulo, J. D., & Lindsay, R. C. (1998). Identification accuracy of children versus adults: A meta-analysis. *Law and Human Behavior, 22*, 549–570.

Pozzulo, J. D., & Lindsay, R. C. (1999). Elimination lineups: An improved identification procedure for child eyewitnesses. *Journal of Applied Psychology, 84*, 167–176.

Prentky, R. A. (1999). Child sexual molestation. In V. B. Van Hasselt & M. Hersen (Eds.), *Handbook of psychological approaches with violent offenders.* (pp. 267–302). New York: Kluwer/Plenum.

Prentky, R. A., & Knight, R. A. (1991). Identifying critical dimensions for discriminating among rapists. *Journal of Consulting and Clinical Psychology, 59*, 643–661.

President's Commission on Law Enforcement and Administration of Justice. (1967). *Toward a just America.* Washington, D.C.: U.S. Government Printing Office.

Press, A. (1988, May 2). Helping the cops and jails. *Newsweek,* p. 67.

Prettyman, E. B. (1960). Jury instructions—First or last? *American Bar Association Journal, 46*, 10–66.

Price, R., & Lovitt, J. T. (1996, October 4). Poll: More now believe O. J. is guilty. *USA Today,* p. 3A.

Pryor, J. B. (1987). Sexual harassment proclivities in men. *Sex Roles, 17*, 269–290.

Pryor, J. B., Giedd, J. L., & Williams, K. B. (1995). A social psychological model for predicting sexual harassment. *Journal of Social Issues, 51*(1), 69–84.

Psychological fitness-for-duty evaluation guidelines. (2004). IACP Police Psychological Services Section: Los Angeles, California. Retrieved July 1, 2005, from www.policepsych.com/fitforduty.pdf

Purkett v. Elem, No. 94802 (1995).

Putnam, F. (2003). Ten-year research update review: Child sexual abuse. *Journal of the American Academy of Child and Adolescent Psychiatry, 42*, 269–278.

Quas, J., & Schaaf, J. (2002). Children's memories of experienced and nonexperienced events following repeated interviews. *Journal of Experimental Child Psychology, 83*, 304–338.

Quay, H. C. (1965). Personality and delinquency. In H. C. Quay (Ed.), *Juvenile delinquency.* Princeton, NJ: Van Nostrand.

Quinsey, V. L. (1984). Sexual aggression: Studies of offenders against women. In D. Weisstub (Ed.), *Law and mental health: International perspectives* (Vol. 1, pp. 84–121). New York: Pergamon Press.

Quinsey, V. L., Harris, G. T., Rice, M. E., & Cormier, C. A. (1998). *Violent offenders: Appraising and managing risk.* Washington, D.C.: American Psychological Association.

Quinsey, V. L., Lalumiere, M. L., Rice, M. E., & Harris, G. T. (1995). Predicting violent offenses. In J. C. Campbell (Ed.), *Assessing dangerousness: Violence by sexual offenders, batterers, and child abusers* (pp. 114–137). Thousand Oaks, CA: Sage.

Quinton, W., Major, B., & Richards, C. (2001). Adolexcents and adjustment to abortion: Are minors at greater risk? *Psychology, Public Policy, and Law, 7,* 491–514.

Radelet, M., & Akers, R. (1996). *Deterrence and the death penalty: The views of the experts.* Available at http://sun.socio.niu, edu/

Raine, A. (2002). Annotation: The role of prefrontal deficits, low autonomic arousal, and early health factors in the development of antisocial and aggressive behavior in children. *Journal of Child Psychology & Psychiatry. 43,* 4, 417–434.

Raine, A., Lencz, T., Bihrle, S., Lacasse, L., & Colletti, P. (2000). Reduced prefrontal gray matter volume and reduced autonomic activity in antisocial personality disorder. *Archives of General Psychiatry, 57,* 119–127.

Raine, A., Meloy, J., & Buchsbaum, M. (1998). Reduced prefrontal and increased subcortical brain functioning using positron emission tomography in predatory and affective murderers. *Behavioral Sciences and the Law, 16,* 319–332.

Raine, A., Phil, D., Mellingen, K., Liu, J., Venables, P. & Mednick, S.A. (2003). Effects of environmental enrichment at ages 3–5 years on schizotypal personality and antisocial behavior at ages 17 and 23 years, *American Journal of Psychiatry, 160,* 1627–1635.

Rainville, G., & Smith, S. (2003). Juvenile felony defendants in criminal courts. *U.S. Department of Justice Bureau of Justice Statistics.* Retrieved September 2, 2005, from http:// www.ojp.usdoj .gov/bjs/

Rainville, J., Sobel, J. B., Hartigan, C. & Wright, A. (1997). The effect of compensation involvement on the reporting of pain and disability by patients referred for rehabilitation of chronic low back pain. *Spine, 22,* 17, 2016–2024.

Ramirez, G., Zemba, D., & Geiselman, R.E. (1996). Judge's cautionary instructions on eyewitness testimony. *American Journal of Forensic Psychology, 14*(1), 31–66.

Randolph, J. J., Hicks, T., & Mason, D. (1981). The Competency Screening Test: A replication and extension. *Criminal Justice and Behavior, 8,* 471–482.

Raskin D. C. (1989). *Psychological methods in criminal investigation and evidence.* New York: Springer.

Rasul v. Bush, 542 542 U.S. 466 (2004).

Rebman, C. (1999). The Eighth Amendment and solitary confinement: The gap in protection from psychological consequences. *DePaul Law Review, 49,* 567–619.

Reckless, W. C. (1967). *The crime problem* (4th ed.). New York: Meredith.

Redding, R. E., Floyd, M. Y., & Hawk, G. L. (2001). What judges and lawyers think about the testimony of mental health experts: A survey of the courts and bar. *Behavioral Sciences & the Law. 19*(4), 583–594.

Redlich, A., Silverman, M., Chen, J., & Steiner, H. (2004). The police interrogation of children and adolescents. In G. D. Lassiter (Ed.), *Interrogations, confessions, and entrapment* (pp. 107–126). New York: Kluwer Academic/Plenum.

Rehnquist, W. (1992). *Grand inquest.* New York: William Morrow & Co.

Reibstein, L., & Foote, D. (1996, November 4). Playing the victim card. *Newsweek,* pp. 64, 66.

Reid, J. E., & Inbau, F. E. (1966). *Truth and deception: The polygraph ("lie-detector") technique.* Baltimore: Williams & Wilkins.

Reid, S. T. (1976). *Crime and criminology.* Hinsdale, IL: Dryden.

Reidy, T. J., Cunningham, M. D., & Sorensen, J. R. (2001). From death to life: Prison behavior of former death row inmates. *Criminal Justice and Behavior, 28,* 67–82.

Reiser, M., & Geiger, S. (1984). Police officer as victim. *Professional Psychology: Research and Practice, 15,* 315–323.

Reiser, M., & Klyver, N. (1987). Consulting with police. In I. B. Weiner & A. K. Hess (Eds.), *Handbook of forensic psychology* (pp. 437–459). New York: Wiley.

Reisner, R., Slobogin, C., & Rai, A. (1999). *Law and the mental health system: Civil and criminal aspects* (3rd ed.). St. Paul, MN: West Publishing.

Reiss, A. J., Jr. (1971). *The police and the public.* New Haven, CT: Yale University Press.

Rembar, C. (1980). *The law of the land.* New York: Simon & Schuster.

Ren, L., Cao, L., Lovrich, N., & Gaffney, M. (2005). Linking confidence in the police with the performance of the police: Community policing can make a difference. *Journal of Criminal Justice, 33,* 1, 55–66.

Repko, G. R., & Cooper, R. (1983). A study of the average workers' compensation case. *Journal of Clinical Psychology, 39,* 287–295.

Reppucci, N. D., & Haugaard, J. J. (1989). Prevention of child sexual abuse: Myth or reality. *American Psychologist, 44,* 1266–1275.

Republican Party of Minnesota v. White, 536 U.S. 765 (2002).

Reske, H. (1996, January). Scarlet letter sentences. *American Bar Association Journal,* pp. 16–17.

Resnick, H. S., Kilpatrick, D. G., Dansky, B. S., Saunders, B., & Best, C. L. (1993). Prevalence of civilian trauma and posttraumatic stress disorder in a representative national sample of women. *Journal of Consulting and Clinical Psychology, 61,* 984–991.

Ressler, R. K., Burgess, A. W., & Douglas, J. E. (1988). *Sexual homicide: Patterns and motives.* Lexington, MA: Lexington Books.

Restrepo, L. F. (1995, April 17). Excluding bilingual jurors may be racist. *National Law Journal,* pp. A21, A22.

Reuben, R. (1996, August). The lawyer turns peacemaker. *American Bar Association Journal, 82,* 54–55.

Rhode Island v. Innis, 446 U.S. 291 (1980).

Ribes-Inesta, E., & Bandura, A. (Eds.) (1976). *Analysis of delinquency and aggression.* Hillsdale, NJ: Erlbaum.

Rich, B. A. (1998). Personhood, patienthood, and clinical practice: Reassessing advance directives. *Psychology, Public Policy, and Law, 4,* 610–628.

Richardson, A., & Budd, T. (2003). Young adults, alcohol, crime and disorder.

Criminal Behaviour & Mental Health, 13, 5–16.

Richey, C. R. (1994). Proposals to eliminate the prejudicial effect of the use of the word "expert" under the federal rules of evidence in civil and criminal jury trials. *Federal Rules Decisions, 154,* 537–562.

Richmond Newspapers, Inc. v. Virginia, 448 U.S. 555 (1980).

Rideau v. Louisiana, 373 U.S. 723 (1963).

Rider, A. O. (1980). The firesetter: A psychological profile. *FBI Law Enforcement Bulletin, 49,* 123.

Riechmann, J. (1985, May 21). Mental illness: Parents of deranged children suffer private tragedies. *Lawrence Journal-World,* p. 6.

Ring v. Arizona, 536 U.S. 584 (2002).

Robbennolt, J. (2000). Outcome severity and judgments of "responsibility": A meta-analytic review. *Journal of Applied Social Psychology 30*(12), 1575–2609.

Robbennolt, J. (2002). Punitive damage decision making: The decisions of citizens and trial court judges. *Law and Human Behavior, 26,* 315–342.

Robbennolt, J. (2003). Apologies and legal settlement: An empirical examination. *Michigan Law Review, 102,* 460–516.

Roberts, C. F., & Golding, S. L. (1991). The social construction of criminal responsibility and insanity. *Law and Human Behavior, 15,* 349–376.

Roberts, C. F., Golding, S. L., & Fincham, F. D. (1987). Implicit theories of criminal responsibility: Decision making and the insanity defense. *Law and Human Behavior, 11,* 207–232.

Roberts, C. F., Sargent, E. L., & Chan, A. S. (1993). Verdict selection processes in insanity cases: Juror construals and the effects of guilty but mentally ill instructions. *Law and Human Behavior, 17,* 261–275.

Roberts, J., & Stalans, L. (2004). Restorative sentencing: Exploring the views of the public. *Social Justice Research, 17,* 315–334.

Roberts, K. (2002). Children's ability to distinguish between memories from multiple sources: Implications for the quality and accuracy of eyewitness statements. *Developmental Review, 22,* 403–435.

Robinson, P. (1982, June 9). Criminals and victims. *New Republic,* pp. 37–38.

Rock v. Arkansas, 107 S.Ct. 2704 (1987).

Roebers, C., & Schneider, W. (2002). Stability and consistency of children's event recall. *Cognitive Development, 17,* 1085–1103.

Roesch, R., & Golding, S. L. (1980). *Competency to stand trial.* Urbana: University of Illinois Press.

Roesch, R., & Golding, S. L. (1987). Defining and assessing competence to stand trial. In I. Weiner & A. Hess (Eds.), *Handbook of forensic psychology* (pp. 378–394). New York: Wiley.

Roesch, R., Zapf, P. A., Eaves, D., & Webster, C. D. (1998). *The fitness interview test* (Rev. ed.). Burnaby, BC: Mental Health, Law, and Policy Institute, Simon Fraser University.

Rogers, J. (1998), Special report: Witness preparation memos raise questions about ethical limits, ABA/BNA *Manual on Lawyers' Professional Conduct, 14,* 48–54.

Rogers, R. (1986). *Conducting insanity evaluations.* New York: Van Nostrand.

Rogers, R. (1988). *Clinical assessment of malingering and deception.* New York: Guilford.

Rogers, R. (1995). *Diagnostic and structural interviewing: A handbook for psychologists.* New York: Psychological Assessment Resources.

Rogers, R., & Ewing, C. P. (1989). Ultimate opinion proscriptions: A cosmetic fix and a plea for empiricism. *Law and Human Behavior, 13,* 357–374.

Rogers, R., & Ewing, C.P. (2003). The prohibition of ultimate opinions: A misguided enterprise. *Journal of Forensic Psychology Practice, 3*(3), 65–75.

Rogers, R., Gillis, J. R., Dickens, S. E., & Bagby, R. M. (1991). Standardized assessment of malingering: Validation of the structured interview of reported symptoms. *Psychological Assessment: A Journal of Clinical and Consulting Psychology, 3,* 89–96.

Rogers, R., Salekin, R. T., Sewell, K. W., Goldstein, A., & Leonard, K. (1998). A comparison of forensic and nonforensic malingerers: A prototypical analysis of explanatory models. *Law and Human Behavior, 22,* 253–267.

Rogers, R., Sewell, K. W., & Goldstein, A. (1994). Explanatory models of malingering: A prototypical analysis. *Law and Human Behavior, 18,* 543–552.

Rogers, R., Tillbrook, C., & Sewell, K. (2004). *Evaluation of Competence to Stand Trial–Revised: Professional manual.* Lutz, FL: Psychological Assessment Resources, Inc.

Rohling, M. L., Binder, L. M., & Langhrinrichsen-Rohling, J. (1995).

Money matters: A meta-analytic review of the association between financial compensation and the experience and treatment of chronic pain. *Health Psychology, 14,* 537–547.

Roman, J., Townsend, W., & Bhati, A. (2003). Recidivism rates for drug court graduates: Nationally based estimates. Retrieved September 1, 2005, from the Office of National Drug Control Policy web site: http://www.whitehousedrugpolicy.gov/

Roman, J., Townsend, W., & Bhati, A. S. (2003) Recidivism rates for drug court graduates: Nationally based estimates, final report (U.S. DOJ document 201229). Washington, CD: The Urban Institute.

Rompilla v. Beard, 2005 WL 141390 (2005).

Roper v. Simmons (2005). Supreme Court, 03–633.

Rose, M. R. (1999). The peremptory challenge accused of race or gender discrimination? Some data from one county. *Law and Human Behavior, 23,* 695–702.

Rose, M. (2003). A voir dire of voir dire: Listening to jurors' views regarding the peremptory challenge. *Chicago-Kent Law Review, 78,* 1061–1098.

Rosen, G. M. (1995). The *Aleutian Enterprise* sinking and posttraumatic stress disorder: Misdiagnosis in clinical and forensic settings. *Professional Psychology: Research and Practice, 26,* 82–87.

Rosen, J. (1996, December 9). The Bloods and the Crips. *New Republic,* pp. 27–42.

Rosenbaum, A., & Gearan, P. J. (1999). Relationship aggression between partners. In V. B. Van Hasselt & M. Hersen (Eds.), *Handbook of psychological approaches with violent offenders: Contemporary strategies and issues* (pp. 357–372). New York: Kluver Academic/Plenum.

Rosenhan, D. L. (1973). On being sane in insane places. *Science, 179,* 250–258.

Rosenthal, R., & Jacobson, L. (1968). *Pygmalion in the classroom: Teacher expectation and pupils' intellectual development.* New York: Holt.

Ross, D., Ceci, S., Dunning, D., & Toglia, M. (1994). Unconscious transference and mistaken identify: When a witness misidentifies a familiar but innocent person. *Journal of Applied Psychology 79,* 918–930.

Rotgers, F., & Barrett, D. (1996). *Daubert v. Merrell Dow* and expert testimony by clinical psychologists: Implications and recommendations for practice. *Professional Psychology: Research and Practice*, 27, 467–474.

Rotter, J. B. (1966). Generalized expectancies for internal versus external control of reinforcement. *Psychological Monographs*, 80(1, Whole No. 609).

Rottman, D., et al. (1998). *State court organization*. Retrieved from http://www.ojp.usdoj.dov/bjs/pub/pdf/sco98.pdf

Rovella, D. (1999, January 18). Man with a mission, *National Law Journal*, p. A1.

Rovella, D. (2000a, December 11). Jurors say brutality, corruption make police less believable. *National Law Journal*, p. A1.

Rovella, D. (2000b, January 10). Unclogging Gideon's trumpet. *National Law Journal*, p. 1.

Rovella, D. (2002, March 1). Survey says jury experience leads to fairness. *The Recorder*, p. 3.

Rowan, C. (1993). *Dream makers and dream breakers*. Boston: Little, Brown.

Rowland, J. (1985). *The ultimate violation*. New York: Doubleday.

Ruben, D. (1995, March). Women of the jury. *Self*, pp. 186–189, 196.

Rubinstein, M. L., Clarke, S. H., & White, T. J. (1980). *Alaska bans plea bargaining*. Washington, D.C.: National Institute of Justice, U.S. Department of Justice.

Ruby, C. L., & Brigham, J. C. (1996). A criminal schema: The role of chronicity, race, and socioeconomic status in law enforcement officials' perceptions of others. *Journal of Applied Social Psychology*, 26, 95–111.

Ruffin v. Virginia, 62 Va. (21 Gratt) 790 (1871).

Runda, J. (1991). *Personal affidavit filed with authors*. Lexington: University of Kentucky Press.

Rush, C., & Robertson, J. (1987). Presentence reports: The utility of information to the sentencing decision. *Law and Human Behavior*, 11, 147–155.

Rushton, J. (1996). Self-report delinquency and violence in adult twins. *Psychiatric Genetics*, 6, 87–89.

Russell, D. E. H. (1984). *Sexual exploitation: Rape, child sexual abuse, and workplace harassment*. Newbury Park, CA: Sage.

Ryan, W. (1970). *Blaming the victim*. New York: Vintage.

Ryerson, E. (1978). *The best-laid plans: America's juvenile court experiment*. New York: Hill & Wang.

Sachs, A. (1989, September 11). Doing the crime, not the time. *Time*, p. 81.

Sack, K. (2001). Research guided jury selection in church bombing trial. Retrieved from http://www.nytimes.com/2001/05/03/national/03CHUR.html

Saks, M. (1997). What do jury experiments tell us about how juries (should) make decisions? *Southern California Interdisciplinary Law Journal*, 6, 1–53.

Saks, M. (2000). The aftermath of *Daubert*: An evolving jurisprudence of expert evidence. *Jurimetrics*, 40, 229–241.

Salekin, R. (2002). Juvenile transfer to adult court: How can developmental and child psychology inform policy decision making? In B. Bottoms, M. Kovera, & B. McAuliff (Eds.), *Children, social science, and the law*. Cambridge: Cambridge University Press.

Salekin, R. T., Rogers, R., & Sewell, K. W. (1997). Construct validity of psychopathy in a female offender sample: A multitrait-multimethod evaluation. *Journal of Abnormal Psychology*, 107, 576–585.

Salekin, R., Trobst, K., & Krioukova, M. (2001). Construct validity of psychopathy in a community sample: A nomological net approach. *Journal of Personality Disorders*, 15, 425–441.

Sales, B. D., & Hafemeister, T. (1984). Empiricism and legal policy on the insanity defense. In L. A. Teplin (Ed.), *Mental health and criminal justice* (pp. 253–278). Newbury Park, CA: Sage.

Sales, B. D. & Shuman, D. W. (1993). Reclaiming the integrity of science in expert witnessing. *Ethics and Behavior*, 3, 223–229.

Salfati, C. G., & Canter, D. V. (1999). Differentiating stranger murders: Profiling offender characteristics from behavioral styles. *Behavioral Sciences and the Law*, 17, 391–406.

Samenow, S. E. (1984). *Inside the criminal mind*. New York: Times Books.

Sanborn, H. (2002, October). The vanishing trial. *American Bar Association Journal*, 87, 24–27.

Sanday, P. R. (1997) The socio-cultural context of rape: A cross-cultural study. In O'Toole, L., Schiffman, Jessica R., et al. (Eds.). *Gender violence: Interdisciplinary perspectives*. (pp. 52–66). New York: New York University Press.

Sandburg, C. (1926). *Abraham Lincoln* (Vol. II). New York: Harcourt Brace.

Sanders, J. (1993). The jury decision in a complex case: *Havener v. Merrell Dow Pharmaceuticals*. *The Justice System Journal*, 16, 45.

Santiago, J. M., McCall-Perez, F., Gorcey, M., & Beigel, A. (1985). Long-term psychological effects of rape in 35 rape victims. *American Journal of Psychiatry*, 142, 1338–1340.

Santobello v. New York, 404 U.S. 257 (1971).

Saxe, L. (1991). Lying: Thoughts of an applied social psychologist. *American Psychologist*, 46, 409–415.

Saywitz, K., & Lyon, T. (1998). *Maltreated children's competence to take the oath*. Paper presented at the International Congress of Applied Psychology, San Francisco.

Saywitz, K., Mannarino, A., Berliner, L., & Cohen, J. (2000). Treatment for sexually abused children and adolescents. *American Psychologist*, 55, 1040–1049.

Saywitz, K., & Nathanson, R. (1993). Children's testimony and their perceptions of stress in and out of the courtroom. *Child Abuse and Neglect*, 17, 613–622.

Scheck, B., Neufeld, P., & Dwyer, J. (2000). *Actual innocence*. New York: Random House.

Scheflin, A. (1972). Jury nullification: The right to say no. *Southern California Law Review*, 45, 168–226.

Schindler ex rel Schiavo v. Schiavo, 2005 WL 713153 (11th Cir. 2005).

Schlossberg, H., & Freeman, L. (1974). *Psychologists with a gun*. New York: Coward, McCann, & Geoghegan.

Schmidt, M., & Reppucci, N. (2002). Children's rights and capacities. In B. Bottoms, M. Kovera, & B. McAuliff (Eds.), *Children, social science, and the law*. Cambridge: Cambridge University Press.

Schneider, B. E. (1987). Graduate women, sexual harassment, and university policy. *Journal of Higher Education*, 58(1), 46–65.

Schretlen, D., Wilkins, S. S., Van Gorp, W. G., & Bobholz, J. H. (1992). Cross-validation of a psychological test battery to detect faked insanity. *Psychological Assessment*, 4, 77–83.

Schul, Y. (1993). When warning succeeds: The effect of warning on success in ignoring invalid information. *Journal of

Experimental Social Psychology, 29, 42–62.

Schuller, R. (1995). Expert evidence and hearsay: The influence of "secondhand" information on jurors' decisions. *Law and Human Behavior, 19*, 345–362.

Schuller, R., & Hastings, P. (2002). Complainant sexual history evidence: Its impact on mock jurors' decisions. *Psychology of Women Quarterly, 25*, 252–261.

Schuller, R., & Klippenstine, M. (2004). The impact of complainant sexual history evidence on jurors' decisions: Considerations from a psychological perspective. *Psychology, Public Policy, and Law, 10*, 321–342.

Schuller, R., McKimmie, B., & Janz, T. (2004). The impact of expert testimony in trials of battered women who kill. *Psychiatry, Psychology and Law, 11*, 1–12.

Schulman, J., Shaver, P., Colman, R., Emrich, B., & Christie, R. (1973, May). Recipe for a jury. *Psychology Today*, pp. 37–44, 77–84.

Schwartz, I., Weiner, N., & Enosh, G. (1998). Nine lives and then some: Why the juvenile court does not roll over and die. *Wake Forest Law Review, 33*, 533–552.

Schwitzgebel, R. L., & Schwitzgebel, R. K. (1980). *Law and psychological practice.* New York: Wiley.

Scoboria, A., Mazzoni, G., Kirsch, I., & Milling, L. (2002). Immediate and persisting effects of misleading questions and hypnosis on memory reports. *Journal of Experimental Psychology: Applied, 8*, 26–32.

Scogin, F., Schumacher, J., Gardner, J., & Chaplin, W. (1995). Predictive validity of psychological testing in law enforcement settings. *Professional Psychology, Research and Practice, 26*, 68–71.

Scott v. Commonwealth, 197 S.W.2d 774 (Ky. 1946).

Scott, C., & Holmberg, T. (2003). Castration of sex offenders: Prisoners' rights versus public safety. *Journal of the American Academy of Psychiatry and the Law, 31*, 502–509.

Scott, E., & Grisso, T. (1997). The evolution of adolescence: A developmental perspective on juvenile justice reform. *Journal of Criminal Law and Criminology, 88*, 137–189.

Scrivner, E. M. (1994). *The role of police psychology in controlling excessive force.* Washington, D.C.: National Institute of Justice. Retrieved June 29, 2005, from http://www.ncjrs.org/txtfiles/ppsyc.txt

Scroggs, J. R. (1976). Penalties for rape as a function of victim provocativeness, damage, and resistance. *Journal of Applied Social Psychology, 6*, 360–368.

Seedman, A. A., & Hellman, P. (1974). *Chief!* New York: Arthur Fields.

Seelau, S. M., & Wells, G. L. (1995). Applied eyewitness research: The other mission. *Law and Human Behavior, 19*, 319–324.

Segell, M. (1997, February). Homophobia doesn't lie. *Esquire*, p. 35.

Sell v. U.S., 539 U.S. 166 (2003).

Seltzer, R., Venuti, M. A., & Lopes, G. M. (1991, September/October). Juror honesty during voir dire. *Journal of Criminal Justice, 19*, 451–462.

Semmler, C., Brewer, N., & Wells, G. (2004). Effects of postidentification feedback on eyewitness identification and nonidentification confidence. *Journal of Applied Psychology, 89*, 334–346.

Sentencing Project (2004). *State rates of incarceration by race.* Retrieved from http://www.sentencingproject.org/pdfs/racialdisparity.pdf

Sewell, J. D. (2005). Book Review: Treating police stress: The work and words of peer counselors. *FBI Law Enforcement Bulletin, 74*(2), 7. Retrieved July 18, 2005, from http://www.fbi.gov/publications/leb/2005/feb2005/feb2005.htm#page7

Shaffer, D. R. (1985). The defendant's testimony. In S. Kassin & L. Wrightsman (Eds.), *The psychology of evidence and trial procedure* (pp. 124–149). Beverly Hills, CA: Sage.

Shannon v. United States, 114 S.Ct. 2419 (1994).

Shapiro, J. P. (1998, November 9). The wrong men on death row. *U.S. News & World Report*, 22–26.

Shapiro, P., & Penrod, S. (1986). Meta-analysis of racial identification studies. *Psychological Bulletin, 100* 139–156.

Shaw, J. S., Garven, S., & Wood, J. M. (1997). Co-witness information can have immediate effects on eyewitness memory reports. *Law and Human Behavior, 21*, 503–523.

Shaw, J., & Skolnick, P. (1995). Effects of prohibitive and informative judicial instructions on jury decision making. *Social Behavior and Personality, 23*, 319–326.

Shaw, J., & Skolnick, P. (1999). Weapon focus and gender differences in eyewitness accuracy: Arousal versus salience. *Journal of Applied Social Psychology, 29*, 2328–2341.

Sheetz, M. (2000). Cyberpredators: Police internet investigations under Florida Statue 847.0135, *University of Miami Law Review, 54*, 405–449.

Sheldon, S. (1994). The role of state bar associations in judicial selection, *Judicature, 77*, 300–305.

Sheley, J. F. (1985). *America's "crime problem": An introduction to criminology.* Belmont, CA: Wadsworth.

Sheppard v. Maxwell, 384 U.S. 333 (1966).

Sheppard, B. H., & Vidmar, N. (1980). Adversary pretrial procedures and testimonial evidence: Effects of lawyer's role and Machiavellianism. *Journal of Personality and Social Psychology, 39*, 320–332.

Sheppard, B. H., & Vidmar, N. (1983, June). *Is it fair to worry about fairness?* Paper presented at the meeting of the Law and Society Association, Denver, Colorado.

Sherman v. United States, 356 U.S. 369 (1958).

Sherman, L. W., & Berk, R. A. (1984). *The Minneapolis domestic violence experiment.* Washington, D.C.: Police Foundation.

Shestowsky, D. (2004). Procedural preferences in alternative dispute resolution: A closer, modern look at an old idea. *Psychology, Public Policy, and Law, 10*, 211–249.

Shulman, K. I., Cohen, C. A., & Hull, I. (2004). Psychiatric issues in retrospective challenges of testamentary capacity. *International Journal of Geriatric Psychiatry, 20*, 1, 63–69.

Shuman, D. (2000). The role of apology in tort law. *Judicature, 83*, 180–189.

Shuman, D. W., & Champagne, A. (1997). Removing the people from the legal process: The rhetoric and research on judicial selection and juries. *Psychology, Public Policy, and Law, 3*, 242–258.

Shuman, D. W., & Sales, B. D. (1999). The impact of *Daubert* and its progeny on the admissibility of behavioral and social science evidence. *Psychology, Public Policy, and Law, 5*, 3–15.

Sickmund, M. (1996). *Minimum transfer age specified in statute.* Office of Juvenile Justice and Delinquency Prevention. Retrieved from http://ojjdp.ncjrs.org

Siegel, A. M., & Elwork, A. (1990). Treating incompetence to stand trial. *Law and Human Behavior, 14*, 57–65.

Sifton, C. P. (1997, November 14). The chief judge likes sentencing guidelines. *National Law Journal*, A24.

Silberman, C. E. (1978). *Criminal justice, criminal violence*. New York: Random House.

Silver, E. (1995). Punishment or treatment? Comparing the lengths of confinement of successful and unsuccessful insanity defendants. *Law and Human Behavior, 19*, 375–388.

Silver, E., Cirincione, C., & Steadman, H. J. (1994). Demythologizing inaccurate perceptions of the insanity defense. *Law and Human Behavior, 18*, 63–70.

Simon, R. J. (1967). *The jury and the defense of insanity*. Boston: Little, Brown.

Simons, D., & Ambinder, M. (2005). Change blindness: Theory and consequences. *Current Directions in Psychological Science, 14*, 44–48.

Singleton, J. V., & Kass, M. (1986). Helping the jury understand complex cases. *Litigation, 12*, 11–13, 59.

Skeem, J. L. & Golding, S. L. (2001). Describing jurors' personal conceptions of insanity and their relationship to case judgments. *Psychology, Public Policy, and Law, 7*, 561–621.

Skeem, J. L., Golding, S. L., Cohn, N. B., & Berge, G. (1998). Logic and reliability of evaluations of competence to stand trial. *Law and Human Behavior, 22*, 519–548.

Skolnick, J. H. (1975). *Justice without trial: Law enforcement in a democratic society* (2nd ed.). New York: Wiley.

Skolnick, J. H., & Bayley, D. H. (1986). *The new blue line: Police innovation in six American cities*. New York: Free Press.

Slade, M. (1994, February 25). Law firms begin reining in sex-harassing partners. *New York Times*, p. B12.

Slater, D., & Hans, V. P. (1984). Public opinion of forensic psychiatry following the *Hinckley* verdict. *American Journal of Psychiatry, 141*, 675–679.

Sloat, L. M., & Frierson, R. L. (2005). Juror knowledge and attitudes regarding mental illness verdicts. *Journal of the American Academy of Psychiatry and Law, 33*, 208–213.

Slobogin, C., Melton, G., & Showalter, S. R. (1984). The feasibility of a brief evaluation of mental state at the time of the offense. *Law and Human Behavior, 8*, 305–321.

Slutske, W., Heath, A., Dinwiddie, S., Madden P., Bucholz, K., Duhne, M.,

Statham, D., & Martin, N. (1998). Common genetic risk factors for conduct disorder and alcohol dependence. *Journal of Abnormal Psychology, 107*, 363–374.

Smith v. State, 686 N.E.2d 1264 (1997).

Smith, C. A., & Farrington, D. C. (2004) Continuities in antisocial behavior and parenting across three generations. *Journal of Child Psychology & Psychiatry. 45*, 230–247.

Smith, P. H., White, J. W., & Holland, L. J. (2003). A longitudinal perspective on dating violence among adolescent and college-age women. *American Journal of Public Health, 93*, 1104–1109.

Smith, S. (1989). Mental health expert witnesses: Of science and crystal balls. *Behavioral Sciences and the Law, 7*, 145–180.

Snibbe, J., Peterson, P., & Sosner, B. (1980). Study of psychological characteristics of a workers' compensation sample using the MMPI and Millon Clinical Multiaxial Inventory. *Psychological Reports, 47*, 959–966.

Snyder, H. N. & Sickmund, M. (1999). *Juvenile offenders and victims: 1999 national report* (Chap. 2). Retrieved September 1, 2005, from the Office of Juvenile Justice and Delinquency Prevention web site: http://www.ncjrs .org/html/ojjdp/nationalreport99/ chapter2.pdf

Solomon, R. C. (1990). *A passion for justice*. Reading, MA: Addison-Wesley.

Solomon, R. M., & Horn, J. M. (1986). Post-shooting traumatic reactions: A pilot study. In J. T. Reese & H. A. Goldstein (Eds.), *Psychological services for law enforcement* (pp. 383–394). Washington, D.C.: U.S. Government Printing Office.

Sommers, S. (2002). *Race and juries: The effects of race-salience and racial composition on individual and group decision making*. Unpublished Ph.D. dissertation, University of Michigan.

Sommers, S., & Kassin, S. (2001). On the many impacts of inadmissible testimony: Selective compliance, need for cognition, and the overcorrection bias. *Personality and Social Psychology Bulletin, 27*, 1368–1377.

Sontag, S. (1978). *Illness as metaphor*. New York: Farrar, Straus & Giroux.

Sorenson, S. B., & White, J. W. (1992). Adult sexual assault: Overview of research. *Journal of Social Issues, 48*(1), 1–8.

Soskis, D. A., & Van Zandt, C. R. (1986). Hostage negotiation: Law enforcement's most effective nonlethal weapon. *Behavioral Sciences and the Law, 4*, 423–436.

Spanos, N. P., Burgess, C. A., Burgess, M. F., Samuels, C., & Blois, W. O. (1999). Creating false memories of infancy with hypnotic and non-hypnotic procedures. *Applied Cognitive Psychology, 13*, 201–218.

Sparf and Hansen v. United States, 156 U.S. 51 (1895).

Sparr, L. (1995). Post-traumatic stress disorder. *Neurologic Clinics, 13*, 413–429.

Spaulding, W. J. (1990). A look at the AMA Guidelines to the evaluation of permanent impairment: Problems in workers' compensation claims involving mental disability. *Behavioral Sciences and the Law, 8*, 361–373.

Spear, P. (2000). The adolescent brain and age-related behavioral manifestations. *Neuroscience and Biobehavioral Reviews, 24*, 417–463.

Spielberger, C. D. (Ed.). (1979). *Police selection and evaluation: Issues and techniques*. Washington, D.C.: Hemisphere.

Spielberger, C. D., Spaulding, H. C., & Ward, J. C. (1978). *Selecting effective law enforcement officers: The Florida police standards research project*. Tampa, FL: Human Resources Institute.

Spielberger, C. D., Westberry, L. G., Grier, K. S., & Greenfield, G. (1980). *The police stress survey: Sources of stress in law enforcement*. Tampa, FL: Human Resources Institute.

Spilbor, J. M. (2004, October 28). *The sexual harassment case against Fox News's Bill O'Reilly: Why winning may be O'Reilly's costliest option*. Retrieved online September 1, 2005, from http://writ.news.findlaw.com/commentary/20041028_spilbor.html

Spill, R., & Bratton, K. (2001). Clinton and diversification of the federal judiciary. *Judicature, 84*, 256–261.

Spohn, C. (2000). Thirty years of sentencing reform: The quest for a racially neutral sentencing process. In J. Horney (Ed.), *Criminal justice 2000: Volume 3. Policies, processes, and decisions of the criminal justice system* (pp. 427–501). Washington D.C.: U.S. Department of Justice, National Institute of Justice.

Sporer, S. (2001). Recognizing faces of other ethnic groups: An integration of theories. *Psychology, Public Policy, and Law, 7*, 170–200

Sporer, S., Penrod, S., Read, D., & Cutler, B. L. (1995). Choosing, confidence, and accuracy: A meta-analysis of the confidence–accuracy relation in eyewitness identification studies. *Psychological Bulletin, 118*, 315–327.

Sprague, J., & Walker H. (2000). Early identification and intervention for youth with antisocial and violent behavior. *Exceptional Children, 66*, 367–380.

State v. Canady, 641 N.W.2d 43 (Neb. 2002).

State v. Cunningham, No. 85342, 2005-Ohio App. LEXIS 3531 (July 28, 2005).

State v. Damms, 9 Wisc.2d 183, 100 N.W.2d 592 (1960).

State v. Dorsey, 539 P.2d 204 (N.M. 1975).

State v. Fuller (2004). 862 A.2d 1130 (N.J.).

State v. Hurd, 86 N.J. 525 (1981).

State v. Johnson, 133 Wisc.2d 307, 395 N.W.2d 176 (1986). Ch8

State v. Lozano, 616 So.2d 73 (Fla. App. 1993).

State v. Michaels, 136 N.J. 299, 642 A.2d 1372 (N.J., 1994).

State of Minnesota v. Mack, 292 N.W.2d 764 (Minn. 1980).

Steadman, H. J. (1979). *Beating a rap? Defendants found incompetent to stand trial.* Chicago: University of Chicago Press.

Steadman, H. J., & Braff, J. (1983). Defendants not guilty by reason of insanity. In J. Monahan & H. J. Steadman (Eds.), *Mentally disordered offenders: Perspectives from law and social science.* New York: Plenum.

Steadman, H. J., Cocozza, J. J., & Veysey, B. M. (1999). Comparing outcomes for diverted and nondiverted jail detainees with mental illness. *Law and Human Behavior, 23*, 615–628.

Steadman, H. J., Deane, D. W., Borum, R., & Morrissey, J. P. (2000). Comparing outcomes of major models of police responses to mental health emergencies. *Psychiatric Services, 51*, 5, 645–649.

Steadman, H. J., Keitner, L., Braff, J., & Arvanites, T. M. (1983). Factors associated with a successful insanity plea. *American Journal of Psychiatry, 140*, 401–405.

Steadman, H., McGreevy, M., Morrissey, J., Callahan, L., Robbin, P., & Cirincione, C. (1993). *Before and after* Hinckley: *Evaluating insanity defense reform.* New York: Guilford.

Steadman, H. J., Rosenstein, M. J., MacAskill, R. L., & Manderscheid, R.

W. (1988). A profile of mentally disordered offenders admitted to inpatient psychiatric services in the United States. *Law and Human Behavior, 12*, 91–99.

Steblay, N. (1997). Social influence in eyewitness recall: A meta-analytic review of lineup instruction effects. *Law and Human Behavior, 21*, 283–298.

Steblay, N., Besirevic, J., Fulero, S., & Jiminez-Lorente, B. (1999). The effects of pretrial publicity on jury verdicts: A meta-analytic review. *Law and Human Behavior, 23*, 219–235.

Steblay, N., & Bothwell, R. K. (1994). Evidence for hypnotically refreshed testimony: The view from the laboratory. *Law and Human Behavior, 18*, 635–652.

Steblay, N., Dysart, J., Fulero, S., & Lindsay, R. (2001). Eyewitness accuracy rates in sequential and simultaneous lineup presentation: A meta-analytic comparison. *Law and Human Behavior, 25*, 459–473.

Steele, W. W., & Thornburg, E. G. (1988). Jury instructions: A persistent failure to communicate. *North Carolina Law Review, 67*, 77–119.

Steffensmeier, D., Ulmer, J., & Kramer, J. (1998). The interaction of race, gender, and age and criminal sentencing: The punishment cost of being young, black, and male. *Criminology, 36*, 763–797.

Steinberg, L., & Scott, E. (2003). Less guilty by reason of adolescence: Developmental immaturity, diminished responsibility, and the juvenile death penalty. *American Psychologist, 58*, 1009–1018.

Stevens, R. (1983). *Law school: Legal education in America from the 1850s to the 1980s.* Chapel Hill: University of North Carolina Press.

Stinson, V., Devenport, J. L., Cutler, B. L., & Kravitz, D. A. (1996). How effective is the presence-of-counsel safeguard? Attorney perceptions of suggestiveness, fairness, and correctability of biased lineup procedures. *Journal of Applied Psychology, 81*, 64–75.

Stith, K., & Cabranes, J. A., (1998). *Fear of judging: Sentencing guidelines in the federal courts.* Chicago: University of Chicago Press.

Stockdale, M. S., Visio, M., & Batra, L. (1999). The sexual harassment of men: Evidence for a broader theory of sexual harassment and sex discrimination. *Psychology, Public Policy, & Law. 5*, 630–664,

Storm, J., & Graham, J. (2000). Detection of coached general malingering on the MMPI-2. *Psychological Assessment, 12*, 158–165.

Stormo, K. J., Lang, A. R., & Stritzke, W. G. K. (1997). Attributions about acquaintance rape: The role of alcohol and individual differences. *Journal of Applied Social Psychology, 27*, 279–305.

Strasser, F. (1989, June 26). Look-alikes win in court. *National Law Journal*, p. 63.

Stratton, T. D., McLaughlin, M. A, Witte, F. M, Fosson, S. E., & Nora, L. M. (2005). Does students' exposure to gender discrimination and sexual harassment in medical school affect specialty choice and residency program selection? *Academic Medicine, 80*, 400–408.

Strauder v. West Virginia, 100 U.S. 303 (1880).

Straus, M. A., & Gelles, R. J. (1988). How violent are American families? Estimates from the National Family Violence Resurvey and other studies. In G. T. Hotaling, D. Finkelhor, J. T. Kirkpatrick, & M. A. Straus (Eds.), *Family abuse and its consequences* (pp. 14–36). Thousand Oaks, CA: Sage.

Streib V. (1983). Death penalty for children: The American experience with capital punishment for crimes committed while under age eighteen. *Oklahoma Law Review, 36*, 613–641.

Strickland v. Washington, 466 U.S. 668 (1984).

Strier, F. (1996). *Reconstructing justice: An agenda for trial reform.* Westport, CN: Quorum Books.

Strier, F. (1999). Whither trial consulting? Issues and projections. *Law and Human Behavior, 23*, 93–115.

Strier, F. (2001). Why trial consultants should be licensed. *Journal of Forensic Psychology Practice, 1*, 69–76.

Strodtbeck, F., James, R., & Hawkins, C. (1957). Social status in jury deliberations. *American Sociological Review, 22*, 713–718.

Strodtbeck, F., & Lipinski, R. M. (1985). Becoming first among equals: Moral considerations in jury foreman selection. *Journal of Personality and Social Psychology, 49*, 927–936.

Studebaker, C. A., & Penrod, S. D. (1997). Pretrial publicity: The media, the law and common sense. *Psychology, Public Policy, and Law, 2/3*, 428–460.

Studebaker, C., & Penrod, S. (2005). Pretrial publicity and its influence on juror decision making. In N. Brewer & K. Williams (Eds.), *Psychology and Law: An empirical perspective* (pp. 254–275). New York: Guilford.

Studebaker, C., Robbennolt, J., Penrod, S., Pathak-Sharma, M., Groscup, J., & Devenport, J. (2002). Studying pretrial publicity effects: New methods for improving ecological validity and testing external validity. *Law and Human Behavior, 26*, 19–42.

Sullivan, C. M., & Bybee, D. I. (1999). Reducing violence using communitybased advocacy for women with abusive partners. *Journal of Consulting and Clinical Psychology, 67*, 43–53.

Sunstein, C., Hastie, R., Payne, J., Schkade, D., & Viscusi, W. (2002). *Punitive damages: How juries decide.* Chicago: University of Chicago Press.

Super, J. T. (1997). Selected legal and ethical aspects of fitness for duty evaluations. *Journal of Criminal Justice, 25*, 223–229.

Surgeon General's Scientific Advisory Committee on Television and Social Behavior. (1972). *Television and growing up: The impact of televised violence.* Washington, D.C.: U.S. Government Printing Office.

Susman, D. (1992). *Effects of three different legal standards on psychologists' determinations of competency for execution.* Unpublished doctoral dissertation, University of Kentucky, Lexington.

Sutherland, E. H. (1947). *Principles of criminology* (4th ed.). Philadelphia: Lippincott.

Sutherland, E. H., & Cressey, D. R. (1974). *Principles of criminology* (9th ed.). New York: Lippincott.

Sutker, P., Davis, J. M., Uddo, M., & Ditta, S. (1995). War zone stresses, personal resources, and PTSD in Persian Gulf returnees. *Journal of Abnormal Psychology, 104*, 444–452.

Swain v. Alabama, 380 U.S. 202 (1965).

Sydeman, S. J., Cascardi, M., Poythress, N. G., & Ritterband, L. M. (1997). Procedural justice in the context of civil commitment: A critique of Tyler's analysis. *Psychology, Public Policy, and Law, 3*, 207–221.

Taber, J. (1988). Gender, legal education, and the legal profession: An empirical study of Stanford law students and graduates. *Stanford Law Review, 40*, 1209–1297.

Tanford, J. A. (1990). The law and psychology of jury instructions. *Nebraska Law Review, 69*, 71–111.

Tanford, J. A. (1991). Law reforms by courts, legislatures, and commissions following empirical research on jury instructions. *Law & Society Review, 25*, 155–175.

Tarasoff v. Regents of the University of California, 17 Cal.3d 425, 551 P.2d 334, 131 Cal.Rptr. 14 (1976).

Tasker, F. (2005). Lesbian mothers, gay fathers, and their children: A review. *Journal of Developmental and Behavioral Pediatrics, 26*, 224–240.

Tasker, F., & Golombok, S. (1997). *Growing up in a lesbian family: Effects on child development.* New York: Guilford.

Taubman, B. (1988). *The preppy murder trial.* New York: St. Martin's.

Taylor, G. (1992, March 2). Justice overlooked. *National Law Journal,* p. 43.

Taylor, S., Jr. (1986, May 6). Justices reject broad challenge in capital cases. *New York Times,* pp. 1, 12.

Taylor, S., Jr. (1987, May 27). Court backs law letting U.S. widen pretrial jailing. *New York Times,* pp. 1, 89.

Taylor, S. E., Klein, L. C., Lewis, B. P., Gruenewald, T. L., Gurung, R. A. R., & Updegraff, J. A. (2000). Biobehavioral responses to stress in females: Tend-and-befriend, not fight-or-flight. *Psychological Review, 107*, 411–429.

Taylor, T., & Hosch, H. (2004). An examination of jury verdicts for evidence of a similarity–leniency effect, an outgroup punitiveness effect or a black sheep effect. *Law and Human Behavior, 28*, 587–598.

Teahan, J. E. (1975). A longitudinal study of attitude shifts among black and white police officers. *Journal of Social Issues, 31*(1), 47–56.

Teahan, J. E. (1975a). Role playing and group experience to facilitate attitude and value changes among Black and White police officers. *Journal of Social Issues, 31*(1), 35–45.

Teahan, J. E. (1975b). A longitudinal study of attitude shifts among Black and White police officers. *Journal of Social Issues, 31*(1), 47–56.

Tebo, M. (November, 2004). Home alone. *American Bar Association Journal 90*, 30.

Tehrani, J., & Mednick, S. (2000). Genetic factors and criminality. *Federal Probation, 64*, 24–28.

Teitelbaum, L. (1991). Gender, legal education, and legal careers. *Journal of Legal Education, 41*, 443–480.

Tennessee v. Garner, 471 U.S. 1 (1985).

Teplin, L. A. (1984). The criminalization of the mentally ill: Speculation in search

of data. In L. A. Teplin (Ed.), *Mental health and criminal justice* (pp. 63–85). Newbury Park, CA: Sage.

Teplin, L. A. (1994). Psychiatric and substance abuse disorders among male urban jail detainees. *American Journal of Public Health, 84*(2), 290–293.

Teplin, L. A., Abram, K. M., & McClelland, G. M. (1996). The prevalence of psychiatric disorder among incarcerated women, I: Pretrial detainees. *Archives of General Psychiatry, 53*, 505–512.

Terman, L. M. (1917). A trial of mental and pedagogical tests in a civil service examination for policemen and firemen. *Journal of Applied Psychology, 1*, 17–29.

Terpstra, D. E., & Baker, D. D. (1987). A hierarchy of sexual harassment. *Journal of Psychology, 121*, 599–605.

Terpstra, D. E., & Baker, D. D. (1988). Outcomes of sexual harassment charges. *Academy of Management Journal, 31*, 185–194.

Terpstra, D. E., & Baker, D. D. (1992). Outcomes of federal court decisions on sexual harassment. *Academy of Management Journal, 35*, 181–190.

Terr, L. (1991). Childhood traumas: An outline and overview. *Journal of Psychiatry, 148*, 10–20.

Thibaut, J., & Walker, L. (1975). *Procedural justice: A psychological analysis.* Hillsdale, NJ: Erlbaum.

Thibaut, J., Walker, L., & Lind, E. A. (1972). Adversary presentation and bias in legal decision making. *Harvard Law Review, 86*, 386–401.

Thomas, A., Bulevich, J., & Loftus, E. (2003). Exploring the role of repetition and sensory elaboration in the imagination inflation effect. *Memory and Cognition, 31*, 630–640.

Thomas, C., Boyer, M., & Hrebenar, R. (2003). Interest groups and state court elections. *Judicature, 87*, 135–149.

Thomas, E. (1991). *The man to see.* New York: Simon & Schuster.

Thompson v. Oklahoma, 487 U.S. 815 (1988).

Thompson, M. (1989, April 3). Misprint. *New Republic,* pp. 14–15.

Thompson, W. C. (1989). Death qualification after *Wainwright v. Witt* and *Lockhart v. McCree. Law and Human Behavior, 13*, 185–215.

Thompson, W. C., Cowan, C. L., Ellsworth, P. C., & Harrington, J. C. (1984). Death penalty attitudes and conviction proneness: The translation of attitudes into verdicts. *Law and Human Behavior, 8*, 95–113.

Thompson, W. C., & Ford, S. (1989). DNA typing: Acceptance and weight of the new genetic identification tests. *Virginia Law Review, 75*, 45–108.

Thornburgh, N. (2005, April 25). When a killer wants to die. *Time*, 43.

Thornton, H. (1995). *Hung jury: The diary of a Menendez juror*. Philadelphia: Temple University Press.

Tierney, K. (1979). *Darrow: A biography*. New York: Crowell.

Tillbrook, C., Mumley, D., & Grisso, T. (2003). Avoiding expert opinions on the ultimate legal question: The case for integrity. *Journal of Forensic Psychology Practice, 3*(3), 77–87.

Tinker v. Des Moines Independent Community School District, 393 U.S. 503 (1969).

Tjaden, P., & Thoennes, N. (2000). *Full report of the prevalence, incidence, and consequences of violence against women* (NCJ13781). National Institute of Justice, Office of Justice Programs: Washington, D.C. Retrieved online September 1, 2005, from http://www.rainn.org/fullnvawsurvey.pdf

Tobey, A. E., & Goodman, G. S. (1992). Children's eyewitness memory: Effects of participation and forensic context. *Child Abuse and Neglect, 16*, 779–796.

Tombaugh, T. (1997). *TOMM: Test of Memory Malingering manual*. Toronto: Multi-Health Systems.

Tonry, M. (1996). *Sentencing matters*. New York: Oxford University Press.

Toobin, J. (1996a, December 9). Asking for it. *New Yorker*, pp. 55–60.

Toobin, J. (1996b, September 9). The Marcia Clark verdict. *New Yorker*, pp. 58–71.

Tooley, V., Brigham, J. C., Maass, A., & Bothwell, R. K. (1987). Facial recognition: Weapon effect and attentional focus. *Journal of Applied Social Psychology, 17*, 845–859.

Toot, J., Dunphy, G., Turner, M., & Ely, D. (2004). The SHR Y-chromosome increases testosterone and aggression, but decreases serotonin as compared to the WKY Y-chromosome in the rat model. *Behavioral Genetics, 34*, 515–524.

Trevethan, S. D., & Walker, L. J. (1989). Hypothetical versus real-life moral reasoning among psychopathic and delinquent youth. *Development and Psychopathology, 1*, 91–103

Tsushima, W. T., Foote, R., Merrill, T. S., & Lehrke, S. A. (1996). How independent are independent psychological examinations? A workers' compensation dilemma. *Professional Psychology: Research and Practice, 27*, 626–628.

Tubb, V., Kassin, S., Memon, A., & Hosch, H. (2000). Experts' views of research on eyewitness testimony after *Daubert*: Kassin et al. (1989) revisited. Paper presented at American Psychology-Law Society, New Orleans.

Tuohy, A. P., Wrennall, M. J., McQueen, R. A., & Stradling, S. G. (1993). Effect of socialization factors on decisions to prosecute: The organizational adaptation of Scottish police recruits. *Law and Human Behavior, 17*, 167–182.

Turkheimer, E., & Parry, C. D. H. (1992). Why the gap? Practice and policy in civil commitment hearings. *American Psychologist, 47*, 646–655.

Turner v. Safley, 482 U.S. 78 (1987).

Turtle, J., & Steblay, N. (2005). *Lineup identification issues with real officers and real cases: Addressing legal, logistical, and lamentable problems*. Paper presented at the meeting of the American Psychology-Law Society, La Jolla, California.

Tyler, T., & Huo, Y. (2002). *Trust in the law: Encouraging public cooperation with the police and court*. New York: Russell Sage Foundation

Underwood, R. (1996) Truth verifiers: From the hot iron to the lie detector. *Kentucky Law Journal, 84*, 597–642.

United States v. American Library Association, 539 U.S. 194 (2003).

United States v. Angelos, 345 F.Supp. 2d 1227 (D.Utah 2004)

United States v. Armstrong, 116 St.C. 1480 (1996).

United States. v. Booker, 125 S.Ct. 735 (2005).

United States v. Burgess, 175 F.3d 1261 (11th Cir. 1999).

United States v. Burr, 24 F.Cas. 49 (D.Va. 1807).

United States v. Dellinger, 475 F.2d 340, 368 (7th Cir. 1972).

United States v. Dixon, 509 U.S. 688, (1993).

United States v. Dougherty, 473 F.2d 1113, 1130–1137 (D.C. Cir. 1972).

United States v. Gementra, 379 F.3d 596 (9th Cir. 2004).

United States v. Jordan, 924 F.Supp. 443 (W.D.N.Y. 1996).

United States v. Lea, 249 F.3d 632. (7th Cir. 2001).

United States v. Masthers, 549 F.2d 721 (D.C. Cir. 1976).

United States v. McVeigh, 918 F. Supp. 1467 (W.D. Okla. 1996).

United States v. Ovalle 136 F. 3d 1092 (6th Cir. 1998).

United States v. Poehlman, 217 F.3d 692 (9th Cir. 2000).

United States v. Salerno, 481 U.S. 739 (1987).

United States v. Santiago-Martinez, 94–10350, 9th U.S. Court of Appeals (1995).

United States v. Scheffer, 118 S.Ct. 1261 (1998).

United States v. Telfaire, 469 F.2d 552 (D.C. Cir. 1972).

United States v. Twigg, 588 F.2d 373 (3d Cir. 1978).

United States v. Wade, 388 U.S. 218 (1967).

U.S. Department of Health and Human Services, National Clearinghouse on Child Abuse and Neglect Information. (2004). *Child abuse and neglect Fatalities: Statistics and interventions*. Retrieved September 2, 2005, from http://nccanch.acf.hhs.gov/pubs/factsheets/fatality.cfm

U.S. Department of Justice (1999). *Eyewitness evidence: A guide for law enforcement*. Washington, D.C.: U.S. Dept. of Justice.

U.S. Equal Employment Opportunity Commission. (1980, November 10). Final amendment to guidelines on discrimination because of sex under Title VII of the Civil Rights Act of 1964 as amended. 19 CFR Part 1604. *Federal Register, 45*, 74675–74677.

U.S. General Accounting Office. (1990). *Death penalty sentencing*. Washington, D.C.: U.S. Government Printing Office.

Ustad, K. L., Rogers, R., Sewell, K. W., & Guarnaccia, C. A. (1996). Restoration of competency to stand trial: Assessment with the Georgia Court Competency Test and the Competency Screening Test. *Law and Human Behavior, 20*, 131–146.

van der Kolk, B. (1997). The psychobiology of posttraumatic stress disorder. *Journal of Clinical Psychiatry, 58*, 16–24.

VanDuyn, A. L. (1999). The scarlet letter branding: A constitutional analysis of community notification provisions in sex offender statues. *Drake Law Review, 47*, 635–659.

Van Dyke, J. (1977). *Jury selection procedures*. Cambridge, MA: Ballinger.

Varela, J. G., Scogin, F. R., & Vipperman, R. K. (1999). Development and preliminary validation of a semistructured interview for the screening of law enforcement candidates. *Behavioral Sciences and the Law, 17*, 467–481.

Verlinden, S., Hersen, M., & Thomas, J. (2000). Risk factors in school shootings. *Clinical Psychology Review, 20*, 3–56.

Victor, T. L. & Abeles, N. (2004). Coaching clients to take psychological and neuropsychological tests: A clash of ethical obligations. *Practice Issues in Forensic Psychology, 35*(4), 373–379.

Vidmar, N. (1994). Making inferences about jury behavior from jury verdict statistics: Caution about Lorelei's lie. *Law and Human Behavior, 18*, 599–618.

Vidmar, N. (1997). Generic prejudice and the presumption of guilt in sex abuse trials. *Law and Human Behavior, 21*, 5–25.

Vidmar, N. (1998). The performance of the American civil jury: An empirical perspective. *Arizona Law Review, 40*, 849–899.

Vidmar, N. (Ed.) (2000). *World jury systems*. Oxford: Oxford University Press.

Vidmar, N. (2002). Case studies of pre- and midtrial prejudice in criminal and civil litigation. *Law and Human Behavior, 26*, 73–106.

Vidmar, N., Gross, F., & Rose, M. R. (1998) Jury awards for medical malpractice and post-verdict adjustments of those awards. *DePaul Law Review 48*, 265–301.

Viljoen, J. L., Roesch, R., Ogloff, J. R. P., & Zapf, P. A. (2003). The role of Canadian psychologists in conducting fitness and criminal responsibility evaluations. *Canadian Psychology, 44*(4), 369–381.

Violanti, J. M. & Aron, F. (1994). Ranking police stressors. *Psychological Reports, 75*(2), 824–826.

Vise, D. A. (1989, August 713). Using a Mafia law to bust high-flying stockbrokers. *Washington Post National Weekly Edition*, p. 20.

Visher, C. A. (1987). Juror decision making: The importance of evidence. *Law and Human Behavior, 11*, 1–18.

Vitale, J. E., & Newman, J.P. (2001). Using the Psychopathy Checklist-Revised with female samples: Reliability, validity, and implications for clinical utility. *Clinical Psychology: Science & Practice, 8*(1), 117–132.

Wagstaff, G (1999). Hypnotically elicited testimony. In A. Armstrong, E. Shepherd, & D. Wolchover (Eds.), *Analysing witness testimony*, (pp. 277–310). London: Blackstone.

Waldo, C. R., Berdahl, J. L., & Fitzgerald, L. F. (1998). Are men sexually harassed? If so, by whom? *Law and Human Behavior, 22*, 59–80.

Walker, L. (1979). *The battered woman*. New York: Harper & Row.

Walker, L. (1984). *The battered woman syndrome*. New York: Springer.

Walker, L., La Tour, S., Lind, E. A., & Thibaut, J. (1974). Reactions of participants and observers to modes of adjudication. *Journal of Applied Social Psychology, 4*, 295–310.

Walker, W. (1989, February 19). In cold DNA. *New York Times Book Review*, p. 11.

Walster, E. (1966). Assignment of responsibility for an accident. *Journal of Personality and Social Psychology, 3*, 73–79.

Waltz, J., Babcock, J. C., Jacobson, N. S. & Gottman, J. M. (2000). Testing a typology of batterers. *Journal of Consulting and Clinical Psychology, 68*, 658–669.

Wambaugh, J. (1989). *The blooding*. New York: Morrow.

Ward, J. (1998, May 18). Boalt boosts minority enrollment by downplaying grades, scores. *National Law Journal*, p. A16.

Ward, S. (2004a, November). Best of both worlds. *American Bar Association Journal, 90*, 34.

Ward, S. (2004b, April). Part-time possibilities. *American Bar Association Journal, 90*, 36.

Ward, S. (2005, February). 2000+ Club stays open 24/7. *American Bar Association Journal, 91*, 32.

Warner, W. J. (2005, April). Polygraph testing: A utilitarian tool. *FBI Law Enforcement Bulletin, 74*, 4. Retrieved online July 26, 2005, from http://vnweb.hwwilsonweb.com

Warren, A. R., Woodall, C. E., Hunt, J. S., & Perry, N. W. (1996). "It sounds good in theory, but . . .": Do investigative interviewers follow guidelines based on memory research? *Child Maltreatment, 1*, 231–245.

Warren, E. (1977). *The memoirs of Earl Warren*. Garden City, NY: Doubleday.

Warshaw, R. (1988). *I never called it rape*. New York: Harper & Row.

Washington v. Harper, 494 U.S. 210 (1990).

Waterman, A., Blades, M., & Spencer, C. (2001). Interviewing children and adults: The effect of question format on the tendency to speculate. *Applied Cognitive Psychology, 15*, 521–531.

Watson, P. (1996). The search for justice—A case for reform in the civil justice system in Britain. *ILSA Journal of International and Comparative Law, 2*, 453.

Wayte v. United States, 105 S.Ct. 1524 (1985).

Weber, N., Brewer, N., Wells, G., Semmler, C., & Keast, A. (2004). Eyewitness identification accuracy and response latency: The unruly 10–12 second rule. *Journal of Experimental Psychology: Applied, 10*, 139–147.

Webert, D. (2003). Are the courts in a trance? Approaches to the admissibility of hypnotically enhanced witness testimony in light of empirical evidence. *American Criminal Law Review, 40*, 1301–1327.

Webster, C. D. (1998). Comment on Thomas Mathiesen's *Selective Incapacitation Revisited*. *Law and Human Behavior, 22*, 471–476.

Webster, C. D., Douglas, K. S., Eaves, D., & Hart, S. D. (1997). *HCR-20: Assessing risk for violence (Version 2)*. Vancouver, Canada, Mental Health, Law, and Policy Institute. Simon Fraser University.

Weeks v. Angelone, 120 S.Ct. 1290 (2000).

Wegner, D. M. (1989). *White bears and other unwanted thoughts: Suppression, obsession, and the psychology of mental control*. New York: Viking Press.

Wegner, D. M. (1994). Ironic processes of mental control. *Psychological Review, 101*, 34–52.

Wegner, D. M., & Erber, R. (1992). The hyperaccessibility of suppressed thoughts. *Journal of Personality and Social Psychology, 63*, 903–912.

Wegner, D. M., Schneider, D. J., Carter, S., III, & White, T. (1987). Paradoxical effects of thought suppression. *Journal of Personality and Social Psychology, 53*, 5–13.

Weinberger, L., Sreenivasan, S., Garrick, T., & Osran, H. (2005). The impact of surgical castration on sexual recidivism risk among sexually violent predatory offenders. *Journal of the*

American Academy of Psychiatry and the Law, 33, 16–36.

Weiner, R. L., Hurt, L., Russell, B., Mannen, K., & Gasper, C. (1997). Perceptions of sexual harassment: The effects of gender, legal standard, and ambivalent sexism. Law and Human Behavior, 21, 71–94.

Weir, J. A., & Wrightsman, L. S. (1990). The determinants of mock jurors' verdicts in a rape case. Journal of Applied Social Psychology, 20, 901–919.

Weissman, H. N. (1985). Psycholegal standards and the role of psychological assessment in personal injury litigation. Behavioral Sciences and the Law, 3, 135–148.

Weitzer, R., & Tuch, S. A. (1999). Race, class, and perceptions of discrimination by the police. Crime and Delinquency, 45, 494–507.

Wells, G. (1978). Applied eyewitness testimony research: System variables and estimator variables. Journal of Personality and Social Psychology, 36, 1546–1557.

Wells, G. L. (1993). What do we know about eyewitness identification? American Psychologist, 48, 553–571.

Wells, G., & Bradfield, A. (1998). Good, you identified the suspect: Feedback to eyewitnesses distorts their reports of the witnessing experience. Journal of Applied Psychology, 83, 360–376.

Wells, G., Charman, S., & Olson, E. (2005). Building face composites can harm lineup identification performance. Unpublished manuscript, Iowa State University.

Wells, G. L., & Lindsay, R. C. L. (1980). On estimating the diagnosticity of eyewitness nonidentifications. Psychological Bulletin, 88, 776–784.

Wells, G. L., Lindsay, R. C. L., & Ferguson, T. J. (1979). Accuracy, confidence, and juror perceptions in eyewitness identification. Journal of Applied Psychology, 64, 440–448.

Wells, G. L., & Loftus, E. F. (1984). Eyewitness research: Then and now. In G. L. Wells & E. F. Loftus (Eds.). Eyewitness testimony: Psychological perspectives (pp. 1–11). New York: Cambridge University Press.

Wells, G., & Luus, C. (1990). Police lineups as experiments: Social methodology as a frame-work for properly conducted lineups. Personality and Social Psychology Bulletin, 16, 106–117.

Wells, G., & Olson, E. (2001). The other-race effect in eyewitness identification:

What do we do about it? Psychology, Public Policy, and Law, 7, 230–246.

Wells, G., & Olson, E. (2003). Eyewitness testimony. Annual Review of Psychology, 54: 277–295.

Wells, G., Olson, E., & Charman, S. (2002). The confidence of eyewitnesses in their identifications from lineups. Psychological Science, 11, 151–154.

Wells, G., Olson, E., & Charman, S. (2003). Distorted retrospective eyewitness reports as functions of feedback and delay. Journal of Experimental Psychology: Applied, 9, 42–52.

Wells, G. L., Small, M., Penrod, S., Malpass, R. S., Fulero, S. M., & Brimacombe, C. A. E. (1998). Eyewitness identification procedures: Recommendations for lineups and photospreads. Law and Human Behavior, 22, 603–647.

Wells, G. L., Wright, E. F., & Bradfield, A. L. (1999). Witnesses to crime: Social and cognitive factors governing the validity of people's reports. In R. Roesch, S. D. Hart, & J. Ogloff (Eds.), Psychology and law: The state of the discipline (pp. 54–89). New York: Kluwer Academic/Plenum.

Westley, W. A. (1970). Violence and the police: A sociological study of law, custom, and morality. Cambridge, MA: MIT Press.

Wetter, M., Baer, R., Berry, D., Smith, G., & Larsen, L. (1992). Sensitivity of MMPI-2 validity scales to random responding and malingering. Psychological Assessment, 4, 369–374.

Wexler, D. B. (1992). Putting mental health into mental health law: Therapeutic jurisprudence. Law and Human Behavior, 16, 27–38.

Whalen v. United States, 346 F.2d 812 (1965).

Wheatman, S. R., & Shaffer, D. R. (2001). On finding for defendants who plead insanity: The crucial impact of dispositional instructions and opportunity to deliberate. Law and Human Behavior, 25(2), 167–183.

Whipple, S. B. (1937). The trial of Bruno Richard Hauptmann. New York: Doubleday.

White, J. W., Lawrence, S., Biggerstaff, C., & Grubb, T. D. (1985). Factors of stress among police officers. Criminal Justice and Behavior, 12, 111–128.

White, J. W., & Sorenson, S. B. (1992). A sociocultural view of sexual assault: From discrepancy to diversity. Journal of Social Issues, 48(1), 187–195.

Whittemore, K. E., & Ogloff, J. R. P. (1995). Factors that influence jury decision making: Disposition instructions and mental state at the time of the trial. Law and Human Behavior, 19, 283–303.

Whren v. United States, 116 S.Ct. 1769 (1996).

Whren et al. v. United States, 517 U.S. 806 (1996).

Widom, C. S. (1989). Child abuse, neglect, and adult behavior: Research design and findings on criminality, violence, and child abuse. American Journal of Orthopsychiatry, 59, 355–367.

Widom, C. S. (1992). The cycle of violence: National Institute of Justice research in brief. Washington, D.C.: U.S. Department of Justice.

Wiener, R. L., & Gutek, B. A. (1999). Advance in sexual harassment research, theory, and policy. Psychology, Public Policy, and Law, 5, 507–518.

Wiener, R. L., & Hurt, L. E. (1999). An interdisciplinary approach to understanding social sexual conduct at work. Psychology, Public Policy, and Law, 5, 556–595.

Wiener, R. L., Hurt, L., Russell, B., Mannen, K., & Gasper, C. (1997). Perceptions of sexual harassment: The effects of gender, legal standard, and ambivalent sexism. Law and Human Behavior, 21, 71–94.

Wiener, R., Rogers, M., Winter, R., Hurt, L., Hackney, A., Kadela, K., et al. (2004). Guided jury discretion in capital murder cases: The role of declarative and procedural knowledge. Psychology, Public Policy, and Law, 10, 516–576.

Wiener, R. L., Wiener, A. T. F., & Grisso, T. (1989). Empathy and biased assimilation of testimonies in cases of alleged rape. Law and Human Behavior, 13, 343–356.

Wiggins v. Smith, 123 S.Ct. 2527 (2003).

Will, G. (1984, January 22). Fitting laws to dynamic society likened to trousers on 10-year-old. Lawrence Journal-World, p. 6.

Willett v. State, 993 S.W.2d 929 (Ark. 1999).

Williams v. Florida, 399 U.S. 78 (1970).

Williams, C. W., Lees-Haley, P. R., & Djanogly, S. E. (1999). Clinical scrutiny of litigants' self-reports. Professional Psychology: Research and Practice, 30, 361–367.

Williams, L. M. (1994). Recall of childhood trauma: A prospective study of women's memories of child sexual abuse. *Journal of Consulting and Clinical Psychology, 62*, 1167–1176.

Williams, W., & Miller, K. S. (1981). The processing and disposition of incompetent mentally ill offenders. *Law and Human Behavior, 5*, 245–261.

Willrich, M. (2003), Boys to men . . . and back again? Revisiting a forgotten experiment in juvenile justice, *Judicature, 86*, 258–62.

Wilson v. United States, 391 F.2d 460 (1968).

Wilson, A. E., Calhoun, K. S., & Bernat, J. A. (1999). Risk recognition and trauma-related symptoms among sexually revictimized women. *Journal of Consulting and Clinical Psychology, 67*, 705–710.

Wilson, J. Q. (1975). *Thinking about crime*. New York: Basic Books.

Wilson, J. Q. (1978). *Varieties of police behavior* (2nd ed.). Cambridge, MA: Harvard University Press.

Wilson, J. Q., & Herrnstein, R. (1985). *Crime and human nature*. New York: Simon & Schuster.

Wilson, J. Q., & Kelling, G. L. (1989, April 24). Beating criminals to the punch. *New York Times*, p. 23.

Wilson, T. (2002). *Strangers to ourselves: Discovering the adaptive unconscious*. Cambridge MA: Harvard University Press.

Wilt, G., Bannon, J., Breedlove, R., Sandker, D., & Michaelson, S. (1977). *Domestic violence and the police— Studies in Detroit and Kansas City*. Washington, D.C.: Police Foundation.

Winick, B. (1985). Restructuring competency to stand trial. *UCLA Law Review, 32*, 921–985.

Winick, B. (1996). Incompetency to proceed in the criminal process: Past, present, and future. In B. D. Sales & D. W. Shulman (Eds.), *Law, mental health, and mental disorder* (pp. 310–340). Pacific Grove, CA: Brooks/Cole.

Winkle, J., & Wedeking, J. (2003). Perceptions and experiences of gender fairness in Mississippi courts. *Judicature, 87*, 126–134.

Winslade, W. J., & Ross, J. W. (1983). *The insanity plea*. New York: Scribner's.

Wise, R. A., & Safer, M. A. (2004). What U.S. judges know and believe about eyewitness testimony. *Applied Cognitive Psychology, 18*(4), 427–443.

Wissler, R., Hart, A., & Saks, M. (1999). Decision-making about general damages: A comparison of jurors, judges,

and lawyers. *Michigan Law Review, 98*, 751–826.

Wissler, R. L., Kuehn, P., & Saks, M. J. (2000). Instructing jurors on general damages in personal injury cases: Problems and possibilities. *Psychology, Public Policy, and Law, 6*, 712–742.

Wissler, R., & Saks, M. (1985). On the inefficacy of limiting instructions. *Law and Human Behavior, 9*, 37–48.

Witherspoon v. Illinois, 391 U.S. 510, 88 S.Ct. 1770, 20 L.Ed.2d 776 (1968).

Witt, P., & Barone, N. (2004). Assessing sex offender risk: New Jersey's methods. *Federal Sentencing Reporter, 16*, 170.

Wolff v. McDonnell, 418 U.S. 539 (1974).

Wolfgang, M. (1958). *Patterns in criminal homicide*. New York: Wiley.

Woocher, F. D. (1986). Legal principles governing expert testimony by experimental psychologists. *Law and Human Behavior, 10*, 47–61.

Wood, J., Schreiber, N., Martinez, Y., McLaurin, K., Strok, R., Velarde, L., et al. (1998). *Child interviewing techniques in the McMartin Preschool and Kelly Michaels cases: A quantitative comparison*. Paper presented at the 1998 American Psychology Law Society, Redondo Beach, California.

Woodrell, D. (1996). *Give us a kiss*. New York: Henry Holt.

Woodworth, M., & Porter, S. (2000). Historical foundations and current applications of criminal profiling in violent crime investigations. *Expert Evidence, 7*(4), 241–264.

Woolard, J. (2002). Capacity, competence and the juvenile defendant: Implications for research and policy. In B. Bottoms, M. Kovera, & B. McAuliff (Eds.), *Children, social science, and the law* (pp. 270–289). Cambridge: Cambridge University Press.

Worden, A., & Carlson, B. (2005). Attitudes and beliefs about domestic violence: Results of a public opinion survey. *Journal of Interpersonal Violence, 20*, 1219–1243.

Wordsworth, A. (2005, January 7). Child-killer unfairly convicted, court rules: Expert witness misled jury in Andrea Yates trial. *National Post, Toronto Edition*, p. A13.

Worsnop, R. L. (1993, February 5). Community policing. *CQ Researcher*, p. 97. Retrieved September 20, 2005, from *CQ Researcher Inc.* database.

Wortley, R. K., & Homel, R. J. (1995). Police prejudice as a function of training and outgroup contact: A lon-

gitudinal investigation. *Law and Human Behavior, 19*, 305–318.

Wright, L. (1994). *Remembering Satan*. New York: Knopf.

Wrightsman, L. S., & Kassin, S. M. (1993). *Confessions in the courtroom*. Thousand Oaks, CA: Sage.

Wyatt, G. E., Guthrie, D., & Notgrass, C. M. (1992). Differential effects of women's child sexual abuse and subsequent sexual revictimization. *Journal of Consulting and Clinical Psychology, 60*, 167–173.

www.abanet.org (2005).

www.florida.gov (2005).

www.nalp.org (2005).

www.whitehousedrugpolicy.gov/enforce/drugcourt (2004).

Yamagmai, D. S. (2001). How can intent be shown in a virtual world in light of the fantasy defense? *Santa Clara Law Review, 41*, 547–579.

Yegidis, B. L. (1986). Date rape and other forced sexual encounters among college students. *Journal of Sex Education and Therapy, 12*, 51–54.

Yochelson, S., & Samenow, S. E. (1976). *The criminal personality: Vol. 1. A profile for change*. New York: Aronson.

Youngjohn, J. (1995). Confirmed attorney coaching prior to neuropsychological evaluation. *Assessment, 2*, 279–283.

Zabin, L., Hirsch, M., & Emerson, M. (1989). When urban adolescents choose abortion: Effects on education, psychological status and subsequent pregnancy. *Family Planning Perspectives, 21*, 248–255.

Zajonc, R. B., & McIntosh, D. N. (1992). Emotions research: Some promising questions and some questionable promises. *Psychological Science, 3*, 70–74.

Zapf, P. A., & Roesch, R. (1997). Assessing fitness to stand trial: Institution-based evaluations and brief screening interview. *Canadian Journal of Community Mental Health, 16*, 53–66.

Zeisel, H., & Diamond, S. S. (1978). The effect of peremptory challenges on jury and verdict: An experiment in a federal district court. *Stanford Law Review, 30*, 491–529.

Zeno, S., Ivens, S., Millard, R., & Duvvuri, R. (1995). *The educator's word frequency guide*. New York: Touchstone Applied Science Associates.

Zernike, K. (2004, June 27). Defining torture: Russian roulette, yes. Mind-altering drugs, maybe. *New York Times*, Week in Review, p. 7.

Zhao, J., & Lovrich, N. (1998). Determinants of minority employment in American municipal agencies: The representation of African American officers. *Journal of Criminal Justice,* 26, 267–277.

Zhao, J., Lovrich, N., & Thurman, Q. (1999). The status of community policing in American cities: Facilitators and impediments revisited. *Policing: An International Journal of Police Strategies and Management,* 22, 74–92.

Zickafoose, D. J., & Bornstein, B. H. (1999). Double discounting: The effects of comparative negligence on mock juror decision making. *Law and Human Behavior,* 23, 577–596.

Zimring, F. (1998). The youth violence epidemic: Myth or reality? *Wake Forest Law Review,* 33, 727–743.

Zinger, I., & Forth, A. E. (1998). Psychopathy and Canadian criminal proceedings: The potential for human rights abuses. *Canadian Journal of Criminology,* 40, 237–277.

Ziskin, J., & Faust, D. (1988). *Coping with psychiatric and psychological testimony* (4th ed., Vols. 1-3). Marina del Rey, CA: Law & Psychology Press.

Photo Credits

Name Index

Subject Index